Latin America and the Global Cold War

The New Cold War History

Odd Arne Westad, *editor*

This series focuses on new interpretations of the Cold War era made possible by the opening of Soviet, East European, Chinese, and other archives. Books in the series based on multilingual and multiarchival research incorporate interdisciplinary insights and new conceptual frameworks that place historical scholarship in a broad, international context.

A complete list of books published in The New Cold War History is available at www.uncpress.org.

Latin America and the Global Cold War

....

EDITED BY
THOMAS C. FIELD JR.,
STELLA KREPP, AND
VANNI PETTINÀ

The University of North Carolina Press Chapel Hill

This book was published with the assistance of Embry-Riddle Aeronautical University.

© 2020 The University of North Carolina Press
All rights reserved
Set in Charis by Westchester Publishing Services

Library of Congress Cataloging-in-Publication Data
Names: Field, Thomas C., Jr., editor. | Krepp, Stella, editor. | Pettinà, Vanni, editor.
Title: Latin America and the Global Cold War / Thomas C. Field Jr., Stella Krepp, and Vanni Pettinà.
Other titles: New Cold War history.
Description: Chapel Hill : The University of North Carolina Press, [2020] | Series: The new cold war history | Includes bibliographical references and index.
Identifiers: LCCN 2019041156 | ISBN 9781469655697 (cloth) | ISBN 9781469684642 (pbk) | ISBN 9781469655703 (ebook) | ISBN 9798890858726 (pdf)
Subjects: LCSH: Cold War. | Latin America—Foreign relations—1948–1980. | Latin America—Politics and government—1948–1980.
Classification: LCC F1415 .L3755 2020 | DDC 980.03—dc23
LC record available at https://lccn.loc.gov/2019041156

Cover art: 1970 poster by Asela Pérez for the Organization in Solidarity with the People of Africa, Asia, and Latin America (OSPAAL). Courtesy of Lincoln Cushing/Docs Populi.

Two of these essays have been previously published in a different form. Chapter 3 first appeared in Spanish as "¡Bienvenido Mr. Mikoyan! Tacos y tractors a la sombra del aceramiento soviético-mexicano, 1958–1964," *Historia Mexicana* 66 (2016): 793–852. Chapter 12 is used here by permission of the University of Pennsylvania Press and first appeared as "A Mexican New International Economic Order?," *Humanity* 9, no. 3 (2018): 389–421.

To Marilyn Young

Contents

Acknowledgments, xi

Introduction, 1
*Between Nationalism and Internationalism:
Latin America and the Third World*
THOMAS C. FIELD JR., STELLA KREPP, AND VANNI PETTINÀ

Part I
Third World Nationalism

1 Brazil and India, 17
   A Brave New World, 1948–1961
   MIGUEL SERRA COELHO

2 Bolivia between Washington, Prague, and Havana, 44
   The Limits of Nationalism, 1960–1964
   THOMAS C. FIELD JR.

3 Mexican-Soviet Encounters in the Early 1960s, 73
   Tractors of Discord
   VANNI PETTINÀ

4 Brazil and Non-Alignment, 100
   Latin America's Role in the Global Order, 1961–1964
   STELLA KREPP

5 Community Development in Cold War Guatemala, 123
   Not a Revolution but an Evolution
   SARAH FOSS

6 Cuba, the USSR, and the Non-Aligned Movement, 148
   Negotiating Non-Alignment
   MICHELLE GETCHELL

7 Argentina's Secret Cold War, 174
Vigilance, Repression, and Nuclear Independence
DAVID M. K. SHEININ

Part II
Third World Internationalism

8 Anti-Imperialist Racial Solidarity before the Cold War, 201
Success and Failure
ALAN McPHERSON

9 Latin American *Tercermundistas* in the Soviet Union, 221
Paradise Lost and Found
TOBIAS RUPPRECHT

10 Cuba, the United States, and the Uses of the Third World Project, 1959–1967, 241
ERIC GETTIG

11 Chile, Algeria, and the Third World in the 1960s and 1970s, 274
Revolutions Entangled
EUGENIA PALIERAKI

12 A Mexican New International Economic Order?, 301
CHRISTY THORNTON

13 Third Worldism and the Panama Canal, 343
Liberating the Isthmus, 1971–1978
MIRIAM ELIZABETH VILLANUEVA

14 Isolating Nicaragua's Somoza, 367
Sandinista Diplomacy in Western Europe, 1977–1979
ELINE VAN OMMEN

Conclusion, 394
The Third World in Latin America
ODD ARNE WESTAD

List of Contributors, 403

Index, 407

Illustrations, Map, and Table

Illustrations

Medley of *Tercer Mundo* journal covers, 1974–1979, 4

Cuban outreach to the Second and Third Worlds, 1959 and 1962, 8

Mexican president Adolfo López Mateos with Soviet vice premier Anastas Mikoyan, 1959, 76

Brazilian president Jânio Quadros awards the Order of the Southern Cross to Cuban envoy Ernesto "Che" Guevara, 1961, 112

Poster for the third anniversary of the Tricontinental, Cuban artist Alfredo González Rostgaard, 1968, 156

Third World leaders and revolutionaries meet at the Tricontinental Conference in Havana, 1966, 263

Dutch poster of solidarity with Nicaragua's Sandinistas, 1979, 376

Map

Latin America, xiv

Table

Documentaries screened by Panama's Grupo Experimental Cine Universitario, 1976, 359

Acknowledgments

This project is the fruit of a multinational, multilingual effort by fifteen scholars whose nationalities and transnational institutional affiliations include ties to sixteen countries throughout Europe and the Americas. Its seed was planted in Bern, Switzerland, where Stella Krepp co-hosted a 2014 workshop on "Latin America in a Global Context," jointly sponsored by the University of Bern and the Brazil-based Gétulio Vargas Foundation. Also funded in part by the Swiss National Science Foundation, this workshop brought Krepp together with Thomas Field Jr. and Vanni Pettinà, all three of whom would be co-editors of this volume, along with two dozen other emerging and established scholars of Latin American history. Workshop participants from countries throughout Europe and the Americas all shared the intellectual goal of analyzing and writing contemporary Latin American history from a more global perspective.

The project germinated at the 2015 conference of the Latin American Studies Association in San Juan, Puerto Rico, where the book's three co-editors presented papers on a panel entitled "Imperial, Transnational, and National Perspectives on 'Development' in Cold War Latin America." The panel led to discussion of a plan to launch a collaborative project to bring Latin American history out of its Western Hemisphere ghetto, to which panel commentator Robert Karl responded that the proposal sounded like an endeavor to "globalize Latin American history while provincializing the study of superpowers like the United States." ¡Bien dicho!

Later that year, the editors put out a worldwide call for abstracts, which resulted in thirty-nine submissions from scholars across the globe; of these we ultimately selected fourteen proposals covering a diverse array of themes and countries. For the final product, we are grateful for helpful conversations with Chuck Grench, Senior Editor at the University of North Carolina Press, copyediting and formatting support from Embry-Riddle graduate students Kara Brennion and Taylor Alvarez, excellent suggestions that helped clarify the volume's argument and scope from two anonymous peer reviewers, additional masterful multilingual copyediting by Didier Coste, and generous critical comments from Julia Sarreal, Alan McPherson, Aaron

Moulton, and Eugenia Palieraki. Embry-Riddle's Interim Dean of Security and Intelligence, Jon Haass, stepped in at the last-minute to provide critical funding for these efforts. Indeed, without support from all three of the editors' home institutions—Embry-Riddle, the University of Bern, and El Colegio de México—this project would have been impossible. We would also like to recognize the institutional and financial support of our contributors' universities: Indiana University, Georgetown University, the U.S. Naval War College, Temple University, the University of Cergy-Pontoise, the University of Exeter, the European University Institute, Trent University, Johns Hopkins University, the London School of Economics and Political Science, Texas Christian University, and the Harvard Kennedy School of Government.

On a personal note, the editors would like to acknowledge the support of their loved ones for tolerating periods of absence and mental distraction that inevitably accompany projects of this magnitude. Thomas would like to mention Milena, Eleanor, and Edmund, who never quite understood why dad was taking time away from the family, and his second monograph, to co-lead an edited book project on Third Worldism. Stella would like to thank Andrej for his support. Vanni would like to acknowledge Ana, Arianna, and Giulio for their patience and love and El Colegio de México for being an incredibly supportive academic institution. All three co-editors benefited from the inspiration and encouragement of the late Marilyn Young, Professor of History at New York University and great scholar of U.S.-Asian relations. To the memory of Marilyn's vision and generosity, this book is dedicated.

Latin America and the Global Cold War

Latin America

Introduction

Between Nationalism and Internationalism:
Latin America and the Third World

•••

THOMAS C. FIELD JR., STELLA KREPP, AND VANNI PETTINÀ

Common ideals of life and organization draw us close to the major nations of the Western bloc. . . . However, at the present juncture . . . it is undeniable that we have other points in common . . . with recently emancipated peoples in Asia and Africa.
—Brazilian President Jânio Quadros, 1961

The fundamental field of imperialist exploitation comprises three underdeveloped continents: America, Asia, and Africa. . . . America, a forgotten continent in the last liberation struggles, is now beginning to make itself heard.
—Argentine-Cuban revolutionary Ernesto "Che" Guevara, 1966

At the 1973 meeting of the Third World Non-Aligned Movement in Algiers, a multinational group of Latin American journalists resolved to launch a new publication focused on what they saw as the global struggle against all forms of imperialism. According to its founders, the new journal aspired to open a window onto the political realities of the Third World, now known as the Global South, a geographical concept forged in the cauldron of the early Cold War. Promising to reinterpret Latin America's sociopolitical struggles as part of broader postcolonial conflicts, the first issue of *Tercer Mundo* (Third World) was published a few months later in Buenos Aires, Argentina, by the socialist press La Línea. Shuttered in 1976 by the military government of Jorge Rafael Videla, *Tercer Mundo* then moved to Mexico City, where for three decades its editors ran a global news network, Cuadernos del Tercer Mundo, until financial hardship led to the team's dissolution in 2005. During its tumultuous existence, the pages of *Tercer Mundo* carried editorial comment and interviews not only with Afro-Asian movement leaders such as Nelson Mandela, Muammar Gaddafi, and Yasser Arafat, but also with Latin American Third Worldists such as Omar Torrijos, Juan Velasco Alvarado, and Fidel Castro. As one of the journal's founding members later described, *Tercer Mundo* "circulated in Spanish, Portuguese, and English in Latin America, Africa, the Middle East, and parts of Asia . . . [and] played a *sui generis* role of promoting South-South dialogue."[1]

The birth of the *Tercer Mundo* journal in the early years of the 1970s coincided not by chance with the rise and fall of Chile's socialist government under Salvador Allende, who unabashedly espoused a Third Worldist ideology and hosted Global South events such as the third meeting of the United Nations Conference on Trade and Development (UNCTAD). In addition, the wide circulation of the journal and its recognition not only in Latin America but also in the broader Third World illuminates the extent to which the Western Hemisphere had become an important interlocutor for Global South leaders, intellectuals, and activists. Further, its forced move from Buenos Aires to Mexico City in 1976 occurred in the wake of Mexican President Luís Echeverría's quest to position his country as a leading figure in the Third World struggle, embodied by Mexico's signal contribution to the UN's passage of the New International Economic Order (NIEO). As such, the rise and fall of *Tercer Mundo* suggest a wider narrative whose conceptual framework, Third Worldism, might allow us to better understand the ebbs and flows of Latin America's varied iterations of Global South ideologies and politics. Its history also serves as a reminder of the potency achieved by the Third Worldist projects in the 1970s, as well as their capacity to link national, regional, and global histories of Latin America.

That many of these projects have been forgotten speaks to both the promises and limits of historical interest in twentieth-century Latin America's broader Third World drama. Like the *Tercer Mundo* journal, the history of what were once powerful interactions between Latin America and the rest of the Global South has faded away, resulting in collective amnesia by scholars of contemporary Latin American history. The lack of sustained attention to Latin American Third Worldism seems especially surprising if one considers the growing scholarly interest in the Cold War in the Global South since 2000. This trend has given rise to a number of excellent new works on the Non-Aligned Movement (NAM), the overlapping trajectories of decolonization and the Cold War, and the rise of Third Worldism in the 1960s and 1970s. Yet few of these studies responds concretely to the historiographical challenge made by Odd Arne Westad in 2005, whose book *The Global Cold War* formulated an innovative intellectual blueprint for writing international histories of the Third World through the prism of three southern continents' shared struggle for postcolonial forms of political and economic sovereignty. Instead, much of the recent Global South literature adopts a narrow political definition of Third Worldism, hemming closely to the formalities of Bandung's Afro-Asian movement, launched in 1955, or to the official membership of the 1961 NAM founded in Belgrade. Taken together, these Afro-Asian and Socialist bloc biases have fueled a persistent "historiographical Monroe doctrine," in which Latin America's varied participation in the Third World movements has been largely neglected. The upshot has been an underappreciation for the multivalent and tricontinental nature of Third World's postwar struggle.[2]

If Cold War historians have declined to fully incorporate Latin America within the emerging literature on the Global South, this lacuna is complemented by a parallel gap in the historiography of the contemporary Western Hemisphere. On the one hand, as Uruguayan scholar Aldo Marchesi posited, Latin American historians have shown a certain reluctance to abandon their nation-specific, domestic narratives regarding each country's political, social, and economic evolution, a geographic exceptionalism evident even in decentered regional scholarship such as a 2008 collection titled *In From the Cold: Latin America's New Encounter with the Cold War*.[3] On the other hand, diplomatic historians persist in their preoccupation with the impacts of U.S. foreign policy in the region. As mirror images of one another, these scholarly canons have fortified the historiographical barrier lying in the southern Atlantic, hobbling attempts to fully incorporate contemporary Latin America within a broader global framework.[4] As historian Lauren Benton put it, hemispheric exceptionalism has pushed the region "off to the side, inhabiting a space that is not so much insignificant as it is simply strange"; Latin America has, in effect, been "the odd region out."[5]

The peculiar evolution of the very concept of the Third World is partially to blame for the underutilization of a Global South framework to describe contemporary Latin America. Coined by French liberal intellectual Alfred Sauvy in 1952, the term "Third World" implicitly drew upon diverse antecedents from "Third Camp" prewar Trotskyists to the nationalist "Third Position" of Juan Domingo Perón's Argentina in the late 1940s. When Sauvy's seminal article appeared in Paris's *L'Observateur*, then a staple of the country's "Third Way" movement of independent liberal-leftists, he reached even farther back to the "ignored, exploited, despised" Third Estate of the French Revolution, which had been "nothing" and then wanted to be "something." Revealing the neologism's presentist bias, Sauvy's 1952 article explicitly

Founded in Buenos Aires in 1974 and relocated to Mexico City after Argentina's 1976 coup, *Tercer Mundo* (Third World) covered political events throughout what is today known as the Global South—Latin America, Africa, the Middle East, and Asia. In its first issue (September 1974), the journal discussed Argentina's nationalist leader, Juan Domingo Perón, events in Peru, the decolonization struggle in Mozambique, dictatorship in Bolivia, and the Middle Eastern conflict. In issue 4 (May 1975), *Tercer Mundo* analyzed "Islamic Socialism" in Somalia, denounced the U.S. economic "blockade" of Cuba, discussed cultural decolonization in Tanzania, and reported on struggles for economic independence in Angola and Panama. Publishing from Mexico City a few years later, the journal's issues 20 and 27 (April 1978 and February 1979) trained its anti-imperialist lens on issues commonly affecting Libya, Morocco (Western Sahara), Zaire (Congo), Mexico, Panama, Ethiopia, Afghanistan, Yemen, Iran, and Cambodia. (Images courtesy of Repositorio Institucional, Universidade Federal Rural do Rio de Janeiro [http://repositorio.im.ufrrj.br:8080/jspui/handle/1235813/540], reprinted with the permission of former *Tercer Mundo* editor, Beatriz Bissio.)

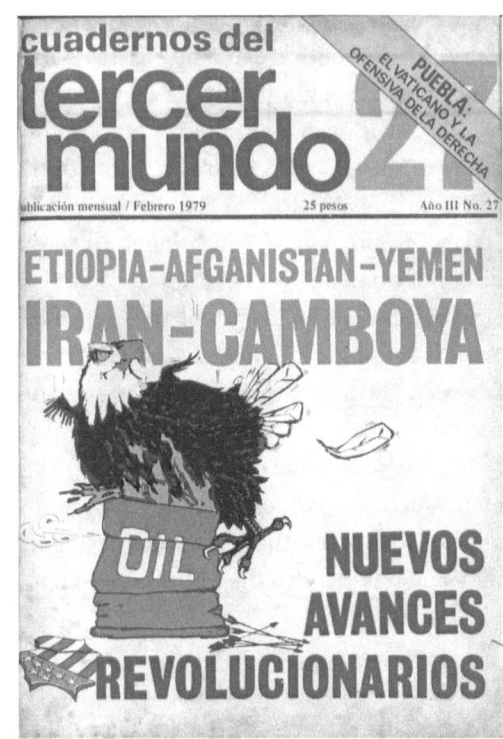

referred to newly independent nations such as India, whose Prime Minister Jawaharlal Nehru soon began to speak of a nonaligned "Third Force" halfway between the emerging bipolar Cold War rivals.[6] As use of the agreed-upon term "Third World" gained increasingly radical political currency, first in French and then in English by the 1960s, pioneering scholars such as Peter Worsley continued to emphasize "newly independent countries" while conceding that the term "could be applied with considerable benefit" to Latin America due to its "shared experience of a colonial past and a continuing 'neo-colonial' present." By the early 1980s, Worsley himself began to advocate for a more expansive definition of "Third World," concluding that any comprehensive analysis of the global postcolonial struggle required the full incorporation of Latin America.[7]

In recent decades, the evolution of historical research on the Global Cold War offered sharper theoretical definitions, which paradoxically reinforced a more inclusive geographic approach to Latin America within a Third World context. One such invitation to the Western Hemisphere came from Vijay Prashad, whose 2007 book incorporated Latin America through the rather totalizing argument that "the Third World was not a place but a project" defined by a politico-economic ideology opposed to all forms of imperialism. Prashad sought to unify a diverse set of experiences under the theme of Third Worldism, delimited conceptually as the struggle for "equality on the world level," yet channeled through a variety of Global South frameworks such as the United Nations General Assembly, UNCTAD, NAM, and Havana's more radical Tricontinental, otherwise known as the Organización de Solidaridad de los Pueblos de África, Asia y América Latina (OSPAAAL, Organization of Solidarity of the People of Africa, Asia, and Latin America). As Prashad recognized, the Cold War catalyzed a certain convergence between Latin American republics and anti-imperialist countries such as Ghana, Yugoslavia, Egypt, and India. This is to say nothing of the region's role as home to some of the most influential theories of economic development, such as *desarrollismo* (developmentalism) and *dependencia* (dependency), which together formed a basis for broad ideological frameworks that would undergird the Third World's opposition to neocolonialism in the 1960s and 1970s.[8]

Following Prashad's work, Global South historians such as Robert Vitalis and Jeffrey Byrne continued to engage in conceptual outreach to Latin America, pioneering a shift away from a discursive analysis of Third Worldism toward empirical studies underwritten by newly available archival resources. Researching African and Asian perspectives on Third Worldism, Vitalis argued that the 1955 Bandung meeting was less racialized and more idea-laden than its subsequent mythology suggests.[9] Writing on Algerian, Cuban, and Yugoslav contributions to early nonaligned radicalism, Byrne echoed Prashad and Vitalis by articulating Third Worldism not just as an institutional scaffolding, "a framework created by political elites in order to achieve political goals," but also as "a doctrine for pragmatic and practicable foreign policies."[10] Drawing on these all-engulfing global definitions, "unbounded by geography," Byrne traced the historical evolution of Third Worldism and its consolidation as a multilateral strategy of "insurgent neutralism," which sought to leverage Cold War rivalries in order to generate political and economic benefits for the Global South.

According to Prashad, Vitalis, and Byrne, it was precisely this new Global South imaginary that enabled the consolidation of a Third World project organized on the inclusive ideological lines of worldwide anti-imperialism, rather than on an exclusively racial divide. During the 1960s Sino-Soviet split, for example, Chinese attempts to impose a racial or geographic definition of Third Worldism alienated elites in North Africa and Latin America, even nationalists who otherwise supported outreach to the Second (socialist) and Third (neutralist) Worlds. Despite Maoist inroads into certain pro-peasant factions of Third World Communists parties, including in Latin America, China's failure to exclude "white" Soviet bloc countries from nonaligned meetings paradoxically paved the way toward fuller globalization of the movement during subsequent years. By highlighting unified ideological definitions of Third Worldism, these scholars thus point toward Latin America's central, even primordial, contribution to the forging of a Third World global ideology. Yet their theoretical coherence sometimes masks a richer political and ideological space that becomes visible when the narrative scope returns to Latin America's local, national, and regional realities.[11]

Through fourteen chapters based on newly available sources from Algeria, Argentina, Bolivia, Brazil, Chile, Cuba, Czechoslovakia, the Dominican Republic, Germany, Guatemala, France, Haiti, India, Mexico, Nicaragua, Panama, Russia, the United Kingdom, and the United States, this book analyzes the connections and interactions that existed between Latin America and the other regions known collectively as the Third World.[12] By incorporating Latin America, on its own terms, into the emerging Global South historiography, this volume embraces a plurality of multidirectional Third World experiences. Concluding that each Latin American invocation of Third Worldism arose from specific and sometimes contradictory theoretical antecedents and national contexts, these chapters describe points of convergence between Latin American countries' interactions with, and participation in, the political and ideological space we call the Third World. Highlighting the particularly Latin American contribution to Third World space, and vice versa, the volume thus facilitates a rediscovery of both geographical concepts, offering a fresh take on a region long cut off from contemporary global historiography. Put another way, the book does more than just discuss Latin America's relations with the broader Third World; it rearticulates Latin American history as Third World history, cataloging the ways that both intellectual constructs—Latin America and the Third World— impacted one another as they merged in the 1960s and 1970s.

In order to historicize and explain the various manifestations of Latin American Third Worldism during the long Cold War, the volume is divided into two conceptual halves, each of them organized chronologically. In Part I, contributors describe a series of cases representative of "Third World Nationalism," ranging from cautious late-1940s diplomatic neutrality to more sustained attempts at Latin American outreach to the Second and Third Worlds during the 1970s and 1980s. Focusing largely on Third Worldism's

In one of the earliest concrete examples of Latin American outreach to the Second and Third Worlds, revolutionary Cuba represented the region's first and most enthusiastic participant in the Third World Non-Aligned Movement (NAM), formally launched in Belgrade in 1961. Two years earlier, Cuban envoy Ernesto "Che" Guevara held friendly meetings, depicted above, with Yugoslov President Josep Broz Tito on the island of Brioni. Later, as the NAM grew in size and ambition, Cuban involvement inspired anti-imperialists while temporarily hampering wider Latin American participation in Third Worldism. Opposite, Cuban leader Fidel Castro hosts the new Algerian head of state, Ahmed Ben Bella, in Havana in October 1962, as Cuban President Osvaldo Dórticos, "Che" Guevara, and others look on. (Above, from Legacy of Konstantin-Koča Popović and Leposava-Lepa Perović, album no. 20, Wikimedia Commons; opposite, courtesy of Keystone-France/Gamma-Keystone via Getty Images.)

potential gains for the nation-state, nationalists even on the political and military Right sometimes sought to harness the power of anti-imperialism for their own ends. In Part II, the volume shifts from strategic (nationalist) themes of resistance, sovereignty, and exceptionalism to transnational conceptual patterns of solidarity, heterogeneity, and inclusion, zooming out to describe a series of mostly left-wing (but also postcolonial and even neoliberal) cases of "Third World Internationalism." This latter trend originated with early twentieth-century anti-imperialist struggles in the Caribbean, but found a particularly strident voice in the 1970s with the radicalization

of Third World demands on everything from raw materials sovereignty and global socialism to the armed liberation of Latin America's remaining colonial and neocolonial spaces.

Part I ("Third World Nationalism") begins with Miguel Serra Coelho's analysis of early Cold War relations between Brazil and India, which reveals the proscribed political possibilities of moderate Third World nationalism while touching on concepts of race, South-South ties, and contested claims to Third World modernity. In chapter 2, Thomas Field identifies similar limitations in Bolivia's sustained outreach to the Soviet bloc and Cuba during the early 1960s, a futile gambit by middle-class nationalists that provoked fierce opposition from the country's entrenched conservative elites. Vanni Pettinà analyzes nationalist Mexico's similarly modest entreaties to the Soviet bloc in chapter 3. Attributing Cold War Mexico's cautious neutrality to its leaders' sincere commitment to national development, Pettinà concludes that neutrality failed to bear fruit thanks to a combination of anti-Communist resistance and a fatalistic acceptance of geographic and economic realities. In chapter 4, Stella Krepp challenges the previous chapters' argument that Latin America's limited Third Worldism in the early Cold War resulted from mere conservative retrenchment, and she employs the Brazilian case to identify a wider, pan-political consensus regarding the region's Western identity.

The last three contributions to Part I reveal how Third World nationalism could cut in several ideological directions. Nationalism takes a turn from moderate to reactionary in chapter 5, where Sarah Foss undercovers the developmentalist origins of Third World nation-building, depoliticization, and authoritarianism. Through an analysis of community development programs in Cold War Guatemala, Foss argues that conservative elites exploited their country's underdevelopment to help shape U.S.-based theories of Third World modernization, while local communitarians subverted and redirected development programs toward their own prerogatives and interests. Shifting to an analysis of the Left in chapter 6, Michelle Getchell interprets revolutionary Cuba's refusal to bind itself to international Communist orthodoxy as evidence of Havana's preference for Third World nationalism. Pointing to Cuba's foreign policy independence and its support for armed revolutionary movements in the Global South, Getchell concludes that Havana's dedication to national liberation contributed to pushing the Soviet Union toward greater acceptance of Third World nationalism at each meeting of anti-imperialist countries during the late 1960s. In chapter 7, David Shenin pivots from Castroism to Peronism to decode what he calls one of twentieth-century Latin America's most "abstruse" iterations of Third Way nationalism. He argues that Argentina's Third Way (later, Third World) identity, long celebrated by local nationalists of many political stripes, masked more banal Cold War cultural and political continuities of pro-U.S. anti-Communism.

Part II ("Third World Internationalism") begins with Alan McPherson's analysis in chapter 8 of how race and language offered both possibilities and obstacles for transnational anti-imperialist solidarity in the Interwar Caribbean. Pointing to the Caribbean roots of Latin America's eventual embrace of Third World internationalism, McPherson's contribution grounds the second half of the book in a set of Global South questions that transcended the bipolar Cold War era, even while they were about to be transformed by it. In chapter 9, Tobias Rupprecht describes the impact of the Soviet Union's intellectual embrace of Latin American anti-imperialism, which began in the 1920s but hit its stride with a wave of *tercermundista* (Third Worldist) visitors to Moscow and Eastern Europe during the Cold War. Analyzing the Soviet bloc travels of indigenous, Communist, and even conservative Catholic *tercermundistas*, Rupprecht argues that these Latin American internationalists articulated their exuberance for Soviet-style Communism through decades-old patterns of anti-imperialist, anti-U.S. rhetoric. Along a similar vein of Communist contributions to Third World internationalism, Eric Gettig reinterprets revolutionary Cuba's obsessive drive to break the confines of the West to forge Latin American ties of solidarity with the Global South in chapter 10. Juxtaposing the conflicting Third World policies of Havana and Washington, Gettig identifies a radicalization of Latin American Third Worldism in the late 1960s, one that provoked fierce opposition from U.S. diplomats everywhere from Bangkok to Cairo.

In chapter 11, in describing how Third World internationalism mobilized state and nonstate actors alike, Eugenia Palieraki leverages the intimacy of postwar Chilean-Algerian relations in order to expand the focus of transnational history beyond its traditional concern with pan-European networks and institutions. In chapter 12, Christy Thornton turns the discussion back to Cold War Mexico, describing how the country's leadership of Third World internationalism in the 1970s arose from decades of anti-imperialist politico-economic praxis. According to Thornton's reading of the Mexican origins of the NIEO, twentieth-century Latin America offered a readymade blueprint for the global postcolonial struggle against economic exploitation and dependency. Miriam Villanueva analyzes cultural Third World internationalism in Panamanian artistic expression in chapter 13, where she describes how the anti-imperialist military government of Omar Torrijos tapped into nonstate solidarity networks to successfully reimagine Panama's decades-long struggle to regain sovereignty over the Canal Zone, one of the region's most persisting and concrete examples of territorial empire. In chapter 14, Eline van Ommen closes the narrative portion of the book by describing how roving Nicaraguan Sandinista diplomats employed the rhetorical framework of Third World internationalism to court sympathetic left-wing and liberal networks in the First World. Acknowledging the salience of Third Worldism in Western European political circles during the late 1970s, van Ommen's contribution also foreshadows the difficulties of maintaining Third World internationalist momentum in an environment of rising neoliberalism in the 1980s and beyond.

Moving past the nationalist/internationalist dyad, Odd Arne Westad contributes the book's forward-looking conclusion, in which he describes how the countries of Latin America and the broader Global South continue to search for a meaningful prism through which to articulate their essentially anti-imperialist alternative to globalization. Calling for a broader reconsideration of Latin American Third Worldism, Westad contextualizes the remarkably short-lived Third World moment, strictly defined, by looking backward to the nineteenth century and forward into the twenty-first. In doing so, Westad suggests that the Global South can serve as a promising framework for future research on Latin American history, one that he hopes will provoke increasingly global narratives of Latin America and the world. Lacking a viable Marxist challenge to capitalist globalization, the future of Latin American foreign relations may well rely on creative intellectual approaches to comprehending the region's efforts to offset U.S. power by globalizing its politics and economics. As these competing iterations of globalization play out, waxing and waning alongside the competing impulses of nationalism and solidarity, research on Latin America's varied Third World experiences offers insights for better understanding the region's past, as well as its possible futures.

Notes

1. Beatriz Bissio, "Bandung, the Nonaligned, and the Media: The Role of the Journal 'Third World' in South-South Dialogue," *Austral: Brazilian Journal of Strategy and International Relations* 4, no. 8 (2015): 21. For more on the journal *Tercer Mundo*, see Nicolás Casullo, "El (Tercer) Mundo es ancho y complejo," *Nexos*, 1 August 1980; Comité Editorial, "Cuadernos del Tercer Mundo, en México," *Proceso*, 14 May 1977.

2. Odd Arne Westad, *The Global Cold War: Third World Interventions and the Making of Our Times* (Cambridge: Cambridge University Press, 2005); quotation from Tanya Harmer, "Review of *The Ideological Origins of the Dirty War* by Federico Finchelstein," *Cold War History* 15, no. 3 (2015): 419.

Scholars making intellectual connections between Latin America and the Third World include Stephen G. Rabe, *The Road to OPEC: United States Relations with Venezuela, 1919–1976* (Austin: University of Texas Press, 1982); Piero Gleijeses, *Conflicting Missions: Havana, Washington, and Africa* (Chapel Hill: University of North Carolina Press, 2001); James Hershberg, "'High-Spirited Confusion': Brazil, the 1961 Belgrade Non-Aligned Conference, and the Limits of an 'Independent' Foreign Policy during the High Cold War," *Cold War History* 7, no. 3 (2007): 373–88; Tanya Harmer, *Allende's Chile and the Inter-American Cold War* (Chapel Hill: University of North Carolina Press, 2011); Thomas C. Field Jr., *From Development to Dictatorship: Bolivia and the Alliance for Progress in the Kennedy Era* (Ithaca, NY: Cornell University Press, 2014); Christine Hatzky, *Cubans in Angola: South-South Cooperation and Transfer of Knowledge, 1976–1991* (Madison: University of Wisconsin Press 2015); Vanni Pettinà, "Global Horizons: Mexico, the Third World, and the Non-Aligned Movement at the Time of the 1961 Belgrade Conference," *International History Review* 38, no. 4 (2016): 741–64; and Anne Garland Mahler, *From the Tricontinental to the Global South: Race, Radicalism, and Transnational Solidarity* (Durham, NC: Duke University Press, 2018).

Global South historians who have engaged in peripheral outreach to Latin America include Vijay Prashad, *The Darker Nations: A People's History of the Third World* (New York: New Press, 2007); Samantha Christiansen and Zachary Scarlett, eds.,

The Third World in the Global 1960s (New York: Berghahn, 2012); Robert Vitalis, "The Midnight Ride of Kwame Nkrumah and Other Fables of Bandung (Ban-doong)," *Humanity: An International Journal of Human Rights, Humanitarianism, and Development* 4, no. 2 (2013): 261–88; Robert J. McMahon, ed., *The Cold War in the Third World* (Oxford: Oxford University Press, 2013); Mark T. Berger and Heloise Weber, *Rethinking the Third World: International Development and World Politics* (Basingstoke, UK: Red Globe Press, 2014); Jeffrey James Byrne, "Beyond Continents, Colours, and the Cold War: Yugoslavia, Algeria, and the Struggle for Non-Alignment," *International History Review* 37, no. 5 (2015): 912–32; Jason Parker, *Hearts, Minds, Voices: US Cold War Public Diplomacy and the Formation of the Third World* (Oxford: Oxford University Press, 2016); Jeffrey James Byrne, *Mecca of Revolution: Algeria, Decolonization, and the Third World Order* (Oxford: Oxford University Press, 2016); and Chen Jian, Martin Klimke, Masha Kirasirova, Mary Nolan, Marilyn Young, and Joanna Waley-Cohen, eds., *The Routledge Handbook of the Global Sixties: Between Protest and Nation-Building* (New York: Routledge, 2018).

For examples of the growing canon of Global South history not directly addressing Latin America, see Robert B. Rakove, *Kennedy, Johnson, and the Nonaligned World* (Cambridge: Cambridge University Press, 2014); Eric Gettig, "'Trouble Ahead in Afro-Asia': The United States, the Second Bandung Conference, and the Struggle for the Third World, 1964–1965," *Diplomatic History* 39, no. 1 (2015): 126–56; Sandra Bott, Jussi M. Hanhimäki, Janick Marina Schaufelbuehl, and Marco Wyss, eds., *Neutrality and Neutralism in the Global Cold War: Between or Within the Blocs?* (London: Routledge, 2016); as well as special journal issues such as "Beyond and Between the Cold War Blocs," *International History Review* 37, no. 5 (2015); "The New International Economic Order: A Reintroduction," *Humanity* 6, no. 1 (2015). See also Jeremy Friedman, *Shadow Cold War: The Sino-Soviet Competition for the Third World* (Chapel Hill: University of North Carolina Press, 2015); and Gregg A. Brazinsky, *Winning the Third World: Sino-American Rivalry during the Cold War* (Chapel Hill: University of North Carolina Press, 2017).

3. Aldo Marchesi, "Escribiendo la Guerra Fría latinoamericana: entre el Sur 'local' y el Norte 'global,'" *Estudos Históricos* 30, no. 60 (2017): 187–202; and Gilbert M. Joseph and Daniel Spenser, eds., *In from the Cold: Latin America's New Encounter with the Cold War* (Durham, NC: Duke University Press, 2008). For other regional histories that retain an air of hemispheric exceptionalism, see Patrick Iber, *Neither Peace nor Freedom: The Cultural Cold War in Latin America* (Cambridge, MA: Harvard University Press, 2015); Greg Grandin and Gilbert Joseph, eds., *Century of Revolution: Insurgent and Counterinsurgent Violence during Latin America's Long Cold War* (Durham, NC: Duke University Press 2010); and Gilbert Joseph and Catherine LeGrand, eds., *Close Encounters with Empire: Writing the Cultural History of U.S.-Latin American Relations* (Durham, NC: Duke University Press 1998).

4. The differences between Latin American and diplomatic narratives can be seen by comparing Greg Grandin, *The Last Colonial Massacre: Latin America in the Cold War* (Chicago: University of Chicago Press, 2004); Hal Brands, *Latin America's Cold War* (Cambridge, MA: Harvard University Press, 2010); and Steven G. Rabe, *The Killing Zone: The United States Wages Cold War in Latin America* (Oxford: Oxford

University Press, 2011). Within Latin America, notable global-minded exceptions to Marchesi's critique are Federico Finchelstein, *The Ideological Origins of the Dirty War: Fascism, Populism, and Dictatorship in Twentieth-Century Argentina* (Oxford: Oxford University Press, 2015) and Martín Bergel, *El Oriente desplazado: Los intelectuales y los orígenes del tercermundismo en la Argentina* (Bernal: Universidad Nacional de Quilmes, 2015).

5. Lauren A. Benton, "No Longer Odd Region Out: Repositioning Latin America in World History," *Hispanic American Historical Review* 84, no. 3 (2004): 423–30.

6. Alfred Sauvy, "Trois mondes, une planète," *L'Observateur*, 14 August 1952, 14. Regarding the hydra-headed evolution of the term "Third World" from Western developmentalist fantasy to revolutionary anti-imperial militancy, see Christopher Kalter, "A Shared Space of Imagination, Communication, and Action: Perspectives on the History of the 'Third World,'" in *The Third World in the Global 1960s*, ed. Samantha Christiansen and Zachary Scarlett (New York: Berghahn, 2012), 23–38. For a boisterous debate regarding the etymology of the term "Third World," see Joseph L. Love, "'Third World': A Response to Professor Worsley," *Third World Quarterly* 2, no. 2 (1980): 315–17; and Laurens Otter et al., "Why Third World? Three Critiques," *Third World Quarterly* 3, no. 3 (1981): 528–31.

7. Peter Worsley, *The Third World* (Chicago: University of Chicago Press, 1964), 215, 285; and Peter Worsley, *The Three Worlds: Culture and World Development* (Chicago: University of Chicago Press, 1984), especially 306–8.

8. Prashad, *The Darker Nations*, xv–xix, 62–74.

9. Vitalis, "The Midnight Ride of Kwame Nkrumah."

10. Byrne, "Beyond Continents," 2.

11. Byrne, "Beyond Continents"; Gettig, "'Trouble Ahead in Afro-Asia.'" For a comprehensive, albeit dated, treatment of China and Latin America, see Cecil Johnson, *Communist China & Latin America, 1959–1967* (New York: Columbia University Press, 1970).

12. Throughout this book, unless otherwise noted, translations of original primary sources are the chapter authors'.

Part I Third World Nationalism

1 Brazil and India

A Brave New World, 1948-1961

MIGUEL SERRA COELHO

This chapter explores the relations between Brazil and India during the first fifteen years of the Cold War era. Encompassing four Brazilian presidencies (Eurico Gaspar Dutra, 1946–51; Getúlio Vargas, 1951–54; João Café Filho, 1954–55; and Juscelino Kubitschek, 1956–61), it explores the diplomatic, economic, and cultural interactions between Brazil and India during a period characterized by a growing global interest in the Third World project. Although lacking a clear policy toward the Afro-Asian world, Brazil recognized the increasing importance of newly independent nations and thus expanded its diplomatic network, especially in the late 1950s under Kubitschek.[1] Conversely, the chapter also considers India's foreign policy toward Brazil and the Western Hemisphere more broadly, during a period that has been described as one of "distant acquaintance" between New Delhi and the countries of Latin America.[2]

Although Brazil and India established diplomatic ties in 1948, their early relations remain understudied. Language barriers, continental distances, and nearly closed archives in the case of India surely contributed to this outcome. In addition, the alleged absence of interactions between the two countries during this period contributed to driving historians away. The few existing studies of Brazilian-Indian relations, though useful, tend to be based on sources of only one country, as is the case with the work of Varun Shani and Anaya Chakravarti.[3] For their part, Jerry Dávila and Williams da Silva Gonçalves approach Brazilian-Indian relations indirectly, through Brazil's support for Portuguese efforts to retain Goa, Daman, and Diu and Brazilian representation of Portugal's official interests in New Delhi.[4]

Based on research in Brazilian, Indian, and Portuguese archives, this chapter aims to shed light on Brazilian foreign policy toward India and ultimately seeks to understand why early ties failed to develop. Particularly, it aims to unveil Brazilian perceptions of, apprehensions about, prejudices against, and interests in India—and, to a certain extent, the Third

World—during a period that preceded the country's so-called independent foreign policy. Additionally, it aims to shed light on India's foreign policy toward Latin America, particularly through New Delhi's efforts to initiate dialogue with the region's largest nation.

Initial Postwar Formalities, 1948–1953

Brazil embraced democracy after World War II. The military leaders deposed the popular dictator Getúlio Vargas, in power since the Revolution of 1930, free and fair presidential and congressional elections took place in 1945, and a liberal-democratic constitution came into force a year later. While maintaining the social gains of the Vargas government, the nascent regime ensured basic civil rights, the rule of law, free and direct state and local elections for the executive and legislative branches, and a free press. Although with several restrictions, such as limitations to the right strike and the denial of the right to vote to illiterate adults (approximately 50 percent of the population), Brazilian society was about to experience a twenty-year period of political and social mobilization that was termed *experiência democrática* (democratic experience).[5]

With a few exceptions, Brazil's postwar foreign policy was aligned with that of the United States. The governments of Eurico Gaspar Dutra (1946–51), Getúlio Vargas (1951–54), and João Café Filho (1954–55) positioned Brazil firmly in the Western sphere of influence led by Washington. Brazil became a member of the Tratado Interamericano de Assistência Recíproca (Inter-American Treaty of Reciprocal Assistance) in 1947 and signed a military assistance agreement with Washington in 1952. The country also repressed domestic communism and actively supported U.S. global interests at the United Nations (UN) as well as in the Organization of American States (OAS). Although it declined to send troops to fight in the Korean War during the years 1950–53, the Brazilian government offered political and diplomatic support and provided the United States with strategic minerals.[6]

While considering itself to be intrinsically anticolonial, Brazil demonstrated little or no interest in the problems of dependent peoples in the immediate aftermath of World War II. Indeed, as Wayne Alan Selcher has noted, Brazil declined to participate in the San Francisco Conference debates on the self-determination documents that became the core of Chapters XI, XII, and XIII of the UN Charter. With few diplomatic and consular representations in the colonial territories as well as absence from the League of Nations, Itamaraty, the Brazilian Ministry of External Relations, did not foresee the demand for independence that was to emerge in the colonies of Asia, Africa, and the Middle East.[7] Though some anticolonial proclamations were made, namely during the Vargas government, Brazil maintained a rather contradictory attitude toward colonialism during these initial years. On the one hand, it sought to be consistent with its anticolonial values by declaring support for the right of self-determination. On the other hand, it supported the colonial powers, especially at the UN, on the grounds that it was necessary to achieve conciliatory solutions.

As Asian states gained their independence from the European colonial metropoles, Brazil usually recognized their sovereignty, although only after the formal recognition of the colonial power. Though with a tight-fitting budget that represented less than 1 percent of the total state budget,[8] Itamaraty opened diplomatic representations in India in 1948, Pakistan in 1951, and both Indonesia and Afghanistan in 1953.

In 1949, roughly one year after his arrival to Rio de Janeiro, Indian Ambassador Minocher Rustom Masani surveyed Brazilian knowledge of his home country.[9] He concluded that, with some exceptions, "India was looked on as a country of Oriental glamour and mystery, a country of maharajas and snake-charmers."[10] Brazilian interest in India was confined to the cultural, social, and spiritual impacts of Mahatma Gandhi and Rabindranath Tagore, while knowledge of India's political aspects and challenges was "exceedingly fitful and sketchy." Only small sections of the official class, politicians, and press had "any point of view at all" about India's policies and international positions. And even these learned Brazilians, Masani seemed to imply, had only a basic notion of what modern India was all about or, more important for him, what it could become in the near future.[11]

Although Masani was surveying Brazilian knowledge of his home country, his conclusions could be easily extended to other parts of Asia. General notions about this vast, distant, and diversified continent amounted to stereotypes and prejudices, and only a small section of the society had any informed vision. This is no surprise, as Brazil did not have departments or centers dedicated to Asia, and most of the information it did gather was obtained through an American or European lens. Besides, there was also a lack of interest in the continent. Except for the establishment of diplomatic legations to Beijing and Tokyo in in the late nineteenth century,[12] Brazilians had done little or nothing to interact with Asia, not least because many of its nations were still under colonial rule.[13]

When Brazil decided to establish diplomatic relations with India in 1948, Itamaraty had more in mind than just a deepening of its knowledge of

Indian realities. Brazilians were moved primarily by international and regional prestige, especially vis-à-vis Argentina, with which it maintained an historical rivalry. Wanting to be the first Latin American country to establish formal relations with India, Brazil set up a legation in New Delhi, which was transformed into a full-scale embassy just a few months later. Brazil was also interested in monitoring Cold War developments in South Asia as many political and military leaders believed that the Cold War would soon turn hot and that India could become ground zero of a new conflagration. Finally, a diplomatic representation in India provided the opportunity to directly request Asian votes for Brazilian candidates in several international organizations and forums.[14]

Brazil's immediate objectives were political and economic. Traditionally, Brazil was politically more linked to the United States and Europe and, to a lesser degree, Latin America, while India was essentially terra incognita for Brazilians. Itamaraty knew that the prospects for trade were limited, since Brazil and India shared similar economies, which were essentially agrarian and industrially underdeveloped. In additional to the virtual lack of large national shipping companies with direct trading routes between South America and South Asia, preference for the U.S. dollar as trade currency had a discouraging effect among Brazilians. Under the circumstances, the Brazilian embassy was essentially meant to create a cordial atmosphere in India and, more importantly, to be the eyes and ears of Brazil in Asia.[15]

The mission of the first Brazilian ambassador to India was thus one of courtesy and observation. Recently promoted to ambassador in 1949, Caio de Mello Franco spent his short, two-year tenure in New Delhi collecting and transmitting information regarding general topics, although without detailed analysis, reflections, or comments. Communism, however, deserved attention. A staunch conservative, Mello Franco regularly dispatched alarming cables about the "red peril," a fact that surely contributed to raising grave concerns in Itamaraty about a possible war. During the year 1950, the ambassador feared the threat of an "atomic-hydrogen storm" in Indochina, labeled the potential occupation of Tibet by Communist China as a "threat" to the fragile equilibrium of Asia, and declared that the political situation in Southeast Asia was headed toward an "outcome that the world has foreseen."[16] These catastrophic views were further influenced by growing Communist activities in India. In 1950, the horrified ambassador reported "communist atrocities" that took place in Hyderabad in which "communists killed more than 2,000 people[;] . . . seized and destroyed villages; and burned and occupied lands and properties."[17]

This initial attitude toward India, blending a lack of interest and knowledge with some Cold War paranoia, prevented Brazilians from following India's foreign policy and economic development achievements properly. Without any constructive or active role to play with regard to the Indian government, the embassy staff devoted most of its time to reporting general material on South Asia and India. Considered a difficult, remote, and ill-equipped post in terms of human and material resources, India was underappreciated within the Brazilian diplomatic milieu, and staff turnover was unusually high. Mello Franco's successor, Ambassador Abelardo Bueno do Prado, who took office in March 1952, bargained for votes and sent general reports before leaving for Zurich four months later, never to return.[18]

For its part, India was motivated mainly by the desire to make friends who might subsequently be converted into votes at the UN. Most likely bearing in mind the conflict with Pakistan over Kashmir in early 1948, the Indian Ministry of External Affairs (MEA) concluded that the absence of contacts with Latin America was a "serious handicap" and emphasized the need for establishing relations "with certain Latin American countries such as Argentina, Brazil, Chile and Mexico, in view of the large voting strength of these countries" at the UN.[19] Struggling, however, with thin staffing levels and a tight budget, the MEA eventually selected Brazil for establishing its first embassy in Latin America, followed by Argentina in 1949 and a legation in Mexico a year later.[20] Being the largest and most populous country in South America, Brazil was an obvious choice. However, it was also noted that the country occupied a position of "special significance" in the region, analogous to that of India in its "own surroundings." The assumption that Brazil—like India—was a potential great power, whose emergence would "mean the shifting of the center of world civilization to the tropical zone," ultimately played a key role in this diplomatic decision. From Rio de Janeiro, Indian diplomats believed, it would also be possible to build up a network of contacts with other South American republics and thus to compensate for the lack of direct diplomatic representation there.[21]

Selecting Brazil also served as a way of trying to meet the challenge of overpopulation in India. Constantly in demand for immigrants, Brazil was perceived as a suitable candidate to receive Indian families, as it was underpopulated (considering its size) and without racial prejudices. Although only forty Indian immigrants lived in Brazil—mainly "illiterate, hardworking farmers, peddlers or railway workers . . . most of them married [to] Brazilian women," the Indian government initially considered the idea of initiating a large-scale emigration to Brazil and instructed its ambassador to approach the Brazilian government with a solution that could be of "mutual interest." How much this prospect was decisive in the choice of establishing relations with Brazil remains uncertain, but evidence suggests that it was an important factor.[22]

Apart from these interests, Brazil was hardly an area of importance to India's foreign policy. Economic interests were virtually nonexistent, as the MEA had concluded in an early 1948 assessment, stating that "there are many points of similarity . . . as both [countries] are industrially underdeveloped . . . and it is unlikely that trade with Brazil will develop to a great extent." Ambassador Masani, in a personal letter to Prime Minister Jawaharlal Nehru, confirmed this assessment, maintaining that "India and Brazil are to a remarkable extent in a parallel condition, and parallels don't meet. Our wants are very much the same and our surpluses not too dissimilar." India's embassy would thus function primarily as a listening post in Latin America.[23]

In contrast with that of the Brazilian government, the Indian diplomacy made some efforts to present India as a "modern twentieth century nation" and to reduce the inaccurate picture that predominated in Brazilian minds. Accordingly, monthly and fortnightly bulletins on general topics such as India's agricultural sector, industrial development, and foreign policy were created and distributed. Exhibitions on India were inaugurated and conferences on Indian poets, such as Tagore, were organized. The Indian embassy fostered good relations with the press, as "they never failed to bring out something special whenever we approach them." The ambassador even visited some Brazilian interior states to promote India. The embassy sponsored an organization—the Sociedade Brasileira de Amigos da Índia (Brazilian Society of Friends of India)—to deepen cultural relations between the two countries. Albeit with budget limitations, India displayed a commitment to promoting itself in Brazil.[24]

These publicity efforts eventually paid off, as the embassy registered a growing interest in the press regarding the international position of India, as well as its foreign policy. Writing in 1953, its press attaché observed that "there were far more press comments on India's policy in this period . . . and much greater discussion among the more knowledgeable newspapermen on India's part in world affairs." These comments revealed, according to the diplomat, that "India's independent foreign policy gained considerable respect [and it is] obvious that newspapers in Brazil had begun to think of India as a power to be reckoned with in world affairs." Moreover, as a result, the embassy started to receive information requests on important subjects such as India's attitude toward Communism and colonial powers, as well as India's efforts to solve the Korean dispute.[25]

Although the press displayed growing respect and interest in India's foreign policy, the same was not true when it came to reporting the so-called case of Goa.[26] Echoing the Brazilian government, the local press did not welcome New Delhi's claims over Portuguese colonial territories in India. Early reports sent to the MEA recognized the possibility that Brazilians would not understand and accept India's claims on Goa, Daman, and Diu. "Even though Brazilians may appreciate India's desire to see the end of foreign settlements on India's soil," one of these reports stated, "it is . . . possible that a certain amount of Brazilian sentiment may range itself behind the historical link between Portugal and Goa." This early assessment proved true when India strengthened its diplomatic campaign for the annexation of Goa and its diplomats realized that this sentiment was indeed strong. "Nehru's statement in the House . . . about the merger of Goa with India evoked strongly worded editorials in the press. . . . Brazilians are Portuguese by origin and in spite of the fact they cut away from Portugal, still have a sense of loyalty to their fatherland." Even the intellectual sphere, among which the embassy had marked credibility, showed signs of great hesitation when the subject was broached. "The hold that Portugal has over the intellectual and cultural strata of the Brazilian populace is somewhat different and has to be experienced to be believed," the embassy stated, and sarcastically underlined: "Scratch a Brazilian and he is a Portuguese."[27]

Despite this disagreement, relations between Brazil and India remained cordial—albeit low key. Interactions were indeed confined to solicitation of votes and the project of an agreement on immigration. However, Brazilians had stressed their preference for immigrants who could be "easily assimilated" and could "fit in [Brazilian] cultural patterns and way of life."[28]

Rising Curiosity, 1954-1955

By late 1953, still under the Vargas government, Ildefonso Falcão was appointed ambassador to India. Falcão was a skilled diplomat and had served before in major diplomatic missions, including consular tenures in Berlin, Cologne, and London, as well as an ambassadorial tenure in Athens. Nevertheless, like his predecessors, Falcão was far from being an ideal candidate: having cut his teeth in Europe and in the Americas, he was not familiar with Indian and Asian affairs.[29] But it may be that his irascible temperament was the decisive factor when Itamaraty was desperate to designate an ambassador to such a difficult, distant, and undesirable diplomatic post.[30]

Itamaraty still considered its embassy in New Delhi both as an observation post and as a contact point with Asia. Now, however, it displayed more curiosity toward India and Asia, requesting more and better quality information. Priority topics included decolonization, geostrategic affairs, Communism, and foreign policy. The embassy also devoted attention to India's development programs. "It is of great importance for Brazil to get to know Nehru's decisions, as well as their results. We have very similar problems and, to solve them, we could use the lessons of the Indian experience."[31] This sudden interest in India can be seen in connection with the Vargas government's development programs, which were based on state-led investment in strategic sectors such as petrochemical, metallurgy, and energy. This interest could also have been a result of an increasing awareness of India's economic and development achievements. As previously mentioned, however, Brazilian diplomatic officials seemed more focused in Cold War dynamics.

Itamaraty started to receive numerous reports sent by Falcão on desired topics, particularly regarding economic development in industries such as coffee that competed directly with Brazilian producers. Moreover, information on local Indian products such as mica and cereals was often dispatched to Rio de Janeiro, which led Itamaraty to become aware of opportunities to diversify its markets. According to the ambassador, there were now direct maritime trade connections available between South America and Asia, while Indian manufacturers and businessmen such as tycoon B. M. Birla were interested in fostering trade with Brazil. "India keeps no traditional markets," Falcão informed Itamaraty in one report, adding, "it buys where it finds lower prices and where the quality of products and delivery deadlines are better." As he wrote in summary, India was a great opportunity, and "Brazil needs to sell."[32]

Despite Falcão's enthusiasm and commitment, he quickly stumbled upon inaction from his home country. Simple requests, such as the appointment of an administrative assistant to collect information or a useful list of Brazilian export companies, were denied. Lack of diplomatic staff and money, as well as the absence of Brazilian businessmen interested in trade with India were common obstacles presented by Itamaraty. Sometimes, Falcão did not even get a reply.[33] In May 1955, for instance, the disillusioned ambassador reported that several attempts of the Indian Rohtas Industries to import Brazilian sugar had been unsuccessful. "At my suggestion, the company sent a letter to the president of the Instituto do Açúcar e do Álcool [Sugar and Alcohol Institute], in order to start a 20,000-ton operation," he stated. "Obtaining no response, they sent four cablegrams that have resulted in the same, that is, no response."[34]

Perhaps more confusing to Falcão was the scarce attention given to his reports, especially to those in which he analyzed India's economic development. While sending a report regarding India's second five-year plan, which he considered to be "of great interest [since] the Indian case is one of the most instructive," Falcão took the opportunity to raise criticism regarding the evident lack of interest in his reports. "It is like if I was flogging a dead horse. The extensive material that I have sent ends a few yards away from the archive, without much attention being paid to it," he fumed. "Otherwise, I am sure I would have received many questions regarding several issues that I have raised without details."[35] Such disregard was due not only to the bureaucratic problems that ravaged Itamaraty but also to the fact that the new João Café Filho government was more conservative in economic and foreign policies than its predecessor.

Falcão's admiration of Indian development programs contrasted, nonetheless, with his sharp rejection of its foreign policy, particularly that of its figurehead Jawaharlal Nehru. If at the beginning of his mission he considered Nehru to belong to a "strain of good fighters, Mahatma Gandhi's favorite disciple," by mid-1954 he had already begun to portray him as a "bad pupil of Mahatmaji . . . who has been committing a series of political felonies which threaten peace, not only in Asia but the whole world."[36] According to the embassy, Nehru was "anti-white" and "anti-Western"; he employed a "sinister picturesque neutral policy" and exhibited an "extreme ambition of leadership, not only regarding the Indian region but also the modern world." The 1955 Conference of Bandung, in his opinion, merely served "to activate [Nehru's] plan of Afro-Asian unity . . . and emphasize the leadership of India among all the countries of this region" as India's "supremacy constitutes the great dream of his personal policy." Although Falcão would later concede that the Afro-Asian conference was a "remarkable happening, of great significance"—not least because from a Western perspective, the conference results were considered quite to be quite moderate and thus a matter for some relief—Falcão immediately underlined Nehru's failure in taking over the leadership.[37] Moreover, he viewed with extreme suspicion Nehru's dual foreign policy: while entertaining relations with the United States, India traded with and courted Communist nations, including the Soviet Union.[38]

Despite his criticism of India's flirtation with Communist nations, particularly with the Soviet Union, Falcão recognized that such policy was paying a dividend, as India was receiving significant aid from Washington. "The Western nations and specifically the United States, court favors from Nehru's India as they would court favors from a brunette sly goodness who refuses to be seduced," Falcão ironically reported. "And why? Assuming that India leans toward communism, they fear . . . that millions of starving Indians join the red hosts." This led Falcão to touch a raw nerve, even for those diplomats who supported alignment with the United States. Despite Brazil's ties to Washington, the country had been "spurned to the inferior status of a poor parent that people are ashamed of inviting home. We are loyal, we ask with a hat in hand, and we received in exchange, most of the time, promises." On the other hand, Falcão furiously reported, India was "doubtful, Machiavellian, audacious, and treacherous" and as a result "she will receive what it [sic] wished for."[39]

As a way of obtaining financial aid from Washington, Falcão proposed a variant of the Indian formula, which many nationalist Brazilians called for: economic rapprochement with the Iron Curtain nations, particularly the Soviet Union, and the establishment of diplomatic relations with Communist China. "The United States reaction would be immediate and, if not, the commercial benefits that we could obtain . . . would allow us to wait for the arrival of U.S. dollars," he wrote to Itamaraty. Besides, "Brazilian products [such as coffee] would find a market and many types of machinery would reach Brazil in more advantageous financial conditions."[40] This audacious suggestion by Falcão went unanswered, like many others sent by the ambassador during his frustrating tenure. The highest echelons of Itamaraty were still occupied by staunch anti-Communists, who brooked little patience for talk about the reestablishment of political or economic relations with the Soviet Union or establishment of diplomatic relations with Communist China.

Falcão's ambassadorship in New Delhi coincided with the escalation of tension between Portugal and India over Goa. In late 1953, the Indian government implemented economic sanctions against the Portuguese territories and created bureaucratic hurdles to hamper the movement of Portuguese officials and citizens. As had so often occurred in the past, the Portuguese regime responded with violent repression and numerous arrests. In early 1954, Itamaraty was informed that the situation was indeed delicate, and it reaffirmed solidarity with Portugal. Sooner or later, this would require some show of solidarity for Lisbon in New Delhi itself.[41]

Indeed, just a few months after the arrival of Ambassador Falcão in New Delhi, Brazil was involved in a rather delicate incident regarding the problem of Goa. Cautioned by the Portuguese ambassador in India, Falcão was informed that Brazil's honorary consul in New Delhi—Jaime Herédia—had organized meetings in the consulate with anti-Portuguese Goan activists. Although Falcão eventually informed Itamaraty, he first decided to admonish the consul regarding what he considered to be an illicit activity. Not only were Brazilian diplomatic and consular staff forbidden to take part in political activities, but Brazil's policy toward Goa was officially defined by Rio de Janeiro. Heredia capitalized on this in order to embarrass the Brazilian government and create a scandal. Presenting his resignation and taking his case to Indian newspapers, he soon became a local hero. The MEA followed by criticizing Itamaraty for its attitude toward the incident. Although both governments eventually swept the episode under the rug, it was clear that disagreement on Goa could become a sticking point between Brazil and India.[42]

When the Indian government countenanced the nationalist occupation of the small Portuguese enclaves of Dadrá and Nagar-Haveli by "peaceful groups" (*satyagraha*) in July and August 1954, diplomatic relations between Rio de Janeiro and New Delhi entered a downward spiral. Falcão received instructions to present a formal protest to the Indian capital, and virtually all the Brazilian embassies in the world were requested to inform the local governments about India's attitude toward the "peaceful" country of Portugal. In Rio de Janeiro, the Indian ambassador was convened for a friendly but tense meeting. According to Sen-Mandi, Brazilians were "really serious about the matter now and wanted something to be done first to ease the tension," since they believed that the situation between Portugal and India could "take a very ugly turn." In addition, the Indian embassy dutifully reported the mass rally organized by the local Portuguese community and the anti-India protests raised by members of Parliament in both the Chamber of Deputies and the Senate.[43] The press, once again, expressed Brazilian indignation against what it considered an intolerable aggression, going so far as to call it a "Hitler- and Mussolini-style Anschluss."[44]

After this "hysterical" reaction, as the Indian ambassador put it, Jawaharlal Nehru sought to take advantage of Krishna Menon's brief visit to Latin American to ease tensions and improve relations. Interestingly, Itamaraty was ready to receive Nehru's envoy, but with a slight nuance: Portuguese Foreign Minister Paulo Cunha was expected in Rio de Janeiro, and the Brazilian government demonstrated a clear willingness to give him priority.[45]

While Menon ended up excluding Brazil from his visit, the Indian government decided to go ahead with the visit of Sarvepalli Radhakrishnan, vice president of India, already scheduled for November 1954. The first Indian statesman to pay a visit to Brazil, the vice president, did not include discussion of the problem of Goa on his agenda.[46]

A more complex stage of relations emerged in 1955, when Brazil assumed the representation of Portuguese interests in India after the rupture of diplomatic relations between the two nations. Although he had no detailed directives, Falcão aimed to play the role of an intermediary between the two parties. Still, he was apparently treated by India as a mere defender of Portuguese colonialism. "After assuming the protection of Portuguese interests, the hostility toward Brazil significantly increased," he reported. "We are now treated . . . with the very same coldness that had been up to now reserved for the Portuguese. . . . we are considered a kind of continuation and surrogate of Portugal." Despite his best efforts, Falcão sensed that India was trying to hamper his mission: for months Indian authorities delayed *de jure* recognition of Brazil as representative of Portuguese interests. Moreover, the Indian government tried to block the reopening of the Brazilian consulate in Bombay, where a colony of around 100,000 Goans lived and worked, in addition to ignoring Portuguese correspondence delivered by the embassy, and in some cases even avoiding interaction with Falcão personally.[47]

Although there are no relevant Indian sources available to cover this particular moment, available evidence suggests that the irascible personality of Falcão, combined with his staunch lusophilia and increasing aversion to Indian authorities, contributed greatly to misunderstandings. Indeed, his reports revealed biased attitudes toward India, which ultimately made him lose credibility both in New Delhi and in Rio de Janeiro. In September 1955, for instance, Falcão held a very tense conversation with Jawaharlal Nehru on the issue of Goa. According to his report, after what he considered to be another unproductive conversation, Falcão stood up and said, "I am sorry, Excellency, to come for the second time in your office and realize the inutility of my mission as ambassador of Brazil. . . . After transmitting with success, the request of my Government, I can only now officially ask for my withdrawal from your country." Perhaps already fed up with Falcão, Nehru replied simply, "Do whatever you think is best."[48] The report on the meeting left a bad impression on Itamaraty, particularly Falcão's suggestion to close the embassy. Nevertheless, he was kept in office for a few more months until newly elected president Juscelino Kubitschek could appoint a new ambassador.⁴⁹ Inadvertently, Falcão had demonstrated to some sectors in Itamaraty that political and diplomatic support for Portuguese colonialism in India could indeed result in serious entanglements.

Kubitschek's Brazil and India, 1956–1961

In 1956, Juscelino Kubitschek de Oliveira (1956–61) was officially sworn in as president of Brazil. Energetic, self-confident, and optimistic, he ran for office with a development plan that promised fifty years of development in five (*50 anos em cinco*). The so-called Programa de Metas (Targets Plan) envisioned significant investments in several strategic sectors of the Brazilian economy: namely, energy, transportation, food, basic industries, and education. Its main objective was to move Brazil beyond its longtime agricultural vocation, away from its chronic underdevelopment, and far from its deep-rooted pessimism. A major symbol of this will-to-modernize was the construction of a new capital—Brasília. Provided for in the constitution since the late nineteenth century, the city was planned from scratch in the late 1950s with the goal of presenting to the world a new Brazil: modern, rational, and organized. Regionally, Kubitschek aimed for his country to lead the way to a more developed, prosperous, and influential Latin America, a hope that would later spread with the arrival of other *desenvolvimentistas* (developmentalists), such as Argentina's Arturo Frondizi and Mexico's Adolfo López Mateos.⁵⁰ Even Brazilian Communist Luis Carlos Prestes praised this bold vision, writing in 1958 that "Kubitschek is the Nehru of South America."⁵¹

Juscelino Kubitschek's foreign policy was essentially focused on issues of economic development. Even before taking office, he visited major political and economic centers such as the United States, Great Britain, the Netherlands, Belgium, France, Italy, and the Federal Republic of Germany, in addition to Spain and Portugal, with which Brazil had a special relationship. Kubitschek's objective was to demonstrate that Brazil's economic development program, which was based largely on private investment, would welcome foreign capital. The highest expression of his economic diplomacy was the launch of Operação Pan Americana (Operation Pan America) following on the heels of U.S. vice president Richard Nixon's disastrous visit to Latin America in 1958, in which an attack on Nixon's motorcade occurred in Caracas, Venezuela. The Operação was a proposal for inter-American cooperation, which sought to attract U.S. economic assistance as a sort of Marshall Plan for Latin America, on the grounds that economic underdevelopment represented fertile soil for the spread of Communism and a threat to hemispheric security.[52]

Although firmly anchored to the West and particularly to the Inter-American System, Kubitschek's Brazil initiated a tepid, albeit remarkable, rapprochement with the nations of the Iron Curtain. Bearing in mind Brazil's economic needs, Itamaraty was forced to set aside its ideological bias and opened trade negotiations in 1958 with Hungary, Poland, and the German Democratic Republic. A year later, after much deliberation and controversy, Brazil even reestablished commercial relations with the Soviet Union. This was not only the product of Brazil's need to expand its markets, especially for coffee exports, but also a result of concrete domestic pressures. Indeed, several political and commercial sectors in the society were concerned that postwar Brazil's "blind" alignment to the United States was not paying off as initially expected. Rapprochement with the Soviet Union, moreover, could work as a way to win concessions in the United States. Kubitschek's initial objective was to reestablish political and diplomatic relations with Moscow, but anti-Communist sentiments were still very strong in Itamaraty. He was thus able only to reestablish trade relations in the late 1950s. President Jânio Quadros would complete this political rapprochement in 1961.[53]

Despite the fact that Brazil maintained a contradictory foreign policy with regard colonialism, tacitly and sometimes openly supporting the European colonial powers while generally claiming to support the granting of independence to colonial territories, Kubitschek took concrete steps toward rapprochement with newly independent nations. Recognizing that the Afro-Asian world was "no longer a mere backyard of the Western countries," Itamaraty opened diplomatic legations in Malaysia, Thailand, South Vietnam, Tunisia, and Morocco in 1959, followed a year later with offices in Ceylon and Ghana.[54] In 1961, when he was in a lame-duck position, Kubitschek initiated the process of establishing diplomatic relations with Senegal, Mauritania, Guinea, Nigeria, the Ivory Coast, Upper Volta, Niger, and Dahomey. These actions were responses not only to the growing political importance of the postcolonial world but also to Brazil's perceived need for building consensus for tackling the problems of economic underdevelopment at the UN and in other international forums.[55] In 1959, Kubitschek invited Indonesia's president, Sukarno, to visit Brazil as part of these same efforts. Increasingly, Brazil also began to envision postcolonial Asia as an attractive market for its exports. In 1959, Itamaraty dispatched an economic mission to Southeast Asia to collect information about the economic structures of the region as well as to investigate the possibilities for trade.[56]

Kubitschek's approach to the postcolonial world was especially visible in his attempt to normalize relations with India. In mid-1956, Itamaraty replaced its ambassador to India, Ildefonso Falcão, whose trustworthiness in the MEA had been weakened by his strongly partisan attitude regarding Goa. In his place, Itamaraty appointed José Cochrane de Alencar, formerly Brazil's first diplomatic representative to India (1948) and most recently its ambassador to Pakistan (1955–56). Like Falcão, Ambassador Alencar was an experienced diplomat with several other important appointments under his belt, including Vienna, London, Canberra, and Stockholm. Alencar, however, was wiser and more balanced, ultimately serving as a pragmatic diplomat who proved to be much less passionate about Brazil's perceived connection to Portuguese colonial assets.

Recognizing the rising importance of India and other postcolonial nations in international affairs, Itamaraty wished to remove the "suspicion of connivance with colonialism" that haunted Brazil's international image. Despite Brazil's claims to be an anticolonial power, the country's UN delegation had consistently supported the colonial powers, frequently abstaining on resolutions that dealt with colonial self-determination. Brazil should now offer its justification for such votes—namely, its desire to secure an atmosphere of equilibrium in which to carry out a peaceful transfer of power in the colonial territories. Resorting to the theories of Brazilian sociologist Gilberto Freyre, who contributed to the myth of Brazil as a "racial democracy,"[57] Itamaraty advised Alencar to emphasize Brazilian society's non-European cultural traits and the supposed nonexistence of racial prejudices in order to downplay suspicions. This became a distinct line of approach in Brazil's diplomacy throughout the 1960s and 1970s, especially in relation to African countries. Through a "courteous" approach toward Indian authorities, Brazilians believed, it would be possible to elucidate Brazil's options in the UN and thus obtain positive political results in the short run.[58] Still without definite policy for Asia, Itamaraty seemed to envisage some kind of collaboration between Brazil and India, based on the two countries' role as active voices against economic underdevelopment. This led Itamaraty to demonstrate a great deal of interest in post-Bandung Afro-Asian developments, and it therefore instructed Alencar to pay "special attention" to this movement. While Cold War neutralism was not an option for Brazil (since Brazil adhered to the Inter-American Treaty of

Reciprocal Assistance but comprised an anti-Communist government, military, and diplomatic staff), the country showed some willingness to send official observers to future Afro-Asian gatherings.[59]

In October 1956, the incoming ambassador met Nehru and Foreign Secretary Subimal Dutt to present credentials and gestures of goodwill. After the disastrous tenure of Falcão, this beginning could prove a new start in Brazilian-Indian relations. Notably, Nehru and Dutt comported themselves with "extreme courtesy," warmly welcoming Alencar and praising the "friendly relationship" between Brazil and India. Both expressed hope that the relationship between the two great nations would not be negatively affected by the fact that Brazil continued to represent Portuguese interests in India. Alencar replied in the same friendly spirit, mentioning that the Brazilian government yearned to strengthen the ties that already bound the two nations and guaranteeing that he would personally invest his "best efforts" to ensure relations between Brazil and Indian government were as "cordial and respectful as possible."[60] Although Falcão had only recently departed, it seems as if both governments were ready to turn the page. To be sure, Goa remained a problem, but the admission of Portugal into the UN in 1955 was a contributing factor to easing the atmosphere between Lisbon and New Delhi, since India exchanged the acts in the terrain for acts in the Fourth Committee (also known as the Special Political and Decolonization Committee).

Bearing in mind his instructions, epitomized by the sentence "Introduce Brazil to India," Alencar reestablished and reinforced diplomatic contacts with India's officials, reported on India's economic and industrial development in detail, and adopted a more impartial posture with regard to Goa. Like his predecessor, however, Alencar was concerned with India's foreign policy and its impact. Refusing to comment on the Cold War's "moral dimension"—clearly bearing in mind an expression used by U.S. Secretary of State Foster Dulles to characterize neutralism—Alencar noted that Nehru "was right when he decided that it would be better not to join one of the two opposing blocks in conflict." "Some argue," he stated in an official letter, "that India has not a single friend. . . . If, however, the success or failure of a policy is measured by its results, it seems to me . . . that [for] the actual position and prestige of this country, [Nehru] appears to have weighed [his decisions] with great sense and much wisdom." Alencar would repeatedly draw the attention of Itamaraty to nonaligned matters throughout his mission in New Delhi (1956–61). Restating Falcão's conclusion from the previous year that India had become a priority while Brazil was struggling to obtain a modicum of useful attention from the United States, Alencar observed that India was receiving a series of indispensable loans from Washington to fund its five-year plans. At the same time, India was also signing trade and cultural agreements with countries such as the German Democratic Republic, Czechoslovakia, Poland, and, of course, the Soviet Union. As a Brazilian diplomat put it, "India continues to negotiate and conclude agreements with everyone, whether Tyrians or Trojans, as long as it could derive maximum benefits from these."[61] To what extent these observations helped the supporters of Brazil's rapprochement with the "Iron Curtain" remains uncertain, but even a casual observer could not deny that neutralism, in practice, was actually paying more dividends than alignment.

On its side, the Indian government had an interest in normalizing relations with Brazil. Accordingly, a July 1956 MEA report expressed some "anxiety to create more cordial relations between India and Brazil." India's former ambassador to Brazil, Raja of Mandi, even suggested that as a preliminary step New Delhi should conclude a cultural agreement with Rio de Janeiro.[62] Although Brazil was not a priority in India's foreign policy, New Delhi was keenly aware of its diplomatic weight. Rio de Janeiro exerted a considerable, and sometimes decisive, influence in Latin America, had significant international prestige, and had already secured a seat on the UN Security Council three times (1946–47, 1951–52, and 1954–55). Besides, Brazil belonged to one of the largest regional groups in the UN, and India had already paid a concrete political price for ignoring it. When the Kashmir issue was discussed and voted on at the Security Council, in which Latin American nations exercised considerable influence, the Argentine delegates had assumed, at certain moments, a partisan attitude against India.[63] The same was true in the case of Portuguese India. Although on a different scale, many Latin American nations had criticized the Indian government for turning a blind eye to the *satyagraha* occupiers in 1954 and 1955.[64]

The MEA was aware of the political as well as the economic and cultural benefits that warm relations with Latin America could provide. Yet constraints on financial and human resources prevented proper diplomatic outreach. Indeed, in 1949 and again in 1952, the question of opening additional missions in Latin American countries was debated in the MEA, resulting in only one additional mission, in Chile, bringing to four the number of Indian diplomatic offices in Latin America, counting Brazil, Argentina, and Mexico. In 1955–56, this question was revisited by the MEA on the grounds that "India [was] assuming more and more responsibilities in international affairs and it [was] important that her point of view is widely known." Once again, the dearth of personnel as well as the tight budget of the Indian Foreign Service prevented the opening of any new missions.[65]

To mitigate this handicap, just after his official visit to the United States in late 1956, Nehru began to contemplate a wide-ranging state visit across South America. After all, he had already been to North America twice and failed both times to follow up with a visit to the hemisphere's southern half. Such idea was not a new one: roughly eight years before, Ambassador Masani had already proposed a whistle-stop tour of several South American states, including Brazil, which he believed could create a "marked and enduring impression" on Latin American governments.[66] Nehru himself had expressed privately on several occasions his great willingness to visit the South American republics, specifically the region's largest and most important states, Brazil and Argentina.[67] During the first half of 1957, Nehru received official invitations from the Chilean and Argentine governments, and he later met Chilean and Peruvian officials in New Delhi.[68] These overtures led the French press to report that Nehru would pay a state visit to several South American countries in 1958, including Argentina and Chile, in order to establish more direct contacts and thus "reinforce the Afro-Asian group in the UN."[69]

These combined developments eventually attracted the attention of the Brazilian government. Itamaraty had initially downplayed the possibility of Nehru's state visit to South American countries, which was reported in several official letters sent by Ambassador Alencar, who requested that Brazil extend an official invitation to Nehru since the country "was the first Latin American nation to establish an embassy" in India years earlier. But when several newspapers in Rio de Janeiro reported the scheduled visit to South America—stressing that Argentina but not Brazil was included in the route—Itamaraty merely requested information from its ambassadors in New Delhi and Buenos Aires. Despite their confirmation of this report, Itamaraty took no action.[70]

In early 1958, Alencar received information indicating that Nehru's visit to South America was still in the works, although he now learned that it was dependent on a Brazilian invitation. Indeed, after a conversation with Miguel Serrano, Chilean ambassador to India, Alencar learned that Foreign Minister Subimal Dutt had confessed that the Brazilian government had not yet extended an invitation. A similar observation was made by another Indian diplomat to his Mexican counterpart. For Alencar, this was the proof that "Nehru's trip to South America will be delayed, for multiple reasons, until Brazil decided to present an official invitation."[71] Although Alencar's assessments might seem exaggerated, a few weeks later Nehru gave his very first interview to a Brazilian newspaper, *Correio da Manhã*, in which he stressed the similarities between Brazil and India, underlined the need for a greater economic and cultural interchange, and ultimately expressed his hope that he and the newspaper's journalist would to meet again soon in "India or Brazil."[72]

Still without any move from Rio de Janeiro, the Indian government finally decided to raise the bar. In June 1958, India's ambassador to Brazil delivered an official invitation to Kubitschek for a state visit to India later that year. This gesture was a way of demonstrating that India was keen on strengthening its ties with Brazil and that it wanted its president to have the honor of being the first Latin American statesman to visit India. By inviting President Kubitschek before any other, India was also revealing that its government considered Brazil to be the most important country in the region for its Third World policy. Although Indian sources are lacking for this period, one should also consider that Nehru wished to send a strong signal to the Brazilian government on the question of his future visit to South America. Indeed, the head of Itamaraty's Political Division, Luis Bastian Pinto, immediately recognized that the Brazilian government "for obvious reasons cannot avoid inviting Nehru to visit Brazil should he come to South America." Alencar, moreover, reported that Kubitschek's invitation was "of high significance," given his proposed Operação Pan America as well as the great Indian interest in achieving rapprochement with Rio de Janeiro.[73]

The Indian invitation, however, unleashed other forces unconnected to Brazil-India relations. Portugal's recently appointed ambassador to Brazil, Manuel Rocheta, rushed immediately to Itamaraty to convey his government's deepest concern. Rapprochement of this kind between Brazil and India, he warned, would be considered a "serious setback" in the historically friendly relationship between Portugal and Brazil. Moreover, the Portuguese diplomat underlined that public association between Brazil and a nonaligned nation could be counterproductive for the success of the Operação Pan Americana. Despite Portugal's entreaties, Itamaraty refused to reject the possibility of a Nehru invitation, even if it considered Kubitschek going forward with a state visit to India later that year improbable.[74]

Domestic forces also mobilized, not just in Itamaraty, but also in Catete, the residence and workplace of presidents, where many sensed that rapprochement could be highly productive for a more "independent" foreign policy. Those connected to economic and trade affairs also lent support for rapprochement with India. Some nationalist Brazilians even hoped for the possibility that an initiation of dialogue with India could lead Brazil into the nonaligned camp. On the other hand, the idea of dialogue with India horrified the more conservative sectors of Itamaraty, as they considered Brazil to be firmly anchored to the West, particularly through the framework of the Inter-American Rio Treaty. These voices were obviously the ones that were also opposed to the reestablishment of relations with the Soviet Union.[75] Pressured by all sides, Kubitschek faced a diplomatic dilemma and refused to make an immediate decision. Alencar, invited to an informal meeting with Nehru, received strict instructions to avoid the issue entirely, allegedly because his government was under "huge pressure" from the Portuguese embassy.[76]

Indeed, domestic conservatives and the Portuguese ambassador eventually combined efforts, agreeing to separately contact the U.S. embassy in Rio de Janeiro. The secretary-general of Itamaraty, a conservative and arch anti-Communist, conveyed his deep concern about a possible rapprochement between Brazil and India, hoping to provoke a reaction from Washington. Portuguese Ambassador Rocheta suggested to U.S. embassy attaché Woodruff Wallner that Kubitschek was being misinformed by his advisors, who falsely claimed that a presidential visit to India would somehow benefit Brazilian and U.S. interests in South Asia. A few days later, Waller confirmed the State Department's disapproval of a Kubitschek visit to India while also rejecting any direct U.S. *démarches*. Such an action, Washington feared, could be regarded as interference by the United States in Brazilian affairs.[77]

Perhaps surprisingly, Kubitschek accepted the invitation.[78] Compelled by his view that it was in Brazil's economic and foreign policy interests, Kubitschek was also aware that the Argentine president, Arturo Frondizi, had just been invited to New Delhi, and Kubitschek wanted to seize the honor of being the first Latin American statesman to visit independent India. A few days later, however, Brazil's ambassador to Washington, Walther Moreira Salles, was persuaded by high-ranking Itamaraty officials to convince Kubitschek of the alleged dangers associated with rapprochement between Brazil and India.[79] Facing congressional elections in October and hoping to avoid unnecessary controversies, Kubitschek backed down. As it turned out, he would eventually visit India in December 1961, but as a senator of the republic rather than as president.[80]

After this failed attempt at a major breakthrough in Brazilian-Indian relations, the two countries returned to the status quo, characterized by low-key interactions. Although many Brazilians looked with sympathy and admiration toward India, Brazil under Kubitschek still considered association with Nehru to be too dangerous. Even in mid-1960, when Brazil had the chance to redeem itself thanks to an interest by Indian National Congress leader Indira Gandhi to include Brazil in the route of her goodwill visit to Latin America, the Brazilians once again ruled out an invitation.[81] Commenting on Itamaraty in early 1961, the Indian ambassador stated that "there is no real interest in Asian and African countries or their problems. . . . Despite its high-sounding and oft-repeated declarations on liberty, democracy, on fighting against colonialism, against racial discrimination, [Itamaraty] is a stronghold of conservatism."[82]

Conclusion

Brazil's interactions with India from 1947 to 1961 show that the South American country demonstrated real interest in Asia. During the immediate postwar years, this interest was driven by Cold War assumptions, followed soon after by a broader Brazilian curiosity in India's model for modernization and Nehru's nonaligned foreign policy. Together, these factors caught the attention of some within Itamaraty and prompted some tepid reappraisals of Brazil's international posture. Early Brazilian ambassadors to India embodied this paradox, with sentiments ranging from envy to admiration, the latter leading to bold suggestions that Brazil might do well to emulate India's dynamic foreign policy. Itamaraty eventually displayed interest in the Bandung movement and notably considered sending an observation mission to forthcoming Afro-Asian summits. Considered within this context, Brazil's participation in the Belgrade meeting of nonaligned nations in 1961 represented the culmination of a process first initiated in 1956.

This is not to say that Brazil was overly willing to engage in an active partnership with neutralist India. Because it was firmly anchored to the Western camp, Brazil's rapprochement with India, and to a certain extent with other postcolonial Asian nations, was limited to specific and "immediate" national interests, particularly the solicitation of votes for Brazil at the UN and other international forums, as well as some loose coordination in the struggle against economic underdevelopment. Political interactions remained scant: mere association with nonaligned nations was still perceived by Brazilian elites as not only immoral but also potentially damaging to the Western effort against Communist advances. Even as some Brazilian officials advocated for close collaboration with India, conservatives retained great influence within Itamaraty, a reality that limited subsequent outreach by both President Jânio Quadros (1961) and President João Goulart (1961–64). Economically, the partnership was also something of a mirage: the distance between the two countries, a persisting information gap, the lack of concrete trade links, and to some extent a lack of political will made further inroads virtually impossible.

For its part, India also demonstrated genuine interest in Brazil. Through a cultural and publicity campaign, Indians sought to project a positive image of their nation, including in the areas of culture, economic development, and foreign policy. The case of Goa deserved additional efforts (and evidence suggests the same was true for Kashmir) in order to rally support from the Brazilian government, media, and public opinion, although without significant success. On balance, India was slightly more interested in rapprochement with Brazil, and with Latin America as a whole, as demonstrated by Nehru's attempts to exchange state visits during Kubitschek's late 1950s government. While more archival research is needed, available evidence suggests that national interests prompted outreach, which, in turn, would accrue benefits such as trade, enhanced international prestige, and expansion of influence elsewhere in the Third World.

Notes

This research was made possible by support provided by the Fundação para a Ciência e Tecnologia and the European University Institute. I would like to thank the editors and the anonymous reviewers. A special thanks to Sofia Tonicher. This chapter is dedicated to the memory of my dearest friend, Thierry Dias Coelho.

1. See José Flávio Sombra Saraiva, *O Lugar da África. A dimensão Atlântica da política externa brasileira (de 1946 a nossos dias)* (Brasília: Editora Universidade de Brasília, 1996), 21–58.

2. Varun Sahni, "India and Latin America," in *Engaging the World: Indian Foreign Policy since 1947*, ed. Sumit Ganguly (Oxford: Oxford University Press, 2016), 380–81.

3. Varun Sahni, "Brazil: Fellow Traveler on the Long and Winding Road to Grandeza," in *The Oxford Handbook of Indian Foreign Policy*, ed. David M. Malone, C. Raja Mohan, and Srinath Raghavan (Oxford: Oxford University Press, 2015), 524–38; Ananya Chakravarti, "Peripheral Eyes: Brazilians and India, 1947–61," *Journal of Global History* 10, no. 1 (2015): 122–46.

4. Jerry Dávila, *Hotel Trópico. Brazil and the Challenge of African Decolonization, 1950–1980* (Durham, NC: Duke University Press, 2010); Williams da Silva Gonçalves, *O Realismo da fraternidade: Brasil-Portugal* (Lisboa: Instituto de Ciências Sociais, 2013).

5. For the period between the Revolution of 1930 and the democratization, see Leslie Bethell, "Politics in Brazil under Vargas, 1930–1945," in *The Cambridge His-*

tory of Latin America, Volume IX. Brazil since 1930, ed. Leslie Bethell (New York: Cambridge University Press, 2008), 3-86. For the process of democratization, see Leslie Bethell, "Politics in Brazil under the Liberal Republic, 1945-1964," in *The Cambridge History of Latin America, Volume IX*, 87-100; and Thomas E. Skidmore, *Politics in Brazil, 1930-1964: An Experiment in Democracy* (Oxford: Oxford University Press, 2007), 48-64. In Portuguese, see Lilia M. Schwarcz and Heloisa M. Starling, *Brasil: Uma biografia* (São Paulo: Companhia das Letras, 2015), and Boris Fausto, *História do Brasil* (São Paulo: Edusp, 2012). For a more detailed account, see, for instance, Ângela Maria de Castro Gomes, Eli Diniz, Aspásia de Alcântara Camargo, Antônio Mendes de Almeida Jr., Ricardo Maranhão, Helgio Trindade, Ítali Tronca, et al., *O Brasil republicano: Sociedade e política (1930-1964)* (Rio de Janeiro: Bertrand Brasil, 1996).

6. See Gerson Moura, *Brazilian foreign Relations: 1939-1950: The Changing Nature of Brazil-United States Relations during and after the Second World War* (Brasília: FUNAG, 2013), 237-300; Mônica Hirst, *The United States and Brazil: A Long Road of Unmet Expectations* (New York: Routledge, 2005), 1-7; Stanley E. Hilton, "The United States, Brazil and the Cold War, 1945-1960: End of the Special Relationship," *Journal of American History* 68, no. 3 (1981): 599-624. In Portuguese, see Amado Luiz Cervo, *Inserção Internacional: Formação dos Conceitos Brasileiros* (São Paulo: Saraiva, 2008), Luiz Alberto Moniz Bandeira, *Presença dos Estados Unidos no Brasil* (Rio de Janeiro: Civilização Brasileira, 2007); Letícia de Abreu Pinheiro, *Política Externa Brasileira, 1889-2002* (Rio de Janeiro: Jorge Zahar Ed., 2004); Amado Luiz Cervo and Clodoaldo Bueno, *História da Política Exterior do Brasil* (São Paulo: Editora Ática, 1992).

7. Wayne Alan Selcher, "The Afro-Asian Dimension of Brazilian Foreign Policy, 1956-1968," PhD diss., University of Florida, 1970, 240.

8. Calculated by the author.

9. On M. R. Masani, see Zareer Masani, *And All Is Said* (New Delhi: Penguin, 2012).

10. M. R. Masani to Nehru, 30 August 1948, File (henceforth F) 2 (4) / 49 AMS (Americas) Division; Indian Embassy in Rio (henceforth IER), "Report on Brazil, Confidential, June 1948-June 1949," 11 September 1949, F 2 (52) AMS 49, National Archives of India (henceforth NAI).

11. M. R. Masani to Nehru, 30 August 1948.

12. Cervo, *Inserção Internacional*, 274.

13. In 1957, the Itamaraty still concluded that Asia was a "huge region that only exists in the headlines. . . . If we exclude India's peculiar case . . . Brazilian missions and consulates in Asia only serve to bargain, from time to time, votes for candidates to the United Nations . . . and to send invitations for conferences." Ministério das Relações Exteriores (henceforth MRE), Memorandum Confidencial, Divisão Política (henceforth [DP]), 3, 3 January 1957, Arquivo do Ministério das Relações Exteriores (henceforth AMRE).

14. Embaixada do Brasil em Nova Delhi (henceforth EMBND) to MRE, Carta-Telegrama (henceforth CT) 12, 24 December 1948; EMBND to MRE, CT 3, 5 January 1959; EMBND to MRE, CT 43, 3 December 1949, all in Arquivo Histórico do Itamaraty (henceforth AHI).

15. EMBND to MRE, Telegrama (henceforth T) 28, 19 September 1950, AHI.

16. EMBND to MRE, CT 21, 16 February 1950, EMBND to MRE, CT 42, 4 May 1959, EMBND to MRE, CT 56, 2 June 1950, AHI.

17. EMBND to MRE, CT 50, 16 May 1950, AHI.

18. EMBND to MRE, CT 8, 20 May 1952, AHI.

19. Ministry of External Affairs (henceforth MEA), Extract of Note by Mr. B. Shiva Rao, 3 February 1948, F 2 (4) / AMS 49, NAI.

20. IER, M. R. Masani to Bajpai, 12 August 1948, F 2 (4) / AMS 49, NAI.

21. IER, "Report on Brazil, Confidential, June 1948–June 1949," and MEA, "Report of Min. E. A. & Commonwealth Relations, 1948–49," 12, Ministry of External Affairs Library, Ministry of External Affairs.

22. IER, Fortnightly Report No. 9, 16 November 1948, F 2 Research & Innovation (henceforth R&I) 48; IER, "Report on Brazil, Confidential."

23. Office of the Economic Adviser to the Government of India, "A note on trade possibilities with Brazil," 20 March 1948, F 2 (4) / AMS 49, NAI.

24. M. R. Masani to Nehru, 27 December 1948, F 2 (4) / AMS 49; EIR, "Fortnightly Report 21," 16 May 1949, F 58 R&I 49; IER, "Annual Press Report (From May to December, 1949)," 27 December 1949, F 3 (5) R&I 50; and "Report on Brazil, Confidential."

25. IER, "Yearly Publicity Report for the Year 1953, Secret," F S54 13514 87, NAI.

26. On Goa, see Sandrine Bègue, *La fin de Goa et de l'Estado da Índia. Décolonisation et Guerre Froide dans le Sous-Continent Indien (1945–1962)*, vols. 1 and 2 (Lisboa: Ministério dos Negócios Estrangeiros, 2007).

27. IER, "Press Report, January–June 1950, Secret," F 3 (5) R&I 50, NAI.

28. IER, "Report on Brazil, Confidential."

29. EMBND to MRE, Ofício (henceforth O) 18, 29 January 1954, AHI.

30. Brazilian *chargé d'affaires* Rodolfo de Souza Dantas summed up the spirit of Brazilian diplomats during their missions in India. When asked by the Itamaraty to give his opinion about the closure of the consulate in Calcutta, Dantas replied:

> Calcutta is, undoubtedly, one of India's major metropolises . . . that provides little comfort to foreigners. . . . The climate is terrible, many times more depressing than Delhi or Bombay. . . . People are extremely poor, with no hygienic habits; they wander the streets . . . like starving dogs. . . . The human scum are afflicted with outbreaks of unparalleled diseases and turn Calcutta into the cradle of almost all epidemics that regularly strike India. Water, vegetables, meat, the air, it all serves as a fertile ground for the most dangerous microbes, and foreigners need to buy canned food from abroad. . . . Cholera, malaria, and smallpox join the communists to make life even more unbearable. Calcutta is the larger red area of the country; one avoids going there as one avoids to visiting an asylum of lepers. (EMBND to MRE, O 23, 7 June 1953, AHI)

31. MRE to EMBND, Despacho (henceforth D) 8, 28 November 1953, AHI.

32. EMBND to MRE, O 129, 25 July 1954, EMBND to MRE, O 130, 26 July 1954, EMBND to MRE, O 113, 30 June 1954, EMBND to MRE, O 133, 28 July 1954, EMBND

to MRE, O 164, 10 September 1954, EMBND to MRE, O 219, 11 November 1954, EMBND to MRE, CT 6, 15 April 1955, AHI.

33. EMBND to MRE, O 119, 6 July 1954, EMBND to MRE, CT 8, 19 May 1955, EMBND to MRE, CT 29, 30 November 1955, AHI.

34. EMBND to MRE, O 133, 11 May 1955, AHI.

35. EMBND to MRE, O 185, 10 June 1955, AHI.

36. EMBND to MRE, O 4, 7 January 1954, AHI.

37. EMBND to MRE, O 112, 26 April 1954, AHI.

38. In June 1955, describing the Indian premier's visit to Moscow, Falcão wrote: "The elusive bird [Nehru], although with a curved beak, ultimately ended up hypnotized by the monstrous Muscovite snake, landing, first, on the red carpet of Moscow and, then, let himself screw in the elastic rings of the poisoning snake. . . . [Nehru] let himself beat and wrap as one of these innocent Amazon's [region] bullocks whose bones are, previously, triturated to be slowly swallowed up by a similarly strong snake." Falcão symbolically compared Nehru to a bird that was "gently" trapped by a snake; in this case, by the Soviet Union. EMBND to MRE, O 193, 23 June 1955, AHI.

39. EMBND to MRE, O [Confidencial] (henceforth [C]) 291, 28 December 1954, Arquivo do Ministério das Relações Exteriores (henceforth AMRE).

40. EMBND to MRE, O [C] 291, 28 December 1954, AMRE.

41. Bègue, *La fin de Goa*, chapters 6 and 7.

42. EMBND to MRE, T [C] 15, 20 April 1954, EMBND to MRE, O [C] 66, 24 April 1954, EMBND to MRE, T [C] 19, 8 May 1954, EMBND to MRE, O [C] 109, 29 June 1954, AMRE.

43. IER, "Reports from Rio, Secret," Monthly Political Report for April 1954, 25 May 1954, Monthly Political Report for May 1954, 5 July 1954, Monthly Political Report for July 1954, 5 August 1954, 13 R&I 54, NAI.

44. "Pró Lusitânia," *O Globo* [Rio de Janeiro, Brazil] 26 July 1954, 5.

45. EMBND to MRE, T [C] 45, 20 August 1954 and EMBND to MRE, T [C] 51, 1 September 1954, AMRE.

46. IER, "Reports from Rio, Secret," Monthly Political Report for November, 1954, 14 December 1954, 13 R&I 54, NAI.

47. EMBND to MRE, O [C] 333, 29 October 1955, AMRE.

48. EMBND to MRE, O [C] 301, 20 September 1955, AMRE.

49. EMBND to MRE, T [C] 41, 6 October 1955, AMRE.

50. Bethell, "Politics in Brazil under the Liberal Republic," 87–164; Skidmore, *Politics in Brazil*, 48–252. In Portuguese, see Claudio Bojunga, *JK. O Artista do Impossível* (São Paulo: Objectiva, 2001).

51. IER, "Annual Reports for 1958, Secret," F 3 (13) R&I 59, NAI.

52. Cervo and Bueno, *História da Política Exterior*, chapter 11.

53. Cervo and Bueno, *História da Política Exterior*, chapters 11 and 12.

54. MRE, Memorandum (henceforth M) [C] [DP] 3, 3 January 1957, AMRE.

55. On Brazilian-African relations, see Dávila, *Hotel Trópico*; Saraiva, *O Lugar da África*; Selcher, "The Afro-Asian Dimension of Brazilian Foreign Policy"; Pio Penna Filho and Antônio Carlos Moraes Lessa, "O Itamaraty e a África: As origens da política

africana do Brasil," *Estudos Históricos* 39 (Janeiro–Junho, 2007): 57–81; Daniel Patrick Aragon, "Brazilian Foreign Policy in Africa, 1961–1976," PhD diss., Auburn University, 2001; Samuel Yaw Boadi-Siaw, "Development of Relations between Brazil and African States, 1950–1973," PhD diss., University of California, 1975; and José Honório Rodrigues, *Brasil e África: Outro horizonte* (Rio de Janeiro: Editora Civilização Brasileira, 1964).

56. Hugo Gouthier, *Presença* (Brasília: Fundação Alexandre de Gusmão, 2008), 247–52.

57. Dávila, *Hotel Trópico,* chapter 1.

58. MRE, M [C] [DP] 239, 20 July 1956, AMRE.

59. MRE, M [C] [DP] 239, 20 July 1956, AMRE

60. EMBND to MRE, T 168, 5 October 1957, AMRE.

61. EMBND to MRE, O [C] 256, 27 September 1957 AHI; EMBND to MRE, O [C] 328, 18 August 1958, AHMRE; EMBND to MRE, O 396, 16 September 1958, AHI.

62. Prime Minister's Secretariat, "Letter from Prof. C. Mahadevan to Prime Minister suggesting the creation of (1) Educational Fellowships for Brazilians and (2) a scheme for emigration of Indians for Brazil," 30 July 1956, F 2 (26) AMS 56, NAI.

63. Sahni, "India and Latin America," 380–81.

64. Venezuela, for instance, issued a formal protest against the Indian government in August 1954. See Miguel Serra Coelho, "The Crisis of Goa between Lisbon, Rio de Janeiro, and New Delhi (1947–1961): The Transnational Destiny of an Empire," PhD diss., European University Institute, 2017.

65. MEA, "The question of opening of new missions in Latin American countries, Secret" 13-1/55 AMS, NAI.

66. M. R. Masani to Nehru, 27 December 1948, F 2 (4) / AMS 49, NAI.

67. EMBND to MRE, CT[C] 45, 23 December 1949, AHI; EMBND to MRE, T Secreto (henceforth [S]) 213, 29 December 1956, AHMRE.

68. EMBND to MRE, CT 52, 16 April 1957, EMBND to MRE, CT 55, 30 April 1957, EMBND to MRE, O [S] 117, 23 May 1957, AMRE.

69. MRE to EMBND, CT 21, 8 May 1957, AHI.

70. EMBND to MRE, T [S] 213, 29 December 1956, AHMRE.

71. EMBND to MRE, O [S] 78, 17 February 1958; EMBND to MRE, O [S] 92, 7 March 1958, AMRE.

72. "Nehru da Índia fala ao Brasil" *Correio da Manhã* [Rio de Janeiro, Brazil] 17 April 1958, 1, 12.

73. MRE, M [DP], 11 July 1958, MRE to EMBND, T [C] 37, 11 July 1958, EMBND to MRE, T [S] 58, 12 July 1958, AMRE.

74. Embaixada de Portugal no Rio de Janeiro (henceforth EPRJ) to Ministério dos Negócios Estrangeiros (henceforth MNE), T, 19 July 1958, EPRJ to MNE, T, 23 July 1958, EPRJ to MNE, T, 24 July 1958, Arquivo Histórico-Diplomático do Ministério dos Negócios Estrangeiro (henceforth AHDMNE).

75. Gonçalves, *O Realismo da Fraternidade,* chapter 9.

76. MRE to EMBND, T [S] 43, 31 July 1958, EMBND to MRE, T 83, 6 August 1958, AMRE.

77. EPRJ to MNE, T, 23 August 1958, AHDMNE.

78. MRE to EMBND, T 53, 26 August 1958, AMRE.

79. EPJR to MNE, T, 30 August 1958, AHDMNE.

80. IER, "Special Report: Political Prospects in Brazil," 20 December 1963, F 101 (7) WII /63, NAI.

81. EMBND to MRE, T 12 6 July 1960, Subimal Dutt to Indira Gandhi, 11 July 1960, F 52 (19) AMS / 60, NAI.

82. IER, "Annual Political Report for 1960," 10 January 1961, F 3 (13) R&I / 61, NAI.

2 Bolivia between Washington, Prague, and Havana

The Limits of Nationalism, 1960–1964

THOMAS C. FIELD JR.

In 1961, Bolivia's national revolution entered its ninth year. Bankrolled since 1952 with hundreds of millions of aid dollars from the United States government, the country's governing Movimiento Nacionalista Revolucionario (MNR, Revolutionary Nationalist Movement) had skillfully avoided Washington's antipathy as it nationalized the largest tin mines in the world and unleashed Latin America's most radical agrarian reform project since the Mexican revolution. Despite occasional State Department outbursts that denigrated the "dictatorship of the Marxist-oriented MNR party," and vitriolic rightwing attacks, such as Senator Barry Goldwater's 1964 campaign pledge to oppose the MNR's "candy-coated despotism," revolutionary Bolivia remained the darling of U.S. foreign policy elites.[1] Hailed by developmentalists in both the Eisenhower and Kennedy administrations as a nationalist bulwark against the encroachment of orthodox Communism in the heart of South America, the middle-class leadership of Bolivia's governing MNR was showered with over $370 million in U.S. financial assistance between 1954 and 1964.[2] Taking stock of Washington's alliance with "revolutionary nationalism" in Bolivia, the U.S. ambassador to La Paz boasted in 1962 that Washington had demonstrated flexibility by tolerating "a good deal of the non-Bolshevik Marxism of a socialist brand," which had gained "such wide currency in the intellectual life of the country" since the MNR's 1952 revolution.[3]

What did a financial alliance with the United States mean for Bolivia's self-styled revolutionary nationalists, who meanwhile courted economic assistance from the socialist countries of Eastern Europe? Was this the consummate Third World ploy, or was Washington's noblesse oblige an imperial kiss of death for Bolivian nationalism? Put another way: How much room for maneuver did revolutionary Bolivia enjoy (or even seek) under the U.S.-backed MNR? Was Bolivia's nationalist party a Third World fraud, wrapping itself in the banner of nonalignment but ultimately selling out to Washington out of economic dependency? Or was its Third Worldism sincere, tempered only by a bourgeois allergy to Communism and a recognition of the geopolitical realities of being a small Latin American country in the polarizing age of Fidel Castro and John F. Kennedy? More broadly, what does the story of Bolivia's dalliance with Third Worldism reveal about the evolution of the Non-Aligned Movement (NAM) in the early 1960s, particularly Latin America's halting role within it?

The extant literature, based on Bolivian and U.S. sources, has provided tentative responses to a few of these questions. We know, for example, that Bolivia's MNR maintained relations with Czechoslovakia and Cuba until just before it was ousted from power by the country's military in 1964, and that MNR leaders even briefly collaborated with Cuban-sponsored guerrilla operations against the military dictatorship in neighboring Peru. We also know that the MNR engaged in extensive economic negotiations with the Soviet bloc and that revolutionary Bolivia's nonaligned pretenses fueled protestations of a right to accept foreign aid from any source.[4] At the same time, Bolivian and U.S. sources reveal the rapid abandonment of these nonaligned postures as U.S. aid reached heroic proportions during President John F. Kennedy's Alliance for Progress. Turning completely against Bolivia's left wing for the first time in 1963, the MNR alienated its most fervent labor supporters and pushed them into armed opposition, in alliance with anti-MNR conservatives and restless military officers who stepped in to restore order in late 1964.[5]

Drawing on newly declassified material from the archives of the Communist Party of Czechoslovakia and the Cuban Foreign Ministry, complemented by newly available diplomatic records from Bolivia and the United States, this chapter adds a global perspective to the story of revolutionary Bolivia's ill-fated Third World gambit in the early 1960s. More than just revealing the impact of U.S. intervention in the Global South, the narrative sheds new light on the evolution of the NAM during the early 1960s and raises fundamental questions about Latin America's fraught position as a region that identified as much with the Third World as with the Cold War West. On a more particular level, this chapter explores the subtle differences in socialist world approaches to Latin American nationalism, particularly the paradoxical relationship between the foreign policies of Prague and Havana, which shared sympathy for the region's growing radicalization but adopted ground-level approaches that differed in both form and substance.

Czechoslovakia, Cuba, and Latin America's Third World

Writing the history of Latin America in a global context leads scholars to three overlapping dilemmas. First, how does one internationalize Latin American history without ending up in bilateral dead-ends, replicating both the promises and limits of traditional diplomatic history, whose archival and ideological foundations occasionally overemphasize the staid duality of U.S. hegemony and Latin American victimhood?[6] Second, what does "global" mean in a region whose elites have long claimed themselves a world apart, in a system encompassing shared values that has taken great pains to quarantine itself from extra-hemispheric influences?[7] Finally, is it possible to resolve these dilemmas without simply writing the United States out of Latin American history, a cure worse than the disease, which can produce narratives of Latin American relations with the extra-hemispheric world that bear little resemblance to the lived experiences of the region's U.S.-centric struggles for social, political, and economic independence?[8] As this chapter demonstrates, a global history of Latin America calls for multiarchival, multinational research that complements (rather than replaces) the documentary record of individual Latin American countries and the superpower to the region's immediate north. In doing so, it reveals the benefits of tracing the loose threads of Latin American attempts to transcend the Inter-American System, even while acknowledging that most of these gambits were partial, halting, and even occasionally deceitful.

One of the best ways to identify Latin America's interest in Third World nonalignment is to explore its relations with the socialist countries of Eastern Europe and Cuba. As the historian Michal Zourek demonstrates in a recent book on Czechoslovak relations with the Latin America, the region's overtures to Eastern Europe mapped neatly onto each country's ties with the related project of Third World neutralism.[9] This phenomenon included Bolivia, Brazil, and Ecuador, which attended the 1961 NAM meeting in Belgrade, followed by Argentina, Chile, Mexico, Uruguay, and Venezuela, which joined Bolivia and Brazil as observers at Cairo in 1964. None of these countries followed Cuba's example by formally joining the NAM, but their participation as observers reflected concrete interest in expanding diplomatic, economic, and cultural relations beyond the Western Hemisphere and across the so-called Iron Curtain. Historian Tobias Rupprecht agrees with this connection, describing in this volume and in his recent book how Latin American intellectuals' interest in the Soviet bloc waxed and waned in direct proportion with their self-identification as part of the Third World.[10]

Cuba's role in the revolutionary politics of its neighbors is well known, but less has been written about Czechoslovakia, which long had "the most active" network of Eastern European missions in Latin America, according to a 1962 report by the U.S. Central Intelligence Agency (CIA). The CIA went on to describe Prague as the Soviet bloc's "chief commercial contact with the area" due to "the respect the Czechoslovaks continue to enjoy as businessmen . . . viewed with less suspicion than those from other bloc countries, who are thought to be more preoccupied with propaganda and subversive activities."[11] It is important to note that this 1962 assessment runs contrary to the secret unfolding of Operación Manuel (1962–ca. 1970), which was a covert program in which the intelligence services of Prague and Havana cooperated to break the Washington-led blockade of Cuba by secretly shuttling Latin American leftists between their home countries and Cuba via the Soviet bloc. The fundamental paradox of Manuel was that Eastern European governments continued their fervent outreach to non-Communist governments in Latin America, a tactic that coexisted uneasily alongside Czechoslovakia's indirect support for Cuban-sponsored armed movements to overthrow the established hemispheric order. This contradiction intensified debates about Latin America's role within the Third World movement, particularly in a revolutionary nationalist milieu such as Bolivia under the middle-class MNR.[12]

As the only Latin American country to officially join the NAM, Cuba, with its advocacy for armed struggle, produced varying levels of elite apprehension about the Third World movement, even among Latin American nationalists whose desire to deepen economic relations with the Soviet bloc remained important manifestations of their adherence to NAM principles. These two approaches to Latin American nonalignment—strict, eastward-leaning diplomatic neutrality pushed by Czechoslovakia, on the one hand, and insurgent anti-imperialism emanating from Cuba, on the other—combined to keep most of Latin America out of the NAM for two decades, thus hamstringing the Third World movement's full geographic potential well into the 1970s. Meanwhile, debates over Cuba and its allies in the East aggravated domestic tensions over the very meaning of Third Worldism, particularly in nationalist countries such as Brazil and Bolivia, where conservative military leaders intervened in 1964 to stamp out their countries' tenuous programs of outreach to the socialist world.

It would be a mistake, nonetheless, to interpret these two approaches as fundamentally opposed to one another. Despite contradictions between the regional tactics employed by Prague and Havana, these major socialist players in Latin America considered themselves to be steadfast allies in the struggle for the region's political and economic independence from the United States. Operación Manuel contained a fundamental paradox, but declassified documents reveal that Prague and Havana interpreted Latin American nationalists such as Bolivia's MNR in a similar manner. The result was an overlapping set of debates over the Latin American middle class, debates that are more thoroughly illuminated through the global lens of the Third World rather than the bipolar, East-West confines of the Cold War.

By bringing in the voices of Czechoslovak and Cuban officials, struggling side by side to maintain a narrow socialist foothold in South America, this chapter points the way to further research on Latin America's sincere efforts to stake out a more independent approach to global politics, with the eventual goal of transcending an Inter-American System that contributed to the region's restricted room for diplomatic maneuver. Watching from the wings as Bolivia's governing MNR party sold out its Third World ideals and threw in its lot with liberal internationalists in Washington and development-oriented generals in La Paz, officials in Prague and Havana expressed varying levels of shock, frustration, and eventually outright hostility (particularly in the case of Cuba) toward the bourgeois nationalism of Bolivia's middle-class leadership.

Revolutionary Bolivia and the Nonaligned Game, 1960–1961

Nonalignment came naturally to the middle-class nationalists who rose to the top of Bolivia's revolutionary coalition in 1952. Formed in the midst of world war in 1942, the MNR gained a strong following in the organized labor movement by ruthlessly criticizing what it viewed as the Bolivian oligarchy's subservient relationship to British and U.S. capitalists. Throughout the war, the MNR and its most outspoken middle-class orator, Víctor Paz Estenssoro, advocated in Parliament for selling tin to the Axis Powers (or threatening to do so) in order to obtain higher prices to fund Bolivia's internal development.[13] The official MNR newspaper, *La Calle*, even peddled in right-wing anti-Semitic nationalism, characterizing the Allied cause as a cosmopolitan, banker, and Jewish conspiracy in league with international Communism.[14] Bolivian Trotksyists similarly condemned the Allies, minus the MNR's bigotry and xenophobia, and eventually forged a revolutionary coalition with MNR politicians and trade unionists, which successfully overthrew the oligarchy in a bloody uprising in April 1952.[15]

The MNR's history of extreme nationalism and anti-Bolshevism helps to explain its subsequent approach to foreign policy as a governing party in the 1950s and 1960s. This included the party's strong opposition to the leftist Guatemalan revolution, its utilitarian approaches to the Third World project and the Communist Second World, its halfhearted tolerance for revolutionary Cuba, and its willing embrace of development assistance from the anti-Communist United States. This meant that, even as the MNR dismantled British capitalist control of Bolivia's tin-mining sector, its bourgeois leadership spurned early 1950s entreaties from the Communist world in favor of its tactical alliance with Washington. Concessions to U.S. capitalists began in the late 1950s, when rampant inflation led President Paz Estenssoro and his successor, Hernán Siles Suazo (1956–60), to open the country's hydrocarbon sector to foreign investors and invite the International Monetary Fund to draw up an austerity plan for stabilizing the country's currency.[16] These measures not only alienated nationalist and leftist workers; they also produced a noticeable distance between Bolivia and ongoing events in revolutionary Cuba.

Tensions were readily apparent between Bolivia's nationalist experiment and more thoroughgoing transformations in Cuba. About a year after the triumph of the 1959 Cuban revolution, Havana's Foreign Ministry complained about "pressure that the Bolivian government has exercised toward certain persons and institutions with the goal of ending their collaboration with our mission and impeding them from organizing events in support of Cuba." In May 1960, the Bolivian foreign minister went so far as to remind the Cuban ambassador in La Paz that while the two country's revolutionary processes "were the same, they take on distinct forms . . . due to the fact that the Cuban revolution has impacted powerful U.S. interests, while the Bolivian process has not." Bolivia's MNR government complained about the circulation of Cuban revolutionary materials in La Paz, saying that the pamphlets and fliers "violate the spirit and letter of Pan-Americanism since they constitute propaganda against a country [the U.S.], and even against the Hemisphere itself." The Cuban government lamented the MNR's cold shoulder, noting that "while there has not been a hostile or aggressive attitude toward the Cuban revolution on the part of the Bolivian government, due largely to pressure from the enormous trade unions, especially the miners," it was still clear that "the government's economic dependency on the United States results in a vacillating attitude with respect to the Cuban revolution."[17]

The return of Víctor Paz Estenssoro to the presidency in late 1960 led many on the Bolivian Left to presume that "a revolution within the revolution was possible." Paz had visited Prague and Belgrade during his interregnal ambassadorship to London (1956–60), and one of his first post-inaugural acts of diplomacy was to dispatch a permanent envoy to Czechoslovakia to finalize agreements for Soviet-bloc economic assistance.[18] To represent revolutionary Bolivia in Prague, Paz Estenssoro selected MNR leftist poet Jorge Calvimontes, who privately revealed to Czechoslovak officials his "full sympathy for Cuba and strong opposition to the United States."[19] In January 1961, this initial MNR foray into Second World diplomacy resulted in a series of economic and cultural agreements, including a tentative offer of an antimony smelter, which were unveiled during a weeklong visit to La Paz by Prague's vice minister of foreign affairs. As the Czechoslovak mission departed, the Bolivian Foreign Ministry privately boasted that Prague viewed this agreement as "just a single aspect of the broad commercial channel that could be established" between the two countries, adding that it had no reason to doubt Prague's assurances that it "did not try to obtain any commitment of a political nature and that [its] proposals were motivated by [its] government's necessity to sell machinery produced by Czechoslovak heavy industry, as well as its desire to cooperate with Bolivia's economic growth."[20]

The CIA was obviously less enamored by revolutionary Bolivia's newfound diplomatic promiscuity, reporting that President Paz was "under heavy domestic pressure" from MNR leftists and trade unions to accept Prague's credit offer as well as a separate aid package of $150 million, which had been announced by a Soviet parliamentary delegation visit to the Bolivian mining camps in December of the previous year. Noting that Paz Estenssoro was simultaneously "seeking an emergency increase in American aid," the CIA suspected that the MNR leader's Second World gambit was aimed at "dramatizing Bolivia's interest in foreign economic help."[21] According to more alarmist agency sources in La Paz, however, President Paz Estenssoro "conveyed the impression that he considers American grant aid . . . a part of ordinary revenues on which his administration can count," and he was thus giving the Second World an "opportunity for political penetration" by "reserving" high-profile extraction projects for the Soviet bloc.[22] The State Department therefore recommended an immediate increase in U.S. aid to Bolivia, fretting that "the Soviets are genuinely interested in establishing a foothold in Latin America" alongside Moscow's burgeoning alliance with Cuba.[23]

If Bolivia's middle-class revolutionaries sought to employ the threat of Second World economic relations to score an increase in U.S. financial assistance, this appeared to be working. In private conversations with White House aide Arthur Schlesinger in February 1961, President Paz Estenssoro distanced his revolution from Cuba's, arguing that the latter "puts land in the hands of the state," while the MNR process "puts land into the hands of the peasants." After Paz Estenssoro offered his view that Cuban leader Fidel Castro "must be eliminated," Schlesinger recorded in his diary the good news—"his words are excellent"—along with the bad—"his actions belie his words"—particularly Paz Estenssoro's lack of interest in taking public his views on Cuba and his continued economic flirtation with the Soviet bloc. Warning President Kennedy that "the loss of Bolivia would be a catastrophe," Schlesinger added his voice in support of an emergency aid package. After three months of negotiations with the United States Agency for International Development (USAID) and the Inter-American Development Bank (IDB), Bolivia signed a $13.5 million aid package for the state-controlled tin-mining sector. Immediately leaked to the public was a list of "Accepted Points of View," harsh conditions imposed by USAID and the IDB that committed the MNR government to abolishing worker representation in mine management, firing 20 percent of the mine workforce, and physically removing Communist Party members from trade union leadership.[24]

Socialist diplomats in faraway Prague and Moscow might have resolved to watch Bolivia fall deeper into a dependent relationship with the United States, but revolutionaries in Havana could ill afford to lose ground among their diminishing cadre of nationalist and leftist friends in the Western Hemisphere. Throughout May and June a fierce debate over USAID's anti-labor conditions roiled the country, and there was a sharp uptick in U.S. military and police assistance to facilitate the impending roundup of dozens of labor leaders opposed to the USAID plan.[25] Refusing to stand idly by while the Bolivian Left faced annihilation, the Cuban Foreign Ministry reevaluated its previous policy of treading carefully in Bolivia so as to "lessen friction with the [Bolivian] Foreign Ministry" and avoid being "accused of intervening in Bolivian domestic politics."[26] Interpreting Bolivia's consideration of USAID's labor conditions as evidence of the MNR Right's "submission to imperialism, its unpopularity, and its actions contrary to the revolutionary process," Cuban diplomats prepared to support "more democratic elements," who "feel a certain sympathy with our process and can be utilized" to resist further concessions to the United States. By providing an unspecified level of "economic support" to MNR leftists and Communist

Party members, particularly in the trade union movement, the Cuban Foreign Ministry believed revolutionary Bolivia could once again be encouraged to adopt policies "in favor of the masses." Havana's ultimate goal was to help coordinate Bolivia's domestic resistance to Paz Estenssoro's deepening reliance on the United States, thus encouraging those local leftists who recognized that "the brotherly people of Bolivia have only one solution for their economic, political, and social problems: armed insurrection which will irrevocably lead the people toward their definitive triumph."[27]

Cuba's strategy of encouraging insurrection by local Communists and MNR leftists rested on the fact that "the majority of the miners and peasants happen to be armed"; many of them also believed their revolution to have been "betrayed" by bourgeois MNR leaders such as Paz Estenssoro. That said, Cuban diplomats recognized that "to move toward the taking of power, it is necessary to create a revolutionary consciousness among the working class and especially in the peasantry." Its specific policies thus included rather moderate proposals to cultivate leftist members of the governing MNR through embassy events and sponsored visits to Cuba that would "improve relations" between the two revolutionary countries. Behind the scenes, Cuba also planned to work with Communist Party members, particularly in the youth and labor movements, who would "form a revolutionary group that would serve as an example of integrity and enterprise in contrast with the *caudillos*" of Paz Estenssoro's MNR machine. According to Havana, it was "necessary to trust only in the Communist Party for the insurrectionary task, because aside from having a political line allied with the work that needs to be done, it is the party that boasts the best human material."[28]

When dozens of Communist trade union leaders were arrested by President Paz's secret police in mid-1961, for no other reason than their opposition to the harsh USAID conditions, Cuba was the only country to lend diplomatic support by hosting the families and allies of the detainees at its embassy in La Paz. In response, right-wing members of the MNR attacked Havana's local installations, plastering their walls with placards that read, "Disgusting Castristas, get out of Bolivia, or you'll end up hung by the lampposts," "Death to Communism," and "Center of the Communist conspiracy against national sovereignty."[29] The conservative press accused the Cuban embassy of intervening in the labor dispute by hosting meetings with striking Communist trade union leaders, leading the Cuban Foreign Ministry to fret that local rightist hostility "could damage Bolivian relations with our country." Havana's diplomats thus breathed a sigh of relief when Paz

Estenssoro's Foreign Ministry notified the press that, despite the controversy, his country's "relations with the revolutionary government of Cuba would continue with absolute normalcy," and Cuba privately praised the MNR government for "not accepting the opinion of [right-wing] outlets for a single minute."[30]

By cracking down on the domestic Left while continuing to respect Bolivia's relations with socialist nations, President Paz Estenssoro's MNR was playing a game familiar to nonaligned Third World leaders. Indeed, throughout the crisis brought on by Bolivia's acceptance of USAID's antilabor conditions, the Paz government continued its high-profile economic diplomacy toward the Soviet bloc. An MNR parliamentary delegation visited Moscow in June 1961, proclaiming "emphatically," for good measure, "that the sympathies of the workers and peasants of Bolivia is with the cause of the Cuban revolution."[31] Later that year, Paz Estenssoro's envoy to Prague "expressed delight" to Czechoslovak officials "that economic relations between our two countries are developing quite well."[32] And in November, Spain's anti-Communist ambassador in La Paz noted that "the Czechoslovak delegation here, blessed with funds and ample resources, carries out an active and effective job of Soviet recruitment, for its activity clearly exceeds its own interests, thus becoming an agent of the USSR."[33]

Bolivian President Paz Estenssoro sought to provoke alarm in Washington through continued flirtation with the Soviet bloc, even as he dedicated his government domestically to President Kennedy's Alliance for Progress. The U.S. State Department took the bait, noting that while Paz's MNR was "basically still oriented toward the free world . . . strong Communist infiltration in the labor movement" meant that "we are faced with an immediate emergency. . . . Soviet pressure is strong [and] the Bolivian government is in a precarious situation." Estimating that Bolivia was the "weakest of all the countries on the continent" and the "prime Soviet target in Latin America," the State Department likened the revolutionary nation to an "undernourished, ill-clad, ill-housed individual who is exposed to tuberculosis." Declaring that "we cannot regard Bolivia as a loss," the Kennedy administration focused on its central goal of curtailing the country's nonaligned pretenses. In short, Washington privately resolved to do "everything we can to prevent Soviet access to the internal affairs of Bolivia."[34]

For Latin American countries receiving U.S. funds under Kennedy's Alliance for Progress, the issue of Cuba was even thornier than that of Eastern Europe. Bolivia's MNR leaders fervently attempted to frame their continuing relations with Cuba as an issue of Third World nonalignment similar to Latin American ties to the socialist states of Eastern Europe. Washington rejected these arguments and instead labored to separate the Cuban issue from the global Third World and to frame it through an inflexible mélange of Pan-American solidarity and Cold War anti-Communism. Revolutionary Bolivia's steadfastness in its relations with Castro's Cuba would soon complicate Paz Estenssoro's Third World game, prompting a level of anxiety in Washington far beyond what he had hoped.

Bolivia's Third World Gambit, 1961–1962

Based on extensive interviews with friends and family of the father of Bolivia's national revolution, I have argued elsewhere that Víctor Paz Estenssoro was a "sincere if flawed nationalist" and a genuine adherent of Third World nonalignment. His son confided that Paz's "points of reference" were nonaligned leaders such as Indonesian President Sukarno, India's Jawalharlal Nehru, and Ghana's Kwame Nkrumah. A journalist close to the Paz Estenssoro wing of the MNR added that President Paz "loved [Yugoslav leader Josep Broz] Tito. He wanted to be a Latin American Tito, to play both sides of the Cold War."[35] For a short period in 1961 and 1962, Paz Estenssoro seemed to be succeeding in his Third World gambit: he had successfully secured a prime place in President Kennedy's Alliance for Progress without breaking off economic negotiations with the Soviet bloc or even considering a diplomatic rupture with Cuba.

In October 1961, Bolivia was one of only four Latin American countries to send delegations to observe the inaugural meeting of the Non-Aligned Movement (NAM) in Tito's Yugoslavia. Heading the Bolivian delegation was Education Minister José Fellman Velarde, an MNR nationalist who was subsequently appointed to lead the Bolivian Foreign Ministry beginning in January 1962. Cuban diplomats, the only Latin Americans to actually sign up to the NAM at Belgrade, had previously disparaged Fellman as a middle-class "enemy of Cuba," but Havana was intrigued by the minister's recent political evolution. Just prior to visiting Belgrade, Fellman had canceled a trip to the United States when his wife (who lacked a visa) was refused boarding by the U.S. airline in La Paz.[36] Fellman subsequently toured Eastern Europe and began work as a correspondent for Havana's *Prensa Latina*, leading the U.S. embassy to fret that the new foreign minister was becoming a "close friend of the Cuban Chargé" and would likely spell difficulty for Washington's plan to erect a hemisphere-wide economic and diplomatic blockade of socialist Cuba.[37]

Throughout early 1962, the U.S. embassy in La Paz leveled fierce pressure against nationalist Bolivia, trying to convince the MNR to join the majority of the hemisphere in breaking relations with Havana. In February, the embassy wrote privately to Foreign Minister Fellman that Cuba's Marxist-Leninism was "incompatible with the Inter-American System," adding that "the government of the United States hopes other countries will join in the effort to achieve, without delay" a decision by the Organization of American States (OAS) "that the present Cuban regime be excluded from participation."[38] U.S. diplomats scoffed at Fellman's public proclamation that relations between Bolivia and Cuba would have nothing to do with "Castro regime, but rather with what the Cubans do or do not do in Bolivia." According to the foreign minister, "Our attitude is not subordinated to other countries, but is always a product of our own decisions arising from national politics."[39] Washington groused that "governments which apparently regard themselves unaffected or less seriously threatened by the Cuban alignment with an extra-continental system and power bloc" should act with "a sense of urgency equal to that which they would feel if they themselves were directly affected." In another private communiqué to the foreign minister, U.S. diplomats returned to alarmist Pan-Americanism, depicting the OAS debate on Cuba sanctions as "perhaps decisive for Inter-American security," thus launching a mostly futile campaign to recruit nationalist Bolivia to join its anti-Castro crusade.[40]

As one of only three postrevolutionary states in Latin America, aside from Mexico and Cuba, Bolivia's neutralist position on the latter soon became the site of an intense proxy war within the country, one that threatened to derail Paz Estenssoro's tenuous Third Worldism by injecting into the country the unwelcome binaries of the Cold War. The Cuban Foreign Ministry, anxious to shore up support for a continuation of normal diplomatic relations, rushed to offer generous scholarships and travel grants to sympathetic Bolivians, particularly members of the left, labor, and youth sectors of the governing nationalist party, along with the much smaller (and decidedly pro-Cuba) Partido Comunista de Bolivia (PCB, Communist Party of Bolivia).[41] Nationalist and Communist Bolivian trade union leaders who visited Cuba in early 1962 returned to deliver emotional vows to defend the socialist island, the first truly "free territory of the Americas." In trade union halls and at national conferences, labor leaders mocked "the imperialists" and their "puppet governments . . . of oligarchic bourgeois creoles, landowners, and traffickers," who characterized Cuba as a "threat to the hemisphere," quipping that it was "considered a threat simply because in Cuba there is progress, honesty, hospitality, and freedom."⁴² At the Eleventh Congress of the Bolivian Mine Workers Federation in mid-1961, one executive committee member launched into a strident apology for revolutionary Cuba, declaring that "we will defend the Cuban Revolution, because to do so means defending the Bolivian Revolution. . . . All those peoples who suffer from the scourge of imperialism pin their hopes on the definitive consolidation of the Cuban Revolution."⁴³

Perhaps the most strident pro-Cuba voice in Bolivia was that of the MNR's youth faction, which in early 1962 pledged "popular solidarity with the historic cause of an entire people rising up in arms against Yankee imperialism" and called for insurrections throughout the region to abolish "the same chains and misery that weigh on the shoulders of all the inhabitants of the Americas." Vowing to put pressure on its governing nationalist party to deepen the Bolivian revolutionary process, the MNR youth declared that Cuba's experiences since 1959 "had objectively demonstrated that oppressed and exploited peoples can obtain their liberation, as long as they struggle in a way that is valiant, resolved, and constant."⁴⁴ Offering its full support for Bolivian workers' struggle against the antilabor conditions required by U.S. aid funds under the Alliance for Progress, the MNR youth wrote to Paz Estenssoro in 1961 that his rightward shift "fills us with shame." Rejecting the infusion of Bolivian politics with Cold War binaries, the nationalist youth declared that "Communism is in the just demands of the workers who cannot live on starvation wages," and its members asked rhetorically, "When will the true revolution arrive?"⁴⁵

Havana's local allies seemed to favor replicating Cuba's radical global approach to liberate Bolivia from U.S.-led Pan-Americanism, but the Cubans themselves sought to reassure MNR leadership as to their benevolent local intentions. Aside from quietly providing assistance to the workers and students on the MNR Left and in the PCB who might eventually take up arms, the Cuban Foreign Ministry also instructed its embassy to adopt a soft public profile, to "attend all official and diplomatic functions" of the MNR government, and to "carry out the task of getting close [*acercamiento*] to Víctor Paz Estenssoro."⁴⁶ In February 1962, Cuban Foreign Minister Raúl Roa wrote to his counterpart, José Fellman, expressing that Havana was "keenly interested in increasing and strengthening the relations of cooperation and friendship between Bolivia and Cuba." Revealing that his ministry was transferring the head of its Latin America division to lead the Cuban delegation in Bolivia, Roa expressed the "profound desire of the [Cuban] revolutionary government that Bolivia accredit an ambassador in Havana," and he concluded by thanking the MNR government for its "gallant position" in defense of Cuba at the OAS.[47]

Given the extent of U.S. aid flowing into revolutionary Bolivia in the early 1960s, it is intriguing to note the subtle contradiction between middle-class MNR leaders' official tolerance of Havana's high-level diplomacy and the persistently more radical pro-Cuba posture of grassroots MNR youth and labor activists. A 22 February 1962 "Manifesto of Solidarity with Cuba" boasted the signatures of a vast majority of MNR trade union and youth leaders and was formally presented to the Cuban embassy by a parliamentary delegation of the governing party. The document, which was also endorsed by the PCB, condemned Washington's treatment of Cuba as "aggression," which reflected First World ignorance of the "fundamental change in the balance of forces in the international scene that is increasingly favorable to National Liberation for colonies and semi-colonies and makes it inevitable that they will achieve their true independence." According to the manifesto, the MNR rank and file would continue to stand up for Bolivia's "interests, dignity, and national honor" by holding fast in defense of the Cuban revolution, a process that "invoked a historical obligation which unites us in the common homeland of Indo-America with Murillo, Martí, Zapata, Juárez, and Albizu Campos."[48]

This growing tension between the MNR government's foreign policy neutralism and its party's radical youth and labor sectors was temporarily papered over by President Paz Estenssoro's strategic penchant for diplomatic theater. Aside from standing by Cuba at the OAS, this also included keeping his party's Left occupied with dramatic displays of outreach to Eastern Europe—showy entreaties that the MNR leader never planned to consummate. In late February, Bolivia's leftist chargé in Prague, Jorge Calvimontes, pleaded with the Czechoslovak Foreign Ministry that "we finally do something in order to see tangible results" in drawn-out trade negotiations between the two countries. Prague's diplomats ruefully observed that "it is a great pity that solid economic relations are yet to be established since we have been waiting for over a year now for the Bolivian economic delegation, already announced many times."[49] In a secret report, Czechoslovakia chalked up "Bolivia's inability to accept loans offered by the USSR and the socialist camp" to the MNR's "more pronounced dependence on the United States of America," particularly under President Kennedy's Alliance for Progress development program. Noting that negotiations over USAID's harsh antilabor conditions "continue to drag on," however, Prague resolved to "advance very carefully, while still aggressively exploiting every opportunity to deepen divisions between Bolivia and the capitalist states led by the USA." According to Prague, Eastern European trade offers to Bolivia should "not be considered so significant from a commercial aspect as much as from the economic aid offered to an underdeveloped country."[50]

In early June 1962, the long-awaited Bolivian parliamentary delegation arrived in Prague, tasked with seeking ways to "achieve a certain degree of independence" in Bolivia's economic relations and (more important from Paz Estenssoro's perspective) to provoke a new wave of fear among Washington negotiators continuing to demand harsh reforms in exchange for U.S. aid funding. Noting "the political importance" of the MNR mission to Prague, the Czechoslovak Foreign Ministry sought to "take appropriate steps . . . [to] maximize the benefit of the Bolivian delegation." The mission succeeded in finalizing its long-stalled offer of an antimony smelter, which Prague believed would galvanize the left sector of the governing MNR and deliver in the process a "bold bite [*tučným soustem*] against the Bolivian reaction."[51] The CIA agreed that "the smelter, which is the Bloc's first developmental assistance to Bolivia, is expected to have considerable political impact."[52]

For nationalist Bolivia, Czechoslovakia's willingness to play the role of Washington's bogeyman was a welcome plot twist. Just days after dispatching his parliamentary delegation to Prague, President Paz Estenssoro sent a parallel mission to Washington, led by two cabinet ministers who shared his Third World vision. Planning to seek U.S. approval for an $80 million Bolivian request under the Alliance for Progress, the mission members told the local press that they were really going to Washington to "find out whether the Alliance was fact or fiction." Unlike the smelter negotiations in Prague, which culminated in five short days, Bolivia's mission to Washington remained mired for eight weeks in disagreements over the USAID conditions. This mostly stemmed from U.S. demands that the governing MNR implement the remainder of the 1961 anti-Communist labor reforms *prior* to additional funds being approved.[53] With Alliance for Progress aid funding stalled, the CIA suggested that the White House take close account of the fact that Eastern European aid "has great appeal in Bolivia," due to the country's "desperate economic need." Consummation of development agreements from the socialist world had previously been "delayed primarily by President Paz," but the CIA warned that these Soviet bloc offers were now being "hotly debated" in Bolivia's trade union halls and Parliament, and that the MNR government was coming "under increasing pressure" to call Washington's hand and prove to the world that its Second World gambit was more than mere bluster.[54]

When the head of Bolivia's mission, Economic Minister Alfonso Gumucio, finally met with White House officials on 18 July, it was clear to Kennedy aide Arthur Schlesinger that the mission leader "bears all the aspects of a man tried beyond endurance until his spirit is substantially broken." Schlesinger begged the Washington bureaucracy to put aside its conditions and approve the $80 million aid package "for the sake of our future relations with Bolivia" and to ensure that Gumucio did not "return to Bolivia a most irritated and discouraged man at the end of the week." The following day, after nearly eight weeks in Washington, Gumucio's mission received word that USAID had approved the entire $80 million request, along with a warning that the new aid package was merely a "test case" that would not be repeated until the Paz Estenssoro government moved forward with the anti-Communist "realignments and reforms that he professes to seek" in the Bolivian trade union movement.[55]

With the Czechoslovak smelter deal in June and the U.S. financial aid package in July, Paz Estenssoro's diplomatic Third Worldism reached its high-water mark. Just as the nationalist leader had hoped, the MNR government's entreaties to Eastern Europe fueled geopolitical anxiety in Washington, which translated into looser purse strings under Kennedy's Alliance for Progress. Meanwhile, Paz Estenssoro continued to defend his country's normal diplomatic relations with revolutionary Cuba, and MNR leftists traveled in droves to the socialist island, where they declared loyalty to Third World principles and shared with Cuban diplomats their recommendations on how to deepen Bolivia's revolutionary process. In Washington, the Cuba issue was radioactive, and U.S. diplomats chafed at their apparent lack of leverage over the governing MNR. Throughout late 1962 and early 1963, Washington redoubled its efforts to convince Paz Estenssoro that his government's toleration of Cuba and its continued flirtations with Eastern Europe combined to represent a "disturbing political issue," sharply incongruent with Bolivia's acceptance of large-scale development assistance under Kennedy's anti-Communist Alliance for Progress.[56]

Radical Bluffs and Fierce Reactions, 1962–1964

In mid-1962, an internal CIA assessment took stock of revolutionary Bolivia's Third World game. Acknowledging that "the government of President

Paz favored postponing acceptance of [Soviet bloc] aid in the hope that Bolivia's aspirations might be realized through the Alliance for Progress," the CIA lamented that "pressure on the government from leftist labor groups" had forced through the Czechoslovak smelter project two months earlier. Worse yet, Bolivia's initial success with Eastern Europe had reopened domestic debate in Bolivia regarding aid from the Soviet Union itself, with MNR leftists now concentrating their efforts on a $150 million offer that had been made by Moscow eighteen months earlier.[57] MNR leftists in parliament wrote to President Paz Estenssoro in August, wondering aloud if "antinational and anti-revolutionary agreements with foreign signatories" in Washington had been conditioned on Bolivia rejecting further aid offers from socialist nations. Asking their party leader, "How can you explain that the offer made by Nikita Khrushchev in 1960 . . . has not yet been accepted?" the MNR politicians added rhetorically: "What powerful forces have prevented, and apparently continue to prevent, the dispatch of a commercial mission to the Soviet Union?"[58]

The left sector of Bolivia's governing MNR had clearly been emboldened by the signing of the Czechoslovak smelter project, but it was U.S. duplicity over the coming weeks that threatened to push Bolivia over the brink to radicalization. The ink had barely dried on Washington's new $80 million aid agreement when the U.S. Treasury Department announced that it would begin selling large quantities of tin from the strategic stockpile held by its General Services Administration. The U.S. ambassador in La Paz complained that the selloff would "probably be construed here as 'dumping,'" and he warned that many Bolivians would see this as an "example of U.S. hypocrisy." According to the U.S. embassy, the scandal put President Paz Estenssoro's "head in [a] political noose," particularly since Paz Estenssoro was scheduled to visit the White House in late September. A trip to Washington in the midst of U.S. tin-dumping could lead to a crisis in which President Paz "could fall or be forced [to] take [a] strongly antagonistic attitude" toward the United States. When the State Department refused to offer Paz Estenssoro any assurance that his visit would lead to an agreement to halt U.S. sales of stockpiled tin, the Bolivian president canceled his trip and even temporarily pulled his country out of future meetings of the OAS.[59]

As if on cue, five members of Moscow's Supreme Soviet arrived in La Paz in September, having been invited by leftist MNR parliamentarians to finalize the long-stalled economic aid offer. When a group of anti-Communist protesters arrived to denounce the Soviet mission, MNR youth cadres attacked them and were soon backed up by Paz Estenssoro's security services operating under the command of MNR labor unions. According to the U.S. embassy, "The brutal actions of the police were undoubtedly ordered to insure that the anticommunist marchers would feel the full weight of police repression and discourage future anticommunist demonstrations."[60] A week later, the U.S. embassy warned Washington that "a crisis in Bolivia's political orientation is near at hand. . . . Evidence [is] piling up that we may well be in the process [of a] complete [MNR] left sector takeover with large-scale Soviet aid." Due to the fact that MNR leftists were pushing rapidly for "advanced stage socialism with greater ties to [the] Soviet Union and at least partial collaboration with the Communist Party," the U.S. embassy called for "serious consideration [of] contingency alternatives" to split Paz Estenssoro from the left sector of his own party and to halt Bolivia's sharp turn to the Left.[61]

President Kennedy responded to these events by placing Bolivia on his Counterinsurgency (CI) Watch List, requiring the U.S. embassy to drum up an "Internal Defense Plan," posthaste. According to the White House committee in charge of coordinating interagency and covert approaches to counterinsurgency in the Third World, Bolivian neutralism had permitted local Marxists to "operate so freely and openly" that "few, if any agencies" of the MNR government were "free of communist influence." The White House agreed that contingency alternatives were necessary to support Paz Estenssoro and split him away from the MNR Left, principally because it worried that "it may not be possible to achieve" the politico-developmental goals of the Alliance for Progress "in time to be effective against the communist threat."[62] The stakes had suddenly been raised in nationalist Bolivia's Third World game. Over the coming months, leftist ascendancy would be matched by a rapid uptick in U.S. covert operations to shore up the Paz Estenssoro government, convince him to abandon his party's left sector, and pressure him to adopt a foreign policy attitude more favorable to his benefactors in Washington.[63]

In October 1962, the Cuban Foreign Ministry noted "the enormous pressure that U.S. imperialism continues to carry out" in Bolivia, lamenting that the MNR government had "practically negated acceptance of socialist camp offers," including potential aid agreements that were Bolivia's only viable hope for "facing up to and resolving its economic crisis." Characterizing Washington's hardline position on Eastern European aid as "blackmail," the Foreign Ministry added that U.S. "imperialism is operating in a violent way to obtain a break with Cuba." According to Havana, the only thing stopping Paz Estenssoro from throwing in his lot completely with the United States was Washington's tin-dumping scandal, coupled with President Paz's realization that outright rejection of Eastern European aid or a break with Cuba would cause his government to "suffer further discrediting among the popular sectors" of the MNR youth and labor left.[64]

As U.S. foreign policy shifted from courting President Paz with economic aid to more militant covert political programs to break him away from the MNR Left, the Bolivian president appeared to manifest fresh interest in deepening his country's relations with Cuba. In early 1963, Paz Estenssoro announced the assignment of an official envoy to Havana, and in February he hosted a meeting at the presidential palace with the head of Cuba's mission in La Paz, Ramón Aja Castro, whom U.S. diplomats disparaged as "the center and coordinating figure in [the] entire Cuban intelligence operations set-up in South America."[65] More risky still, Bolivian Communist Party members recall that their general secretary, Mario Monje, began boasting in March that the PCB's coordination of Cuban-sponsored armed liberation movements now enjoyed a "direct contact to the Presidency." The largest of these covert guerrilla operations was Operación Matraca, in which dozens of Cuban-trained Peruvians received PCB support as they crossed Bolivia on their way to attack the military regime in neighboring Peru. In March, PCB General Secretary Monje told Czechoslovak Communist Party leaders that "Paz Estenssoro was heavily involved, including financial support" for *Matraca* to the tune of $20,000.[66] These funds were apparently given to Paz Estenssoro's Marxist friend, Víctor Zannier, a newspaper editor and Cuban contact who hosted several would-be Peruvian guerrillas at his home in Cochabamba before they were rounded up by unwitting, low-level Bolivian police. One of the Peruvian guerrilla leaders later declared assuredly that the Paz government was "aware of the operation and supported it."[67]

This would have represented a striking shift in MNR policy, which a Cuban intelligence officer chalked up to the rise of "good relations between the Bolivian and Cuban governments" since the U.S. tin-dumping fracas of late 1962.[68] A few weeks after Operación Matraca failed disastrously at Peru's Puerto Maldonado a few miles across the border, Bolivia's Foreign Ministry infuriated the U.S. State Department in mid-June by giving its highest diplomatic decoration, the Condor of the Andes, to Cuban Chargé Aja Castro.[69] For Bolivia's nationalist leader, prone to taking risks in the name of Third World nonalignment, collaboration with Cuban revolutionary operations seems to have been an especially dangerous gamble.

That is, of course, unless the intrigue surrounding Operación Matraca was nothing more than another one of Paz Estenssoro's nationalist bluffs. "The Americans knew everything," Paz's private secretary told me, adding that the U.S. embassy "was informed at every step of the way."[70] The would-be Peruvian guerrillas who had been arrested in Cochabamba were quietly passed to their country's military government "at an unnamed border point," and Peruvian diplomats in La Paz privately praised the Bolivian government's "cooperation" to U.S. embassy officials, pleading that Paz Estenssoro's duplicity with Cuba be "held in strict confidence." The CIA station chief, Tom Flores, was even permitted to participate in the interrogations of several Peruvian guerrillas in Bolivia's Pando province.[71] As PCB General Secretary Monje told the Czechoslovaks, his decision to include President Paz Estenssoro in Matraca "very likely did not sufficiently ensure the operation's confidentiality," principally since it had now appeared that "the American Embassy in La Paz has been informed." PCB Central Committee members later lamented that their faith in Paz Estenssoro "appeared in hindsight to have been erroneous."[72]

As Bolivia's nationalist president betrayed his tenuous allies on the pro-Cuba Left, he meanwhile played similarly insincere games with Eastern Europe. In March 1963, the U.S. embassy reported that the "Czechs have been meeting day and night" with MNR officials in La Paz, who appeared "disposed to accept offer" of an antimony smelter, signed almost a year earlier in Prague but again delayed by President Paz Estenssoro. Privately, the Bolivian president vowed to the U.S. embassy that the "Czech antimony smelter would not go through while he is in office," but U.S. officials worried nonetheless that the "attractiveness [of the] present offer and strong public sentiment for national smelter of any kind, plus his need to have an important showpiece project may compel [the] president to bow to political pressure."[73] In April, the U.S. embassy reported that the Paz government "will continue [to] stall on [the] Czech offer," despite noting that the president would "suffer political setback" as a result.[74] Noting that Prague had offered "substantial concessions" in its attempt to win Bolivian government approval, the U.S. embassy pinned its hopes on their estimation that Paz Estenssoro was letting negotiations proceed merely to "provide a façade of official enthusiasm for a project which has provoked much interest in Bolivia, and whose sudden abandonment might well cause domestic political problems."[75] Local USAID officials, recognizing that there was a lack of appetite in Washington for further funding of the badly behaving MNR, nonetheless did everything they could to "stiffen" Bolivian resistance to Czechoslovak aid projects and to "stall further progress."[76]

The Paz Estenssoro government continued to come under incessant U.S. pressure to move its nationalist revolution "away from both communism and neutralism," in the words of Washington's embassy in La Paz.[77] Throughout 1963, U.S. officials launched a host of overt and covert operations to bolster Paz Estenssoro's repressive security apparatus, "induce [him] to run for a third presidential term," and convince him to make a definitive break with the left sector of his party.[78] According to the U.S. embassy, the stability of a third Paz government would mean a "harder line on Cuba, a harder line on the internal communist problem . . . [and] a harder line on Soviet bloc aid."[79] Indeed it did. Between the launch of his reelection campaign in late 1963 and his fall from power in November 1964, the father of the Bolivian revolution allied his secret police service firmly with the CIA station in La Paz, used USAID weapons to arm strike-breaking MNR peasant militias, dramatically broke with the left sector of the governing party, obtained a third term in the face of a mass abstention of the entire MNR labor movement and all opposition parties, reluctantly broke with Cuba, and sent CIA-armed militiamen to face off with rebellious students and workers seeking a reprise revolution that would return nationalist Bolivia to the Third World promise that once defined the now hollow MNR party.[80]

As Bolivia's twelve-year experiment with middle-class nationalism took a sharp domestic turn to the right in 1963 and 1964, the country's spurned socialist suitors anticipated the worst. In December 1963, the Czechoslovak embassy began to worry that President Paz Estenssoro's local efforts to "weaken the left wing of the ruling MNR" were resulting in "provocations . . . against the trade unions and the PCB, as well as against the diplomatic representations of the socialist states." Unwilling to give up on Bolivia's nationalist workers, Prague resolved to carry out "greater activity" through its local embassy to shore up the embattled MNR trade unions (and indirectly the PCB, which "works through them"), in order to ensure that the labor movement continued to "play a positive role influencing the policy of the current government."[81] As the Czechoslovaks continued to limit their direct funding of local Communists, responding to a May 1964 PCB request with a curt "No way," Prague meanwhile helped to coordinate an increase in Soviet aid to Bolivia's national labor federation, which roughly doubled from $5,000 to $10,000 in 1963.[82]

At the heart of Czechoslovakia's persisting courtship of progressive sectors of the governing MNR was its acceptance of private Bolivian government claims to Prague that Paz Estenssoro was merely "allowing the Right to mobilize and increase its influence" as a "temporary tactic" to win reelection and continue his flexible Third World foreign policy. Prague worried, nonetheless, that the hidden connection between domestic and foreign affairs could complicate Paz Estenssoro's gamble, since his rightward shift was "moving rapidly toward a total alienation from the workers, who . . . are increasingly anti-imperialist and anti-Paz." The Bolivian Left had begun to view Paz Estenssoro as the "White House favorite," with U.S. diplomats publicly fawning over the MNR leader as "the type of 'revolutionary' who can break the momentum of 'communism and Fidelism.'" To halt these developments, Prague hoped the Cuban embassy would join its efforts to support the waning MNR left sector, thus abandoning the "relative passivity" that had defined Havana's foreign policy since the rightward shift began in mid-1963.[83]

If the Czechoslovaks continued to believe in nationalist Bolivia's Third World promise, Cuba had already begun to write off the MNR as a bourgeois fraud, particularly in the wake of the Operación Matraca debacle. According to Havana, Paz Estenssoro's acceptance of USAID's antilabor conditions had "not only guaranteed Paz's reelection" with Washington's support, but also "br[ought] with it the conclusion that the popular forces have been roughly beaten throughout the country, leading to . . . a policy more sold out to the Yankee government." In October 1963, the Cuban Foreign Ministry recognized the futility of Paz Estenssoro's "attempt to balance" domestic anti-Communism with a Third World posture abroad, since "those same [rightist] forces that now support his reelection will maintain their future positions of influence," from which they "will battle against this foreign policy . . . [of] nonalignment." Instead of continuing to play footsie with the governing sectors of the MNR, Cuba's consistent recommendation to its local allies was to begin "preparations for a general or national strike" that would bring about a true revolution in Bolivia, one that would cease to enable "the repressive designs against popular movements that had begun to be applied by the [U.S.] State Department throughout the continent."[84]

Friends of Cuba on the MNR Left had begun to draw similar conclusions by mid-1964. Shortly after Paz's reinauguration in August, leftist workers and students joined with the MNR's traditional right-wing enemies to wage a nationwide insurrection that reached crisis proportions by late October. In the midst of the uprising, Havana's *Bohemia* and *Radio Progreso* declared that Paz Estenssoro was "yesterday a nationalist, today Washington's peon," who had "sold out to imperialism" and now governed over "one of the most hostile regimes toward the Latin American people."[85] While the workers and students initially buckled under the weight of Paz Estenssoro's CIA-supplied secret police, civilian rebels soon began to court military officials, who intervened on 3 November to restore order and depose the duplicitous MNR leader.[86] Two weeks after the coup, the Cuban foreign ministry privately rejoiced at the overthrow of the "demagogic pseudo-revolutionary," Víctor Paz Estenssoro, whose "elimination from the Bolivian political scene" meant that "one of the principle obstacles to the enlightenment and politicization of the Bolivian popular movement has disappeared." President Paz Estenssoro had been "in practice an effective ally of imperialism in the exploitation of the people, contributing in a decisive manner to the stagnation of the revolutionary process in that country."[87] According to the Cubans and their local leftist allies, Paz Estenssoro's vacuous Third World pretense had revealed itself to be a bourgeois dalliance, meant to conceal his domestic project of permitting the U.S.-backed ascendance of the MNR's most reactionary elements.

Conclusion

The story of this Third World gambit and its eventual collapse in the face of Washington's intolerance of true nonalignment in the Western Hemisphere help to elucidate the limits of bourgeois nationalism in the early 1960s. In conversations with the author, Paz Estenssoro's private secretary conceded that the Bolivian president had "sacrificed a portion of his nationalism" to obtain U.S. development funding under Kennedy's Alliance for Progress. In private letters to his family, President Paz Estenssoro defended his decision as a temporary expediency, and he assured his confidants that the time would come when revolutionary Bolivia would "have more room for [international] maneuver."[88]

The failure of revolutionary Bolivia to maintain a nonaligned posture further reveals the subtle differences between socialist foreign policies in Prague and Havana. Both states supported the more radical version of anti-U.S. neutralism emanating from the NAM at Belgrade. But whereas Czechoslovakia preferred to work within the official political structures of Latin American nationalism, Cuba held out hopes for more transformative changes in the Western Hemisphere through popular insurrections against duplicitous bourgeois regimes. Finally, this story points to the need for additional research into the evolution of the Third World movement as it shifted away from the goal of formal decolonization to more radical politico-economic critiques of neocolonialism.

Notes

1. U.S. State Department, "Guidelines for Policy and Operations," 20 April 1962, and Barry Goldwater, 24 October 1963, both quoted in Thomas C. Field Jr., *From Development to Dictatorship: Bolivia and the Alliance for Progress in the Kennedy Era* (Ithaca, NY: Cornell University Press, 2014), xi, 47. For more on U.S. relations with revolutionary Bolivia, see Glenn J. Dorn, *The Truman Administration and Bolivia: Making the World Safe for Liberal Constitutional Oligarchy* (University Park: Penn State University Press, 2011); James F. Siekmeier, *The Bolivian Revolution and the United States, 1952 to the Present* (University Park: Penn State University Press, 2011).

2. United States Agency for International Development, *U.S. Overseas Loans and Grants (Greenbook)*, 2017, https://explorer.usaid.gov/prepared/Total_Economic _and_Military_Assistance_1946–2015.xlsx.

3. U.S. Embassy (La Paz) to Department of State, 8 May 1962, quoted in Field, *From Development to Dictatorship*, 48.

4. Field, *From Development to Dictatorship*, 11–12, 68–74, and 160–64.

5. Field, *From Development to Dictatorship*, chapters 3 through 6.

6. For Latin Americanists rushing to "internationalize" their scholarship and thus break out of their subject countries' nationalist historiographies, diplomatic history offers decades of examples that fuse multinational narrative planes. See Samuel Flagg Bemis, *The Latin American Policy of the United States* (San Diego: Harcourt, 1943); and David Green, *The Containment of Latin America: A History of the Myths and Realities of the Good Neighbor Policy* (New York: Quadrangle Books, 1971). For more recent treatments, see Stephen G. Rabe, *The Killing Zone: The United States Wages Cold War in Latin America* (Oxford: Oxford University Press, 2011); and Greg Grandin, *Empire's Workshop: Latin America, the United States, and the Rise of the New Imperialism* (New York, 2007).

7. Greg Grandin, "The Liberal Traditions in the Americas: Rights, Sovereignty, and the Origins of Liberal Multilateralism," *American Historical Review* 117, no. 1 (2012): 68–91.

8. Regarding the former, see a critique by Paul Kramer, "Power and Connection: Imperial Histories of the United States and the World," *American Historical Review* 116, no. 5 (2011): 1380. For examples of the latter, see Virginia Garrard-Burnett, Mark Atwood Lawrence, and Julio E. Moreno, *Beyond the Eagle's Shadow: New Histories of Latin America's Cold War* (Albuquerque: University of New Mexico Press, 2013); and Hal Brands, *Latin America's Cold War* (Cambridge, MA: Harvard University Press, 2012).

9. Michal Zourek, "Checoslovaquia y el Cono Sur 1945–1989," PhD diss., Universita Karlova v Praze, 2014.

10. Tobias Rupprecht, *Soviet Internationalism after Stalin: Interaction and Exchange between the USSR and Latin America during the Cold War* (Cambridge: Cambridge University Press, 2015). See also Rupprecht's contribution to this volume (chapter 9).

11. Central Intelligence Agency (CIA), "Sino-Soviet Bloc Economic Activities in Underdeveloped Areas," 28 February 1962, CIA Records Search Tool (hereafter

CREST), U.S. National Archives and Records Administration, College Park, MD (hereafter NARA).

12. See Michal Zourek, "Operation MANUEL: When Prague Was a Key Transit Hub for International Terrorism," *Central European Journal of International and Security Studies* 9, no. 3 (2015): 78–98; and Daniela Spenser, "Operation Manuel: Czechoslovakia and Cuba," *Cold War International History Project e-Dossier No. 7* (Washington, DC: Woodrow Wilson International Center for Scholars, 2011), https://www.wilsoncenter.org/publication/operation-manuel-czechoslovakia-and-cuba.

13. Jerry W. Knudson, "The Impact of the Catavi Mine Massacre of 1942 on Bolivian Politics and Public Opinion," *The Americas* 26, no. 3 (1970): 254–76; and Eduardo Ascarrunz Rodríguez, *La palabra de Paz: Un hombre, un siglo* (La Paz: Plural, 2008), 40.

14. Jerry Knudson, *Bolivia, Press and Revolution, 1932–1964* (Lanham, MD: University Press of America, 1986).

15. Herbert Klein, *A Concise History of Bolivia*, 2nd ed. (Cambridge: Cambridge University Press, 2011), 178–208; James Dunkerley, *Rebellion in the Veins: Political Struggle in Bolivia, 1952–1982* (London: Verso, 1984), 1–45; S. Sándor John, *Bolivia's Radical Tradition: Permanent Revolution in the Andes* (Tucson: University of Arizona Press, 2012), especially chapters 3 and 4.

16. Kevin Young, "Purging the Forces of Darkness: The United States, Monetary Stabilization, and the Containment of the Bolivian Revolution," *Diplomatic History* 37, no. 1 (2013): 509–37.

17. Cuban Foreign Ministry, Department B, n.d. [mid-1960], Folder "Bolivia, 1961, ORD," Archivo Central del Ministerio de Relaciones Exteriores [Central Archive of the Foreign Ministry], Havana, Cuba (hereafter MINREX-Cuba).

18. Field, *From Development to Dictatorship*, 6; quotation from Bolivian labor leader Juan Lechín Oquendo, on the same page.

19. Czechoslovak Foreign Ministry, Memorandum of Conversation, 20 September 1960, in "Relations, Czechoslovakia—Bolivia," Inv. č 93, ka 74, Komunistická strana Československa, Ústřední výbor, Kancelář I, Tajemníka ÚV KSČ Antonína Novotného—II. Č, Národní archiv [Central Committee of the Communist Party of Czechoslovakia, General Secretary Antonin Novotny, National Archives], Prague, Czech Republic (hereafter KSČ-Prague).

20. Bolivian Foreign Ministry, 13 January 1961, RV-4-E-53, 1961–1962, Archivo del Minsterio de Relaciones Exteriores y Culto [Archive of the Ministry of Foreign Relations and Culture], La Paz, Bolivia (hereafter RREE-Bolivia).

21. CIA, *Intelligence Bulletin*, 13 January 1961, CREST, NARA.

22. CIA, *Intelligence Bulletin*, 3 February 1961, CREST, NARA.

23. Thomas Mann to George Ball, 14 February 1961, Folder "Bolivia, 1961," Box 2, Lots 62D418 and 64D15, State Department Lot Files (hereafter SDLF), Record Group (hereafter RG) 59, NARA.

24. Arthur Schlesinger Journal Entry, 24 February 1961; and Schlesinger to Kennedy, 10 March 1961, both quoted in Field, *From Development to Dictatorship*, 14. For more on the aid package and its anti-labor conditions, see page 21.

25. Field, *From Development to Dictatorship*, 21–23.

26. Cuban Foreign Ministry, Department B, 22 March 1961, Folder "Bolivia, 1961, ORD," MINREX-Cuba.

27. Cuban Foreign Ministry, Department B, 10 May 1961, Folder "Bolivia, 1961, ORD," MINREX-Cuba.

28. Cuban Foreign Ministry, Department B, 10 May 1961.

29. Cuban Foreign Ministry, Department B, 1 August 1961, Folder "Bolivia, 1961, ORD," MINREX-Cuba.

30. Cuban Foreign Ministry, Department B, 9 June 1961, Folder "Bolivia, 1961, ORD," MINREX-Cuba.

31. Cuban Foreign Ministry, Department B, 11 October 1961, Folder "Bolivia, 1961, ORD," MINREX-Cuba.

32. Czechoslovak Foreign Ministry, Memorandum of Conversation, 2 November 1961, Inv. 93, ka 74, Central Committee (ústřední výbor; hereafter ÚV), Czech Communist Party (komunistická strana československa; hereafter KSČ-Prague).

33. Spanish Embassy to Madrid, 21 November 1961, IDD 177, Fondo 10, Ministry of Foreign Affairs, Archivo General de la Administración, Alcalá de Henares, Spain.

34. U.S. State Department, 10 August 1961, Folder 724.12/8-960, Box 1593, and 29 September 1961, Folder 724.5411/3-161, Box 1594, State Department Central Files (hereafter SDCF), RG59, NARA.

35. Field, *From Development to Dictatorship*, 73; quotations from author interviews with Ramiro Paz Cerruto and Luis Antezana Ergueta, cited on 11.

36. Cuban Foreign Ministry, Department B, 31 August 1961, Folder "Bolivia, 1961, ORD," MINREX-Cuba.

37. Embassy to State, A-1032, 26 June 1963, Folder "POL BOL-CHILE," Box 3831, SDCF, RG59, NARA.

38. U.S. Embassy Aide-Memoire, 6 February 1962, Folder LE-3-R-357, Collection "USEMB-RREE, Parte I," RREE-Bolivia.

39. Cuban Foreign Ministry, Department B, 31 August 1961, Folder "Bolivia, 1961, ORD," MINREX-Cuba.

40. U.S. Embassy Aide-Memoire, 18 January 1962, Folder LE-3-R-357, Collection "USEMB-RREE, Parte I," RREE-Bolivia.

41. For a list of Cuba's friends, see Cuban Foreign Ministry, Department B, 5 January 1962, Folder "Bolivia, 1962, ORD," MINREX-Cuba.

42. José Ninavia to the Bolivian Mine Workers Federation, 14 February 1961, Folder "Bolivia, 1961, ORD," MINREX-Cuba.

43. Mario Torres, cited by Cuban Foreign Ministry, Department B, 11 October 1961, Folder "Bolivia, 1961, ORD," MINREX-Cuba.

44. MNR Youth to Cuban Embassy, 1 January 1962, Folder "Bolivia, 1962, ORD," MINREX-Cuba.

45. MNR Youth to President Paz, 21 July 1961, quoted in Field, *From Development to Dictatorship*, 69.

46. Cuban Foreign Ministry, Department B, 10 May 1961, Folder "Bolivia, 1961, ORD," MINREX-Cuba.

47. Raúl Roa to José Fellman, 22 February 1962, Folder "Bolivia, 1962, ORD," MINREX-Cuba.

48. "Manifiesto de Solidaridad con Cuba," 22 February 1962, Folder "Bolivia, 1962, ORD," MINREX-Cuba.

49. Czechoslovak Foreign Ministry, Memorandum of Conversation, 28 February 1962, Inv. 93, ka 74, ÚV, KSČ-Prague.

50. Czechoslovak Embassy (La Paz) to Foreign Ministry, 24 July 1962, Inv. c 92, ka. 74, ÚV, KSČ-Prague.

51. Czechoslovak Foreign Ministry, Memorandum of Conversation, 5 June 1962, Inv. c 93, ka. 74, ÚV, KSČ-Prague.

52. CIA, "Sino-Soviet Bloc Economic Activities in Underdeveloped Areas," 16 July 1962, CREST, NARA.

53. Field, *From Development to Dictatorship*, 59-60; quotation from Bolivian Minister of Foreign Affairs Roberto Jordán Pando, cited on 59.

54. CIA, "Sino-Soviet Bloc Economic Activities in Underdeveloped Areas," 28 February 1962, CREST, NARA; CIA, Intelligence Bulletin, 23 March 1962; and CIA, "Sino-Soviet Bloc Economic Activities in Underdeveloped Areas," 16 July 1962, CREST, NARA.

55. Field, *From Development to Dictatorship*, 60; quotations of Schlesinger to Dungan, 18 July 1962, and Hansen to Dungan, n.d. [July 1962], both cited on the same page.

56. State Department Bureau of Intelligence and Research, 9 January 1963, Folder "Bolivia, General, 1/63-3/63," Box 10A, National Security Files—Countries (hereafter NSF-CO), John F. Kennedy President Library, Columbia Point, MA (hereafter JFKL).

57. CIA, "Sino-Soviet Bloc Economic Activities in Underdeveloped Areas," 31 August 1962, CREST, NARA.

58. MNR Parliamentarians to President Paz Estenssoro, 20 and 29 August 1962, Presidencia de la República 1009, Archivo y Biblioteca Nacional de Bolivia [National Archive and Library of Bolivia], Sucre, Bolivia.

59. Field, *From Development to Dictatorship*, 61-64; quotations from Ambassador Stephansky to State Department, 13 and 28 August 1962, cited on 62-63.

60. Embassy to State, 22 September 1962, Folder "IPS-1/General/Bolivia, Jan 1962-June 1963," Box 5, Office of Public Safety, Latin America Branch, Country File, USAID, RG286, NARA.

61. Ben Stephansky to Dean Rusk, 22 and 29 September 1962, Folder "Bolivia, General, 8/62-12/62," Box 10, NSF-CO, JFKL.

62. Field, *From Development to Dictatorship*, 65; quotations from Kennedy, National Security Action Memorandum 184, 4 September 1962, and Embassy to State, "Internal Defense Plan," 31 August 1962, both cited on 65.

63. Covert action programs included antiriot police training, arming paramilitary strike breakers, and a panoply of political projects that sought to encourage a pro-MNR, middle-class consciousness among Bolivia's youth, labor, and peasant sectors. See Field, *From Development to Dictatorship*, 76, 84-87, 91-92, 99, 109, 132, 136, and 240n11.

64. Cuban Foreign Ministry, 17 October 1962, Folder "Bolivia, 1962, ORD," MINREX-Cuba.

65. Dean Rusk to Embassy, State 403, Folder "POL BOL-CHILE," Box 3831, and Embassy to State, 22 February 1963, Folder "INCO BOL," Box 3540, SDCF, RG59, NARA. Quotation regarding Aja Castro comes from U.S. Embassy (Santiago) to State Department, 25 March 1963, cited in Field, *From Development to Dictatorship*, 71.

66. Author Interview with PCB leader José Luis Cueto, and Záznam o rozhovoru s prvním tajemníkem KS Bolívie Mario Monjem (Memorandum of conversation with First Secretary of the Bolivian CP Mario Monje), 21 May 1963, both cited in Field, *From Development to Dictatorship*, 72.

67. Héctor Béjar interview with Humberto Vázquez Viaña, cited in Field, *From Development to Dictatorship*, 72. For more on the arrests, see 71–72.

68. Juan Carretero interview with William Gálvez, cited in Field, *From Development to Dictatorship*, 72.

69. Embassy to State, A-1032, 26 June 1963, Folder "POL BOL-CHILE," Box 3831, SDCF, RG59, NARA.

70. Author interview with Carlos Serrate Reich, cited in Field, *From Development to Dictatorship*, 72.

71. Embassy to State, La Paz 1176, 1 June 1963, Folder "CSM BOL," Box 3687, SDCF, RG59, NARA.

72. Author interview with PCB leader José Luis Cueto; Záznam o rozhovoru, 21 May 1963.

73. Stephansky to State, 27 March 1963, Folder "INCO BOL," Box 3540, SDCF, RG59, NARA.

74. Stephansky to State, 4 April 1963, Folder "INCO BOL," Box 3540, SDCF, RG59, NARA.

75. Embassy to State, 23 July 1963, Folder "ECON BOL," Box 3367, SDCF, RG59, NARA.

76. Stutesman to State, 6 June 1963, Folder "INCO BOL," Box 3540, SDCF, RG59, NARA.

77. Stephansky to State, 16 August 1963, Folder "INCO BOL," Box 3540, SDCF, RG59, NARA.

78. State Department, n.d. [1963], Folder "1963 AID Strategy Paper," Box 10, Records Relating to Bolivia, 1961–1975, SDLF, RG59, NARA.

79. Ben Stephansky to Dean Rusk, 8 April 1963, Folder "Bolivia, General, 1/63-4/63," Box 10A, NSF-CO, JFKL.

80. Field, *From Development to Dictatorship*, chapters 3 through 6.

81. Czechoslovak Ministry of Foreign Affairs to First Secretary of the KSC, 2 December 1963, Inv. c. 93, ka. 74, ÚV, KSČ-Prague.

82. Czechoslovak Embassy (La Paz) to KSC (Prague), and written response, 11 May 1964, Inv. c. 93, ka. 74, ÚV, KSČ-Prague (emphasis in the original); and "Guide to the Archives of the Soviet Communist Party and Soviet State Microfilm Collection," December 1963 and January 1964, reel 1.1008, File 29, Fond 89, Hoover Institution, Stanford University.

83. Czechoslovak Ministry of Foreign Affairs to First Secretary of the KSC, 2 December 1963.

84. Ricardo Alarcón (MINREX) to Roberto Lassale (Cuban Embassy, La Paz), 7 October 1963, and MINREX Report, 21 October 1963, Folder "Bolivia, 1963, ORD," MINREX-Cuba.

85. *Bohemia*, 16 and 30 October, and 6 November 1964, and *Radio Progreso*, 31 October 1964, cited in Field, *From Development to Dictatorship*, 163–64.

86. See Field, *From Development to Dictatorship*, chapters 5 and 6.

87. Cuban Foreign Ministry, 18 November 1964, Folder "Bolivia, 1964, ORD," MINREX-Cuba.

88. Author interview with Carlos Serrate Reich, and Paz to son Ramiro, 26 May 1961, both cited in Field, *From Development to Dictatorship*, 73.

3 Mexican-Soviet Encounters in the Early 1960s
Tractors of Discord

VANNI PETTINÀ

In November 1959, Anastas Mikoyan, vice premier of the Union of Soviet Socialist Republics (USSR) and Prime Minister Nikita Khrushchev's close ally, landed in Mexico City to inaugurate a major exhibition of Soviet technical and scientific products. Several meetings with the main political leaders of the country, including President Adolfo López Mateos, were also on the agenda. *Life* magazine, in its photographic coverage of the visit, under the witty title "Mik's Mexican Mix," showed Mikoyan drinking tequila and, later, wolfing down some tacos in a clumsy attempt to counterbalance the intoxicating effect of the agave-based liquor. In the background, one could observe attentive Mexican officials advising the vice premier of the USSR on the best way to enjoy the tequila and, of course, the tacos.

The comic and somewhat inappropriate image of Mikoyan proposed by *Life* in its report could not have been more misleading. The smiles and the ungainly gestures were the façade of the official visit of the most important Soviet politician that a Latin American country had ever received. Mikoyan's presence in Mexico was a key move in the strategy of expansion of the Soviet influence in the Third World, launched by Khrushchev after the death of Stalin. Latin America was included in that plan as early as 1956.[1] On the other hand, the careful attention shown by Mexican officials toward Mikoyan highlighted the importance of the Soviet guest for President Adolfo López Mateos and his strategy of economic and political development at a time when Mexican economic prospects were rather dull. In an analysis of the outcome of Mikoyan's trip, *Time* magazine reported that "crisscrossing Mexico in President López Mateos' twin-motor Fairchild Fokker last week, the Soviet Union's first deputy Premier Anastas Mikoyan sold an image of Russia that was impressive and friendly."[2] Despite the tacos and the tequila, Mikoyan's visit had been very serious business and, up to a point, a success for the bilateral diplomatic relations between the two countries, opening new possibilities driven by a promising expansion of economic and commercial relations between Mexico and the USSR. However, as we shall see, the hopes generated by the visit of the Soviet statesman were not fulfilled by the end of López Mateos's term.

Based on primary sources from archives of the former Soviet Union, the United States and Mexico, this chapter aims to analyze how the climate of enthusiasm of November 1959 waned into much more limited results achieved by 1964.[3] In particular, I will show that for the first time since the beginning of the Cold War in 1947, a number of factors created the conditions for a possible rapprochement between Mexico and the USSR between the late 1950s and the early 1960s. At the same time, I will demonstrate that Mexico's heavy commercial dependence on the United States, as well as internal disagreements in the Mexican political establishment, hampered the process of rapprochement between the two countries. Finally, I will also stress how logistical difficulties and some Soviet naïveté in dealing with Mexican politicians came to limit the projection of Soviet influence in the region.

In order to illustrate the political and logistical problems of the rapprochement, this chapter will analyze the episode of the problematic sale of Soviet tractors to Mexico, one element in a possible economic convergence between the two countries. As we shall see, the economic and political difficulties related to the sale and delivery of tractors clearly show the limitations faced by the Mexican Ostpolitik toward the USSR and vice versa during the early 1960s.

It should also be noted that the late 1950s and early 1960s were crucial for the shaping of a new Mexican Third World identity, and Mexico's relationship with the USSR was part of a broader attempt, carried out during the presidency of López Mateos, to question the country's rigid allegiance to Washington in the context of the Cold War. Thus, López Mateos also sought to develop relationships with some of the most influential leaders of other Third World countries, such as Nehru of India, Sukarno of Indonesia and Tito of Yugoslavia, as well as to define the nature of its possible participation in Third World organizations and groups such as the Non-Aligned Movement.[4] Mexico's *sentimental education* during the early 1960s came to maturity By the 1970s, President Luis Echeverría Álvarez (1970–76) was a leading voice among Third World countries, and Mexico and the USSR signed a treaty of economic cooperation that strengthened their bilateral relations.[5] Although Mexico never completely embraced a Third Wordlist narrative—nor did it break its alliance with the United States—its political relations became much more diversified between the 1960s and the 1970s and a Third World identity progressively became an important component of what could be defined as a hybrid international position—one that, without breaking with the United States, constantly tried to increase the country's margin of autonomy and its convergence with other Third World countries.

The history of the relations between Mexico and the Soviet Union after the Second World War and particularly throughout the 1960s has received little attention from either Mexican or international scholars. Moreover, the scanty research that has been produced on this topic was unable to access Soviet primary sources or combine them with archival material from other countries.[6] More broadly, though, the historiographical gap is a consequence of a general lack of interest in the international history of Mexico during the Cold War and especially in the 1960s.[7] With the notable exception of studies of the relations between Mexico and the Cuban Revolution, this is an unfortunate vacuum, considering that, from 1958 onward, Mexican foreign policy experienced a significant expansion of its geographical radius.[8]

As this chapter will show, the globalization of the country's foreign policy and its rapprochement with the USSR were part of an attempt to diversify Mexican political and commercial relations. The late 1950s were a particularly complex time for economic development in Third World countries. In Mexico, the lack of resources to pursue industrialization, the deficit of its balance of payments, and the volatility of primary commodity markets threatened to disrupt the industrialization process through import substitution (*sustitución de importación*) that the governing Partido Revolucionario Institucional (PRI, Institutional Revolutionary Party) systematically sought to develop after 1946. Mexican foreign policy tried to respond to this situation with a strategy of diversifying its political and commercial relations, which included, among other things, the unprecedented—if incomplete—attempt to raise the level of cooperation with the USSR. In spite of the difficulties involved, the attempt reveals that the political class did not lack a complex and imaginative strategic vision, one that transcended the bilateral relationship with the United States and even Inter-American relations to encompass a genuinely global scale.

The present research aims to reconstruct some crucial aspects of the process of interaction between Latin America, the USSR, and the socialist bloc in the late 1950s and the first half of the 1960s. In the last few years, especially since the publication of Odd Arne Westad's work, historians have shown much greater interest in the relations between the USSR and the

Despite maintaining a close Cold War relationship with its northern neighbor, Mexico frequently sought to assert greater independence over its approaches to trade and foreign policy. Like other moderate nationalists, Mexican president Adolfo López Mateos therefore responded enthusiastically to growing Soviet interest in economic relations with Latin America during the late 1950s. Here López Mateos greets Soviet vice premier Anastas Mikoyan during the latter's goodwill trip to Mexico City in late 1959. (Image courtesy of Instituto Nacional de Antropología e Historia, México.)

Third World. However, Latin American international history has persistently remained focused on the relations between the region and the United States. In spite of recent efforts by such authors as Michelle Getchell and Tobias Rupprecht, the reconstruction of the dynamics of interaction between Latin America and the socialist bloc still lags behind.[9] Seeking to help fill this gap, this chapter documents a serious Mexican-Soviet interest in strengthening commercial and political bilateral relations, as well as the ideological and logistical challenges involved.

Mexico and the Opportunities for Diversification

On 18 November 1959, an Ilyushin-18 turboprop, the latest technological jewel of Soviet commercial aeronautics, landed in Mexico City. On board were Anastas I. Mikoyan and a group of twenty-nine persons that included the wife of the Soviet leader. A crowd of approximately four to five hundred people, headed by Mexico's secretary of foreign affairs, Manuel Tello, received Mikoyan waving red carnations and shouting "¡Viva la Uníon Soviética!"[10]

Mikoyan's Ilyushin landed in a Mexico that had considerably advanced in its process of socioeconomic transformation since the end of the Second World War. As Soledad Loaeza points out, the "Mexican miracle" had dramatically altered the "physiognomy" of the country: "Pipelines, industrial zones, hydroelectric systems, port works, residential areas, labor colonies had been built."[11] Thanks to a successful policy of "import substitution" by industrialization, implemented systematically from the mandate of Miguel Aleman (1946–52) onward, the country saw its gross domestic product (GDP) grow 6 percent per year between 1950 and 1962; the production of goods doubled compared to 1940, and industry came to represent 35 percent of the national product.[12] During these years, the Mexican federal state expanded its regulatory functions and its active participation in industrial promotion, without disregarding the role of private investment. Despite high inequality levels generated by the characteristics of the Mexican development model—economic growth combined with the expansion of the bureaucratic apparatus of the state—the country registered sustained social mobility, evidenced by middle-class growth from 16 to 26 percent of the population between 1940 and the end of 1960s.[13]

However, by the end of the 1950s, the Mexican development model had begun to encounter significant problems. With the decline in export volumes and prices, of cotton and coffee in particular, the balance of payments had become negative, reducing the inflow of foreign exchange necessary for the acquisition of capital badly needed to nourish the industrialization process of the country. According to U.S. data, by 1961, annual GDP growth had fallen to 3.5 percent, an alarming figure for a country with an annual population growth of 3 percent.[14] The López Mateos administration laid the blame for the country's difficulties on the imbalances of the international economic system, which, as a consequence of the protectionism of the economic center of the world and the unfavorable terms of trade for primary goods, hampered the development processes of Third World countries.[15] In fact, at the end of the 1950s, the problem of negative balances of payments caused by the instability of commodity markets or the lack of capital and foreign exchange threatened not only Latin American countries such as Mexico. Nehru's India, for one, was in a similar situation at the beginning of its second five-year plan and, like Mexico, in search of alternative paths to foster its development plans.[16] In the Mexican case, some of the distortions criticized by President López Mateos were inevitably attributable to the trade asymmetry with the United States, Mexico's main trading partner, and called attention to the need to transform this situation of rigid dependency.[17]

As a result of this analysis of the international economic context, the beginning of the presidency of López Mateos was marked by a strategy that aimed to further the nationalization of the economy, in addition to the search for greater commercial diversification. In January 1959, the president issued a decree requiring all government offices, agencies, and state-owned enterprises to use only raw materials of Mexican origin rather than imports. The Mexican private sector had already been subject to a policy of restrictions on its imports, which the decree now extended to the public sector. As emphasized in a note from the U.S. embassy in Mexico, the decree itself was less important than the fact that it showed the zeal with which the new Mexican administration wanted to implement its announced policy of reducing imports to a minimum in support of the industrialization and development needs of the country.[18] The nationalization law of the country's power industry, issued in September 1960, and new legislation that required Mexican companies producing raw or strategic materials to be 51 percent Mexican-owned, completed the internal framework of measures aimed at a nationalization of the economy.[19]

At the international level, the new diversification strategy led Mexico to intensify its interaction with the countries of the region. In January and February 1959, López Mateos made his "grand tour" of Latin America. According to the U.S. embassy in Mexico, the Mexican president visited Venezuela, Brazil, Argentina, Chile, Bolivia, and Peru to promote trade relations between Mexico and Latin America. The entry of Mexico into the Latin American Free Trade Association, created by the Treaty of Montevideo in February 1960, completed the regional framework of the strategy of economic diversification.[20]

The activism of President López Mateos was not limited to the Inter-American sphere. He also sought to develop relations with countries such as Indonesia, India, the Philippines, and Japan. Moreover, the Mexican president, although cautious, drew closer to the Non-Aligned Movement, which sought to make international economic structures more favorable to Third World development processes. At the last minute, Mexico decided not to participate in the Conference of Non-Aligned Countries held in Belgrade during August and September 1961, but it did take part in the Conference on Economic Affairs held in Cairo in 1962 and, under observer status, in the 1964 Second Conference of Non-Aligned Countries.[21]

It was in the context of the Mexican economic downturn and within the framework of the diversification process launched by López Mateos that Mikoyan's visit occurred. Mexican diplomatic documents show an increasing Mexican interest in Soviet engagement with other Latin American countries since at least 1958. Mexican diplomats, for example, closely monitored the process that led to the signing of various trade and credit agreements between Moscow and Buenos Aires in 1958–59. In January 1958, the Ministry of Foreign Affairs asked its diplomatic headquarters in Moscow to explain in detail the terms of the Soviet offer to Argentina of "abundant long-term loans at very low rates" mentioned in a Mexican telegram. Likewise, Mexican diplomats attentively reported the Soviet willingness to provide credit and machinery for the development of the Argentine oil industry, formalized in a commercial agreement in May 1959.[22]

In a long editorial in *Comercio Exterior* (Foreign Trade), a journal published by the state-owned Banco Nacional de Comercio Exterior (BANCOMEXT, National Exterior Commerce Bank), the reasons why Mexico followed the evolution of Argentine-Soviet relations were lucidly clarified. According to the editorialist, "the interest and motivations of several Latin American republics to increase trade volumes" with socialist countries were due to the fact that, after the end of the Korean War, "the traditional markets of some primary products had begun to weaken, and then, with the passage of time, the difficulties of Latin American export trade worsened." The author went on to explain that "recent experience" had shown that the fall in demand for primary products was linked not simply "to the cyclical reduction of economic activity in the major industrial centers of the West, but also to longer-term trends." The relationship with the socialist bloc offered the possibility of "placing part of the exportable goods in new markets" and also receiving "in return for their own sales . . . the fuels and capital goods that were badly needed for economic development."[23]

While Mexico was thus interested in probing whether and to what extent the Soviet Union would support the Mexican diversification strategy, from Moscow's point of view, expanding relations with a country traditionally close to the United States, and in a geographical position of great strategic interest, could represent a significant potential success for the strategy of expansion of Soviet influence in Latin America at the expense of Washington.

The Soviet Exhibition of 1959 and the Approach to Mexico

Soviet analysts had a very accurate reading of the the peculiar characteristics of Mexico's political system and its international place in the world at the end of the 1950s and the beginning of the 1960s. Thus, a report of the Academy of Sciences in 1960 acknowledged the existence of formally democratic institutions and political pluralism, but stated that the real power in the country was held by the president and the PRI. From an economic point of view, Moscow considered that Mexico was "a comparatively developed economy within Latin America" since it did not depend on the sale of a single primary product on the international market. According to Soviet Latin Americanists, its mineral reserves and its production of oil, copper, and silver contributed to a diversified economy. The document also noted the strong impulse given to industrialization, especially in the energy and metallurgical sectors. The high development of both consumer and export agriculture complemented the picture of an economy that the Soviets assessed as relatively diversified and endowed with a complex productive base. At the same time, Soviet Latin Americanists were aware of the extreme levels of poverty and high levels of illiteracy that characterized the country, as well as its heavy commercial and financial dependence on the United States.

At this time, the Mexican state controlled significant parts of the national economy, and López Mateos's administration was determined to raise the levels of industrial and agricultural production by means of further state intervention, despite opposition coming from domestic economic and financial circles, particularly those connected to the United States, and from the American diplomatic establishment itself. According to Soviet diplomats, this domestic policy, coupled with López Mateos's attempt to pursue a more autonomous foreign policy with respect to the United States, had generated "serious differences" between Mexico and Washington especially on issues related to trade and the economy.[24] In one report, Vladimir Bazykin, the

Soviet ambassador to Mexico, stressed the new emphasis placed by the López Mateos administration on the issue of state-led industrialization and the quest for greater independence from the United States:

> Compared with the previous one, the current government of Mexico more consistently seeks the industrialization of the country, and first of all, the development of the oil, metallurgical, electrical, and chemical industries. They see it as a means of gradual liberation from the country's economic dependence on the United States. At the same time, they aim to expand the foreign market by developing trade links with the countries of Europe, Asia, Africa, and Latin America. President López Mateos is in favor of establishing personal contacts with the leaders of other countries and to some extent aspires to leadership in Latin America. In relation to the United States, he takes a more courageous position compared to his predecessors.[25]

The exhibition and Mikoyan's visit offered Moscow an opportunity to exploit U.S.-Mexican tensions and disagreements while potentially giving Mexico economic and trade tools to underpin its state-led economic development process, reduce its dependence on Washington and increase, incidentally, the Soviet influence in the region.

A long report from the U.S. Central Intelligence Agency (CIA) about Soviet strategies in the Third World included a whole section on Mikoyan's visit to Mexico and highlighted how his presence there opened a new phase in the Soviet strategy of approaching Latin America. "The visit of the Vice Premier Mikoyan to Mexico in November in connection with the opening of the Soviet industrial exhibition," the document stated, "marks a new phase in Soviet attempts to take advantage of Latin American economic difficulties in order to expand trade and other types of relations with the Bloc." Moreover, the report emphasized that if Mikoyan had previously focused on promoting trade with the USSR, his interventions had become more political. "His private and public comments in Mexico were directed as much against political as economic aspects of 'colonialism'—U.S. influence in Latin America." For the CIA, the new phase of Soviet policy toward Latin America was directed against "the policies and activities of the United States and of U.S. firms in Latin America" and went hand in hand with "the reiteration of a Soviet interest in increased trade and a willingness to extend, 'without strings,' development credits to Mexico and other Latin American countries."[26]

According to Soviet sources, Mikoyan's visit and the exhibit he inaugurated helped Moscow edge its way into the midst of the political and economic tensions that marked the bilateral relationship between Mexico and the United States during the presidency of López Mateos. In his account of the results of the Soviet exhibition inaugurated in Mexico City in November 1959, the director of the show, A. Shelnov, boasted with great satisfaction that

> the exhibition has been a great success among the business circles of Mexico. During a period of 25 days it has been visited by at least one million people. Among the visitors were politicians and the most important national figures of the country, delegations of union representatives, teachers, students, peasant communities, army and navy, etc., etc. It has received favorable comments in the Mexican press, radio and television, and in this way, has also influenced the mass of Mexicans who have had the opportunity to visit it in person. The attendees have left thousands of enthusiastic comments in the guest book.

The underlying purpose of the exhibition had been to show the advance, progress, and limitless future for which the USSR was destined as a consequence of the socialist revolution and the social and economic changes it had fostered in the country. For this purpose, the Soviet curators had organized the show in a comprehensive manner, complementing sections that displayed the latest advances in science and technology with others dedicated to the history of the USSR and its social, economic, and cultural advances after 1917. As Shelnov recalled, the USSR had organized three major exhibitions in Latin America before 1959—in 1946 in Mexico for the international book fair, and two in Argentina in 1955 and 1957. However, this was the "first Soviet exhibition in Latin American countries that offered wide coverage of different aspects of the life of the Soviet state." Thus, the first section of the exhibition was devoted to a description of the Soviet political system, the geography of the country, the characteristics of the population, and the "huge growth of the economy and culture of the Soviet Union in contrast to prerevolutionary Russia." Mechanical and illuminated maps, surrounded by scale models of commercial airplanes, showed the expansion of the country's electrification and industry, while some photos recalled Khrushchev's trip to the United States in September 1959.

The space dedicated to technology was particularly large, with more than six thousand exhibits. These included "machine tools for the cutting of metals, machinery for the construction of roads, tractors, transport trucks, a truck for oil drilling, motorcycles, mopeds, and other examples of national mechanical engineering, which were of commercial interest." In order to facilitate the understanding of the use of machinery, the Soviet curators included film projections that showed them in action speakers—over 200 units—and headphones providing didactic contents in Spanish.

Of great interest to the public had been the pavilion dedicated to the achievements of Soviet space exploration, which presented natural-scale artificial satellites, scientific instruments launched toward the moon, and the latest advances in missiles. According to Shelnov, from early in the morning to closing time, "the stands with the satellites were surrounded by a large crowd who listened with great attention to the explanations issued through the microphone by a mechanically recorded voice. The Mexicans were simply amazed at the inventions of man."

Another important part of the exhibition, and a great success in terms of audience, was the section devoted to the peaceful uses of nuclear energy, which showed nuclear reactors, particle accelerators, thermonuclear machines, and the nuclear icebreaker *Lenin*.[27]

It would be impossible to list here all the important sections of the exhibition and those that attracted the public. What must be emphasized is that the exhibition was a major effort on the part of the USSR to offer Mexico and Latin America a strong and convincing image of Soviet modernity. As the Soviet ambassador, Bazykin, wrote in a letter to A. Gromyko, the minister of foreign affairs, "The exhibition was very successful . . . and, to a large extent, managed to undermine years of anti-Soviet propaganda, showing what the USSR really is." Bazykin's report also underscored the importance of Mikoyan's presence in Mexico, the warm reception given to him by the Mexican authorities, and López Mateos's willingness to visit the USSR between April and May 1961:

> The visit to Mexico of Comrade A. I. Mikoyan to inaugurate the exhibition on behalf of the Soviet government was of great political importance and helped strengthen our position in Mexico. Comrade Mikoyan was welcomed and bidden farewell at the airport by a larger number of cabinet members than the Japanese Prime Minister Kisi, on his recent state visit to Mexico. For his travels through the country, President López Mateos made the official plane available to A. I. Mikoyan. These gestures of friendship on the part of the president had not occurred during the visits of other distinguished

guests, including heads of governments and states. In principle, President López Mateos accepted the invitation of the Soviet government to visit the USSR. He intends to visit the USSR in April–May 1961.

Additionally, Bazykin commented that the two countries had begun to discuss the possible signing of a bilateral trade agreement that would have made it possible to settle, on a firmer basis, the emerging trade relations between the two countries.[28]

For the USSR, from the second half of the 1950s, the expansion of trade ties represented a strategy aimed at increasing its influence in Third World contexts where Moscow's projection was unstable and dependence on the West was strong. Indeed, Soviet credit lines, which were granted with favorable interest rates and the possibility of exchanging Third World countries' primary goods for Soviet capital and technical assistance in order to accelerate industrialization, made trade relations with Moscow potentially very attractive for these countries. This approach had facilitated the expansion of Soviet influence in West Africa and even in some Latin American countries such as Argentina and Brazil, which had signed commercial treaties with Moscow after 1955.[29]

The optimism that can be seen in Bazykin's analysis was also partly shared by some of the Mexican authorities. In a conversation held at the end of November 1959 with A. P. Malkov, the head of the department of Latin America of the Ministry of Foreign Trade of the USSR, Ricardo J. Zevada, general director of BANCOMEXT, who was a great advocate for the need to diversify Mexican trade, said that "with your exhibition you have achieved a lot to bring consumers closer to Soviet products, and to break the suspicious attitude of Mexican consumers regarding these products that had prevailed here in Mexico for years." Notably, Zevada's interpretation was more nuanced than that of the Soviets, and it was marked by the realism of a Mexican senior official who knew in depth the political and economic reality of his country. "Nothing significant can be changed in a week or two," the director of the bank observed. "It takes time and struggle" to achieve it.[30]

Even more cautious was the Americans' interpretation of the outcome of the exhibition and of how much Mikoyan had achieved through his meetings with the Mexican authorities. In a report sent to Roy Rubottom, an officer with the Latin American affairs bureau of the State Department, Harry Turkel, a specialist in Eurasian affairs, commented that during his meeting with the Mexican authorities Mikoyan had offered a credit line of

$100 million for investments in the oil sector, which had been in the hands of the Mexican state since 1938. According to Turkel, this was not the first time the Soviets offered credit to Mexicans, adding that in the last "two years there have been two or three similar offers," all rejected by Mexico. For Turkel then, "Mikoyan has not achieved much on the economic front in Mexico." The State Department expert on Russia and Asia concluded that having open lines of credit with U.S. bilateral institutions, such as the Export/Import Bank, meant that was not in an emergency situation and that, unless the economic situation of Mexico deteriorated considerably, "a significant increase in Mexican trade relations with the USSR was improbable."[31]

In just a few years, as we shall see, the optimism generated by the success of the Soviet exhibition would give way to the veiled pessimism suggested by Zevada and the doubts of the American diplomats.

Negotiating the Tractors

As Ambassador Bazykin pointed out in his August 1960 report, several official Mexican delegations had visited the USSR (and vice versa) after the end of the exhibition; even more importantly, the two countries had begun to discuss how to restructure bilateral trade by working on a commercial treaty. However, as Zevada had made it clear in his conversation with Soviet officials, it was not going to be an easy task to translate the optimism generated by the exhibition into more tangible bonds between the two countries.

During a meeting between President López Mateos, the Foreign Affairs Minister Manuel Tello, and the members of a Soviet goodwill delegation that visited Mexico in the summer of 1961, some optimism could still be perceived, although elements of concern on the Soviet side were already emerging. According to the Soviets, throughout a conversation described as "warm and friendly," López Mateos had emphasized "the coincidence of Mexican and Soviet Union points of view on several important international affairs." In the same conversation, the Mexican president had recalled that in his last speech in the United Nations, he had referred to "general and complete disarmament, détente, and the strengthening of mutual understanding between all the peoples of the world. The position of Mexico in these matters is firm and unshakeable." In the summer of 1961, the USSR and Mexico probably had some converging points of view on the issues of decolonization, détente, and the construction of mechanisms of cooperation between the nations of the world. However, both President López Mateos and the secretary of foreign affairs had shown more reluctance about taking concrete steps to consolidate the bilateral approach. The Mexican president, citing the need to oversee the municipal and congressional elections, had made it clear that he would not travel, as previously speculated, to the USSR. Instead, he would send the secretary of industry and commerce, Raúl Salinas Lozano.

The conversation with Secretary Tello had been more concrete and indicative of the problems faced by the expansion of trade relations between the two countries. According to the Soviet delegation, "Manuel Tello stated that the Mexican government applauds the expansion of contacts between Mexican officials and those of the USSR. . . . M. Tello pointed out that in the future relations may not only develop in the field of culture, but also in that of commerce. However, he said that in Mexico almost all trade is concentrated in the hands of private companies and that the government has little chance of influencing trade policy." The conclusion reached by the Soviet delegation after these two meetings was that

> the Mexican government is generally interested in maintaining normal relations with the Soviet Union and, because of the positive influence of public opinion, it is willing to expand them to a certain extent, especially in the line of cultural and artistic exchange. With regard to economic and trade relations, taking into account the predominance of U.S. capital in the country's economy, there are in fact no favorable prospects for appreciable development in the short term.[32]

The optimism generated by the exhibition and, more generally, the enthusiasm elicited by Khrushchev's new policies had probably blinded the Soviets to the technical and political obstacles to progress in bilateral relations with Mexico. One indication of these hindrances was the difficulty of simply selling Soviet tractors to Mexico.

In October 1958, the state-owned Soviet company Autoexport, in charge of exporting different types of machinery, had signed an agreement for the sale of seventy-five DT-54 tractors and other agricultural machinery to Mexico.[33] Newspaper reports, such as those published by the local newspaper *El Porvenir* and the national magazine *Jueves de Excelsior*, had speculated on the purchase of these tractors, attributing the initiative to the good offices of former president Lázaro Cárdenas, who, according to different sources, had negotiated the acquisition directly with Moscow.[34] From what Soviet documentation lets us reconstruct and given the lack of Mexican sources, the tractors were originally destined for a group of *ejidos* of the Comarca Lagunera,[35] and another possible sale was being negotiated with the Alianza de Sociedades Locales Colectivas Maximilano López of the Yaqui Valley, Sonora (Alliance of Collective Local Companies Maximiliano López, in the Russian documents the "Maximilian Alliance"). *Ejidos* were a particular kind of communal agricultural lands and had represented the backbone of Lazaro Cárdenas's agrarian reform during the 1930s. The Maximilian Alliance and the *ejidos* of the Comarca Lagunera represented politically active groups, the first led by Ramón Danzós Palomino and the second by Arturo Orona, both of whom belonged to political and trade union groups rooted in the Mexican radical Left.[36] At least since the mid-1950s, as shown in a study by Luis Aboites Aguilar, these groups had fought for the diversification of the cotton market, which the U.S. company Anderson and Clayton monopolized and thus managed to impose low purchase prices.[37] To bypass the monopoly, *ejidos* from Comerca Lagunera and the Yaqui Valley had proposed to sell Mexican cotton on the markets of the socialist bloc, especially in Poland and Czechoslovakia, in exchange for Soviet machinery of various types.[38] The Maximilian Alliance and the Orona group maintained a position of independent trade unionism and, by the end of the decade, left the official Confederación Nacional Campesina (CNC; National Confederation of Peasants). They became closer to the left-wing Movimiento de Liberación Nacional (MLN; National Liberation Movement), founded under the auspices of Lázaro Cárdenas and contributed to the foundation of the Central Campesina Independiente (CCI, Independent Peasant Center).[39] Both the CCI and the MLN were created to challenge the plan of economic modernization launched by PRI governments after World War II. These organizations questioned the social inequality generated by the economic model and the abandonment of communal forms of agricultural production in favor of large tracts of lands devoted to commercial production. In Sonora and the Comarca Lagunera, where the Soviet tractors were headed, the process of land concentration for commercial purpose had been particularly intense, giving rise to strong resistance from local *ejidos* such as those led by Orona and Danzós Palomino.

Moscow, as provided by the contract signed on 25 October 1958, had sent 75 tractors and other agricultural machinery to Mexico. However, in July 1959, four and a half months after their arrival, they were still undelivered. Stored in the customs area of Tampico port facilities, they fed rumors echoed by the Mexican press. An article by Pedro Vazquez Cisneros in the *Jueves de Excelsior*, for example, reported on all kinds of legends about the Soviet machinery in Tampico. According to different accounts, Soviet tractors had turned into scrap metal because they were left out in the open, or they were obsolete old tractors, like those used in Mexican fields in the 1930s. Finally, the article raised the problem of Cárdenas's role in the negotiation and acquisition of the machinery from Moscow.[40]

In February 1959, before the arrival of the tractors in Mexico, the commercial affairs officer of the Soviet embassy in Mexico, K. D. Tikhomirov, accompanied by two engineers from the USSR, held a not very encouraging meeting with all the actors whose interests were involved in the purchase of the tractors. At the meeting were present the Mexican company responsible for the import of the machinery, De Swaan, S. A, and Arturo Orona, described by Soviet documents as the representative of the *ejidal* union of the Province of Cuauhtémoc, together with V. Lopez, whom the documents identify as a representative of the Ejidal Bank.[41] The meeting had evinced a long list of logistical problems for the purchase of Soviet agricultural machinery. In the document, Tikhomirov expressed concern to De Swaan's representatives because the Ejidal Bank had not issued a certificate of payment commitment. However, in the letter delivered to the Soviet company Autoexport, the payout was made dependent on the results of the agricultural work that the *ejidal* units would be able to carry out with the Soviet machines. Moreover, despite the lack of an official payment commitment, the contract provided for a partial transfer of ownership of the tractors to the De Swaan Company. In short, the representatives of the Mexican import company sought to receive the machinery and partial ownership of the same without paying for it immediately and without offering a guarantee of future payment by the Ejidal Bank.

During the negotiation, De Swaan had offered to solve the problem of payment by means of a barter—Mexican cotton in exchange for Soviet machinery—an option successfully used by the USSR in other parts of the Third World to expand its commercial influence. For reasons that are not easy to understand, the Soviet diplomats present at that meeting rejected the proposal somewhat derisively, stating that "Autoexport had not registered at the moment any application for the acquisition of cotton for its customers."[42]

In any case, after a long debate, in which Arturo Orona had largely supported Soviet positions and Lopez had remained silent, a compromise was reached on the basis of which Moscow, without a guarantee from the Ejidal Bank, maintained a reservation of ownership of the tractors that allowed it to recover the merchandise in case it was not paid for.[43] Although the question of the letter of commitment was not resolved during that meeting, other

Soviet documents indicate that, by the spring, the Soviet export company had secured the official commitment of the Ejidal Bank for the payment of the tractors to be delivered to the Comarca Lagunera. Different Soviet sources confirm that Autoexport actually exchanged the tractors and other agricultural machines, worth $2.3 million, for Mexican products, most likely cotton.[44]

This first meeting had shown several problems in the conduct of business transactions between the two countries. First of all, on the Mexican side, the lack of clear support from the Ejidal Bank, which in theory was the public institution responsible for providing the *ejidal* units with financial support for the purchase of tractors, became evident. In turn, on the Soviet side, there was a lack of financial mechanisms and institutions that could contribute to the expansion of trade with Mexico. It is true that the Soviets were willing to hand over the tractors in exchange for a simple payment commitment from the Ejidal Bank. However, a commercial offensive, part of a broader political strategy to get closer to Latin America, needed better planning and more financial instruments to help deal with problematic situations such as that created with the Mexican *ejidatarios* of the Comarca Lagunera or the Yaqui Valley.

The February meeting and the problems manifested in the bilateral negotiations foreshadowed even more difficulties. In fact, as I noted above, once they arrived in Tampico (toward the end of March), the tractors remained at the port facilities for months. In May 1959, in an attempt to understand the real problems of the *ejidos* and the reasons why Soviet machinery remained held in the Mexican port, Tikhomirov, accompanied by the engineer Streltsov, visited the cotton regions of Sonora. There, guided by Ramón Danzós Palomino, the Soviets witnessed the many problems faced by the *ejidal* productive units in the region.[45] In his report, Tikhomirov emphasized the existence of eighty-five *ejidos*, defined by the Soviets as cooperatives, of which between eight and ten were collective farms and the remainder were exploited by individuals. The alliance, composed of an external president and the representatives of each cooperative, was, according to Soviet analysis, the institution in charge of obtaining credits and water supply for irrigation of the fields and, in general, of dealing with and solving all the logistical problems of the cooperatives. Tikhomirov's report revealed that, regarding the purchase of tractors, collective cooperatives, defined by the commercial attaché as the "most progressive form of cooperation among Mexican peasants," had to proceed individually. At the same time, the report emphasized that the *ejidos*, including the collectives, had scarce and outdated machinery and, with almost zero capitalization, were heavily dependent on the credit granted by the Ejidal Bank for the acquisition of new means of production. According to the data provided by *ejidatarios* to Soviet diplomats and specialists, only 20 percent of the land was worked by machinery directly owned by the *ejidatarios*, while the remaining 80 percent used machinery leased from U.S. and Mexican companies. The *ejidos* paid approximately eighty Mexican pesos per day to the companies for the rent, which included the driving and the gasoline of the tractors. Since they had little capital, these amounts were paid through loans granted by the Ejidal Bank at an annual interest rate of 7 to 8 percent. In addition, the Ejidal Bank was also in charge of buying fertilizers, charging a 5 percent commission to the *ejidos*. According to the *ejidatarios*, the purchases made by the Ejidal Bank had to do not with budgetary efficiency but with financial profit, a statement that the Soviets deemed correct.

Regarding the question of the tractors, Tikhomirov had been able to find out that in the state of Sonora they were sold exclusively by American and Canadian companies such as Case, Caterpillar, Ford, John Deere, Oliver, Massy Harry, and the like. There was not a single company from other countries. American companies had a representative office in many cities of the state, and the machinery was shown in well-equipped exhibition halls with all kinds of accessories and parts. These companies generally did not require payment guarantees for the first two or three tractors, whereas for larger purchases they demanded letters of commitment from the two state credit institutes, the Ejidal Bank and the Banco de Crédito Agrícola (the Bank of Agricultural Credit). Payment was usually spread over four years at a 4 percent interest rate. Finally, regarding the credit-granting issue, the Soviet envoys detected political factors that were bound to limit the expansion of Soviet trade with the state as well as the country in general. Sounded out by the Soviets about the possible purchase of tractors from the USSR, *ejidal* representatives admitted that they were not in a position to make a first payment of 20 percent or even 10 percent of the amount because the Ejidal Bank of the region refused to extend credit to the cooperatives to buy Soviet machinery.

In July of the same year, only a few months after the visit to Sonora, Tikhomirov and Ambassador Bazykin had a meeting with the secretary of agriculture and livestock of Mexico, Julián Rodríguez Adame, who confirmed what the *ejidatarios* had already explained about the factors that hindered the expansion of bilateral trade and the release of the tractors from Tampico to the Comarca Lagunera. At that meeting, the Soviets questioned Secretary Adame about why the Soviet machinery had been detained at the port for four and a half months, adding that they had a letter of commitment from the Ejidal Bank for the payment of the merchandise. The point was, Soviet diplomats added, that it was not possible to begin to request and execute payment without previous delivery of the machinery to the *ejidos*. The secretary replied that he would take care of the matter the next day. However, he said that it had been decided to deliver the tractors to areas other than those originally planned. Tikhomirov and Bazykin said they thought it would have been better to concentrate the tractors in adjacent areas to ensure a more efficient use of the machinery and facilitate its maintenance and the distribution of spare parts. Adame retorted sharply that the tractors would be sent to the areas that most needed them. He added that the delay in delivery was due to a political reason: the tractors had not been delivered to the *ejidos* of the Laguna because these were run by Communists and he recommended that, in the future, the Soviets should conduct their transactions on the basis of "purely commercial" reasons and not because they wanted the tractors to be used "by certain people in certain regions."[46]

Soviet sources do not allow us to conclusively document that the delivery of tractors to the *ejidos* linked to the Partido Comunista de México (PCM, Communist Party of Mexico), the MLN, or more independent trade unions such as the CCI reflected a precise Soviet strategy, planned with the help of Cárdenas, to favor those sectors that the Soviets themselves defined as the most progressive in the country. Unfortunately, there are no Mexican sources on this topic available at present. However, the content of *El Porvenir* and the *Jueves de Excelsior*, which attributed Cárdenas a central role in the negotiation of the tractors sale, together with the aforementioned Soviet sources, seem to suggest indirectly that the operation was not without an ideological flavor. The delivery of the tractors to the peasants of the Comarca Lagunera and the Yaqui Valley would have showed that the Soviets were interested in the tractors being delivered to *ejidos*, productive units similar to the *kolkhozes*, governed by political forces ideologically close to Moscow. If we take seriously the words of Secretary Rodríguez Adame, the ideological and political nexus of the commercial operation was, in fact, among the causes of its near failure.

The tractor episode revealed a wide range of ideological and political issues that help to explain the difficulties faced by the process of Mexican-Soviet rapprochement. On the one hand, the retention of the Soviet tractors in Tampico for what turned out to be over eleven months suggests the existence of inner conflicts within the Mexican political establishment with regard to forming closer ties between the USSR and Mexico. A sector of the country's political elite was clearly opposed to the Soviet tractors ending up in *ejidos* politically characterized as Communist or radical leftist or linked to the figure of Cárdenas. The unquestionable anti-Communism of some Mexican political and governmental sectors represented an obvious internal obstacle for the expansion of the relations between the two countries. On the other hand, the incident also betrayed some Soviet naïveté in conducting commercial operations in Mexico. In particular, Moscow underestimated the opposition that an excessively ideologically flavored commercial operation could provoke in a sector of the Mexican political establishment. If Moscow's aim was to increase its influence in Mexico by means of more intense commercial relations, a less ideologically colored operation would have probably been more effective to achieve such an objective.

Beside these political and ideological difficulties, the episode, at a micro level, also points at the logistical problems that the high Mexican dependence on Washington created for the puposes of economic diversification. This dependence—epitomized in this case by the overwhelming presence of U.S. agricultural machinery companies, whose finances were also supported by Mexican credit institutions—obstructed the entry of Soviet equipment. Moscow's own logistical problems, in addition, did not help to overcome what was already an uphill battle for the expansion of its economic influence in Mexico. The fact that, for example, in one of the meetings described above Soviet diplomats chose not use one of their main assets, the possibility of exchanging USSR machinery directly against Mexican primary goods, underlines some limitation on the Soviet side. It is true that, in the end, this particular kind of barter was finally put into practice, but the impression one gets from Soviet sources is that its use was not as straightforward as it should have been.

Another conversation that the magazine editor of BANCOMEXT (Arturo Perera Mena in the Soviet sources) maintained in July 1962 with the correspondent of the Soviet state information agency TASS (A. Pavlenko) provides an indication on a macro level of the dynamics of dependence that slowed down the development of stronger bilateral trade relations.Situations similar to the episode with the tractors continued to generate major difficulties in the process of commercial economic rapprochement between the two countries. Perera Mena confirmed the keen interest on the Mexican side in expanding the relations between the two countries, but he reminded his interlocutor that the main cause of the obstruction of this process was, according to him, "the United States." According to the editor of BANCOMEXT, U.S. companies sold their products to Mexico by installments and on the basis of loans that placed the Latin American country in a position of dependency. Perera Mena clarified that credit lines could be discontinued at any time but that, on the macroeconomic level, the country depended on loans disbursed by the U.S. Treasury and the country's private banks. The Mexican official explained that, for example, the signing of a trade agreement between Mexico and the USSR could cause a "malevolent reaction on the part of the United States," and that a more cautious evolution of relations between Mexico and Moscow—one that would not arouse the neighbor's anger—was therefore advisable.

The rapprochement was more successful when the two parties negotiated economic and trade exchanges involving Mexican public companies. At the end of the López Mateos' term, Mexico and the USSR were able to conclude the sale of ten Soviet oil-well drilling turbines to Petróleos Mexicanos (PEMEX; Mexican Petroleum), the Mexican state-owned oil company. Even if it took time to get the drilling turbines installed and properly working, their sale showed that it was probably easier for the two countries to cooperate when the negotiations involved the public sector rather than the private sector of the Mexican economy. In the public sector, the Mexican government could at least try to diversify the providers of goods. Moreover, in the energy production area, Mexico had more freedom of maneuvering, considering that Washington had remained reluctant to support the development of PEMEX[47] with taxpayers' money ever since the 1938 nationalization of Mexican oil. Even in the public sector, however, Mexico's margins of action were narrow. As we have seen, the López Mateos administration rejected a large Soviet credit line to develop the oil industry, probably out of concern for how the United States might react.

In any case, logistics, economic dependence, ideological polarization within the Mexican political establishment itself, and some degree of Soviet naïveté combine to explain the difficulties that even the sale of a small consignment of Soviet tractors to Mexico could meet. Mexican-Soviet relations had to wait until the 1970s, under the leadership of President Luis Echeverría, to finally gather new momentum.

Conclusion

Between 1959 and 1964, Mexico's interest in developing political and economic relations with Moscow represented a component of a broader strategy aimed at reducing Mexican dependence on the United States. During those years, Mexico tried to modify its Cold War allegiance to the United States and assume a more independent position in terms of the economy as well as international relations. This quest for independence resembled the strategy followed by other Third World countries in those same years. As Jeffery Byrne has observed, by the time of the 1961 Belgrade Conference, the Third World was showing an internal divergence between an insurrectionary approach and a more moderate, development-based interpretation of the role Third Worldism should play as a political movement in the international arena.[48] Countries such as India, for example, embraced the latter course, while nations such as Cuba and Algeria, among others, embraced the former. Mexico never completely cut its allegiance to Washington and, in this sense, the country's Third World identity was closer to that of India, for one. For Mexico, belonging to the Third World meant diversifying trade, increasing economic opportunities, and trying to create a new economic international environment more favorable to economic development projects in the South. This approach would come fully into play during the 1970s, when Luis Echeverría's proposal for a Charter of Economic Rights and Duties of States became Mexico's flagship program for the Third World.

During the 1960s, however, the forging of a Mexican Third World international identity showed limits, which are well epitomized by the difficulties encountered by the López Mateos administration to build a more solid partnership with the USSR. The expectations generated by Mikoyan's trip to Mexico in November 1959, as part of the inauguration of the Soviet scientific and technical exhibition, were never met. Despite his presence, contacts, and conversations, the signing of a trade agreement—the central objective of the Soviet strategy and a crucial instrument for improving economic relations—could not be completed. Even the sale of a few Soviet tractors to the Latin American country proved to be difficult.

The existing documentation does not allow us to assess whether the United States exerted direct pressure on Mexico in order to obstruct the rapprochement with the USSR. What we do know is that the political and economic configuration of the relations with the United States in the context of bipolar confrontation, together with Mexican internal polarization, represented the greatest obstacle to a more substantial level of engagement between Mexico and the USSR. In a way, the same bilateral economic and political structures that President López Mateos made efforts to alter precluded the possibility of implementing a strategy of diversification that would include the USSR. The strong economic and financial integration and interdependence that Mexico and Washington maintained in the mid-1960s made the process of commercial diversification arduous. As emphasized by Harry Turkel in his report to Rubottom, at the macro level, a strong Mexican stability depended on Washington's support channeled through preferential credit lines, such as those granted to the country by the Export/Import Bank or the International Monetary Fund. As Perera Mena argued, developing relations with the main geopolitical competitor of the United States could jeopardize the access to these resources. On the other hand, at the micro level, the Mexican market was too used to the presence of U.S. products to allow an easy replacement of U.S. machinery with Soviet machinery.

This negative picture was made even worse by the rigidity shown by Soviet diplomats. As we have seen, the USSR proposed its products without offering advantageous financial mechanisms or conditions, all elements particularly necessary to seduce a potentially hostile market. Moreover, Soviet diplomats, on some occasions, even seemed to forget the advantages offered by their own commercial strategy, in particular, the use of barter as a mechanism for the trade of goods with Third World countries that had little hard currency. Finally, as we have seen, ideological and political differences that marked the national Mexican political context were coupled with a certain Soviet ingenuousness. In this sense, the political, economic, and logistic difficulties Moscow encountered in its interaction with Mexico, and which the tractors episode epitomizes, seem to confirm Sanchez-Sibony's thesis on the secondary role the Soviet Union played in the Third World, even at the peak of its attempt to incrase its presence in this part of the globe.[49]

Despite the problems encountered at this stage, it can also be argued that without bilateral efforts and coming to terms with the limits and challenges of the late 1950s and the mid-1960s, the greater engagement of the 1970s would have been impossible. In the end, the issues that remained unresolved during the presidency of López Mateos, especially the trade agreement with the socialist bloc, had a better outcome during the 1970s. Thus the 1960s, although not widely researched, are nevertheless essential for the reconstruction of the historical evolution of contemporary Mexico. In particular, it is now clear that those years were crucial for the forging of a new Mexican Third Worldist identity, which with time became an important part of the country's hybrid imaginary as an international player.

Notes

A Spanish version of this piece originally appeared as "¡Bienvenido Mr. Mikoyan! Tacos y tractores a la sombra del acercamiento soviético-mexicano, 1958–1964," *Historia Mexicana* 66 (2016): 793–852.

1. Bevan Sewell, "A Perfect (Free-Market) World? Economics, the Eisenhower Administration, and the Soviet Economic Offensive in Latin America," *Diplomatic History* 32, no. 5 (2008): 841.

2. "Mexico. Russian Headway," *Time*, 7 December 1959, 36.

3. This chapter significantly develops and extends an article that constituted an introduction to previously unpublished Soviet documents: Vanni Pettinà, "Mexican-Soviet Relations, 1958–1964: The Limits of Engagement," Cold War International History Project, e-Dossier 65 (August 2015), https://www.wilsoncenter.org/publication/mexican-soviet-relations-1958-1964-the-limits-engagement#_ftn3.

4. On the Mexican policies of approach to the Third World during the decade of 1960s, see Vanni Pettinà, "Global Horizons: Mexico, the Third World, and the Non-Aligned Movement at the Time of the 1961 Belgrade Conference," *International History Review* 38, no. 4 (2016): 741–64, doi: 10.1080/07075332.2015.1124906.

5. Héctor Cárdenas, *Historia de las relaciones entre México y Rusia* (Mexico City: Fondo de Cultura Económica, 1993), 227.

6. To this date, the historiography on the subject is substantially reduced to a few contributions, published between the 1970s and the 1990s and characterized by the scarce use of primary sources. It is composed of a volume published jointly by the Ministry of Foreign Affairs of Mexico and the Academy of Science of the former Soviet Union, which compiles official bilateral documents produced between 1917 and 1980, and a book by Héctor Cárdenas on the history of bilateral relations, which, however, paid little attention to the 1960s. Finally, an article published in the early 1970s by Blanca Torres analyzes the evolution of trade relations between Mexico and the socialist bloc between 1945 and the late 1960s. Héctor Cárdenas and Alexander Sizonenko, eds., *Relaciones mexicano-soviéticas, 1917–1980* (Mexico City: Secretaría de Relaciones Exteriores, Academia de la Ciencia de la URSS, 1981); Cárdenas, *Historia de las relaciones*; Blanca Torres, "México en la estructura del comercio y la cooperación internacional de los países socialistas," *Foro Internacional* 13, no. 2 (1972): 178–210.

7. Notable exceptions to the lack of studies of international history over the period are, for example, Blanca Torres, *México y el mundo: historia de sus relaciones exteriores*, vol. 7, *De la guerra al mundo bipolar* (Mexico City: Senado de la República, 1991); Mario Ojeda, *Alcances y límites de la política exterior de México* (Mexico City: El Colegio de México, 2001); Lorenzo Meyer, "La guerra Fría en el mundo periférico: El caso del régimen autoritario mexicano. La utilidad del anticomunismo discreto," in *Espejos de la guerra fría: México, América Central y el Caribe*, ed. Daniela Spenser (Mexico City: Porrúa, 2004), 95–118; and Eric Zolov, *The Last Good Neighbor: Mexico in the Global Sixties* (Durham, NC: Duke University Press, 2020).

8. On relations between Cuba and Mexico, see Renata Keller, *Mexico's Cold War: Cuba, the United States, and the Legacy of the Mexican Revolution* (New York: Cambridge University Press, 2015), and "A Foreign Policy for Domestic Consump-

tion: Mexico's Lukewarm Defense of Castro, 1959-1969," *Latin American Research Review* 47, no. 2 (2012): 100-119; Ana Covarrubias, "Las relaciones México-Cuba, 1959-2010," in *Historia de las relaciones internacionales de México, 1821-2010*, vol. 3, *Caribe*, ed. Mercedes de Vega (Mexico City: Secretaría de Relaciones Exteriores, 2011); Ojeda, *Alcances y límites*; Olga Pellicer, *México y la Revolución cubana* (Mexico City: El Colegio de México, 1972).

9. Michelle Denise Getchell, "Revisiting the 1954 Coup in Guatemala: The Soviet Union, the United Nations and 'Hemispheric Solidarity,'" *Journal of Cold War Studies* 17, no. 2 (2015): 73-102; Tobias Rupprecht, "Socialist High Modernity and Global Stagnation: A Shared History of Brazil and the Soviet Union during the Cold War," *Journal of Global History* 6, no. 3 (2011): 505-28, and *Soviet Internationalism after Stalin: Interaction and Exchange between the USSR and Latin America during the Cold War* (Cambridge: Cambridge University Press, 2015).

10. "Mikoyan Arrives in Mexico City," *Chicago Tribune*, 19 November 1959, 3.

11. Soledad Loaeza, "Modernización autoritaria a la sombra de la superpotencia, 1944-1968," in *Nueva Historia General de México*, ed. Erik Velásquez García (Mexico City: El Colegio de México, 2010), 675.

12. "Mexico and the Alliance for Progress," 3 June 1962, Record Group (hereafter RG) 59, 712.00/6-1362, U.S. National Archives and Records Administration, College Park, MD (hereafter NARA).

13. Louise E. Walker, *Waking from the Dream: Mexico's Middle Class after 1968* (Stanford, CA: Stanford University Press, 2013), 3. See also Soledad Loaeza, *Clases medias y política en México: La querella escolar, 1959-1963* (Mexico City: El Colegio de México, 1988).

14. "Mexico and the Alliance for Progress"; Raymond Vernon, *The Dilemma of Mexico's Development: The Roles of the Private and Public Sectors* (Cambridge, MA: Harvard University Press, 1963), 117; Loaeza, "Modernización autoritaria," 665 and 669; Enrique Cárdenas, "La economía en el dilatado siglo XX, 1929-2009," in *Historia económica general de México. De la colonia a nuestros días*, ed. Sandra Kuntz Ficker (Mexico: El Colegio de México, 2010), 517.

15. Pettinà, "Global Horizons," 6-7.

16. On the Indian exchange rate crisis at the beginning of its second five-year plan, see Oscar Sánchez-Sibony, *Red Globalization: The Political Economy of the Soviet Cold War from Stalin to Khrushchev* (Cambridge: Cambridge University Press), 160.

17. In 1965, 64.2 percent of Mexican imports came from the United States, and 71.2 percent of its production was exported to the U.S. market. Pablo González Casanova, *La democracia en México* (Mexico City: Era, 1967), 179, n. 7.

18. "Monthly Economic Summary, January 1959," 13 February 1959, 11, 712-00/2-1359, RG59, NARA.

19. Torres, *México y el mundo*, 138; Loaeza, "Modernización autoritaria," 683-684; "Monthly Economic Summary, January 1959."

20. "Joint Week no. 51-52," 31 December, 1959, 712.00(W)/12-3159, RG59, NARA.

21. Pettinà, "Global Horizons."

22. "Trade Relations between the USSR and Argentina," 17 January, 1958; Mexican Embassy in Moscow, "Untitled," No. 70, 11 January 1958; Political Reports,

"Soviet Equipment and Machinery for the Development of the Argentine Oil Industry," Mexican Embassy in Moscow, 6 June 1959; all in Archivo Histórico Genaro Estrada, Secreteria de Relaciones Exteriores, III/510 (47-0) 959/2-5, III 1933-6, Supplementary Political Reports, General Direction of the Diplomatic Service.

23. "El Comercio de América Latina con los Países Comunistas," *Comercio Exterior*, November 1959, 630–32.

24. "Mexico (Informative Note)," ca. 1960, Fond 645, Opis' 1, Delo 31, 445–50, Russian State Archive of the Economy (hereafter RGAE). See also "Mexico: Politics Ideology and the Economy," 23 June 1964, RAS, Fond 1858, Opis' 1, Delo 109, I, 1–32,; "Information materials on Mexico, (1) Mexico. A brief note," 2 May 1965, Fond 110, Opis' 25, Por, 700, Delo 54, Archives of Foreign Policy of the Russian Federation (hereafter AVP RF).

25. V. Bazykin, "Concerning Soviet-Mexican Relations. Comrade A. A. Gromyko about Mexican-Soviet Relations," 3 August 1960, Fond 110, Informational materials, Item 1, No. 516/OCA, 22–27, AVP RF.

26. "Current Intelligence Staff Study. Soviet Policy toward the Underdeveloped Countries," 28 April 1961, 90, CIA Records Search Tool, https://www.cia.gov/library/readingroom/document/5077054e993247d4d82b6ae7.

27. A. Shelnov, "Report on the Work of the Soviet Exhibition in Mexico Year 1959," n.d. [ca. January 1960], Fond 635, Opis' 1, Delo 392, 1–12, RGAE.

28. V. Bazykin, "Concerning Soviet-Mexican Relations," 23.

29. Alessandro Iandolo, "The Rise and Fall of the 'Soviet Model of Development' in West Africa, 1957–1964," *Cold War History* 12, no. 4 (2012): 689–91.

30. "Memorandum of the Conversation of the Head of the department of Latin America of the Ministry of Foreign Trade of the USSR, Comrade A. P. Malkov, with the governor of the National Bank of Foreign Trade in Mexico, Mr. Ricardo Jose Zevada of November 23 of this year," ca. November–December 1959, Fond 413, Opis' 13, Delo 8510, 63–68, RGAE.

31. Bureau of Inter-American Affairs, Office of Inter-American Regional Economic Affairs, Country and Subject File, Box 1 Arc id2321376, "Your Request Re Information on German Trade Mission to Latin America and Mikoyan's Visit to Mexico," 15 December 1959, RG59, NARA.

32. "Reports on trip to Latin America," Report on Soviet Delegation goodwill trip to Latin American counties," n.d. [c. 1961-62], D. D. Degtyar (1904–1982), Personal Collection, Fond 645, Opis' 1, Delo 31, RGAE.

33. "Report of Comrade K. D. Tikhomirov and B. M. Streltsov on Trip to Obregón City and the Port of Guaymas, State of Sonora, 14–17 May, 1959," 21 May 1959, Fond 413, Opis' 13, Delo 8510, 30–34, RGAE; "Memorandum of the Conversation with the Ministry of Agriculture, Engineer Julián Rodríguez Adame, 31 July 1959," Ref. #368, 4 August 1959, Fond 413, Opis' 13, Delo 8510, 49–51, RGAE; "Memorandum of the Conversation between Comrade K. D. Tikhomirov, Commercial Counselor of the Embassy of the USSR in Mexico, with the Managers (or Directors) of the company 'de Swaan,' S. A., Sheyman y de Swaan, Which Took Place on 7 and 9 February 1959," 20 February 1959, Fond 413, Opis' 13, Delo 8510, 4–5, RGAE.

34. "Poco Comercio con la URSS," *El Porvenir*, April 4, 1959, 1; "Mirador," *Jueves de Excelsior*, 21 May 1959, 6.

35. Comarca Lagunera is the ninth-largest metropolitan area in Mexico, located between two states, Coahuila and Durango.

36. Dolores Trevizo, *Rural Protest and the Making of Democracy in Mexico, 1968–2000* (University Park: Pennsylvania State University Press, 2011), 106.

37. Luis Aboites Aguilar, *El norte entre algodones: Población, trabajo agrícola y optimismo en México, 1930–1970* (Mexico City: El Colegio de México, 2013), 154–55.

38. Aguilar, *El norte entre algodones*, 154.

39. Rodolfo Stavenhagen, *Between Underdevelopment and Revolution: A Latin American Perspective* (New Delhi: Abhinav, 1981), 145; Trevizo, *Rural Protest*, 106.

40. "Mirador," 6.

41. Stavenhagen, *Between Underdevelopment*, 145.

42. "Memorandum of the Conversation between Comrade K. D. Tikhomirov, Commercial Counselor of the Embassy of the USSR in Mexico, with the Managers (or Directors) of the Company 'de Swaan,' S. A., Sheyman y de Swaan," 4–5.

43. "Memorandum of the Conversation between Comrade K. D. Tikhomirov, Commercial Counselor of the Embassy of the USSR in Mexico, with the Managers (or Directors) of the Company 'de Swaan,' S. A., Sheyman y de Swaan," 4–5.

44. "Results of the sales of equipment," 18 (19 sic), 1959, Fond 413, Opis' 13, Delo 8329, RGAE.

45. The name is "Donsos" in Russian in the original Soviet document."Report of Comrade K. D. Tikhomirov and B. M. Streltsov," 30–34.

46. "Memorandum of the Conversation with the Ministry of Agriculture, Engineer Julián Rodríguez Adame, 31 July 1959."

47. Zinaida Ivanovna Romanova, "Economic Cooperation between Latin America and the Countries of the Socialist Camp," n.d. [ca. 1960], Fond 1798, Opis'. 1, Delo 88 ll: 124–36, RAS; "To Deputy Minister Comr. I. F. Semichastnov to Chief of the Protocol Division Comr. I. I. Dokuchaev," 23 June 1964, Fond 413, Opis' 31, Delo 287: 28–29, RGAE.

48. Jeffrey James Byrne, "Beyond Continents, Colours, and the Cold War: Yugoslavia, Algeria, and the Struggle for Non-Alignment," *International History Review* 37, no. 5 (2015): 912–32.

49. Sánchez-Sibony, *Red Globalization*, 125–69.

4 Brazil and Non-Alignment
Latin America's Role in the Global Order, 1961–1964

STELLA KREPP

In the run-up to the first meeting of nonaligned states, set to take place in Belgrade in late 1961, the Brazilian ambassador to Egypt succinctly described Brazil's position as follows: "Even though some of the stands taken until now in the name of positive neutralism correspond to the guidelines of Brazil's independent foreign policy," he conceded, "the special situation of Brazil on the American continent and in the world means that many other theses that have been proposed . . . do no coincide with our national interests."[1] This noncommittal, ambivalent attitude towards the Non-Aligned Movement (NAM) was characteristic not only of Brazil, but of Latin America in general.

Although Brazilians acknowledged the existence of common goals such as development and the renegotiation of the global economic order, Latin American countries apart from Cuba neglected to take a leading role in the NAM during the 1960s, and Brazil provides an illuminating example of this uneasy relationship. Through the case of Brazil, the present chapter will examine three key issues: Latin American membership, the meaning of nonalignment, and distinct notions of a "third way."

Drawing on Brazilian and U.S. documents, the chapter will show how Brasília sought to leverage its independent foreign policy toward participation in the first two meetings of the NAM in 1961 and 1964, with the ultimate goal of bringing Latin America into the Third World. Not a mere bystander, the Brazilian government engaged with nonaligned members on a bilateral level as well as in the United Nations, most notably about the creation of the United Nations Conference on Trade and Development (UNCTAD).

In 1961 and 1962, the Brazilian government actively engaged with the NAM and identified potential partners such as Yugoslavia, but this trend terminated in 1964. Political watersheds in Brazil and Latin America—the polarization of politics, the isolation of Cuba, and the overthrow of the democratic Goulart government by a military coup in 1964—meant a turn away from NAM membership. Tracing this process highlights that domestic and regional contexts had a strong impact on how Brazilian officials related to nonaligned concerns and underscores the "historicity of Third World internationalism" described by Jeffrey Byrne.[2] The present study means to contribute to a new wave of scholarship on the NAM, improving on a narrative that used to focus too exclusively on the figureheads of nonalignment—Jawaharlal Nehru, Gamal Abdel Nasser, and Josip Broz Tito—and often limited itself to the discursive analysis of nonaligned rhetoric instead of dealing more broadly with foreign policy.[3]

The exclusive focus on the architects of the NAM and their ideas has led to neglect of less central actors and themes, among them Latin American participation in the movement. Although some Latin American countries formed part of the NAM and actively participated in its conferences, the region has largely been ignored by scholars interested in the Third World. With the notable exceptions of James G. Hershberg's article on Brazil at the Belgrade meeting and Vanni Pettinà's work on Mexico,[4] research on Latin American relationship to nonalignment remains uncharted territory to this day. Even Cuba's role as an influential member and later leader of the NAM has attracted comparatively little research, owing to the fact that for a long time, Cuban archives were closed but for a few.[5]

This is not to argue that Latin American countries played a central role in the movement. Except for Cuba, they did not in the 1960s. However, a study of the role of Brazil's NAM policy can provide an answer to the question of how to situate Latin America in the history of the Third World, a history otherwise dominated by decolonization and Afro-Asian solidarity. The case of Brazil raises the question of whether the organizing principles of the 1960s—which intimately link the Third World with decolonization and racial solidarity—inform or obscure our understanding of the historical processes of the time. Ultimately, it asks how to inscribe Latin America in the history of the Third World.

Brazil and the Third World

Traditionally, the history of Brazil is presented as separate from that of Hispanic America.[6] Brazil, because of its distinct colonial experience as part of the Portuguese empire and its subsequent transformation into a monarchy and only much later into a republic, is supposed to differ substantially in language, culture, and political institutions from its Spanish-speaking neighbors. African slavery and the plantation system in Brazil also had a deep impact and resulted in a multiracial and multiethnic society. However, since the mid-1950s Brazil had risen to become a regional power in Latin America. This marked a departure from its traditional role as mediator between Washington and Hispanic America toward a more committed and integrative relationship with the rest of Latin America.[7] In sum, Brazil became Latin Americanized during the 1950s.[8]

At the same time, Brazil was becoming increasingly aware of its position as a Third World nation, prompting rapprochement with other Third World countries, particularly in Africa. This shift in political allegiance, initiated in 1958, eventually culminated in Brazil's "independent foreign policy" and the flirtation with neutrality under Kubitschek's successor Jânio Quadros from 1961 onward. In this pursuit, Brazil was not so different from other reformist governments in the region—Mexico, Argentina, or Bolivia—to name but a few. This is why the Brazilian prism helps us to relate the wider Latin American story of these formative years.

The 1950s were a decisive decade not only for Brazil, but also for Latin America as a whole. Under the pressure of severe social and economic problems, Latin American leaders began to turn toward newly independent postcolonial states; they discovered structural similarities with these countries, but also considered them rivals in the global competition for the attention of the First World. With most Latin America nations having achieved independence in the early nineteenth century, the region differed in this respect from the newly independent and postcolonial states that emerged in Africa and Asia in the 1960s. Due to this historical legacy, political and institutional structures in Latin America were comparatively sophisticated. Brazil, for example, could boast a professional diplomatic service, a network of universities, and a semi-industrialized economy. At least in its self-image, Brazil was starting out on a different level.[9]

Another difficulty in identifying with the Third World came from the fact that Latin American elites, predominantly white, considered themselves as an offshoot of European culture and entrenched members of "Western Christian civilization." For Brazil, this attitude translated into a "political and racial democracy" that shared liberal values, Christian beliefs, and an admiration for European culture.[10] The Brazilians argued that their country's unique position was rooted in its singular political and historical trajectory. Consequently, Brazilian policymakers were very hesitant about where Brazil would fit into this changing world order.[11] While they defined themselves as Western, albeit an alternative version, they had been excluded from the official West in the early postwar years, as well as from NATO and a closer alliance with Europe. Yet, they likewise fitted uneasily into the category of the emerging Third World as they often struggled with the postcolonial agenda of the NAM.

Brazil's Independent Foreign Policy

The shift in Brazilian foreign policy toward the Eastern bloc and nonaligned countries was initiated during the presidency of Juscelino Kubitschek, who came to power in 1956. In 1958, Itamaraty (the Brazilian foreign ministry) opened trade negotiations with a range of countries in Eastern Europe—Poland, Czechoslovakia, and Hungary—as well as with the German Democratic Republic. And despite U.S. protestations, Kubitschek reestablished trade relations with the Soviet Union in late 1959. This repositioning was not only ideologically motivated: Brazilian policymakers were very concerned about the creation of the European Common Market and its repercussions on the commercial expansion of Latin America.[12] Thus, as political options with traditional partners were closing off, new partnerships had to be sought. The policy shift was first and foremost motivated by a need to diversify Brazil's economic base and economic relationships both regionally and globally.[13] Yet, Kubitschek also wanted to position his country as a "mediator between first and third world," and he expressed aspirations to make it a leader in the rather amorphous group of emerging Third World countries. The country's history and the fact that it was comparatively advanced, Brazilian officials reasoned, singled it out as an ideal candidate to play this role. After all, Brazil's role in its region was "in a way analogous to that of India in Asia."[14]

In 1961, the newly elected Brazilian President Jânio Quadros continued this trajectory when he announced an "independent foreign policy."[15] Even though his presidency was to be short-lived, his attempt to reorient Brazilian foreign policy both on the regional and the global stages would have long-term consequences. In pursuing relations with the Soviet Union and socialist countries, particularly Yugoslavia, and approaching newly independent African countries, Quadros raised questions about Brazil's traditional alignment with the United States and Portugal.

One such forum to forge new relationships and devise a new policy agenda was the NAM. Despite showing interest in nonaligned concerns, Brazil never assumed formal membership in the NAM. For this reason, scholars have often erroneously assumed that Latin Americans were all but absent from NAM debates. This is far from true. Although Latin American countries did not make it into the official record due to their observer status (with the obvious exception of Cuba as a full member), Brazilian delegations attended the 1955 Bandung conference, as well as the 1961 Belgrade and the 1964 Cairo conferences. Itamaraty also sent observers to the preparatory conferences of Cairo in June 1961 and Colombo in March 1964, respectively. Unlike the actual NAM conferences, which tended to serve as a public platform and made a show of consensus, the preparatory conferences were the locus of agenda-setting where fundamental questions of membership were debated and political landmark decisions were made. This is why Brazilian attendance at the preparatory conferences is significant.

Despite glaring differences, Brazil shared many concerns with official NAM member states: the struggle for economic development and a fairer global economic system, disarmament, denuclearization, and the peaceful settlement of conflicts. The idea of the mediating role of the NAM as a peace broker dovetailed with Brazilian aspirations and its self-image as a regional power. Moreover, the peaceful settlement of conflicts had been a hallowed Inter-American principle for decades.

Lofty proclamations aside, nonalignment offered tangible benefits. In the case of Brazil, it provided an opportunity not only to expand economic relations, but also to form strategic relationships with the purpose of tackling economic underdevelopment and reforming the United Nations. The NAM was particularly useful for forging alliances that would advance Latin American interests in the United Nations and other international organizations, such as the International Monetary Fund and the World Bank, something that had been tried in vain for more than a decade. As Vanni Pettinà has argued regarding Mexico, nonalignment also emerged as a way to win concessions, mainly from the United States.[16] Brazilian officials viewed it as a way to keep the Cold War at bay and to prevent the superpowers from interfering in internal affairs. However, the very pragmatic political approach of Brazil was often at odds with more ideologically driven debates in the NAM.

Despite a measure of convergence, the situation of Latin American countries was undoubtedly quite different from that of recently decolonized nations in Africa and Asia: the Inter-American system constituted a primary political alliance, and these nations were tied to the United States through the Rio Treaty, a mutual defense pact. Moreover, while some objectives of the NAM, most notably those related to development, were of central interest to them, they never perceived the NAM as their most important political forum. Brazilian officials insisted that Inter-American duties came first:

"We are members of the OAS [Organization of American States], and signatories of international agreements that align us unequivocally to this Inter-American regional system, with all the rights and duties that it entails."[17] The Americas had a fully functioning regional system that, despite its drawbacks, provided a forum for vital debates and, crucially, political opportunities to extract concessions from the United States. As such, it would always take precedent over other political communities.

Given Brazil's place in the Inter-American System, its policymakers did not seriously consider a full-fledged membership in the NAM. During those years, Brazil played a pivotal role in the Inter-American System as it took up the leadership in the struggle for political and economic integration as well as for consolidating democratic values in the region. In 1960, a Latin American free trade area was created by the Montevideo Treaty. Although the project would ultimately fail, it showed intensive Latin American efforts to provide regional solutions to the global challenge of economic and political inequality.

As elsewhere in Latin America, Brazil's relationship with the United States also influenced its approach to nonaligned debates. Only months before the first Non-Aligned conference in Belgrade in September 1961, and after a decade of sustained efforts on the part of Brazil, the American nations had officially inaugurated the Alliance for Progress, a hemispheric aid program funded by the United States. From the beginning, Latin American politicians, who ironically dubbed this aid "Fidel's money,"[18] were painfully aware that it came at a political price. In April 1961, the Kennedy administration had aided and abetted the Bay of Pigs invasion in Cuba. This move made abundantly clear what would happen if a Latin American country dared to challenge the United States in the space it considered the American sphere. In other words, one could rattle at the gates of containment, and even try to expand political room for maneuver by bending them, but a political realignment was never an option for Brazil.

This was not just pandering to U.S. wishes but pragmatic calculation. Brazil understood political alignment and envisioned a sort of neutrality in ways that conflicted with more radical views held by countries such as Cuba, Ghana, and Indonesia. Overall, Brazilian foreign policy was driven less by Cold War rationale than by internal debates on Brazil's place in a changing world. Nonalignment in Brazil was an economic rather than a political project. While Brazilian politicians could identify with an "economic Third World" centered on underdevelopment, they were definitely at odds with the idea of a shared cultural or political community.

The Meaning of Non-Alignment and the Question of Membership

In 1961, the Belgrade conference marked the formal birth of the NAM. Locating its ideological roots, however, has proven to be more complicated. Some scholars perceive the Belgrade conference as a successor to the 1955 Bandung conference of Afro-Asian states, yet the connection is tenuous at best.[19] In Bandung, participants had sought to position recently independent nations between the blocs. They professed political nonalignment, mutual respect for each other's territorial integrity and sovereignty, mutual nonaggression, and peaceful coexistence and disarmament, and at the same time demanded a political say in international matters. Yet, while Bandung had been attended mainly by Afro-Asian states, Belgrade was headed by Josip Broz Tito from Yugoslavia, Gamal Abdel Nasser from the United Arab Republic, and, much more hesitantly, Jawaharlal Nehru from India. These leaders envisioned a more inclusive and moderate movement that should cover wide swaths of the Third World, including Latin America. Bandung and Belgrade thus represented both overlapping and competing agendas for a Third World project.

When Tito approached the Brazilian government in 1961 with the idea of a Non-Aligned conference, its first reaction was a mix of keen interest and hesitation. Although generally favorable to the idea of a Non-Aligned conference and appreciative of Tito's and Nasser's endeavors, since they overlapped in part with the "independent foreign policy" of the Quadros government, Brazilian officials remained somewhat puzzled about what that nonalignment actually entailed. This was no surprise as the main proponents of nonalignment were themselves still squabbling over its meaning.

Despite these misgivings, the Brazilians were prepared and willing to engage with nonalignment. The Foreign Ministry sent an observer on an exploratory mission to the preparatory conference that took place in Cairo from 5 to 12 June. Beside Cuba, Brazil was the only other Latin American country to attend, and the ambassador to the United Arab Republic, Araújo Castro was appointed as official observer.[20]

In his detailed reports from the preparatory conference, Araújo Castro remarked that the principle obstacle faced by Latin American countries was the insistence of the hosts that only "nonaligned" countries could participate in the Belgrade conference. But he confessed that this "nonaligned" status remained unclear: it could "refer to the so-called 'active neutralism' practiced by certain Afro-Asian countries" or it could include "those states that, contrary to the members of NATO [the North Atlantic Treaty Organization] and the Warsaw Pact, have no direct military commitments," he explained.[21] The Latin American countries complied with the latter criterion, but clearly violated the former.

It was even more mind-boggling, Araújo Castro noted, that nonalignment was not to be confused with the politics of neutrality.[22] To complicate matters further, neutralism in Brazil and Latin America had different values that resulted from historical experience. It could mean the neutrality of Latin American countries during World War II, as well as policies more along the line of the Peronist policy of equidistance (or third position), or an independent neutral policy like the one espoused by Quadros.

Semantic debates aside, a wholehearted commitment to the Non-Alignment Movement was out of the question, because Latin American countries were clearly aligned with the United States in the Inter-American System, the Brazilians argued. "It is not possible for Brazil to participate directly," given its status, Araújo Castro warned in a report sent as late as May 1961.[23]

Even when applying a flexible interpretation of nonalignment to accommodate distinct political notions and convictions, nonalignment precluded membership in military alliances such as NATO and the Warsaw Pact. Latin American countries, without being formal members of a military alliance, were aligned with the United States as members of the Inter-American System. To make things worse, all twenty Latin American countries had ratified the Rio Treaty, a hemispheric defense pact, and most had bilateral military agreements with the United States. So, while Latin Americans were not in a formal military alliance, they were part of a regional defense mechanism with the United States. Araújo Castro accurately described this dilemma when conceding that Brazil "is not neutral, ideologically it forms part of the West." But, on the other hand, not being a signatory of NATO, Brazil was not part of the "Western bloc" and, whereas Brazil's commitments in the Inter-American System came first, "Brazil was not aligned *against* anyone, but aligned *for* the defense of the hemisphere."[24]

He also expressed his uneasiness about the upcoming Belgrade agenda. The resolutions that were expected at Belgrade, Araújo Castro cautioned, will have a "strong flavor of anticolonial radicalism," which would be difficult for Brazil to accept. In comparison to the more radical countries, Brazil seemed "timid and indecisive," despite the recent inauguration of its independent foreign policy. Maybe, Araújo Castro wondered, it was "preferable to be the most advanced element of a conservative current than to be the most timid and reactionary element in an assembly of radicals."[25]

In fact, there was no need for such exhausting cogitations: Non-Aligned leaders such as Tito, Nasser, and Nehru publicly endorsed Latin American participation, and reassured Latin Americans that the Rio Treaty was not a hindrance. Belgrade was not to be a second Bandung; Tito's and Nasser's objective was to broaden the pool of prospective members. They were particularly keen on Brazil's attendance as a moderating influence and on the grounds of very pragmatic considerations. Since Brazil was a political heavyweight in Latin America and an experienced diplomatic actor, its attendance would lend a certain cachet to the conference. Nonaligned leaders also deemed Brazil an easier political partner than what they perceived as a volatile Cuba. And when it came to more material issues such as furthering trade, Cuba had little to offer.

Tito, in particular, lobbied for Latin American participation, expressing the hope as late as July 1961 that President Quadros himself would attend, because, without Brazil or Mexico, major countries of the continent would not be represented; in this context "Cuba did not count."[26] In conversation with U.S. Ambassador George F. Kennan on the island of Brioni in July, Tito reiterated that "Yugoslavia would be very unhappy if Cuba turned out to be the only Latin American country to be represented."[27] Two weeks later, Kennan reported that the Yugoslavs were seriously displeased with the U.S. opposition to Latin American attendance, a move that amounted in their eyes to a boycott of the conference.

Washington had argued that membership in the Rio Treaty precluded a potential participation of Latin American states in the NAM. However, when the Kennedy government attempted to exert pressure on the Brazilian government, President Quadros publicly attacked the American Ambassador John Moors Cabot for "meddling" in Brazil's internal affairs.[28] This spat with the Kennedy administration played mainly to domestic audiences, to show them that the Brazilian government was now following a truly independent policy. But it also meant that Brazil had to attend in some form to save face.

Whereas relations between Washington and Brasília were souring, Yugoslavia and Brazil were on relatively good terms. In 1959, the Yugoslav government had funded a trade mission to Latin America in order to explore the potential for developing economic relations. The mission ultimately yielded few results because Brazil considered Yugoslav products as substandard, but it did provide a basis for improved relations. In mid-1961,

President Quadros extended an invitation to Tito for an official state visit and expressed interest in closer cooperation. Yugoslavia was selected as the most likely political partner among the nonaligned, one that Brazil saw eye to eye with in a way it could not with recently decolonized countries of Asia and Africa. Neither Yugoslavia nor Brazil fit into that nonaligned mold, and they shared certain superficial similarities: while Tito wished Yugoslavia to be a bridge between the West and the East, Brazil vied to become the link between the First and the Third Worlds.

Although Cuba was adamant about inviting only "truly neutralist countries," it was willing to make an exception in the case of its Latin American neighbors, endorsing the participation of Mexico, Bolivia, Ecuador, and Brazil.[29] Much to his chagrin, Araújo Castro actually had to fend off overtures by the Cuban foreign minister, Raúl Roa, at the preparatory meeting. He was certainly dumbstruck when Roa announced that he had it on good authority that the Brazilian President Jânio Quadros himself would attend the forthcoming conference, along with representatives from several Latin American countries. Abandoning his strict observer position, Araújo Castro intervened: "I cannot permit anyone in this room, even the Foreign Minister of a sister nation, to speak for Brazil."[30] The truth was that while the Brazilian government was still deliberating whether to send a delegation to Belgrade, from the beginning, a visit by Quadros had been out of the question. In a later private talk, Roa confided that the aim of his lie had been to "neutralize actions by Ghana, Guinea, and Mali," which had urged to restrict membership, but that posturing did not endear him to the Brazilians and certainly raised eyebrows elsewhere. On the same day, Yugoslav Ambassador Rato Dugonjic approached Araújo Castro to express his support, confessing that he would have reacted the same way. "We want to know what Brazil thinks but we want to know it from Brazil."[31]

In fact, these skirmishes hinted at a tug of war about who should represent the Latin American voice in the NAM: a radical, pro-Soviet Cuba or a reformist and democratic Brazil. Both Brazil and Cuba laid claim to this role because it lent legitimacy and status to their political actions. The clash between two ideological currents—Third Worldist nationalism and internationalism—was to persist in Latin American engagements with the Third World project in the coming decades.

Yet the organizers of Belgrade clearly favored Brazil over Cuba, as they harbored little sympathy for Castro. The moderates were able to secure invitations for Latin American countries, but the "the elimination of European countries" lobbied for by Cuba, Ghana, Guinea, and Mali could not be averted—a situation that underscored the rifts behind the scenes even before Belgrade.[32]

African countries had a much more critical view of Brazilian participation. While Brazilian diplomats paid lip service to antiracism and anticolonialism in international relations, there was no denying Brazil's "dismal record in the UN regarding colonialism," as Araújo Castro himself conceded. Since the creation of the United Nations, the Brazilian delegation, with one sole exception, had either voted against resolutions condemning colonialism or abstained. Brazil had not been any more vocal about condemning South African apartheid or racial segregation generally.[33] Despite Gilberto Freyre's proclamation of Brazil as a "racial democracy," the country remained a racially stratified society: its diplomats and politicians alike hailed from the Brazilian white elite, who considered themselves to be culturally and racially superior to their African and Asian counterparts.[34]

The story of the first Afro-Brazilian ambassador is edifying here. In 1961, Quadros opened the first sub-Saharan embassy in Accra, Ghana, and appointed his press aide, Raymundo Souza Dantas, an Afro-Brazilian, as ambassador. At that time, the Itaramaty was still almost exclusively white. Souza Dantas' mission was a resounding failure, a "doomed mission" in his own words.[35] Sousa Dantas relates how he was ostracized by the Itamaraty and snubbed by his own staff at the embassy. Even as he was forced to portray Brazil as a racial democracy, which he blatantly felt was not true, his appointment was also criticized in Ghana. João Clemente Baena Soares, head of the Africa Division of the Itamaraty, later recalled that Kwame Nkrumah angrily chided the Quadros government for sending a black ambassador to Africa, a move he considered to be racist. "He should send a black ambassador to Sweden—that would not be racist," he allegedly commented.[36]

African diplomats warned that the test would be the actual votes of Brazil in the United Nations and its stance on the cases of Angola, Congo, and Algeria. If Brazil wished to tighten its relationship with new African countries, Araújo Castro cautioned, it would therefore be "tantamount to abandoning our traditional policies towards France and Portugal." In order to develop a bond with nonaligned nations, Brazil would need to overhaul its attitude toward European colonialism and consider "situating Brazil in the world and defining a Brazilian policy" within a global context.[37] Yet, neither the Brazilian government nor the Foreign Ministry was willing to rethink foreign policy radically.

Belgrade 1961

After much deliberation, Itamaraty decided to send an observer to the Belgrade conference. Wary that that their attendance might be misconstrued by the "propaganda of a few Neutral leaders" as being a full-fledged membership, according to the Brazilian ambassador to Yugoslavia, Itamaraty embarked on a last-minute attempt to convince some of its Latin American neighbors to "deflect and diminish the ire of some US officials."[38] Brazilian officials sent out messages to other Latin American governments to entice them to attend as well. But this attempt to rally a Latin American bloc to attend failed and, in the end, only Ecuador and Bolivia joined the Belgrade conference that took place from 1 to 6 September. In Belgrade, in turn, the halfhearted Latin American participation disappointed and disillusioned its hosts, who began doubting whether courting the Latin Americans was worth the time and effort.

Ultimately, the Belgrade conference was overshadowed by the resignation of President Jânio Quadros on 25 August 1961. Thereafter the political situation was confusing, as military forces were conspiring to frustrate the ascent to power of Vice President João Goulart, because of his alleged leftist sympathies. The turmoil would last until 8 September, when a political compromise was found between the military and the Congress, allowing Goulart to assume the presidency—albeit with reduced executive powers and with the military biding their time in the shadows.

After much hesitation, the Itamaraty finally appointed an official observer, the ambassador to Switzerland, Afrânio de Melo Franco. However, when he arrived in Belgrade, more trouble was awaiting. One hour before the opening of the conference, Yugoslav officials informed him that he was no longer officially accredited after Quadros's resignation. Not only was Brazil disinvited, Melo Franco angrily reported, but the hosts even went to such "extremes of idiocy and indelicacy" as to remove the Brazilian flag.[39] It eventually transpired that the Cuban delegation under President Dórticos had urged the withdrawal of accreditation, charging that Quadros's resignation had been instigated by a military coup and pointblank refusing to recognize the new government. Somewhat embarrassed, Yugoslav officials assured Melo Franco that he was welcome to attend, but only in the capacity of a private observer. Virtually excluded in the first days of the conference, while feverishly trying to resolve the crisis, the Brazilian delegation could not meaningfully engage in nonaligned debates. After an appeal and secret deliberations, Brazil was finally (re)admitted as an official observer,

As one of few Latin American countries to attend the inaugural meeting of the Non-Aligned Movement (NAM), Cold War Brazil's experimentation with independent foreign policies led to some unlikely allies. This reached a crescendo during the short-lived presidency of nationalist Jânio Quadros (1960–1961), who engaged in sustained outreach to the Second and Third Worlds. Here in August 1961, President Quadros decorates Cuba's envoy, Ernesto "Che" Guevara, with membership in the country's chivalric Order of the Southern Cross. Four days later, Quadros resigned under pressure from Brazilian conservatives. (Image courtesy of Arquivo Nacional, Brazil, Public Domain / Arquivo Nacional Collection.)

but this episode put the experience in Belgrade in a negative light and severely tarnished Brazil's relationship with Cuba. Brazil, as the ringleader of the "soft six" had tried to shield Cuba from sanctions in the Inter-American System; it therefore considered this Cuban maneuver not only as backstabbing, but also as proof of the mercurial temper of the Cuban regime.

Between Belgrade and Cairo: Afro-Asianism and Cuba

Brazil's engagement with nonalignment had not been off to an auspicious start. The political turmoil after Quadros's resignation forced the Goulart government to pay close attention to domestic policies in an increasingly polarized Brazil, which was amidst a deepening economic crisis. At the same time, nonalignment took a new direction in which the "nonaligned movement vied with Afro-Asianism as the primary organizing principle in Third World affairs."[40] This had a direct impact on Latin American participation. An Afro-Asian solidarity movement that defined itself explicitly as nonwhite and postcolonial complicated Latin American inclusion.

This situation intersected with feuds between the Soviet Union and China, on the one hand, and China and India, on the other. In 1962, China started to wage "a determined propaganda campaign in Africa that portrayed the Soviet Union as being every bit as neo-imperial as the United States."[41] Seeking to marginalize the Soviet Union, as well as Yugoslavia, the Chinese attempted to define the Third World along racial lines. Even though this recasting of the movement as a racial war ultimately failed, it fueled years of controversial, bitter debates.[42]

Hoping to drive a wedge between the Soviet Union and the Afro-Asian bloc during the Afro-Asian Peoples Solidarity Organization (AAPSO) conference in Tanganyika in March 1963, the Chinese pronounced that "as whites the Russians are going to back the other whites, but we are coloreds and your blood brothers."[43] While some nonaligned members angrily rejected this heavy-handed interference, the Chinese were ultimately successful in securing the exclusion of delegates and observers from "Russia's Eastern European satellites, plus Yugoslavia."[44]

The Latin Americans were not invited either, because "while many African delegates [were] sympathetic to Cuba, they [were] not interested in expansion of AAPSO to include large number of whites [sic]," U.S. sources surmised.[45] Representatives of the Latin American Conference for National Sovereignty, Economic Emancipation and Peace, a leftist group close to Castro, protested indignantly at being denied admission. Appalled by the Chinese attempts to sow discord, Kwame Nkrumah reminded his peers at the AAPSO meeting in September 1963 in Nicosia, Cyprus, that "we are fighting not against race, creed, or color. We are fighting against an economic system which is designed to exploit us and to keep us in a state of perpetual subjection." Thus, he urged, "Afro-Asian solidarity should be reinforced with firm links embracing Latin-American states" because progressive forces existed all around the world.[46]

The Cuban question also contributed to driving a wedge between Latin America and the Afro-Asian movement. Despite Brazilian resistance, Cuba was excluded from the Inter-American System by a controversial decision in early 1962. Major Latin American countries—next to Brazil, Argentina, Mexico, Colombia, Ecuador, and Bolivia—had abstained from this vote and continued diplomatic and economic relations with Cuba. However, Cuban support for guerrilla activities in the region not only incensed right-wing dictatorships in the Caribbean, but also alienated democratic governments in Latin America. Cuban rhetoric and financial and military support threatened to destabilize fraught political coalitions and aggravated political polarization in Latin American societies.

The harsher the drive to isolate and punish Cuba became within Latin America, the more Latin American countries faced opposition within the NAM. Cuba's furious attacks against the United States and Latin American countries, in the forum of the AAPSO as well as in that of the NAM, often met with success. During the AAPSO meeting of March 1963, Afro-Asian nations demanded that Latin American governments stop the "economic blockade illegally forced upon Cuba by North American imperialists."[47] Depicted as stooges of the United States, Latin American countries increasingly came under attack. Whereas some Non-Aligned members took care to distinguish between those that had backed Cuban sanctions and those that had rejected them, many others did not take it into account. The debates on Cuba and an increasingly racialized notion of the Third World made it clear that under the veneer of Third World solidarity, a fundamental mistrust of Latin Americans and their objectives remained. Their professed cultural admiration for everything European, their European heritage, and the fact that they were recipients of U.S. funds through the Alliance for Progress made Latin Americans suspicious in Afro-Asian eyes. In many ways, thus, moderate governments such as Brazil's that advocated for conciliation were caught in the middle of ideological battles.

The Second Non-Aligned Conference, Cairo 1964

By 1964 the tide had turned. In Latin America, from the Argentine coup in 1962 onward, democratic governments were toppled one after another by a wave of coups d'état that swept bureaucratic-authoritarian regimes into power. The 1964 coup in Brazil topped the high-water mark.[48] In March that year, the Brazilian military overthrew the democratically elected Goulart government. The new military government under Castello Branco pursued a staunch anti-Communist line and adopted a foreign policy that dovetailed with U.S. political interests in Western Hemisphere affairs. As Foreign Minister Juracy Magelhães glibly noted in 1966: "What is good for the United States is good for Brazil."[49] The diplomats whose action had been crucial in the formulation of the Brazilian independent foreign policy of the early 1960s were forced to leave after the military coup. With the military in power, the leverage of security agencies, such as the Serviço Nacional de Informações (SNI, National Intelligence Service) increased. As a civilian ministry, the Itamaraty, in turn, lost some of its influence. This change in the political climate of Brazil affected its stance with regard to nonalignment.

Shortly after the coup, the Brazilian regime broke diplomatic relations with Cuba and helped push through economic sanctions against the Castro regime. In July 1964, the OAS mandated that all American states—including those that had not done so previously—sever diplomatic ties and "suspend all their trade"—a move that amounted to full-scale economic sanctions.[50] Although some were against the embargo, they followed suit, because resolutions under the Rio Treaty were binding. Thus, with the notable exception of Mexico, Cuba was now economically and politically ostracized within Latin America.

The years since 1961 had also brought major changes within the NAM. The original twenty-five members at Belgrade had nearly doubled to forty-six member-states. The number of observers had also sharply risen from three to ten, most of them representing Latin American countries. As African states gained in numbers, the NAM took a more radical direction. Since 1961 the movement had continuously "shifted to the left," as a U.S. observer critically remarked.[51] Particularly after the failure of a second Afro-Asian conference, the radical members regrouped in the Non-Aligned forum to pressure for their political interests. The Cold War had likewise turned "hot" again, with violent struggles in the Congo and the Portuguese colonies in Africa, as well as the Americanization of the Vietnam War.

With the new political climate in Brazil, and in Latin America more generally, the U.S. State Department nursed hopes that the Brazilian military government would opt out of attending Non-Aligned conferences. In the run-up to the Cairo conference, U.S. officials had been instructed to "discourage Hemisphere attendance," yet to do so "quietly and discreetly, in order to minimize the possibility of criticism from the so-called 'unaligned countries' on the grounds that we are preventing the success of the conference."[52] Given that members of the Inter-American System, including the United States, were "bound together by a body of agreements," Latin American participation was judged "incongruous," especially given the "hemispheric ostracism of Cuba."[53] Intriguingly, Washington and Havana agreed on this point, as the Cuban delegate similarly charged that Latin American states did not meet the membership criterion, because they were "aligned with U.S. imperialist policy of subversion and world domination."[54]

Originally, the Cairo conference had been scheduled before the UNCTAD that was to take place later that year. However, some scheduling problems frustrated the original aim to work out a unified unaligned position to better negotiate a reform of the global economic system during UNCTAD discussions. Instead, the UNCTAD coincided with the preparatory Non-Aligned meeting in Colombo. Despite Yugoslav and Indian endeavors to make economic development the central theme of Non-Alignment in years to come—an interpretation that particularly appealed to Latin Americans—they failed to dominate the political agenda in 1964. This came as a blow to Brazilians, for whom UNCTAD and the renegotiation of the global economic order had been a clear priority.

Although the regime change in Brazil was viewed critically, Non-Aligned leaders reached a compromise "to accept both Cuba and Brazil at Conference."[55] Brazil was eventually invited to attend the 1964 Cairo conference, and the military junta sent an observer. In addition to Brazil, invitations had been extended to another nine Latin American and Caribbean countries—Cuba, Jamaica, Trinidad and Tobago, Bolivia, Mexico, Chile, Uruguay, Venezuela, and Argentina—most of which sent only observers, not official delegations, possibly in deference to U.S. wishes. Cuba, however, had fiercely opposed Latin American attendance and had attempted to leverage the Preparatory Committee to counteract Latin American "maneuvers" and in particular to "unmask Venezuelan activities against the Cuban revolution."[56] This move was a payback for Venezuelans initiating OAS sanctions against Cuba, which were successful in July 1964.

This time around, the Brazilian diplomats were much more circumspect. Detailed communications before the Cairo conference from a range of embassies show how the NAM had alienated Brazilians. In June 1964, the ambassador in Cairo urged the Foreign Ministry to speak with other Latin American chancelleries to coordinate their policy, fearing that failing that, "one or few Latin American voices will be overwhelmed, totally, by the choir of Afro-Asians with an anti-Western ideological tendency."[57]

In a lengthy report, Sérgio Armando Frazão, the recently appointed Brazilian ambassador to the United Arab Republic who doubled up as observer at the Cairo conference, cast a critical light on the debates. The focus on decolonization as "the first preoccupation of the Non-Aligned Movement" reflected the political priorities of African nations. The Non-Aligned forum had thus been reduced to "Afro-Asian questions."[58] The bigger idea of a "third force" had been sidelined in favor of shortsighted belligerent rhetoric, he noted. This "agitated flood of words" and radical demands made even a Non-Aligned pioneer such as Tito look like "a rancid conservative."[59] Many of the core themes of the Cairo conference—decolonization, antiracism and the rejection of Apartheid, as well as the struggle against "neocolonialism"—did not resonate with Brazilians.

Moreover, because of their alleged support of Cuban ostracism from the Inter-American System, Latin American members were attacked as "accomplices in the imperialist strategy" of the United States.[60] As a result, a cultural rift emerged. Brazilian diplomats huffily commented that many of the Non-Aligned recommendations, such as the one on the peaceful settlement of conflicts, were nothing new and had actually been commonplace in Latin America for many decades. "There is a complete lack of knowledge of Latin American diplomatic traditions," Armando Frazão reprovingly noted. In this confusion of "realities, ideas and generalizations" regarding Latin America, it was no surprise that misunderstandings ensued.[61]

Other Latin American observers shared the disappointment expressed by Brazil. A Mexican senator compared the meeting of foreign ministers that took place shortly before the actual conference to a "bad session [of the] Mexican Chamber of Deputies."[62] Even the representative of the newly independent Jamaica, Egerton Richardson, complained about African intransigence and blamed it for the deeply disappointing result of Cairo.[63] Evaluating the Cairo conference in early 1965, the Ambassador of Trinidad and Tobago to the United States, Ellis Clarke, commented that the very aggressive, anti-European rhetoric of African states, which he described as "un-Western," had opened a gap between African and West Indian nations.[64]

From the beginning, Brazil and Latin America had very uneasily fit into the postcolonial narrative of the NAM. African attacks on foreign investment as "neocolonialism" and increasingly angry rhetoric put Latin Americans off, as these attacks were in direct opposition to their efforts to develop and secure private and public capital under the Alliance for Progress. As Non-Aligned debates increasingly focused on the fight against colonialism, they felt more and more on the margins of the movement.

Conclusion

In the nascent phase of the NAM, Brazil had shown avid interest because the movement reflected its political concerns. By 1964, seismic shifts in Latin America and the radicalization of Non-Aligned politics meant that paths were diverging. Ultimately, the 1964 military coup and the subsequent rapprochement with the United States put an end to Brazilian flirtation with the NAM.

Brazilians actively participated in debates on a "third way," but for them it was centered on economic development and the renegotiation of the global economic world order. As much as Brazilian elites talked about nonalignment, there was always a clear understanding that this was not a feasible political option for Brazil. They perceived themselves to be Western, both culturally and politically. Nonalignment for Brazilians, as for many other Latin American politicians, was about expanding their room for political maneuver vis-à-vis the United States.

Despite this divergence of interests, nonaligned themes continued to resonate in Brazil and had far-reaching repercussions. And Brazil's engagement with nonalignment or wider Third World solidarity did play out in the nonaligned movement itself within the United Nations, in debates on UNCTAD, the group of 77, and the Organization of the Petroleum Exporting Countries. In the end, this is where Brazilians felt they belonged: in an economic Third World.

Notes

1. Telegrama da Embaixada no Cairo, 20 May 1961, Documentos Sigilosos, Embaixadas A–K, 1960–61 (Box 47), Archive of the Brazilian Foreign Ministry (hereafter AMRE).

2. Jeffrey James Byrne, "Beyond Continents, Colours, and the Cold War: Yugoslavia, Algeria and the Struggle for Non-Alignment," *International History Review* 37, no. 5 (2015): 912–32.

3. Robert Vitalis has argued for a new history of nonalignment that would replace "exaggerated accounts of metropolitan power and the indistinguishable portraits of Nasser, Nehru and Nkrumah" and instead "recognize the competing national state-building projects and regional state-systemic logics." Robert Vitalis, "The Midnight Ride of Kwame Nkrumah and Other Fables of Bandung (Ban-doong)," *Humanity* 4, no. 2 (2013): 261–88. Nataša Mišković, Harald Fischer-Tiné, and Nada Boškovska, eds., *The Non-Aligned Movement and the Cold War: Delhi-Bandung-Belgrade* (London: Routledge, 2014); Robert Rakove, *Kennedy, Johnson, and the Nonaligned World* (New York: Cambridge University Press, 2014); Frank Gerits, "'When the Bull Elephants Fight': Kwame Nkrumah, Non-Alignment, and Pan-

Africanism as an Interventionist Ideology in the Global Cold War (1957–66)," *International History Review* 37, no. 5 (2015): 951–69. Sandra Bott, Jussi M. Hanhimäki, Janick Marina Schaufelbuehl, and Marco Wyss, eds., *Neutrality and Neutralism in the Global Cold War: Between or Within the Blocs?* (London: Routledge, 2016); Vijay Prashad, *The Darker Nations: A People's History of the Third World* (New York: New Press, 2007).

4. James G. Hershberg, "High-Spirited Confusion: Brazil, the 1961 Belgrade Non-Aligned Conference, and the Limits of an 'Independent' Foreign Policy during the High Cold War," *Cold War History* 7, no. 3 (2007): 373–88; Vanni Pettinà, "Global Horizons: Mexico, the Third World, and the Non-Aligned Movement at the Time of the 1961 Belgrade Conference," *International History Review* 38, no. 4 (2016): 741–64. See also Eric Zolov, "Non-Alignment and Student Protest in 1968 Mexico," in *1968 in Europe and Latin America*, ed. A. James McAdams and Anthony Monta (Notre Dame, IN: University of Notre Dame Press, forthcoming).

5. Rozita Levi, "Cuba and the Nonaligned Movement," in *Cuba in the World*, ed. Cole Blasier and Carmela Mesa-Lago (Pittsburgh, PA: University of Pittsburgh Press, 1979), 147–51.

6. Leslie Bethell, "Brazil and 'Latin America,'" *Journal of Latin American Studies* 42, no. 3 (2010): 457–85.

7. As Ambassador Henrique Rodrigues Valle commented in 1961, Brazil "is playing a role opposite to what it had become accustomed to, from an interpreter of the United States in Latin America, it has become the advocate of Latin Americans vis-à-vis the northern power." As quoted in Stanley E. Hilton, "The United States, Brazil, and the Cold War, 1945–1960: End of the Special Relationship," *Journal of American History* 68, no. 3 (1981): 623.

8. See also Alexandre Moreli's and Boris Le Chaffotec's work on the Unión Latina, an attempt to unite Latin America, France, and Spain under the banner of *latinidad*. Alexandre L. Moreli and Boris Le Chaffotec, "Countering War or Embracing Peace? Dialogues between Regionalism and Multilateralism in Latin America (1945–1954)," *Culture and History Digital Journal* 4, no. 1 (2015).

9. Debates on the awkward place of Latin America in the world order continue to this day, both in academic and public discourse. Some scholars have therefore claimed that Latin America as a region belongs neither to the West nor to the Third World, but constitutes a category of its own—a "Fourth World of Development," as Howard Wiarda framed it. Howard Wiarda, *Politics and Social Change in Latin America: Still a Distinct Tradition?* (Boulder, CO: Westview Press, 1992), 6. Lauren Benton, "No Longer Odd Region Out: Repositioning Latin American in World History," *Hispanic American Historical Review* 84, no. 3 (2004): 423–30.

10. Address of Foreign Minister Francisco de Negrão de Lima, 5 July 1958, EAP emb 1958.05.27, Centro de Pesquisa e Documentação de História Contemporânea do Brasil (hereafter CPDOC).

11. Charles Hale describes how Latin American culture "emerged within the broader confines of Western European culture." Charles Hale, "Political Ideas and Ideologies in Latin America, 1870–1930," in *Ideas and Ideologies in Twentieth-Century Latin America*, ed. Leslie Bethell (Cambridge: Cambridge University Press,

1996), 133. Joseph L. Love, *Crafting the Third World: Theorizing Underdevelopment in Rumania and Brazil* (Stanford, CA: Stanford University Press, 1996), 5.

12. First Report of the Brazilian Delegation of the Committee of 21 by Cleantho Paiva Leite, 10 May 1959, EAP emb 1958.05.27, CPDOC.

13. Instructions for the Brazilian Delegation of the Committee of 21, drafted by the Economic Department of Itamaraty, Setor Econômico, October 1958, EAP emb 1958.05.27, CPDOC.

14. Hershberg, "High-Spirited Confusion," 381.

15. Jânio Quadros, "Brazil's New Foreign Policy" *Foreign Affairs* 40, no. 1 (1961): 19–27.

16. Pettinà, 759.

17. Telegram, 9 May 1961, Folder Politica Internacional 900.1 (00), AMRE.

18. Lester D. Langley, *America and the Americas: The United States in the Western Hemisphere* (Athens: University of Georgia Press, 1989), 245.

19. Vijay Prashad and Robert C. Young draw a direct connection, but as Robert Vitalis has rightly argued, Bandung and Afro-Asianism was a rival movement to nonalignment. Prashad, *The Darker Nations*; Robert C. Young, *Postcolonialism: A Historical Introduction* (Malden, MA: Blackwell, 2012). Vitalis, "The Midnight Ride," 277.

20. According to G. H. Jansen, twenty-one governments had sent representatives. These included Algeria, Tunisia, Egypt, Ghana, Guinea, Mali, Sudan, and Ethiopia from Africa; Saudi Arabia, Lebanon, Afghanistan, Indonesia, India, Burma, Ceylon, Cambodia, and Laos from Asia and the Middle East. The only European country was Yugoslavia. G. H. Jansen, *Afro-Asia and Nonalignment* (London: Praeger, 1966).

21. Telegram for Embassy Belgrade, 30 June 1961, Folder Politica Internacional 900.1 (00), AMRE.

22. Relatório do Observador do Brasil à Reunião Preliminar de Conferência de Chefes de Estado a Govêrno de Países Não-Alinhados, 15 June 1961, Folder Politica Internacional 900.1 (00), AMRE.

23. Telegram, 9 May 1961, Folder Politica Internacional 900.1 (00), AMRE.

24. Relatório do Observador do Brasil à Reunião Preliminar de Conferência de Chefes de Estado a Govêrno de Países Não-Alinhados, AMRE. Emphasis in the original.

25. Relatório do Observador do Brasil à Reunião Preliminar de Conferência de Chefes de Estado a Govêrno de Países Não-Alinhados, AMRE.

26. Telegram, 29 July 1961, Folder Politica Internacional 900.1 (00), AMRE.

27. As quoted in Hershberg, "High-Spirited Confusion," 379.

28. Hershberg, "High-Spirited Confusion," 376.

29. Relatório do Observador do Brasil à Reunião Preliminar da Conferência de Chefes de Estado e Gôverno de Países Não-Alinhados, AMRE.

30. Remarks by J. A. Araújo Castro, observer of Brazil, Annex 2, Relatório do Observador do Brasil à Reunião Preliminar de Conferência de Chefes de Estado a Govêrno de Países não-Alinhados, June 1961, Politica Internacional 900.1 (00), AMRE.

31. Relatório do Observador do Brasil à Reunião Preliminar da Conferência de Chefes de Estado e Gôverno de Países Não-Alinhados, AMRE.

32. Telegram to Embassy Delhi, 11 July 1961, Folder Politica Internacional 900.1 (00), AMRE.

33. Relatório do Observador do Brasil à Reunião Preliminar da Conferência de Chefes de Estado e Gôverno de Países Não-Alinhados, AMRE.

34. Gilberto Freyre, *The Masters and the Slaves: A Study in the Development of Brazilian Civilization* (Berkeley: University of California Press, 1986).

35. Raymundo Souza Dantas, *África difícil: missão condenada* (Rio de Janeiro: Editôria Leitura, 1965).

36. As quoted in Jerry Dávila, *Hotel Trópico: Brazil and the Challenge of African Decolonization, 1950–1980* (Durham, NC: Duke University Press, 2010), 46.

37. Relatório do Observador do Brasil à Reunião Preliminar da Conferência de Chefes de Estado e Gôverno de Países Não-Alinhados, AMRE.

38. As quoted in Hershberg, "High-Spirited Confusion," 374.

39. Relatório do Observador do Brasil à Conferencia dos Chefes de Estado de Governo dos Países Não Alinhados, 7 September 1961, Folder Politica Internacional 900.1 (00), AMRE.

40. Byrne, "Beyond Continents, Colours, and the Cold War," 913.

41. Byrne, "Beyond Continents, Colours, and the Cold War," 913.

42. Jeremy Friedman, *Shadow Cold War: The Sino-Soviet Competition for the Third World* (Chapel Hill: University of North Carolina Press, 2015); Lorenz Lüthi, *The Sino-Soviet Split: Cold War in the Communist World* (Princeton, NJ: Princeton University Press, 2008).

43. Telegram from Dar-es-Salam, 5 February 1963, Political Section (POL) 8 Neutralism/Non-Alignment, Central Foreign Policy Files, 1963, Box 3793, U.S. National Archives and Records Administration, College Park, MD (hereafter NARA).

44. Telegram from Dar-es-Salam., NARA.

45. Airgram from Department of State, 11 January 1963, POL 8 Neutralism/Non-Alignment, Central Foreign Policy Files, 1963, Box 3793, NARA.

46. Airgram Embassy Accra to Department of State, 3 October 1963, POL 8 Neutralism/Non-Alignment, Central Foreign Policy Files, 1963, Box 3793, NARA.

47. Telegram from Dar-es-Salaam, 14 February 1963, POL 8 Neutralism/Non-Alignment, Central Foreign Policy Files, 1963, Box 3793, NARA.

48. In 1964, of the nineteen Latin American member-states, only Costa Rica, Colombia, Venezuela, Uruguay, Chile, Peru, and Mexico had civilian governments and were at least superficially democratic.

49. "Entrevista concedida ao Diário Popular, de Lisboa, sobre as relações luso-brasileiras," JM pi Magelhães, J. 1966.08.24/3, CPDOC.

50. Resolution I Applications of Measures to the Present Government of Cuba, OEA/Ser. F/II.9, Columbus Memorial Library (hereafter CML).

51. Telegram AmEmbassy Paris, 23 October 1964, POL 8 Neutralism/Nonalignment, Central Foreign Policy Files, 1964–66, Box 1828, NARA.

52. Airgram circular to all American Republics (ARA) posts, 30 July 1964, POL 8 Neutralism/Nonalignment, Central Foreign Policy Files, 1964–66, Box 1829, NARA.

53. Airgram to all American diplomatic and consular posts, 30 July 1964, POL 8 Neutralism/Nonalignment, Central Foreign Policy Files, 1964-66, Box 1829, NARA.

54. Telegram from Department of State, 28 October 1964, POL 8 Neutralism/Nonalignment, Central Foreign Policy Files, 1964-66, Box 1829, NARA.

55. Airgram from Belgrade, 6 August 1964, POL 8 Neutralism/Nonalignment, Central Foreign Policy Files, 1964-66, Box 1829, NARA.

56. Posición de Cuba ante el Comité Preparatorio de la Conferencia de los No-Alienados, n.d., Box MNOAL 1949-1964, Archive of the Cuban Foreign Ministry (hereafter MINREX). The folder includes in-depth reports on each Latin American delegation.

57. Folder Secreto, Telegram from Embassy in Cairo, 8 July 1964, AMRE.

58. Relatório "II Conferência da Cúpula dos Estados Nao-alinhados," 21 October 1964, AMRE.

59. Relatório "II Conferência da Cúpula dos Estados Nao-Alinhados."

60. Relatório "II Conferência da Cúpula dos Estados Nao-Alinhados."

61. Relatório "II Conferência da Cúpula dos Estados Nao-Alinhados."

62. Telegram from Cairo, 3 October 1964, POL 8 Neutralism/Nonalignment, Central Foreign Policy Files, 1964-66, Box 1829, NARA.

63. Conference Telegram from New York, Plimpton, 23 October 1964, POL 8 Neutralism/Nonalignment, Central Foreign Policy Files, 1964-66, Box 1828, NARA.

64. Airgram, United States Delegation at the United Nations, 22 Jan 1965, POL 8 Neutralism/Nonalignment, Central Foreign Policy Files, 1964-66, Box 1828, NARA.

5 Community Development in Cold War Guatemala
Not a Revolution but an Evolution

SARAH FOSS

Human development indicators in Cold War Guatemala were abysmal. In a world increasingly obsessed with defining modernity in statistical terms, underdevelopment was supposedly easy to measure, diagnose, and cure.[1] In the 1950s, Guatemala's numbers told a depressing story. Illiteracy levels were at 71.9 percent of the population, life expectancy was forty years, and only 2.17 percent of the landholders owned an incredible 72.21 percent of all arable land, causing Guatemala's largely rural population to barely survive using subsistence mono-agriculture on tiny plots.[2] Beyond the measures of mass poverty and wealth disparity, Guatemala experienced high levels of political instability; by the 1960s, leftist movements were mounting a guerrilla war against the state.

Guatemalan newspapers regularly discussed the nation's underdeveloped status, identifying it as a national embarrassment. These articles remarked on the success that other "Third World" countries, such as the Philippines, India, and Pakistan, had experienced in using community development programs to curb instability and combat poverty. Naturally, in these articles, government officials and social scientists recommended a similar trajectory for Guatemala. They argued that through local participation in community development projects, Guatemala would peacefully transition from its underdeveloped status to a fully democratic, capitalist society, experiencing "not a revolution, but an evolution."[3]

In this chapter, I suggest that while the Guatemalan political elite sought stability, it desired a stability that ensured their continued rule, even at the expense of democracy and in favor of authoritarianism.[4] Looking at Guatemala's National Program of Community Development, which was officially launched in 1964 and dispatched teams across the country to bring about this evolution, and more importantly, prevent the spread of revolution, the chapter focuses on one of these sites, the community of Tactic, and explores the interplay between project planners' use of a Third World identity to consolidate power and local actors' ability to undermine project goals in pursuit of their own interests.

In the early 1950s, U.S. foreign policy took a significant turn toward utilizing covert operations to interfere in other country's internal affairs, secretly supporting a coup that overthrew Iran's nationalist government under Mohammad Mossadeq and Guatemala's socially reformist government under Jacobo Árbenz. U.S. interference in domestic politics throughout the Global South would continue to mark U.S. Third World policy.[5] In Guatemala, the U.S. Central Intelligence Agency (CIA) collaborated with a Guatemalan military colonel to overthrow the democratically elected government of Árbenz in 1954, due to his alleged ties to international Communism.[6] In the immediate aftermath of this coup, the U.S. State Department viewed Guatemala as "a political, social, and economic laboratory. . . . The success or failure of this experiment by the first country in the world to overthrow the Communist yoke will be a major factor in determining the future course of Latin American affairs."[7] Eager to make Guatemala a success story, the Eisenhower administration poured financial assistance into the country, and later administrations continued to do so through the U.S. Agency for International Development (USAID), with a heavy focus on large-scale infrastructure projects such as highways and ports.[8]

Guatemalan development was intended to showcase the success of First World modernization theory, which positively correlated capitalist economic development with democratic political stability. As such, it would blatantly challenge the centralized rural and urban industrialization that the Soviet Union had effectively demonstrated in other Third World countries, such as Kazakhstan's Virgin Lands agricultural modernization project, and through economic aid to Chile for projects such as urban housing and deep-sea fishing programs.[9] The case of Guatemala thus illustrates the high stakes of the international development game for control over the Third World.[10]

Recent histories of development tend to focus on the ways that Cold War superpowers utilized development as a means to amass influence over the contested Third World, highlighting the continuities and ruptures in development policies across different political moments and geographical contexts.[11] Western modernization theories imbued the Third World with an unquestioned sense of being "a world perceived as both materially and culturally deficient."[12] In so doing, modernization theory actually redefined the concept of the Third World from simply being a recently decolonized and politically nonaligned area to identifying it more broadly as a primordial and backward space in need of the First World's guidance. Conceived in this way, the Third World was linked to a homogeneous status of underdevelopment, with modernization theory establishing "the most explicit and systematic blueprint ever . . . for reshaping foreign societies" in a way that "supplied not only a sense of the 'meaning' of postwar geopolitical uncertainties, but also an implicit set of directives for how to effect positive change in that dissilient world."[13] Thus, modernization theory created acceptable ways of thinking about and labeling the countries and peoples of the world. Within this broader conception of the Third World, Guatemala, while tied closely with the United States and experimenting with U.S. modernization policies, was unequivocally part of the Third World.

In Guatemala and throughout the Third World more broadly, economic development took various forms, from large-scale infrastructure projects and extensive systems of credit to small loans and community development projects. As the idea of community development gained traction and legitimacy, "a strange pattern . . . emerged within the foreign aid apparatus." Adherents of modernization theory "gravitated toward centers of power," while those more supportive of a localized approach, the communitarians, worked at "the sites of implementation."[14] Therefore, a top-down, national plan of community development, designed to be a one-size-fits-all formula for what modernizers saw as homogeneous, backward, traditional societies, could take on very different meanings and see drastically varied results at the local level. While other studies have considered Guatemala's history of development from the perspective of cultural change within the context of globalization or in terms of natural resource management and environmental history, I suggest that placing the history of community development in Guatemala within a Third World modernization framework elucidates the ways that international history and local practices shaped one another and connected small Guatemalan Mayan communities to larger trends in Third World development politics.[15]

As the various layers in this history reveal, the United States heavily invested in securing a foothold in this strategically important Central American nation, viewing Guatemala as the geographic place where the First World could demonstrate the success of its modernization model. Guatemalan political elites used (and abused) their identity as a Third World nation to consolidate their own power, much as local political elites elsewhere in the world did.[16] In drawing attention to Guatemala's underdeveloped status and linking this with the plight of the broader Third World, the political elite presented community development projects as strictly humanitarian endeavors, devoid of political meaning and implication. Community development became an important tool of governance in Cold War Guatemala, which eventually allowed the military to gain complete control of the state. The result was a seemingly paradoxical combination of "democratic" development and dictatorship that took place elsewhere in Latin America, including Bolivia and Brazil.[17] In many ways, the modernizing development project helped Guatemalan elite to consolidate tyranny. However, at the same time, this modernizing project met resistance when actually implemented in communities like Tactic, Alta Verapaz. Local actors, the communitarians, who were well aware of international politics, utilized the opportunities top-down development provided to pursue their own goals in their community, not adhering to bipolar geopolitical constraints, but instead crafting an alternative model of development and citizenship.

This chapter proceeds in two sections. First, it situates the history of community development in Tactic, Guatemala, within its national and international historical moments. Second, it considers Guatemala's Program of Community Development, which had sites in towns throughout rural Guatemala, including Tactic. This section analyzes a single program that experts created with the model of modernization theory in mind, but that local actors implemented according to the community's wishes, not the central government's agenda. A brief conclusion revisits the central theme of this chapter, namely how the employment of a Third World identity allowed Guatemalan elites to use development as a tool of governance and how individuals exercised their agency in resisting and challenging this homogenizing vision.

Historical Context

Across the globe, both U.S. and Soviet development experts sought to achieve a "fundamental *structural* change," believing that the world order would tilt in their respective favor as more and more underdeveloped nations in the Third World adopted their specific model for this change.[18] Both the U.S. and Soviet models of development were based on a universal and linear path toward a defined notion of progress, and both positioned Third World countries at a lower stage. The question was which path these strategically important, resource-rich nations would take.[19] In the wake of sweeping decolonization, the newly created nations, in a sense, were considered blank slates for one of the superpowers to inscribe direction and guidance.

Though not part of the post–World War II decolonized world, Guatemala, and much of Latin America, shared commonalities with these nations, as they too struggled to overcome the neoimperialist tendencies of the First World, particularly in terms of economic independence.[20] From 1944 to 1954, Guatemala successively elected two democratic governments that pursued an agenda that sought to increase Guatemalan economic and political independence from the United States, most controversially through land reform. Due to the supposed increasing Communist infiltration of the government and the expropriation of United Fruit Company land, a CIA-supported coup, led by Colonel Carlos Castillo Armas, overthrew Guatemala's democratic government in 1954.[21]

According to the counterrevolutionary regime, Guatemala's underdeveloped status left it dangerously teetering between two paths to modernity: that of democracy and capitalism, as exhibited by the United States, and that of Communism, as manifested by the Soviet Union. For many Guatemalan elites and the U.S. government, Guatemala had just been "liberated" from the dangerous throes of Communism, but as long as Guatemala remained "underdeveloped," this threat would not subside. From the U.S. perspective, as well as that of the Guatemalan elites, ordinary Guatemalans' expectations of accessing more material resources were certainly rising, yet as the brief experiment with reform had demonstrated, if unchecked, Guatemala would drift toward the Left and endanger U.S. and its own national security. Guatemala needed to develop, but in a way that would support a slow evolution, dictated from above, not a more radical revolution that immediately responded to demands from below.[22] This model resonated with the United States' modernization project, and the counterrevolutionary government began closely collaborating with U.S. experts to devise what it believed to be an appropriate, safe strategy for Guatemala's development.

While other Latin American countries had more flexibility in networking with the Non-Aligned Movement or seeking economic aid from Second World sources, due to the 1954 coup that had "liberated" Guatemala from "Communism," it was much trickier for Guatemala to pursue that option.[23] Vice President Richard Nixon stated in August 1955, "This is the first instance in history where a Communist government has been replaced by a free one. The whole world is watching to see which does the better job."[24] Determined to prove the validity of the First World path to modernity, the United States was figuratively and literally invested in the success of Guatemala's modernization. Pouring money and resources into the country, U.S. experts helped to craft the first of Guatemala's five-year development plans, thus charting the "appropriate" course for Guatemalan development and ensuring that the country fell firmly within the orbit of the First World. With pressure from the U.S. embassy in Guatemala, the economic consulting firm Klein & Saks, which had reportedly "done an 'outstanding job in Peru,'" had representation on Guatemala's National Economic Planning Council, in order to "act as watch dog to help the new and inexperienced administration avoid making serious blunders in the economic field" and to "get closer to the Guatemalan government."[25]

Colonel Castillo Armas, the first counterrevolutionary president, welcomed U.S. aid and informed the population that they must adapt to the structural changes occurring in Guatemala's economy and society as a result of the development plans. In a presidential speech on 19 July 1957, he cautioned, "Guatemalans must recognize the large changes that are occurring in this country and must incorporate themselves into this new attitude that they have been hoping for, because those who do not understand this will be the failures of tomorrow." This "new attitude" was precisely his government's slogan of "Nueva Vida," which mandated that the modern Guatemalan citizen must have faith in him- or herself, work hard, and capitalize on state provided opportunities to personally improve both spiritually and materially. Most importantly, adopting this new life provided through state development programs was not optional.[26]

Castillo Armas was assassinated in 1957, and his successor, Miguel Ydígoras Fuentes, also tied development to national security, pointing to the Guatemalan government's desire to align with the United States. In addition, Ydígoras signaled the reality that without U.S. economic aid, the country's popular classes could very well turn to Second World sources for guidance. For instance, in 1959, Ydígoras Fuentes wrote one of his annual New Year letters to President Eisenhower, complaining about the fall in international coffee prices. With the loss of nearly $26 million in revenue, the Guatemalan government was unable to improve citizens' lives and fulfill its promises. Requesting aid from the United States, Ydígoras concluded by writing, "The common enemy, Communism, will not invade us from outside but flourishes among our hungry people. Khrushchev is waiting at the door."[27] Clearly, Ydígoras positioned Guatemala on the side of the First World while also warning that without U.S. aid, Guatemala would quickly fall outside of the First World's orbit. Here Ydígoras invoked the Third World strategy of nonalignment, demonstrating his willingness to obtain funds for national development from either superpower, although revealing his preference for U.S. sources of aid. Guatemala, like other Third World nations, was up for grabs in the geopolitical game.

Guatemalan political elites had much to gain in adopting the First World's model of modernization—military and humanitarian aid, international legitimacy, and political backing. They used their Third World nation status to gain access to these important resources, which allowed them to consolidate their power, although not without serious and repeated contestation. Strong nationalist tendencies also forced the political elite to mask this acceptance of the U.S. model and instead justify it based on purely national terms in order to avoid being labeled as simply another stooge of what was popularly perceived to be the United States' imperialist tendencies. Guatemalan political elites faced an interesting dilemma. To stay in power and quash any political dissidence, this military government desperately needed First World grants and loans, yet they also had to justify their actions in terms of national wellbeing so as to not appear to be completely subservient to First World interests.

In 1959, the Cuban Revolution succeeded and subsequently inaugurated the first Communist regime in the Western Hemisphere. Just over one hundred miles from the U.S. mainland, Cuba immediately changed the importance of Latin America in the Cold War. Just a year later, Guatemala, approximately nine hundred miles away, faced a growing leftist insurgency, presenting the possibility of a second Cuba in the West. On 13 November 1960, a group of young soldiers, disenchanted with the government's corruption and inability to improve living standards, launched an attack on the Matamoros Barracks in the capital of Guatemala City. Their manifesto explained their justification in rising up against the very institution that they were supposed to serve and their belief that the military should serve the interests of the people writ large, not the state: "We are in the mountains fighting to the death for those who are hungry, for the land that none other than John F. Kennedy is asking to be given to our peasants."[28] While the government successfully stopped this rebellion, those remaining from the rebelling faction founded the Movimiento Rebelde 13 de Noviembre (MR-13) and continued the insurgency in the eastern part of the country.[29]

In 1963, partly due to President Ydígoras' inability to quickly end MR-13 activities and also because former revolutionary-era president Juan José Arévalo had announced his candidacy for the upcoming election and was leading in the polls, a military coup overthrew Ydígores Fuentes in his final days as president. Colonel Enrique Peralta Azurdia assumed the presidency in March 1963.³⁰ A declassified memo from the U.S. embassy in Guatemala on 21 January 1963, explicitly stated that if Arévalo were to return to office, he would "likely serve the Communist purpose well again, turning his country away from friendly relations with the United States, and away from a constructive role in the Alliance for Progress for which he has no apparent understanding or sympathy."³¹ Due to the widespread popularity that Arévalo's reformist politics still enjoyed throughout the country and the guerrilla insurgency, Peralta Azurdia's regime understood that the large-scale infrastructure projects were not effectively changing the daily lives of Guatemala's impoverished rural population and as a result failed to convince the majority that the First World modernization development model was the appropriate path for Guatemala.

During the 1960 U.S. presidential campaign, Kennedy released a press statement justifying his proposals for widespread economic development programs in Latin America, writing, "Although the Cold War will not be won in Latin America—it may well be lost there."³² Adolf Berle, who would become an architect for Kennedy's Alliance for Progress, revealed in his diary in January 1961, that "eight governments may go the way of Cuba in the next six months unless something is done."³³ Recognizing the impact that a First World–oriented Latin America would have on U.S. success, Kennedy's administration began pouring funds into the region. Significantly, Kennedy's international development model focused on projects at the community level.³⁴ Thus it is not surprising that his foreign aid program for Latin America, the Alliance for Progress, was supportive of localized development projects, a turn from the previous administration's emphasis on large-scale infrastructure.

Moreover, many Guatemalans recognized that it would take decades for the expected benefits of the large-scale infrastructure projects to trickle down to Guatemala's rural masses, so community development projects became the means to efficiently and cost-effectively improve rural life. State plans for community development had begun elsewhere in the Third World in the 1950s, with the intention of being a top-down program that could effectively translate the modernizing goals of the national government into tangible projects and changes in mentalities at the local level. For example, India received the first U.S.-sponsored pilot community development project, setting up a holistic village-level project of agricultural modernization, hygiene campaigns, and infrastructure development in Etawah.³⁵ In 1956, the Philippines inaugurated the Presidential Assistant on Community Development, a national program of community development largely inspired by the Etawah project.³⁶ And in Peru, from 1952 to 1966, the Cornell-Peru Project studied the community of Vicos, an inefficient rural *hacienda* in the Andes, cultivated by indigenous peasants, in an effort to devise and assess strategies for modernizing Peruvian highland agriculture and addressing the land tenure crisis.³⁷

In 1963, Guatemalan also began advocating for a plan of community development, positioning this model as the means guide the countryside toward support of the governing regime, one strongly aligned with the United States. For example, Guatemalan social scientist Víctor Manuel Navarro published a series of articles about the philosophy of community development, calling this broad project a means to "reconstruct the world," meaning that over three-fourths of the world, Guatemala included, faced the same principal problems of inadequate housing and clothing, hunger, and illiteracy.³⁸ One remedy for this unacceptable state of "underdevelopment" was for the Guatemalan state, in the words of the Pan-American Union Director of Community Development, to "establish the basis of a strategic plan in America to produce not a revolution but rather an accelerated evolution based upon the conscience and participation of the people."³⁹ Community development could increase collective economic productivity and facilitate participation as active democratic citizens. Such a project would not come without considerable investment in time and money, but Guatemalan and U.S. policymakers believed it could be a means to transform the mentalities and realities of rural Guatemalans and direct them toward capitalism and democracy. The Program of Community Development (DESCOM) was intended to breathe new life into rural communities, effectively bringing them on board with the state's modernization program and in so doing, allowing the military to consolidate its rule and power.

Program of Community Development (DESCOM)

In 1964, the Guatemalan government created DESCOM based on recommendations from the 1961 Punta del Este conference. The conference's charter established the Alliance for Progress, pledging to "accelerate economic and social development" by eradicating illiteracy, improving rural housing, and establishing more public health programs, all with the end goal of strengthening the hemisphere's democratic institutions.⁴⁰ Ironically, it was Peralta's authoritarian military government that created DESCOM; as a result, from its inception, community development in Guatemala had a complicated relationship with democracy.

Under the Secretary for Social Wellbeing, DESCOM started with a monthly budget of nearly $7,500 and one regional center, located in Chimaltenango. By 1966, the program had rapidly expanded, with centers in Chimaltenango, Jalapa, and Zacapa. In the same year, the military allowed elections, believing that their candidate, Colonel Juan de Dios Aguilar de León, would win. In a surprising election that saw the two right-wing parties split the share of the right's vote, the more progressive party, the Partido Revolucionario, and its candidate, Julio Méndez Montenegro, emerged victorious.[41] However, the army prevented congressional ratification of this unexpected result until Méndez Montenegro signed an accord with the military that allowed them to name the Minister of Defense, maintain executive control over the armed forces, and continue, without oversight, the war against the guerrillas.[42] Therefore despite having a democratically elected government that proclaimed to be the third government of the revolution, state repression, particularly in eastern departments, escalated, with Colonel Carlos Arana Osorio's forces killing an estimated 10,000 people between 1967 and 1968.[43]

Yet rural development initiatives continued, and in 1967, DESCOM had a budget of $1.5 million and had moved directly under the secretary of the presidency.[44] During the next ten years, development existed alongside repression in the countryside, even as the military resumed authoritarian rule until 1985. New guerrilla organizations emerged in 1972 and began a second phase of the civil war, shifting the theater westward into the indigenous highlands where the violence eventually reached genocidal levels, killing over 200,000 and displacing 2.3–3 million, the majority being Maya.[45] Yet despite the violence, DESCOM's work continued, as the government perceived this program to be a way to cheaply and efficiently bring economic progress and anti-Communism to the countryside.[46]

By the 1970s, DESCOM operated throughout the country as the civilian counterpart to the Army's Civic Action programs, which were development projects in regions of recent guerrilla insurgency. The Guatemalan government adopted the same two-prong approach that President John F. Kennedy had proposed a decade earlier for U.S. foreign policy—namely, that countries adopt long-term economic development plans while in the short term ensuring national security through military strength, if necessary. The United States was prepared to simultaneously offer nations economic loans and military assistance through USAID, and Guatemala took full advantage of this offer.[47] Although DESCOM's program objectives were couched in terms of democratic participation, DESCOM provided a means for the state to extend its presence into the countryside and work to transform the diverse rural indigenous population into predictable, controllable, homogeneous modernized citizens.[48]

U.S. foreign aid supported development and dictatorship as the Guatemalan elite, particularly the military, used their Third World status to gain funds. In doing so, many Guatemalans believed, these elite lined their own pockets and consolidated their own positions of authority. While direct evidence of corruption does not exist, newspaper articles regularly critiqued the Alliance for Progress and USAID for failing to provide the necessary oversight to ensure proper use of funds. In the words of one congressional representative, the obtained money should go directly to schools, hospitals, and other needs, not to the military government because "it will go to the pockets of the functionaries."[49] In order to contest the messianic messages and promises of improved quality of life that the guerrilla organizations were disseminating in the countryside, the government expanded the activities of DESCOM, believing that community development could prevent rural Guatemalans from joining these leftist movements by changing the mentalities and the material conditions of the population.[50]

A series of training booklets that the Pan-American Union's Department for Social Affairs created clearly outline the philosophy of community development and its ability to establish stable, democratic nations. Guatemala was not the only Latin American country to have a comprehensive state-led community development program, as Venezuela, Colombia, Brazil, Ecuador, Peru, Haiti, and Mexico also implemented similar projects.[51] The goal was to help populations reach their full human potential as quickly, and as cheaply, as possible.[52] For these development practitioners, "full human potential" meant that individuals used their energy effectively and in cooperation with one another to improve infrastructure, pursue capitalist ventures, and gradually acquire wealth. Argentine Professor Ezequiel Ander-Egg, who had advised DESCOM in its nascent stages, explained that Guatemala, like much of the Third World, was experiencing a "revolution of rising expectations." However, this revolution presented policymakers with two options: "democratic revolution or a bloody and deadly revolution."[53] Community development had the potential to form a political consciousness and an inclination toward informed democratic participation. Otherwise, the population would become the cause of "major conflict and social and political disorganization."[54] DESCOM would effectively combat Communism through "directing mankind toward liberty and toward a better destiny," as defined by the state, and by the First World.[55]

While improving infrastructure was certainly a central objective of DESCOM, changing the recipients' psychology was key. This was not a new idea generated in Guatemala's community development program; rather, it had been applied elsewhere in the world, reflecting an acceptance of a broader contemporary global conversation about community development.[56] For example, in the aftermath of World War II, a film for U.S. troops occupying Japan emphasized this psychological component of development, stating, "These brains, like our brains, can do good or bad things, all depending on the kinds of ideas that are put inside."[57] It was up to the experts to determine which ideas to inscribe upon the recipients of development projects. Thus, Y. C. James Yen's International Institute for Rural Reconstruction, with programs in the Philippines, Thailand, Ghana, Colombia, and Guatemala, sought to transform local mentalities by helping communities to organize and establish committees to collectively solve local problems in yet another example of this pervasive belief that psychological transformation was a key component of any community development project.

DESCOM ascribed to this dual emphasis of development, believing that practical projects not only would propel a community to a higher stage of development but would also achieve the mental transformations necessary for forging a local democracy. Through inculcating communities with a sense of social responsibility and the tools to effectively organize themselves, DESCOM could "help people to acquire the necessary attitudes, habits, and points of view to effectively and democratically participate in the solution of problems for the local, regional, and national community."[58] Not only this, but communities would gain important self-empowerment after successfully organizing and completing a project. According to MIT economist Wilfred Malenbaum, backwardness was not really "a lack of resources but rather an inability to use them."[59] Though Malenbaum was not specifically referring to the Guatemalan context, when applied to Guatemala, this statement's underlying philosophy takes on racist tones, coding all indigenous rural regions as needing nonindigenous guidance. Through the intervention and humanitarian efforts of DESCOM, rural Guatemalans could be taken out of this backward condition and, through the patient instruction of urban, white project leaders, learn how to effectively utilize their resources and improve their lives.

Through DESCOM, training materials proclaimed, Guatemala could join other Third World nations on the path to modernity and stable democracy. These pamphlets positioned the project as one guided by the tenets of the

United Nations and cited India, Pakistan, Indonesia, Iran, the Philippines, Thailand, Peru, Venezuela, Colombia, and Ecuador as states with successful community development models. Although several of these turned toward authoritarianism shortly after these materials were published,[60] presumably they were listed as models due to their political allegiance with the United States. Even so, any overt political discourse was absent from the pamphlets. Created in the United States, they attempted to strip community development of its political ideology and instead present it as a universal model that could bring peace and prosperity to all parts of the globe. Community development positioned democracy and liberalism as humanitarian and as the natural form that social relations should take, conveniently ignoring the fact that the United States supported nondemocratic governments with substantial amounts of development aid as long as they were anti-Communist. Community development had become the peaceful means to transform the Third World into close allies of the United States.

In 1971, amid the recent and reportedly fraudulent election of Colonel Carlos Arana Osorio and the immediate state of siege that he declared in the country, DESCOM began working in Tactic. The guerrilla insurgency in the east intensified, as did military repression in some rural areas.[61] At the same time, the Guatemalan countryside experienced an escalation of development projects. While the military's Civic Action programs concentrated on the eastern parts of the country, in areas of recent insurgency, DESCOM operated in areas that did not have a significant guerrilla presence, including Alta Verapaz, the department where Tactic is located. On 19 June 1971, members from DESCOM's Local Center No. 10 met with the municipal leadership and representatives from each of Tactic's villages to create the Municipal Committee of Programming, the entity tasked with receiving petitions from communities, prioritizing these, and establishing DESCOM's schedule of projects.[62] Project coordinator Emilio Vásquez Robles's understanding of the relationship between DESCOM and its host communities is worth quoting at length because it underscores the staff's belief that their work was purely humanitarian and beneficial to the communities:

> Everything was coordinated, coordinated in a way that didn't feel like an impact to the community [*punching fist into hand repeatedly as he said this*], but rather was a help that they, well, would accept, that the team had arrived there to work, through health, education, and the economy. We were never rejected, we never felt like it was a blow [*un golpe; punching fist again*], that a strange team had arrived

to the community, but rather in the investigations that we did, in the meetings with the leaders, we explained what our work was and that we hadn't come to alter the community's way of life but rather had come to bring some help from the government to the community, in order to improve their community, in order to develop their community.[63]

Through careful coordination, thoughtful preliminary study, and several meetings with local leaders, DESCOM staff worked in these communities and brought, from Vásquez's perspective, humanitarian help from the central government, which thus extended its reach, for better and for worse, into rural Guatemala.

Because a central goal was to promote integral development and empower communities to utilize their own resources to realize their own improvement, DESCOM leaders organized communities and quickly deferred daily oversight of projects to local committees. Like teams in other parts of the country, Tactic's DESCOM team consisted of five members: an adult educator, a nurse, a home educator, a social worker, and an agronomist. Based in the municipal center of Tactic, they traveled almost daily to nearby villages to organize locals into Community Improvement Committees. Once formed, these committees presented proposals and project designs for DESCOM to approve and finance. DESCOM operated in Tactic until 1981, when the local center was transferred to Lanquín in northern Alta Verapaz.[64]

During the decade that DESCOM worked in Tactic, it pursued a variety of projects but focused heavily on developing potable water systems and modernizing agricultural methods. Safe drinking water and a varied diet would improve the nation's health, and healthier people would have more energy to pursue economic and social activities. Because U.S. foreign policy focused on developing a strong middle class by breaking the feudal relationships so prevalent in rural Latin America, creating a strong class of agricultural entrepreneurs was critical to modernization's success. Particularly for Guatemala, doing so meant the integration of a majority Maya population that traditionally practiced subsistence agriculture into the national capitalist economy. Improving nutrition was central to achieving this goal and had been a priority of the Guatemalan government for some time. At a 1958 U.S. presidential breakfast where Secretary of State John Foster Dulles had criticized what he perceived to be the poor work ethic of Guatemala's indigenous peoples, Guatemalan physician Mariano López Herrate retorted, "Mr. Secretary, I respectfully submit that if you had the anemia of most of our Latin American workers you wouldn't even be at breakfast this morning."[65] This link between nutrition, public health, and economic productivity continued into the 1970s and guided DESCOM activities in infrastructure and agricultural modernization projects.

In April 1972, the village of Chiacal, just outside Tactic's municipal center, organized an improvement committee with the explicit goal of "realizing distinct activities, of a socio-cultural character for the development of the village so that they can foster a better means of life."[66] For this community, development was simply a way to acquire a higher standard of living. Solving the community's lack of access to drinking water was the Chiacal committee's main objective. In 1974, Chiacal's residents organized work crews to pipe water from a distant spring, located on an estate up the mountain, several kilometers away. The piped water then reached several closed tanks in the village center, replacing the open wells that the community was currently utilizing. These open wells could collect only rainwater, not freshwater, and besides, they were dangerous, as several people had fallen into them and drowned. DESCOM staff negotiated with the estate owner to secure access to this water source and provided the concrete pipes necessary for the project. Community members provided the labor. Decades later, Rogelio Bin Quej, a seventy-two-year-old widowed farmer and the only living member of the local committee, proudly recalled his community's efforts to solve this problem that for years had plagued their health. For weeks, he said, work crews rotated every eight days so that each person contributed his efforts to the project while still having adequate time to tend to his crops and provide sustenance for his family. Men worked to dig the ditches and place the pipes while women provided food and drink to the workers. In the end, they created a potable water system that was replaced only in the early 2000s with an updated system that piped water to every home. Bin has carefully guarded his diploma of service that DESCOM awarded to him on the project's completion date, 6 June 1974, which he proudly displays as evidence of his community service.[67]

As seen in this example, DESCOM worked in Tactic to first organize committees and then acquire the necessary resources to complete practical development projects. Providing safe and accessible drinking water was a central project of DESCOM, as this could significantly reduce disease and allow residents to reallocate the time they typically spent walking to these distant water sources into other activities. However, these projects were about more than piped water. In organizing the committees, DESCOM staff hoped to demonstrate that communities could improve their position through more efficient appropriation of local resources and manpower, thus instilling self-confidence, motivation, and a strong collective work ethic. This model of providing materials and then requiring the community to actually complete the work allowed DESCOM's team to oversee more projects and extend its reach to additional communities. DESCOM projects geared toward agricultural modernization and crop diversification tell a similar story. Globally, Malthusian fears of overpopulation had combined powerfully with a recognition of insufficient food supplies to generate what is now termed the "Green Revolution," referring to the efforts of development planners, agronomists, and scientists to figure out ways to feed the world through improved agricultural techniques, modified seeds and crop varieties, and more efficient transportation.[68] The Guatemalan peasantry barely survived on subsistence agriculture, with many having to supplement familial earnings with seasonal labor on the coastal plantations that grew Guatemala's key export crops. Extremely unequal land tenure patterns were the primary explanation for the rural peasantry's inability to grow enough food for survival. According to the 1964 Guatemalan agrarian census, 87.4 percent of Guatemala's farms were too small to provide work and food for a peasant family, and these small farms covered only 18.6 percent of Guatemala's arable land.[69] However, land reform presented too political of a solution; instead, development experts focused on agricultural modernization, blaming the peasants' "traditional" cultivation methods for insufficient harvests.

DESCOM in Tactic adhered to this agricultural diversification and improvement model. Even though the department of Alta Verapaz had one of the highest rates of expropriated territory during Guatemala's short-lived land reform from 1952 to 1954, at no point was land reform an option for DESCOM, as it would drastically alter the local status quo. Rather, DESCOM proposed technical training in modern cultivation techniques that would theoretically produce higher crop yields. Training materials told DESCOM staff that agriculture could be considered "developed" when farmers were simultaneously completing three economic functions: that of worker, administrator, and capitalist. Understanding the male-led household to be the basic economic unit, the model farmer provided sustenance for his family through his own labor, on his own land. At the same time, his productivity required employees, whom he managed effectively. This agriculture entrepreneur also sold excess produce and actively accumulated wealth, which he used to improve his agricultural ventures and provide opportunities for his dependents.[70] Such a model of agricultural modernization would serve to maintain the status quo by not upsetting current land tenure patterns, and at the same time, it would draw the rural peasantry into the national and global capitalist market, an important goal of First World modernization.

Municipal residents remember DESCOM efforts to shape local agrarian practices and attempts to transform them into model farmers. In 1972, DESCOM implemented its village garden and crop diversification programs in Tampó, Pasmolón, and Chiacal, introducing new crops such as carrots, wheat, and cabbage. Social promoters and DESCOM's home economics instructors taught local women new recipes that used these unfamiliar vegetables in an attempt to improve rural nutrition. Rogelio Bin recalls that during this time, he began growing mandarin tomatoes that he sold at the municipal market, thus increasing his family's income. Alberto Bin, a shop owner, and Heriberto Isem, a farmer, remember the community garden and the beehives that DESCOM oversaw in Pasmolón, recounting that gardening was part of the school curriculum and students took produce home to their families. DESCOM's agricultural expert also taught residents alternative cultivation methods, distributed new types of hybrid seeds, and introduced products such as chemical fertilizers, insecticides, and herbicides. When local residents donated land, DESCOM staff planted experimental fields to demonstrate how modern agricultural practices could provide a higher yield at harvest.[71]

However, not all attempts at agricultural modernization were quickly accepted or applied. DESCOM staff member Gladys Gamboa recalls that although people received seeds and insecticides for free, they were at times hesitant to abandon cultivation techniques that they had learned from their families. Former mayor Carlos López remembers that although DESCOM recognized and respected the sacredness that Maya culture attributed to corn, their efforts to change agricultural practices had mixed results. DESCOM staff tried to teach farmers to plant their crops in rows rather than digging holes for individual seeds and also tried to encourage farmers to plant crops other than corn and beans. While some farmers did accept these suggestions, others maintained that years of experience had convinced them that their traditional methods were best.[72] A farmer in Chiacal said that at first they used the fertilizers that DESCOM provided; however, they quickly realized that these fertilizers, while perhaps increasing their crop yield, were harming the soil, so they abandoned this practice.[73] These oral histories convey the importance that tradition held for rural farmers and their hesitation over changing their cultivation patterns.

Recipients of DESCOM projects celebrated the infrastructure development that occurred in their community but at the same time were less inclined to accept "improvements" in sociocultural areas such as agriculture. Residents did not identify the top-down modernization project of the state as the solution to their problems. While grateful for government financing, local residents took a much more communitarian approach, often seeking "development *without* modernization."[74] Alberto Bin and Heriberto Isem maintained that more serious issues, such as access to land, went unresolved. Development projects, according to these men, were full of corruption and were used as a way of winning votes.[75] Tactiqueños were not completely malleable nor were they willing to alter their lives because a government program suggested alternative behaviors. Even though community development, in many ways, helped the military to consolidate their authoritarian rule, it by no means suffocated local agency. Tactiqueños participated in development as far as they wished, but they collectively refused to completely mold their lives into what the Guatemalan state desired. In the process, both the modernizers and the communitarians (re)created their Third World identity as they daily negotiated the complex layers in international development programs.

Conclusion

Throughout the Western Hemisphere, development experts believed in the power of community development. By employing specialists, channeling projects through international institutions, and framing development as strictly a humanitarian endeavor, they attempted to strip it of all its political content. Oral histories of former DESCOM staff confirm this interpretation of development, as these projects are etched in their memories as apolitical, benevolent endeavors that had a positive impact on Tactic. These men and women tirelessly dedicated their careers to a low-paying job, that, to paraphrase one educational promoter, had a daily start time, but did not have a fixed end time.[76] They traveled almost daily, often on foot or on horseback, to remote communities with the goal of using their expertise to alleviate the widespread poverty in Guatemala's countryside. These communitarians, alongside the villagers with whom they worked, challenged the modernizing aspects of the state's community development program, tailoring it instead to the local context and allowing for some resistance.

In short, local practitioners allowed communities to develop largely on their own terms. Local histories of development reveal how participants were not bound by geopolitical constraints. Their Third World identity was a lived experience, as they daily pursued alternative models of development that better resonated with local customs and practices. In this regard, the state's effort to create a homogenous, modernized citizenry failed.

The program's planners in Guatemala City justified the need for finances for these programs, as well as the very existence of these projects throughout the countryside, in terms of Guatemala's economic underdevelopment, which they considered to be a national embarrassment and the responsibility of the state to remedy. By positioning Guatemala as a country in limbo, with dissatisfied masses who would turn toward Communism if that ideology offered them a better material future, Guatemalan political elites made development an issue of national security and by extension, hemispheric security. By making economic development directly related to continued official Guatemalan support of First World politics, they ensured a steady stream of U.S. and international development aid that allowed the government—which for much of DESCOM's history was a military regime— to consolidate power and maintain an appearance of goodwill in the countryside through what they portrayed as humanitarian efforts.

As part of the broader Third World, Guatemala's experience with community development informs our understanding of development history and its connections, parallels, and disjunctions across the Global South. The nations of the Third World were those believed to be in need of economic development assistance, and while the Cold War was certainly about military escalation and nuclear proliferation, it also was a struggle for defining development and a model for modernity and modern citizens. Localized histories of development, rooted in administrative buildings in Third World capital cities and in town plazas in the Third World's countryside, allow us to draw global connections that trace the ways in which both elites and popular classes negotiated the changes that development initiatives brought to their lives.

Notes

1. Nick Cullather, "The Foreign Policy of the Calorie," *American Historical Review* 112, no. 2 (April 2007): 337–38.

2. Sexto Censo de Población, 1950, 39, Archivo General de Centroamérica (hereafter AGCA); Silvia Quick, *Guatemala*, Country Demographic Profiles (Washington, DC: U.S. Department of Commerce, 1977), 6; "Algunos rasgos de la realidad

agraria en Guatemala," Colección Mario Payeras-Yolanda Colóm, Doc. 004, 5, Archivo del Centro de Investigaciones Regionales de Mesoamérica (hereafter CIRMA).

3. "Da Confianza del Programa de Desarrollo de la Comunidad," *El Imparcial*, 31 May 1965.

4. Nick Cullather, *Illusions of Influence: The Political Economy of United States–Philippines Relations, 1942–1960* (Palo Alto, CA: Stanford University Press, 1994); Nick Cullather, *The Hungry World: America's Cold War Battle against Poverty in Asia* (Cambridge, MA: Harvard University Press, 2010).

5. Odd Arne Westad, *The Global Cold War: Third World Interventions and the Making of Our Times* (Cambridge: Cambridge University Press, 2007), 122.

6. Piero Gleijeses, *Shattered Hope: The Guatemalan Revolution and the United States, 1944–1954* (Princeton, NJ: Princeton University Press, 1991); Stephen Schlesinger and Stephen Kinzer, *Bitter Fruit: The Story of the American Coup in Guatemala*, rev., exp. ed. (Cambridge, MA: Harvard University Press, 2005). In particular, see chapter 10 for a history of the failed attempt by the Arbenz government to buy arms from Czechoslovakia as the United States had refused to sell arms to Guatemala since 1948.

7. U.S. Congress, House of Representatives, Committee on Foreign Affairs, Special Study Mission to Central America on International Organizations and Movements, 84th Congress, 1 Session, rpt. 1155, 1955, 16, quoted in Stephen M. Streeter, *Managing the Counterrevolution: The United States and Guatemala, 1954–1961* (Athens: Ohio University Press, 2000), 137.

8. See Streeter, *Managing the Counterrevolution*, for an excellent historical analysis of U.S. foreign aid and Guatemalan development during the Eisenhower administration.

9. Westad, *The Global Cold War*, 66–72; "Soviet Experts Assisting Chile: High-Level Mission Arrives to Develop Aid programs," *New York Times*, 27 January 1972, http://www.nytimes.com/1972/01/27/archives/soviet-experts-assisting-chile-highlevel-mission-arrives-to-develop.html?nytmobile=0.

10. Westad, *The Global Cold War*, 396.

11. Joseph Morgan Hodge, "Writing the History of Development (Part 1: The First Wave)," *Humanity* 6, no. 3 (2015): 429–63; Joseph Morgan Hodge, "Writing the History of Development (Part 2: Longer, Deeper, Wider)," *Humanity* 7, no. 1 (2016): 25–174; Westad, *The Global Cold War*, 3.

12. Michael E. Latham, *Modernization as Ideology: American Social Science and "Nation Building" in the Kennedy Era* (Chapel Hill: University of North Carolina Press, 2000), 5.

13. Arturo Escobar, *Encountering Development: The Making and Unmaking of the Third World* (Princeton, NJ: Princeton University Press, 2012), 4–6; Nils Gilman, *Mandarins of the Future: Modernization Theory in Cold War America* (Baltimore, MD: Johns Hopkins University Press, 2003), 5.

14. Daniel Immerwahr, *Thinking Small: The United States and the Lure of Community Development* (Cambridge, MA: Harvard University Press, 2015), 54.

15. John T. Way, *The Mayan in the Mall: Globalization, Development, and the Making of Modern Guatemala* (Durham, NC: Duke University Press, 2012); Sheldon

Annis, *God and Production in a Guatemalan Town* (Austin: University of Texas Press, 1987); Douglas Brintnal, *Revolt against the Dead: The Modernization of a Mayan Community in the Highlands of Guatemala* (New York: Gordan and Breach, 1979); Luis Solano, *Contextualización histórica de la Franja Transversal del Norte (FTN)* (Huehuetenango, Guatemala: CEDFOG, 2012); Edward F. Fischer, *Broccoli and Desire: Global Connections and Maya Struggles in Postwar Guatemala* (Stanford, CA: Stanford University Press, 2006).

16. For one such example, see Bradley Simpson, *Economists with Guns: Authoritarian Development and U.S.-Indonesian Relations, 1960–1968* (Palo Alto, CA: Stanford University Press, 2010).

17. Thomas Field, *From Development to Dictatorship: Bolivia and the Alliance for Progress in the Kennedy Era* (Ithaca, NY: Cornell University Press, 2014); Ruth Leacock, *Requiem for Revolution: The United States and Brazil, 1961–1969* (Kent, OH: Kent State University Press, 1990).

18. Michael E. Latham, *The Right Kind of Revolution: Modernization, Development, and U.S. Foreign Policy from the Cold War to the Present* (Ithaca, NY: Cornell University Press, 2011), 56. Emphasis in original.

19. Westad, *The Global Cold War*, 92.

20. See Lars Schoultz, "Providing Benevolent Supervision: Dollar Diplomacy," in *Beneath the United States: A History of U.S. Policy toward Latin America* (Cambridge, MA: Harvard University Press, 1998), chapter 11, for an account of U.S. intervention in foreign economic affairs in Latin America.

21. Nick Cullather, *Secret History: The CIA's Classified Account of Its Operations in Guatemala, 1952–1954*, 2nd ed. (Stanford, CA: Stanford University Press, 2006).

22. Latham argues that this trend characterized the official U.S. stance toward the Third World in *The Right Kind of Revolution*, 32.

23. Cole Blasier, *The Giant's Rival: The USSR and Latin America*, rev. ed. (Pittsburgh, PA: University of Pittsburgh Press, 1987; Roger Hamburg, "The Soviet Union and Latin America," in *The Soviet Union and the Developing Nations*, ed. Roger E. Kanet (Baltimore, MD: Johns Hopkins University Press, 1974), 179–213.

24. Quoted in *This Week*, 7 August 1955, and cited in James Dunkerley, *Power in the Isthmus: A Political History of Modern Central America* (London: Verso, 1989), 425.

25. Streeter, "The Failure of 'Liberal Developmentalism,'" 393; Memorandum of Conversation, Subject: Guatemala: IBRD and Klein & Saks Missions, 24 April 1956, Documentos Desclasificados (hereafter DES), No. 367, CIRMA; Memorandum of Conversation, Subject: Guatemala: Relations between Klein & Saks Mission and American Embassy, 24 April 1956, DES No. 362, CIRMA.

26. Ministerio de Economía, *Política económica del gobierno de liberación: Reunión con los sectores de la iniciativa privada* (Ministerio de Economía: Guatemala, C.A., 1957), 13, 22.

27. Streeter, *Managing the Counterrevolution*, 131.

28. "We Are Officers of the Guatemalan Army," November 13 Rebel Movement, translated by Greg Grandin, in *The Guatemala Reader: History, Culture, Politics*, ed. Greg Grandin, Deborah T. Levenson, and Elizabeth Oglesby (Durham, NC: Duke University Press, 2011), 250.

29. Ralph Lee Woodward Jr., *A Short History of Guatemala* (Guatemala: Editorial Laura Lee, 2008), 146.

30. Stephen G. Rabe, *The Most Dangerous Area in the World: John F. Kennedy Confronts Communist Revolution in Latin America* (Chapel Hill: University of North Carolina Press, 1999).

31. Memorandum to Mr. McGeorge Mundy, Subject: "Guatemala," 21 January 1963, DES, 734, CIRMA.

32. Speech in Tampa, Florida, 18 October 1960, Campaign Speech File, Pre-Presidential papers, John F. Kennedy Library, cited in Rabe, *The Most Dangerous Area in the World*, 14–15.

33. Adolf A. Berle, *Navigating the Rapids, 1918–1971: From the Papers of Adolf A. Berle* (New York: Harcourt Brace Jovanovich, 1973), 729, quoted in Rabe, *The Most Dangerous Area*, 22.

34. The Peace Corps clearly illustrates this localized approach. Immerwahr, *Thinking Small*, 138–44, and Latham, *Modernization as Ideology*, 109–50, both consider the historical importance of the Peace Corps to U.S. development history, with Immerwahr proposing a more communitarian understanding of this project while Latham maintains that the Peace Corps only helped to fulfill the modernization mission abroad.

35. See chapter 3, "Peasantville" in Immerwahr, *Thinking Small*, for a discussion of the Etawah project. See also Nicole Sackley, "Village Models: Etawah, India, and the Making and Remaking of Development in the Early Cold War," *Diplomatic History* 37, no. 4 (2013): 749–78, for a discussion about the transnational processes of attributing various meanings and memories to the Etawah project.

36. See chapter 4, "Grassroots Empire," in Immerwahr, *Thinking Small*, for a discussion of the Filipino community development program.

37. Jason Pribilsky, "*Indigenismo*, Science, and Modernization in the Making of the Cornell-Peru Project at Vicos," *Diplomatic History* 33, no. 3 (2009): 405.

38. Víctor Manuel Navarro, "Filosofía del desarrollo de la comunidad, ideario y principios I," *El Imparcial*, 30 December 1963.

39. "Valiosa opinión de Ospina Restrepo sobre desarrollo de la comunidad" *El Imparcial*, 26 June 1965.

40. José R. Castro, "Desarrollo de la comunidad," *El Imparcial*, 6 December 1965; "Declaration of Punta del Este: 17 August 1961, in *Inter-American Relations: Collection of Documents, Legislation, Descriptions of Inter-American Organizations, and Other Material Pertaining to Inter-American Affairs*, comp. Barry Sklar and Virginia M. Hagen (Washington, DC: U.S. Government Printing Office, 1972), http://avalon.law.yale.edu/20th_century/intam15.asp; Ministerio de Gobernación de Guatemala, *Decreto Ley 296*, 24 November 1964.

41. Juan José Arévalo, the first president of the Revolution, had belonged to the Partido Revolucionario. Initially Mario Méndez Montenegro, Julio's brother, was the PR candidate, but when he was mysteriously assassinated, Julio, dean of the law school at the National University, took his place as the candidate.

42. Dunkerley, *Power in the Isthmus*, 448–49.

43. Ian F.W. Beckett, *Modern Insurgencies and Counterinsurgencies: Guerrillas and Their Opponents since 1750* (London: Routledge, 2001), 172.

44. "Cuadro comparativo de presupuesto para 1966," Administrative Records of the Secretaría de Bienestar Social, Paquete 1, Tomo 4, Año 1964–1968, AGCA; Departamento Personal, Planillas de Sueldos, January–June 1965, Archivo de la Secretaría de Bienestar Social (hereafter SBS); Ministerio de Gobernación de Guatemala, Acuerdo Gubernativo de 3 November 1967. The Quetzal was pegged 1:1 to the U.S. dollar during this time.

45. Megan Bradley, "Forced Migration in Central America and the Caribbean: Cooperation and Challenges," in *The Oxford Handbook of Refugee and Forced Migration Studies*, ed. Elena Fiddian-Qasmiyeh, Gil Loescher, Katy Long, and Nando Sigona (Oxford: Oxford University Press, 2014), 666.

46. Dirección de Desarrollo de la Comunidad, *3 años de labor intensiva de la Dirección de Desarrollo de la Comunidad de la Presidencia de la República en beneficio de los habitantes de las comunidades rurales del país* (Guatemala, C.A.: September 1981).

47. John F. Kennedy, "Letter to the President of the Senate and to the Speaker of the House Transmitting Bill Implementing the Message on Foreign Aid," 26 May 1961, in *John F. Kennedy: 1961; Containing the Public Messages, Speeches, and Statements of the President, January 20 to December 31, 1961*, Public Papers of the Presidents of the United States. (Washington, DC: Office of the Federal Registrar, National Archives and Records Service, General Services Administration, 1962), 407.

48. This argument follows James C. Scott's work on legibility in *Seeing Like a State: How Certain Schemes to Improve the Human Condition Have Failed* (New Haven, CT: Yale University Press, 1998), 2–3.

49. "Críticas, lo que falta en la práctica," *El Imparcial*, 27 August 1963; "Promesas y La Alianza," *El Imparcial*, 13 November 1964; "No todo es alabanzas," *El Imparcial*, 26 August 1968; "Los silencios de Guatemala," *El Imparcial*, 7 January 1966.

50. Jennifer Schirmer, *The Guatemalan Military Project: A Violence Called Democracy* (Philadelphia: University of Pennsylvania Press, 1999), 36–39; Ministerio de Defensa Nacional, *Acción Cívica* (Guatemala, 1962); Mario Payeras, *Los días de la selva* (La Habana, Cuba: Casa de las Américas, 1980); "Programa de Guatemala considerado el mejor concluido en proyección social," *El Imparcial*, 19 June 1965; "Será sede de Desarrollo de la Comunidad," *El Imparcial*, 24 November 1964; "Análisis de problemas en lo económico, social, político," *El Imparcial*, 28 October 1970.

51. Searches in worldcat.org for these Pan-American Union training booklets revealed that they were published throughout these countries. A couple of newspaper accounts in Guatemala also indicate regional conferences where Latin American countries met to discuss their respective community development programs: "Del discurso del Dr. Restrepo: Desarrollo de la Comunidad; el Gobierno y Pueblo, en Acción," *El Imparcial*, 18 June 1965; "Guatemala Encabeza Desarrollo de la Comunidad en América; Constancias en la II Reunión Regional," *El Imparcial*, 21 June 1965.

52. Luis Lebret, *Desarrollo y civilizaciones*, Colección Bienestar Social y Desarrollo de la Comunidad, No. 4 (Guatemala, C.A.: 1964), 9.

53. Ezequiel Ander-Egg, *El desarrollo de la comunidad en la planificación y ejecución del desarrollo nacional*, Colección Bienestar Social y Desarrollo de la Comunidad, No. 8 (Guatemala, C.A.: 1964), 11–12.

54. Ander-Egg, *El desarrollo de la comunidad*, 26; Manfred Max-Neef, *El desarrollo de la comunidad y la programación nacional de desarrollo*, Colección Bienestar Social y Desarrollo de la Comunidad, No. 7 (Guatemala, C.A.: 1964), 33.

55. "Desarrollo de la comunidad estudia el Dr. R.W. Poston," *Prensa Libre*, 2 June 1965; "Colaboración mutua en mes," *El Imparcial*, 24 February 1966.

56. See chapter 3, "A Continent of Peasants," in Cullather, *The Hungry World*.

57. U.S. Army film, 1945, quoted in John W. Dower, *Embracing Defeat: Japan in the Wake of World War II* (New York: Norton, 2000), 215, quoted in Westad, *The Global Cold War*, 24.

58. Secretaría de Bienestar Social (hereafter SBS), *Programa integral de desarrollo de la comunidad para Guatemala de la Jefatura de Gobierno*, Colección Bienestar Social y Desarrollo de la Comunidad, No. 3 (Guatemala, C.A.: 1964), 19.

59. SBS, *Programa Integral de Desarrollo*, 16.

60. SBS, *Programa Integral de Desarrollo*, 11–14.

61. Dunkerley, *Power in the Isthmus*, 444.

62. Libros de Actas, No. 8, Acta No. 252, 19 June 1971, Archivo Municipal de Tactic (hereafter AMT).

63. Emilio Vásquez Robles, interview by author, Cobán, Guatemala, 3 September 2016.

64. Gladys Gamboa de Fernández, interview by author, Tactic, Guatemala, 1 September 2016. The informant is not completely certain about this date, but other interviews confirmed that DESCOM's work diminished in the early 1980s due to the civil war and then ceased after it left in the early 1980s. Municipal records from this decade that could confirm this date no longer exist.

65. "Memorandum from the President's Special Assistant (Schlesinger) to President Kennedy, 10 March 1961, *Foreign Relations of the United States, 1961–1963*, Vol. 12, *American Republics*, ed. Edward C. Keefer, Harriet Dashiell Schwar, and W. Taylor Fain III (Washington, D.C.: Government Printing Office, 1996), Document 7, https://history.state.gov/historicaldocuments/frus1961-63v12/d7; Streeter, *Managing the Counterrevolution*, 80.

66. Libros de Actas, No. 9, Acta 16–72, 13 April 1972, AMT.

67. Rogelio Bin Quej, interview by author, Chiacal, Guatemala, 24 September 2016. In an interview conducted by my research assistant, Aracely Cahuec, with Enrique Tun, in Chiacal, Guatemala, on 17 September 2016, Tun narrated a similar experience in working on this project. Tun and his wife participated directly in the project, and his uncle was on the local committee; "592 Obras realizadas por Desarrollo de la Comunidad," *El Imparcial*, 16 April 1975, 5.

68. Nick Cullather, *The Hungry World*, 8.

69. Shelton H. Davis and Julie Hodson, *Witness to Political Violence in Guatemala: The Suppression of a Rural Development Movement* (Boston, MA: Oxfam America, 1982), 45, Doc. 2555, Inforpress, CIRMA.

70. Lynn Smith and George Foster, *Los aportes de la sociología y de la antropología para el desarrollo de la comunidad*, Series Colección Bienestar Social y Desarrollo de la Comunidad (Guatemala, C.A.: 1964), 20–21.

71. Libros de Actas Varias, No. 9, Acta 44 de 17 October 1972, AMT; Gladys Gamboa de Fernández, interview by author; Lesli Magdalena Guzmán, interview by author, Tactic, Guatemala, 1 September 2016; Carlos Salomon López Cantoral, interview by author, Tactic, Guatemala, 2 September 2016; Heriberto Isem, interview by author, Pasmolón, Guatmala, 24 September 2016; Otilia Isem Sierra, interview by author, Tactic, Guatemala, 23 September 2016; Alberto Bin, interview by author, Pasmolón, Guatemala, 24 September 2016; Rogelio Bin Quej, interview by author; María Hercilia Cantoral Hernández, interview by author, Tactic, Guaemala, 24 September 2016.

72. Carlos López Cantoral, interview by author.

73. Enrique Tun, interview by Aracely Cahuec, Chiacal, Guatemala, 17 September 2016.

74. Immerwahr, *Thinking Small*, 58; emphasis added.

75. Heriberto Isem, interview by author; Alberto Bin, interview by author.

76. Ofilia Isem Sierra, interview by author.

6 Cuba, the USSR, and the Non-Aligned Movement
Negotiating Non-Alignment

MICHELLE GETCHELL

Fidel Castro was never content with confining his ambitions to as small a stage as Cuba. Immediately after the triumph of the 26th of July movement, he held up the Cuban Revolution as an example for the rest of Latin America and the Third World. On 3 January, a mere two days after Batista fled the country, Castro delivered a speech in Santiago declaring that "all of America is watching the course of the fate of this revolution."[1] As early as November 1959, Assistant Secretary of State Roy Rubottom observed that Castro not only rejected the U.S. conception of hemispheric solidarity—which envisioned the Western Hemisphere as a united, anti-Communist front under the firm leadership of the United States—but also favored "a greater role for Latin America, if possible under Cuba's leadership, in world affairs, though not as a component part of the Western community of nations, but rather as an independent force, associated closely with the Afro-Asian bloc."[2]

Castro did seek a leadership role in the burgeoning Non-Aligned Movement (NAM), not merely to further his own personal ambitions, but also for strategic purposes. U.S. opposition to the Cuban Revolution, undeniable after the April 1961 Bay of Pigs invasion, was a powerful goad to Castro's efforts to establish and strengthen relations with Third World leaders. Moreover, the outcome of the Cuban Missile Crisis had starkly revealed that the Soviet protective umbrella was leaky at best. After Soviet Premier Nikita Khrushchev had denied Castro's request for an open and public arms deal, preferring instead to cloak the stationing of nuclear missiles on Cuban territory in secrecy and thereby present U.S. leaders with a fait accompli, he then bargained away those missiles, without even deigning to consult the Cubans.[3] In return for the withdrawal of the weapons, the Soviets secured U.S. President John F. Kennedy's pledge not to invade Cuba—a pledge that Castro considered worthless, given the Kennedy administration's open and obvious hostility to the Cuban Revolution. Becoming a part of the NAM was thus not only consistent with Castro's worldview but also served as a strategy to shore up the Cuban Revolution and prevent it from becoming isolated in the international arena. Yet Castro's international ambitions and aspirations to Third World leadership frequently conflicted with Cuba's role as Soviet ally.[4]

Cuban foreign policy was among the most significant sources of tension with the Soviets. Cuban support for violent revolutionary movements in the Western Hemisphere contradicted the line of the Soviet Communist Party (CPSU), which emphasized peaceful coexistence with the United States and rejected the armed struggle. The Cuban Revolution and the deepening of the Sino-Soviet split radicalized Communist parties and national liberation movements in many parts of the Third World, threatening Moscow's claims to revolutionary leadership.[5] In the interest of appeasing the Cubans and smoothing out contentious theoretical disputes, the Soviets developed a series of doctrinal compromises aimed at bolstering Soviet-Cuban solidarity and preventing the Cubans from foraying into Peking's ideological camp. These compromises continued to emphasize the peaceful path, while endorsing armed struggle in those Latin American countries where the Cubans were providing the bulk of their assistance to guerrilla forces.[6] The Cuban leadership viewed its support for revolutionary movements in the Western Hemisphere as critical to Cuban national security, which they saw as being constantly threatened by real (and imagined) U.S. aggression. Though the Cubans had never toed the "peaceful coexistence" line, after the Cuban Missile Crisis they viewed it as a fundamental betrayal of Third World interests and shorthand for the imperialist collusion that had sold out the Cuban Revolution.[7]

As Cuba's increasing dependence on the Soviet Union became obvious to Latin American leaders, and as the Kennedy administration sought to facilitate economic and political reforms through the Alliance for Progress, the aim of Castro's foreign policy shifted from toppling regional dictators to the less laudable goal of discrediting reformist regimes in the hemisphere.[8] Cuba had many reasons for supporting the national liberation movements battling such regimes: doing so was consistent with the Marxist-Leninist view that revolution on a worldwide scale was inevitable, it gave Cuba more authority and leverage in its relations with the communist world, and it enhanced Cuban prestige in the Third World, which would help Castro break out of the diplomatic, economic, and political isolation imposed by the United States.[9] The Soviets, however, had identified many of these regimes as relatively independent of U.S. political influence or at least striving for such independence; therefore, Castro's support for subversive movements aimed at toppling these governments undermined Soviet efforts to reestablish and strengthen state-to-state relations with them. Moreover, attempts to use Cuba's leadership position in the NAM in order to enhance Soviet prestige were sometimes counterproductive.

On the basis of archival and published sources from the NAM, Cuba, and the former Soviet Union, this chapter advances a bold reinterpretation of Cuba's role in the world. It argues that the radical turn in Cuban foreign policy was the result of Castro's attempts to pursue Cuban national interests in the context of a Cold War superpower rivalry that largely defined the international system. This rivalry imposed constraints upon the policy choices of actors such as Castro while paradoxically opening up opportunities for such actors to manipulate the system in pursuit of goals that long predated the emergence of the Cold War—namely, goals of political, economic, and social justice. Castro's attempts to balance his commitments as Soviet ally with leadership of the NAM were not wholly successful. Though he was able to negotiate continued aid from the Soviet Union and assert an independent foreign policy stance when he felt Cuban security interests were at stake, the Soviet-Cuban relationship was rocky at best, and Communist Cuban leadership of the NAM damaged the movement's international reputation as a vehicle for the interests of the truly nonaligned. In addition to bringing new archival evidence to bear on this topic, this chapter also uses this evidence to reinterpret the scholarly literature on the NAM, Cold War Latin America, and Cuban foreign policy. Though the experience of Latin America in the Cold War is the subject of a good deal of recent scholarship, the literature on the NAM and Cuban foreign policy is still underdeveloped.[10] Moreover, we continue to suffer from a very limited understanding of how Latin America as a region came to be identified as a part of the Third World. This chapter suggests that Castro himself, through his efforts to spread the revolution in the Western Hemisphere and adopt a leadership position in the NAM, played a significant role in the process by which Latin America became considered part of the Third World.

Cuba, the Third World, and the Non-Aligned Movement

In the earliest days of the revolution, Fidel Castro and Che Guevara demonstrated a desire to position Cuba as a leader of the Third World. Che believed that in order to consolidate the Cuban Revolution, its leaders should "go out fighting in the international arena."[11] Anticipating that the United States would adopt any conceivable measure to isolate Cuba from its neighbors in the Western Hemisphere, Castro and Guevara sought to strengthen relations with Third World leaders in Africa and Asia. In the summer of 1959, Che was dispatched on an international tour that included stops in many Third World capitals. The purpose of the trip was not merely to indicate Cuban interest in strengthening ties with the countries of the developing world, but also to utilize Third World outreach in order to make contact with representatives of the Soviet bloc.

Reflecting the cultural and ideological cleavages that would fracture Third World solidarity, Che clashed with other Non-Aligned leaders. Egyptian president Gamal Abdel Nasser, for instance, was not amused by Che's wild-eyed radicalism, and diplomats in Yugoslavia did not appreciate his "beatnik" appearance.[12] His meeting with Indonesian Prime Minister Sukarno was abruptly terminated when Che nonchalantly dismissed him as a "*latifundista* [landowner]."[13] Despite these personal affronts, Che's trip allowed him to enter into discussions with the Soviets, while apparently leaving the U.S. administration in the dark about what was transpiring. U.S. policymakers seem not to have grasped the significance of the trip for the positioning of the Cuban Revolution at the vanguard of the emerging NAM.[14]

The guidelines for membership in the NAM were established in June 1961 at the Cairo Preparatory Committee and stipulated that the country in question should adhere to an independent policy based on the principles of peaceful coexistence, should "consistently support" national independence movements, and should not be a member of any "multilateral military alliance." If the country did have a bilateral military agreement or remained party to a multilateral defense pact, those arrangements should not have been "deliberately concluded in the context of great power conflicts." Moreover, if the country "has conceded military bases to a foreign power, the concession should not have been made in the context of great power conflicts."[15]

According to these guidelines, Cuba's membership in the movement was dubious. Although the country was not a member of the Warsaw Pact, it had concluded military agreements with the USSR in the context of the Cold War. However, if this criterion was applied strictly, most Latin American candidates for the NAM would be disqualified because they had signed onto the Rio Pact.[16] The only basis upon which Cuba's claim to nonalignment could be challenged was on the willingness of Cuban leaders to permit the Cold War superpowers to construct military bases on the island. Though Cuba welcomed the stationing of Soviet-supplied nuclear missiles on its territory in 1962, and then again in 1970, when Soviet nuclear missile submarines were allowed to operate out of Cienfuegos, these episodes were considered by the Cubans to be "ephemeral in nature." And since Castro did not "willingly play host" to the U.S. naval base at Guantanamo, Cuba's claim to NAM membership did not suffer from the presence of foreign military bases on Cuban soil.[17]

At the first NAM summit in Belgrade in 1961, Cuba was the only official Latin American member-state in attendance, though Bolivia, Brazil, and Ecuador sent observers.[18] Cuba's invitation to attend the 1961 Belgrade summit was based on Third World solidarity engendered by the failed Bay of Pigs invasion and Third World support for the removal of the U.S. military base at Guantanamo. In the early years of the movement, Cuban officials were careful to distance themselves from too close an association with the Soviet Union and did not begin to actively champion Soviet international positions until the late 1960s and early 1970s.[19] Nevertheless, even at this early stage, some members of the movement, particularly the Yugoslav delegation, sought to balance Cuba's anticipated anti-U.S. hostility by inviting other Latin American countries to attend.[20]

The Belgrade Declaration lauded "the peoples of Latin America" for their "increasingly effective contribution to the improvement of international relations," affirmed Cuba's right to "freely choose" its own social and political system, and condemned the U.S. naval base at Guantanamo as an affront to Cuban sovereignty.[21] Notably, the Belgrade Declaration did not mention the United States by name, though the Beijing-backed Afro-Asian People's Solidarity Organization (AAPSO) sent a statement to the conference praising "the valiant fight of the Cuban people against U.S. imperialism" and expressing hope that the NAM would "take concrete steps" to "expose and defeat the manoeuvres [sic] of the Colonial powers . . . supported by U.S. imperialism."[22]

On 16 September 1961, Soviet leader Nikita Khrushchev sent a letter to Cuban President Osvaldo Dorticós, in which he described the importance of the Non-Aligned summit in Belgrade. "To a significant degree," Khrushchev pointed out, "the views of the Soviet government on the current international situation coincide" with those of the Non-Aligned countries.[23] He mused that it was virtually impossible "not to be happy" that the neutral nations, with a combined population "representing *one-third of humanity*," had "raised their voice in defense of peace" and "decisively repudiated militaristic policies."[24] Considering that the "entire foreign policy" of the socialist bloc, which contained "*another one-third of humanity*," was focused on the "struggle to prevent war," this left the remaining one-third of humanity—the warmongers—outnumbered by a factor of two to one.[25] The emergence of the NAM was thus a welcome development indeed.

At the Twenty-Second Congress of the CPSU, in October 1961, Khrushchev emphasized the struggles of the decolonizing world. Touting the "revolutionary struggle" of the peoples of Asia, Africa, and Latin America, Khrushchev was convinced that "the 1960s will go down in history as the years of the complete disintegration of the colonial system." Yet "remnants" of the colonial system remained; Khrushchev singled out the U.S. military base at Guantanamo as evidence of U.S. neo-imperialism.[26] The Soviet premier heralded the significance of the countries "often called neutralist," expressing the conviction that "the basic issues of world politics can no longer be settled without regard for their interests."[27] As one scholar has suggested, Khrushchev's formulation of the significance of Cold War neutralism was that it represented a form of anti-imperialism; therefore, the foreign policy goals of the neutralist states coincided with the political views of the socialist bloc.[28]

On 23 May 1963, Castro and Khrushchev worked out a theoretical compromise on the thornier issue of armed struggle. This compromise was crucial to shoring up Soviet-Cuban solidarity after the rupture in relations following the Cuban Missile Crisis. After refusing Castro's request for a public arms deal, Khrushchev then negotiated the withdrawal of Soviet-supplied nuclear weaponry, without even bothering to consult the Cubans. The episode, which sparked an anti-Soviet backlash in Cuba, suggested to Castro that Moscow was an unreliable ally that prioritized good relations with the American imperialists over support for its socialist brethren. The compromise was also vital if the Soviet Union was to maintain its claim to leadership of the socialist world in view of the ideological threats posed by Chinese and Cuban radicalism. The Cuban and Chinese Revolutions had more in common with each other than either had in common with the Bolshevik Revolution. And both Mao Zedong and Fidel Castro believed that as the revolutionary leaders of agrarian, colonized, and underdeveloped countries, they had more to offer Third World revolutionary leaders than the Soviets did. The Soviet-Cuban joint communiqué stated that "the question of the peaceful or non-peaceful road to socialism in one country or another will be definitely decided by the struggling peoples themselves."[29] This theoretical shift was interpreted by orthodox Communist parties as a confirmation of their nonviolent tactics, while allowing Castro to continue Cuban support for guerrilla groups in the Western Hemisphere. The year after the issuance of the joint communiqué, he was already back to trumpeting the "inevitability" of the armed struggle.[30]

In the fall of 1963, Che Guevara published an article on guerrilla warfare. The piece, a slap in the face to the Soviet party line on the peaceful path to power, asserted "the necessity of guerrilla action in Latin America as the central axis of the struggle."[31] Then, in a speech in November, Che called for the Cuban people to demonstrate solidarity with the people of Vietnam, not out of an altruistic sense of "proletarian internationalism," but because Vietnam was "the great laboratory of Yankee imperialism," where the troops "are being trained . . . that one day will be able to defeat our guerrillas—ours in all America."[32] While Che's view was clearly a Manichean one, pitting the forces of colonialism and imperialism against the righteous struggles of the mythical "people," this speech can also be read as a tacit rebuke to the Soviet Union, which in the minds of the more radical Cuban leaders was not doing enough to support its socialist brethren in the Third World.

By 1964, Cuban support for armed guerrilla movements in the hemisphere had become a major source of tension in the Soviet-Cuban alliance. The Soviets, for their part, were frustrated with Castro's revolutionary ambitions, as they tended to complicate relations with other Latin American countries and to impede efforts at détente with the United States.[33] Castro and other Cuban leaders did not hesitate to sharply criticize the Soviets, whom they deemed opportunistic and eager to pander to U.S. interests. The Cubans also rebuked the Soviets for being too stingy in their aid to Third World countries and not doing enough to help their struggling Third World allies—not just Cuba, but North Korea and North Vietnam as well.[34]

The 1964 summit of the NAM was held in Cairo in October and the list of Western Hemisphere countries sending observers expanded dramatically. Argentina, Bolivia, Brazil, Chile, Jamaica, Mexico, Trinidad and Tobago, Uruguay, and Venezuela all sent observers to Cairo. The summit convened mere months after the Organization of American States (OAS) had adopted a resolution mandating that all member-states sever diplomatic and consular relations with Cuba and suspend all trade and sea transportation, except for humanitarian purposes.[35] The aftermath of the Cuban Missile Crisis had witnessed not only an increase in anti-Cuban sentiment in the Western Hemisphere, but also a growing aversion to the ways in which the Cold War superpower struggle continued to dominate U.S. relations with Latin America. Many Latin American leaders were dissatisfied with both Cuba and the United States, and this was partially reflected in their rising interest in Non-Alignment.[36]

Though the bulk of the summit was devoted to the African independence struggle, the Cairo Declaration drew attention to the case of Puerto Rico and condemned all "manifestations of colonialism and neo-colonialism in Latin America."[37] The statement on the U.S. naval base at Guantanamo went further than it had in the Belgrade Declaration, which had described it as a "North American" base and merely acknowledged Cuban opposition to it, noting that its presence affected Cuban sovereignty. Reflecting the influence of the Cuban delegation, the Cairo declaration urged the United States "to negotiate the evacuation of this base."[38]

In November, a conference of Latin American Communist parties was held in Havana, symbolizing Cuban leadership of the region's Communists. Moscow availed itself of the opportunity to assail the Chinese and to block Beijing's ideological influence. Present at the conference were doctrinaire Communists loyal to the Soviet party line, and while the CPSU sent observers, the Chinese Communist Party did not. The proceedings were thus buffered against Chinese and even *fidelista* ideological heresies.[39] The final communiqué issued by the conference exhorted Latin American revolutionaries to strengthen the "unity of the international communist movement," which can be read as a statement of support for the USSR in its dispute with the Chinese, who believed that revolutionary forces could succeed only by rejecting the "revisionism" of the Cubans and Soviets.[40] A compromise was reached on the issue of armed struggle, which was approved in the case of six countries. The Communist parties would support the "freedom fighters" of Colombia, Guatemala, Haiti, Honduras, Paraguay, and Venezuela, while the parties of the other countries would continue to follow peaceful means.[41]

After a year of aggressive Cuban support for guerrilla movements throughout the continent—and not only in countries approved in the late 1964 Communist Party agreement—the Havana-based Afro-Asian-Latin American Peoples' Solidarity Organization (OSPAAAL) convened its inaugural summit in January 1966. Also known as the Tricontinental Conference, the idea had germinated at the most recent meeting of the Afro-Asian Peoples' Solidarity Organization (AAPSO) in Accra, Ghana, in May 1965. Prompted by radical African states such as Algeria, AAPSO devoted special attention to Latin America, and its delegates decided to launch the broader OSPAAAL organization in Havana the following year.[42]

The introduction to the conference proceedings clearly stated that the historic goal of the meeting was to unite "the two great contemporary currents of the World Revolution," the socialist revolution spearheaded by the USSR and the "parallel current of the revolution for national liberation." It

Often contrary to the wishes of its allies in Moscow, revolutionary Cuba rejected moderate nonalignment throughout the 1960s, adopting a more radical position that culminated in the 1966 launch of the Organización de Solidaridad de los Pueblos de Africa, Asia y América Latina (OSPAAAL, Organization of Solidarity of the Peoples of Africa, Asia, and Latin America). Commonly known as the Tricontinental, OSPAAAL created a series of iconic images typically including a map, images of a face or fist of a revolutionary fighter, and a rifle. Produced for the third anniversary of the Tricontinental's January 1966 launch, this late 1968 poster by Cuban artist Alfredo González Rostgaard suggests the global scope of Havana's independent foreign policy and its linkage of Latin America's anti-imperial struggle with similar movements elsewhere in the Global South. (Image courtesy of Lincoln Cushing / Docs Populi.)

was noted as especially appropriate that the meeting place was in Havana, because the Cuban Revolution was "in effect the concretization [sic] of the union of these two historic currents."⁴³ Cuba was thus recognized as the tangible link between the socialist bloc and the Third World. The text of the conference reflected the strong influence of the Cuban delegation, with repeated references to the machinations of Yankee imperialism and a description of the OAS as the "Yankee Ministry of the Colonies."⁴⁴ The central references to the Soviet Union in the conference proceedings and declarations were laudatory, praising the Russian Revolution and crediting the socialist bloc with providing crucial support to the national liberation movements of the Third World.

The Tricontinental Conference took place during a period of heightened Sino-Cuban conflict, and Castro's opening remarks included explicit criticisms of the Chinese leadership.⁴⁵ Soviet aims for the conference were to enhance Cuba's prestige in the Third World while undermining China's.⁴⁶ Yet the Cubans continued to promote armed struggle as the only means of achieving revolutionary socialism and to make statements that were implicitly critical of the Soviets. Che Guevara sent a message to the conference, which focused on the plight of the Vietnamese people, whom he characterized as "forgotten" and "tragically alone." In a more direct critique of the USSR, Che blamed not only "U.S. imperialism," but also "those who . . . hesitated to make Vietnam an inviolable part of the socialist world."⁴⁷ Insisting that the peoples of Asia, Africa, and Latin America "must answer imperialist violence with revolutionary violence," the conference asserted that "the effective channel to reach victory is armed insurrection."⁴⁸

Castro's speech at the closing session of the conference echoed these themes. "Sooner or later," he asserted, "the peoples will have to fight, arms in hand, for their liberation."⁴⁹ The Cuban leader's hostility toward the OAS was reflected in a resolution declaring that the OAS "has no juridical or moral authority whatsoever to represent the Latin American continent."⁵⁰ The conference further resolved "to lend the most determined assistance to the revolutionary movements in Colombia, Venezuela, Peru, Panama, Ecuador and other Caribbean and South American countries."⁵¹ In Castro's view, any Latin American government that adhered to the principles of the Inter-American System—principles that were designed as a mere smokescreen for Yankee imperialism—was by definition a puppet government serving the ends of U.S. monopolies and local oligarchs.

In August, the Soviet Foreign Ministry prepared a report on the U.S. government's "aggressive actions" against Cuba, which involved a propaganda campaign aimed at discrediting the Tricontinental. Secretary of State Dean Rusk had informed Congress that the Havana conference "reflects the strengthening of terrorist and subversive activity."[52] The Soviet Foreign Ministry also reported on the successful use by the United States of the OAS to further its anti-Castro agenda. The OAS had been used as a mechanism to pressure the countries of the Western Hemisphere into isolating Cuba. Moreover, the United States continued to push for the creation of "permanent armed forces," under the auspices of the OAS, to use as a "tool in the struggle against the national liberation movement in Latin America."[53] This reflected the Cuban view of the creation of the Inter-American Peace Force and its deployment in the Dominican Republic the previous year. The Tricontinental had issued a resolution "condemning the so-called Inter-American Peace Force" as "the armed counter-revolution of Yankee imperialism," which, through the "participation of the Latin American puppet troops," was "disguised as Latin American."[54] The prominence of the issue in the Soviet Foreign Ministry report suggests that to a significant extent, Cuban fears and preoccupations remained central to Soviet perceptions of U.S.-Latin American relations.

In an environment of rising Soviet discomfort over Cuba's persisting support for armed liberation movements in Latin America, in January 1967, Castro and Dorticós penned a letter to the general secretary of the CPSU, Leonid Brezhnev, chairman of the Supreme Soviet, Nikolai Podgorny, and chairman of the Council of Ministers, Alexei Kosygin. The letter affirmed the loyalty of Cuba to the Soviet Union, assuring the Soviet leaders that the "friendship and cooperation between our peoples will continue to strengthen in the joint struggle against the reactionary and exploitative forces oppressing the peoples of Asia, Africa, and Latin America."[55] Dorticós and Castro expressed their strong desire for "the unity of all progressive and revolutionary forces of the world in their struggle for the utter annihilation of U.S. imperialism," and for the "definitive victory of the communist and socialist cause."[56] These statements were aimed at reassuring the Soviets of Cuban friendship in the face of the ongoing tensions over Havana's Latin American activities and Cuba's previous critical statements regarding the USSR's lack of revolutionary zeal.

Two months later, Castro vehemently denied that Cuba was a Soviet "satellite" and proclaimed that he would "never ask anyone's permission . . . be it in ideology or in domestic or foreign affairs." He even expounded upon the real meaning of Communism, arguing that in the context of the Western Hemisphere, "what defines a communist is . . . action in the armed revolutionary movement."[57] Clearly, Castro recognized that his reliance on Soviet largesse contributed to the labeling of Cuba as "Soviet satellite." Yet he chafed under that label and the circumscribed independence of action it implied; seeking through reassurances to the Soviets to keep the aid flowing, Castro reiterated Cuba's independent orientation for international consumption.

The first meeting of the Latin American Solidarity Organization (OLAS), which emerged from the Tricontinental Conference, was held in Havana in August 1967. The Cubans envisioned the conference as an opportunity for the revolutionary movements of the hemisphere to "strengthen their solidarity and renew for the benefit of world public opinion the accusations against the growing American imperialist domination of Latin America and the complicity of the native oligarchies in this repression."[58] Just as the Cubans were preparing for the opening of the conference, Soviet Premier Alexei Kosygin paid them a visit to warn against the regime's insistence upon the armed struggle and its continued provision of support for violent revolutionary movements in Latin America.[59] Kosygin's visit did not yield the anticipated results. Castro used the conference to snub the Soviets, by ensuring that most delegations were headed by non-Communist revolutionary leaders and by issuing provocative statements that were clearly aimed at Moscow. Arguing that "there is a much broader movement on this continent than the movement composed simply of the communist parties in Latin America," Castro defiantly declared that "we shall judge the conduct of organizations, not by what they claim they are, but by . . . their conduct." In case that was too subtle, Castro responded to those who claimed that socialism could be achieved peacefully with the retort that "this is a lie, and those who say in any place in Latin America that they are going to achieve power peacefully will be deceiving the masses."[60]

The USSR had hoped to use Cuba to raise its prestige and increase its influence in Latin America and the Third World and had provided generous subsidies to the Cuban Revolution. Now Castro was blatantly rejecting the idea of solidarity with the Latin American Communist parties and developing his own international organization, thereby discrediting the Soviet Union among the non-Communist revolutionary movements in Latin America and the Third World.[61] OLAS did not last long, however, but was folded into the Organization for Solidarity with the Peoples of Africa, Asia, and Latin America (OSPAAAL). Moreover, subsequent events contributed to a rapprochement between the Cubans and the Soviets.

The Death of Che Guevara and Cuban-Soviet Rapprochement

Che Guevara's attempts to establish a *foco* in Bolivia, from which it was hoped that the revolutionary struggle would spread throughout South America, was a major source of tension in the Cuban-Soviet relationship. Castro had apparently sent Che to Bolivia without consulting the Soviets, and his decision was frowned upon in the Kremlin. Che's efforts in Bolivia threatened Soviet attempts at détente with the United States, which was more important to Moscow than fomenting guerrilla warfare in South America. Soviet Premier Alexei Kosygin met with U.S. President Lyndon Johnson in New Jersey in June 1967, and apparently, an exchange of acrimonious letters between Brezhnev and Castro had prompted Kosygin to visit Havana on the eve of the OLAS conference before returning to Moscow.[62] Though Kosygin's efforts to bring Castro to heel were apparently unsuccessful, the failure of Che's mission in Bolivia finally catalyzed rapprochement between Cuba and the USSR.

Che's attempts to establish a *foco* in Bolivia ultimately came to naught, and there were several reasons for this failure. He was thoroughly unprepared for the level of acrimony between himself and Mario Monje, the secretary general of Bolivia's Communist Party. The tension between Monje and Guevara reflected the broader doctrinal dispute between radical revolutionaries and orthodox pro-Soviet Communist parties over the proper source of leadership for the revolution. For orthodox Communists like Monje, the army was a tool to be controlled by the party, whereas for Che, the idea of subordinating his military leadership to the political leadership of the party was anathema.[63] For Monje to accept Che's leadership of the Bolivian struggle would entail revising his entire theoretical approach and sacrificing party leadership of the struggle to a ragtag band of foreign guerrillas. In addition to their failure to account for the opposition of orthodox Communists, Castro and Guevara also underestimated the strength of Bolivian nationalism. The widespread lack of support for revolution among the Bolivian peasantry was a reality check for the Cubans, who had posited their own revolutionary experience as the model for the rest of Latin America. They failed to consider that conditions in rural Bolivia were far from what they had been in 1950s Cuba.[64]

Moreover, Che had been an even more vehement critic of Soviet policies than Castro. In March 1964, he had delivered a speech to the UN Conference on Trade and Development (UNCTAD), in which he chided the socialist bloc for the terms of trade offered to underdeveloped countries. Observing that "the socialist camp has developed uninterruptedly," he lamented that "in contrast to the rapid rate of growth of the . . . socialist camp [. . .] the unquestionable fact is that a large proportion of the so-called underdeveloped countries are in total stagnation."[65] Thus, he suggested that the socialist countries, with their highly developed industrial economies, had more in common with the capitalists than with the underdeveloped world. In February 1965, at the second seminar of the AAPSO, he openly censured the Soviet Union for not doing enough to support decolonizing countries. Arguing that the development of such countries was the responsibility of the socialist bloc, he implied that the USSR had eschewed its international obligations. The socialist countries, due to the terms of trade based on world market prices, were "accomplices of imperialist exploitation." Che argued that "the socialist countries have a moral duty to end their tacit complicity with the Western exploiting countries."[66]

Che's capture and execution by the Bolivian armed forces were virtually ignored in Moscow. The only public demonstration to commemorate Che's life was a rally by a small group of Latin American students from Moscow's Patrice Lumumba People's Friendship University. Soviet news media continued to sneer at the brand of revolutionary "adventurism" exemplified by Guevara, and a month after his execution, the general secretary of the CPSU, Leonid Brezhnev, gave a speech in which he declared that socialist revolutions should be launched only in countries where the necessary objective conditions for revolution had already been fulfilled. The message was clearly a reference to Che's failure in Bolivia. Orthodox Communist parties in Latin America followed suit, issuing denunciations of armed struggle and declaring their loyalty to the CPSU line.[67]

The death of Che and the obliteration of the nascent Bolivian *foco* he had nurtured, combined with guerrilla defeats in Guatemala, Colombia, and Venezuela, contributed to a very slow but gradual improvement in Cuba's relations with the USSR. Though Castro continued to aid revolutionary movements in the Western Hemisphere, he was more selective in determining which movements to support, and he watered down his fiery rhetoric about the inevitability of the armed struggle.[68] In November 1967, Cuban Foreign Minister Raúl Roa sent a telegram to his Soviet counterpart, Andrei Gromyko, expressing confidence that "friendly relations and mutual cooperation between Cuba and the USSR," along with the "support rendered to all peoples struggling for liberation," would remain an "important contribution in our struggle against imperialism, colonialism, and neocolonialism."[69]

However, two weeks later, the Soviet embassy in Havana reported that the Cubans were continuing to espouse the armed path. The Communist daily *Granma* had emphasized the significance of the "armed struggle against imperialists and exploiters." The publication of Cuba's National Association of Small Farmers had also printed an article lauding the Bolshevik Revolution, noting its significance for the peoples of Latin America, especially of Venezuela, Bolivia, and Colombia, where "with weapons in hand they battle against imperialism and the reactionary oligarchs for their freedom."[70] Virtually "all [press] materials" had focused on the "role and significance of the armed uprising in the fulfillment of the October revolution and accordingly, emphasized the importance and applicability of the armed struggle of the peoples of the modern era."[71] If the Soviets were looking for indications that Castro had moderated his stance in the aftermath of Che's capture and execution, such expressions were certainly not reassuring.

The Cultural Congress of Havana, held from 4 to 12 January 1968, provided the Soviets with further evidence that Castro had not moderated his position in the aftermath of Che's death. Cuban President Dorticós delivered the inaugural address to the congress, in which he declared that "noble revolutionary violence had to play an inevitable and decisive role . . . in that climb of man to the summit of his true liberation."[72] Mere weeks later, Castro made another display of Cuban independence from the Soviets. Aníbal Escalante had returned to Cuba in 1964 after a brief exile in Czechoslovakia and had resumed leadership duties in the Cuban Communist Party. In January 1968, behind closed doors, Fidel and Raúl Castro prosecuted the pro-Soviet "micro-faction" of the party, delivering a clear message to Moscow that it no longer had any Communist allies in Havana with whom it could intrigue against Fidel.[73] The timing of the exposure of the micro-faction coincided with the anniversary of José Martí's birthday and thus was symbolic of Cuban strivings toward national independence and sovereignty. Developments later in the year, however, would constitute a turning point in the Cuban-Soviet alliance, and Castro would begin to take active measures to improve relations with his patrons in the Kremlin.

The watershed moment was the crushing of the Prague Spring. Though Castro supported the Soviet invasion, he also continued to tacitly chastise Moscow for its unwillingness to provide military support to the peoples of North Vietnam, North Korea, and Cuba itself. By refusing to condemn the invasion, Castro was signaling to the Soviets that he would support their foreign policy line. However, his speech was not a wholehearted endorsement of Soviet policy; indeed, it contained several veiled criticisms of Moscow. Yet the occasion did represent a turning point, after which Soviet-Cuban relations were much closer and less contentious.

Castro would never really abandon his emphasis on the armed struggle, and he would continue to promote the necessity of revolutionary violence even after the election of Salvador Allende in Chile vindicated the CPSU line. Nevertheless, during the early 1970s, Cuban foreign policy became more moderate and aimed less at fomenting violent revolutions than at reestablishing traditional diplomatic and political relations with Latin American countries and reintegrating into the Inter-American community. By the mid-1970s, Cuba had largely broken out of the diplomatic and political isolation imposed by the United States. The coming to power of Allende in Chile, as well as the military coup that brought General Juan Velasco to power in Peru, marked the beginning of a progressive alliance in Latin America. Castro also modified his support for revolutionary movements in the hemisphere and became more open to bargaining with Latin American leaders. As a result, several Latin American countries reestablished diplomatic ties with Cuba and signed trade agreements.[74]

The Latin American governments had excluded Cuba from their caucus in the United Nations, but in 1969 Cuba was elected to a vacant spot in the U.N. Development Program's Council. Cuba had also been excluded from membership in the Group of 77, a caucus for less developed countries within the UN Conference for Trade and Development. In 1971, at the initiative of the Peruvian government and with the backing of the nonaligned countries, Cuba was admitted to membership in the group.[75] In 1972, Cuba became a member of the Council for Mutual Economic Assistance, the Soviet-led economic assistance organization comprising the socialist bloc countries. Later in the year, the Soviets and the Cubans signed a series of trade, economic, and financial agreements, in which generous credits and the restructuring of Cuban debt featured prominently.[76] Cuba's economic dependence on the USSR at this point was almost total, and as a result, Castro moderated his anti-Soviet rhetoric and subdued his hostility toward regional Communist parties. Cuban support for the Soviet international agenda manifested in the United Nations and especially in the NAM.

The 1973 summit of the NAM in Algiers provided the occasion for Castro to demonstrate solidarity with the Soviets. Whereas previous Cuban delegates had deemphasized their country's status as Marxist-Leninist, Castro declared up front that Cuba was a Marxist-Leninist state and expressed his gratitude to the Soviets, without the efforts of whom "the end of colonialism would have been absolutely impossible."[77] Castro put forth the "natural ally" thesis, which held that the Soviet Union and the Communist bloc were the natural allies of the NAM. It was a difficult sell. Influential states such as Yugoslavia, India, Tanzania, and Algeria rejected the thesis in favor of the concept of "equidistance"—a refusal to endorse one side or the other in the Cold War, thus remaining equally distant from both superpowers. The "two imperialisms" theory, moreover, which was spearheaded by the Chinese and viewed the United States and the Soviet Union as morally equivalent, was held by many Non-Aligned states, with Algeria and Libya among its strongest advocates. Castro strenuously repudiated the theory of two imperialisms, extolling the "glorious, heroic, and extraordinary services that the Soviet people have rendered to humanity."[78] Indeed, as others have pointed out, for Castro to accept the "two imperialisms" theory would "suggest that he is exchanging one imperialism for another."[79] Despite being unable to convince his colleagues of the natural ally thesis, Castro did succeed in removing any direct condemnation of the USSR from the official conference statements.[80] Moreover, the Algiers summit marked the advent of the NAM as a reliably anti-U.S. voting bloc in the United Nations.[81]

In the statement's various resolutions and declarations, the United States was repeatedly singled out for special condemnation. The Soviet Union was not mentioned by name, except for once in the context of a laudatory statement on the progress of East-West détente.[82] The head of the AAPSO delegation to the conference, moreover, delivered an address in which the "false theory about 'superpowers'" was denounced as an attempt to smear the socialist bloc with the imperialist label, when in fact the socialist states had proffered "multilateral and disinterested aid" to Third World national liberation forces.[83] The Soviets rejected the view that had emerged among many in the underdeveloped world that the main schism of the times was not between East and West but between North and South, between the rich industrialized countries and the poor underdeveloped ones. To accept the latter view would be to acknowledge that the Soviet Union was in fact a rich, industrialized country and was therefore far removed from the daily challenges of the underdeveloped Third World. This points up a dilemma in the Soviet approach to the Third World. On the one hand, the Soviet Union touted its industrial development as a model for the nations of the Global South. On the other hand, the extent of that industrial development suggested that Moscow was perhaps out of touch with Third World realities. This was a dilemma the Soviets were never quite able to resolve.

Fidel Castro became the chairman of the NAM in 1979, and the sixth summit was held in Havana that September. Though Castro would maintain his leadership position until 1983, the Havana summit represented the apex of Cuban influence in the movement. In his opening speech, he castigated the Chinese as "new allies" of U.S. imperialism and charged both China and the United States with having "contrived the repugnant intrigue" that Cuba would attempt to convert the NAM into an "instrument of Soviet policy." Castro thanked the Soviet Union enthusiastically for providing crucial support to Cuba in its revolutionary struggle against Yankee imperialism, and he credited the "glorious October Revolution" with having "started a new age in human history."[84]

The Havana Declaration reflected Castro's preoccupations and priorities. The declaration expressed "particular satisfaction" with the "expansion of nonalignment in Latin America and the Caribbean" and "profound satisfaction" with the first NAM meeting to be held in Latin America.[85] Special attention was accorded to Latin America, which had taken its place alongside its "African and Asian brothers and sisters" in the struggle against imperialism. At the Belgrade summit in 1961, Cuba had been the only Latin American country with membership in the movement, and only three Latin American countries had sent observers. By the time of the Havana summit, twenty-one Latin American and Caribbean countries were represented in the movement, either as permanent members or as observers.[86]

The 1979 Havana summit was not what critics of the NAM expected. Preparations for the summit were plagued by tensions between the radical faction headed by Cuba, with the support of Angola and Vietnam, and the more moderate faction headed by Yugoslavia, with the support of Indonesia and Somalia. Tito and Yugoslavian Foreign Secretary Josip Vrhovec disparaged the "natural ally" thesis and advocated a stance of "passive neutrality," which implied the maintenance of "equidistance" between the two Cold War superpowers.[87] On the second day of the summit, Tito delivered a speech urging the members of the movement to eschew bloc politics in favor of true nonalignment.[88] The radicals within the movement did not carry the day, and indeed, the Cubans ultimately jettisoned the "natural ally" thesis, recognizing that it tarnished their Non-Aligned credentials.

The Soviet invasion of Non-Aligned Afghanistan, moreover, put the Cubans in an extremely difficult position. They had gone on record as touting the USSR as a benevolent protector and ally of the NAM, a stance that became untenable after the Soviet invasion. Some Non-Aligned member-countries even called for Cuba to be ousted from the movement, arguing that Cuban actions had proved that the country was a "Soviet agent."[89] The Chinese spearheaded an attack on Cuban "splittism" [sic] and contrasted Cuban servility to the USSR with Yugoslavia's genuine independence and respect for nonalignment.[90] The Yugoslavs, for their part, condemned the "small group of nonaligned countries" that was "linking itself ever more closely with the Warsaw Pact."[91] "Having identified itself so closely with the USSR," one scholar observes, "[Cuba] now had to pay the cost of that identification."[92] The sinking of Cuban chances to occupy the UN Security Council seat reserved for a member-country of the NAM was one such cost.[93]

During Cuba's tenure as chairman of the NAM, the Soviets attacked the concept of "equidistance" that had been championed by more moderate members of the movement anxious to maintain equal distance from both superpower blocs. Boris Ponomarev, the head of the Central Committee's International Department, complained in October 1980 of attempts to split the movement, and Yevgeni Primakov, a Third World foreign policy specialist, criticized the striving for "equidistance."[94] In 1983, the presidium of AAPSO issued a statement to the NAM conference at Nicosia, Cyprus, in which the theory of "equidistance" between the two Cold War superpowers was disparaged because "the socialist community has proved to have a stand of friendship and alliance to the liberation movement," while "the imperialist powers are, per force, the enemy that should and must be combated and defeated."[95]

Though the prestige and credibility of the NAM had been damaged during the years of Cuban leadership, most members remained confident that the transfer of the presidency to India would reinvigorate the movement.[96] At the NAM summit in New Delhi in 1983, Castro changed his tune. He failed to so much as mention the Soviet Union by name, and he lauded the achievements of national liberation as those of the NAM alone. Of course, Castro did not go so far as to criticize the USSR or to embrace the concept of "equidistance" or the theory of "two imperialisms." Nevertheless, considerations of Cuban prestige and reputation within the movement demanded a more moderate approach. Having been denounced for his subservience to Soviet international policies, and especially the invasion of Non-Aligned Afghanistan, Castro undoubtedly sought to reassure the more moderate members of the movement that Cuba was not a Soviet satellite, but was indeed truly nonaligned.

Conclusion

Fidel Castro's aspirations for Third World leadership complicated Cuba's relationship with the Soviets. The Cuban Missile Crisis had ruptured the Cuban-Soviet alliance and exposed the reality of Soviet great-power chauvinism, proving that in times of crisis, Moscow would have no qualms about sacrificing the goals and interests of its Third World allies to the necessity of maintaining cooperative relations with the United States. Moreover, Castro's support for revolutionary movements in Latin America had been a source of tension in the Cuban-Soviet relationship even before the Missile Crisis. Such support directly contradicted the CPSU line, which asserted that peaceful coexistence did not preclude socialist revolution and that the best way to achieve the latter was through the concerted efforts of regional Communist parties. Though ultimately the breach was repaired and the Cubans became consistent defenders of the Soviet Union in the United Nations and the NAM, this was reflective of Castro's unwillingness to antagonize his revolution's patrons in a changed situation of Cuban economic dependence on the USSR. Nevertheless, Castro attempted to straddle the line between dependence and sovereignty, asserting Cuban independence and leadership and thereby antagonizing the Soviets, but never to the point that the relationship was irreparably ruptured.

The Soviets, for their part, while attempting to use Cuba's Third World standing to their own advantage, found that this complicated relations with other Third World countries and especially with the democratic reformist governments of Latin America, which struggled to combat guerrilla movements inspired (and often financed) by the Cubans. As Cuba scaled back support for these subversive groups and was gradually reintegrated into the Inter-American community, Cuban relations with both the Soviets and the governments of Latin America improved. Yet the attempts of the Cuban leadership to draw the NAM into a closer relationship with the socialist bloc ultimately led to a loss of credibility and prestige within the movement. Many in the moderate camp recognized that the "natural ally" thesis would undermine the movement's claims to nonaligned status, and after the Soviet invasion of Afghanistan, such a stance became completely untenable. Ultimately, Castro was unable to successfully juggle the demands of loyalty to his Soviet patrons and the assertion of Cuban autonomy and leadership of the Third World.

Notes

1. "Fidel Castro Speaks to Citizens of Santiago," speech by Fidel Castro, Santiago, 3 January 1959, Castro Speech Database, http://lanic.utexas.edu/project/castro/db/1959/19590103.html.

2. Quoted in Lars Schoultz, *That Infernal Little Cuban Republic: The United States and the Cuban Revolution* (Chapel Hill: University of North Carolina Press, 2009), 105.

3. For more on this, see Sergo Mikoyan, *The Soviet Cuban Missile Crisis: Castro, Mikoyan, Kennedy, Khrushchev, and the Missiles of November* (Washington, DC: Woodrow Wilson Center Press, 2012).

4. Jorge Domínguez has argued that when Cuba's status in the Nonaligned Movement conflicted with its obligations to the Soviets, the latter took precedence. See Domínguez, *To Make a World Safe for Revolution: Cuba's Foreign Policy* (Cambridge, MA: Harvard University Press, 1989), 219.

5. For more on the impact of the Sino-Soviet split on the Third World, see Jeremy Friedman, *Shadow Cold War: The Sino-Soviet Competition for the Third World* (Chapel Hill: University of North Carolina Press, 2015).

6. For more on the compromise between the armed struggle and the peaceful path in the Western Hemisphere, see Jacques Lévesque, *The USSR and the Cuban Revolution: Soviet Ideological and Strategical Perspectives, 1959-1977* (New York: Praeger, 1978), 96-101.

7. James G. Blight and Philip Brenner, *Sad and Luminous Days: Cuba's Struggle with the Superpowers after the Missile Crisis* (Lanham, MD: Rowman & Littlefield, 2007), 96.

8. D. Bruce Jackson, *Castro, the Kremlin, and Communism in Latin America* (Baltimore: Johns Hopkins University Press, 1969), 16.

9. Domínguez, *To Make a World Safe for Revolution*, 146.

10. Recent scholarship on Cold War Latin America includes: Hal Brands, *Latin America's Cold War* (Cambridge, MA: Harvard University Press, 2010); Virginia Garrard-Burnett, Mark Atwood Lawrence, and Julio E. Moreno, eds., *Beyond the Eagle's Shadow: New Histories of Latin America's Cold War* (Albuquerque: University of New Mexico Press, 2013); Gilbert M. Joseph and Greg Grandin, eds., *A Century of Revolution: Insurgent and Counterinsurgent Violence during Latin America's Long Cold War* (Durham, NC: Duke University Press, 2010); Gilbert M. Joseph and Daniela Spenser, eds., *In from the Cold: Latin America's New Encounter with the Cold War* (Durham, NC: Duke University Press, 2008); Renata Keller, *Mexico's Cold War: Cuba, the United States, and the Legacy of the Mexican Revolution* (New York: Cambridge University Press, 2015); and Stephen Rabe, *The Killing Zone: The United States Wages Cold War in Latin America* (New York: Oxford University Press, 2012). Most works on the Nonaligned Movement published during the Cold War can be described more accurately as propaganda than as scholarship. Recent scholarly work on the Nonaligned Movement includes: Sandra Bott and Jussi M. Hanhimäki, eds., *Neutrality and Neutralism in the Global Cold War: Between or Within the Blocs?* (New York: Routledge, 2015); Michelle Getchell and Rinna Kullaa, "Endeavors to Make Global Connections: Latin American Contacts and Strategies with Mediterranean

Non-Alignment in the Early Cold War," *Südosteuropäische Hefte* 4, no. 2 (2015): 25–35; Rinna Kullaa, *Non-Alignment and Its Origins in Cold War Europe: Yugoslavia, Finland and the Soviet Challenge* (London: IB Tauris, 2012); Mark Atwood Lawrence, "The Rise and Fall of Nonalignment," in *The Cold War in the Third World*, ed. Robert J. McMahon (New York: Oxford University Press, 2013), 139–55; and Robert B. Rakove, *Kennedy, Johnson, and the Nonaligned World* (New York: Cambridge University Press, 2013). On the subject of Cuban foreign policy, Piero Gleijeses has published two excellent volumes based on unprecedented access to Cuban archives: *Conflicting Missions: Havana, Washington, and Africa, 1959–1976* (Chapel Hill: University of North Carolina Press, 2003), and *Visions of Freedom: Havana, Washington, Pretoria, and the Struggle for Southern Africa, 1976–1991* (Chapel Hill: University of North Carolina Press, 2013).

11. Quoted in Jon Lee Anderson, *Che Guevara: A Revolutionary Life* (New York: Grove Press, 1997), 423.

12. Simon Reid-Henry, *Fidel and Che: A Revolutionary Friendship* (New York: Walker Publishing Company, 2009), 203–6.

13. Reid-Henry, *Fidel and Che*, 209.

14. Robert Rakove has shown that the Eisenhower administration "balanced uneasily between expressions of sympathy for newly decolonized states and annoyance at their refusal to choose sides in the Cold War" and that "the 1950s were years of ambivalence for the United States in its dealings with the nonaligned world"; Rakove, *Kennedy, Johnson, and the Nonaligned World*, xx.

15. Mannaraswamighala Sreeranga Rajan, *Nonalignment and Nonaligned Movement: Retrospect and Prospect* (New Delhi: Vikas, 1990), 8.

16. Wayne S. Smith, *Castro's Cuba: Soviet Partner or Non-Aligned?* (Washington, DC: Woodrow Wilson International Center for Scholars, 1984), 1.

17. Smith, *Castro's Cuba*, 2.

18. On Latin America and the nonaligned world, see Getchell and Kullaa, "Endeavors to Make Global Connections"; James G. Hershberg, "'High-Spirited Confusion': Brazil, the 1961 Belgrade Non-Aligned Conference, and the Limits of an 'Independent' Foreign Policy during the High Cold War," *Cold War History* 7, no. 3 (2007): 373–88; Vanni Pettiná, "Global Horizons: Mexico, the Third World, and the Non-Aligned Movement at the Time of the 1961 Belgrade Conference," *International History Review* 38, no. 4 (2016): 741–64; and Christopher M. White, *Creating a Third World: Mexico, Cuba, and the United States during the Castro Era* (Albuquerque: University of New Mexico Press, 2007).

19. Roy Allison, *The Soviet Union and the Strategy of Non-Alignment in the Third World* (New York: Cambridge University Press, 1988), 70.

20. Getchell and Kullaa, "Endeavors to Make Global Connections," 29.

21. "Declaration of the Heads of State or Government of Non-Aligned Countries, Belgrade, September 1961," in *Main Documents Relating to Conferences of Non-Aligned Countries: From Belgrade, 1961 to Georgetown, 1972* (Georgetown, Guyana: Ministry of Foreign Affairs, 1972), 8, 11.

22. Message from the Afro-Asian People's Solidarity Organization (AAPSO) to the First Summit Conference of Non-Aligned Countries in Belgrade, in *AAPSO and*

Non-Alignment: Documents, 1961–1983 (Cairo: Permanent Secretariat of AAPSO, 1983), 6, 7.

23. Letter to Cuban President Dorticós from Khrushchev, September 16, 1961, Fond 104, Opis' 16, Papka 8, Delo 9, List 40, Foreign Policy Archive of the Russian Federation (hereafter AVPRF).

24. Letter to Cuban President Dorticós from Khrushchev, September 16, 1961, emphasis in original.

25. Letter to Cuban President Dorticós from Khrushchev, September 16, 1961, emphasis in original.

26. Nikita Khrushchev, "Report of the Central Committee to the XXII Congress of the CPSU, October 17, 1961," in *Diversity in International Communism: A Documentary Record, 1961–1963*, ed. Alexander Dallin (New York: Columbia University Press, 1963), 10.

27. Khrushchev, "Report," 16.

28. Allison, *The Soviet Union and the Strategy of Non-Alignment in the Third World*, 23.

29. Jackson, *Castro, the Kremlin, and Communism*, 21.

30. Jackson, *Castro, the Kremlin, and Communism*, 22.

31. Che Guevara, "Guerrilla Warfare: A Method," *Cuba Socialista*, no. 25 (September 1963), in *Venceremos! The Speeches and Writings of Ernesto Che Guevara*, ed. John Gerassi (New York: Macmillan 1968), 273.

32. Che Guevara, "On Solidarity with Vietnam," speech at the Ministry of Industry, 20 November 1963, in *Venceremos! The Speeches and Writings of Ernesto Che Guevara*, ed. John Gerassi (New York: Macmillan 1968), 289.

33. Piero Gleijeses, *The Cuban Drumbeat: Castro's Worldview: Cuban Foreign Policy in a Hostile World* (London: Seagull Books, 2009), 12.

34. Gleijeses, *The Cuban Drumbeat*, 14.

35. O. Carlos Stoetzer, *The Organization of American States* (Westport, CT: Praeger, 1993), 282.

36. For more on the Latin American response to the missile crisis, see Renata Keller, "The Latin American Missile Crisis," *Diplomatic History* 39, no. 2 (2015): 195–222.

37. "Programme for Peace and International Cooperation," Cairo, October 1964, in *Main Documents Relating to Conferences of Non-Aligned Countries: From Belgrade, 1961 to Georgetown, 1972* (Georgetown, Guyana: Ministry of Foreign Affairs, 1972), 21.

38. "Programme for Peace and International Cooperation," 28.

39. Jackson, *Castro, the Kremlin, and Communism*, 28. See also Appendix A in William E. Ratliff, *Castroism and Communism in Latin America, 1959–1975* (Washington, DC: American Enterprise Institute, 1976), 195.

40. Jackson, *Castro, the Kremlin, and Communism*, 35.

41. Jacques Lévesque, *The USSR and the Cuban Revolution* (Westport, CT: Praeger, 1978), 103.

42. "The First Tricontinental Conference, Another Threat to the Security of the Inter-American System," a study prepared by the Special Consultative Committee

on Security at its Sixth Regular Meeting, 2 April 1966, 11–13 (OAS Official Records, Pan American Union, 1966).

43. Introduction, *First Solidarity Conference of the Peoples of Africa, Asia, and Latin America* (Havana: General Secretariat of OSPAAAL, 1966).

44. "Antecedents and Objectives of the Movement of Solidarity of the Peoples of Africa, Asia, and Latin America," in *First Solidarity Conference of the Peoples of Africa, Asia, and Latin America* (Havana: General Secretariat of OSPAAAL, 1966), 10.

45. Domínguez, *To Make a World Safe for Revolution*, 69.

46. Lévesque, *The USSR and the Cuban Revolution*, 116.

47. Ernesto Che Guevara, "Message to the Tricontinental," in *Venceremos! The Speeches and Writings of Ernesto Che Guevara*, ed. John Gerassi (New York: Macmillan 1968), 415.

48. "Antecedents and Objectives," 22.

49. Speech Delivered by Major Fidel Castro Ruz, Prime Minister of the Revolutionary Government and First Secretary of the Communist Party of Cuba, in the Closing Session, *First Solidarity Conference of the Peoples of Africa, Asia, and Latin America* (Havana: General Secretariat of OSPAAAL, 1966), 169–70.

50. "Resolution on the OAS," in *First Solidarity Conference of the Peoples of Africa, Asia, and Latin America* (Havana: General Secretariat of OSPAAAL, 1966), 71–72.

51. "Resolution on Aid to the Revolutionary Struggle of the Peoples of Colombia, Venezuela, and Peru," in *First Solidarity Conference of the Peoples of Africa, Asia, and Latin America* (Havana: General Secretariat of OSPAAAL, 1966), 104–5.

52. Briefing on U.S. Aggressive Actions in Relation to Cuba—USA Department of Soviet Foreign Ministry, 23 August 1966, Fond 104, Opis' 21, Papka 17, Delo 14, List 11, AVPRF.

53. Briefing on U.S. Aggressive Actions in Relation to Cuba—USA Department of Soviet Foreign Ministry, 23 August 1966, Fond 104, Opis' 21, Papka 17, Delo 14, List 16, AVPRF.

54. "Resolution Condemning the So-Called Inter-American Peace Force and the Governments that Support It," in *First Solidarity Conference of the Peoples of Africa, Asia, and Latin America* (Havana: General Secretariat of OSPAAAL, 1966), 69–70.

55. Telegram to Comrade Brezhnev, General Secretary of the Communist Party of the Soviet Union, Comrade Podgorny, Chairman of the Supreme Soviet, and Comrade Kosygin, Chairman of the Council of Ministers, from Osvaldo Dorticós and Fidel Castro, January 24, 1967, Fond 104, Opis' 22, Papka 18, Delo 9, List 1, AVPRF.

56. Telegram to Comrade Brezhnev.

57. Quoted in Jackson, *Castro, the Kremlin, and Communism in Latin America*, 114.

58. Text of questionnaire prepared by OLAS Organizing Committee, reprinted in "The First Conference of the Latin American Solidarity Organization, July 28–August 5, 1967," A Staff Study Prepared for the Subcommittee to Investigate

the Administration of the Internal Security Act and other International Security Laws of the Committee on the Judiciary of the United States Senate (Washington, DC: U.S. Government Printing Office, 1967), 28.

59. Richard Gott, *Cuba: A New History* (New Haven, CT: Yale University Press, 2005), 232–33.

60. Fidel Castro Speech at LASO Closing Session, 11 August 1967, Castro Speech Database, http://lanic.utexas.edu/project/castro/db/1967/19670811.html.

61. Lévesque, *The USSR and the Cuban Revolution*, 132.

62. Henry Butterfield Ryan, *The Fall of Che Guevara: A Story of Soldiers, Spies, and Diplomats* (Oxford: Oxford University Press, 1998), 62.

63. Ryan, *The Fall of Che Guevara*, 65.

64. Ryan, *The Fall of Che Guevara*, 156–57.

65. Ernesto Che Guevara, "Freedom of Competition or 'A Free Fox among Free Chickens'?," address to the Geneva Trade and Development Conference, 25 March 1964, in Fidel Castro and Che Guevara, *To Speak the Truth: Why Washington's 'Cold War' against Cuba Doesn't End* (New York: Pathfinder, 1992), 103.

66. Che Guevara, quoted in Smith, *Castro's Cuba*, 18.

67. Ryan, *The Fall of Che Guevara*, 164.

68. See Gleijeses, *Conflicting Missions*, 220–21.

69. Telegram to Soviet Foreign Minister Gromyko from Cuban Foreign Minister Raúl Roa Garcia, 6 November 1967, Fond 104, Opis' 22, Papka 18, Delo 9, List 27, AVPRF.

70. Soviet Embassy in the Republic of Cuba, 21 November 1967, Cuban press coverage of the 50th anniversary of the Great October Socialist Revolution (press review), Fond 104, Opis' 22, Papka 18, Delo 9, Listy 30–31, AVPRF.

71. Soviet Embassy in the Republic of Cuba, Listy 32–33.

72. Dorticós, quoted in "Cultural Congress of Havana," Study Prepared by the Special Consultative Committee on Security against the Subversive Action of International Communism at Its Tenth Regular Meeting (Washington, DC: General Secretariat of the Organization of American States, 1968), 14.

73. Blight and Brenner, *Sad and Luminous Days*, 135–37.

74. Domínguez, *To Make a World Safe for Revolution*, 225.

75. Domínguez, *To Make a World Safe for Revolution*, 222.

76. Nikolai Zaitsev, "The Soviet Union, Russia, and the Latin American Countries: Major Issues in Trade and Economic Cooperation," in *The Soviet Union's Latin American Policy*, ed. Edmé Domínguez Reyes (Gothenburg, Sweden: Göteborgs Universitet, 1995), 55–70.

77. Quoted in Smith, *Castro's Cuba*, 26.

78. Quoted in Leon Gouré and Morris Rothenberg, *Soviet Penetration of Latin America* (Miami, FL: University of Miami Press, 1972), 73.

79. Gouré and Rothenberg, *Soviet Penetration*, 74.

80. Smith, *Castro's Cuba*, 27.

81. Richard L. Jackson, *The Non-Aligned, the UN, and the Superpowers* (New York: Praeger, 1983), 28.

82. Jackson, *The Non-Aligned, the UN, and the Superpowers*, 44.

83. Speech by the Head of the AAPSO Delegation at the 4th Summit Conference of Nonaligned Countries in Algiers, in *AAPSO and Non-Alignment: Documents, 1961–1983* (Cairo: Permanent Secretariat of AAPSO, 1983), 19–20.

84. Castro's Opening Speech to the 6th Summit Conference of Non-Aligned Countries, 3 September 1979, Castro Speech Database, http://lanic.utexas.edu/project/castro/db/1979/19790903.html.

85. "Havana Declaration," 3–7 September 1979, in *Summit Declarations of Non-Aligned Movement, 1961–2009* (Kathmandu: Institute of Foreign Affairs, 2011), 118, 119.

86. "Havana Declaration," 119. Western Hemisphere member-states were Argentina, Bolivia, Cuba, Grenada, Guyana, Jamaica, Nicaragua, Panama, Peru, and Trinidad and Tobago. Belize was accorded special status, and Brazil, Colombia, Costa Rica, Dominica, Ecuador, El Salvador, Mexico, St. Lucia, Uruguay, and Venezuela sent observers.

87. Jackson, *The Non-Aligned, the UN, and the Superpowers*, 30.

88. James Daniel Ryan, *The United Nations under Kurt Waldheim, 1972–1981* (Lanham, MD: Scarecrow Press, 2001), 143.

89. Quoted in Allison, *The Soviet Union and the Strategy of Non-Alignment in the Third World*, 72.

90. Quoted in Allison, *The Soviet Union and the Strategy of Non-Alignment*, 72–73.

91. Quoted in Jackson, *The Non-Aligned, the UN, and the Superpowers*, 201.

92. Smith, *Castro's Cuba*, 35.

93. Jackson, *The Non-Aligned, the UN, and the Superpowers*, 33. See also Ryan, *The United Nations under Kurt Waldheim*, 144–45.

94. Allison, *The Soviet Union and the Strategy of Non-Alignment*, 47.

95. Statement of the AAPSO Presidium Committee on Non-Alignment, 22–23 January 1983, Nicosia, Cyprus, in *AAPSO and Non-Alignment: Documents, 1961–1983* (Cairo: Permanent Secretariat of AAPSO, 1983), 86.

96. Statement of the AAPSO Presidium Committee on Non-Alignment, 36.

7 Argentina's Secret Cold War

Vigilance, Repression, and Nuclear Independence

DAVID M. K. SHEININ

Among historians and in Argentine popular culture, Argentina has generally been cast as having positioned itself outside a Cold War strategic framework; as the proponent of President Juan Perón's *tercera posición* (third position) from 1946 to 1955, charting a dynamic, independent path in international affairs; and after 1954, outside periods of military rule, as the inheritor of that third position. The story is more disorderly, though, as illustrated by a 1974 trade arrangement through which Argentina may or may not have broken the U.S. economic blockade of Cuba. Through a new Argentine-Cuban trade agreement that year, Chevrolet Argentina, the U.S.-capitalized Argentine subsidiary of the American auto giant, sold the Cuban government a few dozen pick-up trucks built in Argentina. Chrysler Argentina sold nine thousand Dodge 1500s. Ford Argentina sent one thousand F-7000 trucks and fifteen hundred Falcons. As a preamble to the trade agreement, Perón waxed eloquent in a letter to Cuban president Fidel Castro, framing the sale as a mark of Latin American unity, their shared revolutionary voice, and Third World development.[1]

The military government in Brazil protested the sales as a violation of an Organization of American States (OAS) resolution committing all member states to suspend trade with Cuba. Washington saw things differently. The U.S. Treasury Department had issued the Argentine subsidiary firms waivers that allowed each to bypass the embargo (about which Brazilian authorities knew and with which they disagreed). Earlier that year, the Argentine government had seen an opportunity to jumpstart car exports. For Chrysler alone, the agreement with Cuba doubled foreign sales against 1973 figures. Before the waiver, Argentine Foreign Minister Alberto Vignes announced that the embargo would have to be set aside. If no waiver were issued, the American subsidiary companies would be forced to sell cars directly to the Argentine government that, in turn, would transfer them to

Cuba. In that event, the U.S. car subsidiaries would lose valuable government export subsidies.[2]

Why did Washington agree to the waiver and to what seemed Vignes's threat? The public Argentine position echoed Perón's comments to Castro, invoking Latin American solidarity, Argentine nationalism, and a third way—Argentina's third position—linking Argentina, through Peronism, to other "revolutionary" movements in developing countries. But Washington knew better. Vignes had told them so. In October 1973, in a private meeting at the Waldorf Astoria in New York, the Argentine foreign minister told U.S. Secretary of State Henry Kissinger that Argentina would work with the United States in all areas. "Public opinion," he pointed out, "is highly sensitized and euphoric. . . . Therefore, while this euphoria may have certain negative reflections, it can also be channeled to positive ends." Peronism, Vignes was stating delicately, was both populist and highly emotional. He was careful not to opine specifically on Peronist street politics but wanted Washington to know that Perón meant his public pronouncements to be taken in Washington with a grain of salt. Bilateral relations were crucial to Argentina, as it moved to resolve a chronic trade deficit with the United States. In that context, Argentina was desperate for scrap iron for industrial production, which included the auto sector. Kissinger probed. Why had Argentina offered Cuba $200 million in credit? It was strictly business Vignes answered. "Cuba knows that Argentina is *justicialista* and anticommunist."[3]

How did Cuba *know* when Perón was telling Castro the reverse while framing it in the language of Argentina's *tercera posición*? Like U.S. officials, Cubans watched as Perón's government shifted hard right politically. On 25 September 1973, the Montoneros—a leftist, Peronist revolutionary group with strong ties to Cuba—assassinated centrist Peronist labor leader José Ignacio Rucci, the general secretary of the Argentine Confederación General de Trabajo. Perón was appalled. Days later, trying to convince congressional deputies to vote in favor of tough-on-crime reforms to the Penal Code, Perón asked, "Are we going to allow ourselves to be killed? They killed the general secretary of the Confederación General de Trabajo. They're killing at will and we're sitting around with our arms crossed because we don't have a law in place to counter them." On 19–20 January 1974, a second leftist revolutionary group, the Ejercito Revolucionario del Pueblo, attacked a military base in the province of Buenos Aires. Perón instructed the armed forces to annihilate the revolutionary Left, to exterminate the guerrillas (whom he called psychopaths).[4]

In the seeming chasm between Vignes's affirmation of anti-Communist, pro–United States Argentine foreign and economic policies, and Perón celebrating Third World *desarrollismo* and strong ties to his fellow "revolutionary" Fidel Castro, Vignes reinforced key components of Argentine foreign and strategic relations throughout the Cold War. Argentina frequently distanced itself from both Soviet and United States strategic, economic, and policy orbits. That stand, though, was not a set of policy imperatives. Perón's third position was an ambiguous rehashing of *justicialista* dictums that never confined Argentina to stated policy. On global social problems, Perón wrote, "The third position, between individualism and collectivism, is the adoption of an intermediate system whose basic instrument is social justice."[5] It never became less abstruse. At the same time, the third position was just that, a diplomatic position that might publicly and ostensibly frame policy, but that was not policy itself. During and after Perón, Argentine Cold War interests frequently dovetailed with those of Non-Aligned Movement members and in other "third way" contexts. However, those points of contact, even when they generated tense relations with the United States, cannot be viewed through a Third World or third way lens. They never jeopardized a vital, largely consistent pro-Washington foreign policy.

Why didn't Washington balk over the car sales to Cuba? Kissinger took Vignes at his word. While his stance had been framed publicly as a threat to Washington, U.S. ambassador in Argentina Robert C. Hill read the Argentine position as Vignes had cast it to Kissinger in less menacing terms. Hill and other U.S. diplomats and policymakers understood that Perón had staked out a center-right political agenda. Bearing in mind Argentina's fragile economy, Hill urged that Washington approve the Argentine-Cuba trade deal in order to maintain strong ties with Argentina. Cuban authorities also closely watched the Argentine government's toughening stand on the revolutionary Left. Soon after the 1976 coup d'état in Argentina, the Cuban ambassador in Buenos Aires told Argentine military authorities that while Cuba had intervened in many countries in support of leftist revolutionaries, Argentine military intelligence would find no such activity in Argentina among the revolutionary Left reviled by Perón. Cuba told the new Argentine *junta* that it saw the coup d'état as a "necessary change."[6]

The broken trade embargo is a faithful reflection of Argentine foreign policy during the Cold War. This goes for periods of *peronista* governance (1946–55 and 1973–74) most closely identified with a nationalist, third way stand, as it does for periods military rule, short-lived limited democratic governments, and democratic government after 1983. Argentina often demonstrated sympathy for Third World causes. However, Argentina framed an interest in strong ties with developing nations by strong, consistent pro–United States strategic and commercial biases and interests. This chapter explains Argentina's Cold War in four sections. The first shows the ways in which Argentines have written and read their history after 1945, setting aside continuities in policymaking across dramatic political shifts, the extent of U.S. influence on Argentina, and the Cold War as a formative set of problems. The second section argues that close economic ties with Washington coupled with long-standing anti-Communist policies, foreign and domestic, were the basis for Argentine Cold War foreign policy. The third documents the related problem of Argentina's independent nuclear foreign policy as motivated by economic gain and international leadership. The final section charts Argentina's late Cold War push for an end to the nuclear arms race while developing a missile program.

Disrupting Chronologies

Argentina's relationship with the United States is key to understanding the limited significance of Perón's third way and related foreign policy initiatives in the Third World during the Cold War. In that context, four dominant historical narratives have obscured the ways in which Argentina's Cold War was closely linked to U.S. cultural, political, and strategic leadership. Scholars have routinely argued that, after 1945, Argentina charted an anti-American foreign and economic policy without ever falling under a Soviet orbit—starting with Perón's third position. This view was regularly reproduced in middle-class intellectual circles.[7] Coupled with Argentina's distance from violent Cold War conflict hotspots, such as El Salvador and Guatemala, this approach reaffirmed the argument that Argentina remained apart from Cold War power politics and cultural determinants. A parallel de facto historical narrative holds that the Cold War touched the Argentine polity only episodically.[8] This derives in part from an approach to Cold War Argentina in parameters set by the brutalization of subject peoples in the Caribbean basin through U.S.-sponsored state terror, and as such, relevant to Argentina only peripherally. Finally, Argentine historiography has organized political and other narratives to stress severe breaks from government to government—through *peronismo*, military rule, and post-dictatorship democracy—in a manner that marginalizes Cold War continuities as of limited relevance to Argentine historical processes.[9]

The other story is one of continuities. It highlights a historical narrative running apart from, in parallel to, and sometimes at odds with dominant historical accounts that establish severe chronological breaks along political lines. While in no way altering the significance of Argentina's dramatic political and social upheavals in 1955, 1966, 1973, 1976, and 1983, this chapter holds that dominant narratives have allowed the significance of those jarring, transformative shifts to overshadow key continuities. The latter include the force of anti-Communism in government domestic and foreign policies, the long-standing importance of U.S.-Argentine political, economic, social, and cultural ties, and the emergence of an independent Argentine nuclear policy.

Some building blocks of Argentina's cultural Cold War have been documented by historians Isabella Cosse (on the impact in Argentina of the translation and dissemination of Dr. Benjamin Spock's writings),[10] Karina Felitti (on evolving sexualities in the 1960s),[11] and Carlos Scolari (on the influence of Robert Crumb on political and social cartooning in the serial *Fierro* in the 1980s),[12] among many others.[13] Yet none evokes historian Penny Von Eschen's dictum that cultural exchange "was the commodity that closely pursued the quintessential Cold War commodities, oil and uranium, along with many others critical to America's seductive abundance."[14] While some authors provide evidence of the connection between U.S. cultural and social influences and larger historical developments in Argentina, none highlights those influences as a key problem in and of itself.

This is sometimes a function of the powerful scholarly and popular commitment to the idea that Argentina's foreign cultural influences were European in the first instance. In 2016, I asked former Teatro Colón artistic director Darío Lopérfido about high cultural U.S. influences in Argentina during the Cold War. He rejected the notion; Argentina's inspirations came from across the Atlantic. But in short order, Lopérfido recalled with evident pleasure the brilliant performances of Tennessee Williams plays in Buenos Aires decades ago, and how the writing of Lillian Hellman had shaped his thinking on the intersections of politics and the arts. Jessye Norman, he added, would be performing at the Colón in 2017. Norman had first graced that stage as a young diva in 1978.[15]

The force of U.S. cultural sway as a Cold War phenomenon tied to U.S. economic power remains apart from how authors have charted Argentine historical narratives, and how deeply those influences have penetrated local cultural strata. In the long-standing primacy of the Ford/Chevrolet rivalry, for example, in Turismo Carretera (rally car racing)—launched by racing legends Juan Manuel Fangio (in his Chevy) and Oscar Alfredo Gálvez (in his Ford)—the notion that those two car brands were from the United States and that the automakers capitalized over the long term on their racing teams' successes to achieve enormous commercial, economic, and even sinister Cold War political advances has simply never been addressed. Nor have the commercial, economic, and cultural meanings of those brands and their marketing. The Cuban auto sales agreement is a footnote by comparison. The Ford and Chevy brands *became* Argentine, through dictatorship and democracy.[16]

A lasting cultural manifestation of Cold War Argentine atomic fears was the Objeto Volador No Identificado (OVNI, Unidentified Flying Object) subculture. Its narrative contours rigorously follow larger, transnational Cold War story lines. It marks Argentina's enormous distance from third way international politics in its profoundly U.S. story lines. OVNI culture penetrated well beyond loyal followers into mainstream media reports, inexpensively produced paperbacks (most by U.S. authors), genre magazines, and legions of witnesses. While Argentina developed its own nuclear program, atomic fears as expressed through OVNI culture were a reaction to the threat of nuclear weapons—absent in Argentina. Here as elsewhere, the United States became a cultural and scientific reference point. Waves of Argentine OVNI sightings—in 1947 and 1978 for example—corresponded to equivalent waves in the United States.[17]

The historian Mark Wasserman wondered aloud whether my purpose in arguing that Argentina was not an antagonist of the United States and that U.S. cultural influences exerted defining Cold War–era influences in Argentina was to assert the existence of a hegemonic imperialism.[18] The answer is no. Argentina has a place in how we understand the Cold War in Latin America that is strongly influenced by historical change in the United States, that is not marginal to the hemispheric Cold War by virtue of its having been outside core struggles in the Caribbean basin, and that extends past the episodic. That place is both unique and all at once reflective of the transnational Cold War. The geographical and theoretical marginalization of Argentina as a hot Cold War site and the historical treatment of the Cold War as episodic are evident in a seminal study of what editors Gilbert M. Joseph and Daniela Spenser call the "Latin Americanization" and "transnationalization" of the Cold War conflict.[19] In removing the problematizing of the hemispheric Cold War from the limited sphere of U.S. foreign policy experts, the chapters in *In From the Cold: Latin America's New Encounter with the Cold War* (Durham: 2008) include one focused on Argentina. While Ariel C.

Armony's excellent "Transnationalizing the Dirty War: Argentina in Central America" is strong historical analysis, it is distinctive among volume chapters and representative of how Argentina's Cold War has been cast. Unlike other chapters in the book, "Transnationalizing the Dirty War" combines an exclusive focus on dictatorship, not democracy, with an externalizing of the Cold War—in this case, the notable but relatively insignificant Argentine military incursion into Central America. Here, the Argentine Cold War is constructed entirely from the outside in a National Security Doctrine–inspired military regime and how it fits into the emerging Central American conflagrations of the 1980s. The Cold War becomes a foreign phenomenon in Argentina.[20]

If Cold War Argentina spanned democracy and dictatorship, incorporated powerful U.S. influences, reflected connections between politics, policy, and culture, and demonstrated continuities across a period not normally constructed as driving Argentine historical processes—1945–90—what can that period tell us about Argentina's past? Cold War Argentina is a period that, through defining continuities, reshapes Argentine historical narratives. Without erasing the obvious dictatorship-democracy dichotomies, the Argentine Cold War prompts a rethinking of the severity of extant chronological markers and boundaries. Cold War Argentina reflects powerful U.S. influences. But they are often, though not always, *influencias argentinizadas*, like the hybridizing of Ford and Chevy from classic American brands into Argentine cultural markers through rally racing. In addition, recasting Argentine history as Cold War Argentine history reshapes how we might approach Argentine politics, policies, and international strategy through a Cold War lens.

"With the United States, but Not for the United States"

In considering the foreign policies of *peronismo*, particularly through 1955, scholars have rehearsed the self-asserted *peronista* "third position" as a guiding framework, characterized by a policy stand at odds with both the Soviet Union and the United States, and with a strong component of hostility toward the latter.

That approach has masked a strong current of anti-Communism, framed as a Cold War problem. In 1951, as the Argentine government exercised a public, third position foreign policy, in secret it outlined policy and action far more in keeping with U.S. Cold War strategic positions. In March 1951, the Defense Ministry issued a secret position paper calling for the Argentine government to press for an end to "Chinese communist aggression" and for the development of a public government position more clearly in keeping with that stand. In response, Under-Secretary of Foreign Relations Guillermo R. Spangenberg argued that the Cold War was now the key determinant of Argentine international ties. Argentina could no longer see itself as in any way neutral. A war between "East and West" was coming, imagined privately by Argentine policymakers as two clear-cut binaries: Communism versus anti-Communism, and the "East" versus "Western Civilization." Argentina had developed a military strategic plan, the "Fórmula Media." When the new world war came, the Argentine Navy would deploy to join U.S.-led expeditionary forces, the Army would maintain internal security and "repress fifth columns," and the Air Force would preserve air sovereignty in the face of possible Communist aggression. This came long before the advent of National Security Doctrine thinking in Washington.[21]

These tenets guided Argentine strategic policymaking for decades. They disarm a popularly held notion that Argentina was a dogged antagonist of the United States. In the context of longstanding anti-Communism—reinforced by U.S.-influenced Argentine government responses to the Korean War and the 1954 Guatemala crisis—Argentina held to three additional priorities through the end of the Cold War. First, Argentina sought stronger economic ties with the United States. It is part of Argentine nationalist history and lore that during his first presidency (1946–51), Perón imposed economic impediments on commercial and financial relations with the United States. True enough, but at the same time Argentina pursued stronger business ties with the United States in many areas. Moreover, policymakers in both countries understood that there was progress here, despite the commonly known barriers.

Second, while Argentina asserted its independence as a strong diplomatic third way, that independence was nuanced and tended toward good relations with the United States. Third, where Argentina asserted policy independence from Washington, it did so only on matters that would not fundamentally shake sound bilateral ties. Argentina took strong and consistent positions, for example, at the United Nations and in other forums on the need for an international redistributive economic politics as both just and as an antidote to Communist advances. This last, most consistent area of Argentine policy between 1945 and 1955 was largely divorced from the first two. As Argentina came closer to U.S. positions on the first two, its consistent backing for the third became more hollow and more rote. As such it anticipated the failures of Operación Panamericana in the late 1950s and the Alliance for Progress in the 1960s.

In the late 1940s, despite commercial tensions between Argentina and the United Sates, both saw barriers as negotiable. Dozens of U.S. companies continued to function unimpeded in Argentina. For many, business grew quickly. Coca-Cola S.A. opened its first Argentine plant in 1942, its second in 1948, and its third in 1954. In the case of General Motors Argentina, while import restrictions curtailed manufacturing at its San Martín plant, in response, the company switched gears by winning new lucrative Argentine government contracts for school desks, doors, windows, steel cabinets, and more. In 1944, E. R. Squibb & Sons Argentina reached an agreement with the Argentine government, which blocked importation of penicillin as long as Squibb Argentina could supply the country's requirements. Over the next decade, Squibb increased output of the drug by 6,000 per cent over its initial production in 1945. In 1952, the company built the first commercial pharmaceutical research laboratory in South America.[22]

The United States' demand for beryllium, a key component of metal alloys in weapons systems and in the burgeoning nuclear sector, grew rapidly in the late 1940s and early 1950s. It typified continuity in the U.S. consumption of Argentine raw materials. In 1947, the New York–based Foote Mineral Company advised the U.S. Commerce Department of an unexpected opportunity to export the resource from Argentina. While there had been no beryllium imports from Argentina the previous year and though the government-controlled Argentine Trade Promotion Institute (IAPI) purchased all beryllium and fixed prices for export, the U.S. Commerce Department saw an opportunity. Strategically important Argentine beryl ore was now available for purchase by the United States.[23] Private negotiations advanced despite a supposed Argentine embargo on beryllium exports to the United States. A year later, Argentine and U.S. authorities continued to negotiate a beryllium purchase in return for the sale to Argentina of Geiger counters. Both the U.S. State Department and the Argentine Foreign Relations Ministry were marginal to negotiations conducted by the U.S. Commerce Department, the U.S. Atomic Energy Commission, the Argentine Army, and the Argentine War Ministry. In 1952 and 1953, exports of beryllium to the United States resumed in part as a result of negotiations and military contacts that dated back to the late 1940s.[24]

On matters of regional and global strategy, Argentina's long-standing independent foreign policy deferred to U.S. guidance on the question of international Communism. Throughout the first *peronista* presidencies,

Argentina read U.S.-Argentine relations and U.S. global strategy as shaped in part by imperial, interventionist American ambitions. At the same time, Argentina's vocal challenges to that imperialist tendency were often pro forma. Far more significant was Argentina's adherence to the Inter-American Treaty of Reciprocal Assistance (1947), which the Argentine Foreign Ministry acknowledged privately in 1947 to be "a military alliance."[25] From that point forward, the Argentine government gradually aligned its strategic thinking more with that of the United States, viewing a Communist peril in increasingly severe terms. Argentina read the United States agenda for the planned Fourth Meeting of Consultation of Foreign Ministers of the American Republics (1951) as a major transformation of the Inter-American Treaty of Reciprocal Assistance into an even more explicitly military alliance for both defensive and now *offensive* purposes. The American push came in response to the outbreak of the Korean War, to which Argentina's reaction was unequivocally in support of the United Nations, at odds with "international Communism," and "For the western world." Argentina again balanced independence of action with alignment toward the United States. In confronting the international Communist menace, Argentine positions threaded a policy needle "with the United States, but not for the United States."[26]

In November 1953, Argentina reasserted its long-standing position that states should be free to recognize military dictatorships when such governments came to power under the "norms of international law." That same month, Argentina registered what it described as its unwavering support for the principal of nonintervention.[27] However, the Guatemalan crisis transformed Argentine foreign policy in the latter stages of the second Perón presidency toward an even harder anti-Communist line. In early 1954, many Argentines followed the Guatemalan crisis closely. Dozens protested U.S. intervention in Central America to Argentine authorities—from residents of Barrio Candiotti in the city of Santa Fe to the Asociación de Estudiantes, Ciencias Económicas, Concordia (Entre Ríos) to the Communist Party–affiliated Unión de Mujeres de la Argentina (Ciudad Evita branch).[28] On 25 June 1954, the Guatemalan ambassador to Argentina, Manuel Galich, wrote to the Argentine Foreign Ministry describing a slaughter on par with Guernica the day before: "Modern planes . . . mounted a criminal attack against civilian populations in Chiquimula, Gualán and Zacapa, dropping trinitrotoluene bombs and machine gunning helpless people."[29] It made no difference. At the Tenth Inter-American Conference in 1954, Argentina defined its firmest pro–United States, anti-Communist line to date. It abstained from the crucial vote condemning Guatemalan Communism. In the fog of McCarthyist America, U.S. policymakers read this as hedging. But the abstention came as a reflection of Argentina's pro-Washington independence. A vote otherwise would have been read in Argentina as an abrogation of Argentina's commitment to anti-intervention in the Americas. The abstention was, nevertheless, a remarkable step back from decades of strong, condemnatory language on U.S. intervention in the hemisphere.

The Argentine delegation to the 1954 Caracas conference held that international aggression could not be reasonably defined in that various international conventions had failed to come up with an objective designation on meaning.[30] The delegation went on to argue that the problem of aggression was of *limited importance*; as a practical matter it would always fall to the OAS to assess any supposed aggression when it arose. At Caracas, Argentina played a central role in *removing* lingering obstacles to U.S. anti-Communist intervention. In addition, Argentina argued for "the impropriety of applying the collective security [components of the Rio Pact] in response to cases of aggression that might be covered by United Nations accords."[31] In the aftermath of United Nations support for the United States during the Korean War, Argentine policymakers found that body a more reliable arbiter of international aggression than the Rio Pact.

During the 1960s and 1970s, anti-Communist precepts rather than an ostensible third position guided Argentine policy in the Middle East in a manner that transcended the shifts from democratic to military governments in Argentina. Publicly, the Argentine diplomatic position was often one of moderation and what Argentine diplomats termed an "equidistant" approach in policy between Arab and Israeli interests. Privately, some of Argentina's most relied-upon diplomats in the field characterized regional conflicts as primed in the first instance by Soviet-American confrontation. Advising the foreign ministry in 1969, the Argentine chargé d'affaires in Syria, Raúl Lascano, conceived of regional problems as deriving from how the superpowers pressed their regional clients. Moreover, he argued that a next Middle East fracas would most likely be the result of Soviet or American reactions to an expansion of Chinese power in the region and Chinese backing of the Palestinian Fedayeen.[32]

The Cold War framing of Argentine policy was evident in diplomatic approaches elsewhere but also in what the Foreign Ministry did with those on-the-ground interpretations and reports. In 1967, the Argentine ambassador in South Korea, Alejandro A. Galarce found laughable a suggestion from UN Secretary General U Thant that the United States stop its bombing campaign in North Vietnam without a quid pro quo from the North Vietnamese or the Viet Cong. "This . . . ignores," he wrote, "that the only means of stopping the Communist advance or bringing about an end of the war is to destroy through bombing the centers of support for the Red Army." Galarce squared Argentina's geopolitical circle with Lascano's views by arguing that should it win its initiatives in the Southeast Asian conflict, China would move to assert "predominance" over the Middle East.[33]

A key architect of Argentina's late 1960s Middle East strategy took it all in. Ambassador to the United Nations José María Ruda privately linked his country's interests in the Middle East to equivalent Cold War interests in Southeast Asia when he reported to his superiors in Buenos Aires in 1968 that the risk of war in Cambodia had diminished thanks to Prince Norodom Sihanouk's pro–United States position and to the effectiveness of the U.S. bombing campaign in Laos (known at the time in diplomatic circles) as the only force blocking further Communist advances in the region.[34]

The persistence of Cold War anti-Communism in Argentine foreign policy and strategy dovetailed with a domestic equivalent that transcended democratic and dictatorial regimes. In 1951, the Argentine government identified "vigilance and repression" as a first domestic priority in confronting Communism.[35] In 1959 and 1960, a high point of post–World War II Argentine democratic governance, Argentine policing and justice retained strong Cold War anti-Communist operating precepts dating not only from the recent Revolución Libertadora, but also from the period of *peronista* governance before 1955. Argentine authorities regularly detained purported Communists for unspecified crimes. In August 1960, for example, the president of the Chamber of Deputies, Federico Monjardín, complained to Interior Minister Alfredo Roque Vítolo that federal police had detained two Communist Party members in Luján without cause. Late at night, police had stormed their homes, breaking windows and doors with submachine guns at the ready. Both suspects were apprehended. One of those sought climbed out of bed and surrendered immediately, but was still subjected to blows as reported by neighbors. Several days later, the two were released without charges having been laid. Then a few days after that, at 11:00 A.M., police went after them again, this time in the manner of grim Keystone Kops. Monjardín told the interior minister that anybody in Luján could have told the police where the two were that morning. Instead, several police vehicles raced about town, sirens blaring until they finally settled inexplicably on the offices of the newspaper *El Civisimo*, which they entered—guns at hand—and ransacked. Having published for forty years as an organ of the centrist Unión Cívica Radical Party, *El Civismo* was targeted, a police officer stated eventually to the incredulous newspaper director, because there had been reports that it was publishing Communist propaganda.[36]

Pan-Global Nuclear Policy

Atomic policy expressed each of Argentina's Cold War policy priorities and reflected the highest level of consistency and continuity across the period. Beginning in the mid-1940s, Argentine leaders, like their equivalents in Canada, France, and other countries, viewed nuclear power as a path to modernity. They imagined it might power a dynamic naval fleet and as a necessity for expanded industry. Most important, they saw the international dissemination of Argentine nuclear technology as a route to strategic influence. From the 1960s forward, Argentina's Cold War position on nuclear development was anathema to the United States. Argentine authorities held to a distinction between bellicose and nonbellicose nuclear programs. Theirs was peaceful. It had no relevance to weapons systems. Successive U.S. administrations took a different view, never shaped by any specific action taken by Argentina. All nuclear programs, including Argentina's, had military potential and as such, marked a threat to the international Cold War strategic order. Before 1990, the two countries were never able to reconcile these competing viewpoints. This prompted low-intensity diplomatic tensions at times, but nothing equivalent to the concerns Washington held with regard to India or Pakistan in similar contexts or the issues that almost brought Chile and Argentina to war in the late 1970s. The nuclear standoff between the two countries was marginal to how bilateral relations unfolded. Beginning in the 1960s, Argentine authorities began to target other developing nations as markets for nuclear technology, products, and education.

Argentine governments adopted a set of foreign policy positions that shaped clear boundaries on their independence. Argentina tacitly and often practically backed U.S. Cold War positions on international Communism. Those positions dovetailed with domestic anti-Communism, but did not preclude Buenos Aires from adopting diplomatic positions critical of the United States. While Argentine leaders saw their adherence to the Rio Pact as making them part of a U.S.-led military alliance, they also saw the practical benefits to diplomatic independence. Each of these elements, along with a developmentalist foreign policy, shaped the country's nuclear foreign policy. After 1980, such initiatives were explicitly packaged as a Third World, "Sur-Sur" outreach. However, throughout the Cold War, profit, economic advantage, and a boost to the Argentine technology sector drove Argentine nuclear policy. Argentina sold to whoever was interested in buying.

Longstanding nonadherence to the Nuclear Non-Proliferation Treaty (NPT) (effective 1970) did not signify that Argentina was a proliferator of nuclear arms or that it favored proliferation. While it was ostensibly designed to block the proliferation of nuclear weapons and while treaty adherents took the position that the accord governed only arms, Argentina held that the treaty discriminated against nonnuclear powers in their potential for the development of nonbellicose nuclear programs. Article 18 of the Treaty for the Prohibition of Nuclear Weapons in Latin America and the Caribbean (Treaty of Tlatelolco, 1968) preserved the right of nonnuclear powers to conduct nuclear explosions toward peaceful uses of atomic energy, a right prohibited by the NPT. Privately, Argentine authorities were more nuanced than in their public stand against NPT. They recognized that there was practical merit to the NPT failure to distinguish between bellicose and nonbellicose nuclear explosions. A 1975 memorandum from the Ministry of Foreign Relations Department of International Organizations (United Nations Division), for example, noted that the NPT prohibition on nuclear explosions of any sort made sense when bearing in mind the recent nuclear explosion in India. Publicly there was no Argentine reconciling the India case with the fact that the NPT proscription limited a nonbellicose nuclear option for Argentina. According to the Argentine permanent representative to the United Nations in 1968, "The key dilemma presented by [the NPT] is how to achieve a balance between an effective guarantee of national security, to which we all have a right, while at the same time creating an instrument that will not function as a barrier to nuclear development in our countries"—that is, underdeveloped countries. Argentina felt the effects of the India explosion in 1974. Before then, it enjoyed somewhat open technological and scientific assistance from more developed countries. After the explosion, Canada was among several countries to restrict the transfer of nuclear technology. The result, for Argentina, was some loss of economic and development opportunities over the short and medium terms.[37]

As a matter of Cold War policy, Argentines identified three dimensions of nonproliferation: "vertical," "geographical," and "horizontal." The first two spoke not to a shared nuclear interest with other developing countries but to a long-term Argentine sense of hypocrisy on the part of the five nuclear powers and Argentina's distance from proliferation. Vertical proliferation marked the exponential growth of nuclear arsenals among the great powers. Geographical proliferation represented the dissemination of nuclear weapons by the great powers outside their national territories in those of their dependencies, other states, or air and maritime space outside of great power national jurisdictions. Horizontal proliferation was what concerned the United States and other strong advocates of nonproliferation agreements. It covered the ambiguous—and in the opinion of Argentine leaders, undemonstrated—likelihood that new nuclear arms players might emerge among nation-states that previously did not have such weapons. Advanced as a panacea by its advocates, the NPT not only ignored the first two categories, it legitimized them. Only one clause in the NPT concerned vertical proliferation. Clause 6 determined that the nuclear powers promised nothing more than to negotiate in good faith on the end of the nuclear arms race and disarmament—a process that bore little fruit in the two decades between the signing of the treaty and the end of the Cold War.[38]

There was no middle ground on the disparate Argentine and U.S. approaches to nuclear arms and proliferation. While the 1974 Indian explosion of a nuclear device proved to Americans that horizontal proliferation was real, Argentines privately reached the same conclusion and, at the same time, took it as an indication of the reverse. It was an exceptional event. That there was only one explosion of this sort after NPT demonstrated that horizontal proliferation was a fantasy even as the great powers added thousands of weapons to their arsenals. For successive Argentine governments the way to prevent horizontal proliferation was simple: end the nuclear arms race and dissolve the barriers to the free and open transfer of nuclear technology and know-how for the peaceful development of nuclear energy. Argentines complained publicly and privately that limits placed by the United States and Canada on nuclear technology transfers to Argentina after India's first nuclear explosion in 1974 had had a deleterious impact on the Argentine atomic sector. But that impact was minimal. And there were benefits. Those limits accelerated Argentina's push to nuclear self-sufficiency and scientific advancement, not to sharing nuclear secrets with other developing countries or easing tensions with their chief rival in the sector, Brazil. Thus they contributed, for example, to the Argentine decision to develop the capacity to enrich its own uranium, and then to produce its first batch on the eve of democracy's return in 1983. Argentine nuclear physicists, chemists, and engineers continued to work at an advanced scientific level, often in academic and other collaborations with their colleagues in the United States. Perhaps more important, Argentine policymakers saw no contradiction in opposing U.S. policy on nuclear proliferation and at the same time advancing strategic positions that conformed to U.S. Cold War strategic stands.

The transition from dictatorship to democracy in 1983 marks the most striking of the chronological narrative breaks in how Argentines imagine their past. It is also the key point through which nuclear policy remained unchanged in larger contexts of global strategy, much of which continued to draw implicitly and explicitly on 1950s anti-Communist precepts. By 1980, Argentina had a commercial nuclear reactor in operation (Atucha at 334 MWe) and a second under construction (Embalse at 600MWe). The Argentine government had plans for four more plants to come on line by 1990. That they were not built had less to do with the transition to democracy three years later than with the shift away from nuclear power in many countries, including Canada and the United States, as the 1970s oil crisis subsided.

In 1977, the Argentine National Atomic Energy Commission (CNEA) designed and built an experimental reactor in Lima, Peru. Argentine leaders hoped the Peru project would establish Argentina as a leading nuclear power with a mandate to assist other developing countries to develop nuclear technologies. Argentina planned to equip Peru with an infrastructure of nuclear science and technology that would include the production of radioisotopes, a disposal system for nuclear waste, and the training of technical staff to operate all facilities. The 1977 bilateral contract ensured that Peruvian professionals would take part in each stage of the project from design to reactor commissioning. In addition, then, to a more common turnkey contract, Peru would emerge with a nuclear research center, as well as a local team of technicians to run the national nuclear project.[39]

Through the 1980s, the Peru venture was a model for Argentine foreign atomic policy and a centerpiece for late–Cold War Argentine international relations. Nuclear ties were meant to foster business opportunities and good bilateral relations with other countries across political divides, without prejudice to a pro-U.S. strategic foreign policy. Argentina opened and maintained strong nuclear ties with nations from every region and every political bloc. Where Argentina balked at establishing nuclear ties, it did so for narrow pragmatic purposes. In the late 1970s, for example, nuclear cooperation with South Africa was filtered through familiar and consistent geostrategic reasoning. In reference to apartheid and the occupation of Namibia, Argentina found the political situation in South Africa "delicate." The Argentine-assisted development of South Africa's nuclear sector would engender apprehension in the United Nations, in France, and in the United

States. It would produce "totally negative consequences" for Argentina among governments that had expressed support for Argentina's military government. To support the South African nuclear program presented a threat of criticism on human rights in the international community. The decision by the military government, then, to back away from atomic cooperation with South Africa had nothing to do with the evils of apartheid, but rather with concerns over isolation in the international community.[40]

After 1983, the Argentine government identified a strong position in favor of nuclear disarmament in conjunction with an effort to "recover the confidence of the international community" lost during the military dictatorship. That narrative of disarmament referenced a strategic position going back to the 1950s, Argentina's active participation since 1969 in the Conference on Disarmament, and the nation's membership in the Non-Aligned Movement (NAM), where, along with India and Mexico, Argentine leaders had helped define the NAM's position on atomic weapons.[41] Nothing had changed here in the 1983 transition to democracy. The Argentine government continued to seek nuclear markets and partnerships on the same policy premises as in the past, with no bearing on its geopolitics or its support for disarmament.

In keeping with excellent ties to the Soviet Union during the dictatorship, Argentina maintained ongoing relations with the Soviet Union on nuclear matters through the 1980s. From 1981 to 1985, Argentina bought tube-laminating machines from the Soviet Union for the building of reactor fuel tubes to hold enriched uranium. In 1981, the Argentine government acquired five tons of heavy water from the Soviet Union to help power its Canadian-built Atucha I commercial nuclear plant. In 1982, Argentina contracted with the USSR for the enrichment of uranium for use in the reactor it had built in Peru and for the experimental reactor at the Centro Atómico Ezeiza, outside Buenos Aires. In 1988, Argentina negotiated for the acquisition of a further two tons of heavy water.[42]

In 1987, Argentina and Syria opened conversations on nuclear cooperation and exchanged nuclear delegations. In 1988, working with the Argentine government, the state-owned Investigaciones Aplicadas S.E. offered the Syrian government a contract to build a turnkey commercial nuclear reactor similar to one the company had recently built for Algeria.[43] Argentine leaders saw an opportunity that, once again, was strictly business. The fall of President Jacques Chirac in 1989 brought an end to France's interest in building a reactor in Syria, as did political turmoil in the USSR. Syria welcomed the Argentine pitch.[44] In 1985, Argentina and China signed a fifteen-year agreement fomenting the transfer of technology, equipment, and personnel destined exclusively for the peaceful production of nuclear energy. The agreement was modeled on a similar agreement negotiated in 1985 by the United States and China. For Roberto M. Ornstein, CNEA director of international affairs, the hook for China was Argentina's offer of what he wrote in English as "on the job training"—Argentine technicians and scientists training their Chinese equivalents in the design, project management, construction, and technology transfer in the building of commercial nuclear reactors.[45]

The End of the Cold War: When Is a Missile Not a Missile?

The end of the Argentine Cold War was encapsulated in Argentina's push for leadership among nations working on nuclear disarmament and, at the same time, on the development of missile systems with the capacity to carry conventional and nuclear payloads. While Argentine officials played an increasingly important role among nonaligned nations advocating for disarmament, their meetings with officials from the USSR and United States to demand arms reduction were often undemanding. In 1983, in the shadow of US-USSR arms control negotiations and the killings of Indian prime minister Indira Gandhi and Swedish prime minister Olof Palme, Sweden, Argentina, India, Mexico, Greece, and Tanzania opened discussions among the "Group of Six" on reducing or eliminating missiles in Europe and on an aggressive nuclear arms reduction program. The other Group of Six members shared Argentina's refusal to follow U.S. pressures on arms reduction by region, emphasizing global solutions and a new issue of demilitarizing outer space. Five years later, however, Swedish Prime Minister Ingvar Carlson expressed the group's disappointment that Moscow and Washington had by and large ignored them, particularly with regard to their advocacy of a complete ban on nuclear weapons testing.[46]

There is no evidence that the Group of Six altered how the great powers or other nations developing nuclear weapons proceeded with their arms programs or that they had any illusions about doing so. When Argentine officials met with their U.S. and Soviet counterparts in the 1980s, their statements on arms reduction were made and received as an obligatory formality, much in the way Soviet officials had chided Argentina in the late 1970s on human rights. In September 1988, Soviet and Argentine foreign ministry officials met for an annual bilateral private meeting on disarmament. It was a recital of official positions, not a conversation. On the December 1987 signing of the first nuclear disarmament treaty between the United States and the Soviet Union specifically targeting the elimination of all intermediate-range missiles, Argentina expressed its approval and itemized further weapons reductions that were needed. The Soviets responded simply by noting that any intermediate-range missile reductions were conditional on the two sides reaching a new agreement on cruise missiles launched from warships and on nuclear weapons in space. Argentina halfheartedly pressed the Soviets on wrapping up longstanding negotiations on a comprehensive agreement for the elimination of nuclear weapons.[47]

While Argentina pressed the great powers on disarmament, the Argentine military had begun to develop the Cóndor II rocket. In April 1987 and September 1988, with greater concern than had ever been shown for Argentina's nuclear program, the United States held multilateral meetings with Canada, the United Kingdom, France, Italy, Germany, and Japan on the Cóndor II. In response to the rocket project, they agreed on restrictions on technology transfers to Argentina with possible military applications. U.S. Secretary of State George Schultz held further meetings with his equivalents from the Soviet Union, China, and Brazil, as well as with Argentine Foreign Minister Dante Caputo. U.S. Defense Secretary Frank Carlucci met with his Argentine equivalent Horacio Jaunarena to express concerns. This was the first time that United States and Argentine defense ministers had met one on one during the Cold War.[48]

Argentine authorities recognized the fine line they were walking between the peaceful and the bellicose. In 1988, Ministry of Foreign Relations, Department of Nuclear Affairs (DIGAN) director Roberto García Moritán privately addressed accusations that the Condor missile program had crossed that line. The missile program had developed an Argentine capacity to build a rocket for peaceful purposes that "technically, is not a missile." García Moritán understood the nuance. Like Argentina's nuclear program, the Condor program was a peaceful one in terms of stated intent and track record. The rockets, Argentina maintained, were for the deployment of meteorological and communications satellites. It escaped nobody's attention that the program had the financial and technical backing of the Egyptian government, itself a beneficiary of massive U.S. military aid. But García Moritán also reasoned that the program was never a secret: it was covered widely in academia and the media and exhibited at the 1987 Argentine Air Force celebration of its seventy-fifth anniversary. Egyptian help on the Condor project was in part a quid pro quo for progress on a bilateral nuclear agreement that would include Argentine technical expertise in the building of a nuclear reactor.[49]

Conclusion

Perón's rise showed some of the hallmarks of two other nationalist leaders espousing third way foreign policies, Gamal Abdel Nasser and Charles De Gaulle. At the same time, Perón differed from the Egyptian, the French, and other third way nationalist models on lines in the sand over which Argentina would not cross—and in proximity to the United States. Those lines distinguish Argentina's far more tepid flirtation with a third way from that of the others. The latter generated more severe breaks with the United States, more lasting policy shifts, military conflict or the threat of international strategic crisis, and perhaps most significantly, and as a consequence of those actions, changes in important international followings and global leadership roles. Argentina's international positions might as reasonably be compared with those of Canada as those of third way exponents. A middle power with a mixed economy like Canada, Argentina cultivated relations with Third World nations often as a path toward more agricultural sales and other economic advantages, but in addition in a manner often independent of the United States; Canada was similar in its strong relations with revolutionary Cuba and Nicaragua, for example. For each, conflicts with the United States on economic and political matters were brief, of little significance to Washington, and against a backdrop to generally strong bilateral ties. Both nations highlighted human rights as a policy priority during the final decade of the Cold War. While there was no Argentine parallel to the significance of Canada's membership in NATO, Argentina never deviated from an anti-Communist strategic position in line with that of Washington.[50]

Perón shared the nationalism and anti-elitism of another military officer who led a political revolution at roughly the same time, Egypt's Nasser. Both charted political movements that linked modernity to international leadership, Third World solidarity, and populist revolution primed in significant measure by an industrial working class. But Nasser's willingness to confront imperial power militarily during the Suez Crisis and the Arab nationalist policies that led to Egypt's political union with Syria had no equivalent in Argentina. Moreover, while Nasser's economic program—focused on the expropriation of large landholders and the buttressing of state capitalism—functioned for almost two decades as a "frenetically action-oriented"[51] strategic basis for his Third World nationalism, Argentina never advanced economic confrontation with the great powers as policy, over an extended time period.[52]

Like De Gaulle, Perón imagined a continental bloc of nations free of U.S. influence. But while Perón had some success in regional labor diplomacy,[53] it was very limited in comparison with the impact of De Gaulle's withdrawal of France from NATO. Like France (and Canada), Argentina developed a nuclear sector in the 1940s and 1950s capable of a weapons program. Unlike France (though much like Canada), Argentina's atomic goals never veered toward weapons production (much less a nuclear test) and, as a consequence, never contributed to advancing an equivalent to De Gaulle's international stature as a strategic antagonist of the United States. Part of what De Gaulle, Nasser, and other third way exponents sought was what Gaullists called national *grandeur*. In the end, this may be the most significant distinction between Argentina and nations that followed a successful third path during the Cold War. Without the international status, read by multiple measures, of De Gaulle or Nasser, Argentina's *tercera posición* remained a vague statement of intent.

Notes

1. "Cuando Perón le vendió autos a Fidel (y Brasil se enojó)," *Autoblog*, 30 November 2016, http://autoblog.com.ar/2016/11/30/cuando-peron-le-vendio-autos-a-fidel-y-brasil-se-enojo; "Cuando Perón rompió el bloqueo," *Página/12*, 16 March 2003, https://www.pagina12.com.ar/diario/cultura/7-17650-2003-03-16.html.

2. Doc. no. 1974BUENOS00435_b, U.S. Embassy, Argentina, to U.S. Secretary of State, 18 January 1974, Wikileaks, wikileaks.org/plusd/cables/1974BUENOS00435_b.html. [19 May 2017]; José Bodes and José Andrés López, *Perón-Fidel Línea Directa: Cuando la Argentina rompió el bloqueo a Cuba* (Buenos Aires: Ediciones Deldragón, 2003), 91–104.

3. U.S. Department of State, Memorandum of Conversation, "U.S.-Argentine Relations," Alberto Vignes, Henry Kissinger, Neil Seidenman, Waldorf-Astoria Hotel, New York, 5 October 1973, Box 2092, Subject-Numeric File, 1970–1973, Record Group (RG) 59, U.S. National Archives and Records Administration, College Park, MD (hereafter NARA); David M. K. Sheinin, "Making Friends with Perón: Developmentalism and State Capitalism in U.S.-Argentine Relations, 1970–1975," *Federal History* 5 (January 2013): 111–12.

4. "Cuando Perón habló de 'exterminar uno a uno' a los guerrilleros," *Clarín*, 18 January 2009, www.clarin.com/ediciones-anteriores/peron-hablo-exterminar-guerrilleros_0_S18epAqRaYl.

5. "Esta es la tercera posición," in *Perón Mediante: Gráfica peronista del periodo clásico*, ed. Guido Indij (Buenos Aires: La Marca, 2006), 223.

6. Doc. no. 1974BUENOS02392_b, U.S. Embassy, Argentina, to U.S. Secretary of State, 3 April 1974, Wikileaks, wikileaks.piraattipuolue.fi/plusd/cables/1974BUENOS 02392_b.html; David M. K. Sheinin, *Argentina and the United States: An Alliance Contained* (Athens: University of Georgia Press, 2006); Ezequiel F. Pereyra, Director of External Politics, Argentine Foreign Relations Ministry, "Entrevista del Director General de Política Exterior con S. E. Embajador de Cuba," 24 April 1976, 419-B, Archivo del Ministerio de Relaciones Exteriores y Culto, Buenos Aires (hereafter AMREC).

7. Carlos Escudé, *El estado parasitario: Argentina, ciclos de vaciamiento, clase política directiva y colapso de la política exterior* (Buenos Aires: Lumiere, 2005); Mario Rapoport and Noemí Brenta, "La gran inundación," *Página/12*, 26 March 2013; David M. K. Sheinin, "Peripheral Anti-Imperialism: The New Revisionism and the History of Argentine Foreign Relations in the Era of the Kirchners," *Estudios Interdisciplinarios de América Latina y el Caribe* 25, no. 1 (2014): 63–84.

8. Leandro Morgenfeld, *Relaciones peligrosas: Argentina y Estados Unidos* (Buenos Aires: Capital Intelectual, 2012); Mario Rapoport and Claudio Spiguel, *Relaciones tumultuosas: Estados Unidos y el primer peronismo* (Buenos Aires: Emecé, 2009).

9. See for example, Germán Ferrari, *1983, el año de la democracia* (Buenos Aires: Planeta, 2013); Horacio Gaggero, Alicia Iriarte, and Humberto Roitberg, *Argentina, 15 años después: de la transición a la democracia al menemismo, 1982–1997* (Buenos Aires: Proyecto Editorial, 2000).

10. Isabella Cosse, *Pareja, sexualidad y familia en los años sesenta* (Buenos Aires: Siglo Veintiuno, 2010), 184.

11. Karina Felitti, *La revolución de la píldora: Sexualidad y política en los años sesenta* (Buenos Aires: Edhasa, 2012).

12. Carlos A. Scolari, *Historietas para sobrevivientes: Comic y cultura de masas en los años 80* (Buenos Aires: Colihue, 1999), 249–93.

13. Matias Raña, *Guerreros del cine: Argentino, fantástico e independiente* (Buenos Aires: Fan, 2010); Mabel Bellucci, *Historia de una desobediencia: Aborto y feminismo* (Buenos Aires: Capital Intelectual, 2014), 297–313; Valeria Manzano, *The Age of Youth in Argentina: Culture, Politics & Sexuality from Perón to Videla* (Chapel Hill: University of North Carolina Press, 2014).

14. Penny M. Von Eschen, "'Satchmo Blows Up the World': Jazz, Race, and Empire during the Cold War," in *"Here, There and Everywhere": The Foreign Politics of American Popular Culture*, ed. Reinhold Wagnleitner and Elaine Tyler May (Hanover, NH: University Press of New England, 2000), 164.

15. Author's interview with Darío Lopérfido, December 12, 2016, Buenos Aires.

16. Jorge Ezequiel Sánchez, *El fenómeno TC* (Buenos Aires: Clarín, 2004); Irma Emiliozzi, *Los Emiliozzi: De la historia a la leyenda* (Buenos Aires: Claridad, 2015); "Chevrolet busca un campeonato," *Corsa*, 92 (January 23, 1968): 4–7.

17. Javier García Blanco, *Humanoides. Encuentros con entidades desconocidas* (Buenos Aires: Edaf del Plata, 2003), 97–100.

18. Comment to the author by Mark Wasserman, 5 March 2016, Philadelphia.

19. Gilbert M. Joseph, "What We Now Know and Should Know: Bringing Latin America More Meaningfully into Cold War Studies," in *In From the Cold: Latin*

America's New Encounter with the Cold War, ed. Gilbert M. Joseph and Daniela Spenser (Durham, NC: Duke University Press, 2008), 7.

20. Ariel C. Armony, "Transnationalizing the Dirty War: Argentina in Central America," in *In from the Cold: Latin America's New Encounter with the Cold War*, ed. Gilbert M. Joseph and Daniela Spenser (Durham, NC: Duke University Press, 2008), 134–68.

21. José Humberto Sosa Molina, Minister of Defense, to Hipólito Paz, Minister of Foreign Relations, 16 March 1951; Ministry of Defense, "La Junta Interamericana de Defensa, 16 March 1951; Grupo de Trabajo No. 2, minuta 1, 23 February 1951; Minuta 2, 28 February 1951, File: "Estudio Técnico-Militar," all in Working Group No. 1, File IV, AMREC.

22. No. IRI. ARG. 4. U.S. United States Information Service (USIS), "USIS Survey in Economic Field," 15 November 1955, Box 1, Field Research Reports, 1953–82, Entry 1007B, RG 306, NARA.

23. U.S. Department of State, "Argentine Beryl," 13 May 1947, File 21, Box 25, Atomic Energy Matters, 1944–52, RG 59, NARA.

24. Horace T. Reno, "Beryllium," in United States Bureau of Mines, *Minerals Yearbook: Metals and Minerals, 1954*, vol. 1 (Washington, DC: U.S. Government Printing Office, 1958), 221–27. U.S. Department of State, "Radioactivity Detectors for Argentina and Beryl for the United States," June 7, 1948, File 21, Box 25, Atomic Energy Matters, 1944–52, RG 59, NARA; A. A. Welles, United States Atomic Energy Commission, to R. Gordon Arneson, Special Assistant to the Under Secretary of State for Atomic Energy Affairs, "Argentine Embargo on Beryl," 5 October 1948, File 21, Box 25, Atomic Energy Matters, 1944–52, RG 59, NARA; D. H. Hershberger, Treasurer, The Brush Beryllium Company, to Otto Tolderlund, Minerales y Metales, 7 December 1951, File 21, Box 25, Atomic Energy Matters, 1944–52, RG 59, NARA.

25. Ministerio de Relaciones Exteriores y Culto (hereafter MREC), "Política de los Estados Unidos de América con respect a la Argentina," 1947, Memorandums, 1947–48, 36, AMREC.

26. MREC, "Reunión de Consulta de los Ministros de Relaciones Exteriores de las Republicas Americanas," 21 December 1950, IVa. Reunión de Ministros de Relaciones Exteriores de las Repúblicas Americanas, Comisión Especial, No. 8, AMREC.

27. José Carlos Vittone, Embajador Argentina ante la Organización de Estados Americanos (OEA), "Recapitulación de los aspectos más importantes de la política sustentada por el gobierno argentine en la OEA," 28 December 1953, 554, AMREC; 160, José Carlos Vittone, "Informe complementario, s/recapitulación de intervenciones argentinas en la O.E.A.," 8 April 1954, 554, AMREC.

28. Unión de Mujeres de la Argentina, Filial Ciudad Evita, to Perón, June 1954; Residents of Barrio Candioti to Remorino, June 1954; Asociación Esdudiantes, Ciencias Económicas, Concordia, to Remorino, June 1954, 15c, División Estados Americanos, AMREC.

29. No. 454, Galich to Remorino, 25 June 1954, Caso Guatemala, OEA, 2174, AMREC.

30. MREC, Departamento de Organismos Internacionales y Tratados, "Quinta Reunión de Consulta de Ministros de Relaciones Exteriores," 7, 1956, AMREC.

31. MREC, Departamento de Organismos Internacionales y Tratados, "Quinta Reunión de Consulta de Ministros de Relaciones Exteriores."

32. No. 61, Lascano to Foreign Relations Ministry, 8 July 1969, Crisis del Medio Oriente; No. 651/155, José María Ruda to Foreign Relations Ministry, 7 May 1969, Conflicto Árabe-Israelí, Refugiados Palestinos, 1969, Packet 26, Box 5, AMREC.

33. No. 5, Galarce to Nicanor Costa Méndez, "Empeoramiento de la situación en Asia," 22 May 1967, File 37, Box 8, AMREC.

34. No. 87/8/108, Ruda to Costa Méndez, 17 January 1968, "Informar" problemas fronteras Laos, Camboya," Cuestiones del Sudeste de Asia, 1966–72, File 37, Box 8, AMREC.

35. No. 5, Departamento de Política, MREC, IV Reunión de Consulta, 19 January 1951, No. 5, 3, AMREC.

36. Monjardín to Vítolo, 29 August 1960; Juan Enrique Olivella to Director de Coordinación Federal, Policía Federal, 29 August 1960, File 85, Box 139, Secretos, Confidenciales, y Reservados, Ministry of the Interior, Archivo Intermedio, Archivo General de la Nación (henceforth AI-AGN), Buenos Aires.

37. MREC, Department of International Organizations (United Nations Division) to Eastern Europe Division, "Visita Embajador Tsarapkin," 10 July 1975, 110, Noproliferación de armas nucleares, AMREC.

38. No. 67, Asuntos Nucleares y Desarme, Ministerio de Relaciones Exteriores y Culto (MREC), to Argentine Embassy, Ottawa, "Adelanto lineamientos de la política argentina sobre T.N.P.," 13 May 1985, 26, Dirección General De Asuntos Nucleares (DIGAN), AMREC.

39. Comisión Nacional de Energía Atómica (CNEA), Argentina, "Possibilities of Cooperation in the Nuclear Field Offered by the Argentine Republic," 1980, 3, Movimiento de Países No Alineados (NOAL), AMREC.

40. Carlos Ortiz de Rozas, Comisión Desarme, MREC, to Subsecretario de Relaciones Exteriores, "Consulta efectuada por la Comisión Nacional de Energía Atómica," January 15, 1979; A. J. A. Roux, President, Atomic Energy Board (South Africa), to Carlos Castro Madero, President, CNEA, 28 September 1978, 25, DIGAN, MREC.

41. MREC, "Sentido de la Iniciativa de las Seis Naciones Para la Paz y el Desarme," n.d. [1988], 15, DIGAN, MREC.

42. No. 610.000-925/88, Roberto Ornstein to Sub-Secretariat of International Cooperation, MREC, 10 August 1988, 43, DIGAN, AMREC.

43. No. 010289/89, García Moritán to Argentine Embassy, Syria, "Siria-Relación nuclear-visita director Comisión," 14 March 1989, 15, DIGAN, AMREC; No. 010673/1989, Guyer to DIGAN, "Presentación oferta argentina p/suministro invest. nuclear," 28 September 1989, 15, DIGAN, MREC; No. 010069/89, García Moritán to Secretaría de Estado de Asuntos Multilaterales y Espaciales, 24 August 1989, 15, DIGAN, AMREC; José María Trillo, Argentine Chargé d'Affaires, Damascus, to Enrique J. Candioti, Director General, Seguridad Internacional y Asuntos Estratégicos, MREC, 12 December 1990, 15, DIGAN, AMREC.

44. No. 010378/90, Trillo to DIGAN, "Requerir información estado bilateral en temas nucleares," 4 January 1990, 15, DIGAN, AMREC.

45. Roberto O. Cirimello, Development Manager, and Enrique E. García, Manager, Heavy Water Projects, CNEA, "Desarrollo Nuclear de la República Popular China," n.d. [1988], 15 DIGAN, MREC; 575/86, Adolfo Saracho, Director, Nuclear Affairs, MREC, to Secretaría de Estado de Relaciones Internacionales, "Compra Agua Pesada a China Popular," 2 October 1986, 79, DIGAN, AMREC; 610.000-1088/85, Roberto M. Ornstein, Director, International Affairs, CNEA to DIGAN, 28 August 1985, 79, DIGAN, MREC; 610.000-1047/85, Ornstein to DIGAN, 20 August 1985, 79, DIGAN, MREC.

46. Andrés Ortega, "Los 'seis' aprueban hoy una declaración que pide prohibir las pruebas nucleares," *El País* (Madrid), 21 January 1988, http://elpais.com/diario/1988/01/21/internacional/569718004_850215.html; Carlos Quirós, "Alfonsín y 'la cumbre' de Nueva Delhi. Otro llamado a la paz," *Clarín* (Buenos Aires), 18 January 1985.

47. No. 967/88, DIGAN, "Consulta política anual con la cancillería soviética sobre temas de desarme," 29 September 1988, 43, DIGAN, MREC.

48. García Moritán, "Sugerir Tratamiento Tema Espacial con los E.E.U.U.," 19 October 1988, 43, DIGAN, MREC; García Moritán, "Sugerir tratamiento tema especial en próxima reunion entre señores Caputo y Schultz," 5 October 1988, 43, DIGAN, MREC.

49. No. 959, García Moritán to Cabinet of the Foreign Minister, "Relación con la República Árabe de Egipto en los usos pacíficos de la energya nuclear," 26 September 1988, 43, DIGAN, MREC.

50. Maurice Vaïsse, *La puissance ou l'influence? La France dans le monde depuis 1958* (Paris: Fayard, 2009), 104–07.

51. Tarek Osman, *Egypt on the Brink: From Nasser to the Muslim Brotherhood* (New Haven, CT: Yale University Press, 2013), 53.

52. Steven A. Cook, *The Struggle for Egypt* (New York: Oxford University Press, 2012), 42–69.

53. Ernesto Semán, *Ambassadors of the Working Class: Argentina's International Labor Activists and Cold War Democracy in the Americas* (Durham, NC: Duke University Press, 2017), 15, 108.

Part II Third World Internationalism

8 Anti-Imperialist Racial Solidarity before the Cold War
Success and Failure

ALAN McPHERSON

"On the international scene there has now appeared a new actor: solidarity," said Dominican Tulio Cestero in late 1919, as the end of the Great War provoked both elation and disillusionment at the peace it had wrought. "No nation, no people, can realize by itself its destiny." To Cestero, "nationality" encompassed transnational identity, especially among Spanish-speaking Latin Americans. "We are citizens of twenty nations," he said, "but in one language, with the same soul, we feel nationality."[1]

Did they, though, "feel nationality"? More importantly, did they do anything about it? Political leaders in the interwar years in Latin America often declared their racial unity and devotion to one another despite separation by national borders, and historians should take seriously their desire to forge a common identity. When based on mere claims of shared cultural traits rather than interests, however, Latin Americans' actions were often not able to match their rhetoric.

This chapter finds both success and failure in about equal measure in Latin American racial thought and activism when trying to end U.S. military occupations in Haiti (1919–34) and in Cestero's own country, the Dominican Republic (1916–24). People of African heritage in both republics of Hispaniola were greatly affected by the landing of U.S. Marines, including tens of thousands who migrated from the West Indies. Their many grievances against the racism of U.S. occupiers translated into transnational political action through the United Negro Improvement Association (UNIA), European publics, and alliances with African Americans. Pan-Africanism was partly spurred by the occupations, and, though its role in actually *ending* occupations remained minimal, antiracism pointed to larger patterns of identity and transnational solidarity against empire that were the primary causes of withdrawal. This story of identity formation through imperialism, however, cannot be complete without examining the substantial limits and failures of pan-Africanism in Hispaniola, based partially on Dominicans' and Haitians' own racial ideas. Ethnic "oneness" was in no way as accepted by Latin American leaders as Cestero might have hoped. Even Cestero did not fully buy his own rhetoric.

This clear-eyed look at anti-imperialist solidarity at the apex of U.S. military power in the region may be most helpful as a comparison and contrast to the rest of this volume, where the focus lies almost entirely on the Cold War. We might assume too easily that racial solidarity with the rest of the developing world came naturally to Latin Americans or that anti-imperialism was always effective. Moreover, major political moments such as World War II and the Cuban Revolution caused major shifts in Latin America's shared identity, bringing about fundamental breaks with the more racist interwar years.

・・・・・・

This chapter's purpose is not to analyze the racism of empire, as scholars have covered the topic exhaustively. It is appropriate to remind ourselves, however, that pervading almost all interactions between occupiers and occupied was the marker of race.[2] The racism of U.S. occupiers toward Haitians is well known, but the occupiers were also nearly uniformly contemptuous of all nonwhite, non-Protestant, or non-English-speaking Latin Americans. Marines often called Dominicans "spigs" or "niggers," even more so in the east, where there was more mixed and African blood.[3] There were clear political implications in this racism. "The negro race," said John Russell, the head of the Haitian occupation, "will always require inspection by white men." "The only power the Haitian recognizes is force."[4]

Relations between men and women further heightened racial tensions. The Marines at first discouraged white U.S. wives from accompanying their husbands to Haiti in order to minimize opportunities for friction.[5] When wives were allowed in 1916, tensions arose, mostly at dances.[6] "When a Haitian gentleman asked an American woman to dance," reported the *New York Times*, "he usually was met with a polite excuse, only to see her a few minutes later dancing off with an American."[7] Marines also treated black women as either jezebels or mammies, lascivious or asexual. In Port-au-Prince, a city of 100,000, there were 147 registered saloons or dance halls, and prostitutes operated out of all of them.[8] Yet, as one Marine recalled decades later, the "thought of intermarriage" with Haitian women was "horrifying."[9]

In response to such pervasive racism, Haiti certainly presents a successful case of pushback—though one undercut by Haitians' other racial perceptions. Generally, investigator Carl Kelsey found that Haitians showed "no subserviency [sic] in their attitude toward the whites."[10] Haitians rarely fought back physically because military courts protected U.S. whites. Instead, they used their own courts in which judges and juries regularly sided with Haitians against whites.[11] In one typical case, a Haitian lawyer defended his client against an airtight case of theft by saying, "It is not the poor negro who is guilty . . . it is the white man. . . . But why, by an absurdity of the law, is it necessary that the American escape from Haitian [justice]?" After seventeen minutes of deliberation, the jury pronounced the defendant not guilty and the court broke out in applause.[12]

U.S. racism also helped change the way Haitians thought about race and their connections to other peoples of color. By the late 1920s, some Haitian intellectuals developed their own version of black empowerment. This flourished a few years later in France under the names *négritude* or *noirisme*, partly in response to what Dantès Bellegarde called the "white dictatorship."[13] The agenda of these intellectuals was primarily to recognize the positive contributions of Africa to Haitian culture, but some individuals also aimed to dehumanize whites. Émile Roumer, founder of one of the central vehicles of *noirisme*, *La Revue Indigène*, explained that "the racial principle of *l'Indigène* consisted in recognizing only two races: *homo sapiens* and the human excrement that is the WASP [White Anglo-Saxon Protestant]."[14]

Jean Price-Mars set the intellectual tone for the new generation in a more genteel fashion. The son of a deputy, a cousin of a former president, and himself a physician and former minister to Paris, Price-Mars was fully of the elite, except that he was "a pure black man" and seriously explored Haiti's racial identity.[15] In 1904 Price-Mars had visited the Centennial Exposition in St. Louis and been shocked by its primitivist treatment of Filipinos. He was also disgusted by segregation. Yet, he attended Booker T. Washington's Tuskegee Institute and showed interest in bringing its agricultural techniques to Haiti. Price-Mars returned to Haiti denigrating the superiority complex of mulattoes and other elites and preaching an embrace of the black peasantry and its practices such as farming and Vodou. His masterwork was *Ainsi parla l'oncle* (1928).[16]

Some of the new generation's concerns, coinciding with the rise of a transnational *noirisme*, were largely literary and consisted mostly of an effort to pull away from classical French influences.[17] For this reason, U.S. occupiers paid little mind to Price-Mars and his ilk; nor did they care about

Haitian art.[18] However, another purpose of *Ainsi parla l'oncle* and *La Revue Indigène* was to build up solidarity against occupation by reminding Haiti of its unique and meaningful blend of African and Western virtues.[19] Among the many new rebels of *noirisme* were well known anti-occupation activists Léon Laleau, Alfred Nemours, Ernest Chauvet, Georges Léger, and Clément Magloire.[20]

Haitians' growing identification with the African Diaspora led to meaningful transnational networks of solidarity against occupation. Among U.S. citizens, African Americans played a disproportionate role in transforming nation-based anti-occupation movements into transnational crusades. Haiti was a major concern for a diverse group of African American leaders, from Communists such as Cecil Briggs of the African Black Brotherhood to capitalists including the Tuskegee Institute's Robert Moton and feminists such as Addie Hunton. In 1919, Hunton founded the International Council of Women of the Darker Races (ICWDR) in order to investigate the lot of Haitian women and children. Those traveling, writing about, or otherwise defending Haiti were a veritable who's who of postwar black America. In 1919, Madam C. J. Walker allied with A. Philip Randolph to found the short-lived but important International League of the Darker Peoples to oppose the occupation. Margaret Murray Washington, the wife of Booker T., presided over the ICWDR. Visitors to the black republic included some of the brightest lights of the Harlem Renaissance and 1920s civil rights—Langston Hughes, Zora Neale Hurston, William Scott, and Arthur Spingarn. They linked the cause of Haitian independence to larger struggles for racial justice.[21]

James Blackwood wrote to the U.S. chief of the Haitian Gendarmerie to denounce its abuses in Haiti: "I am an American citizen, though of the colored race, which means that I am little, or not at all regarded at home; yet I cannot help to be loyal to the mother country [Haiti]."[22] Blackwood's letter demonstrated that, for African Americans, patriotism meant pressuring their nation to meet its own standards. The only African American working for the occupation in Haiti, Napoleon Marshall, became a critic of it and helped connect Haitians and U.S. citizens.[23] Back in the United States, 143 members of a Harlem church asked for the recall of the U.S. head of the occupation after reading an article in the *Courrier Haïtien*.[24] The African Episcopal Church in New York, under Haitian native Reverend John Hurst, also spoke out for the five hundred or so New Yorkers from Haiti.[25] Through much of the 1920s, Joseph Mirault, a Sleeping Car porter, wrote tirelessly to U.S. officials and prominent African Americans to promote the cause of a free Haiti.[26]

More than any other group, the National Association for the Advancement of Colored People (NAACP) contributed to making Haiti a pan-African cause for solidarity.[27] From 1915 on, the NAACP's co-founder, W. E. B. Du Bois, whose grandfather hailed from Haiti, editorialized against the occupation.[28] Du Bois urged President Woodrow Wilson to send African Americans instead of whites if an occupation had to occur and called on "we ten million Negroes" to write the president. In the following years, the NAACP denounced human rights violations in Haiti.[29] When three Haitian delegates presented a memoir to the U.S. government in 1921, Moorfield Storey, the NAACP's white former president and last president of the Anti-Imperialist League, was there and wrote to Secretary of State Charles Evans Hughes.[30] Haitian anti-imperialists also used the NAACP's New York office as their headquarters.[31] In 1923, Perceval Thoby and Georges Sylvain used their friendship with Spingarn, also of the NAACP, to seek justice when President Louis Borno persecuted editors.[32] By the mid-1920s, therefore, African Americans were deeply intertwined with anti-imperialism in the Caribbean—far more than whites.

The individual who most contributed to this solidarity was James Weldon Johnson, hired in 1916 as the NAACP's first black field secretary. With a great-grandmother from Haiti, facility in Spanish and French, formative days in France, and diplomatic experience in Venezuela and Nicaragua, Johnson felt a kinship to Latin America.[33] Like many African Americans, he originally thought that strategic interests justified the Haitian occupation. But the constitution of 1918 imposed on Haiti changed his mind. Johnson also wanted to enlarge the scope of the NAACP by making it more international, and Haiti served that very purpose.[34]

Johnson headed to Haiti in March 1920 and stayed for two months.[35] He talked to Marines—some of whom, while drunk, admitted to the worst abuses. He also met with the most prominent Haitian activists, which, in turn, prompted the rebirth of the Patriotic Union (UP). One Haitian later boasted that Johnson's resulting articles were "the almost literal translation" of the notes he gave the African American.[36] Johnson would stay in contact with Haitians, especially UP founder Georges Sylvain, and even helped create a U.S. branch of the UP in 1923.[37] Johnson's resulting exposés in *The Crisis* and *The Nation* and his speeches got the attention of the U.S. public.[38] He made arguments that shocked progressive consciences—namely, that economic interests had plotted the invasion of Haiti and that atrocities and racism ran rampant. Often explicit was a comparison to U.S. Southern traditions of underdevelopment, disfranchisement, and lynching.[39]

Johnson also did arguably more than anyone to insert Haiti into U.S. presidential politics. His trip to Haiti was partly motivated by politics since, as a member of the Republican National Advisory Committee, he asked for Theodore Roosevelt's advice before boarding his ship.[40] It is also likely that the Republican Party financed the trip in order to dig up a scandal against Democrats.[41] Additionally, the NAACP polled African Americans in 1920 on their concerns, and Haiti ranked number four. So, to cement the alliance between the GOP and blacks, Johnson set up a meeting with candidate Warren Harding on 9 August 1920 in Marion, Ohio. The meeting prompted the candidate to make a front-page speech on 28 August denouncing "the rape of Haiti and Santo Domingo" and forcing Democrats to respond.[42]

This pan-African effort also included a non-black entity, *The Nation* magazine. This anti-imperialist force since the War of 1898 played perhaps as weighty a role as Johnson and the NAACP, often in collaboration with them.[43] It was one of few U.S. publications, black or white, that spoke out against the Dominican intervention during World War I.[44] It also uniquely served to join together the resistance to both occupations by helping to found, along with Johnson and the UP, the Haiti-Santo Domingo Independence Society and house its headquarters in *The Nation*'s New York offices.[45] Following the Johnson articles, some Haitians founded *La Nation* in 1920, a newspaper that reproduced articles from the New York magazine.[46]

By as early as 1920, results of this solidarity began to show. Largely because of the work of Johnson and *The Nation*, the majority of U.S. publications swung from pro-occupation to anti-occupation.[47] Occupation officials stopped trusting visiting U.S. journalists and began spying on them.[48] The Marine Corps also began fearing a newfound spunk in the Haitian press, which they explained "partly as a reflection of race disturbances and agitation in the United States."[49] Such a comment was a testament to the effectiveness of the transnational pan-African solidarity stirred up by U.S. occupations in Hispaniola.

The problems and limitations encountered by this network, however, were as substantial as its achievements. Race proved as much of an anticoagulant as it was a glue for solidarity networks in the Caribbean and between the Caribbean and the United States.

The Dominican Republic largely stood in the way of a solidarity network in Hispaniola itself. Haiti's neighbor harbored few advocates of pan-Africanism. Most Dominicans who resisted the occupation in newspapers and politics were whites or mulattoes, and they identified with Europe rather than with the African Diaspora. Dominican elites did enlist a racial discourse in the cause of anti-imperialism, but, devastatingly for solidarity, it was in the service of persuading the U.S. invaders of their similarities instead of their differences. Dominicans' blood was mixed—their own 1920 census showed that half were mulatto, one quarter white, and the remaining quarter black.[50]

Elite Dominicans, disproportionately white, consequently used the trope of "civilization" to distinguish themselves from their neighbors and expressed shock at the possibility of being considered at the same level as Haitians. As U.S. troops first disembarked in Santo Domingo in 1916, four Dominicans explained to the U.S. minister that Dominicans were "not a semi-barbaric race needing to be civilized by canons."[51] One of the most persistent advocates for withdrawal, Tulio Cestero, wrote President Wilson that his country had fought a nineteenth-century war against Haiti for its independence "on behalf of the prevalence of the white race and with the same unswerving will they conserve religion, language, and the racial attributes bequeathed by the Spanish founders."[52] In 1921, another Dominican wondered why occupiers "treated us as though we were Negroes from the Congo."[53] He might as well have said "Haiti."

Haiti, meanwhile, had its own conflicted racial identity that acted against solidarity in that its color line was drawn even more sharply than in the Dominican Republic. There, racial difference coincided with class and culture. Occupiers were often perplexed by the differentiations Haitians made between mixed-race and African-phenotype Haitians, or, as Haitians said at the time, between "yellows" and "blacks." The so-called line was, in fact, more of a ladder with many confounding rungs as Haitians constructed a vast array of miscegenation formulas—4 for Indians, 10 for whites, and 14 for blacks.[54] Many African Americans who visited were shocked at the pervasiveness of inter-Haitian racism. "It was in Haiti that I first realized how class lines may cut across color lines within a race, and how dark people of the same nationality may scorn those below them," wrote Langston Hughes in his memoir. "I hated this attitude."[55] Educator Robert Moton and other African Americans came back from the black republic even saying "that the dividing line between mulattoes and negroes is more sharply drawn than between the whites and negroes in the south of the United States."[56] Because of mulatto-black relations, wrote former Haitian president Sténio Vincent, "too many Haitians became hypnotized by race and thus relegated the Nation to a secondary consideration."[57] Many others agreed that the color line undermined political stability, observing that mulatto-led governments tended to be thrown out by blacks and vice-versa.[58] U.S. occupiers did little to discourage this state of affairs. Some reinforced it by assuming that light-skinned Haitians were more competent and honest in government and appointed them disproportionately to positions of influence. President Sudre Dartiguenave, appointed by the Marines in 1915, was the first mulatto president since 1879, and three others followed.[59]

These ideological perceptions eventually scuttled some efforts to resist occupations via pan-African solidarity. In the early decades of the twentieth century, Marcus Garvey's United Negro Improvement Association (UNIA) ran successful chapters throughout the circum-Caribbean. In the Dominican Republic, however, U.S. and Dominican racism sealed its fate. The context lay in a labor dispute that predated occupation. Dominican political elites and U.S. occupiers both disliked Haitians and other black workers, yet sugar corporations needed the labor, and the occupation welcomed corporations as agents of globalized development. A legal tug of war thus ensued. In 1912, before the occupation, Santo Domingo required authorization to introduce non-Spanish-speaking workers into the country and declared Spanish the official language. In 1919, the occupation countered by giving the mostly dark-skinned *braceros* temporary residency, effectively nullifying the requirement for authorization and prompting migration around the southern Dominican town of San Pedro, where most sugar plantations were located. Since English-speaking blacks outnumbered Haitians there, it was a logical place for the establishment of one of the first UNIA chapters in the Caribbean in December 1919.[60] The San Pedro UNIA was a mutual aid society "for all Negroes irrespective of nationality." It took care of its ailing, buried its dead, and taught its illiterates.[61]

The occupation still shut it down, not because the UNIA opposed the occupation but rather because of accusations of Bolshevism and anti-white racism.[62] A white Episcopal minister, Archibald Beer, told occupation authorities, "The negroes are as jealous as can be of one another and continual trouble and contention arises." Accusing them of unspecified labor agitation, he also charged them, without a trace of irony, of "Klu [sic] Klux Klan methods."[63] In September 1921, the San Pedro police burst into UNIA headquarters, arrested its leaders, and deported them for "not observing an irreproachably moral and legal conduct according to law."[64]

In Haiti, the UNIA also made a brief appearance, but its solidarity activism there gained even less traction. There is mention of a UNIA-connected business established in the summer of 1920 but no record of its success.[65] For "Haitian Independence Day" on 26 October 1924, the elite's Georges Sylvain allied with the UNIA to parade banners marked "Down with the Occupation, Long live Haiti," "Long live the Negro Improvement Society," and "Long live Government of the People, by the People, and for the People." Occupation authorities reported that 90 percent of attendees were "of the lowest class" and that in Cap-Haïtien, a town of twenty thousand, only two hundred took part.[66] The crowds were exclusively black and urban, meaning that peasants, mulattoes, and the elite stayed away. In a sign of the continuing class- and culture-based divisions that plagued Haiti, a Cap paper, *Les Annales Capoises*, denigrated Garvey as a "workman who does not possess . . . that beautiful Latin culture, that civilization of which we are so proud and which distinguishes us from all the other Negroes in the world."[67]

The UNIA's failure in the so-called Black Republic reflected not only its color line but also Haitians' structural difficulties and poor strategic choices in finding common ground with others in the hemisphere. Despite their occupation lasting thirteen years longer than the Dominican one, Haitians enjoyed far fewer transnational connections. The UP, which Johnson inspired, devoted most of its energies to funding ineffectual trips for its delegates. From March to May 1921, Pauléus Sannon, Sténio Vincent, and Perceval Thoby were in the United States and presented the UP's report to the U.S. press, the Republican Party, the Department of State, and the Senate Foreign Relations Committee.[68] In August, Vincent returned to Washington to give a statement at Senate hearings.[69] The UP report was well argued and specific. Unlike Dominican reports, though, it advocated quick withdrawal and no U.S. supervision of a transition, indicating that Haitians accepted none of the reforms advocated by Washington.[70] The radical stance of the Haitian resistance earned it much less traction with U.S. audiences.[71]

A few years later, Dantès Bellegarde, twice Haitian delegate to the League of Nations in Geneva, had an equally frustrating experience. Since Haiti was nominally sovereign during the occupation, it carried on diplomacy but in a muted fashion. Bellegarde broke with the pattern by making passionate speeches in Europe, especially in 1924 and 1930, which drew more attention from Europe than any other Haitian action. President Borno recalled Bellegarde so as to silence him, but Bellegarde persisted.[72] In 1924, the League of Nations accredited him despite protests from his own government.[73] A speech in Lyon on 1 July to a pacifist organization garnered applause for "several minutes, punctuated by cries of 'Bravo!'" and, when he returned to Port-au-Prince, Bellegarde received more of the same.[74]

Haitian efforts, however, failed to obtain much from the international community. Woodrow Wilson himself admitted that he had occupied the republic partly because, in the rest of Latin America, Haitians, "being negroes[,] . . . are not regarded as of the fraternity!"[75] In the 1920s, Haitian anti-occupation activist Pierre Hudicourt went to the United States, Peru, Cuba, and to the Fifth Pan-American Conference in Chile, but was escorted out of the conference.[76] A lone State Department bureaucrat met with him, and, Hudicourt, wishing not to disappoint the UP, lied that the president and secretary of state had received him on his return home.[77] In Geneva, British delegates, with U.S. assistance, diluted a request for the immediate withdrawal of troops to instead simply reaffirm Haiti's nominal independence.[78] The Quai d'Orsay also refused to advocate for Haiti on the technicality that Haiti was independent and could fend for itself.[79] Perhaps for these reasons, Le Nouvelliste called Bellegarde's 1924 speech a "moral victory."[80] It was little else.

One of the reasons for Haitians' difficulty in raising support from abroad was the expense. The UP's major fundraising drive in 1920–21 raised less than ten thousand dollars.[81] Dominicans raised over ten times that in just one week.[82] In 1925, the UP began another subscription drive, but after several weeks the town of Jacmel had raised only $50, Aux Cayes $100, and a few other towns nothing at all.[83] Unlike Dominicans, Haitian diplomats abroad largely toed the line of occupied Port-au-Prince.[84] There was not yet much of a Haitian community in New York and even less of one in Florida. Even Paris was quiet, despite the prominent Haitians there. (Italy's invasion of Ethiopia in 1935 would more directly awaken French *négritude* intellectuals to anti-imperialism.[85]) Only The Nation's editor, Garrison Villard, made an effort to welcome the Haitians to the United States in 1921.[86] The *Courrier Haïtien* took notice of how the Dominicans were better organized with an "intelligent, tireless" network of solidarity active in Europe and the Americas.[87] The *Courrier*'s editor, Joseph Jolibois Fils, himself spent September 1927 to March 1930 touring Latin America, but encountered widespread indifference, some of which was based on language and race.[88] Costa Ricans said that "his color and his complete appearance are against him. . . . He speaks Spanish so brokenly as scarcely to be able to make himself understood. . . . Even those who know French in this country have difficulty in understanding him."[89] As a U.S. officer noted in 1922, in contrast to the Dominican Republic, "no criticism has been directed in Latin-America against the action of the United States Government in intervening in Haitian affairs."[90]

Latin American discrimination, to be sure, was also based on race. One particular incident is telling. Years after the occupation of his own country was over, Afro-Dominican rebel Gregorio Urbano Gilbert left his homeland to join the struggle of Augusto Sandino in Nicaragua. When Gilbert tried to board a vessel for Central America, none would take him because he was "colored." He finally found passage to Belize but jumped off the ship when it briefly stopped in Honduras. There he met Nicaraguan guides who, he said, treated him as an inferior, overcharged him, and tried to lose him in the woods. When he finally got to Sandino's camp, on 13 October 1928, he was called a "Haitian." In this case, racism backfired. While it may have discouraged Gilbert, it also kept him motivated to fight segregationist U.S. soldiers. Sandino's troops eventually accepted him as "the Dominican." Sandino even promoted him to captain within three weeks and made him his Dominican liaison.[91]

Even when not facing foreigners' racism, Haitians failed to find common cause with potential allies abroad. The color line they had drawn at home between "yellows" and "blacks" extended to all African Americans precisely because of their propensity to ignore color gradations when advocating social reforms. Haitian elites wanted little to do with cross-class efforts or sensibilities. When William Scott, an African American painter, visited in the 1920s, he was shocked that no Haitian painter had taken the rich natural beauty of the island as a subject. Haitian artists were instead stuck in a formalism inherited from premodern Europe and unable to appreciate abstraction or realism. In 1932, when a U.S. lieutenant named Perfield put on an exhibit of his own clearly reminiscent of the Ashcan School, Port-au-Prince newspapers derided it for portraying "the most villainous kind of Haitians, sometimes poor and sickly." President Borno, buckling under elite pressure, deported Perfield.[92]

The Haitian elite also negatively associated vocational training with African Americans, an antipathy most in evidence during the visit of the Moton Commission, which President Herbert Hoover sent to Haiti in mid-June 1930 to recommend changes to Haitian education. African Americans dominated the commission, starting with its head, Robert Moton.[93] In response to the announcement of the commission's coming, Raoul Lizaire, the Haitian chargé in Washington, feared that African Americans would recommend "a program of agricultural and vocational rather than cultural education."[94] The Moton Commission, which no Haitian took seriously, was to reform an area that no Haitian wanted reformed.

The commission went ahead with its work for twenty-four days in Haiti and gave its report to Hoover on 1 October 1930. It concluded that private, religious education was elitist and unsuited to the needs of the country. Yet it sympathized "with the Haitian view point concerning the charge that the

[U.S.-dominated educational] service is over-staffed and extravagant." The report's sixty-one recommendations advocated a third way—namely, public education for all, with a centralized system, higher salaries, more farm and educational programs, a national university and library, foreign study, Haitian rather than U.S. administrators, and more.[95] The Department of State said the report was badly informed and made no announcement to the public when it was published in April 1931. No recommendation saw the light of day.[96] No Haitian protested.

These internal and external challenges to establishing pan-Africanism in Hispaniola during times of occupation resulted clearly in the prolongation of the occupations, especially in Haiti. The main reason why the Dominicans moved toward independence in 1922 while the Haitians did not until the early 1930s was the judgment by U.S. policymakers and observers that Haitians were unprepared for self-government, primarily because of their race. In typical remarks, the Latin-American Division urged the Department of State "to distinguish at once between the Dominicans and the Haitians. The former, while in many ways not advanced far enough on the average to permit the highest type of self-government, yet have a preponderance of white blood and culture. The Haitians on the other hand are negro for the most part, and, barring a very few highly educated politicians, are almost in a state of savagery and complete ignorance. The two situations thus demand different treatment."[97]

A U.S. Senate committee agreed that "early withdrawal of or drastic reduction in the American marine occupation force in Haiti would be followed certainly by brigandage and revolution."[98] A half-decade later, at a Pan-American conference in Havana attended by Charles Evans Hughes, the U.S. secretary of state faced a barrage of criticism from Latin American delegates for the U.S. practice of occupation. This disapproval, however, was directed primarily toward the ongoing occupation in Nicaragua, not the then thirteen-year-old one in Haiti. The secretary seemed to sense that Latin Americans' racism compelled them to agree on the degenerate nature of Haitian politics and, therefore, with the occupation. "We would leave Haiti," he promised them, "at any time that we had reasonable expectations of stability, and could be assured that withdrawal would not be the occasion for a recurrence of bloodshed."[99] By 1935, a year after the Haitian withdrawal, even the NAACP criticized openly Haitians for their lack of civic freedoms. Haitian elites shot back that "here no one any longer bothers about" jailed journalists and accused African Americans of being manipulated by Haitian Communists.[100] In 1942, Howard University historian Rayford Logan visited Haiti for the second time since 1934 and noted a growing disenchantment with democracy. "I was especially struck," wrote Logan, "by the frequency with which I heard the statement: 'What Haiti needs is a dictator like [Dominican Rafael] Trujillo.'"[101]

Yet despite these very real impediments to pan-Africanism in Hispaniola, we should not forget nor minimize the meaningful efforts to forge and spread a pan-African identity among those who resisted occupation, and the substantial—if indirect—results of those efforts. Scholars such as Robin Kelley, Penny Von Eschen, Andrew Zimmerman, and Michael Goebel have been exploring the many connections that African Americans, Africans, and Europeans nurtured in the first half of the twentieth century, and how those connections impacted U.S. and other imperialist interests in the Americas.[102] They have demonstrated that pan-Africanism, first, was a unique literary movement, and, second, that its waves built upon one another—weak during World War I but growing mightier in the interwar years. This resulted in a multivocal, multidirectional set of networks that deeply impacted the politics and culture of the Atlantic world. The French intellectuals who developed *négritude* into a full intellectual movement in the 1930s, for instance, owed a debt to the Haitians of the previous decade.

The Haitian occupation, especially, might have continued for another generation had African Americans and pan-Africanist Haitians not combined their energies to pressure Washington to end its foolish adventure. When major events such as World War II and the Cuban Revolution further questioned the traditional racism of Latin American elites in the Caribbean and the rest of Latin America, racial solidarity advocates could have pointed to the interwar years of occupation for examples to emulate as well as to avoid.

Notes

1. My translation. "Palabras pronunciadas por Tulio M. Cestero el 5 de julio en Nueva York," *Letras*, 11 August 1918, 7, Archivo General de la Nación (hereafter AGN), Santo Domingo, Dominican Republic.

2. Historians have noted how anti-imperialism has long had a racial and ethnic component. See, for instance, Thomas Miller Klubock, "Nationalism, Race, and the Politics of Imperialism: Workers and North American Capital in the Chilean Copper Industry," in *Reclaiming the Political in Latin American History: Essays from the North*, ed. Gilbert M. Joseph, (Durham, NC: Duke University Press, 2001), 232.

3. Bruce J. Calder, "Caudillos and *Gavilleros* versus the United States Marines: Guerrilla Insurgency during the Dominican Intervention, 1916–1924," *Hispanic American Historical Review* 58, no. 4 (1978): 664.

4. Russell, memo to Forbes, Port-au-Prince, 13 March 1930, Folder Russell, John H., 13-14 March 1930, Box 1073, President's Commission for Study & Review of Conditions in Haiti, Herbert Hoover Library, West Branch, Iowa.

5. Randolph Coyle, United States Marine Corps (hereafter USMC), "Service in Haiti," *Marine Corps Gazette,* December 1916, 343; Dana G. Munro, *Intervention and Dollar Diplomacy in the Caribbean 1900-1921* (Princeton, NJ: Princeton University Press, 1964), 358-59.

6. Hans Schmidt, *The United States Occupation of Haiti, 1915-1934* [1971], repr. with a foreword by Stephen Solarz (New Brunswick, NJ: Rutgers University Press, 1995), 136.

7. Harold N. Denny, "Haiti—A Problem Unsolved. IV. Heredity that Hampers Agreement," *New York Times,* 2 July 1931; Dossier 14, Haiti, Amérique 1918-1940, Correspondance Politique et Commerciale 1914-1940, Archives Diplomatiques, Ministère des Affaires Étrangères, Paris, France.

8. Emily G. Balch, ed. *Occupied Haiti* [1927] (New York: Garland, 1972), 119.

9. Brig. Gen. Ivan W. Miller, USMC, oral history, by Thomas E. Donnelly, 10 December 1970, 24, Marine Corps Audiovisual Research Archives, Marine Corps Base, Quantico, Virginia.

10. Carl Kelsey, "The American Intervention in Haiti and the Dominican Republic," *Annals of the American Academy of Political and Social Science* 100 (March 1922): 123-24.

11. Alan McPherson, "The Irony of Legal Pluralism in U.S. Occupations," *American Historical Review* 117, no. 4 (2012): 1149-72.

12. [Shepard?], Intelligence Report, Cap-Haïtien, 22 July 1926, Folder Intelligence Reports Nord 2 of 2, Box 1, Intelligence Reports from the Department of the North, 1926-27, Record Group 127 (hereafter RG 127), U.S. National Archives and Records Administration, Washington, D.C. (hereafter NARA I).

13. My translation. Dantès Bellegarde, *L'occupation américaine d'Haïti: ses conséquences morales et économiques* (Port-au-Prince: Chéraquit, 1929), 20.

14. My translation. Roumer cited in Michel J. Fabre, "La *Revue Indigène* et le mouvement nouveau noir," *Revue de littérature comparée* 1 (January-March 1977): 32.

15. Magowan, Memo to Henderson, 5 May 1931, File A2898, Reference 15093, Foreign Office 371, Public Record Office, Kew, UK.

16. Magdaline W. Shannon, *Jean Price-Mars, the Haitian Elite and the American Occupation, 1915-1935* (New York: St. Martin's Press, 1996), 27, 7-20; Roger Gaillard, *Les blancs débarquent,* vol. 4, *La République autoritaire, 1916-1917* (n.p., 1981), 220; Jean Price-Mars, *Une étape de l'évolution haïtienne* (Port-au-Prince: La Presse, n. d.).

17. David Nicholls, "Ideology and Political Protest in Haiti, 1930-1946," *Journal of Contemporary History* 9, no. 4 (October 1974): 3-26; Michel-Philippe Lerebours, "The Indigenist Revolt: Haitian Art, 1927-1944," *Callaloo* 15, no. 3 (1992): 711-25; Matthew J. Smith, "Shades of Red in a Black Republic: Radicalism, Black Consciousness, and Social Conflict in Postoccupation Haiti, 1934-1957," PhD diss., University of Florida, 2002, 24-25.

18. Shannon, *Jean Price-Mars,* 71.

19. Nicholls, "Ideology."

20. Georges Corvington, *Port-au-Prince au cours des ans*, vol. 5, *La capitale d'Haïti sous l'occupation, 1915-1922* (Port-au-Prince: Henri Deschamps, 1984), 220.

21. Anne R. Winkler-Morey, "Good Neighbors: Popular Internationalists and United States' Relations with Mexico and the Caribbean Region (1918-1929)," PhD diss., University of Minnesota, 2001, 87-103; Emily S. Rosenberg, *Financial Missionaries to the World: The Politics and Culture of Dollar Diplomacy 1900-1950* (Durham, NC: Duke University Press, 2003), 127; Lerebours, "Indigenist Revolt," 713-14.

22. Blackwood, letter to Wise, Port au Prince, 22 September 1919, Folder Complaints from Citizens (1918-19), 1 of 3, Box 1, General Correspondence of Headquarters, Gendarmerie d'Haiti 1916-1919, RG 127, NARA I.

23. Munro, memo to White, Washington, 19 April 1929, 838.00/2523, Central Decimal Files Relating to Internal Affairs of Haiti, 1910-1929, RG59, National Archives and Record Administration, College Park, MD (hereafter NARA II); Rosenberg, *Financial Missionaries*, 127.

24. Lawson, Petition to Coolidge, New York, 14 December 1925, 838.00/2178, Central Decimal Files Relating to Internal Affairs of Haiti, 1910-1929, RG 59, NARA II.

25. "Bishop Hurst Calls for Haitian Inquiry," *New York Times*, 10 November 1920, 3.

26. Munro, memo to White, 19 May 1924, 838.00/2024, Central Decimal Files Relating to Internal Affairs of Haiti, 1910-1929, RG 59, NARA II.

27. The NAACP did not completely ignore the Dominican Republic. It prepared a full day of activities on its behalf for its August 1922 convention in New York City; Robison, memo to Department of Foreign Relations, Santo Domingo, 25 May 1922, Legajo 120, 1920-1922, Fondo Gobierno Militar, AGN.

28. W. E. B. DuBois, "Hayti," *The Crisis* 10, no. 6 (1915): 291.

29. DuBois, "Hayti," 291; *Le Nouvelliste*, 20 October 1915, cited in Roger Gaillard, *Les blancs débarquent*, vol. 3, *Premier écrasement du cacoïsme: 1915* (n.p., 1981), 153; Leon D. Pamphile, *Haitians and African Americans: A Heritage of Tragedy and Hope* (Gainesville: University Press of Florida, 2001), 104, 122. One such letter was Williams, telegram to Wilson, Cincinnati, 8 February 1916, 711.38/66, U.S.-Central Decimal Files Relating to Internal Affairs of Haiti, 1910-1929, RG 59, NARA II.

30. Storey, letter to Hughes, Boston, 6 June 1921, 838.00/1780, Central Decimal Files Relating to Internal Affairs of Haiti, 1910-1929, RG 59, NARA II; Robert D. Johnson, *Ernest Gruening and the American Dissenting Tradition* (Cambridge, MA: Harvard University Press, 1998), 37.

31. Brenda G. Plummer, "The Afro-American Response to the Occupation of Haiti, 1915-1934," *Phylon* 43, no. 2 (June 1982): 139.

32. Arthur Spingarn, "Under American Rule in Haiti," *The World*, 7 February 1925. A similar case was that of Jolibois Fils: Thoby, letter to Spingarn, Port-au-Prince, 1 May 1923, Folder Thoby, Perceval (On Haiti) 1923-27; Sylvain, letters to Spingarn, Port-au-Prince, 30 May and 12 June 1923, Folder Sylvain, Georges (On Haiti) 1923-24, and undated; Thoby, letter to Spingarn, Port-au-Prince, 4 July 1923, Folder Thoby, Perceval (On Haiti) 1923-27, all in Box 4, Papers of Arthur B. Spingarn, 1850-1968, Manuscripts Division, Library of Congress, Washington, D.C.

33. James W. Johnson, *Along This Way: The Autobiography of James Weldon Johnson* [1933] (New York: Da Capo Press, 2000).

34. Eugene Levy, *James Weldon Johnson: Black Leader, Black Voice* (Chicago: University of Chicago Press, 1973), 202–3.

35. Biographers disagree on the point; see Levy, *Johnson*, 204; Pamphile, *Haitians and African Americans*, 109. But Johnson himself said he was in Haiti from 21 March to 21 or 22 May 1920, in U.S. Congress, Senate, *Hearings before a Select Committee on Haiti and Santo Domingo*, 67th Congress, 1st and 2nd sessions, 1921 (Washington: U.S. Government Printing Office, 1922), 1:779.

36. My translation. B. Danache, *Le président Dartiguenave et les Américains*, 2nd ed. (Port-au-Prince: Les Editions Fardin, 1984), 9.

37. Leon D. Pamphile, "The NAACP and the American Occupation of Haiti," *Phylon* 47, no. 1 (1986): 118; Plummer, "The Afro-American Response," 132.

38. James W. Johnson, "The Truth about Haiti: An N.A.A.C.P. Investigation." *The Crisis*, September 1920, 217–24; James W. Johnson, "Self-Determining Haiti II: What the United States Has Accomplished," *The Nation*, 4 September 1920, 265–67.

39. Johnson, "Haiti and Our Latin-American Policy," speech delivered at the "World Tomorrow Dinner," New York City, 31 March 1924, in *In Search of Democracy: The NAACP Writings of James Weldon Johnson, Walter White, and Roy Wilkins, 1920–1977*, ed. Sondra Kathryn Wilson (New York: Oxford University Press, 1999), 113.

40. Plummer, "The Afro-American Response," 132.

41. Levy, *James Weldon Johnson*, 203.

42. Harding cited in Lars Schoultz, *Beneath the United States: A History of U.S. Policy toward Latin America* (Cambridge, MA: Harvard University Press, 1998), 255; Pamphile, "NAACP," 94, 113–14; Richard B. Sherman, "The Harding Administration and the Negro: An Opportunity Lost," *Journal of Negro History* 49, no. 3 (1964): 156; Kenneth J. Grieb, *The Latin American Policy of Warren G. Harding* (Fort Worth: Texas Christian University Press, 1976), 2.

43. Rosenberg, *Financial Missionaries*, 124.

44. Joseph R. Juarez, "United States Withdrawal from Santo Domingo." *Hispanic American Historical Review* 42, no. 2 (1962): 153.

45. Robert Debs Heinl Jr. and Nancy Gordon Heinl, *Written in Blood: The Story of the Haitian People 1492–1971* (Boston: Houghton Mifflin, 1978), 469; Grieb, *Harding*, 69.

46. Entry for 27 November 1920, Russell, USMC, daily diary report, 29 November 1920, 838.00/1725, Central Decimal Files Relating to Internal Affairs of Haiti, 1910–1929, RG 59, NARA II.

47. John W. Blassingame, "The Press and American Intervention in Haiti and the Dominican Republic, 1904–1920," *Caribbean Studies* 9, no. 2 (1969): 42.

48. Williams, letter to Snowden, Santiago, 17 December 1920, Folder 4, Admiral Snowden Personal File, Box 30, Military Government of Santo Domingo, Record Group 38, NARA I.

49. Unsigned memo, Washington, DC, 24 June 1921, Folder Haiti opns Reports, Intelligence Summaries (1920–21), Box 3, General Correspondence, 1907–1936, RG 127, NARA I.

50. Bruce J. Calder, *The Impact of Intervention: The Dominican Republic during the U.S. Occupation of 1916–1924* (Austin: University of Texas Press, 1984), xxvii.

51. My translation. Vicente Galván, Conrado Sánchez, Manuel A. Patin Maceo, and Lirio H. Galván, "Al Señor Ministro Americano," in *Vetilio Alfau Durán en Anales: escritos y documentos*, ed. Arístides Incháustegui and Blanca Delgado Malagón (Santo Domingo: Banco de Reservas, 1997), 544–46.

52. Cestero, letter to Wilson, Washington, 1 April 1920, Legajo Papeles 1919–1920, Tomo 1, Archivo de Tulio Cestero, Fondo Antiguo, Universidad Autónoma de Santo Domingo, Santo Domingo, Dominican Republic.

53. Statement of Perez, U.S. Senate, *Hearings before a Select Committee on Haiti and Santo Domingo*, 2:967. See also Fabio Fiallo et al., "A los extranjeros residents en el territorio nacional," Santo Domingo, 19 June 1921, in *Vetilio Alfau Durán en Anales: Escritos y documentos*, ed. Arístides Incháustegui and Blanca Delgado Malagón (Santo Domingo: Banco de Reservas, 1997), 609.

54. Sténio Vincent, *En posant les jalons . . .* Tome 1 (Port-au-Prince: Imprimerie de L'État, 1939), 21–23.

55. Langston Hughes, *The Collected Works of Langston Hughes*, vol. 13, *Autobiography: I Wonder as I Wander*, ed. Joseph McClaren (Columbia: University of Missouri Press, 2003), 59, 61.

56. Phillips, letter to McCormick, Washington, 13 July 1923, 838.00/1950, Central Decimal Files Relating to Internal Affairs of Haiti, 1910–1929, RG 59, NARA II.

57. My translation. Vincent, *En posant*, 152, 153.

58. "La question de couleurs," wrote Danache, "c'est la seule qui nous émeuve véritablement et qui soit capable de nous porter aux injustices les plus criantes, aux pires extrémités" (*Le président*, 20); Brig. Gen. Lester A. Dessez, USMC oral history, by Thomas E. Donnelly, 16 June 1970, 94, Marine Corps Audiovisual Research Archives, Marine Corps Base, Quantico, Virginia.

59. James G. Leyburn, *The Haitian People* [1941] (New Haven, CT: Yale University Press 1966, 1941), ix.

60. Humberto García Muñiz and Jorge Giovannetti, "Garveyismo y racismo en el Caribe: El caso de la población cocola en la República Dominicana," *Clío* (Dominican Republic) 168 (July–December 2004): 127–34.

61. Van Putten, letter to Secretary of Interior and Police, San Pedro de Macorís, 23 December 1919, Legajo 43, 1919, Fondo Secretaría de Estado de Interior y Policía, AGN.

62. Hennessy, letter to Secretary of Interior and Police, San Pedro de Macorís, 6 February 1921, Legajo 405, 1921, Fondo Secretaría de Estado de Interior y Policía, AGN.

63. Beer, letter to Moses, San Pedro de Macorís, 13 September 1921, Legajo 420, 1921, Fondo Secretaría de Estado de Interior y Policía, AGN.

64. My translation. Warfield, memo to the Departement of Foreign Relations, 28 April 1922, Legajo 90, 1922, Fondo Secretaría de Estado de Interior y Policía, AGN; Fuller, letter to Van Putten, Santo Domingo, 27 December 1919, Legajo 43, 1919, Fondo Secretaría de Estado de Interior y Policía, AGN; De Jesús Lluveres, memo to Peguero, San Pedro, 24 January 1922, Legajo 90, 1922, Fondo Secretaría de Estado

de Interior y Policía, AGN; Military Governor, memo to the Department of the Interior and Police, 22 March 1922, Legajo 90, 1922, Fondo Secretaría de Estado de Interior y Policía, AGN.

65. Russell, daily diary report, 12 July 1920, 838.00/1651, Central Decimal Files Relating to Internal Affairs of Haiti, 1910-1929, RG 59, NARA II.

66. My translation. Russell, letter to Hughes, 31 October 1924, 838.00/2049, Central Decimal Files Relating to Internal Affairs of Haiti, 1910-1929, RG 59, NARA II; Scott, letter to Kellogg, 27 October 1925, 838.00/2165, Central Decimal Files Relating to Internal Affairs of Haiti, 1910-1929, RG 59, NARA II; Brenda G. Plummer, *Haiti and the United States: The Psychological Moment* (Athens: University of Georgia Press, 1992), 123; Russell, letter to Hughes, 11 November 1924, 838.00/2051, Central Decimal Files Relating to Internal Affairs of Haiti, 1910-1929, RG 59, NARA II.

67. *Les Annales Capoises*, 30 October 1924, cited in Pamphile, *Haitians and African Americans*, 132.

68. Agel, letter to Minister of Foreign Affairs, Port-au-Prince, 15 March 1921, Dossier 4, Haiti, Amérique 1918-1940, Correspondance Politique et Commerciale 1914-1940, Archives Diplomatiques, Ministère des Affaires Étrangères, Paris, France; Sannon, Vincent, and Thoby, letter to Hughes, Secretary of State, New York, 13 April 1921, 838.00/1765, Central Decimal Files Relating to Internal Affairs of Haiti, 1910-1929, RG 59, NARA II; Pamphile, "NAACP": 96-97.

69. U.S. Senate, *Hearings before a Select Committee on Haiti and Santo Domingo*, 1:3-4.

70. A summary is in "Haitian Delegates Want Us to Get Out," *New York Times*, 9 May 1921, 17.

71. Welles, letter to Schoenrich, 16 April 1921, Folder Haiti 1920-1922, Box 178, Sumner Welles Papers, Franklin D. Roosevelt Library, Hyde Park, New York.

72. Mercer Cook, "Dantes Bellegarde," *Phylon* 1, no. 2 (1940): 132, 130. See also Interview with Bellegarde, "Latin America Against the Hegemony of the United States," *Le Temps* (Port-au-Prince), 20-21 September 1927, in Russell, Letter to Secretary of State, 27 October 1927, 838.00/2412, Central Decimal Files Relating to Internal Affairs of Haiti, 1910-1929, RG 59, NARA II.

73. Cook, "Dantes Bellegarde," 130.

74. "Defends Our Haiti Action," *New York Times*, 3 July 1924, 17; Russell, letter to Hughes, Secretary of State, 1 October 1924, 838.00/2040, Central Decimal Files Relating to Internal Affairs of Haiti, 1910-1929, RG 59, NARA II.

75. Cited in Munro, *Intervention*, 54.

76. D'Arcy M. Brissman, "Interpreting American Hegemony: Civil Military Relations during the United States Marine Corps' Occupation of Haiti, 1915-1934," PhD diss., Duke University, 2001, 293.

77. Hudicourt, letter to Coolidge, Washington, 21 May 1925, 838.00/2119, Central Decimal Files Relating to Internal Affairs of Haiti, 1910-1929, RG 59, NARA II; Hudicourt, letter to Kellogg, Secretary of State, Washington, 21 May 1925, 838.00/2114, Central Decimal Files Relating to Internal Affairs of Haiti, 1910-1929, RG 59, NARA II; Russell, letter to Kellogg, Secretary of State, 20 June 1925, 838.00/2131, Central Decimal Files Relating to Internal Affairs of Haiti, 1910-1929,

RG 59, NARA II; Merrell, letter to Kellogg, Secretary of State, 18 July 1925, 838.00/2143, Central Decimal Files Relating to Internal Affairs of Haiti, 1910–1929, RG 59, NARA II.

78. "La République de Haiti demande à être libérée des troupes américaines," *Le Nouvelliste*, 24 July 1924, and "Une grande victoire morale—détails sur l'action de Bellegarde," *Le Nouvelliste*, 29 July 1924, both in Folder Newspaper Clippings (1–28Jul24), Box 3, Records of the First Provisional Brigade in Haiti, 1915–1934, RG 127, NARA I.

79. "Rejects Plea for Haiti," *New York Times*, 25 March 1925, 33.

80. "Une grande victoire morale."

81. Corvington, *Port-au-Prince au cours des ans*, 213.

82. Welles, memo to Hughes, Secretary of State, Washington, 24 March 1921, 838.00/1833, Central Decimal Files Relating to Internal Affairs of Haiti, 1910–1929, RG 59, NARA II.

83. Russell, letter to Kellogg, Secretary of State, Port-au-Prince, 13 November 1925, 838.00/2169, Central Decimal Files Relating to Internal Affairs of Haiti, 1910–1929, RG 59, NARA II; biography of Thoby, unsigned and undated, 838.00/2585, Central Decimal Files Relating to Internal Affairs of Haiti, 1910–1929, RG 59, NARA II.

84. There was one possible exception: Abel Théard, the chargé in London. See Delage, letter to Minister of Foreign Affairs, Port-au-Prince, 20 September 1919, Dossier 9, Haiti, Amérique 1918–1940, Correspondance Politique et Commerciale 1914–1940, Archives Diplomatiques, Ministère des Affaires Étrangères, Paris, France.

85. Michael Goebel, *Anti-Imperial Metropolis: Interwar Paris and the Seeds of Third World Nationalism* (Cambridge: Cambridge University Press, 2015), 171.

86. Corvington, *Port-au-Prince au cours des ans*, 214.

87. My translation. "La leçon d'un échec," *Le Courrier Haïtien*, July 1924, in Folder Newspaper Clippings (1–28Jul24), Box 3, Records of the First Provisional Brigade in Haiti, 1915–1934, RG 127, NARA I.

88. For more, see Alan McPherson, "Joseph Jolibois Fils and the Flaws of Haitian Resistance to U.S. Occupation," *Journal of Haitian Studies* 16, no. 2 (2010): 120–47.

89. Cohen, G-2 report, 11 October 1928, 838.00/2489, Central Decimal Files Relating to Internal Affairs of Haiti, 1910–1929, RG 59, NARA II.

90. Welles, memo, [13 February?] 1922, 838.00/1845, Central Decimal Files Relating to Internal Affairs of Haiti, 1910–1929, RG 59, NARA II.

91. My translation. Gregorio Urbano Gilbert, *Junto a Sandino* (Santo Domingo: Universidad Autónoma de Santo Domingo, [1979?]), *passim* 17–43, 269–73. Sandino, pronouncement, El Chipotón, 5 November 1928, and Sandino, credential, El Chipotón, 13 February 1930, both in E-001, C-002, 000070, Collección ACS (Augusto César Sandino), Centro de Historia Militar, Managua, Nicaragua.

92. Lerebours, "Indigenist Revolt," 713–14.

93. Apart from Moton, the commissioners were Dr. Mordecai W. Johnson, President of Howard University; Professor Le M. Favrot, Field Agent of the General Education Board; B. F. Hubert, President of the Georgia State Industrial College, and

Dr. W. T. B. Williams, Dean of the College at Tuskegee and Field Agent of the Jeanes and Slater Boards. Five others accompanied the party. Among the commissioners only Favrot was white. R. R. Moton letter to Hoover, 20 February 1930, Folder Countries—Haiti Haitian Commission, Moton Commission, Box 989, Presidential Papers, Herbert Hoover Library, West Branch, Iowa.

94. Cited in Pamphile, *Haitians and African Americans*, 124.

95. "Digest of the Report of the United States Commission on Education in Haiti, by G. Lake Imes, Secretary of the Commission," Department of State, press release, 29 November 1930, Folder Report of Investigation 10 March 1919–13 March 20, Haiti, Geographical Files, Reference Branch, Marine Corps History Division, Marine Corps Base, Quantico, Virginia.

96. Munro, telegram to Secretary of State, Port-au-Prince, 13 December 1930, Folder Munro, Dana G. 1929–30, Box 8, Francis White Papers, Herbert Hoover Library, West Branch, Iowa; Shannon, *Jean Price-Mars*, 94–95.

97. Mayer, letter to Hughes, 30 July 1921, 839.00/2451, Central Decimal Files Relating to Internal Affairs of the Dominican Republic, 1910–1929, RG 59, NARA II.

98. Cited in "Urges Maintaining Our Troops in Haiti," *New York Times*, 27 June 1922.

99. Hughes cited in Donald B. Cooper, "The Withdrawal of the United States from Haiti, 1928–1934," *Journal of Inter-American Studies* 5, no. 1 (1963): 86.

100. "Haitians Protest N.A.A.C.P. Resolution." *The Crisis*, October 1935, 298.

101. Rayford Logan et al., "The Contributions of Negroes in the Dominican Republic, Haiti, and Cuba to Hemispheric Solidarity as Conditioned by the Agrarian Problems in Each," 1942, Folder 16, Box 166-37, Rayford D. Logan Papers, Moorland-Spingarn Research Center, Howard University, Washington, D.C.

102. Robin D. G. Kelley, *Freedom Dreams: The Black Radical Imagination* (Boston: Beacon Press, 2003); Penny Von Eschen, *Race Against Empire:* (Ithaca, NY: Cornell University Press 1997); Andrew Zimmerman, *Alabama in Africa: Booker T. Washington, the German Empire, & the Globalization of the New South* (Princeton, NJ: Princeton University Press, 2010); Michael Goebel, *Anti-Imperial Metropolis: Interwar Paris and the Seeds of Third World Nationalism* (Cambridge: Cambridge University Press, 2015).

9 Latin American *Tercermundistas* in the Soviet Union

Paradise Lost and Found

TOBIAS RUPPRECHT

It was midnight when the Peruvian journalist and self-professed *poeta del pueblo* Gustavo Valcárcel entered his Moscow hotel room in the autumn of 1963. As the hotel music system started playing "The Internationale," he stepped on the balcony, looked upon "the capital of world socialism, illuminated by lights and the future" and was overwhelmed with emotion. Bathed in tears, Valcárcel shared this epiphany with his wife: "With one of the many hammers and sickles with which the firmament is studded, I have engraved a letter: Violeta, we have not fought in vain! I have seen the accomplished reality of all our dreams!" Back in his room, he wrote—on paper—several emphatic poems about the USSR and the future of a socialist Latin America that would emulate the Soviet example. Upon his return to Peru, Valcárcel extolled the superiority of the Soviet model of modern society in successive publications throughout the 1960s. The apparent feats of this socialist utopia included its state-led economic and technological development, its free education and health care systems, women's rights, family values, architecture, and "progressive" arts. For his homeland to prosper, Valcárcel, in a chapter titled "Kasajstan: Un ejemplo para América Latina,"[1] suggested necessary reforms that would take their cue from Soviet Central Asia.

Not only in Peru, but all over Latin America, the ideological conflict between the United States and the Soviet Union was reflected in intellectual debates over how to organize modern societies. Most traditional Latin American elites continued to perceive Communism as a serious threat to the political, ethical, and cultural foundations of their societies. For many intellectuals, however, Marxism in the 1950s still constituted a valid model for understanding the continent's many problems. The increasing feeling of insurmountable backwardness and old resentments against the "Yankees" in the North led many to develop an anti-imperialist identification with (post-)colonial nations and socialist movements in Asia and Africa. The 1960s came to be the decade of *tercermundismo* (Third-Worldism) in Latin America. *Tercermundistas* all over the Americas reached out to like-minded fellows of the Global South, who had formed the loose Non-Aligned Movement in the wake of the 1955 Afro-Asian conference in Bandung. The struggle of nationalists in Algeria and Indochina radicalized leftists all over the Americas, and some of them eventually took up arms against the governments of their respective states.

It is usually assumed that this generation of Latin American intellectuals and political activists had lost all interest in the motherland of state socialism, the Soviet Union. According to Jorge Castañeda, it seemed too bureaucratic to them, too repressive, too grey, and, in the light of its invasions of Hungary in 1956 and Czechoslovakia in 1968, it appeared as one more northern imperialist power.[2] "I put them all in the same bag," Andre Gunder Frank recalled in his memoirs about Soviet and Western development models.[3] This chapter, based on an analysis of Latin American travelogues and Soviet memoirs, will show that this generalization reflects a zeitgeist of the 1990s rather than the views of many Latin Americans during the Cold War.

Current scholarship on Latin American intellectuals during the Cold War is certainly correct in its claim that after the Cuban Revolution Havana became a more important point of reference than Moscow. And the revolutionary Left did find fault with the cautious Soviet concept of peaceful coexistence.[4] But travel reports of *tercermundistas* who visited the USSR from the 1950s to the 1970s do not support the view that "Latin American intellectuals had lost all interest in the Soviet Union by the early 1960s."[5] This chapter will demonstrate that Latin Americans who developed an anti-Western sense of belonging with the Third World in the 1960s were still susceptible to the lure of certain features of the Soviet state and could even advocate the implementation of these policies in their home countries. Accounts of the history of the Cold War in Latin America, it will be argued, have too readily put aside the Soviet Union, as a political and intellectual point of reference.[6] A look at non-Western historical sources on encounters between the Second World and the Third World from the 1940s to the 1980s supports this view and helps to avoid an anachronistic retroprojection of the failure of state socialism. In the process, it may also contribute to understanding the contemporary perception by intellectuals worldwide of this alternative path to modern society.

Paradise Lost? The Latin American Intelligentsia and Stalinist Socialism

From early on, the Soviet Union had fascinated the Latin American intelligentsia. Communist parties in most Latin American countries were founded and dominated by poets and artists. Yet only a few of them had the chance to see the first socialist state with their own eyes before Stalin's death. The Mexican muralist painters Diego Rivera and David Siqueiros had made short visits in 1927. Others, mostly Mexicans and Brazilians, went in the course of the 1930s.[7] They were very much part of a community of Western "fellow travelers"[8] to the Soviet Union, and, like many Europeans, most of them hailed Stalin and his ostensible achievements. The Mexican novelist José Revueltas proclaimed after a 1935 trip to a Comintern congress: "I adore Stalin more than anything else on earth." His compatriots Vicente Toledano, Víctor Manuel Villaseñor, José Muñoz Cota, and José Mancisidor labeled their pilgrimages to Stalinist Moscow "travels to the future of the world." Octavio Paz, later an ardent critic of totalitarianism, wrote letters full of admiration for the Soviet project. And Siqueiros was even involved in one of the attempts on the life of Stalin's arch enemy, Leon Trotsky, in Mexico City in 1940.[9]

During the early Cold War, many Latin American leftist intellectuals maintained their admiration for the dictator and his realm. The Argentine novelist and journalist Alfredo Varela wrote a four-hundred-page ode on the Soviet Union after his 1948 trip, praising Stalin as "the greatest man of our epoch."[10] The Chilean poet Pablo Neruda made his first trip to the Soviet Union in 1949, which inspired him to write many rightfully forgotten poems ("Pushkin, you were the angel / of the Central Committee"[11]). In his 1973 memoirs, Neruda reflected on his metaphysical experience of the Soviet state: "Nature seemed to finally form a victorious unity with the human being."[12] The Ecuadorian author Enrique Gil Gilbert, the Cuban poet Nicolás Guillén, the Puerto Rican-Mexican novelist José Luis Gonzales, and the Uruguayan Jesualdo Sosa traveled together through Eastern Europe during late Stalinism and held forth about the transcendent metaphysical significance of what they saw happening in the Soviet Union, contrasting ostensibly free life under socialism with the sad state of serfdom in their home countries.[13]

Jorge Amado, Brazil's most famous and cherished author of the twentieth century, went to the USSR for the first time in 1951, when he was awarded the Stalin Peace Prize. His extensive travelogue, *O mundo do paz*, was yet another paean on every aspect of the Soviet system, including its policies in Eastern Europe.[14] His Cuban friend Nicolás Guillén, another Stalin Prize winner, summed up in his memoirs his impressions from his first of at least ten trips to the USSR.[15] Like Amado, most other Latin American visitors to the Stalinist Soviet Union went to see the utopia they expected to find. Their ideas and expectations were similar to those of their Western European and Mexican colleagues in the 1930s; in a rhetoric of redemption and utopianism, they took as real the world that was staged for them. With the notable exception of the Peruvian Víctor Haya de la Torre, whose early fascination with the USSR faded after a 1931 visit, the majority of Latin American visitors to the USSR under Stalin hailed the dictator and his apparent economic and political achievements for the Soviet Union and the world.

Nikita Khrushchev's revelation of some of Stalin's crimes in 1956, the Soviet invasion of Hungary the same year, and the suppression of the Prague Spring in 1968 are usually presented as the cornerstones of a loss of faith in the Soviet alternative by the international Left, but this chronology is more accurate regarding Western intellectuals than the Latin Americans. Jorge Amado was one of the few who developed a more critical stance towards the Soviet Union in 1956. Disappointed by the news from Moscow and by the lack of reaction amongst his Brazilian comrades, he left the Communist Party that year. He also protested against the treatment of the disgraced Soviet author Boris Pasternak in 1960 ("even though I did not like the novel [*Doctor Zhivago*]") and, many years later in his memoirs, showed deep regret for his earlier naïve praise of Stalin. Nevertheless, he still felt "linked to the Soviet Union like through an umbilical cord." He returned there many times and remained in close contact with Soviet writers while politically supporting Fidel Castro's Cuba and campaigning for Third World interests instead of the USSR.[16]

However, the admiration of most other Latin American intellectuals of that generation for the Soviet Union remained unshaken. With Khrushchev's reforms, some of them, who had been excluded under Stalin, were accepted back into the ranks of the Communist movement. José Revueltas, readmitted into the Mexican Communist Party at the beginning of 1956, dutifully supported the Soviet invasion of Hungary and made a second trip to the USSR in 1957. "With the death of Stalin in 1953, socialism took on new dimensions of hope," he remembered. "There was a newly recaptured glamour of international communism as a political strategy."[17] Diego Rivera, too, was readmitted to the party, from which he had been excluded since 1929 under the somewhat obscure reproach of being a "Trotskyite." His memoirs, written shortly after his readmission in 1954, included all-encompassing praise of the Soviet Union.[18] His lifelong rival, Siqueiros, who had visited Rivera's Moscow sickbed during a Soviet trip in 1956, had been a Stalinist from the very beginning and remained a loyal friend of the Soviet Union until the end of his life: "I reiterate, for what remains of my life," he declared shortly before his death in 1974, "my intention of fidelity to the party and to proletarian internationalism."[19]

Indeed, the shockwaves of 1956 hardly affected most Sovietophile Latin Americans. The Argentine essayist María Rosa Oliver, who was in Moscow a year later to receive the Lenin Peace Prize, rehashed the flimsy Soviet explanations of a Hungarian fascist counterrevolution supported by the capitalists through Radio Free Europe.[20] For the Ecuadorian writer Pedro Jorge Vera, who was personally received by Khrushchev when he visited the USSR in the early 1960s, Moscow was still "the symbol of our ideals of justice."[21] Joaquín Gutiérrez, a Costa Rican story-teller, novelist, and author of a famous book for children, defended Stalin—"thirty per cent bad, seventy per cent good"[22]—even after a 1967 trip to Moscow; in Brezhnev he saw the man to solve some of the problems that Khrushchev had been unable to fix. Whatever new directions its leaders took, Neruda remained a faithful friend of the Soviet Union until the end of his life. He refused to comment on the invasion of Czechoslovakia and did not stand up for the threatened dissident Alexander Solzhenitsyn.[23] Vera Kutejščikova, a Soviet Latin Americanist and official Soviet guide for many Latin American visitors, noted in late 1956 that "most of my Mexican friends [are] glowing with socialist ideas; in me, they saw the representative of a state that had implemented these ideas. Soviet society was in their eyes a paradise, and I was their guide to this paradise."[24] Neither the official revelation and acknowledgment of some of Stalin's crimes nor the invasion of Hungary chipped away at the fascination that most leftists of that generation had for the Soviet Union.

In contrast, a younger generation of socialist intellectuals of international fame from the late 1950s were much more critical of the USSR (although they initially displayed the same kind of blind enthusiasm for revolutionary Cuba). This was the generation of the "Latin American Boom," internationally influential and commercially successful authors such as Carlos Fuentes, Mario Vargas Llosa, and Gabriel García Márquez. Fuentes had great hopes in Khrushchev's "Thaw" policies as he perceived them during a 1963 visit—but, he no longer saw the USSR as a source of inspiration for Latin America. In 1968, when the USSR invaded Czechoslovakia, Fuentes traveled to Prague, together with García Márquez and the Argentine novelist Julio

Cortázar; all of them wanted to show their support for the Czech reformist socialists. García Márquez, although affiliated with the Colombian Communist Party from 1955, was indeed very critical of the Soviet Union from the beginning of his political activism. In 1957, after some failed attempts to procure a visa, he finally managed to get to Moscow under the pretext of being an accordion player in a Colombian folklore band. In his travelogue, he acknowledged some improvements of living conditions in the Soviet Union, but described the country overall as a rather drab and uninspiring place.[25] Márquez and other Latin American leftist intellectuals of his generation and background no longer saw the Soviet Union as a utopian paradise or a source of solutions for Latin American concerns. Their upbringing in their countries' upper or upper middle classes connected them closely to Western Europe and its literary traditions; Western views of Latin American intellectual life thus became focused on them. But many other Latin American writers and political activists, who were from less privileged backgrounds and less connected to Western Europe and North America and who were spiritually oriented toward the Third World, still saw the USSR model as a viable alternative to Western modernity well into the 1970s.

Paradise Found? *Tercermundismo* and Anti-Westernism in Latin America and the Soviet Union

Tercermundismo, the self-identification of Latin American intellectuals with the Third World, coincided with the Soviet discovery of what was then commonly called "the underdeveloped countries" in the mid-1950s. The early Cold War saw not only the gradual loss of Western leftists' hopes in the Soviet Union, but also more intense, and rather successful, Soviet attempts to present their country in a positive light to the Third World. Policymakers and internationalist-minded pundits tried to forge bonds based on a shared sense of anti-imperialism, rather than on the struggle for Communist world revolution. As part of a huge charm offensive toward Africa, South Asia, the Middle East, and Latin America, Soviet (front) organizations invited Third World intellectuals to the USSR.[26] The upper crust of Latin American leftist intelligentsia met in Moscow for a 1957 World Youth Festival: Nicolás Guillén, the novelist Carlos Augusto León, and the poet Pedro Dona from Venezuela were official guests, as were the playwright Saulo Benavente, the composer Gilardo Gilardi, the pupeteer and poet Javier Villafañe, and the authors Juan Gelman and María Rosa Oliver from Argentina. Jorge Amado was there along with his Guatemalan friend Miguel Angel Asturias. From

Mexico came the playwright Emilio Carballido, from Chile the poet Praxedes Urrutia, from Bolivia the poet Jorge Calvimontes.[27] And, for the then internationally unknown Gabriel García Márquez, the festival provided a pretext to sneak in as an accordion player in a folklore combo.

This influx of Latin American cultural figures visiting the Soviet Union at the same time was an exception, but many more were officially invited, or went on their own initiative, throughout the 1950s, 1960s, and 1970s. Moreover, twenty-three Latin Americans were awarded the Stalin/Lenin Peace Prize between 1950 and 1985, usually receiving it during a ceremony in Moscow.[28] Conspicuously, even more writers and artists from less developed and smaller countries of the Americas were invited to the Soviet Union. Professional guides took care of them—among them, some three thousand Spaniards, refugees of the Spanish Civil War, who still lived in Moscow in the 1950s and provided a great pool of native speakers. Additionally, an increasing number of specially trained staff in internationalist organizations could speak fluent Portuguese or Castilian and showed their guests all around Moscow, Leningrad, Kiev, and other regions and republics of the Soviet Union.[29] Some of the visitors' travel expenses were paid; some made considerable (albeit not exportable) Soviet money selling the translation rights of their works to Soviet publishers. Others came out of their own interest and on their own budget. They met with Soviet cultural figures and went on tour programs that often led them on long journeys through the entire USSR. They visited city administrations, schools, universities, ministries, sanatoriums, hydroelectric power plants, or whatever they asked to be shown, without being subjected to Soviet access restrictions for foreigners.

A common feature of these visits were trips to the Central Asian and Caucasian republics. The Moscow-led modernization of this "domestic Third World" indeed dominated Soviet self-representation toward Latin Americans. Journals, radio broadcasts, and large exhibitions in Latin America reported broadly on the progress, under Soviet tutelage, of these former agrarian, "backward," and "feudal" regions. The chief officers of Soviet internationalist organizations were usually from these republics: a group of the Supreme Soviet that traveled to Bolivia in 1960 was led by the Kazakh Communist Party boss; a group that went to Brazil, Ecuador, Mexico, and Cuba was led by the head of the Supreme Soviet, a Georgian. The Armenian composer Aram Khachaturian headed the Soviet-Latin American Friendship Society, the Azeri Raúf Gadžiev the Cuban-Soviet Institute. Khrushchev himself pointed out the role model of Soviet republics for developing countries. He also motivated his choice of Anastas Mikoyan as his "agent for Cuba": he was a native-born Armenian and he had experience in the "modernization" of the Caucasus.[30] The model of a non-Western, state-led path to industrial modernity had replaced proletarian world revolution as Moscow's main ideological export to the Third World.

Valcárcel's reflections on Kazakhstan as a role model for Latin America reveal that these Soviet images of development could still have an impact on Latin Americans in the 1960s. None of the Latin American visitors saw this Soviet modernization of the periphery critically, as an act of "imperialism" in its own right. On the contrary, many of them readily adopted this rather colonial attitude: after his trip to Central Asia, the Argentine writer Rodolfo Ghioldi, in a book that he called *Uzbekistan. El espejo*,[31] described the recent history of Central Asia as a perfect model of what needed to happen in his homeland. When the Paraguayan Communist activist Efraín Morel was taken on a trip to the Caucasus, the ancient advanced civilizations that had fallen victim to (tsarist) imperialism reminded him of his own people, and the ostensibly anti-imperialist Soviet alternative met with his unconditional approval.[32] Many other lesser-known Latin American visitors to the Soviet Union throughout the 1960s were still taken in by the country they were presented with. The fast and egalitarian modernization of formerly backward agrarian societies, the education, health care, and public transport systems impressed many visitors from less privileged backgrounds and with a *tercermundista* outlook. Emphasizing the appreciation of intellectuals in the Soviet Union and common anti-Western cultural values, the guides from Soviet internationalist organizations did an excellent job of instilling a pro-Soviet stance among the visitors. The tenor of travelogues by Latin Americans to the Soviet Union in the 1950s, 1960s, and 1970s was predominantly positive. Many who came with neutral views went back home with a rather positive opinion of the USSR. Conflicts and problems did nevertheless occur during the guided visits. Translators reported arrogant and bumptious behavior on the part of their protégés as well as embarrassing situations when terrible service in restaurants and hotels threatened to destroy the positive impressions carefully built up.[33]

Still, well into the 1970s, Valcárcel's enthusiastic reports from the Soviet Union were representative of most Latin American travelers' accounts. Following contemporary Soviet party doctrine, Valcárcel denounced the past "excesses of Stalin's personality cult." Beyond that, however, he drew an over-optimistic picture of the Soviet model as the future of mankind. In the perception of some *tercermundistas*, industry, agriculture, and education were blossoming in the USSR. Rents were low, income high, the women free, all children healthy and happy. Schools and universities, as well as health care and sanatoriums, were free. Soviet youth, they reported, patriotically loved their national cultures. Valcárcel was amazed by the spirit of resistance to "decadent formalism" that prevailed in Soviet art. Unlike Amado, he approved the treatment of Pasternak; he denounced the Hungarian insurgents as a bunch of fascists, and praised Soviet support for the Third World. At a parade for the cosmonauts Yuri Gagarin and German Titov, Valcárcel sat next to Pablo Neruda on Red Square, together with the Chilean feminist activist Olga Poblete de Espinosa, the Haitian poet René Depestre, and the Costa Rican writer Joaquín Gutiérrez. In this illustrious company, he experienced another epiphany and eventually summed up his trip, the first of several, as "one of the most intensive emotional experiences of [his] life."[34]

The *tercermundista* fascination with the Soviet Union continued even after the reformer Khrushchev was ousted in 1964 and despite the fact that his successor, Leonid Brezhnev, reduced the generous Soviet engagement with Third World countries and activists. In 1965, Valcárcel returned to Moscow to see his son, whom he had sent to study in the Soviet Union. After all his writings in praise of Khrushchev's accomplishments on the occasion of his first two trips, Valcárcel was initially a bit skeptical about the new Soviet leadership, but quickly bought into the official explanation that Khrushchev had stepped down for health reasons. In yet another lengthy book, Valcárcel went on about the exemplary character of the Soviet state—including the above-mentioned chapter on Kazakhstan as a role model for Peru: both countries, Valcárcel argued, had a population of around eleven million, among them "large masses of indigenous people" who had long lived in poverty. Thanks to the Soviet modernization of the 1930s, Valcárcel continued, an end had been put to the backwardness of the Kazakhs, their economic underdevelopment, and their illiteracy, without going through the painful phase of capitalism. Now, ten thousand schools and thirty-eight universities provided free education in several languages. The agricultural output, exploitation of minerals, and industrial production had multiplied hundredfold. Art and culture allegedly blossomed in the modern cities. Unlike Peru, Kazakhstan had made huge progress from the same starting level. In this unfavorable comparison, Valcárcel saw the reason why Peru banned travel to the Soviet Union.[35]

Any criticism of Soviet internal repression and aggressive foreign policy was just "massive counterpropaganda against the USSR," explained Carlos Fonseca, another Latin American visitor, who had grown up under extremely poor conditions in his native Nicaragua. Fonseca, the future founder and leader of the Frente Sandinista de Liberación Nacional (FSLN), had been awarded a travel grant to the World Youth Festival in Moscow when he was leader of a Marxist student group in Managua. Years later, full of nostalgia, he would remember his first stay in the Soviet Union in a book called *Un Nicaragüense en Moscú*.[36] "I thought I was dreaming," he wrote of Moscow. All the Soviet citizens he met were highly educated and well-dressed, Fonseca claimed; students were paid, and no one was unemployed. Even in villages, libraries were better than the biggest one in Managua, he reported, and religion and the press were ostensibly completely free. Defending Stalin against international blame, the Nicaraguan explained Khrushchev's position in one of his speeches as an erroneous translation: *criticism*, he lectured his readers, actually meant critical acknowledgment in Russian! The events in Hungary, he added, just as in the official Soviet depiction, were attempts at a fascist putsch. Upon returning to Nicaragua, Fonseca was arrested, interrogated, and eventually fled to Cuba. He underwent training as a guerrilla fighter but remained an ardent supporter of the Soviet Union until his death in the mountains of Nicaragua in 1976 during the violent struggle against the National Guard.

Gabriel García Márquez and Carlos Fuentes, internationally known cultural figures linked to Western literary circles, may no longer have had such a positive opinion of the USSR in the 1960s and 1970s. But those "fellow travelers" who identified with the Third World and indigenous groups continued the old leftist tradition of embracing the Soviet Union as an anti-Western socialist utopia. Several other reports by Latin American *tercermundista* visitors to the post-Stalinist Soviet state confirm this observation. The Bolivian novelist, poet, and indigenous activist Jesús Lara wrote most of his literary work in Quechua, his native language; much of it was translated and circulated in Eastern Europe and the Soviet Union. He hailed the Soviet Union as the "land of the new man" in a travelogue by this title.[37] His compatriot, the writer Fausto Reinaga, reported from the "red utopia" in a similar vein. From a poor *campesino* family, he had not learned to read and write until the age of sixteen, but later became Bolivia's most influential indigenous intellectual. On the brink of losing his faith in Marxism due to the extreme sectarianism of the Bolivian workers' movement, he had long felt the need to see the Soviet Union to refresh his ideals. "Even if I risk to die on the way, I have to get to Russia," he said. He could not afford the travel costs of a trip to Moscow for the World Youth Festival of 1957, but eventually, the Bolivian president himself, Hernán Siles Zuazo, of the ruling Movimiento Nacionalista Revolucionario (MNR), contributed to the financing of his trip.

Reinaga's odyssey to Moscow, his views on the Western colonial empires, his encounters with other Latin Americans, and his assessment of the Soviet Union illustrate the *tercermundistas*' anti-imperialist and anti-Western outlook on the world at the time. In Brazil, Reinaga was appalled by the racist attitudes he perceived against the black population. Stuck without money in Buenos Aires, he was supported by Argentine intellectuals for weeks before they finally bought him a ticket to Europe. He crossed the Atlantic and on his way had a glimpse of the "French imperial system" in Senegal as well as "fascism in power" in Spain. "It caused nausea and I was completely disillusioned with Europe," Reinaga recalled.[38] From Spain, he took a ship to Genoa, a train to Stuttgart and Leipzig, and finally arrived in Moscow after a week-long journey. The title of his book on the Soviet Union, *El sentimiento mesiánco del pueblo ruso*, might sound like a condemnation of Red imperialism, but in fact, it was the opposite: Reinaga applauded to every aspect of Soviet life he was presented with. He was deeply impressed by the technological feats, atomic energy, and factories, the health care and education systems, and the ubiquitous rhetoric of peace. Like his hosts, Reinaga excoriated the United States on every occasion—and returned to Bolivia confident again in his Marxist ideals: "I came with some petit bourgeois doubts, but I left enthusiastically with an assignment and a clear worldview."[39]

This lingering idealistic view of the USSR during the Cold War as a flawless utopian society was typical of a group of Latin American visitors who shared certain features: they all came from humble backgrounds, mostly from the poorest countries of the Americas, as did the Bolivians Lara and Reinaga and the Nicaraguan Fonseca. They identified strongly with the indigenous people of their home countries, or more broadly with what Frantz Fanon called the "wretched of the earth," much as the Peruvian Valcárcel and the socialist writer Fernando Benítez did. The latter traveled many times to the Soviet Union, where he shared his knowledge as a renowned expert on the indigenous tribes in his native Mexico.[40] Due to the circumstances in which they had grown up, these visitors were often impressed by Soviet self-representation: Soviet living standards around the 1960s were indeed better than those of the average person in their home countries. The fact that Latin American critics of the Soviet system were usually white upper-middle-class men made their allegations unreliable to some of the *mestizo* authors, who often explicitly penned their praise of the

Soviet Union against more critical assessments of Soviet Communism by the white middle-class novelists of the "Latin American Boom" generation.

In the long run, the admiration of the *indigenistas* and *tercermundistas* for the Soviet Union faded, too: like Haya de la Torre in the 1930s, many drifted away from Soviet-style Communism with its focus on industrialization and rational progress to a specific brand of Latin American indigenous socialism. Lara left his Communist Party because it followed the Moscow party line of a nonviolent path to socialism and for that reason had not supported Che Guevara in the armed struggle in the Bolivian jungle. Reinaga was arrested right after his return to Bolivia, where the local Communists made no move to help him. After his release, he went on a pilgrimage to Machu Picchu, the mountain site of an ancient Inca town, and, as originator and mentor of *indianismo*, founded the first indigenous party, the Partido de Indios Aymaras y Keswas (PIAK), later renamed the Partido Indio de Bolivia (PIB). Benítez and many other indigenous writers eventually classified the Soviet Union as belonging to what they considered the camp of European imperialists. Manuel Scorza, a guerrilla fighter in Chile and Peru and an *indigenista* writer, dedicated a chapter of his last novel, *La danza inmóvil*, to the disillusion of Peruvian Communists with the Soviet Union. But these views emerged only in the 1980s. They should not be projected on the mindsets of the 1960s and 1970s, when a fascination for the Soviet Union was still widespread amongst *tercermundistas* all across the Americas.

Conservative and Catholic Variants of Anti-Westernism

The common denominator of Soviet and Latin American *tercermundistas* was not so much Communism as embodied in the party, but a shared sense of anti-imperialism or anti-Westernism. This is why a group that is not usually included in accounts of foreign visitors to the Soviet Union joined their ranks: conservative Catholics. In fact, the groups overlapped. Fausto Reinaga, for instance, was not only a militant *indigenista* Marxist, but also a pious, anticlerical Christian who hailed Moscow as "the new Jerusalem" and felt "like Lazarus after Jesus' healing" when he saw Lenin in his mausoleum.[41] The poet Roque Dalton, a future guerrilla fighter in his native El Salvador, was a devout Christian when he went to Moscow for the 1957 World Youth Festival, attracted to the Soviet Union for its "redemptive promise of a just society."[42] The "messianic sentiment of the Russian people," as Reinaga put it, attracted more than just socialists. Many conservative Catholics saw their own traditional values better preserved in the Soviet Union than in their own societies, which were undergoing rapid changes under the influence of the United States. Failing to grasp the reality of ongoing antireligion campaigns in the USSR of the 1950s and 1960s, most of these Latin American visitors affirmed that freedom of faith prevailed in the country and that the persecutions of believers in earlier periods of Soviet Communism, acknowledged by some, were long over.

The Colombian educationist Agustín Nieto Caballero was a practicing Catholic who traveled to the Soviet Union in 1959. After hearing the news of the successful flight of the *Sputnik*, he wanted to study the education system that had made possible that "historic leap of the Russian people." His report *El secreto de Rusia* was published as a series of articles in the newspaper *El Tiempo* and as a book that had several print runs. High-ranking Soviet officials had introduced Nieto Caballero to the Soviet educational system, to schools, universities and libraries, and organized visits to research institutes. Nieto Caballero had been deeply impressed. He considered education in the Soviet Union "excellent"—and found interesting reasons for its success: Soviet students were so bright, Nieto Caballero claimed, because they were not exposed to sexual lures, as everything even mildly erotic was prohibited. There were hardly any taverns, bars, and restaurants, he noted with puritanical delight, and newspapers did not feature gossip and scandal. The Catholic Nieto Caballero believed he had found "a new religion [in the Soviet Union], the religion of work," and he concluded: "The materialist ideology of the Soviet man is intimately impregnated with bourgeois Christian morality." He found plenty of parallels between his *ora et labora* attitude and Soviet policies: "Soviet ideals and goals are like our Christian ones, this is something capitalism is lacking," he felt, and he approved certain limitations on freedom of expression in the USSR: "Ugly degenerations of modern art should not be tolerated!"[43] The pious Colombian Catholic summed up his impressions of the Soviet Union: "The Russian people, whom we find so remote from us physically and spiritually, are nevertheless, even if we would never have believed that this could be possible, giving lessons to us, lessons of purity, of honesty, of love of study, of tenaciousness in the most difficult endeavors and humble conduct."[44]

Nieto Caballero was not the only Latin American Catholic who nourished these peculiar sympathies for the Soviet Union. Ironically, while white middle-class leftists turned their back on the USSR in the 1960s, some of their political adversaries at home took an interest in what they perceived as a genuinely conservative state. Alberto Dangond was a man of many vocations, a trained lawyer and a producer of television shows. He was also a practicing Catholic and represented the Partido Conservador in the Colombian parliament. In early 1967, he toured the Soviet Union and wrote a book about his experience, *Mi diario en la Unión Soviética. Un conservador en la U.R.S.S.*, in which the staunch Catholic conservative praised the motherland of atheist socialism to the skies. Dangond, who was a beneficiary of the standard tour program through the Soviet Union, was impressed, like many others before him, by hydroelectric power plants, railway stations, and universities. During his stay in Leningrad, he found the breadth and quality of cultural life fantastic, saying, "I am ashamed of Bogotá compared to it. This is a great conservative system. There is no lack of order, no anarchy, no lack of discipline! . . . Everyone respects the authorities, order and discipline! These hierarchies in the Soviet Union correspond perfectly with the nature of man, it is authoritarian and at the same time wonderfully dynamic and vital within a jurisdictional order and universal consent."[45]

What makes Dangon's report particularly interesting is the list of similarities he found between Soviet Communism and his understanding of Catholic values. During a stint in Minsk, he was invited to debate population policies and birth control—and found only like-minded people: "I am radically anti-communist, this is the truth," Dangond warned, "but, being a Catholic and patriotic Colombian conservative from a small underdeveloped tropical nation, I have met here, in the capital of communist Belorussia, a government official who says exactly the same things and thinks the same as myself, with the same human warmth!" Dangond explained he had always thought that Marxism wanted to destroy the family, but now in the USSR he saw precisely the opposite: "The application of Marxism in the Soviet Union has produced . . . a practice of morals, social life and a development of the human being which are easily identifiable with our best and most valued Christian, Catholic ideals." In the late 1960s, some Latin American conservatives thus found Soviet puritanism and authoritarianism more appealing than what they saw as the West's moral and cultural decline.[46] While proponents of Liberation Theology attempted to reconcile Christianity and socialism, these other Latin American Catholics praised the antiliberal conservatism of the Soviet state.

Gonzalo Canal Ramírez, a Colombian novelist, professor of sociology, and a Christian politician, wrote a rather similar account of his 1968 trip to Moscow, where he was received as a guest of the Soviet state press agency. While Canal Ramírez conceded that religion had been suppressed in the early days of the revolution, he defended these measures as a somewhat overzealous anticipation of the Second Vatican Council. Now in the late 1960s, according to him, religion was completely tolerated, but the real faith of the people was the belief in the Soviet state and its ideology. Art was considered a religion now, he explained, and the Russians prayed in countless museums, orchestra halls, cinemas, and on the radio. Canal Ramírez saw close parallels between Christian catechism and the values of Soviet society: a strong belief in an idea and a high esteem for work, collectivism, intolerance towards enemies of the faith and parasitical behavior, and appreciation of the family allegedly characterized both Soviet Communism and Latin American Catholicism. Canal Ramírez saw Lenin as a modern Redeemer and compared his April Theses to the gospel. Thanks to their political and moral order, he believed, all Russians were cheerful and optimistic, highly educated and yet modest. "What impressed me most," he summed up, "was not the technological achievements, the hydropower, the spaceships, but the new man as Lenin created [sic] him. . . . This new man, his cultural, and moral values, is the great strength of the Soviet Union."[47]

Throughout the 1960s and 1970s, many Latin American visitors perceived the Soviet Union under Brezhnev to be a successful conservative state, without the moral debauchery they thought was undermining the West. While the uncritical celebration of the USSR in the style of Nieto Caballero, Dangond, and Canal Ramírez was not representative of Colombian or Latin American Christians, mystical Catholicism, the hope of redemption, and anti-Western sentiments led some conservative Catholics to believe that the Soviet Union was, if not a perfect place, at least preferable to the soulless United States and Western Europe. All the travelogues described here share a deep contempt for the decadent and immoral West, its materialism, its incomprehensible modern art and music, its increasing sexual license, and its confused and disoriented youth, with their excesses, drug abuse, and superficial pastimes. The Soviet internationalist organizations, catering to this new interest and the concerns of their Christian visitors, occasionally included representatives of Soviet churches in their host programs. "The socialist regime is, above all, humanitarian," they had a Georgian Orthodox priest tell the Brazilian journalist Nestor de Holanda, "We Christians and communists belong together."[48] Yet, judging by the impressions of Latin American Catholics in their travelogues, many of them were less interested in the churches of the Soviet Union than in the ideology of the state itself, an ideology in which many perceived Christian elements and a common dislike of modern Western moral values and cultural tastes.

Conclusion

Gustavo Valcárcel's dream of a socialist America, and of a Peru that would follow the path of Kazakhstan, never materialized. While several populist nationalists, and even military dictatorships built good political and military relations with Moscow, the view of the USSR as a redeeming utopia was mostly limited to intellectual and artistic circles. Some changed their minds during the Cold War, but most Latin American visitors to the USSR were still susceptible to the lure of certain characteristics of the Soviet state and advocated their implementation in their home countries, but the internationally known writers of the "Boom" generation, mostly white middle-class men who dominated the Western perception of Latin American intellectual life, were no longer particularly interested in the Soviet Union as a role model to emulate. The revelation of Stalin's crimes, the persecution of intellectuals within the Soviet Union, and the invasions of Hungary in 1956 and Czechoslovakia in 1968 put an end to the remaining idealist illusions about the Soviet state for most Latin Americans of their generation and background, as it had done for their European counterparts. For the radical minority in Central and South America who supported guerrilla warfare, the Soviet Union and its concept of peaceful path to socialism were no longer a valid point of reference either.

Soviet efforts to win Latin Americans over during the Cold War were not all in vain, however. The anti-Western *tercermundistas* were still very interested in certain achievements and features of the Soviet state. Two main lines of interest are salient in the travelogues of Latin American visitors to the Cold War Soviet Union. One was their interest in a non-Western development pattern. Travelers were impressed by the state-led build-up of Soviet infrastructure, especially in the "domestic Third World" of Central Asia and the Caucasus, as well as by the education and health systems and by industrial output and technological achievements. These successes were particularly impressive for visitors from less developed countries, or from less privileged personal backgrounds. The oft-noted absence of dire poverty and starvation, or the supply of running hot water in all buildings hardly impressed any Western visitor in the 1960s—but, for someone from rural Bolivia or Central America, these were signs of a successful, egalitarian type of modernization. Unlike Western visitors, who usually came to see the Soviet Union out of sheer curiosity, the *tercermundistas* usually sought inspiration for the improvement of living conditions in the countries they came from. The second line of interest was directed against the West as well, but with an antimodern angle. From the 1960s, conservative and indigenous Latin American Catholic authors identified more and more with what they perceived as an antimaterialist spirit in the Soviet Union. Latin American conservatives with an anti-Western bias felt close to what they saw as traditional family values and laws in the USSR, and praised its resistance against debilitating cultural influences from the United States.

As opposed to most Western "fellow travelers," Latin American visitors to the Soviet Union constantly drew parallels with and pondered on the differences between the Soviet Union and their home countries. The Colombian poet María Mercedes Carranza called this "the secret appeal of socialism." She was well aware of the many downsides of life in the Soviet Union, but argued in a conversation with a French diplomat, who bitterly complained about life in the sad and grim country in 1977: "I see all this with very different eyes—the eyes of an underdeveloped country that gyrates in an orbit of influence which dominates it economically. Ours is a very different case from Europe. . . . I recommend you always write two letters back to Paris, one from your perspective, and one that corresponds to our point of view. We do not care about the spies and the grain trade. Our problems are of a very different nature. . . . In the Soviet Union, at least, no one suffers from hunger, they have enough doctors and they have erased illiteracy and prostitution."[49]

The overwhelmingly positive perception of the Soviet Union by its Latin American visitors until the late 1970s does not justify sweeping conclusions about a generally naïve view of the USSR in Latin America. This chapter has only presented the views of those who actually traveled to the USSR in the 1950s, 1960s, and 1970s and wrote about their experience. Writers with a more critical view of the Soviet Union tended not to go there in the first place. However, what the travelogues of Latin American visitors to the Cold War Soviet Union do make clear is that, at least for an influential minority of writers, artists, and political activists from all over the Americas, the Soviet Union remained an important intellectual and political point of reference for much of the Cold War period. Their positive perception of the country resulted, in part, from lavishly funded and well-conducted programs for foreigners, but it was also based on their respect for a state without the huge social inequalities the visitors knew in their home countries—a state with a sound infrastructure, free health care, free and good education, functional public transport, and the apparently peaceful coexistence of people of different ethnic backgrounds. Finally, and this was perhaps the most important criterion for the *tercermundistas*, the Soviet Union stood for a successful non-Western, ostensibly anti-imperialist type of state that, for a while, managed to cope with the challenges of a modern society while defying the influence of the United States.

Notes

1. Gustavo Valcárcel, *Medio siglo de revolución invencible: Segunda parte de "Reportaje al futuro"* (Lima: Ediciones Unidad, 1967), 50–64; Gustavo Valcarcel, *Reportaje al futuro: Crónicas de un viaje a la U.R.S.S.* (Lima: Perú Nuevo, 1963), http://gustavoyvioletavalcarcel.blogspot.com/2009/02/biografia-y-obra-de-gustavo-valcarcel.html. This chapter is based on a more extensive analysis of Soviet–Latin American encounters during the Cold War in my book *Soviet Internationalism after Stalin: Interaction and Exchange between the USSR and Latin America during the Cold War* (Cambridge: Cambridge University Press, 2015).

2. Jorge Castañeda, *Utopia Unarmed: The Latin American Left after the Cold War* (New York: Vintage, 1994), 177.

3. Andre Gunder Frank, "The Underdevelopment of Development," in *The Underdevelopment of Development. Essays in Honor of Andre Gunder Frank*, ed. Sing Chew and Robert Denemark (New York: Sage, 1996), 26.

4. Patrick Iber, *Neither Peace Nor Freedom. The Cultural Cold War in Latin America* (Cambridge, MA: Harvard University Press, 2015), esp. 116–43; Renata Keller, "Don Lázaro Rises Again: Heated Rhetoric, Cold Warfare, and the 1961 Latin American Peace Conference," in *Beyond the Eagle's Shadow: New Histories of Latin America's Cold War*, ed. Virginia Garrard-Burnett, Mark Lawrence, and Julio Moreno (Albuquerque: University of New Mexico Press, 2013), 129–49.

5. Claudia Gilman, *Entre la pluma y el fusil: Debates y dilemas del escritor revolucionario en América Latina* (Buenos Aires: Siglo Veintiuno, 2003), 68.

6. Among the few exceptions are: Germán Alburquerque, *La trinchera letrada. Intelectuales latinoamericanos y Guerra Fría* (Santiago de Chile: Ariadna, 2011); Sylvia Saítta, *Hacia la revolución: Viajeros argentinos de izquierda* (Buenos Aires: Fondo de Cultura Económica, 2007).

7. L. Chejfec, "'Čtoby rasskazat' pravdu o SSSR': Pervye latinoamerikanskie delegacii v Sovetskom Sojuze," *Latinskaja Amerika*, no. 12 (1982): 73–83.

8. David Caute, *The Fellow Travelers: Intellectual Friends of Communism* (New Haven, CT: Yale University Press, 1988).

9. Vera Kutejščikova, *Moskva-Meksiko-Moskva: Doroga dlinoju v žizn'* (Moskva: AkademProekt, 2000), 89–90, 115, 134; David Siqueiros, *Me llamaban el Coronelazo: Memorias* (México DF: Grijalbo, 1977), 369; José Mancisidor, *Ciento veinte días* (México DF: Editorial México Nuevo, 1937); Vicente Lombardo Toledano and Victor Manuel Villaseñor, *Un viaje al mundo del porvenir* (México DF: Publicaciones de la Universidad obrera de México, 1936).

10. Alfredo Varela, *Un periodista argentino en la Unión Soviética* (Buenos Aires: Ediciones Viento, 1950), 167.

11. Pablo Neruda, "En la Unión Soviética," *Cuadernos de la Fundación Pablo Neruda* 37 (1999): 29–37.

12. Pablo Neruda, *Confieso que he vivido*, Biblioteca Pablo Neruda (Barcelona: Plaza & Janés, 2001), 237.

13. Neruda, *Confieso*, 285–87.

14. Jorge Amado, *O mundo da paz: União Soviética e democracias populares* (Rio de Janeiro: Editorial Vitória, 1951).

15. Nicolás Guillén, *Páginas vueltas: Memorias* (La Habana: Unión de Escritores y Artistas de Cuba, 1982), 348–50.

16. Jorge Amado, *Navegação de cabotagem: Apontamentos para um livro de memórias que jamais escreverei* (Lisboa: Editora Record, 1992).

17. Kutejščikova, *Moskva-Meksiko-Moskva*, 123; Sam L. Slick, *José Revueltas* (Boston: Twayne, 1983), 169. With his 1964 novel *Los errores* (*The Mistakes*), however, Revueltas renounced Soviet-style communism finally and for good. Dedicated to the memory of the executed Hungarian reform Communist Imre Nagy, it contraposed idealistic militants to party dogmatists in 1930s and 1940s Mexico and described the mirror images of the Moscow purges in the ranks of the Mexican party. José Revueltas, *Los errores* (Mexico DF: Fondo De Cultura Economica, 1964).

18. Diego Rivera and Gladys March, *My Art, My Life: An Autobiography* (New York: Citadel, 1960).

19. Philip Stein, *Siqueiros: His Life and Works* (New York: International Publishers, 1994), 322; 373; Siqueiros, *Me llamaban el Coronelazo*, 458.

20. Hebe Clementi, *María Rosa Oliver*, Mujeres Argentinas (Buenos Aires: Planeta, 1992).

21. Pedro Jorge Vera, *Gracias a la vida: Memorias* (Quito: Editorial Voluntad, 1993).

22. Joaquin Gutiérrez, *La URSS tal cual* (Santiago de Chile: Nascimento, 1967), 17.

23. Paul Hollander, *Political Pilgrims: Western Intellectuals in Search for the Good Society* (Piscataway, NJ: Transaction Publishers, 1997), 72.

24. Kutejščikova, *Moskva-Meksiko-Moskva*, 29f.

25. Gabriel García Márquez, *De viaje por los países socialistas: 90 días en la "Cortina de Hierro"* (Bogotá: La Oveja Negra, 1982). The book edition came out only after a year-long struggle with the publishing house, but later became a bestseller, with at least seven editions during the decade. See Dasso Saldívar, *García Márquez: El viaje a la semilla, la biografía*, ABC, biografías vivas (Barcelona: Folio, 2005), 354–58.

26. Rupprecht, *Soviet Internationalism after Stalin*, 22–72.

27. N. N., "'Prekrasnaja vosmožnost': Beseda s kubinskim poetom Gil'enom," *Molodež' mira* 4 (1957): 15.

28. They were Heriberto Jara Corona (1950), Jorge Amado (1951), Eliza Branco (1952), Pablo Neruda (1953), Baldomero Sanin Cano (1954), Nicolás Guillén (1954), Lázaro Cárdenas (1955), Maria Rosa Oliver (1957), Fidel Castro (1961), Olga Poblete de Espinosa (1962), Oscar Niemeyer (1963), Miguel Ángel Asturias (1965), David Alfaro Siqueiros (1966), Jorge Zalamea (1967), Alfredo Varela (1970–71), Salvador Allende (1972), Enrique Pastorino (1972), Luis Corvalán (1973–74), Hortensia Bussi de Allende (1975–76), Vilma Espín Guillois (1977–78),

Miguel Otero Silva (1979-80), Líber Seregni (1980-82), Luis Vidales (1983-84), and Miguel d'Escoto (1985-86).

29. Kutejščikova, *Moskva-Meksiko-Moskva*, 260-64.

30. Aleksandr Fursenko, *Prezidium CK KPSS: 1954-1964, Archivy Kremlja* (Moskva: Rossijskaja Političeskaja Enciklopedija, 2003), 884-903.

31. Rodolfo Ghioldi, *Uzbekistan: El espejo* (Buenos Aires: Editorial Fundamentos, 1956).

32. Rupprecht, *Soviet Internationalism after Stalin*, 65.

33. Rupprecht, *Soviet Internationalism after Stalin*, 188.

34. Rupprecht, *Soviet Internationalism after Stalin*, 161

35. Valcárcel, *Medio siglo*, 50-64, 182-87.

36. Carlos Fonseca, *Un nicaragüense en Moscú* (Managua: FSLN, 1980).

37. Mario Lara, "Jesús Lara (1898-1980): Homenaje," *Marxismo Militante* 24 (1998): 79-83.

38. Fausto Reinaga, *El sentimiento mesiánico del pueblo ruso* (La Paz: Ediciones SER, 1960), 38.

39. Reinaga, *El sentimiento mesiánico*, 137-38.

40. Rupprecht, *Soviet Internationalism after Stalin*, 164-65.

41. Reinaga, *El sentimiento mesiánico*, 29.

42. Luis Alvarenga, *El ciervo perseguido* (San Salvador: Dirección de Publicaciones e Impresos, 2002), 40-44

43. Agustín Nieto, *El secreto de Rusia* (Bogotá: Antares, 1960), 16, 32, 58-64.

44. Nieto, *El secreto de Rusia*, 64-65.

45. Alberto Dangond, *Mi diario en la Unión Soviética: Un conservador en la U.R.S.S.* (Bogotá, 1968), 41, 139.

46. Dangond, *Mi diario en la Unión Soviética*, 156, 179.

47. Gonzalo Canal Ramírez, *La Unión Soviética: Reto Moral* (Bogotá: Imprenta y Rotograbado, 1969), 11, 38, 69, 76-77, 140, 175.

48. Nestor de Holanda, *O mundo vermelho: Notas de um Repórter na URSS* (Rio de Janeiro: Editora Pongetti, 1962), 26.

49. Marìa Mercedes Carranza, "El discreto encanto del socialismo," *Nueva Frontera* 127 (1977): 23-24.

10 Cuba, the United States, and the Uses of the Third World Project, 1959–1967

ERIC GETTIG

In modern international history, revolutionary states have often faced tension between engaging commercially and diplomatically with the world as it is, in order to consolidate the revolution, and seeking to transform that world by spreading the revolution's ideals. The revolutionary government of Cuba faced this tension in its relations with the Third World after January 1959.

Historical scholarship on Cuban relations in the Third World has focused on Cuban support for revolutionary movements and governments in Latin America and Africa.[1] We have very few analyses—and none based on archival documents—of Cuba's diplomatic engagement with Third World internationalism.[2] Historians have not yet conducted sustained research to determine Cuba's role in the major forums of what Vijay Prashad calls the "Third World project," such as the Non-Aligned Movement (NAM), the United Nations (UN), and the Group of 77 (G-77) developing countries arising from the UN Conference on Trade and Development (UNCTAD).[3]

This scholarly neglect is regrettable and surprising, because revolutionary Cuba decisively shaped the terms under which the rest of Latin America associated with the Third World project, not only through its material support for revolution, but also through its diplomacy. Cuba's impact was both direct, by influencing how Latin American peoples and governments acted toward the Third World and its emerging institutions, and indirect, as Cuba became a primary driver of the United States' corresponding efforts to shape Latin American engagement with the Third World.

This chapter examines the early years of revolutionary Cuba's engagement with the Third World project. While acknowledging Cuba's efforts to "export revolution" by inspiring and materially supporting revolutionaries in Latin America and Africa, it focuses on a neglected side of Cuban internationalism: Cuba's diplomatic engagement in major conferences of Third World governments. In particular, it examines Cuba's failed effort to convene a "Conference of Underdeveloped Nations" in Havana in 1960 and Cuba's participation in the first two Non-Aligned summits, at Belgrade, Yugoslavia in 1961 and Cairo, Egypt in 1964. To do so, the essay draws on documents from Cuba's Ministry of Foreign Relations (Ministerio de Relaciones Exteriores, abbreviated MINREX) from its archive in Havana and the private papers of a Cuban ambassador. It also uses declassified U.S. documents from the National Archives and presidential libraries, as well as documents from the archives of the British Foreign Office and the Mexican Secretariat of Foreign Relations (Secretaría de Relaciones Exteriores, SRE).

These documents, particularly the Cuban records, which are analyzed here for the first time, illuminate the extent to which Cuba and the United States worked at opposite purposes in their approach to the Third World project and Latin America's participation. Both governments viewed Latin America's relationship to the Third World largely—sometimes almost exclusively—with reference to their bilateral relationship to each other. Their goals for the direction of Third World internationalism and Latin America's place therein were almost mirror images, and both parties, especially the Cubans, often saw their attempts to influence the Third World project as a zero-sum game.

From Eisenhower through Kennedy and Johnson, U.S. administrations pursued three principal goals regarding Cuba, Latin America, and the Third World. First, Washington worked to isolate Cuba from the rest of the Third World. Second, it sought to isolate Latin America from the Afro-Asian world to the extent possible, to prevent a drift toward "neutralism" that could weaken the U.S.-led "Inter-American System." Third, U.S. administrations tried to channel the Third World project toward thematic and institutional frameworks nonthreatening to U.S. interests, and thus especially toward questions of economic development addressed through UN-sponsored forums.

The Cuban government pursued essentially opposite goals. Cuba sought, first, to maximize Third World solidarity in order to demonstrate that it was not isolated. Second, Cuba sought to draw Latin America closer to Afro-Asia, often by creating or contributing to new international forums not under Washington's influence, a policy that positioned Cuba as a bridge between continents and a potential leader of a tri-continental movement. Third, Cuba sought to radicalize Third World internationalism, to define it as militant and uncompromising anti-imperialism, and to draw the Second and Third, nonaligned and socialist worlds together, hoping thereby to defeat U.S.-led imperialism once and for all.

Underdevelopment: Cuba's First Foray into Third World Internationalism

The abortive "Congress of Underdeveloped Countries" has been essentially lost to history, but it was a major diplomatic initiative of the Cuban government, amidst a volatile, formative half-year period in the revolution's domestic and foreign relations. Coming less than five years after the Asian-African Conference at Bandung and more than a year before the inaugural Non-Aligned conference at Belgrade, it was, moreover, the first significant move—by the Cuban government or any other—to draw Latin American, African, and Asian governments together under a common framework.

The new government's first outreach to the Afro-Asian world came when Ernesto "Che" Guevara took a three-month tour of the Mediterranean and Asia, visiting Egypt, India, Burma, Japan, Indonesia, Ceylon, Pakistan, Iraq, and Yugoslavia as the head of a Cuban "Good-Will and Economic Mission" between June and September 1959. At a time when Cuba's agrarian reform was beginning to bring it into conflict with U.S. landowners and Washington, the mission had both political and economic motives. In addition to establishing or strengthening diplomatic relations with the emerging Non-Aligned world, Guevara and his team of economic advisers sought to study their hosts' approaches to land reform and industrialization and to negotiate trade agreements to help Cuba diversify its export markets for sugar and its suppliers of capital and manufactured goods.[4] In the Non-Aligned capitals of Cairo, New Delhi, and Belgrade, Che expressed Cuba's interest in the Bandung principles and his hosts' independent foreign and domestic policies, lamenting that Cuba, bound by the 1947 Rio Treaty and the Organization of American States (OAS), had not been able to exercise similar independence.[5] In Ceylon Guevara ventured that Cuba now had more in common with the "Bandung powers" than with dictatorial Latin American neighbors such as Nicaragua. The State Department's intelligence branch saw Che's mission as "initiating a new phase in Cuban foreign relations."[6]

State's analysts were essentially correct. In an article published upon his return, Guevara began positioning Cuba as a model for the economic and political liberation not only of Latin America but also of Africa and Asia. Cuba, Che wrote, was "an ally across the sea" for "the hundreds of millions of Afro-Asians" struggling, like their Latin American brethren, for liberation.[7] At a press conference discussing his trip, Che argued that Cuba should adopt "a third position" in the Cold War, like that of the majority of underdeveloped countries. Those countries, he said, "understand our revolution," and their "solidarity" was an important new factor in international affairs. To strengthen these connections, Che ventured, the Cuban government should host a "Congress of Under-Developed Countries."[8]

The idea for such a conference had originated with Cuba's Foreign Minister Raúl Roa García (hereafter "Roa"), according to his son, Raúl Roa Kourí (hereafter "Roa Kourí"), himself a career diplomat who served at the time as Cuba's alternate delegate to the United Nations. According to Roa Kourí, father and son had been "very interested" in the Bandung Conference's potential as the basis for "a third way" between the capitalist West and communist East.[9] The elder Roa, he recalls, was also inspired by the 1948 book *The Geography of Hunger* by the Brazilian social scientist Josué de Castro, which identified hunger and underdevelopment caused by plantation monoculture and mono-export economies as the root cause of sociopolitical upheaval in the Global South. The book provided Roa a framework to connect Cuba's social ills, rooted in sugar monoculture, with the development problems elsewhere in the Americas, Asia, and Africa. De Castro recommended economic development through the diversification and modernization of agriculture by adjusting the terms of trade to benefit primary-product-exporting countries and fostering industrialization—an agenda consistent with that being articulated at the UN's Economic Commission for Latin America and with the reformist and liberal currents of the coalition that would soon launch the Cuban Revolution.[10] De Castro's prediction that communism and capitalism would "converge" toward "organizing production to satisfy the fundamental needs" of all people likely appealed to Roa, who by this point had had a long career in leftist activism but was not a member of, or much associated with, Cuba's Communist Party.

Roa's appointment as foreign minister in summer 1959 coincided with Guevara's mission and Cuba's outreach to the Afro-Asian and Non-Aligned worlds. It also came at the peak of the Cuban leadership's identification of the revolution as being guided by neither capitalism nor communism, but rather a vaguely defined "humanism."[11] In the fall of 1959, Roa began to put these aspirations into action. In a late September speech at the UN, Roa—echoing de Castro's *Geography of Hunger*—blamed Latin America's political problems on underdevelopment and argued that "the great problem of the world" was being forced to choose between a capitalism "that kills people through hunger" and a communism "that solves the economic problems, but suppresses freedom." The "humanist" Cuban Revolution, he said, would transcend this dilemma, bringing (as Fidel often assured at the time) "bread with freedom, bread without terror."

Taking stock of Cuba's new orientation, Roa declared that "Cuba is today, for the first time in her history, effectively free, independent, and sovereign" in its foreign and domestic policies. In a world divided into two Cold War camps, there was, Roa observed, "a third group, with much more moral than material force, that hopes to serve as a bridge between the two." Cuba, he acknowledged, "figures, through its historical tradition, its geographical location, and its international obligations, in the so-called western group." But his government, he went on, "does not admit or accept . . . that it is ineluctably necessary to choose between the capitalist and the communist solution. There are other paths and other solutions of pure democratic character; and Cuba has now found its own path and its own solution to its problems, which is the path and solution of the Latin American peoples and which . . . connects her to the underdeveloped peoples of Africa and Asia."[12] Speaking at the UN again on 3 December, Roa officially announced his government's intention to convene a Conference of Underdeveloped Countries in Havana "as soon as possible."[13]

By late 1959 Cuba's move toward an independent or third position had begun to concern U.S. officials, who worried also about domestic developments in Cuba. Several moderate ministers were replaced by leftists; seizures of agricultural and mineral properties accelerated; elections were postponed seemingly indefinitely; known or suspected Communists gained strong influence in managing the economy and military. The government's denunciations of U.S. imperialism sharpened, and Cuba broke with the West at the UN by backing Algeria's independence movement and abstaining on the annual vote to seat the Communists rather than the Nationalists of Taiwan as China's delegation. "It is increasingly evident that the Castro Government is following a deliberate planned course hostile to the United States and apparently designed to establish a Tito-like state with an ostensibly neutral position in the cold war," Assistant Secretary of State for Latin American affairs Roy Rubottom wrote in late November.[14] State's intelligence bureau concluded soon after that "Cuban leaders envision the establishment of a Latin American bloc which will unite forces with the underdeveloped nations of Asia and Africa. It is becoming increasingly apparent, however, that the Cuban concept of a middle road is one in which a strong stand against the western powers is coupled with an almost total lack of criticism of the Sino-Soviet bloc."[15]

By mid-December U.S. officials resolved to counter Cuba's overtures to the Afro-Asian and nonaligned worlds and to wall off the rest of Latin America. "The theme of 'positive neutralism' and rapprochement with the Afro-Asian bloc are all the rage within Fidel Castro's governing clique," Rubottom wrote to the European and Near East and South Asian bureaus, citing the commercial and diplomatic outreach in Asia and the Mediterranean, visits to Cuba by the Egyptian and Yugoslav foreign ministers, and the China vote at the UN. Moreover, he wrote, "the Cuban regime in a variety of ways is trying to promote neutralism in Latin America" by sponsoring international student, labor, and youth conferences and federations that were "Communist-infiltrated 'neutralist' and 'third position'" in orientation and were expected to pressure Latin American governments to soften their pro-U.S. and anti-Communist positions on domestic and international issues.

The implications, for Rubottom, were global. Pronouncing himself "disturbed" by the warmth with which Nasser and Tito had welcomed Castro into the emerging nonaligned camp, he considered it important to remind such leaders that "the ability of the United States to view neutralism in the Near East and South Asia with understanding and forbearance has been affected to an important degree by the unity of all the American Republics which has provided us with essential support on key security issues, such as the China question." By embracing a regime that was undermining the unity of the Western Hemisphere under U.S. leadership, "the neutralists may well also be . . . undermining our ability to view certain aspects of their own positive neutralism with forbearance." Rubottom asked for "measures [that] might be taken to dampen the enthusiasm of neutralist governments" for Cuba, suggesting "both informal diplomatic approaches and *unattributed* propaganda exposing the realities of the Cuban situation and the Communist participation in the neutralist drive."[16]

The proposed Congress of Underdeveloped Nations became a focal point in this effort. Starting in January 1960, Havana and Washington engaged in a global diplomatic struggle, publicly and secretly, over the conference. High-level Cuban delegations fanned out across the world to build support for the initiative; partnering with Brazil and other Latin American governments, U.S. officials worked—successfully—to undermine it.

Four Cuban delegations visited Europe, Asia, Africa, and Latin America in the first three months of 1960 to make Cuba's case for the conference. Roa himself led a delegation to Morocco, Tunisia, Egypt, Greece, and Yugoslavia.[17] Cuba's ambassador-designate to India, Eugenio Soler, headed a mission to the Middle East and Asia.[18] Carlos Lechuga and Leví Marrero, ambassadors to Chile and the OAS, respectively, visited every Latin American republic except the Dominican, Nicaraguan, Paraguayan, and Haitian dictatorships, with which Cuba had no diplomatic relations.[19] In March, military officer William Gálvez led a delegation to Ghana, Guinea, and the Ivory Coast.[20] These missions coincided with a move to establish relations with over a dozen African and Asian states.[21] Cuban records of the Roa, Soler, and Gálvez missions are not available. But Marrero and Lechuga's forty-seven page report to Roa on their Latin American mission gives an inside account of Cuban efforts to launch the conference, of its significance for Cuban and Latin American engagement with the Third World, and of U.S. and Latin American resistance to this project.

Publicly and in private sessions, Roa, Marrero and Lechuga, and other Cuban officials insisted that the conference was strictly economic in nature, with no political motive or the intention to create a global "third force."[22] A memo presented to the Latin American ambassadors in Havana and delivered by Lechuga and Marrero to each host foreign minister proposed seven broad and uncontroversial topics for the congress to address: stabilizing global commodity prices; expanding international trade; regional economic integration; strengthening multilateral lending institutions' assistance to developing countries; agrarian reform; industrialization; and UN technical assistance to developing countries. The suggested goal of the congress was to draft a "Charter of Economic Rights of Peoples." The conference, the Cubans suggested, had the approval and logistical support of the UN Secretariat.[23]

U.S. officials, nevertheless, were suspicious. The U.S. embassy advised in a 5 January cable that the conference "poses danger of weakening [the] fabric of inter-American cooperation and solidarity" if many Latin American governments attended. From the U.S. point of view, "It would be highly desirable to have LA governments throw cold water on [the] proposal on [the] grounds [that] their development problems [are] not comparable to those confronting Asian and African countries and [the] long tradition [in the] American family of nations to seek solution [to] their problems through mutual effort." Such a cold reception "would be [a] serious blow" to Cuba's government "and further isolate it in hemispheric official and public opinion."[24] Officials in Washington agreed, and on 6 January the State Department cabled its embassies in Latin America that it believed that the Cubans' real goals were to "secure wider recognition, prestige, and status" for the revolution, to "obtain support and allies for neutral position in East-West struggle," and to "provide [a] forum for continuation [of] charges against US of colonialism, economic exploitation, [and] political domination." For these reasons, and the overall downward trend in U.S.-Cuban relations, the Department hoped that the congress would not be held or "that if held it will be poorly attended and result in failure."[25]

Instructed to raise, at their discretion, any arguments that might persuade their host governments, U.S. diplomats abroad began working against the conference. An *aide-memoire* to Mexico's foreign minister from the U.S. ambassador on 12 January—just after Marrero and Lechuga left Mexico for Guatemala—provides one example, repeating verbatim the alleged "real purposes of the Conference" from the secret cable of 6 January. A mostly Afro-Asian conference, the note also suggested, could not effectively address Latin America's unique developmental context and challenges; holding it without UN or OAS support would "harm" both organizations and "serve only to confuse and delay" their existing development efforts.[26]

U.S. officials were not alone in their hostility. As early as 4 January—just after Roa left for the Mediterranean, and two days before the proposal was even presented to Latin American ambassadors in Havana ahead of Lechuga and Marrero's departure for Mexico and points south—Brazil's Foreign Minister Horacio Lafer had reached out to the U.S. embassy in Rio de Janeiro. Lafer explained Brazil's opposition to a congress that, he indicated, "could benefit only Communists" and proposed that Brazil and the United States work together to discourage attendance, particularly by Latin American states.[27]

The United States responded to the Brazilian initiative with cautious enthusiasm. Washington cabled the embassy in Rio that the "Department shares Brazilian Foreign Minister's concern" about the conference "and agrees on desirability of influence designed to discourage attendance." Egypt became an early target. Hoping that Brazil could persuade Cairo that the rest of Latin America did not support Cuba's initiative, and that if Nasser were cool to the congress other Arab and African governments would follow his lead, the cable instructed the embassy to urge Lafer to have Brazil's diplomats express their views to the Egyptians. However, the cable acknowledged, "US Government must move carefully" given its testy relationship with Cuba, its status as an uninvited outsider, and the fact that the Cubans were likely to exploit for propaganda purposes any evidence that the United States was working to undermine the conference. It was, therefore, "of utmost importance that our concurrence in or knowledge of measures being taken by Brazil . . . not become known."[28] On his own initiative, Manoel Pio

Correa, chief of the Foreign Ministry's political section, spoke along these lines to Egypt's ambassador on 7 January, but got the impression that Brazil would have more success influencing Latin American rather than Middle Eastern governments.[29]

By mid-January U.S. diplomats in Latin America and around the world were making what Rubottom called "a frontal attack" against the conference.[30] While not commenting publicly, U.S. officials were stressing in private that the initiative threatened the political and economic interests of the United States and the entire hemisphere.[31] Furthermore, they were coordinating with their Brazilian counterparts in capitals as far away as Bangkok to try to influence governments' views of the initiative.[32]

Within Latin America, the contest pitted Cuba against Brazil and the Southern Cone countries, backed by the United States. Pio Correa told the U.S. ambassador in Rio that Argentina and Chile had agreed with Brazil to jointly oppose the conference and persuade other Latin American governments not to attend.[33] Marrero and Lechuga perceived this influence once they reached the South American half of their tour. The Mexican and Panamanian governments had already agreed in principle to attend, while the Guatemalans, Salvadorans, and Hondurans had received the ambassadors' presentation in polite but noncommittal fashion.[34] But Marrero and Lechuga wrote to Roa that upon reaching Colombia on 18 January, "for the first time in our journey we encountered in Bogotá formal objections to the initiative. . . . These objections, as we managed to confirm later in our visits to the Foreign Ministries of Rio de Janeiro, Buenos Aires, and Santiago de Chile, seem to have a common patron." While the government of Venezuela, the next stop on their tour, agreed to attend, they wrote, "From Brazil onwards we encountered ever-stronger resistance to the initiative, gathering furthermore the impression that in more than one previous opportunity the Brazilian Foreign Ministry had promoted the initiatives and purposes of the United States among the South American foreign ministries."[35]

While Brazil and the United States were both working against the conference, it is important to note the evidence that Brazil did so for its own reasons, and not out of deference to Washington, as the Cubans believed. As noted above, it was Lafer who reached out to the State Department about coordinating against the conference, not the other way around. The Brazilians' chief motive appears to have been concern that Cuba's proposed congress would derail their own development initiative, Operaçao Panamericana (Operation Pan-America, OPA), which President Juscelino Kubitschek had been promoting since 1958 to a reluctant Eisenhower administration.[36] Marrero and Lechuga reported that "despite all the effort of our arguments insisting that the Havana Conference supported, in a concentric manner, Operation Panamericana and that it would elevate it to the world stage, making the struggle for development on the continental level more effective," the Brazilians saw the initiatives as contradictory, not complementary and viewed Afro-Asian commodity exporters as "competitors" rather than comrades. Several Andean and Southern Cone governments, notably those of Ecuador and Colombia, were likewise concerned that the proposed congress would undermine OPA and other development activities under the OAS aegis.[37] As the controversy over the Havana conference continued, Lafer and other Brazilian and Argentine officials pressured Herter and Rubottom to move to implement OPA and other OAS activities in order to sap the energy from revolutionary movements in the hemisphere. The Havana conference had become a form of leverage.[38]

Of the hemisphere's leading governments, only Mexico and Venezuela agreed, along with Panama, to attend the conference, while declining to co-sponsor it. Both did so, furthermore, on the condition that a majority of Latin American states would also attend. Mexican enthusiasm diminished rapidly when it became clear that the UN Secretariat was not, in fact, supporting the conference, as Cuba had been suggesting.[39] At a time when the *New York Times* reported that "it is an open secret at the United Nations that the United States is discouraging participation in the conference,"[40] the Mexican government ignored a Cuban request that Mexican delegates at the UN lobby the secretary-general's staff to reconsider.[41]

Roa visited Caracas in late March to seek further Venezuelan support. Publicly, the resulting communiqué reiterated that Venezuela "accepted [the invitation] in principle."[42] But in a private letter to his Cuban counterpart, Osvaldo Dorticós, Venezuelan President Rómulo Betancourt warned that his country's attendance was conditioned on being joined by a majority of Latin American governments: "We here believe that, even if a large number of Asian and African representatives were to attend, if the majority of Latin American representatives were absent, the event would be, not a success, but rather a failure."[43] As Betancourt wrote privately to one of his coalition partners, attending as one of the few Latin Americans at a mostly Afro-Asian conference in the Western Hemisphere "would contribute to the opening of a rift among the countries of our own language, located in the American geographical orbit and having problems and preoccupations similar to those of Venezuela."[44] But the rest of Latin America either declined outright or avoided responding to the initiative. In early June, Venezuela's foreign minister reportedly urged Roa and Dorticós to abandon the project.[45]

Yugoslavia's Tito endorsed the conference, but the Cubans did not invite the nonaligned Communist state so as to avoid awkward questions about the less-developed Eastern European allies of Moscow.[46] In Asia and Africa, committed support came only from the most militantly anticolonial nonaligned governments. Nasser agreed in January to co-sponsor the conference, though Egyptian enthusiasm for this step later waned.[47] Indonesia's Sukarno, the first head of state to visit revolutionary Cuba, issued a joint statement with Castro in May reiterating Indonesia's support for the congress.[48] Kwame Nkrumah of Ghana and Sékou Touré of Guinea also indicated their support. But the other African and Asian governments that were consulted—a group that included most of the pro-Western and nonaligned states but excluded China, North Korea, and North Vietnam—remained either hostile or uncommitted.[49] State Department analysts concluded that "the essentially negative response on the part of every Latin American and several Afro-Asian governments . . . amounts to a serious rebuff for Castro."[50]

For Cuba, the lesson of the initiative was to show who the revolution's real friends were. Marrero and Lechuga reported to Roa upon the conclusion of their tour that "our direct observation of the social and economic realities of the Latin American countries permits us to confirm that the oligarchies that govern almost all of the Latin American countries feel seriously threatened by the popularity that the objectives of the Cuban Revolution have achieved among the masses. For this reason they are reluctant to cooperate with any measure that might be considered tending to praise and consolidate our Revolution." Politically, they wrote, "The traditional political parties of the Latin American nations move constantly against our Revolution. The only real political contribution that we have observed comes from the popular and liberal parties and most especially from their youth," as was the case of the center-left parties in Venezuela, Peru, and Chile, and the leftist Frente Nacionalista led by presidential candidate Jânio Quadros in Brazil.[51] The Mexican and Venezuelan governments, supportive in principle, proved unwilling in practice to lobby on Cuba's behalf. Before Havana abandoned the initiative entirely in late July 1960, U.S. officials saw signs that the Cubans were moving to invite nongovernmental delegations—from opposition parties, youth or labor movements, or other groups—to represent countries whose governments opposed the congress.[52]

The failure of the Underdeveloped Nations Conference, therefore, distanced Cuba from other Latin American governments, pushing it toward the sort of leftist regional and tri-continental youth, labor, and "people's" organizations and conferences that would proliferate in Havana for the rest of the decade and that would culminate in the militant revolutionary Tricontinental Conference in 1966 and the Latin American Solidarity Organization conference in 1967.[53] As early as late March 1960, Castro announced that Cuba was no longer constrained by its commitments under the OAS system. "We do not feel bound by this [Rio] treaty," he told a televised audience.[54]

It also revealed Cuba's affinity with the left wing of the emerging nonaligned world, in Indonesia, Egypt, and the radical West African states. In September 1960, as U.S.-Cuban relations collapsed and Cuba went about nationalizing all U.S. property and reorienting its economy toward the socialist bloc, Castro made his celebrated visit to the UN. While he famously embraced Soviet leader Nikita Khrushchev, he also deepened ties to the nonaligned leaders present; these talks were the seeds of Cuba's participation in the NAM conferences.[55]

Cuba and the Non-Aligned Movement, 1961–1964

A comprehensive account of Cuba's participation in the NAM, which peaked with Havana hosting the movement's sixth summit in 1979, is not possible here. The partial declassification of relevant Cuban Foreign Ministry files, however, provides new insight into Cuba's approach to the NAM in the 1960s.[56] These documents, in the context of other available sources, reveal that Cuban objectives toward the movement from early 1961 through late 1964 were quite consistent, even as other events profoundly unsettled Cuba's relations with Latin America and the Soviet Union.

In April 1961, Nasser and Tito included Cuba among the invitees to a conference in Cairo in June to prepare for the first Non-Aligned summit. Their interactions with the Cubans at the UN the previous autumn, when the groundwork for the summit was laid, had been positive. More spectacularly, Castro's forces had defeated the U.S.-sponsored Cuban exile invasion at the Bay of Pigs just days before the invitations were issued on 26 April. Castro had declared the Cuban Revolution socialist, but had concluded no formal alliance with Moscow. His prestige as an independent anti-imperialist nationalist leader was at its peak.[57]

Perhaps due to post-invasion turmoil at home, Cuba's preparations for the 5 June preparatory conference appear to have been haphazard. As late as 21 May the embassy in Cairo complained that it had neither instructions nor even confirmation that Cuba would attend.[58] But two weeks later, Roa, leading Cuba's delegation in Cairo, boldly proposed that Havana host the summit, since Cuba was now "the center of resistance to United States imperialism."[59] The published conference report says only that Yugoslavia was chosen as host over Egypt and Cuba "after a short discussion."[60] Writing in 1966, the Indian diplomat and journalist G. H. Jansen added that "the idea of Cuba was greeted in total silence."[61] Despite two years of outreach to the Afro-Asian world, Cuba had a long way to go before it would become a leader of the incipient NAM.

Cuban officials' views of the Third World and Havana's place therein are presented in a thirty-six-page MINREX paper written in August 1961, between the Cairo preparatory talks and the Belgrade summit. After tracing the history of Afro-Asian gatherings since 1955, the paper declared that Cuba's participation in the Non-Aligned conference "marks a new era in the collaboration of the underdeveloped countries, removing it from the purely Afro-Asian framework to extend it to Latin America" and building on the "solidarity" that had grown since Cuba began voting with the Afro-Asian states on colonial and development issues at the UN in 1959. "The essential interests of the Afro-Asian countries and the Latin American countries coincide," the paper asserted. Economically and socially, they shared problems of underdevelopment, inequality, and neocolonial exploitation by foreign capital. Politically, colonialism lingered in the Americas in Puerto Rico, the Guyanas, and the Panama Canal Zone, as it did in Africa and Asia; Cuba was punished for its independent foreign policy just as Laos and other Afro-Asian states were. Simply put, the three continents "have a principal common enemy: imperialism," especially U.S. imperialism. Accordingly, the paper concluded, "the path to the common victory" was to strengthen diplomatic, economic, and cultural ties and mutual support among the peoples of the three continents. This emerging, united Third World, moreover, had a natural ally: "The Afro-Asian and Latin American peoples today can count on the inestimable aid of the socialist countries. No more can the imperialists determine the course of history thanks to the existence of the socialist world. If to this is joined the unified solidarity of the Afro-Asian and Latin American peoples, colonialism in all its forms will endure briefly, impotent before the forces of socialism, national liberation and peace."[62]

In Cuban diplomats' view by the second half of 1961 there was, therefore, no contradiction—as Castro's detractors often alleged—between Havana's close economic and political ties to the Soviet Union and the socialist camp, on one hand, and its membership in the NAM, on the other. Cuban officials saw nonalignment as synonymous with their revolution's independence and anti-imperialism. Cuban participation in the NAM was intended to advance the process that would connect Latin America to Asia and Africa *and* to the socialist world. In the near term, support from both the Second and Third Worlds was desirable, even essential, to shield Cuba from U.S. efforts to isolate and destroy the revolution; in the long term, the two worlds' shared anti-imperialism would provide the means to fully defeat U.S.-led imperialism.

For this reason, Roa had pushed successfully at Cairo to secure invitations to Belgrade for other Latin American governments, a move welcomed by the Egyptian, Yugoslav, and Indian governments for their own reasons.[63] Bolivia, Ecuador, Mexico, and Brazil under its new president, Quadros—four of the Latin American governments most sympathetic toward Cuba at this time—were invited to the summit, while more hostile neighbors such as Venezuela (Betancourt and Castro having fallen out completely) and the conservative Central American governments were not. Cuba could therefore hope to demonstrate that it was not isolated as the only Latin American exponent of nonalignment and independence from the United States, without too great a risk of being openly criticized by its neighbors.[64]

As several historians have demonstrated, Washington vigorously opposed Latin American attendance. While the John F. Kennedy administration tended to be tolerant of nonalignment in newly independent Asia and Africa, it was hostile to any drift toward "neutralism" by established allies, especially in Latin America. U.S. diplomats assiduously discouraged Latin American governments from attending the Belgrade parley. In the end, Mexico declined to participate, while Bolivia, Ecuador, and Brazil sent observers only.[65] U.S. policy thereby confirms the Cubans' belief that Washington sought to divide Latin America from the rest of the Third World—the latest episode in a long tradition of trying to insulate the Western Hemisphere from Old World influences, going back to the conception of the Monroe Doctrine in the 1820s.

A MINREX paper on Cuba's objectives, written between the preparatory talks in June and the start of the Belgrade summit on September 1, develops Cuba's goals in more detail and shows that the struggle with the United States dominated the country's approach to nonalignment, but not to the exclusion of a wider worldview. Cuba's "essential objective" was to "obtain the support of the Afro-Asian countries in condemning North American imperialism in its systematic policy of all types of aggression against Cuba." The Cubans hoped to see the conference "condemn imperialism, such that the fundamental weight of this just measure falls on the United States." Specifically, Cuba's delegates were to secure the conference's condemnation of U.S. violations of Cuban air and naval space; of the "subversion and harassment" the United States perpetrated against Cuba directly and by supporting counterrevolutionaries; of the U.S. policy of economic "discrimination and aggression" against Cuba; and of the presence of foreign military bases, such as the Guantánamo Bay naval station, in the former colonial world. Along with these items specific to Cuba, the ministry also hoped to secure resolutions condemning apartheid in South Africa and racial discrimination everywhere (including the United States), endorsing the People's Republic for the China seat at the UN, and supporting the independence movements in Portuguese Guinea, Angola, Southwest Africa, British Guiana, and Puerto Rico. The concept of "peaceful coexistence," Cuba asserted, was "one and indivisible" and should apply not just to relations among the great powers but also between them and small countries.[66] Cuban objectives, therefore, were at once particular to itself and global in scope.

Dorticós and Roa, leading Cuba's delegation to Belgrade, fought for these positions both publicly and in private sessions.[67] Addressing the conference, Dorticós noted that Cuba had worked for two years to make nonaligned and underdeveloped countries' voices heard on the world stage and took the opportunity "to draw special attention to that initiative of the Cuban Government . . . to convene an international meeting of the under-industrialized countries." As head of the only full Latin American delegation, Dorticós reminded the attendees "that the problems of the struggle against imperialism and for the liquidation of colonialism and neocolonialism take place not only in Asia and in Africa, but also in Latin America." This movement's ultimate goal, Dorticós argued, must be "the liquidation of colonialism, of neocolonialism and of imperialist exploitation," which could come only by abandoning "diplomatic dissimulation" and confronting their concrete expressions in the policies of the imperialist powers, chiefly the United States, whose aggressions Dorticós catalogued indignantly.[68] The *New York Times* reported that both in tone and on specific issues, Dorticós's address was the most confrontational toward the United States and closest to Soviet positions of all.[69] This also held true behind the scenes. Roa later told MINREX officials that he and Dorticós had "moved among different delegations to slow down [Western] propaganda" against the Soviet nuclear-weapons test conducted just before the summit, helping soften speeches and avert resolutions that would have criticized Moscow's policy.[70]

Cuban diplomats deemed Belgrade a success. The conference declaration stated that the Guantánamo base "affects the sovereignty and territorial integrity" of Cuba. In addition to the general statement upholding countries' right of self-determination without outside "intimidation, interference, or intervention," Cuba secured a specific statement that "the participating countries believe that the right of Cuba as of any other nation to freely choose their political and social systems in accordance with their own conditions, needs, and possibilities should be respected."[71] A MINREX assessment concluded that on issues specific to Cuba and its struggle with the United States, Belgrade was "a scene of victory for our cause."[72]

Equally encouraging were the prospects for relations between the Third World and the socialist world. The MINREX Yugoslavia desk concluded that even where some resolutions fell short due to Indian or Yugoslav efforts to moderate or block them, the general sentiments and specific positions of most delegations on Cold War and colonial issues—including UN reform, the definition of peaceful coexistence, Algerian independence, and recognition of East Germany—"coincide in their fundamentals with the points of view of the socialist camp." The Cuban delegation's efforts, in tandem with those of Indonesia, Ghana, and especially Guinea and Mali, were judged to have "played a decisive role in the achievement of these positive results."[73]

Most importantly, "the imperialists" and their Non-Aligned collaborators, chiefly moderate India and "revisionist" Yugoslavia, "failed in their attempts to define and bind together a neutral 'third bloc' and to define it as being in opposition to 'the two blocs,' a well-known definition that would situate the USSR and the socialist camp in the same position as the imperialists."[74] This "specter" of equivalence and equidistance between imperialism and socialism, Roa reported, had been roundly opposed, as was crucial for Cuba's interests.[75] Instead, another MINREX paper concluded, "The leaders present at Belgrade made it clear that they are not in favor of the integration of the so-called 'third position,' that this does not apply where there are no neutral men nor neutral states. Simply put, the peoples that went to Belgrade represented but one camp, that of the peoples all over the world with no possibility but condemnation for the imperialist system, and not of adopting a neutral posture towards it." This attitude, the author predicted, "will permit the countries present at Belgrade to unite themselves with the socialist countries and dictate the majority opinion" at future UN General Assembly sessions, where the Second and Third World anti-imperialist camp, if united, held a commanding majority. All of this, of course, represented a defeat for the United States.[76]

The period between the first NAM summit in Belgrade in September 1961 and the second summit in Cairo in October 1964 would, however, sorely test Cuba's efforts to bridge the Second and Third Worlds and the four continents of Asia, Africa, (Eastern) Europe and (Latin) America. First, Cuba's promotion of militant revolution at home and abroad soured its relations with its Latin American neighbors. In December 1961 Fidel declared that he was, and would always be, a Marxist-Leninist, an ideology that was to guide the building of a unified revolutionary party-state and the construction of socialism and eventually communism in Cuba. This ideological program combined with charges that Cuba was supporting subversive movements in several Latin American countries led the OAS to vote, narrowly, to suspend Cuba in January 1962.[77]

Soon after, Khrushchev proposed stationing Soviet nuclear missiles in Cuba, which Castro accepted both as a means of deterring an expected U.S. invasion and as Cuba's strategic contribution to global socialism. The two governments, in secret, signed an agreement providing Cuba a Soviet guarantee against U.S. aggression, intending to make this military pact public along with the missiles once the latter were operational and Khrushchev visited Cuba at the end of 1962.[78] The ensuing Missile Crisis, when exposure of the missiles by the United States revealed that Castro and Khrushchev had provocatively escalated the Cold War nuclear confrontation, further distanced Cuba's government from those of Latin America; the OAS called unanimously for the missiles' withdrawal, and Castro's strongest regional critics, such as Betancourt, used the crisis to call for further action against Havana.[79] The discovery in late 1963 of a cache of weapons buried on a Venezuelan beach—supplied, Betancourt said, by Havana to bolster Venezuela's left-wing insurgency—provided the final straw for Cuba in the hemisphere: in July 1964, the OAS called on all members who had not already done so to sever diplomatic, commercial, and travel connections with Cuba. Though Mexico (and nonmember Canada) did not comply, Cuba's isolation in the Americas had reached its most severe point.[80]

Meanwhile, Khrushchev's decision—made without consulting the Cubans—to withdraw the missiles in exchange for Kennedy's pledge not to invade Cuba and to withdraw U.S. missiles from Turkey infuriated the

Cuban leadership and much of the Cuban public, none of whom trusted Kennedy's word. Their secret defense pact was essentially voided without ever being announced, and the undiscovered Soviet tactical nuclear weapons and combat troops were removed, leaving Cuba indefensible against a U.S. invasion. The Cubans could never fully trust that Moscow would come to their aid from afar against the United States if it meant risking superpower war. Soviet documents reveal that the Cuban leadership continued pushing in 1963 for a formal military alliance, but Khrushchev refused, believing that Castro was too unreliable to join the Warsaw Pact or a bilateral alliance and that such a public commitment would only assist anti-Castro propagandists.[81] A further source of acrimony was Havana's adherence to a revolutionary foreign policy, whose emphasis on immediate, armed struggle in Latin America and elsewhere contradicted Moscow's position of peaceful competition with the capitalist states and the gradual building of socialism in the underdeveloped world. Sino-Soviet competition in the Third World exacerbated this tension, as the Cubans, despite being dependent on Soviet aid and trade, were ideologically and tactically closer to the more militant Chinese. For these and other reasons, Cuban-Soviet relations remained delicate into 1968.[82]

Cuba therefore approached the second Non-Aligned summit in Cairo in the fall of 1964 in a precarious position. It was estranged from the United States and Latin America and branded a de facto member of the Soviet bloc because of its Marxism-Leninism and economic dependence on Moscow. But from Cuba's point of view, Moscow's commitment was unreliable. They shared diplomatic and political interests and trade deals; but while their military agreements provided Cuba with Soviet weapons and technical assistance, they did not bind Moscow to defend Cuba as an ally.[83] Cuba's relationship with the nonaligned and the imperative to reconcile the Second and Third Worlds and push both in a radical anti-imperialist direction, had therefore become simultaneously more important and more challenging.

Throughout the buildup to the second summit in Cairo, Cuba's claim to Non-Aligned status was more contested than in 1961. In late January 1964, as Nasser and Tito prepared to issue invitations, Roa wrote to Castro that "the African ambassadors [in Havana] take Cuba's participation as a given, as do the socialist ones."[84] The Chinese ambassador told Roa's deputy that Beijing urged Cuba and the other "countries of the left" within the NAM to participate "with the goal of encouraging the Conference toward the revolutionary and anti-imperialist struggle."[85] But officials of some NAM members, including India, Saudi Arabia, Morocco, Yugoslavia, and even Ghana, questioned, sometimes obliquely and sometimes directly, Cuba's claim to Non-Aligned status.[86] The Soviet missiles, Cuba's chargé in Cairo reported, were the main point raised in these arguments.[87] In the end, the sponsors Tito, Nasser, and Srimavo Bandarainake of Ceylon decided to invite all those who had attended Belgrade, thereby grandfathering in Cuba. The decision, ratified at the preparatory ministers' meeting in Colombo, resolved to add all other independent Arab and African states and others, including Latin Americans, on a case-by-case basis.[88] The State Department noted ruefully that South American countries facing Cuban-backed or -inspired insurgencies, especially Venezuela, had the strongest case for disputing Cuba's claim to Non-Alignment with international Communism, but that their delegates, as nonvoting observers, were reluctant to force the issue.[89]

The U.S. view was unambiguous. By 1964 the Johnson administration had arrived at a hierarchy of desirable thematic and institutional frameworks for Third World internationalism: it supported a Third World organized around the concept of economic development and centered on the UN, followed less desirably by what they termed a "genuine" nonalignment independent of and equidistant from both superpowers and their allies and working toward peaceful and (from the U.S. point of view) constructive solutions to the Cold War, colonialism, and underdevelopment. Militant revolutionary anti-imperialism of the Cuban and Chinese varieties, as embodied in Havana's vision for the NAM and Beijing's project for a "Second Bandung" conference, were to be opposed above all.[90] So, too, was any drift toward "neutralism" by U.S. allies, especially in Latin America, and so U.S. diplomats again discouraged all OAS members from associating themselves with Cuba, and weakening the OAS and UN, by attending the Cairo summit. All U.S. overseas posts were instructed in July to argue that Cuba's participation would delegitimize the entire NAM, being "a travesty on 'nonalignment' label" that raised "serious doubts as to real motives and validity of avowed conference objectives."[91] Despite these arguments, Argentina, Bolivia, Brazil, Chile, Mexico, Uruguay, and Venezuela all ended up attending as observers.

For Cuba, the objectives remained mostly the same as in 1961, with a few additions given the changing international context. The fundamental objective was again securing the maximum solidarity for Cuba and condemnation of the United States for its various coercive actions in the diplomatic, economic, military, and covert spheres, reaffirming the resolutions taken at Belgrade. The new goals included gaining the conference's condemnation of the OAS actions against Cuba and its endorsement for Cuban admission to the newly formed G-77 at the UN, where the Latin American caucus was blocking its membership.[92] Having once again opposed—unsuccessfully, this time—an invitation to Venezuela, which had led the OAS charge against Cuba, Havana hoped to question the Venezuelan government's right to attend and to secure a resolution endorsing the "national liberation movement" there, along with those in Vietnam, Portuguese Africa, the Congo, British Guiana, and Puerto Rico.[93]

As U.S. intelligence analysts reasoned, "Cuba's interest in pressing its claim to 'nonaligned' [and not Soviet client] status and its desire to take a position of leadership among underdeveloped countries in the 'anti-imperialist revolution' are goals that may be difficult to reconcile."[94] In one example, Roa, unbeknownst to Washington, proposed to his Indonesian counterpart Subandrio to hold a meeting of "like-minded"—that is, militantly anti-imperialist and Communist-backed or pro-Communist—foreign ministers in Cairo to coordinate on the eve of the summit; but Subandrio, Roa reported, declined, arguing that creating a new "bloc" *within* the NAM was not "politically appropriate."[95] Such a leftists' caucus would likely have alienated more moderate NAM members.

The attendance of Venezuela highlights this central dilemma for Cuba in its militant approach to the NAM at this time of maximum vulnerability. Cuba's diplomats had made clear that they considered Venezuela's invitation "an unfriendly act" against Cuba.[96] "Our opposition [to Venezuela's claim to nonalignment] is even more unyielding [*irreductible*] after the Meeting of Ministers of the OAS, in which it played the repugnant role of North American imperialism's attack dog" in pushing for sanctions on Cuba, Roa wrote in August. He instructed that in discussing the upcoming summit with host governments, "attacking Venezuela will be the primary issue."[97]

Fearing that Dorticós and Roa would disrupt the proceedings over the presence of the Venezuelan observer or the issue of the Venezuelan insurgents' legitimacy, Egyptian, Indian, and Yugoslav diplomats all warned Cuba's representatives in Cairo not to threaten the entire summit over what was, to them, a minor and parochial issue. "Cuba should understand," the Yugoslavs chided one embassy official, "that [the Cubans] are not the only ones attending the Conference."[98] Upon arriving in Cairo, Roa took pains to reassure his Yugoslav and Egyptian counterparts that Cuba's objections to Venezuela's presence would be appropriately diplomatic. Cuba's case, moreover, "is not local, nor even regional, but rather of global character," Roa argued, since the OAS actions were, he alleged, preparing the ground for a U.S. invasion that would violate the UN Charter and threaten the entire postwar global order.[99] In the event, Cuba's "unyielding" opposition had its limits. Dorticós and Venezuela's delegate each cast doubt on the other's nonalignment; the Cubans walked out at the start of the Venezuelan's speech, but did not quit the conference entirely, and matters escalated no further.[100]

Dorticós again made the case for Cuba's view of nonalignment as revolutionary anti-imperialism. Cuba, he told the conference, had the right to participate since it was uncommitted to any military bloc. However, he explained, "this does not mean for Cuba, and should not mean for any country participating here, a neutral position" in world affairs. Rather, Dorticós elaborated, "We reject equidistance" in the binary struggles of the contemporary international scene: peace versus war; political and economic independence versus imperialism, colonialism, and neocolonialism; social equality versus racial discrimination; development versus exploitation. Lasting peace, he argued, would be possible only "when the last remnant of exploitation . . . and imperialist domination disappears from the face of the Earth."[101]

The second NAM summit had a more left-leaning and militant tenor than the first, focusing more on anti-imperialism than on themes of world peace, disarmament, or development. The final declaration affirmed the Cuban positions that "peaceful coexistence is an indivisible whole" and that "imperialism, colonialism, and neo-colonialism constitute a basic source of international tension and conflict." It urged that "all necessary political, moral, and material assistance be rendered to the liberation movements" in Africa, Palestine, and the Arabian Peninsula. It also "condemn[ed] the manifestations of colonialism and neo-colonialism in Latin America" and upheld Latin American and Caribbean peoples' right to self-determination, particularly in British Guiana, the French possessions, and Puerto Rico. The U.S. embargo against Cuba was criticized as "contrary to the principles of international law and peaceful coexistence," and the Guantánamo base was unambiguously labeled "a violation of Cuba's sovereignty and territorial integrity."[102]

Both the Cuban and U.S. foreign services considered the Cairo summit another success for Havana's diplomacy. In his notes on the outcome, Roa concluded that Cuba had achieved "the approval, without objections or reservations, of the questions referring to Cuba" and, more broadly, "acceptance of all the principles and proposals supported by Cuba."[103] State Department analysts likewise concluded that the summit had a "generally anti-Western tone," with the United States and its allies criticized explicitly for specific policies while the Soviet bloc was subjected to no similar treatment. "As presently constituted," one analysis concluded, "the nonaligned movement should be regarded as useful from the Soviet Union's point of view," given the Second and Third Worlds' convergence on anti-imperialism and the success of the NAM's leftists—Ghana, Guinea, Mali, Algeria, Indonesia, and Cuba—in contesting the moderating influence of India, Yugoslavia, and Egypt. The Cubans, meanwhile, "probably are right in their jubilant conclusion that they have 'arrived' among the nonaligned," given that their presence at the meeting was largely uncontested, their views of nonalignment were largely accepted, and their specific complaints against the United States were endorsed again.[104] Choosing to look beyond Cuba's hemispheric ostracism, Roa called U.S. efforts to isolate Cuba a "spectacular failure" and concluded that "Cuba's international position today is more solid than ever: it not only has the fraternal support of the socialist camp, but also the active backing of the forty-seven countries that attended the Conference, formally committed to make the principles and declarations formulated in Cairo into tangible reality."[105]

Conclusion

Cuba's international position by the mid-1960s, therefore, exemplifies the tension between pragmatic engagement and revolutionary transformation. Years of diplomatic outreach to the Third World had made the country an accepted and influential voice in the NAM, whose positions on global issues of the Cold War, anti-imperialism, and peaceful coexistence and on the local issue of U.S.-Cuban relations increasingly agreed with Cuba's. And yet, Cuba's revolutionary fervor and Marxism-Leninism at home and support for revolutionary insurrection abroad had isolated it from practically all of Latin America and led to the failure of its Conference of Underdeveloped Countries initiative and its exclusion from the OAS and the G-77 and Latin-American caucuses at the UN.

Three conferences held in Havana between December 1964 and August 1967—the first a secret meeting of Latin American Communist parties, the second the Tricontinental Conference in January 1966, and finally the OLAS conference—demonstrated Havana's unwavering commitment to the armed struggle, particularly in Latin America. The Tricontinental and OLAS conferences associated Cuba with the Communist-front Afro-Asian People's Solidarity Organization (AAPSO), and pushed this organ-

The limits of national liberation under the framework of moderate nonalignment during the early 1960s encouraged to the growth of more radical forms of anti-imperialism. In January 1966, supported by Marxist and militant revolutionary organizations throughout the Third World, Cuba launched the Organización de Solidaridad de los Pueblos de Africa, Asia y América Latina (OSPAAAL, Organization of Solidarity of the Peoples of Africa, Asia, and Latin America). Known as the Tricontinental, OSPAAAL brought the leaders of radical Third World states together with armed liberation movements throughout the Global South. Here on the dais sit (from left to right), Ghanaian Vice President John Tettegah; Secretary General of Egypt's Afro-Asian Writers' Association Yousseff El-Sebai; Cuban officials including Defense Minister Raúl Castro, Prime Minister Fidel Castro, President Osvaldo Dórticos, and Foreign Minister Raúl Roa; Pedro Medina Silva, Vice President of Venezuela's National Liberation Army; and the second-in-command of the Vietcong, Nguyen Van Tien. (Image courtesy of Keystone-France/Gamma-Keystone via Getty Images.)

ization, too, into yet more militant channels that made even Moscow and Cairo, to say nothing of the governments of the Western Hemisphere, uncomfortable.[106]

Ideologically, there was no contradiction for the Cuban leadership in endorsing the *via armada* of revolutionary liberation and socialism, on the one hand, and nonalignment, on the other. But Cuba paid a steep price for this revolutionary ardor. The U.S. embargo and covert program continued to harass the island. Leftist militancy in Latin America empowered reactionaries to prosecute relentless counterrevolutionary campaigns against leftist enemies—real or exaggerated—from Mexico to the Southern Cone, leaving right-wing and military forces in control of most of the region by the end of the decade.[107] And Cuba's militancy continued to strain its relations with Moscow, which was seeking deeper commercial and diplomatic relations with many of the same Latin American governments Castro hoped to see overthrown. Only by winding down its support for armed revolution in Latin America, particularly after Che Guevara's martyrdom in Bolivia in 1967, did Havana begin to repair its relations with its neighbors and with Moscow and to reverse its hemispheric isolation.[108] Gradually reestablishing its diplomatic relationships in Latin America in the early 1970s would allow Cuba to take fuller advantage of its position in the NAM and to aspire to play the leading role in bridging continents within the Third World and working to unite the Global South and the socialist world in the 1970s, a role its policymakers had in fact envisioned for the country since 1959.[109]

Notes

1. Jonathan C. Brown, *Cuba's Revolutionary World* (Cambridge, MA: Harvard University Press, 2017); Piero Gleijeses, *Conflicting Missions: Havana, Washington, and Africa, 1959–1976* (Chapel Hill: University of North Carolina Press, 2002); Piero Gleijeses, *Visions of Freedom: Havana, Washington, Pretoria, and the Struggle for Southern Africa, 1975–1991* (Chapel Hill: University of North Carolina Press, 2013).

2. In the 1970s and 1980s, political scientists showed some interest in the topic. Jorge I. Domínguez, *To Make a World Safe for Revolution: Cuba's Foreign Policy* (Cambridge, MA: Harvard University Press, 1989), 219–47; Rozita Levi, "Cuba and the Non-Aligned Movement," in *Cuba in the World*, ed. Cole Blasier and Carmelo Mesa-Lago (Pittsburgh, PA: University of Pittsburgh Press, 1979), 147–51.

3. Vijay Prashad, *The Darker Nations: A People's History of the Third World* (New York: New Press, 2007): xv.

4. Jon Lee Anderson, *Che Guevara: A Revolutionary Life* (New York: Grove Press, 1997), 423–30.

5. U.S. Embassy (hereafter USE) Cairo, embassy telegram (hereafter embtel) 3846, 1 July 1959, Folder 350, Box 98, USE Havana Classified General Records 1940–1961, Record Group (hereafter RG) 84, U.S. National Archives and Records Administration, College Park, MD (hereafter NARA); "Declaraciones del Che en Bombay," *Diario de la Marina* (hereafter *DDLM*), 18 July 1959; "Negocia Guevara Relaciones Diplomáticas con Indonesia," *DDLM*, 31 July 1959; Embassy of the United Kingdom (hereafter UKE), Belgrade letter 10337 to Foreign Office (hereafter FO) Southern Department, 26 August 1959; AK 10392/1, FO 371/139427, United Kingdom National Archives (hereafter UKNA); translation of article in *Borba* (Belgrade), 22 August 1959, Folder "Che en la ONU," Fondo Ernesto Che Guevara, Archive of the Ministerio de Relaciones Exteriores, Havana (hereafter MINREX).

6. Department of State (hereafter DOS) Bureau of Intelligence and Research (hereafter INR), Intelligence Information Brief 187, "'Che' Guevara and Cuba's Mission to Afro-Asian Countries," 12 August 1959, Folder 350, Box 98, USE Havana Classified General Records 1940–1961, RG84, NARA. Had U.S. officials known that Che had met secretly with Soviet KGB officers stationed in certain cities on his tour, they would likely have taken an even weightier view of his mission. Anderson, *Che Guevara*, 428–29.

7. Ernesto 'Che' Guevara, "América desde el balcón afroasiático," *Humanismo* (September/October 1959), http://www.cubadebate.cu/opinion/2014/01/27/america-desde-el-balcon-afroasiatico-un-articulo-del-che-poco-divulgado/#.WLIaHxiZOi4.

8. Quoted in "Lo que pretendemos es una planificación industrial," *Revolución*, 15 September 1959, 1.

9. Author's interview with Raúl Roa Kourí, Havana, 7 February 2017.

10. Josué de Castro, *The Geography of Hunger* (Boston: Little, Brown, 1952). First published in Portuguese as *Geografia da Fome* in 1948, the book had been translated into Spanish, English, French, Italian, and Russian editions published abroad by the mid-1950s.

11. Lillian Guerra, *Visions of Power in Cuba: Revolution, Redemption, and Resistance, 1959–1971* (Chapel Hill: University of North Carolina Press, 2012), 37–134, esp. 59.

12. "Texto completo del discurso de Raúl Roa," *Revolución*, 25 September 1959, 1. See also "Cuba en la ONU," *Carteles* 40, no. 40 (1959): 21.

13. "En Cuba: Los países del hambre," *Bohemia* 52, no. 3 (1960): 69–70; "Cuba Promoting '3D Bloc' Parley," *New York Times*, 3 January 1960, 7.

14. Roy R. Rubottom Jr. (Assistant Secretary of State for Latin American Affairs), memo to the Undersecretary for Political Affairs, "Developments on the Cuban Political Scene in November," 27 November 1959, Folder "Cuba September–December 1959," Box 1, American Republics Affairs (hereafter ARA) Assistant Secretary Subject Files, 1959–1962, Lots 62D418 and 64D15, RG59, NARA.

15. Hugh S. Cuming Jr. (DOS-INR), "The Present Situation in Cuba and Outlook through 1960," 11 December 1959, Folder "Cuba General 1960 (2 of 2)," Box 3, ARA-Caribbean and Mexican Affairs, Subject Files 1957–62, Lot 63D67, RG59, NARA.

16. Rubottom memo to European (Kohler) and Near Eastern Affairs (Hart) Bureaus, "Cuba and 'Positive Neutralism,'" December 21, 1959, Folder "Cuba September–December 1959," Box 1, ARA Assistant Secretary Subject Files, Lots 62D418 and 64D15, RG 59, NARA, emphasis in original.

17. "En Cuba: Los países del hambre"; "En Cuba: Esfuerzo y Trabajo," *Bohemia* 52, no. 4 (22 January 1960): 65.

18. USE Baghdad (Jernegan), embtel 1719, 28 January 1960, and USE Tehran (Wailes), embtel 1710, 3 February 1960, both in Folder 310 (Conf of Under-Dev Countries 1959–1960), Box 94, USE Havana Classified General Records 1940–61, RG84, NARA (hereafter cited as Folder 310, Box 94, RG84, NARA).

19. Leví Marrero and Carlos Lechuga, letter to Roa, enclosing "Informe sobre la Misión realizada por los Embajadores Marrero y Lechuga," n.d. [ca. 18 February 1960],

papers of Carlos Lechuga, private archive of Lillian Lechuga, Havana. This report is cited hereafter as "Informe." I am grateful to Lechuga's daughter Lillian for sharing this document with me.

20. USE Accra (Flake), embtel 676, 10 March 1960, Folder 310, Box 94, RG84, NARA.

21. In December Cuba announced that it had established relations with Ghana and Tunisia, upgraded its mission in the Philippines to embassy status, and initiated talks to establish relations with Libya, Sudan, Ethiopia, Guinea, Liberia, Yemen, Iraq, Iran, Jordan, Afghanistan, Burma, Thailand, Laos, Cambodia, the Malay Federation, Indonesia, Australia, New Zealand, and Ireland. USE Havana (Daniel Braddock, Chargé a.i.) despatch 1038, 28 January, 1960, 637.00/1-2860, Box 1329, Central Files 1960–63, RG59, NARA.

22. "En Cuba: Los países del hambre"; "Proyección de la Reunión de los Países Subdesarrollados," *Revolución*, 11 January 1960, 6; Marrero and Lechuga, "Informe."

23. A copy of the memo is included in Marrero and Lechuga, "Informe." See also USE Havana (Braddock), embtel 1571, 6 January 1960, Folder 310, Box 94, RG84, NARA; Mexican Embassy (hereafter EmbaMex) Havana (Ambassador Gilberto Bosques) memo to Secretaría de Relaciones Exteriores (hereafter SRE), "Iniciativa Cubana para Conferencia Países Sub-Industrializados," 6 January 1960, XII-606-/8, SRE Archive, Mexico City (hereafter SREMEX).

24. USE Havana (Braddock), embtel 1560, 5 January 1960, Folder 310, Box 94, RG84, NARA.

25. DOS (Acting Secretary C. Douglas Dillon), telegram 878 to all ARA posts, Athens, Belgrade, and twenty-five African and Asian posts, 6 January 1960, Folder 310, Box 94, RG84, NARA.

26. USE Mexico, "Aide-Memoire" to Foreign Minister Manuel Tello, 12 January 1960, XII-606-/8, SREMEX.

27. USE Rio de Janeiro (Ambassador John M. Cabot), embtel 981, 4 January 1960, Folder 310, Box 94, RG84, NARA.

28. DOS (Dillon), Department telegram (hereafter deptel) 761 to USE Rio (repeated Cairo, Havana), 7 January 1960, Folder 320 (Cuba January 1960), Box 123, USE Rio Classified General Records 1941–1963, RG 84, NARA.

29. USE Rio (Cabot), embtel 1009, 9 January 1960, Folder 310, Box 94, RG84, NARA.

30. Memorandum of Discussion at the 432nd Meeting of the National Security Council, 14 January 1960, in *Foreign Relations of the United States, 1958–60*, vol. 6, *Cuba* (Washington, DC: Government Printing Office, 1991), document 423 (hereafter cited as *FRUS* with years, volume, and document number).

31. Memorandum of Discussion at the Department of State—Joint Chiefs of Staff Meeting, 8 January 1960, *FRUS 1958–60*, 6:419. Operations Coordinating Board, "Activity Report," January 11, 1960, Folder "OCB 319.1 Activity Report (File #6) (3)," Box 10, National Security Council Staff Papers 1948–61, White House Office File, Dwight Eisenhower Presidential Library, Abilene, KA.

32. DOS memorandum of conversation (hereafter memcon), Leonard Unger (DCM, USE Bangkok) with Faust Cardona (Chargé, Brazilian Embassy Bangkok), 23 January 1960, Folder 310, Box 94, RG84, NARA.

33. USE Rio (Cabot), embtel 1116, 28 January 1960, Folder 310, Box 94, RG84, NARA.

34. Marrero and Lechuga, "Informe"; SRE [Tello?], "Memorandum para información del Señor Presidente," 12 January 1960, XII-606-/8, SREMEX; USE Guatemala City (Corrigan), embtel 278, 13 January 1960, USE San Salvador (Kalijarvi), embtel 178, 14 January 1960, USE Tegucigalpa (Newbegin), embtel 309, 16 January 1960, and USE San José (Willauer), embtel 254, 18 January 1960, all in Folder 310, Box 94, RG84, NARA.

35. Lechuga and Marrero, "Informe."

36. Stephen G. Rabe, *Eisenhower and Latin America: The Foreign Policy of Anti-Communism* (Chapel Hill: University of North Carolina Press, 1988), 108–10.

37. Lechuga and Marrero, "Informe."

38. DOS memcon, "Operation Pan America and XI Inter-American Conference," Herter, Rubottom, and Boonstra with Lafer and Brazilian Ambassador Moreira Salles, Washington, 18 March 1960, Folder 311 ("Operation Pan America 1959–60"), Box 95, USE Havana Classified General Records 1940–61, RG84, NARA; ARA briefing paper, "President's Good Will Trip to South America: Quito Conference and the Alternatives," 11 February 1960, Folder "Briefing Papers Cuba 1960 (2 of 3)," Box 2, ARA/Coordinator of Cuban Affairs Subject Files, Lot 63D91, RG59, NARA

39. SRE [Tello?] "Memorandum para Información del Señor Presidente," 12 January 1960; Tello letter 120590 to Roa, 12 January 1960, Jorge Castañeda (Dirección General de Organismos Internacionales), memo 120419 to Chargé, Misión Permanente of Mexico at UN, 25 January 1960, and Amb. Eduardo Espinosa Prieto (Rep. Alterno, EmbaMex UN), letter to Tello, 2 February 1960, SRE circular telegram (hereafter cirtel) 120468 to all Latin American embassies, 5 April 1960, all in XII-606-/8, SREMEX; USE Mexico City (Hill), airgram G-124, 13 January 1960, Folder 310, Box 94, RG84, NARA.

40. Thomas J. Hamilton, "Most Latins to Shun Cuban Economic Parley," *New York Times*, 7 March 1960, 1.

41. Amb. Eduardo Espinosa y Prieto (Chargé, EmbaMex UN), despatch 560 to SRE, 16 May 1960, Espinosa telegram 85 to SRE, 18 May 1960, and despatch 569, 19 May 1960, enclosing Manuel Bisbé (Cuban Ambassador to UN), note #184 to Luís Padilla Nervo (Mexican Ambassador to UN), 17 May 1960, and SRE (Castañeda) instruction #122486 to Espinosa, 26 May 1960, all in XII-606-/8, SREMEX.

42. "Declaración Conjunta de los Ministros de Relaciones Exteriores de Cuba y Venezuela," Caracas, 31 March 1960, Folder "Venezuela 1960 Ordinario," Fondo Venezuela, MINREX.

43. Rómulo Betancourt letter to Osvaldo Dorticós, 30 March 1960; Tomo XXXVII, Complemento D, Rómulo Betancourt Papers, Fundación Rómulo Betancourt, Caracas.

44. Betancourt letter to Rafael Caldera, 30 March 1960; Tomo XXXVII, Complemento D, Rómulo Betancourt Papers, Fundación Rómulo Betancourt, Caracas.

45. USE Caracas (Sparks), embtel 968, 10 June 1960, 737.00/6-1060, Box 1603, CDF1960-3, RG59, NARA.

46. USE Buenos Aires (Ambassador Willard Beaulac), memcon, Cecilio Morales (Economic Director, Pan American Union), with Beaulac, 1 February 1960, Folder 310, Box 94, RG84, NARA.

47. USE Cairo (Anschuetz), embtel 2192, 19 January 1960, Folder 310, Box 94, RG84, NARA; UKE Havana letter 11212/60 to FO-A, April 5, 1960, AK 11316/3, FO 371/148247, UKNA.

48. Marrero, cable #129 to Cuban Embassy in Washington and Cuban missions to OAS and UN, 16 May 1960, with text of joint communiqué signed by Castro and Sukarno on 13 May, Legajo 35, Expediente 639, Fondo MINREX, Archivo Nacional de Cuba, Havana; "Coinciden Indonesia y Cuba en su posición anticolonialista," *Revolución*, 14 May 1960, 1; "Cuba no está sola," *Revolución*, 14 May 1960, 2;

49. DOS-INR, paper "INR Contribution to NIE 85-2-60 Subject: The Situation in Cuba," 2 May 1960, U.S. Declassified Documents Online, http://tinyurl.gale.com/tinyurl/C44TH9.

50. DOS-INR, paper "INR Contribution to NIE 85-2-60 Subject."

51. "Conclusiones del informe de los Embajadores Carlos Lechuga y Leví Marrero," in Marrero and Lechuga, "Informe."

52. DOS (Herter) circular telegram 989, 6 February 1960 (no addressees appear on this copy of the cable, but it likely went to all ARA posts and most African and Asian posts), DOS (Henderson), airgram CA-8872 to all ARA posts, 26 April 1960, both in Folder 310, Box 94, RG84, NARA.

53. On these conferences see Brown, *Cuba's Revolutionary World*, 216-22.

54. Castro quoted in Lars Schoultz, *That Infernal Little Cuban Republic: The United States and the Cuban Revolution* (Chapel Hill: University of North Carolina Press, 2009), 117.

55. G. H. Jansen, *Afro-Asia and Non-Alignment* (London: Faber & Faber, 1966), 283-84.

56. These documents were created at the working and planning levels, by ambassadors in the field and, mostly, by regional bureaus and vice-ministers in Havana, the ministry's policy-planning section (the Instituto de Política Internacional), and Foreign Minister Roa and his assistants. Documents created by and for senior figures including Fidel and Raúl Castro, Dorticós, and Guevara either remain classified at the MINREX or are in the archive of the Council of State, which is not open to researchers.

57. Jansen, *Afro-Asia*, 280-84. On the foundations of the first summit, see Lorenz M. Lüthi, "Non-Alignment, 1946-1965: Its Establishment and Struggle against Afro-Asianism," *Humanity* 7, no. 2 (2016): 208-10.

58. Cuban embassy (hereafter EmbaCu) Cairo (Ambassador Armando G. Rivera), despatch 94 to MINREX, 21 May 1961, Fondo Asuntos Multilaterales, Serie 22: Movimiento de los Países No Alineados, MINREX. The three boxes from this

series dealing with the period 1961–64 are unnumbered. Documents are often undated, and folders often untitled. More precise citations are not possible.

59. "Roa Asks Neutrals to Meet in Havana," *New York Times*, 7 June 1961, 5.

60. "Informe Final de la Reunión Preparatoria de la Conferencia de Jefes de Estado o Gobierno de Países No Alineados," 12 June 1961, Serie 22, MINREX. This document is also published as "Report, Preparatory Meeting of Representatives of the Non-Aligned Countries, Cairo, June 5-12, 1961," in *The Third World without Superpowers: The Collected Documents of the Non-Aligned Countries*, ed. Odette Jankowitsch and Karl P. Sauvant (Dobbs Ferry, NY: Oceana Publications, 1978), 1:33–39.

61. Jansen, *Afro-Asia*, 289–90. Jansen's based his book on his experience in India's foreign service and on interviews with fellow nonaligned diplomats.

62. MINREX, "Informe Sobre el Colonialismo y el Neocolonialismo," 16 August 1961, Serie 22, MINREX.

63. Whereas Havana hoped that Belgrade would pull Latin America to the Left, India's Jawaharlrl Nehru saw broad Latin American participation as a way to moderate the conference's politics. Ryan A. Musto, "Non-Alignment and Beyond: India's Interest in Latin America, 1961-72," *Diplomacy & Statecraft* 29, no. 4 (2018): 613–37.

64. Cuba's role here is synthesized from Jansen, *Afro-Asia*, 286–90; Vanni Pettiná, "Global Horizons: Mexico, the Third World, and the Non-Aligned Movement at the Time of the 1961 Belgrade Conference," *International History Review* 38, no. 4 (2014): 741–64; CIA Office of Current Intelligence (hereafter OCI) Weekly Summary OCI #0287/61, 6 July 1961, CIA Electronic Reading Room, https://www.cia.gov/library/readingroom/docs/CIA-RDP79-00927A003200110001-6.pdf; CIA, OCI, memo, "The Nonaligned Nations Conference," August 7, 1961, Declassified Documents Reference Service database (hereafter DDRS).

65. Pettiná, "Global Horizons"; James G. Hershberg, "'High-Spirited Confusion': Brazil, the 1961 Belgrade Non-Aligned Conference, and the Limits of an 'Independent' Foreign Policy in the High Cold War," *Cold War History* 7, no. 3 (2007): 373–88; Robert B. Rakove, "Two Roads to Belgrade: The United States, Great Britain, and the First Nonaligned Conference," *Cold War History* 14, no. 3 (2014): 337–57; Robert B. Rakove, *Kennedy, Johnson, and the Non-Aligned World* (Cambridge: Cambridge University Press, 2013), 70–72.

66. "Objetivos de Cuba en la Conferencia de Países No Alineados," n.d. [August 1961], Serie 22, MINREX.

67. The available Cuban documents do not address why Dorticós, rather than Prime Minister Castro, the Revolution's dominant leader, represented Cuba at Belgrade in 1961 and Cairo in 1964. Concerns over domestic security in Cuba and/or Castro's safety abroad may have been factors. A Cuban diplomat in Europe told the CIA that Roa had told him that Castro canceled his plans to attend the Cairo summit for fear that Cuban exiles and the CIA would stage an attack in Cuba in order to influence the upcoming U.S. election; CIA Intelligence Information Cable, "Fidel Castro's Concern that Cuban Exiles Will Mount a Provocative Attack against Cuba before the United States Election," 13 October 1964, Document 69, Folder "Cuba

Exile Activities, Volume 1 11/63-7/65 (2 of 3)," Box 22, National Security Files (hereafter NSF), Country File, Lyndon B. Johnson Library, Austin, Texas (hereafter LBJL). It is also possible that the sober, lawyerly Dorticós was considered a better advocate in speeches and working sessions for Cuba's intended self-presentation—as an aggrieved and unbowed, but dignified and reasonable, socialist and anti-imperialist country—than the charismatic but mercurial Castro, and a better complement to the often pugnacious Roa. As historian Hugh Thomas observed a few years after these events, Dorticós gave the revolutionary government "stability, continuity, and formality on the occasions that such things were needed"; Hugh Thomas, *Cuba: The Pursuit of Freedom* (New York: Harper & Row, 1971), 1234.

68. "Texto del discurso pronunciado por el Presidente de Cuba, Doctor Osvaldo Dorticós Torrado, en el debate general de la Conferencia de Países no Alineados, en Belgrado, el 2 de septiembre de 1961," Serie 22, MINREX.

69. Paul Hofman, "U.S. Is Denounced by Cuban at Talks," *New York Times*, 3 September 1961, 3.

70. MINREX, Dirección de Asuntos Afro-Asiáticos, "Recuento de la charla de Raúl Roa sobre las interioridades de la Conferencia de Belgrado—Despacho del Ministro," 30 October 1961, Serie 22, MINREX.

71. Quotations from "Declaration: First Conference of Heads of State or Government of Non-Aligned Countries," 6 September 1961, in Jankowitsch and Sauvant, *Third World*, 3–7. Cuba's main obstacle in securing these specific resolutions was India. MINREX, Dirección de Asuntos Afro-Asiáticos, "Recuento de la charla de Raúl Roa."

72. MINREX paper, "Conferencia de los Países No Alineados en Pactos Militares (Belgrado, Septiembre de 1961)," n.d. [between 5 and 19 September 1961], Serie 22, MINREX.

73. Dirección de Países Socialistas, Departamento A (Yugoslavia), "Informe Semanal: Conferencia de Países No Alineados en Bloques Militares," n.d. [ca. 5 September–mid-September 1961), Serie 22, MINREX.

74. Dirección de Países Socialistas, Departamento A (Yugoslavia), "Informe Semanal."

75. MINREX, Dirección de Asuntos Afro-Asiáticos, "Recuento de la charla de Raúl Roa."

76. MINREX paper, "Conferencia de los Países No Alineados en Pactos Militares."

77. Schoultz, *That Infernal*, 174–75; Thomas C. Wright, *Latin America in the Era of the Cuban Revolution* (Westport, CT: Praeger, 2001), 60–61.

78. James G. Blight and Philip Brenner, *Sad and Luminous Days: Cuba's Struggle with the Superpowers after the Missile Crisis* (Lanham, MD: Rowman & Littlefield, 2002), esp. 35–43 (on the 1962 military pact). Blight and Brenner's account is based largely on the text of a secret speech that Castro made to the Cuban party leadership in 1968, explaining the origins and course of the Missile Crisis and the vagaries of Cuban-Soviet relations, in which Castro included the text of the pact.

79. Renata Keller, "The Latin American Missile Crisis," *Diplomatic History* 39, no. 2 (2015): 195–222.

80. Schoultz, *That Infernal*, 226–29; Wright, *Latin America*, 60–61.

81. Aleksandr Fursenko and Timothy Naftali, *One Hell of a Gamble: Khrushchev, Castro, and Kennedy, 1958–1964* (New York: Norton, 1998), 325–34.

82. Blight and Brenner, *Sad and Luminous Days*; Brown, *Cuba's Revolutionary World*, 73–101. On the Sino-Soviet context see Jeremy Friedman, *Shadow Cold War: The Sino-Soviet Competition for the Third World* (Chapel Hill: University of North Carolina Press, 2015), 60–147.

83. Dorticós reminded the MINREX during preparations for the 1964 NAM summit that "Cuba is a non-aligned country in the sense that it does not have military pacts with other countries. The military agreements with the USSR cover technical assistance. Cuba has no commitments to any bloc of any sort"; Roa, letter to Ambassador Armando Entralgo (EmbaCu Accra), 17 March 1964, Serie 22, MINREX.

84. Roa, memo to Fidel Castro, 24 January 1964, Serie 22, MINREX.

85. Vice-Ministro Arnol Rodríguez Camps, memo to Roa, "Conferencia Afro-Asiática, Conferencia de Países No Alineados," n.d. [ca. May 1964], Serie 22, MINREX. This undated document refers to events as late as the 10–15 April preparatory meeting for the Afro-Asian conference.

86. EmbaCu Belgrade (Hernández), embtel 17, n.d. [late January/early February 1964], and embtel 30, n.d. [February 1964], EmbaCuba New Delhi (Ortega), embtel 3-C, n.d. [late January/early February 1964], Agustín Canoura Valdés (Chargé a.i., EmbaCu Colombo), despatch to Roa, "Entrevista con el Embajador de la República Árabe Unida," 4 September 1964, all Serie 22, MINREX.

87. José Antonio Arbesú (Chargé a.i., EmbaCu Cairo), confidential despatch to Roa, "Conferencia de Países No Alineados," 10 August 1964, Serie 22, MINREX.

88. "Preparatory Meeting for the Cairo Summit: Report and Communiqué, Colombo, 23–28 March 1964," in Jankowitsch and Sauvant, *Third World*, 65–71.

89. Thomas L. Hughes (Director, INR), memo to Rusk, INR-40, "The Non-Aligned Conference, the Communist Powers, and the US," 2 October 1964, DDRS.

90. Eric Gettig, "'Trouble Ahead in Afro-Asia': The United States, the Second Bandung Conference, and the Struggle for the Third World, 1964–65," *Diplomatic History* 39, no. 1 (2015): 126–56.

91. DOS, cirtel CA-1212 to all posts, 30 July 1964, enclosed in William J. Jorden memo to Robert Komer, 30 July 1964, Document 23, Folder "Non-Aligned Conference Cairo October 1964," Box 44, Robert W. Komer File (hereafter RWKF), NSF, LBJL.

92. Cuba failed to join the G-77 at its founding in June 1964, and the Latin American states, which excluded Cuba from their caucus at the UN after the OAS resolution of July 1964, thereafter blocked its adherence. Cuba's representative to the UN organs in Geneva called Cuba's exclusion from the G-77 "dangerous" and even "fatal insofar as international congresses and conferences go"; MINREX memcon, "Reunión Celebrada en el Hotel Nilo Hilton el 29 de Septiembre para Conocer los Puntos de Vista de los Compañeros Presentes en Relación con la II Conferencia de los Países No Alineados," Roa, Enrique Camejo Argudín (Cuban representative to UN in Geneva), José Luís Pérez (Ambassador, Belgrade), Luís García Guitar (Ambassador, Cairo), Arbesú, and Luís Rodríguez Chaveco (First Secretary, EmbaCu Cairo), September 29, 1964, Serie 22, MINREX. Cuba did not join the G-77 until 1971; Domínguez, *To Make a World*, 222.

93. "Proyecto de Objetivos en la Segunda Conferencia de Países No Alineados," n.d. [ca. 25 August, as indicated by the date-received stamp], Serie 22, MINREX.

94. Hughes, Research Memorandum INR-41, "Latin American Participation at the Cairo Non-Aligned Conference," September 28, 1964, Document 19, Folder "Non-Aligned Conference Cairo October 1964," Box 44, RWKF, NSF, LBJL.

95. "Entrevista del Dr. Raúl Roa con el Dr. Subandrio, Ministro de Relaciones Exteriores de Indonesia," n.d. [ca. 30 September 1964], Serie 22, MINREX.

96. "Informe Sobre la Reunión Preparatoria de la Conferencia de Países No Alineados," 6 May 1964, enclosed in Ricardo Alarcón (chief, Latin America Division), letter to Ambassador Carlos Olivares Sánchez (EmbaCu Moscow), May 6, 1964, Serie 22, MINREX.

97. Roa letter to Olivares Sánchez, August 6, 1964, Serie 22, MINREX. Identical instructions were sent on this date to Cuba's embassies in Brussels and Cairo, and most likely to all other posts as well.

98. MINREX, memcon, "Reunión Celebrada en el Hotel Nilo Hilton el 29 de Septiembre para Conocer los Puntos de Vista de los Compañeros Presentes en Relación con la II Conferencia de los Países No Alineados," Roa, Enrique Camejo Argudín (Cuban representative to UN in Geneva), José Luís Pérez (Ambassador, Belgrade), Luís García Guitar (Ambassador, Cairo), José Antonio Arbesú (Counselor, EmbaCu Cairo), Luís Rodríguez Chaveco (First Secretary, EmbaCu Cairo), 29 September 1964, Serie 22, MINREX.

99. "Informe de la Entrevista del Dr. Raúl Roa con el Ministro de Relaciones Exteriores de la RAU," n.d. [ca. 30 September 1964] (quotation), "Conversación con el Ministro Yugoslavo Kocha Popovich," n.d. [ca. 30 September 1964], both Serie 22, MINREX.

100. Dorticós said that Venezuela and other OAS members except Mexico were "accomplices of imperialistic strategy" for supporting U.S. policy against Cuba; "Speech of Osvaldo Dorticós Torrado, President of Cuba," in *Conference of Heads of State and Government of Non-Aligned Countries, Cairo, 5–10 October 1964* (Cairo: Ministry of National Guidance Information Administration, 1964), 228–38. The Venezuelan observer stated that Cuba had "aligned herself with an ideological and political system which differs from our own concepts"; "Speech of Octavio Lapage, Venezuela," in *Conference of Heads of State and Government of Non-Aligned Countries, Cairo, 5–10 October 1964* (Cairo: Ministry of National Guidance Information Administration, 1964), 322–23. The walkout was reported in Sergio Pineda, "Apoya México las Metas de Libertad y Justicia de los Países No Alineados," *Hoy*, 10 October 1964, 1.

101. "Speech of Osvaldo Dorticós Torrado."

102. "Second Conference of Heads of State or Government of Non-Aligned Countries: Program for Peace and International Cooperation, Cairo, 5–10 October 1964," in Jankowitsch and Sauvant, *Third World*, 44–59.

103. Untitled document, n. d. [ca. 11 October 1964], Serie 22, MINREX (hereafter Roa, "Notes"). This document—which includes typed and handwritten notes on the conference—is unsigned, but the author lists the rest of Cuba's delegation before ending the list with "*y este prójimo* [and this fellow]," and reports Roa's declarations to the press in the first person.

104. Hughes, memo to Rusk, INR-50, "The Non-Aligned Conference at Cairo," 16 November 1964, Document 4, Folder "Non-Aligned Conference Cairo—October 1964," Box 44, RWKF, NSF, LBJL.

105. Roa, "Notes."

106. On these conferences see Brown, *Cuba's Revolutionary World*, 216–22; David Kimche, *The Afro-Asian Movement: Ideology and Foreign Policy of the Third World* (New York: Halstead Press, 1973), 126–213.

107. Brown, *Cuba's Revolutionary World*; Stephen G. Rabe, *The Killing Zone: The United States Wages Cold War in Latin America* (New York: Oxford University Press, 2012), 59–174.

108. Blight and Brenner, *Sad and Luminous Days*; Tanya Harmer, "Two, Three, Many Revolutions? Cuba and the Prospects for Revolutionary Change in Latin America, 1967–1975," *Journal of Latin American Studies* 45, no. 1 (2013): 61–89.

109. The evidence reviewed here makes the argument that Cuba did not begin trying in earnest to actively draw the nonaligned world closer to the Soviet bloc until the 1970s untenable. See Levi, "Cuba and the Non-Aligned Movement."

11 Chile, Algeria, and the Third World in the 1960s and 1970s

Revolutions Entangled

••

EUGENIA PALIERAKI

In December 1972, the Chilean President Salvador Allende delivered a speech at the United Nations General Assembly in New York and then, on his way to Moscow, made a stopover in Algiers.[1] Alberto Gamboa, the director of the main Chilean left-wing newspaper, *Clarín*, also present, wrote, "Here the contrast to New York is striking. The enthusiasm, the affection and understanding that the Algerian people and the Government have expressed ... are extraordinary ... [and] overwhelmingly friendly!"[2] This friendship and affection expressed a strong affinity and shared values. But how did Chile and Algeria—two very distant countries from a geographical, cultural, and historical standpoint—connect to each other?

Based on French and Spanish-language sources,[3] this chapter aims to clarify the relevant historical links between Chile and Algeria, and more precisely, between their left-wing and progressive movements and governments from the 1950s to the 1970s. Until now, the foreign relations of the Chilean left-wing parties have been explored mainly on a continental level or in relation to Western and Eastern European countries. This also applies to Allende's Popular Unity from 1970 to 1973, a period of unprecedented internationalization of the national political scene.[4] As for Algeria, its Third-Worldist policy in the 1960s and 1970s is a rapidly growing field of inquiry.[5] Here, the Third World itself provides a critical framework. The concept of "Third World," developed by the French geographer Alfred Sauvy in 1952, clearly implied that during the postwar era, Third World countries would drive world revolution in the same way that the Third Estate ignited the French Revolution. Even though it has a rather negative meaning today, "Third World" had a very positive connotation until the early 1980s.[6] Although its most common definition is geographical—the Third World usually designates the decolonized African and Asian territories and, in some cases, Latin America—it is actually a political construction, embracing the revolutionary community that the postwar "wretched of the earth" supposedly formed.[7]

Until this community emerged in the 1950s, there were hardly any links between Chile and Algeria. Thereafter, the left wing in both Chile and the Algeria felt they belonged to it. It can be thus argued that the political bonds between these two countries in the postwar era should mainly be explained *via* the Third World framework—the Third World not as an abstract entity, but as a performative concept. Through the example of the relations between Chile and Algeria during the Cold War period, this chapter examines the mechanisms, the material means, and the agency that formed the Third World as a coherent and meaningful political space, or, in the words of the French political scientist Lilian Mathieu, as a new "universe of practice and autonomous meaning."[8]

While this case study covers a hitherto unexplored field of inquiry, it also engages with two existing and interrelated historiographical debates. The first concerns the "relational approaches" of global history and *histoire croisée* (connected or entangled history), and the second concerns New Cold War history with its emphasis on the role played by "Third World" countries during the Cold War. Indeed, this research is fully aligned with the main epistemological contributions made by global and entangled history.[9] That includes on the one hand the questioning of Western-centered and nation-centered visions, the critique of a cultural transfer approach, and the emphasis on the links tying different geographical and cultural areas together.[10] On the other hand, the "relational approaches" to twentieth-century history have focused mainly on social or cultural history, paying little attention to the political field. In this sense, the history of international relations, political sociology, and political science offer solid theoretical bases for approaching political objects from a transnational perspective.[11] Yet the majority of transnational approaches to politics have taken a limited interest in regions other than Western Europe and the United States. Moreover, they have focused almost exclusively on international institutions and abandoned historical actors such as nation-states or noninstitutionalized agency.[12] Thus, this chapter—with its focus on both informal transnational activism and on "peripheral" regions and nation-states—will address some key issues that have been neglected by "relational approaches."

Despite a certain criticism expressed here, it must be noted that "relational approaches" have brought new perspectives on numerous historical objects and periods, among which are Cold War Latin American political history. Whereas starting with the 1970s, the postwar political history of Latin America has been viewed mainly as a reflection of the Cold War,[13] recent studies have heralded a more balanced view and have questioned the premise that Latin American political history during the Cold War was exclusively a local reproduction of the global struggle between the two superpowers.[14] This new vision of the Latin American 1960s and 1970s owes a great deal not only to "relational approaches," but also to New Cold War history, which shares a few basic premises: the emphasis on agency rather than structures; the relevance of state ideology, which cannot be summed up as a mere defense of economic interests; and the recognition of the vital role played by regions other than the "First" and the "Second" worlds.[15] Logically, the last premise has produced a renewed interest in the Third World and in Latin America, even if a bipolar Cold War lens remains salient for many scholars.[16] Some have sought to counterbalance this view, not always sufficiently supported by archives and fieldwork,[17] while other specific attempts to present the history of Third World have paid little attention to the circulations and connections between geographical and cultural areas.[18] Through an examination of the connections between two constituent parts of the Third World, Chile and Algeria, this chapter aims to rethink the Cold War period through a Third World lens, giving priority to intra–Third World relations.

"Geography is a social and ideological construction, susceptible to alteration during primordial periods," claims Jeffrey Byrne in his book on Algeria and the Third World.[19] Indeed, the 1960s and the 1970s, a period of unprecedented transnationalization of the political scene, was a "primordial" one for the Third World. Geographic distances seemed to matter less and less for its countries and peoples. Within the Third World, an increasing number of activists traveled from one country to another and from one continent to another to assist revolutionary movements, to attend military or intelligence training, or to seek refuge from dictatorial right-wing regimes. The idea of a common emancipatory struggle for the defense of their nations against colonial and neocolonial powers grew stronger among these activists. The emancipation of the Third World had a double meaning for its protagonists: the strengthening of its nation-states and, at the same time, the creation of a new political space through the convergence of Third World countries into a single transnational community.

As anthropologists have recently argued, the nation-state and transnationalism are in no way incompatible, and in several cases, nation-states have been fortified through transnational networks.[20] Additionally, Third

World nation-states emerged as major players in the postwar international stage due to the construction of a transnational community rather than the formation of separate nation-states. To a large extent, this community was based upon global militant networks. During the postwar period, not only were Third World nation-states and revolutionary transnationalism intertwined, but they also helped reduce the impact of the Cold War on global political dynamics.

But why focus on the Algerian and the Chilean cases? The radical characteristics of its Liberation War and its aftermath established Algeria as an emblematic case of anticolonial struggle. In addition, after its independence in 1962, Algiers became a global revolutionary city: on the one hand, it was a hub for activists from Africa, the Americas, Asia and Europe, and thus a place of meetings and circulation of ideas; on the other hand, it was a provider of financial and military support for revolutionary movements. Finally, Algeria was one of the first Arab countries to establish solid long-term ties with the Latin American Left. The Algerian Front de Libération Nationale (FLN, National Liberation Front) regime had strong similarities with Allende's Unidad Popular (UP, Popular Unity, 1970–73). The Algerian FLN was a local version of socialism based on the combination of nonalignment and economic nationalism, while, at the same time, it was claiming a global outreach. As for Allende's peaceful and democratic "Chilean road to socialism," it aspired to become a model for Latin American and eventually other Third World countries. Moreover, Chile had one of the largest and most dynamic Arab communities in Latin America, a community that played a prominent role in connecting Chile with the Arab World.[21]

The ties between Algeria and Chile, and specifically between the Algerian FLN and the Sociality Party of Chile, developed gradually in the late 1950s and 1960s. After the 1973 coup in Chile and the establishment of a military regime, these links persisted thanks to Algeria's solidarity with Chilean political exiles from 1973 to 1990, when, in Chile, democracy was restored and the diplomatic relations between the two countries reestablished. The interstate relations were established in 1962, the year of Algeria's independence. In 1963, Alessandri's right-wing government opened a Chilean embassy in Algiers. At that time, it was the first and only Chilean embassy in Africa. Until the late 1960s, it and the Cuban embassy were the only two Latin American embassies in Algiers. Although the role of the Chilean embassy diminished during the Christian Democrat presidency (1964–70), it became important again under the Allende government.

This chapter focuses on the years 1956–73, from the creation of the Chilean Committee for the Self-Determination of Algeria in 1956 to the military coup and the overthrow of Allende in 1973 and its aftermath. The first section analyzes the links between the two countries, through the Chilean-Arab diaspora and different transnational militant networks during the pre-independence period. The second section shifts to the post-1962 period and focuses more precisely on the role of the recently decolonized Algeria, as well as of Cuba in the making of Chilean-Algerian relations. The third and fourth sections focus on the 1963–73 period and on the institutionalized means of building these relations. The third section addresses the opening of a Chilean embassy in Algiers, which inaugurated interstate relations initially determined by Cold War politics. The fourth section focuses on Allende's assumption of office in November 1970, which resulted in the partial abandonment of the Cold War mindset as far as Chile's foreign policy was concerned and in the development of diplomatic relations between Chile and Algeria based on links between the FLN and the UP. These relations were maintained and transformed in the aftermath of the 1973 Chilean coup and the Chilean resistance to Pinochet's dictatorship.

Between Alterity and Proximity: The First Encounters

The first Chilean connections with pre-independence Algeria were created through the Arab diaspora, as well as through militant networks, which often overlapped. The Arab community in Chile was one of the largest in Latin America. Exceeding 14,000 people in the early 1940s, its members came mainly from Palestine, Syria, and Lebanon.[22] They created a vast network of social clubs and associations across Chile. They had newspapers in Arabic and in Spanish, the most important one being the weekly magazine *Mundo Árabe*, which began publication in the 1930s and was distributed across Latin America.

It was originally within the Chilean Arab community—though also supported by left-wing and center political parties—that the Comité Chileno Pro-Autodeterminación de Argelia (Chilean Committee for the Self-Determination of Algeria) was created in 1956. This was the first and main association in Chile supporting Algeria's independence from France.[23]

However, it was not the first Chilean committee in support of an Arab nation's independence: there had been one to support Syrians, as well as a very active Palestinian committee. The Comité Pro-Autodeterminación de Argelia was presided over by some of the leading figures of the Arab community, who, until the 1950s, were active mostly in the Chilean center political parties. Algeria's fight for independence represented an ideological change toward a more progressive political stance within the Chilean Arab community. This change was partly a result of political events in the Arab world, including the 23 July revolution in Egypt, the Suez crisis, and the rise of Pan-Arabism, in addition to the beginning of the Algerian war for independence in 1954. *Mundo Árabe* became fiercely pro-Nasserite in the mid-1950s and expressed increasingly anti-imperialist and anticolonial views, some of them overtly revolutionary.

Radicalization was also a generational issue. The older generation participating in Comité chileno pro-autodeterminación de Argelia was rather conservative and almost exclusively of Arab descent. This included the committee's president, Marco Antonio Salum, who was a deputy for the populist Partido Agrario Laborista (Agrarian Labor Party) led by General Carlos Ibáñez del Campo and Omar Rumié Vera, a successful real estate agent. By contrast, the younger generation participating in the committee—most of them students—were not necessarily bound by an Arab identity; rather, they were overwhelmingly affiliated with either the Socialist Party of Chile or Trotskyite groups, and, to a lesser extent, with the Communist Party. The Chilean Socialist Party was, in fact, sympathetic to both Socialist and Non-Aligned regimes around the globe.[24] For instance, one of the main leaders of the Socialist Party, Raúl Ampuero, participated in the 1961 Non-Aligned Conference in Belgrade, where the Algerian FLN was present. Ampuero was also one of the first Chilean party leaders to visit Algeria, in 1963, after receiving an official invitation from Ahmed Ben Bella, the first Algerian President.[25]

The significant presence of Trotskyites in the Socialist Party also contributed to the party's interest in the Algerian war and the socialist regime established in 1962. Most of these Trotskyites were followers or sympathizers of Michel Pablo, the Fourth International's secretary general, who encouraged participation in broad alliances and left-wing parties, a policy also known as "entryism." More broadly, in the aftermath of World War II, the Fourth International played a key role in crafting global solidarity with African and Asian national liberation movements, but also in the foundation of "New Left" revolutionary movements in Latin America. Moreover, the Fourth International contributed greatly to the establishment of contacts between the three continents and to the creation of the Third World.

In the late 1950s, Pablo and his closest collaborators within the Trotskyite Fourth International became strongly involved in the Algerian cause. In addition to political and public expressions of support for the independence struggle, they secretly organized a weapons factory for the FLN in Morocco, where among the skilled workers were several Argentinian Trotskyites.[26] They also attempted to counterfeit French currency, a clandestine operation that led to Pablo's arrest.[27] After the 1962 independence, Algerian president Ben Bella had a close relationship with Pablo, who had settled in Algeria in 1962 and stayed there to promote workers' and peasants' self-management economy (*autogestión*).[28] During the UP years, Pablo moved for a short time period to Chile, where he also promoted *autogestión* in the country's factories.

But links between the Chilean Trotskyites and Algeria did not wait for Pablo's visit to Chile; they traced back to the Comité Chileno Pro-Autodeterminación de Argelia. Its main solidarity activities were a combination of conventional and more radical actions, reflecting the generation gap between its members. These activities included fundraising for the FLN[29] and open letters to the president of the Chilean Republic urging him, albeit in vain, to back United Nations resolutions on Algeria's right to self-determination, but also interrupting Congress sessions using firecrackers and loudly chanting slogans in favor of the Algerian independence.[30] They also included hosting FLN leaders and delegations in Chile. Such was the case of Alfred Berenguer, a Catholic priest of Spanish descent and an icon of the Algerian struggle for independence. After being expelled from Algeria, Berenguer found refuge in Santiago in 1959, when he spent six months in the residence of a wealthy woman connected to the committee.[31]

In 1960, the Gouvernement Provisionel de la République Algérienne (GPRA; Provisional Government of the Algerian Republic)—the government-in-exile of the FLN—was cornered by the French after a bloody six-year war and having trouble obtaining the support of Algeria's neighbors. In search of new allies, the GPRA turned to sub-Saharan Africa and Latin America.[32] From 9 to 15 October, a GPRA delegation campaigning in Latin American made a stopover in Chile. There, Benyoussef Benkhedda, the GPRA's and the delegation's head, met with the Chilean Committee for Algeria's Self-Determination, which also arranged meetings with several members of Parliament and senators.[33]

A year before that, in February 1959, only a month after the Cuban revolution, the Union Générale des Étudiants Musulmans Algériens (UGEMA; General Union of Muslim Students of Algeria), which was attached to the FLN, attended the pro-Western International Students Conference meeting in Lima. Immediately after that, the UGEMA delegation went on a Latin

American tour and visited Chile. Invited there by the Federación de Estudiantes de Chile (Student Federation of Chile), which was then dominated by the Christian Democrats, UGEMA members also met with the youth section of the Chilean Committee for the Self-Determination of Algeria and with a significant number of young Socialists and Communists.[34] The FLN's ideological ambiguity and its constant search for balance between East and West were apparent during the UGEMA's Latin American tour.[35] Either way, the message that the UGEMA conveyed in the Chilean press immediately after the pro-West Lima meeting was all but moderate: "In this land of Simon Bolivar and San Martin, these legendary figures who held the continent's liberation on the edge of their sword freeing it from the powerful Spanish rule, the struggle for freedom takes on singular importance."[36]

Nor were some of the solidarity actions carried out by the younger left-wing members of the committee moderate. When the French novelist and De Gaulle's minister of cultural affairs, André Malraux, visited Latin America and Chile in September 1959 in order to campaign against Algerian independence, a group of young pro-Algeria students energetically opposed Malraux's talk,[37] as witnessed by Eduardo Salum, future ambassador to Algeria under Allende's UP and head of the youth front of the Chilean Committee for Algerian Self-Determination:

> When André Malraux arrived in Chile in order to ask for Chile's vote in the United Nations [in favor of the French position], we—the youth section of the Chilean pro-Algerian Committee—organized a counter-demonstration during Malraux's talk at the University of Chile. . . . In the upper part of the room, there was a sort of balcony. . . . When I shouted "Long live free Algeria!" . . . Patricio Figueroa [a Trotskyite activist] set off a firecracker. The old ladies who were downstairs, so snobby, so frenchified, started yelling, "This is a terrorist attack against Malraux!" . . . Of course, Malraux's talk was suspended. . . . Our counter-demonstration was a complete success![38]

More importantly, the pro-Algerian Chileans believed that in order for the peripheral and underdeveloped nation-states to defend their rights, they should integrate into supranational entities; this was reflected in the idea of pan-Arabism underlying the Algerian struggle.[39] As for the Algerians, their Latin American circuit was a highly formative experience. Indeed, it was the GPRA's Latin American expedition that gave rise to a new perception of the Third World, one that brought Latin America closer to the recently decolonized countries. This perception of a revolution of independence that needed to be both political and socioeconomic, already present in Nasser's *Philosophy of the Revolution* and in the work of the nineteenth-century Cuban independentist José Martí, was later updated by Marxism and the Cuban Revolution.[40] This is how Benyoussef Benkhedda, the aforementioned head of the GPRA and founder of the FLN's newspaper, *El Moudjahid*, summarized what the FLN had learned in Latin America: "The lesson we can learn from Latin America . . . is extremely useful. A century and a half ago, these countries gained their 'independence' . . . However, that decolonization was nothing more than an illusion . . . British and later American colonialism fostered division . . . in order to bring Latin America under their sway. Since 1940, the whole continent struggles for its 'second independence,' a true independence . . . that is, a revolution in two stages, first political liberation, then economic and social."[41]

Faraway, So Close: Algeria, Cuba, and the Chilean 1960s

Understandably, the first connections between the Algerian FLN and the Chilean political scene, which dated from the late 1950s, developed through nonstate networks. The informal—mainly militant, and to a lesser extent diasporic—networks maintained their importance even after the creation of an Algerian state in 1962, and despite the establishment of diplomatic relations between the two countries in 1963. During the period under examination, the main connections between Algeria and Chile were anchored within civil society and ideologically marked by a Third-Worldist revolutionary transnationalism.

However, two changes took place in the post-1962 period, following the independence of Algeria. Before 1961–62, support for the Algerian cause came generally from progressive militants and the Arab diaspora. But from 1962 onward, broader and much more direct bonds developed between Chilean and Algerian civil societies. In Chile, an increasing number of individuals (activists, intellectuals, and professionals) and collectives (political organizations, informal networks) developed an interest in Algeria, and several traveled there.

Mass media and air travel facilitated the coming closer of the two countries. Even though these technological and material advances may appear devoid of any political dimension, they were highly politicized. Recently decolonized and Non-Aligned countries were fully aware of the political significance of mass media. For instance, during UGEMA's tour in Latin America in 1959, its leaders saw the lack of publicity for the FLN as one of the main obstacles to widespread support across the continent. As they noted, all relevant information published in nondiasporic Latin American press was sourced through the Agence France Presse and other pro-French press agencies.[42] Non-Aligned countries thus felt the need to create independent press agencies or to count on amicably inclined ones. Thus, in December 1961, the GPRA created its own press agency, the Algérie Presse Service. Even though its press dispatches rarely reached Chile directly, the Yugoslavian press agency Tanjug and the Cuban *Prensa Latina* ensured that Algerian news appeared in the Chilean left-wing press.[43]

As for air travel, much to the distress of the United States, the independent Algerian state decided to purchase its aircraft from socialist countries.[44] In exchange, the USSR turned Algiers's airport into a mandatory refueling stop for Aeroflot's long-distance flights, mainly the ones connecting with the American continent. Serving, in addition, as a bridge between Africa and the Mediterranean, the Algerian capital city became a "global city."[45] In the 1960s and 1970s, it also became a hub for radical political movements and regularly hosted political conferences, such as the Non-Aligned Summit in September 1973, a few days prior to the Chilean military coup.[46]

Algiers, moreover, became a meeting point for socially and politically sensitized professionals. Professional activity and political commitment were intertwined ever since the French colonized Algeria in the 1830s, when qualified jobs were generally reserved for non-Muslim populations. From independence onward, Algeria consistently suffered from a massive braindrain. Thus, for the Algerian independent state, the replacement of white-collar professions was a highly political matter, inseparable from economic development and political self-determination.[47] This is why from 1962 onward, Algeria invested considerable energy into the organization of international conferences and meetings of engineers, educators, journalists, legal practitioners, doctors, and other professionals. In addition to attracting professionals, these events served to develop cooperative ties with other Third World countries that had a lesser need for white-collar labor force.[48]

Those international meetings, both militant and professional, also offered the participants a unique opportunity to discover the host country, learn about political and social changes taking place there, and describe its achievements when they returned home. Educating public opinion further promoted a new closeness between two geographically distant countries. Indeed, every time a Chilean delegation attended an international meeting in Algeria, the Chilean press published interviews and detailed descriptions of the country, concerning not only Algeria's modern history, culture, and customs but also its forms of political and social organization. And, vice versa, when Algerian politicians or professionals visited Chile or when Chilean dignitaries were present on the Algerian soil, extensive articles and radio and TV shows were dedicated to Chile, its history and political news.[49]

In the early 1960s, Cuba became increasingly influential in Chilean-Algerian relations. Cuba became a mediator between Chile and Algeria on several occasions. Along with Algeria, Cuba also hosted international conferences and was indeed a favorite meeting place for activists and political leaders from all over the world. At the 1966 Tricontinental Conference in Havana, for instance, the Socialist and the Communist Party represented Chile, while the then-minister of foreign affairs of Algeria, Abdel Aziz Bouteflika, represented his country.[50] From 1962 onward, the progressive Chilean press relied on the Cuban press agency for information on Algeria and, more generally, on Africa.

More importantly, Cuba served as a reference point that allowed the Chilean public opinion (mostly left-wing, but not exclusively) to better grasp Algerian politics. Algeria was constantly compared to Cuba; and thus, Cuba translated Algerian politics that initially seemed extremely remote and exotic to a political project with which the Latin Americans were familiar. These comparisons were initiated in Cuba, and only later reproduced, through *Prensa Latina* articles, in other Latin American countries. Jorge "Papito" Serguera, Cuba's ambassador in Algeria under the Ben Bella presidency, noted how in Cuba, "we considered the Algerian revolution as a process very similar to our own revolution . . . [as] a twin [revolution]: they took place at the same time and they lasted more or less the same [time]. . . . The [Algerian] Army of National Liberation [fought] against the French Armed Forces; and [M26] Ejército Rebelde against the Armed Forces of the Cuban state. . . . In both cases, first-rank foreign powers supported the peoples' enemies."[51]

Such comparisons were also made in the Chilean press. For instance, after the appointment of Ben Bella as head of state, the Chilean newspapers published numerous articles comparing him to Fidel Castro.[52] The socialist Victor Barberis wrote on that occasion: "Ben Bella demands nothing more than the effective exercise of the right for self-determination that Algeria has won, eliminating forever every remnant of imperialist domination. . . . [This can occur] thanks to the revolutionary Armed forces, which are—as in Cuba—the only true guarantor that the revolution will not become a palace coup and that the profound political and social reforms that the Algerian people have accomplished by the magnitude of their sacrifice will take place."[53] Barberis thus reiterated the idea that, for recently decolonized countries, revolution should be at the same time political and socioeconomic, a double revolution. But he also noted that the revolutionary forces of Cuba and Algeria were guerrilla fighters—that is, civilians, a people in arms.

Both Cuba and Algeria had experienced revolutionary and/or decolonization processes. Afterward, they also continued to conduct international relations mostly through informal militant networks. Both Algeria and Cuba hosted clandestine or exiled revolutionary organizations that they recognized as the sole legal and legitimate representatives of their nations and took solidarity and brotherhood with these as the basis for Third World relations. As a 1962 FLN article put it, "History . . . gave us a special place in the Arab world, of which we are and desire to be an integrated part. However, this primary solidarity forms part of a much broader solidarity, the solidarity built between us and the peoples of Africa and Latin America, who are engaged in the same struggle for total emancipation. This is the historic significance of our Revolution."[54]

This Third-Worldist conception was thus based not so much on "classical" interstate relations as on relations among states created through revolution or between such states and revolutionary organizations elsewhere. It might, however, be useful to remember that for the Latin American Left in the 1960s and 1970s, revolution was not necessarily an armed and violent opposition to the state. Rather, they thought that the road to socialism could be traveled nonviolently, or as a combination of legal and violent means. In the case of the relations between Algeria and Chile, this distinctive feature of the Algerian state's foreign policy—that is, privileging relations with revolutionary organizations or revolutionary governments—explains why Algeria's favored links with Chile involved Chilean left-wing parties from the 1960s to the 1980s.

Chile: From Ally of Cold War Superpowers to Friend of the Non-Aligned

In parallel with the militant links between Algeria and Chile, formal diplomatic relations also developed between the two countries from 1963 to the 1973 Chilean military coup. However, there is a considerable difference between the 1963–70 and the 1970–73 interstate relations. Before 1970 and Allende's elections, diplomatic relations between Algeria and Chile were marked by the Cold War; after Allende's election, they became relations between two states that defined themselves as Third-Worldist and revolutionary. Indeed, in the interstate relations between Algeria and Chile after 1970, it was not career diplomats but the informal activist networks that had supported the Algerian fight for independence in the late 1950s that started playing a major role at the Ministry of Foreign Affairs. Further, as these relations developed, both countries also sought independence from Cold War superpowers and dominant socioeconomic and political models.

The pre-1970 diplomatic relations between Chile and Algeria can thus help us grasp the Third-Worldist facet of Allende's foreign policy through the contrast they present with the latter. In May 1963, Chile opened an embassy in Algiers. It was a year after Algeria's independence and only two months after the establishment of diplomatic relations between the two countries. This embassy in Algiers was also assigned the diplomatic mission for Morocco and Tunisia, Algeria's neighboring countries and ex-protectorates of France, with which Chile had established relations in 1961. In the 1960s, the opening of an embassy, especially in a very distant country, entailed considerable costs that a country such as Chile often found difficult to cover. This, combined with the fact that the socialist orientation of Ben Bella's government was exactly opposite the conservative politics of Jorge Alessandri, president of Chile from 1958 to 1964, suggests that the Chilean state saw the new embassy as serving important priorities and geostrategic goals. According to confidential reports of the Chilean Ministry of Foreign Affairs, Chile not only acknowledged the increasing international importance of the independent African states but also wanted their support in the United Nations, mainly regarding the dispute with Bolivia concerning the binational River Lauca.[55] Indeed, the embassy in Algiers was to act as Chile's liaison with sub-Saharan Africa. In addition, Alessandri's government saw in Chile's presence in Africa an opportunity to closely follow its immediate competitors' economic activity, since Chile was, like most African countries, mainly an exporter of raw materials.[56] Diplomacy was thus instrumental to a rather classic form of rivalry between countries producing primary commodities.[57]

At the same time, however, Alessandri's ministry of foreign affairs reminded the first ambassador in Algeria that one of his main missions was to defend the principles of self-determination, peace, and democracy that Chile and the Western world stood for. That being said, this rhetoric also masked the connection between the opening of the Chilean embassy in Algiers and Cold War dynamics. Even though it was never explicitly stated in the Chilean foreign ministry's confidential reports, the Chilean embassy was implicitly presented as a proxy for the United States, tasked with informing on all "suspicious activities" and with serving as a counterweight to Non-Aligned and socialist countries.[58] In a confidential report, the first Chilean Ambassador, Eugenio Velasco Letelier formulated in these terms his visit to the United States, and his meeting with representatives of the State Department: "The Assistant Secretary General insisted on the State Department being extremely satisfied with Chile's initiative to establish relations with the newest states of Northern Africa, especially with Algeria, because . . . until then in Algiers there was only one Latin American Embassy, the Cuban."[59] In addition, the first confidential report transmitted to the ambassador in Algeria specified that one of his main goals should be the scrutiny of Algeria's relations with the USSR and with the United Arab Republic—the latter because a pan-Arabic union would be a threat to stability in Northern Africa and the Middle East, the former out of concern with economic but mostly military "help" that Algeria was receiving from the USSR.[60]

The choice of Eugenio Velasco Letelier as the first Chilean ambassador to Algeria may have been related to a desire to balance the anti-Communist orientation of Alessandri's foreign policy, given that Velasco was a member of the Radical Party, which dominated the 1930s and 1940s Popular Front governments. However, despite his ideological differences with Alessandri's government, Velasco was very close to the Alessandri family. Arturo, the president's elder brother, was Velasco's professor and mentor in law school.[61] Thus, Velasco was faithful to the Alessandri government's Western-oriented international policy, even as his progressive political beliefs were expected to facilitate his connections with the Algerian government.

But, while the United States looked favorably on the opening of the Chilean embassy in Algiers, Velasco's priorities changed from following Soviet activity in Algeria to focusing on Cuba. One reason for this is that Velasco quickly noted that Algeria had much closer relations with China and Cuba than with the USSR. Not only did the Cuban ambassador, Jorge Serguera, enjoy personal and ideological affinity with Ben Bella, but *Prensa Latina* significantly influenced the view of the Algerians—both government and people—of Latin America.[62] In the case of Chile, it systematically attacked the Chilean government on the government's pro-US political stance. That this view was negative was especially worrisome to Velasco, who was concerned about the impact it could have on Algeria's diplomatic relations with other Latin American states. More generally, Velasco was alarmed by the influence Cuba had gained across the African continent, mostly thanks to Algerian mediation.[63]

At the same time, recognition of this influence led the Chilean ambassador to perceive Cold War dynamics as much more polycentric than he did when he was still in Chile. Velasco's reports give a clear view of how he gradually came to doubt the effectiveness of a binary view of global politics and the division of the world into two camps. Even though he remained hostile to Cuba, his effort to understand what was initially incomprehensible to him—the sympathy the Algerians had for Cubans—led him to question his binary vision of the Cold War period. "The friendship and the sympathy for Cuba and its revolution are very pronounced both within the Algerian government and the people. To this contributes . . . in a very special way the belief that Cuba symbolizes a small but courageous country that heroically stood up against the United States in order to free itself from imperialism and to build its own economic future in complete freedom. This attitude allowed Cuba to put up with all kinds of sacrifices."[64]

In late 1964, the Christian Democrat candidate Eduardo Frei won the presidential elections in Chile. Velasco was replaced by a Christian Democrat intellectual and diplomat, Humberto Díaz Casanueva, a few months before the violent overthrow of Ben Bella and the July 1965 military coup led by Houari Boumediene. Toward the end of his mission in Algeria, Velasco's political stance had become Third-Worldist and overtly anticolonial and anti-imperialist. Velasco's reports became more and more friendly with regard to the Algerian government and its president, and more and more convinced of the capital role that Algeria was destined to play:

> Nowadays, Africa is the most interesting place in the world. And in Africa, Algeria holds a uniquely important place. It is . . . the bridge between the Old World and the nascent states. The fact that it controls a big part of the Southern coast of the Mediterranean Sea; its potential wealth and power and especially, its large repository of oil; its resolute policy, neutralist at the international level, and socialist within Algeria; Ben Bella's extraordinary leadership and its growing influence on many neighboring countries have converted Algeria into a nervous center for world politics.[65]

While it is difficult to measure the effect of Velasco's analyses on the Chilean Foreign Ministry, they do reflect a considerable shift in the way certain public servants and ministry officials and diplomats conceived world political geography in the 1960s, as well as the increasing relevance they attached to Algeria, and more generally recently decolonized countries. They also reflect a process of radicalization quite similar to the abovementioned process experienced by the Arab diaspora in the late 1950s—namely, the gradual adoption of a Third-Worldist stance by a wide spectrum of political organizations, ranging from guerrilla movements to center parties. In a way, Velasco's reports on Ben Bella are a preview of the Allende-Boumediene relations. In one of their private conversations, Ben Bella reported to Velasco that one of Algeria's main global goals was to obtain the broadest possible consensus among Third World countries, a consensus based on promoting economic development and cooperation.[66] Although Ben Bella was overthrown by Boumediene in 1965, the view he had expressed in 1964 was very similar to Boumediene's outlook once he became head of state. It is that same attitude that Boumediene and Allende would maintain in their collaboration from Allende's rise to power in 1970 to the 1973 coup.

Boumediene's Algeria and Allende's Militant Diplomacy

After coming to power in 1965, Boumediene expressed interest in developing Algeria's relations with Chile and its Christian Democrat government, even though the seat of the Algerian embassy in South America remained in Buenos Aires and Algeria did not open up a new embassy in Chile. However, the Christian Democrats did not consider Algeria a priority. The reasons are not specified in the Foreign Ministry reports, but after Díaz Casanueva's departure from Algeria in 1968, the embassy was managed by several chargés d'affaires in fast succession.

This situation changed dramatically with Allende's coming to power. From 1970 to 1973, the Algerian and Chilean governments developed a strong relationship. In May 1972, Chérif Belkacem, the second most powerful man in the Boumediene government, visited Chile and extended an official invitation to Allende.[67] Allende visited Algeria some months later, in December 1972.[68]

Those governmental and official relations were based upon the crystallization of a Third-Worldist ideology, which existed since the late 1950s in a fragmented form and stemmed from previous militant links between the Algerian FLN and the Chilean Socialist Party. The person appointed UP Ambassador in Algiers, Eduardo Salum, perfectly embodied these links. Salum was not a career diplomat, but a socialist intellectual of Arab origin, whose elder brother was a leading figure of the 1950s Chilean solidarity movement with the FLN. Eduardo Salum was appointed ambassador by the Socialist Party's Political Commission.[69] The main political parties of the UP, the Communist and the Socialist Parties, appointed ambassadors to embassies according to their respective political affinities. For instance, the Communist Party named the Chilean ambassador to Moscow, whereas the Socialists appointed the Chilean ambassador to Rome. Hence, the choice of Eduardo Salum demonstrated the Chilean socialist government's desire not only to deepen interstate relations, but also to develop a more profound ideological bond with Algeria. Allende's government, mainly the Socialist Party, attached high political importance to the country. For them, Algeria was a bridge allowing Chile to connect with Africa and Asia in spite of its geographical confinement.[70] The importance that the Socialist Party attached to Algeria was a direct reflection of its conviction that the political center of the world was gradually shifting from Europe to African countries, such as Algeria, or to Asian countries, such as Vietnam.

As for Algeria's motivations, according to the main FLN publication, *El Moudjahid*, Algeria's interest in Allende's Chile stemmed partly from older political links.[71] However, the Algerian government was also attracted by certain features of the UP, which, according to the FLN, were the embodiment of Third World politics. More precisely, Allende's Chile embodied supranational unity and solidarity through its commitment to regional integration, the same project Algeria was promoting through the Organization of African Unity and pan-Arabism. Moreover, after Allende's election and U.S. reactions to it, Chile had become a new center for anti-imperialist struggle. For Algeria, anti-imperialism was but the other side of anticolonialism: "Working relentlessly to 'demolish the French colonial order,' Algeria claimed a leading role in 'the process of demolition of imperialism' in general. All the ideology that *El Moudjahid* disseminated since June 1956, was profoundly influenced by Frantz Fanon and advocated the confluence of the struggles of all the colonized, in order to promote new solidarities which could moderate the imperialist powers."[72]

Furthermore, Allende and Boumediene shared a common conception of what Third-World revolution and revolutionary governance should be like: both focused their discourse on the necessity of obtaining "true independence," perceived as being the result of an efficient economic policy and state control over natural and human resources. As the Chilean ambassador said when presenting his credentials: "The destinies and trajectories of our two governments touch one another. We both prepare the ground for the construction of socialism, by adopting measures to regain our national wealth. This is the only way to secure absolute sovereignty, impossible to obtain if there is still economic dependency. National political autonomy is not enough for securing peoples' development."[73]

Both Boumediene's and Allende's governments advocated for national control over raw materials (copper in Chile, oil in Algeria), for land reform, and for workers' and peasants' self-management. In this respect, the need for qualified personnel (technicians, doctors and nurses, teachers, agronomists, engineers) in the main economic sectors and activities was apparent, especially in Algeria.[74] Thus, cooperation agreements that included the transfer of qualified personnel from Chile to Algeria were signed between the two countries.[75]

Additionally, both countries were actively engaged in international forums that promoted similar economic policy. In the 1960s, Algeria had been one of the most committed sponsors of the United Nations Conference on Trade and Development (UNCTAD), a forum where countries producing raw material could defend their commodities by pressuring industrialized countries to maintain the price level of primary commodities. In April 1972, Chile hosted the UNCTAD III. Its candidacy was supported by Algeria,[76] whose delegates were also present in Santiago and tried to obtain consensus among the participants both on a common Third World economic policy—that was to be approved a year later in Algiers' UNCTAD—and on solidarity with Vietnam.[77]

As Nicole Grimaud points out, the Algerian Third-Worldist and nationalist economic policy aimed to create a Third World consensus.[78] According to the Boumediene government, an economic consensus would be much easier to extrapolate later on to the political field: "[Algeria's] aim was to bypass political barriers by putting forward demands related to [economic] development. However, the long-term goal was to gradually bring Third World countries together around a radical political agenda."[79] This explains why an important part of the cooperation and coordination between the FLN and the UP concerned Latin American exiles, mostly Brazilian, who had abandoned their homeland after the 1964 military coup, and their free circulation between the two countries.[80] As the Chilean Ministry of Foreign Affairs archives and FLN publications demonstrate, both Boumediene's Algeria and Allende's Chile focused their discourse on their common belonging to a broader community, the Third World. Thus, solidarity with other national liberation movements (a category that also included movements resisting to right-wing dictatorships) was a moral and political obligation.[81]

Hence, as soon as the news of the Chilean coup broke, the Algerian government, like other governments in Latin America, Africa, Asia, and Eastern Europe, interrupted its diplomatic relations with Chile, now represented by a military junta. But the Algerian case was rather unique, in the sense that Allende's ambassador was maintained at his position and was recognized by Boumediene's government as the sole legitimate and legal representative of the Chilean nation.[82] It was he who represented Chile in Algerian official ceremonies and who remained the respondent on matters related to Chilean politics until his departure from Algiers to Milan in December 1976.

Furthermore, Algeria hosted an important number of Chilean political exiles, in particular, technicians, engineers, agronomists, doctors, nurses, and teachers. Those professionals were invited by Boumediene's government to settle in Algeria and to contribute to the country's efforts at economic and technological development. The settlement of the Chilean political exiles in Algeria was, in many ways, the perpetuation of the militant diplomacy of 1970–73 and the fulfillment of the cooperation agreements signed between the two heads of state before 1973.[83]

Conclusion

In the late 1950s, personal and organizational links were established between the Chilean Left and the Algerian FLN, thanks to the Arab diaspora in Chile and mostly to militant transnational networks that actively supported the Algerian national cause. After independence, the relations between the Algerian government and Chilean left-wing parties became tighter, as they were both seeking solidarity and Third World economic and political integration. In this process, several mediators, among them Cuba, played a key role. In addition, the opening by the right-wing government of Jorge Alessandri of a Chilean embassy in 1963 in Algiers led to the development of interstate relations, as well as to recognition of the importance for the Cold War era of Third World dynamics. In 1970, with Allende's coming to power the militant and the institutional logics converged entirely. After the 1973 Chilean coup, despite the breaking off of diplomatic ties, the militant and institutional bonds consolidated throughout the Political Unity period were maintained thanks to the Algerian state's support of Chilean political exiles in the framework of Third World solidarity.

Through the study of the postwar Chilean-Algerian relations, this chapter has demonstrated that the gradual forging of links between the two nations must be placed within the nascent Third World dynamics. As discussed, we cannot understand Cold War Chilean history exclusively through the country's relations with the United States and/or the USSR. The Third World—and thus Chile's relations with countries and political organizations that situated themselves in the Third World—are equally relevant. Moreover, by studying the interchange of revolutionary ideas, practices, and activists between Chile and Algeria from the 1950s to the 1970s, this chapter contributes to the ongoing debate on the meaning, content, and material reality of the "Third World" without limiting it to its relations with the United States and the Soviet Union.

Notes

1. Allende was president of Chile and head of the Popular Unity Government (1970–1973) until the 11 September military coup and the establishment of a dictatorship, led by Augusto Pinochet, that ended with the return to democracy in 1990.

2. Alberto Gamboa, "En el aeropuerto, un gran letrero: 'El cobre de Chile seguirá siendo de Chile,'" *Clarín*, 6 December 1972, 24

3. More precisely, this chapter builds on the extensive examination of the 1950s–1970s Chilean and the 1960s–1970s Algerian press, the Archives of the Chilean Ministry of Foreign Affairs, the magazines and journals that the Chilean political exiles published in Algiers in the post-1973 period, and more than twenty extensive interviews with Chilean left-wing activists connected to Algeria.

4. See for instance Heraldo Muñoz and Joseph Tulchin, eds., *Latin American Nations in World Politics* (Boulder, CO: Westview Press, 1984); Augusto Varas, ed., *Soviet–Latin American Relations in the 1980s* (Boulder, CO: Westview Press, 1987); Joaquín Fermandois, *Mundo y fin de mundo: Chile en la política mundial, 1900–2004* (Santiago: Ediciones Universidad Católica de Chile, 2015).

5. When it comes to Algeria's links with Latin America, only Ben Bella's relations with Cuba have been examined so far. See Piero Gleijeses, *Conflicting Missions: Havana, Washington and Africa, 1959–1976* (Chapel Hill: University of North Carolina Press, 2002), 30–52; and Jeffrey James Byrne, *Mecca of Revolution. Algeria, Decolonization and the Third World Order* (Oxford: Oxford University Press, 2016).

6. The term "Third World" is undoubtedly an ideological and political construction. But as noted by Samantha Christiansen and Zachary A. Scarlett, "although the term Third World may be outmoded today—replaced by the vague (and equally questionable) Global South—we stand by its value as a historical idea of vital importance during the Cold War. Discarding the term would be to erase a historical situation that did indeed play a central role in the global protest movement of the 1960s." Christiansen and Scarlett, eds., *The Third World in the Global 1960s* (New York: Berghahn Books, 2013), 3. Indeed, the activists, governments, and institutions that I study use the term "Third World" broadly.

7. This is an allusion to the title of Frantz Fanon's book *The Wretched of the Earth* (London: Penguin, 1963). Born in Martinique, the psychiatrist and Marxist Frantz

Fanon became a leading figure of the Algerian revolution of independence. Prefaced by Jean-Paul Sartre, *The Wretched of the Earth* illustrates Fanon's vision of revolutionary violence. It became an important ideological reference for the 1960s and 1970s Latin American New Left.

8. Lilian Mathieu, "L'espace des mouvements sociaux," *Politix* 77, no. 1 (2007): 131–51.

9. For instance, Dominic Sachsenmaier, "Global History and Critiques of Western Perspectives," *Comparative Education* 42, no. 3 (2006): 451–70. Michael Werner and Bénédicte Zimmermann, "Penser l'histoire croisée: Entre empirie et réflexivité," *Annales. Histoire, Sciences Sociales* 1 (2003): 7–36.

10. Pierre-Yves Saunier, "Circulations, connexions et espaces transnationaux," *Genèses* 4, no. 57 (2004): 110–26; Caroline Douki and Philippe Minard, "Histoire globale, histoires connectées: un changement d'échelle historiographique?," *Revue d'Histoire moderne et contemporaine* 54, no. 5 (2007): 20.

11. For instance, the concept of "interstitial space" is particularly suited for the analysis of historical processes situated in different geographical scales. Thibaud Boncourt, "Acteurs multipositionnés et fabrique du transnational. La création du European Consortium for Political Research," *Critique internationale* 59, no. 2 (2013): 17–32; Thibaut Rioufreyt, "Les passeurs de la 'troisième voie.' Intermédiaires et médiateurs dans la circulation transnationale des idées," *Critique internationale* 59, no. 2 (2013): 33–46.

12. Kevin Funk, "How Latin America Met the Arab World: Toward a Political Economy of Arab–Latin American Relations," in *Latin American Foreign Policies towards the Middle East. Actors, Contexts, and Trends*, ed. Marta Tawil Kuri (New York: Palgrave MacMillan, 2016), 11–36.

13. For instance José Rodríguez Elizondo, *Crisis y renovación de las izquierdas: de la Revolución Cubana a Chiapas, pasando por el "caso chileno"* (Buenos Aires: Andrés Bello, 1995); Jorge Castañeda, *La utopía desarmada. Intrigas, dilemas y promesa de la izquierda en América Latina* (Buenos Aires: Ediciones Ariel, 1993); Enrique Ros, *Castro y las guerrillas latinoamericanas* (Miami: Ediciones Universal, 2001).

14. For a critical view of this historiographical approach, see Tanya Harmer and Alfredo Riquelme, eds., *Chile y la Guerra Fría Global* (Santiago: Ril, 2015).

15. The two reference publications are Odd Arne Westad, ed., *Reviewing the Cold War: Approaches, Interpretations, Theory* (London: Frank Cass, 2000); and Odd Arne Westad, *The Global Cold War* (Cambridge: Cambridge University Press, 2007).

16. Matthew Connelly, "Taking Off the Cold War Lens: Visions of North-South Conflict during the Algerian War for Independence," *American Historical Review*, 105, no. 3 (2000): 739–69; Robert J. McMahon, ed., *The Cold War in the Third World* (New York: Oxford University Press, 2013); Peter L. Hahn and Mary Ann Heiss. eds., *Empire and Revolution: the United States and the Third World since 1945* (Columbus: Ohio State University Press, 2000).

17. Jason C. Parker, "Decolonization, the Cold War, and the post-Columbian era," in *The Cold War in the Third World*, ed. Robert J. McMahon (New York: Ox-

ford University Press, 2013), 124-38; Thea Pitman and Andy Stafford, "Introduction: Transatlanticism and Tricontinentalism," *Journal of Transatlantic Studies* 7, no. 3 (2009): 197-207.

18. See, for instance, Christiansen and Scarlett, *The Third World*; and Kare Dubinsky, Catherine Krull, Susan Lord, Sean Mills, and Scott Rutherford, eds., *New World Coming: The Sixties and the Shaping of Global Consciousness* (Toronto: Between the Lines, 2009).

19. Byrne, *Mecca of Revolution*, 5.

20. See for instance Tricia M. Redeker Hepner, "Transnational Governance and the Centralization of State Power in Eritrea and Exile," *Ethnic and Racial Studies* 31, no. 3 (2008): 476-502. Hepner shows that "the Eritrean state utilizes its transnational capacities not to expand socio-political participation and rights or to enable foreign/global economic interventions, but rather to limit, control and repress them" (478).

21. Donald W. Bray, "The Political Emergence of Arab-Chileans, 1952-1958," *Journal of Inter-American Studies* 4, no. 4 (1962): 557-62; Brenda Elsey, *Citizens and Sportsmen: Fútbol and Politics in Twentieth-Century Chile* (Austin: University of Texas Press, 2011), chapter 4.

22. Ahmad Hassan Mattar, *Guía social de la Colonia Arabe en Chile: Siria, Palestina, Libanesa* (Santiago: Club Palestino; Ahues Hermanos, 1941), 379.

23. Cecilia Baeza and Elodie Brun, "La diplomacia chilena hacia los países árabes: entre posicionamiento estratégico y oportunismo comercial," *Estudios Internacionales*, 171 (2012): 61-85.

24. Marie-Noëlle Sarget, *Système politique et Parti Socialiste au Chili. Un essai d'analyse systémique* (Paris: Édition de L'Harmattan, 1994), 324-25; Óscar Waiss, *Chile vivo. Memorias de un socialista (1928-1970)* (Madrid: Ediciones Fuenlabrada, 1985).

25. "La potencia de Ben Bella," *Ercilla*, 13 November 1963, 23; "Invité par le président de la République, Raul Ampuero, secrétaire général du Parti socialiste chilien, est arrivé à Alger," *Alger Républicain*, 11 October 1963, 1.

26. Sylvain Pattieu, *Les camarades des frères. Trotskistes et libertaires dans la guerre d'Algérie* (Alger: Éditions Casbah, 2006); Sylvain Pattieu, "Le 'camarade Pablo,' la IVe Internationale et la guerre d'Algérie," *Revue Historique*, 619, no. 3 (2001), 695-729; Piero Gleijeses, *Conflicting Missions*, 30-52; Dimitris Livieratos, *L'Usine invisible de la révolution algérienne. Mémoires d'un trotskiste grec* (Athens: Asini, 2012); Roberto Muniz, interview by Eugenia Palieraki, Algiers, 19 October 2012.

27. Pattieu, "Le 'camarade Pablo,'" 708-14.

28. Michel Raptis ("Michel Pablo"), *Le dossier de l'autogestion en Algérie* (Paris: Anthropos, 1967).

29. For instance, in December 1960, the Chilean Committee had raised $11,000 for the FLN. "Des Parlementaires Chiliens s'adressent au G.P.R.A.," *El Moudjahid* 71, 29 January 1961, in *El Moudjahid: Un Journal de Combat, 1956-1962* (Alger: Anep, 2011), 3:405. See also "Apoyo a la causa argelina," *Mundo Árabe*, 15 October 1960, 1-2.

30. Apoyo a la causa argelina," 1–2.

31. Eduardo Salum Yazigi, interview by Eugenia Palieraki, Milan, 18 July 2016. See also From: Embassy of Chile in Algeria/Eugenio Velasco Letelier (Amb.), To: Ministry of Foreign Affairs/Political Division, "Informa sobre importante conversación con el Presidente Ben Bella," 10 October 1964, 2, Confidential Report no. 16, *1964—Argelia*, Fondo Histórico del Ministerio de Relaciones Exteriores (hereafter MFA).

32. Byrne, *Mecca of Revolution*, 71–72.

33. "Misión de la República argelina vino a explicar a Latinoamérica la realidad francesa en Argelia," *Mundo Árabe*, 15 October 1960, 1–2.

34. *El Moudjahid* 41, April 1959, in *El Moudjahid: Un Journal de Combat*, 2:262.

35. On UGEMA's ambiguous stance towards the United States and the USSR, see Karen Paget, *Patriotic Betrayal: The Inside Story of the CIA's Secret Campaign to Enroll American Students in the Crusade against Communism* (New Haven, CT: Yale University Press, 2015), 158–64.

36. *El Moudjahid* 41, 262.

37. C. de B., "Las contradicciones de M. André Malraux," *Mundo Árabe*, 26 September 1959, 7.

38. Interview with Salum Yazigi. See also "Que el Sr. Malraux se defina como escritor o como ministro," *Mundo Árabe*, 9 September 1959, 1–2.

39. C. de B., "Las contradicciones," 7; Todd Shepard, "A l'heure des 'grands ensembles' et de la guerre d'Algérie. L' 'Etat-nation' en question," *Monde(s). Histoire, Espaces, Relations* 1 (May 2012): 113–34.

40. Nasser's *Philosophy of the Revolution* was translated into Spanish by *Mundo Árabe* and published in Chile and Latin America in 1954. According to Nasser, the countries undergoing decolonization had to achieve a double revolution: a political one by separating themselves from the metropolis, and, at the same time, a social and economic one to break away from all economic dependency. In other words, the revolution had to be at once anticolonial and anti-imperialist or anti-neocolonial. Gamal Abdel Nasser, *The Philosophy of the Revolution* (Buffalo, NY: Smith, Keynes & Marshall, 1959).

41. Benyoussef Benkhedda, "Impressions d'une tournée latino-américaine," *El Moudjahid* 76, 5 January 1961, in *El Moudjahid: Un Journal de Combat*, 3:405. This is also reminiscent of Kwame Nkrumah's conception of neocolonialism. Nkrumah was both an important ally of and an ideological reference for the FLN. On Ghana's postcolonial foreign policy, see Willard Scott Thompson, *Ghana's Foreign Policy, 1957–1966: Diplomacy Ideology, and the New State* (Princeton, NJ: Princeton University Press, 1969). On Nkrumah's political thought see, for instance, Saïd Bouamama, "Kwame Nkrumah," in *Figures de la révolution africaine. De Kenyatta à Sankara*, ed. Saïd Bouamama (Paris: La Découverte, 2014), 182–201.

42. *El Moudjahid* 41, 262.

43. Tanjug's dispatches were used mainly by the socialist press (namely, by the journal *Noticias de Última Hora*), whereas both the socialist and the communist press were using the Cuban *Prensa Latina*'s dispatches.

44. Byrne, *Mecca of Revolution*, 235.

45. Sabine Dullin and Pierre Singaravélou, "Le débat public: Un objet transnational?," *Monde(s). Histoire, Espaces, Relations* 1 (May 2012): 23.

46. "Carta del Presidente a Boumedienne: Debe ser estimulado aflojamiento de tensiones," *La Nación*, 2 September 1973, 35.

47. On Algeria's economic and social situation and the brain drain following the country's independence, see Mohamed Harbi and Benjamin Stora, eds., *La guerre d'Algérie. 1954-2004. La fin de l'amnésie* (Paris: Laffont, 2004), and Jean-Louis Miège and Collette Dubois, eds., *L'Europe retrouvée. Les migrations de la décolonisation* (Paris: L'Harmattan, 1994).

48. For instance, the Third International Meeting of journalists in 1963, as well as the International Conference on Education in April 1965 took place in Algiers. A Chilean delegation attended both events.

49. See, for instance, the reports published by the communist journalist Hernán Uribe and the educator Crisólogo Gatica: Hernán Uribe, "Líder africano habla para *El Siglo*. Ben Bella: llevaremos hasta su término la construcción del socialismo en Argelia," *El Siglo*, 29 September 1963, 13; Crisólogo Gatica, "Argelia debe seguir el camino del socialismo. Entrevista a Crisólogo Gatica," *El Siglo*, 6 June 1965, 4.

50. Roger Faligot, *Tricontinentale. Quand Che Guevara, Ben Barka, Cabral, Castro et Hô Chi Minh préparaient la révolution mondiale (1964-1968)* (Paris: La Découverte, 2013).

51. Jorge Serguera Riverí ("Papito"), *Caminos del Che: datos inéditos de su vida* (México, DF: Plaza y Valdés, 1997), 94.

52. For instance, "¿Ben Bella es un nuevo Castro?," *Ercilla*, 25 July 1962, 11; and "Ben Bella es el Fidel Castro argelino; triunfal marcha hacia Reforma Agraria," *Clarín*, 26 July 1962, 2.

53. Víctor Barberis, "Por una Argelia socialista," *Noticias de Última Hora*, 11 July 1962, 2.

54. "Nation arabe et Révolution algérienne," *El Moudjahid* 89, 16 January 1962, cited by Nicole Grimaud, *La politique extérieure de l'Algérie* (Paris: Karthala, 1984), 190-91.

55. From: Ministry of Foreign Affairs/Political Division, To: Embassy of Chile in Algeria/ ugenio Velasco Letelier (Amb.), "Instrucciones al Sr. Embajador Extraordinario y Plenipotenciario de Chile en Argelia, Marruecos y Túnez, Don Eugenio Velasco Letelier. Estrictamente confidencial," 31 May 1963, 3-6, *1963—Argelia*, Fondo Histórico del MFA. The River Lauca is a binational river that originates in Chile but empties into a Bolivian lake. In the 1930s, Chile used part of the flow to better irrigate the Chilean valley of Azapa, thus considerably reducing the quantity of water that reached the Bolivian Altiplano and endangering this region's agriculture.

56. Mostly copper which was also produced by Zambia (Northern Rhodesia until 1964) and Zaire.

57. From: Ministry of Foreign Affairs, "Instrucciones al Sr. Embajador Extraordinario y Plenipotenciario de Chile," 9-11.

58. From: Ministry of Foreign Affairs, "Instrucciones al Sr. Embajador Extraordinario y Plenipotenciario de Chile," 3 and 6-8.

59. From: Embassy of Chile in Algeria/Eugenio Velasco Letelier (Amb.), To: Ministry of Foreign Affairs / Political Division, "Informa sobre misiones cumplidas," 7 July 1963, 2, *1963—Argelia*, Fondo Histórico del MFA.

60. From: Ministry of Foreign Affairs, "Instrucciones al Sr. Embajador Extraordinario y Plenipotenciario de Chile," 7–8.

61. "Homenaje a Eugenio Velazco Letelier," *Anales de la Facultad de Ciencias Jurídicas y Sociales* 14 (January, 1972), www.analesderecho.uchile.cl/index.php/ACJYS/article/view/4317/4207.

62. "The misconception on what happens in Latin America and in Chile is serious. The view that [the Algerians] have on the New World is exclusively the one the Cubans want them to have"; From: Eugenio Velasco Letelier (Amb.), To: MFA/Political Division, "Informe sobre situación en Argelia," 10 August 1964, 10, Informe no. 7, *1964—Argelia*, Fondo Histórico del MFA. From: MFA/Political Division, To: Eugenio Velasco, "Acusa recibo oficios confidenciales nos. 9, 10 y 11," 10 October 1964, 1, *1964—Argelia*, Fondo Histórico del MFA, where the ministry tries to reassure Velasco, who is extremely preoccupied with the Algerian government's retaliation on the Chilean Embassy after the interruption of Chile's diplomatic relations with Cuba.

63. From: Eugenio Velasco Letelier (Amb.), To: MFA/Political Division, "Informa sobre actividades cubanas en Argelia," 13 June 1964, Confidential Report no. 62/4, *1964—Argelia*, Fondo Histórico del MFA.

64. From: Eugenio Velasco Letelier (Amb.), To: MFA/- Political Division, "Informa sobre reacción producida en Argelia con la ruptura de relaciones con Cuba," 31 August 1964, 1, Confidential Report no. 8, *1964—Argelia*, Fondo Histórico del MFA.

65. From: Eugenio Velasco Letelier (Amb.), To: MFA/Political Division, "Formula algunas observaciones generales sobre política internacional en relación con Argelia y África," 2 September 1964, 1, *1964—Argelia*, Fondo Histórico del MFA.

66. From: Eugenio Velasco Letelier (Amb.), To: MFA/Political Division, "Informa sobre importante conversación con el Presidente Ben Bella," 10 October 1964, 4, Confidential Report no. 16, *1964—Argelia*, Fondo Histórico del MFA;. From: Eugenio Velasco Letelier (Amb.), To: MFA/Political Division, "Informa sobre entrevista con el Presidente Ben Bella," 6 April 1964, 1-2, *1964—Argelia*, Fondo Histórico del MFA.

67. "Dijo Ministro Belkacem: Pueblo de Argelia espera visita del Presidente Allende," *La Nación*, 31 May 1972, 1; "Ministro del Consejo de la revolución de Argelia en Santiago," *La Nación*, 30 May 1972, 8; "Ministro argelino se entrevistó con Allende," *Noticias de Última Hora*, 31 May 1972, 24.

68. From: Eduardo Salum Yazigi (Amb.), To: MFA/Political Division, "Escala del Presidente Salvador Allende en Argelia," 7 December 1972, Confidential Report no. 152/26, *1972—Argelia*, Fondo Histórico del MFA. See also "Estamos como camiseta y espalda con Argelia," *Clarín*, December 7, 1972, 10.

69. Salum's candidacy was supported by Clodomiro Almeyda, Allende's Minister of Foreign Affairs. Interview with Salum Yazigi.

70. See, for instance, From: MFA/Political Division, To: Eduardo Salum Yazigi (Amb.), "Acusan recibo de ofi n°66/54 y 67/55 sobre visitas a Argelia del Vice-Presidente del Consejo de Estado de la República Popular del Congo y el Presidente de Camerún," 6 October 1971, Report no. 21826, *1972—Argelia*, Fondo Histórico del MFA.

71. For instance, in 1972, the members of the ex-Comité Chileno Pro-Autodeterminación de Argelia, Luis Karque, Tawfik Rumie, and Marco Antonio Salum, were invited to Algeria on the tenth anniversary of the country's independence. From: Eduardo Salum Yazigi (Amb.), To: MFA/Political Division, "Delegación chilena a las festividades de la Independencia," 19 July 1972, Confidential Report no. 93/16, *1972—Argelia*, Fondo Histórico del MFA.

72. Grimaud, *La politique extérieure*, 263.

73. From: Eduardo Salum Yazigi (Amb.), To: MFA/Political Division, "Presentación de Cartas Credenciales," 27 July 1971, 2, Confidential Report no. 42:8, *1972—Argelia*, Fondo Histórico del MFA.

74. From: Eduardo Salum Yazigi (Amb.), To: MFA/Political Division, "Entrevista con Ministros de la Información, Agricultura y Telecomunicaciones," n.d. [July 1971], Confidential Report no. 53/9, *1971—Argelia*, Fondo Histórico del MFA. From: Eduardo Salum Yazigi (Amb.), To: MFA/Economic Division, "Visita técnica chilenos de ENAP en Argel," 22 June 1971, Report no. 31/26, 22 June 1971, *1971—Argelia*, Fondo Histórico del MFA.

75. From: Eduardo Salum Yazigi (Amb.), To: MFA/Political Division, "Entrevista con Ministros de la Información, Agricultura y Telecomunicaciones," July 1971, 1–2, Confidential Report no. 53/9, *1971—Argelia*, Fondo Histórico del MFA. From: Eduardo Salum Yazigi (Amb.), To: MFA/ Political Division, "Ref. Visita del Sr. Alberto Martínez 8ª Feria Internacional de Argel," 10 September 1971, Confidential Report no. 65/11, 1*1971—Argelia*, Fondo Histórico del MFA. From: MFA/- Political Division, To: Eduardo Salum Yazigi (Amb.), 3 March 1972. Confidential Report no. 701, *1972—Argelia*, Fondo Histórico del MFA. From: Eduardo Salum Yazigi (Amb.), To: MFA/Political Division, "Delegación ENAP," 11 April 1972, Confidential Report no. 40/6, *1972—Argelia*, Fondo Histórico del MFA.

76. One of the most important missions the new Chilean ambassador had to carry out in 1971 was to lobby the Algerian government in order to obtain Algeria's vote for Chile hosting the UNCTAD Conference in 1972. From: MFA/Economic Division, To: Eduardo Salum Yazigi (Amb.), "Despacho inmediato,"4 March 1971, *1971—Argelia*, Fondo Histórico del MFA.

77. "Argelia apoya causa del pueblo vietnamita," *La Nación*, 12 May 1972, 12.

78. Grimaud, *La politique extérieure*, 266.

79. Grimaud, *La politique extérieure*, 266.

80. See numerous articles of *El Moudjahid*, January 1970; From: MFA/South American Department, To: Carlos Souper (Chargé d'Affaires), 9 January 1971, Cable n° 1, *1971—Argelia*, Fondo Histórico del MFA; From: MFA/ Political Division, To: Eduardo Salum Yazigi (Amb.), "Solicita instrucciones sobre solicitud de inmigración," 9 November 1971, Confidential Report no. 91/15. *1971—Argelia*, Fondo Histórico del MFA.

81. Salum Yazigi, "Presentación de Cartas Credenciales," 2–3.
82. Interview with Salum Yazigi.
83. On the Chilean exile in Algeria, see Eugenia Palieraki, "Broadening the Field of Perception and Struggle: Chilean Political Exiles in Algeria and Third-World Cosmopolitanism," *African Identities*, 16, no. 2 (2018): 205–18, in *Revolutionary Cosmopolitanism: Africa's Positionality and International Solidarities (1950s–1970s)*, ed. Eugenia Palieraki and Sarah Fila-Bakabadio.

12 A Mexican New International Economic Order?

CHRISTY THORNTON

Just nine months into his presidency, in October of 1981, Ronald Reagan stepped off a plane into the sweltering autumn sunshine in the resort city of Cancún, Mexico, to deliver the coup de grâce to the already faltering effort to create a New International Economic Order (NIEO). On disembarking in Cancún, where the North-South Summit on Cooperation and Development was to take place over the following days, Reagan shared an embrace with Mexican President José López Portillo, who had spearheaded the effort to convene the summit together with the Austrian Chancellor Bruno Kreisky.[1] But the U.S. president's professions of friendship with the leaders of what had come to be called the "developing world" belied the message he would deliver: not only would there be no consideration of any redistribution of global wealth, as the Brandt Commission Report had urged the year before; there would be no further "global" negotiations on the matter, either.[2] Instead, Reagan repeated his insistence on the "magic of the marketplace," a refrain he had repeatedly used since taking office, arguing that "massive transfers of wealth" would not "somehow miraculously produce new well-being."[3] The prospect of reordering the global economy to take into consideration the needs of the developing world was all but dead. As López Portillo would put it, "Tragic paradoxes were raised in Cancún that could not be solved."[4]

It was a sad irony that the already wounded NIEO project faced its final blow in Mexico, for Mexican leaders had been among its fiercest champions—and of the ideas underpinning it. It was, in fact, Mexico's previous president, Luis Echeverría, who had proposed one of the NIEO's core documents: the Charter of Economic Rights and Duties of States, adopted by the United Nations (UN) General Assembly in 1974 after more than two years of negotiations. For many scholars, the charter is a consummate document of the 1970s: conceived in the context of the collapse of the Bretton Woods monetary system and the energy crisis surrounding the Organization of the Petroleum Exporting Countries (OPEC) oil embargo, the charter and the

NIEO more broadly have been interpreted in recent scholarship as emerging at a moment of political possibility, when the decolonizing groundswell of newly independent states entering the UN system encountered a crisis in the capitalist world economy, which resulted in a call for a new kind of global economic imaginary. But while the form the NIEO and the charter took within the structures of the UN was undoubtedly embedded in the political-economic specificities of its time, the particular tenets of this imaginary actually had deeper roots. Although the proximate influence was obviously the 1960s agenda of the UN Conference on Trade and Development (UNCTAD), under the ideological leadership of Argentine economist Raúl Prebisch, the underlying principles actually date all the way back, as scholars have recently noted, to the Mexican revolutionary constitution of 1917.[5] Indeed, if we pull this single thread from the fabric of the Charter of Economic Rights and Duties of States, we unravel a decades-long history of Mexican advocacy for precisely the economic ideas codified in the charter—a history that both predates our traditional periodization of political struggles over international governance and development and widens our geographic understanding of where and by whom those struggles were fought.

That it was Mexico's president who both proposed and was the fiercest advocate of the Charter of Economic Right and Duties of States— frequently referred to in Mexico as the *Carta Echeverría*—was not an accident.[6] In fact, the charter represented the culmination of decades of advocating such rights and duties by Mexican politicians, economists, and diplomats in international fora: during the Paris Peace Conference in 1919, within the Pan-American Union in 1923, at the 1933 Inter-American Conference at Montevideo, in the planning for the Bretton Woods Conference in 1944, at the 1948 UN conference at Havana that was to have created an International Trade Organization, and beyond, into the era of UNCTAD and the finally the NIEO. In each of these moments, Mexican actors seized on moments of crisis and reform to project a developmentalist vision outward and to argue for new systems of international governance. The charter was, then, shaped in profound and heretofore unexamined ways by the political, social, and economic ideas that emerged from the Mexican Revolution and the postrevolutionary governments that carried its legacy into the international arena. In insisting on the fundamental premise of juridical equality of states, large and small, the right of those states to maintain sovereignty over economic decision-making, and the organization of the global economy for the mutual benefit of rich and poor nations, the 1974 charter directly echoed each of these earlier interventions made by Mexican experts on behalf of what were variously termed the "smaller," "weaker," "debtor," or "less-developed" states. The roots of the New International Economic Order had long been nurtured in Mexican soil.

. . . . . .

Despite this legacy, we know relatively little about the particularly Mexican foundations of the New International Economic Order. Renewed interest in the NIEO has emerged in the context of a larger turn toward global history, and particularly within an emerging subfield that could loosely be categorized as "histories of the global"—that is, research about historical projects that were themselves avowedly, explicitly globe-spanning. This new work, building on existing themes in transnational and international history, seeks to examine how the international and the global were conceived by historical actors, and how institutions and organizations for their governance were imagined and built. This emerging field brings together the robust historiography of international institutions such as the League of Nations and the vast UN system with a growing body of scholarship on the norms, ideological projects, and legal frameworks, such as human rights, global governance, and development, which have guided those institutions.[7]

A central concern of much of this new historiography of the global has been to read its subjects, long viewed through a North Atlantic lens, "from the outside in," as Erez Manela puts it, using sources and perspectives from those "on the margins."[8] Thanks to this new scholarship, the exchange between center and periphery—of activists, diplomats, and intellectuals; the ideas with which they analyzed their world; and the policies they put in place to shape it—is now more frequently understood not as a one-way diffusion from the West to the rest, but a multidirectional and reciprocal process unevenly structured by power relations. The achievements of this path-breaking scholarship are to be celebrated, as it has opened new avenues of historical inquiry and offered new and exciting explanatory frameworks for historical change not only in what we now call the Global South—an imprecise but expansive term used to refer to the world beyond Europe and the United States—but in the Global North, as well.[9]

But even as renewed interest in the history of the global has pushed scholars to take seriously interventions from the South, a curious divide has emerged in this literature: Latin America is frequently left off the maps scholars have drawn.[10] Latin America was, of course, a region colonized by European powers, ruled using imperial systems of control and resource extraction, and decolonized in fierce wars of independence.[11] In fact, Latin America came into being as a kind of prototype of the modern interstate system, a community of nations simultaneously challenging and affirming one another's right to existence through their shared commitment to republicanism and anti-imperialism.[12] But by the late twentieth century, the region would come to form an integral part of the Third World: independent, unaligned, and indebted. Despite this, however, there has been a marked tendency to leave Latin America out of new histories of the global, even where actors and ideas from Africa, Asia, and the Middle East have been centered.[13] The distance between these regions of the world is perhaps less geographical, however, than chronological, deriving from the century or more between their struggles for decolonization. In this emerging literature on global institutions and ideas, there is an apparent incommensurability of the decolonizing world in Africa, Asia, and the Middle East with the formally sovereign but economically and politically weak states of Latin America.[14]

The imperative toward global history, as Sebastian Conrad has noted, is motivated not only by moving beyond the nation-state as the container of history but also by decentering Europe as the driver of that history.[15] In the push to decenter, however, much of this new literature—produced largely by scholars trained in European history—nonetheless replicates particular understandings of the relationship between Europe and its colonial peripheries, leaving Latin America largely beyond the frame. When Latin Americans do appear, their ideas and actions are frequently painted either as derivative of European antecedents, and therefore as not distinctive or, conversely, written off as simple pawns of a hegemonic United States, whose power is already always constituted and largely uncontested. In Samuel Moyn's highly influential *The Last Utopia*, for example, much-lauded Latin American interventions in the midcentury codification of human rights at San Francisco merely "reflected long since globalized European practices in the first place."[16] In Giuliano Garavini's impressive and wide-ranging *After Empires*, Latin Americans play a distinctly more active role, but the story is still one in which representatives of the Non-Aligned Movement in 1961 could find themselves "offering admission" in Belgrade to a "Latin America whose states had been considered to that point almost as culturally dependent arms of the Western powers."[17] Considered by whom, we aren't told, but presumably it wasn't Latin American intellectuals, diplomats, or revolutionaries themselves, who had a long history of contention with the United States and other great powers.

Other work notes the importance of Latin American contributions to, for example, ideas about global governance—drawing on a dynamic and growing body of scholarship about Latin American contributions to international law—but leaves these episodes for area-studies scholars to detail.[18] Mark Mazower, for instance, acknowledges in *Governing the World: The History of an Idea*, that "South Americans such as ... Carlos Calvo and Alejandro Alvarez were important pioneers of the new international law, and Pan-Americanism itself emerged as an alternative to the ossified hierarchies and rivalrous alliances of Europe"—but despite this assertion, these experiences remain peripheral to the story he tells.[19] To argue for the noninclusiveness and European focus of the League of Nations, for example, Mazower notes that of the forty-seven countries in attendance at the first League Assembly meeting, only four were from Asia and none from the Middle East.[20] He fails, however, to note that fully sixteen of the countries represented—more than one-third—were from Latin America, as compared with twenty-one from Europe.[21] Similarly, Glenda Sluga's concise but influential *Internationalism in the Age of Nationalism* examines many of the diverse contexts for twentieth-century internationalist activism, including Black internationalism, Gandhian anti-colonialism, and Japanese regional internationalism, but makes only fleeting reference to the long experience of multilateral cooperation, contestation, and institution-building in the Western Hemisphere.[22] In Sluga's account, the Universal Postal Union comes in for considerably more discussion than the Pan-American Union, which merits not a single mention, despite being a forum for intergovernmental negotiations that predated the league and presaged many of the great debates on multilateralism that would define the twentieth century. This marginalization of the Pan-American Union is, is fact, something of a conventional wisdom: the *Routledge History of International Organizations* describes the Universal Postal Union's work at length, but dismisses much of the international cooperation and contestation of the Pan-American Union as "specialized."[23] For many scholars—including, frequently, Latin Americanists ourselves—the long history of inter-American cooperation and contestation is insufficiently international, relegated to the "merely" regional.

Even some scholarship that is grounded in the analytical terrain of the Third World itself marginalizes, dismisses, or leaves out Latin America altogether. A recent special issue of the *International History Review* on Non-Alignment, for example, that sought to look "Beyond and Between the Cold War Blocs," featured not a single article on Latin America.[24] In another example, Roland Burke's recent article about the struggle for economic and social rights in the 1960s sets up two antagonists in the battle he describes: the Western democracies, on the one side, and Africa, Asia and Middle East—as the constitutive parts of the Third World—on the other.[25] The Latin Americans appear in this story only cursorily, when it is noted that "Latin American and communist states pressed the newer rights *with the greatest vigor*."[26] That this would be so makes sense, of course, given that economic and social rights have been at the core of Latin American liberalism since at least independence and were especially central to Latin American international interventions in the twentieth century, as Greg Grandin has argued.[27] But here, the Latin American contribution to the struggle for a more expansive social rights regime within the United Nations is left unexamined, marginal *even* to a story told from the perspective of the Third World. A final example comes in Erez Manela's groundbreaking *The Wilsonian Moment*, which traces "the international origins of anti-colonial nationalism" in a broad swath of the globe, looking at Egypt, India, Korea, and China. Left unexamined, however, are those places where Wilsonian ideals were actively belied in practice: the countries in Latin America and the Caribbean occupied by Marines sent by Wilson himself. In fact, the "universal moral authority" of Wilsonian self-determination was questioned not only by African Americans fighting racial subjugation in the United States, but also by Latin Americans grappling with continued U.S. military and economic intervention in their countries—something recognized by prominent African American thinkers of the time.[28]

So despite the fact that much of Latin America, Africa, Asia, and the Middle East shared the experiences of colonial rule, economic subordination, and the struggle for decolonization and self-determination, and despite the fact that actors from these varied regions would come together to form the fractious political project of the Third World, much of the new historiography of the global renders these regions of the world all but impossible to understand together, in relation to one another and to the Global North. Actors and ideas travel through Bandung and Belgrade, but only rarely Bogotá or Buenos Aires. There is too frequently in this literature, then, an apparent "decolonization divide," resulting in an inability to cross the chronological and historiographic barrier between the regions of the Global South.[29]

Perhaps this decolonization divide is the reason the new literature on the NIEO has similarly deemphasized the importance of Latin America, even while highlighting the interventions of actors from Africa, Asia, and the Middle East. The 2015 special issue of *Humanity* devoted to the New International Economic Order, and the publication of Vanessa Ogle's "States' Rights against Private Capital" a year earlier, brought a wealth of new scholarship on the NIEO, sparking new debate about the project and the era.[30] Essays in the issue highlight the intervention of actors from Tanzania and Algeria, the socialist bloc and the United States, as well as those from institutions such as OPEC, the World Bank, and British nongovernmental organizations (NGOs). Certainly, Latin American actors are far from absent in this work—Raúl Prebisch, Luis Echeverría, Hernán Santa Cruz, and Che Guevara all make appearances in the empirical details of the essays, as do other figures. Mexico City appears as the setting for a transnational struggle over women's rights and how they would be best achieved. And the work of Latin American delegations at the 1948 Havana Conference, in UNCTAD and the UN Economic Commission on Latin America (ECLA), and within the struggles over the NIEO at the UN General Assembly, is duly noted. One essay even observes, in a single sentence about the legal project of the NIEO, "This project had a long history, which extended back to disputes between the United States and Mexico regarding the rights of U.S. investors," but leaves those disputes largely unexplored.[31] In failing to uncover the specifically Latin American contributions to the NIEO moment, this new literature overemphasizes the novelty of the arguments being put forward and misses the conceptual roots of the NIEO in earlier moments of Latin American, and particularly Mexican, internationalism. As detailed below, for example, the notion that states had both *rights* and *duties* in the world economy had motivated Latin American internationalism since well before the existence of the United Nations.[32] The language of "interdependence" in the international economy was one that the Latin Americans used forcefully to argue for global economic change in the 1930s.[33] And the idea of "states' rights against private capital" was a core principle of the Mexican Constitution of 1917, one that motivated its outward projections in the decades that followed. These are the deeper roots of the NIEO, uncovered in the Mexican archives.

· · · · · ·

Of course, Mexican experts were far from alone in their advocacy for an international order that was more fair to what were variously called the "weaker," "poorer," or "debtor" countries of the world—by necessity, these campaigns were multilateral and coalitional.[34] The ideas that would come to be embodied in the Charter of Economic Rights and Duties of States in the early 1970s had circulated widely for years, forming the basis for debates across the Global South and even for what Johanna Bockman has called "socialist globalization."[35] And in addition to ongoing debates within UNCTAD and the Group of Seventy-Seven (G-77), Mexican experts drew on a long history of Latin American interventions in the realm of international law, taking inspiration from the Calvo and Drago doctrines, which sought to subject foreigners and their capital to local law, in advocating their own principles for foreign affairs, such as the Carranza and Estrada doctrines.[36] In moments of crisis in the world economic system of the twentieth century, then, Mexican diplomats, economists, and political figures consistently carried out their campaigns for the creation or reform of international regimes and institutions in close cooperation with representatives from other countries, both in Latin America and beyond.

There were, however, important ways in which Mexico occupied a unique position in the rapidly changing international order of the twentieth century: in its proximity to the United States, which resulted in a sustained history of economic, diplomatic, and intellectual engagement with the rising hegemon; in its status as an increasingly important oil producer, and one that had defied the United States and Great Britain in nationalizing its petroleum industry; and, perhaps most importantly, in the legacy of Mexico's fractious social revolution, from which subsequent governments all claimed to derive their legitimacy, providing a continuity across administrations of markedly different political orientations. Relying on these factors, Mexican authorities repeatedly asserted and affirmed a historical duty to lead the other poor, weak, and debtor states in the international arena. (And in fact, Mexico's self-styled leadership frequently resulted in the serious irritation of other states with whom they were to have been allied.) The ideas and institutions promoted by Mexico were not unique, then, but Mexico consistently played a crucial role in the struggle to turn such ideas into actions and institutions—indeed, into a new international economic order, even before it was given such a name.

While examining any single episode in the history of Mexican campaigns to realign the international order in which the country found itself might reveal only marginal or fleeting influence, taken together, they reveal a larger pattern. From the beginning, Mexico's campaigns turned on the struggle for economic sovereignty, the need for equitable representation in international institutions, and the rights of weaker and indebted countries in the global system. Recognizing that Mexico, and countries like it, lacked domestic capital and were therefore reliant on foreign investment and foreign markets, Mexico's postrevolutionary government began to chart a path toward a developmentalist future that focused not only on *national* development strategies in agriculture and industry, but also sought to rectify the *international* conditions in which such strategies were necessarily embedded. As Mexican officials sought to create a state-guided, developmental, mixed economy at home—always pushed and pulled by the social forces of labor, the peasantry, and the business classes, domestic and international—they also sought to scale up such a model. Their vision was an international economic architecture that, they argued, would distribute the gains of global capitalism more evenly and therefore prevent the recurrence of crises not only in the poor countries, but in the rich ones, as well.

These efforts began even before the military phase of the Mexican revolution truly ended—and just as the first global organizations of the twentieth century were being crafted. Beginning in 1919, the leader of the victorious Constitutionalist faction of the revolution, Venustiano Carranza, intervened in the debates about the creation of the League of Nations to argue for the juridical equality of states, large and small, and for their right to sovereignty over economic decision-making. Carranza had set forth an eponymous doctrine of international affairs that closely paralleled U.S. President Woodrow Wilson's vision for the world, but derived its force from Mexico's revolutionary redefinition of property rights.[37] The 1917 constitution had declared that "private property is a privilege created by the Nation" and argued that this privilege would be constrained by the "public interest" and managed by the state "to ensure a more equitable distribution of public wealth."[38] This conception of property rights underpinned Mexico's international political program, and Mexican experts argued that their vision was not a *rejection* of Wilsonian liberalism, but rather an *extension* of its principles into the realms of collective economic and social rights. It also, of course, represented a claim to the substantial subsoil resources represented in Mexico's oil fields, over which Mexico would clash with richer countries for decades.[39] Carranza's program included an end to secret diplomacy; absolute nonintervention in the internal affairs of other nations; the formal equality of foreign and national individuals—and corporations—before the law; and complete equality among nations and mutual respect for their sovereignty.[40]

Despite the basic underlying congruence of some of their ideas, however, Carranza's doctrine would clash forcefully with Wilson's plans for the League of Nations.[41] After a roaring debate within the United States, Republican critics of the League—anxious that the new organization might foreclose any future U.S. intervention to recover losses in Mexico—convinced

Wilson that the only way to guarantee ratification of the League Covenant in the Senate was to include an explicit recognition of the Monroe Doctrine within the document.[42] When Wilson announced his amendment to the covenant, Carranza's reaction was swift. In a bombshell interview published in the United States, Carranza declared that Mexico did not recognize the validity of the Monroe Doctrine and argued that, if all sovereign nations were juridically equal, there was no need for Wilson's amendment: "There is no Monroe Doctrine for strong nations and there would be no necessity for such doctrine for [the] benefit of weak ones if [the] principle of equality is adhered to," he told a U.S. journalist. The League as negotiated did not establish "a perfect equality for all nations and races," he argued, and he went on: "The Mexican government has proclaimed as fundamental principles of its international policy, that all the states of the globe should have the same rights and the same obligations."[43] After Carranza's declaration, it was clear to Wilson's critics in Congress that the covenant's protection of the Monroe Doctrine was an insufficient guarantee of U.S. privilege. If the negotiations over the League represented the first time that the United States had attempted to reconcile unilateral prerogative with multilateral legitimacy, Carranza's critique laid bare the contradictions from the very beginning.

Carranza soon dispatched representatives throughout the hemisphere as part of a concerted effort to bring other Latin American countries on board with his vision. Over the next few years, even after the deaths of both Wilson and Carranza, Mexican diplomats would continue their quest to enshrine the principle of equality of nations in multilateral institutions. In the context of ongoing negotiations with international creditors and diplomatic pressure from the great powers, Mexican representatives used a reform effort at the fifth Inter-American Conference, at Santiago, Chile, in 1923, to codify their ideas about absolute sovereignty and the juridical equality of states into the statutes of the one interstate organization to which the United States and Mexico both belonged: the Pan-American Union. If the Union had to that point functioned as what many Latin Americans saw as "the colonial division of the Department of State," such an impression was underscored by two rules in Union governance: its presidency was reserved for the U.S. secretary of state, and its governing board was made up only of the diplomats formally recognized by Washington, residing in the U.S. capitol.[44] Because the Mexican government, now under president Álvaro Obregón, had not been formally recognized by the Harding administration (which hoped to force Mexico to recognize the property rights of U.S. oil companies), Mexico had been excluded from the governing board's planning of the Santiago conference—and therefore didn't send official delegates to the meeting.

During the conference, however the Mexican chargé d'affaires in Santiago, Carlos Trejo y Lerdo de Tejada—whom, despite not being a formal delegate, the Chilean president called the "most important person at the conference"—organized a group of delegates, including the representatives of Cuba, Costa Rica, and Venezuela, among others, into what he called the *bando latinoamericano*.[45] The group introduced a series of proposals to radically reorganize the Union's governance structure: the United States should no longer have the exclusive right to control which countries had representation on the governing board, they argued, and, what's more, the presidency and vice-presidency should be rotating, not automatically vested in the U.S. secretary of state.[46] After a protracted debate on the reform proposals, the U.S. representative, Henry Fletcher, was forced by Latin American insistence to largely accept the position taken by the *bando latinoamericano*.[47] In the end, the new governance rules adopted at Santiago included the right of representation for all members at all international conferences, the ability to appoint a special representative to the governing board in the case of nonrecognition in Washington, and the right of the members of that board to elect their president and vice-president. In asserting the formal equality of sovereign nations within international institutions and insisting on their rights to participate in decision-making structures, Mexico had established a principle it would continue to pursue all the way up through the NIEO.

If debt had been an underlying issue structuring Mexico's international relations in the 1920s—a decade when bankers' and bondholders' groups deployed massive international pressure to try to recoup defaulted loans from the Mexican government—it would become a global issue after the dislocations of the Great Depression. At the 1933 World Economic Conference in London, Mexico's Alberto J. Pani joined those arguing for the necessity of international economic coordination to overcome the financial crisis. But after Roosevelt thwarted any possibility of cooperation in London, Mexican economists and diplomats looked to the upcoming Inter-American Conference in Montevideo, Uruguay, to lay out their plans for new vision of the world economy. Having witnessed Pani's surprisingly forceful interventions in London, a British Foreign Office staffer reported to his superiors that it was likely that the Montevideo conference was to bring a contest "between Argentina and Mexico for the theoretical leadership of Latin America." In such a contest, he continued, "Argentina has the resources, Mexico the theories."[48]

At Montevideo, Mexico put forward its theories forcefully, once again assuming a self-appointed leadership role (much to the chagrin of the Argentine delegation, which fought Mexico's proposals). Mexico's foreign minister, José Manuel Puig Casauranc, issued a series of proposals for a wholesale reform of the system of international debt and credit and rallied support from other Latin American countries with a rousing speech in which he called for "a new legal and philosophic conception of credit" based on a recognition of international finance not as a technical economic science, but as a reciprocal, international social relation.[49] Just as borrowers needed creditors to lend to them, Puig argued, the lenders needed borrowers to make productive use of their surplus capital. Despite this interdependent relationship, however, the poorer countries were robbed of their sovereignty over economic decision-making—meaning, Puig argued, that the credit form itself had become an ordering principle for international politics. He proposed a series of interventions to rectify this order, including an explicit recognition of the Drago doctrine, a debt moratorium, a bi-metalist international monetary system, and the creation of an international bank that would oversee currency stabilization and channel capital to productive investments in Latin America. The implications of his new conception of credit, Puig argued, were global: his plans should help in establishing "a procedure that we wish to be continental, that may perhaps come to have some effect of a *universal* order."[50] Such an order would be devised four decades later, of course, in the Carta Echeverría.

As the conference came to a close, U.S. Secretary of State Cordell Hull managed to postpone any binding discussion of Puig's proposals by putting them off for a subsequent financial conference that never occurred. But the ideas that underwrote them would resurface quickly in a campaign to create an the Inter-American Bank (IAB), which was, as one scholar put it, "the first international organization to be formally negotiated whose central mandate included the promotion of international development"—a mandate that came not from the United States or Europe, but from Latin America.[51] The creation of the IAB was, then, a key moment in making concrete the vision Puig had laid out in Montevideo. Mexican treasury official Eduardo Villaseñor detailed the specifics for the bank at a meeting of finance ministers in Guatemala in 1939: the IAB, he said, would be an international agency that would prevent the financial predations of private bankers, stabilize foreign exchange systems, and, crucially, "act as a channel for the investment of capital which will promote sound economic development in the American Republics." Once again, the protection of economic sovereignty for the poor nations was key; Villaseñor argued that the bank would have to "avoid in all cases the aspect of hegemony or privilege that [foreign] investment could represent in the internal economy" of the debtor countries.[52]

By the late 1930s, and particularly after key nationalizations of oil in Mexico and Bolivia, Latin American insistence had convinced U.S. officials that they would need to play an active role in the development of the proposed bank, in order to ensure U.S. interests were protected.[53] Treasury official Harry Dexter White, who had been arguing for increased U.S. aid to both China and Latin America, promoted the IAB to Treasury Secretary Henry Morgenthau by insisting not only that such a multilateral institution would reduce the risk of default, but also that with such a bank, "the charge of dollar diplomacy would be absent."[54] The United States was learning from the criticisms that had been leveled against it—and it would seek to take those lessons beyond the hemisphere. As he looked to the postwar order, for instance, Assistant Secretary of State Adolf Berle thought the IAB might serve as a "laboratory study" for the kind of international economic planning would be necessary after WWII ended.[55] Under the direction of White, Treasury officials worked with Latin American experts and with representatives from the State Department and the Federal Reserve to draw up a charter and bylaws for the bank. The proposed bylaws took up nearly all of the original proposals of the Mexican planners, establishing a bank whose purpose was to "facilitate the prudent investment of funds and stimulate the full productive use of capital and credit," as well as to stabilize currencies; increase trade in the Western Hemisphere; facilitate research, data collection, and technical advising; and promote "the development of industry, public utilities, mining, agriculture, commerce and finance" in the Americas.[56] Finally, Puig's vision for "a new legal and philosophic conception of credit" was on the verge of being operationalized.[57]

The Inter-American Bank, however, faced severe opposition from private banking interests in the United States, and congressional representatives friendly to Wall Street managed to delay ratification of the bank's charter long enough to prevent the institution from coming into being in the early 1940s (though Mexican officials would continue to argue for its creation until 1948). In the United States, attention turned to the creation of the new, global financial institutions that would govern the world economy after the war. As Eric Helleiner has argued, Harry Dexter White would take with him all of the lessons learned in the IAB negotiations—as well as negotiations with Mexico and other countries under the rubric of the Treasury Department's Exchange Stabilization Fund—as he set out to create those new institutions: the World Bank and the International Monetary Fund (IMF).[58] In those negotiations, Mexican representatives continued to argue for the rights of small states—and the duties of rich ones—within the international financial system and the organizations that governed it. As the Mexican delegation prepared for the Bretton Woods conference, a headline in Mexico City summed up their plans: "Mexico Will Seek Voice and Vote for the Weaker Nations at the Monetary Meeting."[59]

For Harry Dexter White, the proximity to and long experience with Mexican experts such as Antonio Espinosa de los Monteros, who had been at Harvard with White and had negotiated many bilateral agreements on behalf of Mexico, was crucial.[60] Of course, White recognized the need for buy-in from the Latin Americans to sell his plans on a world stage, but he also drew from his experiences in the IAB and Exchange Stabilization Fund negotiations in developing his understanding of the problems of global finance. Over the course of the years preceding the Bretton Woods conference, Espinosa and his colleagues had repeatedly emphasized to White the need for a mechanism that would provide long-term capital to the developing countries, not simply short-term commercial credits for small-scale investment projects. In interagency planning for Bretton Woods, White explicitly referenced Espinosa's demands and detailed how the proposed institutions would provide such capital.[61] White's insistence on Latin American participation in the planning and execution of the conference scandalized many in Great Britain, including John Maynard Keynes, whose assessment of the conference as "the most monstrous monkey-house assembled for years" is a well-known dismissal of the presence of so many representatives from Latin America.[62] Less well-known, but more direct, was the assessment of another British Treasury official, who wrote to a colleague, "It is also silly to make the pretense that the Mexicans (even though their representative in July was, I understand, a graduate of the London School of Economics) and the Brazilians would discuss 'at the expert level' a document which the American Treasury was endorsing," in the way that Dutch and Belgian experts might. He concluded dismissively, "Their function is to sign in the place for the signature."[63]

Mexican officials had made clear to White, however, "that small countries have interests and responsibilities no less than the large countries," and that if the institutions they were building were to be, indeed, multilateral, they must not benefit only a few countries at the expense of the majority.[64]

Espinosa de los Monteros would explicitly argue at the conference against rules for the IMF and the World Bank that would allow the rich countries to force "smaller countries [to] change their laws and perhaps even their constitutions"—an unacceptable violation of sovereignty.[65] It was, therefore, on these questions of economic sovereignty that Mexico's interventions at the conference turned. During the conference, Mexico joined with other countries to advocate for a series of measures: recognizing the responsibility of creditor nations, as well as debtors, for resolving financial disequilibria; protecting sovereignty over currency valuation decisions; guaranteeing adequate voting power for the developing countries, so that the United States could not unilaterally make policy without the smaller states; obtaining adequate representation for Latin Americans among the IMF executive directors; and ensuring that the World Bank would not focus exclusively on European reconstruction, but would include the development of the poorer nations.[66] And in the end, the Mexican vision for an institution that would provide long-term development financing was fully integrated into the design of the bank and was one of the institution's most innovative features.[67] But while Mexico and its allies were able successfully negotiate provisions for each of these features into the chartering documents for the new institutions, it remained to be seen if the World Bank and the IMF would actually function to the benefit of the developing countries.

Even Mexican experts who had participated in the negotiations and were therefore seen as supporters of the new institutions quickly made their concerns clear. In 1945, economist Víctor Urquidi, who had been a central figure on the Mexican delegation, published an analysis of the new institutions in which he noted that as they were constituted, they "didn't attack the root of the problem of investments for world economic development."[68] And so Mexican advocacy for a more just international economic system continued. Near the end of the Bretton Woods conference, the final meeting of the Third Commission (which was chaired by Mexican Finance Minister Eduardo Suárez) had considered two important topics: the creation of an "international agreement on maintaining high employment" and consideration of "trade and its relation to other financial policies."[69] While these issues were not addressed in depth at Bretton Woods, they would be taken up just a few years later, at the 1948 UN Conference on Trade and Employment in Havana. There, Mexico's foreign minister, Ramón Beteta, worked diligently with representatives from countries such as Cuba and Australia to include provisions on commodity prices and labor protections in the charter of a proposed International Trade Organization (ITO).[70] After four contentious months of negotiations, a charter was drawn up for the ITO that included some, but not all, of Mexico's proposals. But as in the case of the Inter-American Bank, the U.S. Congress never ratified the ITO charter, and the organization came to be substituted by the General Agreement on Tariffs and Trade (GATT), a supposedly temporary agreement between the advanced countries of the world that lasted almost half a century. While many Latin American countries joined GATT, Mexico refused and did not become a party to the agreement until the mid-1980s.

The failure to create an ITO reflected the sea change in geopolitics that occurred between 1944 and 1948, as new U.S. Cold War priorities shifted international concerns away from full employment and anything resembling international economic redistribution. Mexican officials sought to adapt to this new reality, and the path to import-substituting industrialization (ISI), meant to lessen the country's dependence on foreign goods, became clear. But the pursuit of what was called "stabilizing development" was not a total retreat from the attempt to change the international systems within which Mexico and the other developing countries pursued their national strategies.[71] Parallel to the negotiations at Bretton Woods, Mexico had argued at Dumbarton Oaks, Chapultepec, and San Francisco for the rights of what were called the "small countries" within the new United Nations organization and proposed language for a Declaration of the Rights and Duties of Nations, which was deemed a "substantial contribution toward the progressive development of international law" by the General Assembly in 1949.[72] That proposal both crystalized much of the previous three decades of activism and prefigured the Carta Echeverría in crucial ways, including arguing for all countries' "right to develop materially and spiritually" and promoting the principle of nonintervention, about which the Mexicans noted that their intentions were in a draft "expressly referring to political and economic intervention."[73]

As UN agencies and bodies proliferated, Mexican officials continued to argue for these principles in the various reform efforts that shaped the practices and policies of the organization throughout the 1950s. In the aftermath of the Bandung conference in the fall of 1955, Jorge Castañeda, who would go on to be Mexico's ambassador to the UN, wrote, "Lately, our governments have come to realize that the independence of colonial peoples is already an important economic problem which will become more acute in the future."[74] The question of the role of Latin America in what had not yet consolidated into the Third World was, then, already on the table. So even as the Mexican government ramped up ISI, Mexican economists and diplomats participated actively in negotiations in the 1950s on Latin American economic integration and continued to argue for changes to the international financial system. Mexican economic experts were crucial in the creation of institutions such as the long delayed Inter-American Development Bank, which was finally chartered in the late 1950s after Brazil's Juscelino Kubitschek and Argentina's Arturo Frondizi took up the cause, and the Latin American Free Trade Association, which was chartered in 1960 to foster complementarity and reciprocity (and not simply open markets) in Latin American trade.[75]

In the 1960s, as the shape of the postcolonial world became clearer and the first "development decade" got underway, Mexican officials would more forcefully begin to ally themselves with the Third World. Presidents Adolfo López Mateos (1958–64) and Luis Echeverría (1970–76) would undertake well-known diplomatic campaigns to this end, with what Vanni Pettinà has called the "urge to hasten the creation of a fairer international context for Third World countries' development aspirations."[76] But below the level of presidential diplomacy—and even during the interregnum of the decidedly more conservative Gustavo Díaz Ordaz (1964–70)—Mexican state officials continued their campaign to promote not just the rights of the developing countries, but the responsibilities of the rich countries, as well. Through institutions such as ECLA and UNCTAD, as well as within the World Bank and the IMF, economists such as Víctor Urquidi spent the 1960s waging a campaign with other representatives from around the world who argued for reform of the international monetary system.[77] Urquidi and his colleagues continuously warned—as he had in 1945—that not only did the international financial institutions still not provide the resources for development that the Third World needed, but also that they lacked the capacity to force the rich countries to confront the disequilibria their policies introduced. Such fears proved justified when the United States undertook unilateral action in August 1971, suspending gold convertibility, levying a 10 percent surcharge on imports, and devaluing the dollar, thereby reducing the purchasing power of Third World reserves. Mexico, which sent nearly two-thirds of its exports to the United States, worried that it would be particularly hard hit by the new U.S. policy.[78] In response to this new moment of crisis, therefore, Mexico's president would not only draw on the ongoing struggles over reform of the international monetary system, but would in fact summon the entire long history of Mexican advocacy for a fairer world economy in the quest to create a new international economic order.

● ● ● ● ● ●

The long history outlined above was the deeper context for the plans that Echeverría would promote for a Charter of Economic Rights and Duties of States. That it was Luis Echeverría who led the charge for a kind of global economic justice has always been seen as something of a contradiction, as the other policy for which he is best known was the violent repression of student and guerrilla movements at home. How could he champion the cause of the Third World—lending support to leaders like Allende and Castro, flirting with the Non-Aligned Movement, establishing diplomatic relations with the Peoples' Republic of China—all while waging a dirty war against those fighting for justice within his own country?[79] In fact, the struggle over the Charter of Economic Rights and Duties of States reveals the basic coherence of his domestic and foreign policies. Throughout the campaign for what would become the charter, Echeverría used the threat of leftist insurgency, both within Mexico and throughout the Third World, to argue that his agenda represented a kind of responsible, reformist middle ground in a revolutionary world. Drawing on an exceptionalist narrative about the legacy of Mexico's non-Communist social revolution, Echeverría tried to head off rebellious discontent through economic and social reforms that would make revolution less attractive, both at home and abroad. Where such reform was not enough, repression of student and guerrilla movements and cooperation with CIA surveillance of Cubans would prove, to the United States above all, that Mexico was crucial international interlocutor.[80] As had been the case throughout the long history of Mexican developmentalism and internationalist advocacy surveyed above, Echeverría's reforms—democratic opening of and increased state intervention in the economy at home and a new global economic framework abroad—were intended to save capitalism from succumbing to its contradictions.

Echeverría debuted his ideas about the world economy at the 1971 UN General Assembly, convened just weeks after the United States closed the gold window. The Mexican president began his speech to the assembly by reaffirming the similarities between Mexico's own struggle against colonialism and the struggles of the recently decolonized world, putting Mexico in the ranks of the "majority of the world," up against the powerful nations, whose own economic progress had "caused an unbalanced stratification of the world community."[81] He argued that the experiences of Latin America, and of Mexico in particular, had demonstrated that the achievement of formal independence and political sovereignty was insufficient for the achievement of justice, and he expressed the hope that "after the era of political decolonization through which we have lived, there comes another, of economic decolonization." To achieve this, he called for a "basic reorganization of economic relations among nations."

Back in Mexico City, Echeverría aide Porfirio Muñoz Ledo assembled a small team of experts to design such a reorganization, and their vision was debuted just a few months later at the third UNCTAD conference in Santiago, Chile.[82] Decrying the failure of the industrialized world to meet the aid goals set out by the first "development decade" and noting the success that the Marshall Plan had brought to Europe, Echeverría told the gathered delegates that "there now needs to be a second process of the massive transfer of resources, directed this time to the periphery, that will correct many of the current economic distortions and open the path to shared prosperity for all nations."[83] Achieving this prosperity, he declared, would require a Charter of Economic Rights and Duties of States. He then outlined the basic tenets of such a charter in his speech:

> Freedom to dispose of natural resources; the right of every nation to adopt the economic structure it considered most suitable and to treat private property as the public interest required; renunciation of the use of economic pressures; subjection of foreign capital to domestic laws; prohibition of interference by supranational corporations in the internal affairs of States; abolition of trade practices that discriminated against the exports of non-industrial nations; economic advantages proportionate to levels of development; treaties guaranteeing stable and fair prices for basic products; transfer of technology; and greater economic resources for long-term untied aid.[84]

He concluded this list of principles with a warning: "The solidarity we demand," he said, "is a condition of survival." He argued that there could never be stability if the majority of the peoples of the world found themselves impoverished and discontented: "Our people," he noted, "are aware that their misery produces wealth for others."[85]

In response to Echeverría's proposal, the conference created an international working group charged with drawing up a draft of the charter.[86] The working group, initially made up of thirty-one countries and eventually expanded to forty, would include representatives from both industrialized and developing countries, both socialist and capitalist.[87] Echeverría's proposal now had a global mandate, and back in Mexico, the team that had initially proposed the idea began to draw up a first draft of the charter for the working group to consider.[88] The Mexican draft drew on ideas that had been circulating in Third World forums, including the 1962 Cairo Declaration of Developing Countries and the 1967 Charter of Algiers. But it placed more emphasis than those previous documents on the responsibilities of the rich countries for the ongoing economic crisis, even going to so far as to call for the "structural adjustment" of the developed countries' economies.[89]

In order to obtain such an adjustment, Muñoz Ledo reasoned, echoing Mexico's interventions at the UN in 1949, it would be necessary that "international law and its codification should be progressively developed."[90] That is, the Charter of Economic Rights and Duties of States should move international law *forward* from its presently accepted norms. This was supported by figures such as the renowned Chilean jurist Hernán Santa Cruz, who considered the Mexican proposal an extension of the principles codified in the Universal Declaration of Human Rights into the economic sphere.[91] At the first working-group meeting, in Geneva in February of 1973, Mexico's Sergio González Gálvez stressed the need for the working group to consider "not only norms of *lex lata* [current law], but also of *lex ferenda* [future law]," as well. For the Mexican representatives, the fight was for the creation of international law that governed the world as it should be, not simply as it was.[92]

The positions taken by the industrialized countries, however, consistently sought to confine the charter's draft within their own understandings of the existing principles of law, particularly with regard to the rights of the developing countries to regulate foreign investment.[93] The U.S. and International Chambers of Commerce and the American Bar Association lobbied strongly against any version of the charter that did not carve out adequate protections for international law, and they held sway with important members of the developed country delegations.[94] Given this fundamental disagreement, the first working-group meeting managed during the two weeks of negotiations to produce only a draft outline that contained numerous alternative suggestions included for each article. The meeting was judged by its chair, Mexico's Jorge Castañeda, to have been "extraordinarily difficult and turbulent."[95] The second working-group meeting in June of 1973 advanced the draft somewhat, but it still included a long series of seemingly irreconcilable proposals. The group sought an extension of its mandate from the Trade and Development Board at UNCTAD and agreed to hold two additional negotiating sessions, one in Geneva in February of 1974 and then in Mexico City in June.[96]

Throughout the negotiations, Echeverría undertook a worldwide campaign to promote the charter personally. On his first trip, he tried to woo skeptical officials in London, Brussels, and Paris before making his way to Moscow, where Leonid Brezhnev offered enthusiastic backing for the charter—particularly for the draft's emphasis on nondiscrimination against countries with different socioeconomic systems.[97] From Moscow, Echeverría traveled to China, where the government of Zhou Enlai agreed to undertake the "maximum efforts" for the formulation of the charter.[98] He would later make another trip to Europe, stopping in Salzburg, Munich, Bonn, Rome, and Vienna, as well as in Belgrade, where he met personally with Josip Tito, who offered his "full support" for the charter.[99] In addition, he toured South America, meeting with the presidents of Ecuador, Argentina, Peru, Brazil, and Venezuela, with whom he discussed the idea of creating primary producers' cartels for Latin American exports.[100] He also met multiple times with U.S. officials, including Nixon and Kissinger, to whom he made explicit his strategy of positioning Mexico as the responsible reformist in a world threatened by revolution. After reminding Nixon of his own effectiveness at quashing internal rebellion within Mexico—something U.S. embassy staff noted he did at every meeting—Echeverría put it bluntly: "If I don't take this flag in Latin America," he told Nixon, "Castro will."[101] By playing up the destabilizing threat represented by those to his left, he was positioning Mexico's plans—modeled on what he called "capitalist solutions of a mixed type"—as the responsible way to head off social conflict and therefore attempting to make the economic vision represented by the charter indispensable to a skeptical United States.[102]

In addition to push-back from the industrialized world, Mexico's attempts to position themselves as the responsible middle ground revealed serious division among the developing countries themselves. At a meeting of the foreign ministers of the Non-Aligned Countries in Georgetown, Guyana, just after the Santiago UNCTAD conference, Algeria's Abdelaziz Bouteflika had laid out one important axis of disagreement, arguing pointedly that "the road of Third World economic emancipation does not run through UNCTAD."[103] And even within Latin America, the more radical governments of Peru, Chile, and Cuba had used ongoing negotiations about reforming the international monetary system to argue that the reform of existing institutions such as the IMF would be insufficient—instead, they declared, the Third World needed new global financial structures altogether.[104] Mexico faced skepticism, then, from those in the Third World who sought a more revolutionary path forward. Nevertheless, in 1973, when the Algerian government called for a special session of the UN General Assembly to address not just the spiraling energy crisis but "raw materials and development" more broadly, the Mexican government enthusiastically supported the effort.[105]

Mexican officials broadly understood the special session's agenda on development as complimentary to, if not derivative of, the effort to create a Charter of Economic Rights and Duties of States, and they thought that the session's final declaration would be an important means of advancing the charter. In fact, the background paper laying the groundwork for the special session was prepared in the February 1974 charter working-group meeting in Geneva, which meant that the issues to be discussed closely mirrored the language of the draft charter as it was being negotiated.[106] During the session, the Mexican representative served on a six-member ad hoc committee that worked to bring the G-77 countries into agreement. In addition, Mexican delegates worked hard to drum up support for the charter; the Foreign Ministry noted that at least twenty-three countries had publicly voiced support for it in the general debate. A memo for Echeverría from the Foreign Relations Ministry after the special session noted that the NIEO declaration represented an "important advance and a convergence of positions" between the various countries, which it was hoped would facilitate the task of the final working-group session in Mexico City only a few weeks later.[107] The draft worked out by the ad hoc committee of the G-77 was remitted to the plenary session as unanimous, though in plenary the United States, members of the European Community, and Japan all registered reservations to the text, with the United States and the United Kingdom making special mention of international law.[108] Nevertheless, the resolution was adopted by the General Assembly without a vote and therefore carried the imprimatur of unanimity.

Despite initially supporting the effort, Mexico's Foreign Minister Emilio Rabasa soon came to realize that the NIEO declaration may have had the effect of making the passage of the charter itself more difficult. In response to the increasing militancy of the Third World, particularly once the OPEC oil embargo was underway, U.S. Secretary of State Henry Kissinger had devised what he called a "New Dialogue" with Latin America, hoping to peel off regional allies from the Third World coalition. Such a move reinforced the position of Mexico as a mediator between the industrialized countries and Third World radicals, and Mexican officials attempted to take advantage of this space. In addition to the ongoing official working-group negotiations and Echeverría's own ceaseless worldwide advocacy of the charter, Mexican officials had been undertaking sidebar negotiations with two legal advisors to the U.S. State Department, Carlyle Maw and Stephen Schwebel. By the end of the third working-group meeting, Rabasa noted that the Mexican and U.S. teams had "agreed upon a formula" regarding language around nationalization and multinational corporations, which would be the basis on which they would enter into negotiations in the fourth and final session.[109] Indeed, in the final working-group session, the Mexican and U.S. teams worked to introduce compromise language about the issue of international law, secretly ghostwriting an alternative to the charter's controversial Article 2—on permanent sovereignty over natural resources, nationalization, and the regulation of multinational corporations—which was then introduced by the Philippine representative as his own.[110] The NIEO declaration as passed in the special session, however, went beyond this compromise language. When Rabasa met with Kissinger in Washington in August of 1974 (just after Nixon had resigned), Rabasa argued that by not abstaining from or voting against the NIEO resolution, the United States had emboldened what he called the "unaligned" countries and that it would therefore need to compromise further. But Kissinger stuck to the compromise they had already reached. At a later meeting, he argued, "We want a charter consistent with the Maw-Rabasa agreement but we cannot go beyond that. We do not want to elaborate principles of international law to be used against us."[111]

Despite his refusal to compromise further, however, Kissinger had come to see support for the charter as an important means of keeping Mexico in the U.S. orbit. He was frustrated that others in the U.S. government could not see the geopolitical logic at stake: he accused Maw and Schwebel of legalistic nitpicking and told those who championed the business interests aligned against the charter, such as Republican Senator Charles Percy of Illinois (himself the former head of Bell and Howell Corporation), that U.S. businessmen were "morons" who could not see that the charter, as conceived, would actually have little impact on them in practice.[112] President Ford, for his part, seemed to get Kissinger's strategy: meeting at the U.S.-Mexico border in October of 1974, Ford surprised the assembled reporters, as well as the Mexican president, by saying that the charter "had very great merit and support." Echeverría seized on Ford's remarks, telling reporters, "actually this is a complete change from what it was before, and this is very valuable support."[113] While the U.S. delegation to the UN released a statement a few days later indicating that there had not, in fact, been a change in its position, Echeverría's remarks were enough to stir up great controversy in the United States, not least among the business class. The National Foreign Trade Council, representing some six hundred U.S.-based multinational firms, released a statement saying that the charter "would seriously deter if not fully shackle foreign private investment."[114] The chorus of business-class opposition was growing louder.

In late November, the final deliberations got underway at the General Assembly in New York. It was clear that, given the compromise reached with the U.S. representatives, Mexico's original efforts at the creation of *lex ferenda*, codifying the international law for the world as they wished to see it, would remain an unfinished project at the General Assembly. But Mexican representatives had come up with a justification for the success of the charter, despite this failure: Mexico's Jorge Castañeda argued that the charter had, "in a certain sense, the character of a constitution, that should only set forth basic principles."[115] So, Castañeda argued, just as the Mexican constitution of 1917 had required enabling legislation to nationalize petroleum or effect land reform, so would the charter require, over the coming years, just that sort of international codification. Once again, Mexico mobilized its own historical legacy as a guide for its global vision.

The last few days of furious negotiation turned on how the industrialized countries would vote: the Europeans had made clear that they hoped to abstain, rather than voting against the charter, shielding themselves without having to go too far. Kissinger wanted the United States to abstain, as well, but others on the U.S. delegation—especially Deputy Secretary of State Robert Ingersoll, Senator Percy, and UN Ambassador John Scali—continued to argue on behalf of the business class that explicit protection for international law was necessary to preclude a no vote. After France introduced a resolution to postpone the vote, the G-77 countries introduced further compromises, deciding for instance to drop a reference to the "codification and progressive development" of international economic law.[116] They hoped this and other changes would be sufficient to bring the developed country skeptics around, but to no avail. In the final vote, Japan and a number of the European countries abstained, while Belgium, Denmark, Luxembourg, West Germany, the United Kingdom, and the United States voted no.

After the vote, Kissinger was exasperated. Excoriating Percy and Scali, he told an incredulous Rabasa, "Assuming you're not going to quote me, I think our people behaved very badly."[117] Kissinger later worried to his staff that "Echeverría, who was always basically a third-worlder, is going to be unloosed"—and therefore that rather than an ally who sought to temper the most radical demands emanating from Latin America and the Third World, Mexico might instead lend its weight increasingly to efforts against U.S. interests.[118] Indeed, it now seemed that Mexico had a broad set of allies: from Afghanistan to Zambia, 120 countries voted in favor of the charter, and it therefore passed overwhelmingly. Rabasa noted in his remarks after the vote that those voting yes "represented 3.2 billion people, on five continents."[119] The Mexican representatives could now claim that the majority of the world had spoken, and it had done so with Mexico's voice.

・・・・・・

Of course, by ensuring that the compromise language worked into the charter would have no binding legal power, the industrialized countries insulated themselves from the demands of what they saw as a surprisingly unified Third World. As a result, the NIEO and the charter are largely remembered as failures. The period that followed saw the birth of an entirely different new international economic order, presaged by Reagan's visit to Cancún, based in the neoliberal tenets that came to be codified in the Washington Consensus. Mexico itself would be emblematic of this change: when Mexico defaulted on its international debts in 1982 and subsequently turned to the IMF for assistance, the structural adjustment programs that followed marked the true end of the Mexican revolutionary process. But if, as Nils Gilman has recently argued, the NIEO should be thought of not as a failure, but as what Jennifer Wenzel has termed an "unfailure"—a failed project that can "live on as prophetic visions, available as an idiom for future generations to articulate their own hopes and dreams"[120]—then that idiom should be traced all the way back through the long history of Mexican interventions in the international arena, through the lineage that led to Echeverría's advocacy of the charter.

The Charter of Economic Rights and Duties of States echoed and realized fifty years of Mexican campaigning for an international order that would harness global capitalism to an agenda of social and economic justice. The document's fundamental insistence that "all states are juridically equal" was a reformulation of Carranza's assertions about the "principle of equality" in international relations a half-century earlier. The charter's argument that states had equal decision-making rights within international institutions directly paralleled the reforms of the Pan-American Union that Trejo y Lerdo orchestrated in 1923. Its insistence on economic sovereignty and its vision for a world economic system based in reciprocity drew directly from the arguments of Pani and Puig at the London and Montevideo conferences in the 1930s. Echeverria's invocation of an "identity of interests" in reform directly echoed the Mexican planners who had called for the creation of an Inter-American Bank and had written in 1931 that such a bank would create what they called a "solidarity of interests."[121] The charter's focus on the right to development drew from the insistence of Espinosa and Urquidi on the centrality of these issues at Bretton Woods. And its vision of the role of trade in development drew from the proposals Beteta had pursued in the negotiations over an international trade organization in 1948. Indeed, the entire struggle to codify international economic law was a direct echo of an argument Beteta had made in 1940, defending this agenda: "As Mexico questioned the sacredness of a profit-making system based on an absolute right of private property, in her Agrarian Reform and in her Labor Laws—to mention but two of her fundamental reforms—she could not accept without reserve the so-called 'principles of international law' which often were but means to protect that very system and absolute right which foreigners might not have at home, but which they expected to enjoy in the small countries where they had made their investments, as much as in the colonies belonging to their powerful fatherlands."[122] This refusal to accept the principles of international law was, as demonstrated above, not just rhetorical: it was made manifest in repeated campaigns to reform those laws and institutions that governed the international economy during the twentieth century.

This legacy, however, is one that has been all but ignored in the recent scholarship, even as the NIEO has been subject to renewed study. Because the NIEO resolution was passed first and because it did not receive any negative votes, we remember the charter as largely derivative of the NIEO effort, when in fact the historical record shows the reverse was true. Overlooking this chronology, as well as prior moments of Latin American struggle, as influences on the emergence of the NIEO causes us to misidentify what precisely is novel in that 1970s moment and therefore to misapprehend both where the struggle came from and how it was understood by the United States as a world economic power in a moment of crisis. The argument made by Vanessa Ogle, for example, for the centrality of the "role and function of trade, private capital, and foreign direct investment" in our understandings of the history of development is indispensable.[123] But by insisting that "states rights vs. private capital" and that "permanent sovereignty over natural resources" were novel political concepts of the 1960s, her analysis overlooks Latin America's long fight against economic imperialism, which took U.S. and European capital as its target. Moreover, it also overlooks the centrality of the Mexican Revolution's radical redefinition of property rights—and its long struggles over control of its petroleum industry—as its most important manifestation.[124] Mexican and other Latin American economists and diplomats had identified the problems of the organization of international finance as early as the 1920s and 1930s, and in proposing the reforms outlined above, they attempted to preclude many of the inequities that would motivate the call for a new international economic order.

Uncovering this history helps us to see international projects such as the NIEO not as novel products of postwar decolonization, but as culminations of projects of modernization from below, originating in the decades before World War II. Rather than locating the emergence of demands for "development-related rights" and the "corresponding obligations of developed countries and the international community as a whole" in the early 1970s, the story outlined above reveals the origins of the project of international development as emanating from Latin America and in postrevolutionary Mexico in particular.[125] This perspective centers the importance of *economic* sovereignty as a necessary counterpart to *territorial* sovereignty—indeed, as a major constitutive part of self-determination. Nationalist leaders of newly decolonized countries in Africa and Asia would come to stress the importance of economic sovereignty in the 1960s and 1970s, but it had been a central impetus for Latin American nationalism and internationalism in a much earlier period.[126] As we now know, the postrevolutionary Mexican state's internationalist project was animated by many of the same aspirations (and, it should be said, suffered many of the same contradictions) that would emerge later in other regions of the world in the process of decolonization. Centering economic sovereignty and self-determination, rather than political decolonization, in the history of the twentieth century might provide a new and more accurate periodization of the emergence of the project of not just the New International Economic Order, but of the Third World itself.

Notes

The author would like to thank Samuel Moyn and Nils Gilman for their helpful feedback, as well as the anonymous reviewers at *Humanity*, where this piece originally appeared in 2018. In addition, comments by the participants of the Weatherhead Initiative on Global History seminar at Harvard University, especially Arne Westad, Angélica Márquez-Osuna, Sven Beckert, and Quinn Slobodian, as well as additional feedback from Thomas Field, Vanni Pettinà, Stuart Schrader, Erez Manela, Giuliano Garavini, and Vijay Prashad, were invaluable. Research for this piece was supported by a Lewis Hanke Postdoctoral Award from the Conference on Latin American History (CLAH).

1. María Luisa González Marín, "México ante el diálogo Norte-Sur," *Foro Internacional* 24, no. 3(95) (1984): 327–40.

2. Walter Goldstein, "Redistributing the World's Wealth: Cancun 'Summit' Discord," *Resources Policy* 8, no. 1 (March 1982): 40.

3. Howell Raines, "Reagan Meets with Chinese and Mexican Leaders," *New York Times*, 22 October 1981; Ronald Reagan, "Remarks to Reporters upon Departure for the International Meeting on Cooperation and Development in Cancun, Mexico," 21 October 1981, *The Public Papers of the President: Ronald Reagan, 1981–1989*, Ronald Reagan Presidential Library.

4. José López Portillo, "Las Naciones Unidas en la encrucijada," *Comercio Exterior* 32, no. 11 (1982): 1244.

5. Nils Gilman, "The New International Economic Order: A Reintroduction," *Humanity: An International Journal of Human Rights, Humanitarianism, and Development* 6, no. 1 (2015): 3; Antony Anghie, "Legal Aspects of the New International Economic Order," *Humanity* 6, no. 1 (2015): 150.

6. See César Sepulveda, "El sentido y el alcance de la Carta de Derechos y Deberes Económicos de los Estados," in *Estudios en Honor del Doctor Luis Recaséns Siches*, ed. Fausto E. Rodríguez García (México DF: Universidad Nacional Autónoma de México, Facultad de Derecho, Instituto de Investigaciones Jurídicas, 1980), and John Toye and Richard Toye, *The UN and Global Political Economy Trade, Finance, and Development* (Bloomington: Indiana University Press, 2004), 239–42.

7. Exemplary work that fits in the "histories of the global" frame includes Glenda Sluga and Patricia Clavin, eds., *Internationalisms: A Twentieth-Century History* (New York: Cambridge University Press, 2016); Susan Pedersen, *The Guardians: The League of Nations and the Crisis of Empire* (New York: Oxford University Press, 2015); Marc Frey, Sönke Kunkel, and Corinna R. Unger, eds., *International Organizations and Development, 1945–1990* (Houndmills, Basingstoke, Hampshire, UK: Palgrave Macmillan, 2014); Glenda Sluga, *Internationalism in the Age of Nationalism* (Philadelphia: University of Pennsylvania Press, 2013); Patricia Clavin, *Securing the World Economy: The Reinvention of the League of Nations, 1920–1946* (New York: Oxford University Press, 2013); Mark Mazower, *Governing the World: The History of an Idea* (New York: Penguin Press, 2012); Daniel Maul, *Human Rights, Development, and Decolonization: The International Labour Organization, 1940–70* (Houndmills, Basingstoke, Hampshire, UK: Palgrave Macmillan, 2012); Giuliano Garavini, *After Empires: European Integration, Decolonization, and the Challenge from the Global South 1957–1986* (Oxford: Oxford University Press, 2012); Samuel Moyn, *The Last Utopia: Human Rights in History* (Cambridge, MA: Belknap Press of Harvard University Press, 2010); Roland Burke, *Decolonization and the Evolution of International Human Rights* (Philadelphia: University of Pennsylvania Press, 2010); Mark Mazower, *No Enchanted Palace: The End of Empire and the Ideological Origins of the United Nations* (Princeton, NJ: Princeton University Press, 2009); Erez Manela,

The Wilsonian Moment: Self-Determination and the International Origins of Anticolonial Nationalism (New York: Oxford University Press, 2007); and Akira Iriye, *Global Community: The Role of International Organizations in the Making of the Contemporary World* (Berkeley: University of California Press, 2002), among others. Human rights and development have become subfields of their own. For a review of recent debates in human rights history, see Christopher McCrudden, "Human Rights Histories," *Oxford Journal of Legal Studies* 35, no. 1 (1 March 2015): 179–212. For a recent review of literature on development, see Joseph Hodge, "Writing the History of Development (Part 1: The First Wave)," *Humanity* 6, no. 3 (2015): 429–63, and "Writing the History of Development (Part 2: Longer, Deeper, Wider)," *Humanity* 7, no. 1 (2016): 125–74.

8. Manela, *The Wilsonian Moment*, 6.

9. Of course, the turn toward the global is not without its skeptics. See especially Frederick Cooper, "What Is the Concept of Globalization Good For?," *African Affairs* 100, no. 399 (2001): 189–213, and, more recently, "How Global Do We Want Our Intellectual History to Be?," in *Global Intellectual History*, ed. Samuel Moyn and Andrew Sartori (New York: Columbia University Press, 2013), 283–94.

10. This is not to argue that Latin America has not figured in broader histories of transnational or global processes: from World Systems theory to postcolonial studies, many scholars have made the case for the centrality of Latin American commodities, markets, ideas, and movements to countless world historical processes and events. But even in much Latin Americanist scholarship, we tend not to argue for the "global" impact of interstate and transnational processes: *region* remains the dominant analytic frame for the international, and Pan- and Inter-American movements and processes are often regarded as *merely* regional and therefore insufficiently international. For an example of a regional engagement with the League of Nations, see Alan L. McPherson and Yannick Wehrli, eds., *Beyond Geopolitics: New Histories of Latin America at the League of Nations* (Albuquerque: University of New Mexico Press, 2015).

11. Latin American engagements with postcolonial theory have generated a vast and much debated literature that has long sought to understand the place of Latin America in broader world systems. See, for example, Mabel Moraña, Enrique Dussel, and Carlos A. Jauregui, eds., *Coloniality at Large: Latin America and the Postcolonial Debate* (Durham, NC: Duke University Press, 2008); Walter Mignolo, "Delinking: The Rhetoric of Modernity, the Logic of Coloniality and the Grammar of De-Coloniality," *Cultural Studies* 21, no. 2 (2007): 449–514; Aníbal Quijano, "Coloniality of Power, Eurocentrism, and Latin America," *Nepantla: Views from South* 1, no. 3 (2000): 533–80; Aníbal Quijano and Immanuel Wallerstein, "Americanity as Concept: Or the Americas in the Modern World-System," *International Social Science Journal* 131 (1992): 549–57.

12. Michel Gobat, "The Invention of Latin America: A Transnational History of Anti-Imperialism, Democracy, and Race," *American Historical Review* 118, no. 5 (1 December 2013): 1345–75; Greg Grandin, "The Liberal Traditions in the Americas: Rights, Sovereignty, and the Origins of Liberal Multilateralism," *American Historical Review* 117, no. 1 (1 February 2012): 68–91.

13. There are, of course, important exceptions to this trend, such as Vijay Prashad, *The Darker Nations: A People's History of the Third World* (New York: New Press, 2008), and Odd Arne Westad, *The Global Cold War: Third World Interventions and the Making of Our Times* (New York: Cambridge University Press, 2005). This volume also seeks to address connections across regions.

14. The problem posed by Latin America for these new concepts of the global also appears in a series of recent methodological volumes. Sven Beckert and Dominic Sachsenmaier, eds., *Global History, Globally: Research and Practice around the World* (New York: Bloomsbury, 2018), bucks the trend somewhat, as it is grounded in scholarship emerging from the various regions of the world and therefore includes a chapter on how Latin American scholars have understood the place of their region in world historical processes by the Brazilian historians Rafael Marquese and João Paulo Pimenta. But in Julian Go and George Lawson, eds., *Global Historical Sociology* (Cambridge: Cambridge University Press, 2017), which outlines an exciting research agenda that combines history, historical sociology, and international relations, there is scant mention of Latin America, even while other regions receive in-depth case studies. In Samuel Moyn and Andrew Sartori, eds., *Global Intellectual History*, the crucial ideas that circumnavigated the earth to make meaning of the concepts of the global and the universal make only one brief stop in the Western Hemisphere outside the United States, in revolutionary Haiti (though in his reply to Moyn and Sartori, Frederick Cooper evokes Garcilaso de la Vega, signaling further intellectual exchanges to be examined. Cooper, "How Global Do We Want Our Intellectual History to Be?," 290.) In Margrit Pernau and Dominic Sachsenmaier, eds., *Global Conceptual History: A Reader* (New York: Bloomsbury, 2016), "encounters leading to the transformation of concepts" do not occur in the Western Hemisphere at all.

15. Sebastian Conrad, *What Is Global History?* (Princeton, NJ: Princeton University Press, 2016).

16. Moyn, *The Last Utopia*, 66.

17. Garavini, *After Empires*, 25.

18. An overview of Latin American interventions in international law is provided by Jorge L. Esquirol, "Latin America," in *The Oxford Handbook of the History of International Law*, ed. Bardo Fassbender and Anne Peters (New York: Oxford, 2012). For further work on the topic, see Juan Pablo Scarfi, "In the Name of the Americas: The Pan-American Redefinition of the Monroe Doctrine and the Emerging Language of American International Law in the Western Hemisphere, 1898-1933," *Diplomatic History* 40, no. 2 (2016): 189-218; Arnulf Becker Lorca, "International Law in Latin America or Latin American International Law? Rise, Fall, and Retrieval of a Tradition of Legal Thinking and Political Imagination," *Harvard International Law Journal* 47, no. 1 (2006): 283-305; Liliana Obregón, "The Colluding Worlds of the Lawyer, the Scholar and the Policy Maker: A View of International Law and Foreign Policy from Latin America," *Wisconsin International Law Journal* 23, no. 1 (2005): 145-72; and Teresa Davis, "The Continent of Peace: Sovereignty, Empire and Internationalism in Latin America, 1914-1939," PhD diss., Princeton University, in progress. This chapter takes up Mark Mazower's expectation that "much more will certainly be written from the vantage point of what was once known as

the Third World to reframe the version of history told here." Mazower, *Governing the World*, xviii.

19. Mazower, *Governing the World*, 9. He recognizes, additionally, that "the South American contribution to the League and the United Nations, to postwar global debates about development and neoliberalism, begins . . . in a nineteenth-century hemispheric counterdiplomacy that unified North and South in a common if uneasy embrace against European diplomatic hegemony" (9). But even a quick survey of the relationship between the United States and Latin America in this period reveals that there is a great deal more contention in the "common if uneasy embrace" than is allowed here. While U.S. power was undeniably preponderant in, for example, the Pan-American Union, it was far from uncontested. It is by paying closer attention to those contests that we can discover how the United States came to understand both the advantages and dangers of multilateralism and international cooperation and reveal how U.S. actors saw institutions such as the Pan-American Union as a laboratory for working out more expansive forms of international association.

20. Mazower, *Governing the World*, 254. Mazower counts the total number at forty-eight, but Honduras did not send a representative to the first meeting. In addition, Persia was, in fact, in attendance, and its representative, Emir Zoka-Ed-Dowleh, argued passionately for the "representation of all the peoples who form the human race" in the assembly. See League of Nations, *Records of the First Assembly: Plenary Meetings* (Geneva, 1920), 568, and Arnulf Becker Lorca, *Mestizo International Law* (New York: Cambridge University Press, 2014), 272.

21. Representatives from Argentina, Bolivia, Brazil, Chile, Colombia, Costa Rica, Cuba, Guatemala, Haiti, Nicaragua, Panama, Paraguay, Peru, El Salvador, Uruguay, and Venezuela were in attendance at the first League Assembly meeting; League of Nations, *Records of the First Assembly*. An analysis of the history of the idea of governing the world should take seriously the presence of these countries not as multilateral fig-leaves covering the bare pretentions of U.S. or European power but as internationalist interlocutors continuously defining the boundaries within which the great powers would have to reconcile multilateral liberalism with unilateral prerogative.

22. Sluga, *Internationalism in the Age of Nationalism*.

23. This is due, as we shall see, to the notion that the "United States obviously acted as the regional hegemon" within the Pan-American Union, therefore, apparently, rendering the Pan-American Union's internationalism inferior to that of telegraphers and postal services. See Bob Reinalda, *Routledge History of International Organizations: From 1815 to the Present Day* (New York: Routledge, 2009).

24. See the special issue "Beyond and Between the Cold War Blocs," ed. Janick Marina Schaufelbuehl, Sandra Bott, Jussi Hanhimäki, and Marco Wyss, *International History Review* 37, no. 5 (2015).

25. Roland Burke, "Some Rights Are More Equal than Others: The Third World and the Transformation of Economic and Social Rights," *Humanity* 3, no. 3 (2012): 427–48.

26. Burke, "Some Rights Are More Equal than Others," 428; emphasis mine.

27. Grandin, "The Liberal Traditions in the Americas."

28. Manela, *The Wilsonian Moment*, 26. Critics such as James Weldon Johnson, in fact, honed their critique of U.S. production of racial inequality through recourse to analysis of the occupation of Haiti. See Mary Renda, *Taking Haiti: Military Occupation and the Culture of U.S. Imperialism, 1915–1940* (Chapel Hill: University of North Carolina Press, 2001). My thanks to Stuart Schrader for emphasizing this point.

29. As H. Reuben Neptune points out, "decolonization" has been used to refer, as well, to independence of the United States, and it was only with the rise of the Cold War and the move from an "old and new" world schema to a "first, second, third" one that the United States lost its affinity with, as he puts it, "Argentina and Haiti, for example," and thereby "precluded the presumption of commensurability across the hemisphere." H. Reuben Neptune, "The Irony of Un-American Historiography: Daniel J. Boorstin and the Rediscovery of a U.S. Archive of Decolonization," *American Historical Review* 120, no. 3 (2015): 941.

30. Nils Gilman, "The New International Economic Order: A Reintroduction," *Humanity* 6, no. 1 (2015), http://humanityjournal.org/issue6-1/the-new-international-economic-order-a-reintroduction/; Vanessa Ogle, "State Rights against Private Capital: The 'New International Economic Order' and the Struggle over Aid, Trade, and Foreign Investment, 1962–1981," *Humanity* 5, no. 2 (2014): 211–34.

31. Antony Anghie, "Legal Aspects of the New International Economic Order," *Humanity* 6, no. 1 (2015): 150.

32. This idea of obligations, of *duties* as important as *rights*, has been largely forgotten in the history of international governance, as Samuel Moyn reminds us. See Moyn, "Rights vs. Duties," *Boston Review*, 16 May 2016, https://bostonreview.net/books-ideas/samuel-moyn-rights-duties.

33. Victor McFarland, "The New International Economic Order, Interdependence, and Globalization," *Humanity* 6, no. 1 (2015): 217–33. A resolution on the creation of a Pan-American economic organization passed in 1931, for example, explicitly recognized the "interdependence" of the economies of the Western Hemisphere. See Pan-American Union, *Fourth Pan-American Commercial Conference: Final Act with Annexes and a Summary of the Work of the Conference* (Washington, DC: Pan-American Union, 1931).

34. The multilateral strategies employed by weak states in the global system has been characterized by political scientists as "meta-power behavior" and "soft-balancing." Stephen D Krasner, *Structural Conflict: The Third World against Global Liberalism* (Berkeley: University of California Press, 1985); Robert Pape, "Soft Balancing against the United States," *International Security* 30, no. 1 (2005): 7–45. For the application of "soft-balancing" to historical cases in Latin America, see Max Paul Friedman and Tom Long, "Soft Balancing in the Americas: Latin American Opposition to U.S. Intervention, 1898–1936," *International Security* 40, no. 1 (2015): 120–56.

35. Johanna Bockman, "Socialist Globalization against Capitalist Neocolonialism: The Economic Ideas behind the New International Economic Order," *Humanity* 6, no. 1 (2015). On Third-World coalitional politics, see Stephen Krasner, *Structural Conflict: The Third World against Global Liberalism* (Berkeley: University of California Press, 1985). Krasner theorized that this sort of activity was typical of

weak states that were seeking to promote new international regimes and institutions through what he calls "meta-power behavior." For the role of Latin American economists and experts in promoting international economic regulation within the League of Nations structure in the 1920s and 1930s, see José Antonio Sánchez Román, "América Latina y los orígenes de la regulación económica internacional," *XV Encuentro de Latinoamericanistas Españoles*, November 2012 (Madrid: Trama Editorial), 1461-72.

36. The Estrada Doctrine called for the diplomatic recognition of all governments on the principle that nonrecognition was a form of intervention and a violation of sovereignty. See Amelia M. Kiddle, *Mexico's Relations with Latin America during the Cárdenas Era* (Albuquerque: University of New Mexico Press, 2016), 16.

37. Indeed, the Mexican government was at pains throughout the conference to stress how closely its program for international affairs paralleled that promoted by Wilson. See especially "El Senado de México desea la participación de nuestro país en la Liga de Naciones," *El Universal* (México DF), 18 March 1919.

38. Constitution of Mexico, Article 27, reproduced in Gilbert M. Joseph and Timothy J. Henderson, *The Mexico Reader: History, Culture, Politics* (Durham, NC: Duke University Press, 2009), 398-401.

39. The literature on revolutionary Mexico's oil politics is substantial, but is almost always examined from a bilateral perspective and rarely examines Mexico's multilateral diplomacy. A few key works are Lorenzo Meyer, *Mexico and the United States in the Oil Controversy, 1917-1942* (Austin: University of Texas Press, 1977); Jonathan Brown, *Oil and Revolution in Mexico* (Berkeley: University of California Press, 1993); and Linda Hall, *Oil, Banks, and Politics: The United States and Postrevolutionary Mexico, 1917-1924* (Austin: University of Texas Press, 1995). More general works on revolutionary and postrevolutionary foreign policy tend to focus on Mexico's "revolutionary nationalism" to the exclusion of internationalist tendencies; an exception is Roberta Lajous Vargas, *Historia mínima de las relaciones exteriores de México (1821-2000)* (México DF: El Colegio de México, 2012), which situates Mexican foreign relations in their international context. The best general studies include Friedrich E. Schuler, *Mexico between Hitler and Roosevelt: Mexican Foreign Relations in the Age of Lázaro Cárdenas, 1934-1940* (Albuquerque: University of New Mexico Press, 1998); Daniela Spencer, *The Impossible Triangle: Mexico, Soviet Russia, and the United States in the 1920s* (Durham, NC: Duke University Press, 1999); Stephen R. Niblo, *War, Diplomacy, and Development: The United States and Mexico 1938-1954* (Wilmington, DE: Scholarly Resources, 1995); Friedrich Katz, *The Secret War in Mexico: Europe, the United States, and the Mexican Revolution* (Chicago: University of Chicago Press, 1981), Mark T. Gilderhus, *Diplomacy and Revolution: U.S.-Mexican Relations under Wilson and Carranza* (Tucson: University of Arizona Press, 1977), and Robert Freeman Smith, *The United States and Revolutionary Nationalism in Mexico, 1916-1932* (Chicago: University of Chicago Press, 1972). More recently, works that have looked to Mexico's relations with the rest of Latin America or with international institutions have been more multilateral in focus. See Kiddle, *Mexico's Relations with Latin America during the Cárdenas Era*; Renata Keller, *Mexico's Cold War: Cuba, the United States, and the Legacy of the Mexican Revolution*

(New York: Cambridge University Press, 2015); Fabián Herrera León, "México En La Sociedad de Naciones: Modernización Y Consolidación de Una Política Exterior, 1931–1940," PhD diss., El Colegio de México, 2010, and Pablo Yankelevich, *La Revolución Mexicana en América Latina: Intereses políticos e itinerarios intelectuales*. (México DF: Instituto de Investigaciones Dr. José María Luis Mora, 2003).

40. "Don Venustiano Carranza, al abrir el Congreso de sus sesiones ordinarias el 10. de Septiembre de 1918," *Los presidentes de México ante la Nación: Informes, manifiestos y documentos de 1821 a 1966*, vol. 3 (Mexico DF: XLVI Legislatura de la Cámara de Diputados, 1966). As Friedrich Katz has pointed out, "In these statements he anticipated some of the principles of the Bandung conference in the 1950s, which stressed the solidarity of the underdeveloped countries and called on the great powers not to interfere in their domestic affairs"; Katz, *The Secret War in Mexico*, 498.

41. This congruence was frequently invoked by Mexican politicians, such as Juan Sánchez Azcona, who argued in the Mexican Senate that "the principal tendencies of the international politics of President Wilson are the same as those which on solemn occasions President Carranza has made known as the current Mexican international policies, with the applause of the entire nation." See "El Senado de México desea la participación de nuestro pais en la Liga de Naciones," *El Universal* (México, DF), 18 March 1919.

42. In the long discussion of the text of the amendment, Wilson insisted that the doctrine be mentioned by name, but repeatedly rejected the idea, raised by the French and others, that it might be explicitly defined. He reiterated his interpretation of the League as an extension and protection of the doctrine and told the other members of the commission that he was introducing the language "by way of concession" to his critics at home. David Hunter Miller, *Drafting the Covenant* (New York: G.P. Putnam's Sons, 1928), 444.

43. Secretaria de Relaciones Exteriores, Memorandum, 22 April 1919, L-E-1845 (1), Archivo Histórico de la Secretaria de Relaciones Exteriores de México (hereafter SRE); Telegram, Robert H. Murray to the New York "World," 8 May 1919, United States Department of State, *Foreign Relations of the United States 1919: The Paris Peace Conference, Vol. II* (Washington DC: Government Printing Office, 1942), 547.

44. This characterization is mentioned in Samuel Guy Inman, *Inter-American Conferences 1826–1954: History and Problems*, ed. Harold Eugene Davis (Washington, DC: University Press, 1965), 101.

45. Inman's impression was confirmed by numerous other observers, such as the Mexican chargé d'affaires in Havana, who reported that Cuban delegate Manuel Márquez Sterling had praised Trejo y Lerdo, "who is said to have captured the great sympathies of President Alessandri, the intellectual circles, and the press." See Mariano Armendáriz del Castillo (La Habana) a Alberto J. Pani, 2 June 1923, L-E-191, SRE. Of course, as was often the case, support for the reforms was not unanimous, and most notable among the Latin American opponents was Chile's Augustín Edwards, that country's longtime ambassador in London who had been recently been elected president of the General Assembly of the League of Nations in Geneva. His

arguments, however, carried little weight with the reformers: when Edwards tried to insist to Cuba's Carlos Agüero that the Pan-American Union's stability and prestige rested on the leadership being vested in the United States and not turned over to a Latin American, Agüero replied, "Tell me, Mr. Edwards, how is it, then, that League of Nations did not collapse with you as president?" Trejo y Lerdo, Mexican Legation in Chile, "Informe sobre la Quinta Conferencia Panamericana: Tercera Parte—Carácter General de la Conferencia," May 1923, L-E-194, SRE.

46. Trejo y Lerdo, Mexican Legation in Chile, "Informe sobre la Quinta Conferencia Panamericana." The stakes were quite clear from the beginning: the *New York Times* reported that the proposal brought up "the question of North American control" of the Pan-American Union. See "Delay Endangers Latin Arms Plan," *New York Times*, 11 April 1923.

47. Fletcher's defeat was palpable when he cabled to Secretary of State Hughes: "After a week of protracted negotiation I believe this is the best possible solution and that any further attempt at mediation would be unwise and unsuccessful." Fletcher to Hughes, 24 April 1923, Record Group (RG) 43, Entry 133, Box 2, National Archives and Records Administration, College Park, MD (hereafter NARA).

48. Cover attachment to Thompson to Foreign Office, 4 October 1933, Foreign Office Files (FO) 371/16530, British National Archives (hereafter TNA). On the long history of debt crises in the region, see Carlos Marichal, *A Century of Debt Crises in Latin America: From Independence to the Great Depression, 1820-1930* (Princeton, NJ: Princeton University Press, 1989), 203. The only country to avoid default on federal loans by the time the Montevideo conference convened was Argentina, although the Mexicans were quick to point out that even there, payments had been suspended on provincial and municipal loans. See Jose Manuel Puig Casauranc, "Memorandum para ampliar—en un terreno personal y no official—la plática de Puig, de esta mañana, con el señor Embajador Daniels," 14 September 1933, L-E-210 (I), SRE.

49. Jose Manuel Puig Casauranc, *Remarks on the Position Taken by Mexico at Montevideo* (México DF: Ministry of Foreign Affairs, 1934), 24. Puig's vision had three important implications: first, that repayment should be premised on a state's capacity to pay (and therefore that the practice of taking on further debt simply to meet existing repayment obligations should be abandoned); second, that there should be some mechanism for disciplining not just debtors but creditors, as well, for their role in generating financial imbalance; and finally, that the ultimate responsibility for the smooth operation of the system credit must fall to the state and be regulated through cooperation between states. Puig's "new legal and philosophic conception of credit" was, in many ways, an international version of what Keynes would come to call, in the *General Theory*, a "somewhat comprehensive socialization of investment"; John Maynard Keynes, *The General Theory of Employment, Interest, and Money* (London: Macmillan, 1936), 377. But the Mexican insistence on the capacity to pay drew explicitly not from Keynes, but from Pierre Jaudel, whom Secretary of Foreign Relations staffer Luis Sánchez Pontón saw as the intellectual progenitor of the Dawes Plan. See Luis Sánchez Pontón, "Las Deudas de

Guerra y su Influencia en la Crisis Economica Presente," Universidad Nacional Autónoma de México, 1933, L-E-254, SRE.

50. Puig, *Remarks on the Position*, 30; emphasis added.

51. Eric Helleiner, *Forgotten Foundations of Bretton Woods: International Development and the Making of the Postwar Order* (Ithaca, NY: Cornell University Press, 2014), 53.

52. Villaseñor's Guatemala proposal is detailed in Eduardo Villaseñor, "Problemas financieros y de comercio interamericano," *El Trimestre Económico* 8, no. 31 (1941): 355–97.

53. For this argument, see David Green, *The Containment of Latin America: A History of the Myths and Realities of the Good Neighbor Policy* (New York: Quadrangle, 1971), 60–72.

54. White to Morgenthau, "Proposed Inter-American Bank," 28 November 1939, RG 56, Treasury Records of the Assistant Secretary for Monetary and International Affairs, Chronological File, Box 3, File 14, NARA.

55. Memorandum of conversation, 25 January 1940, Re: Proposed Inter-American Bank, in Franklin D. Roosevelt Presidential Library, Morgenthau Diaries, Volume 237, 21–25 January 1940, 266, quoted in Helleiner, *Forgotten Foundations*, 71.

56. Inter-American Financial and Economic Advisory Committee, *Convention for the Establishment of an Inter-American Bank* (Washington, DC: Government Printing Office, 1940).

57. Berle himself echoed this when he wrote in 1941 that the new institution represented "complete departure from the nineteenth-century form of development." Rather, he said, the bank "should be the beginning of a system in which finance is the servant of exchange and development . . . in direct contrast to the older system, which insisted that the development and the commerce must serve finance, or it could not go forward"; Adolf Berle, "Peace without Empire," *Survey Graphic* 30, no. 3 (March 1941): 107.

58. Helleiner, *Forgotten Foundations of Bretton Woods*, 77.

59. "Mexico Pedirá Voz y Voto para los Países Débiles, en la Junta Monetaria," *Excelsior* (México, DF), 14 June 1944.

60. For a more detailed treatment of Mexican interventions at Bretton Woods, see Christy Thornton, "Voice and Vote for the Weaker Nations: Mexico's Bretton Woods," in *Global Perspectives on the Bretton Woods Conference and the Post-War World Order*, ed. G. Scott-Smith and J. Simon Rofe (London: Palgrave MacMillan, 2018), 149–65.

61. "Memorandum of a Meeting on the International Stabilization Fund," 25 May 1943, RG 56, Memoranda of Conferences held in Harry Dexter White's Office, 1940–1945, Entry 360T, Box 20, NARA.

62. Keynes to Sir David Walley, 30 May 1944, cited in John Maynard Keynes, *The Collected Writings of John Maynard Keynes*, ed. Elizabeth S Johnson and D. E Moggridge, vol. 26 (Cambridge: Royal Economic Society, 1978), 42.

63. Sir Wilfred Eady to Padmore, 12 January 1944, Treasury Files, Papers of Lord Keynes, T247/27, TNA.

64. White to Morgenthau, 23 June 1944, RG 56, Records of the Secretary of the International Monetary Group–Records of the Bretton Woods Agreements, 1938–46 (BWA), Box 1, NARA.

65. "Commission I International Monetary Fund Fifth Meeting: Transcript," 14 July 1944, 10:00 A.M., in *The Bretton Woods Transcripts*, ed. Kurt Schuler and Andrew Rosenberg (New York: Center for Financial Stability, 2012).

66. Eduardo Turrent y Diaz, *México en Bretton Woods* (México DF: Banco de México, 2009).

67. Helleiner, *Forgotten Foundations of Bretton Woods*, 63–66.

68. Víctor L. Urquidi, "Elasticidad y rigidez de Bretton Woods," *El Trimestre Económico* 11, no. 44(4) (1945): 595–616. This is one reason why Mexican experts such as Villaseñor continued to advocate for the creation of the Inter-American Bank, even after the Bretton Woods institutions came into being.

69. "Commission III: Other Means of International Financial Cooperation, Third (Final) Meeting: Transcript," 20 July 1944, in *The Bretton Woods Transcripts*, ed. Kurt Schuler and Andrew Rosenberg (New York: Center for Financial Stability, 2012).

70. Mexico's draft on labor can be found at United Conference on Trade and Employment, "Draft Charter, Mexico: Proposed Amendments," E/CONF.2/11/Add.28, GATT Documents, World Trade Organization; Beteta's correspondence with Mexican president Miguel Alemán and other officials is in Fondo Miguel Alemán Valdés, 433/216, Archivo General de la Nación (Mexico) (hereafter AGN). For more on this, see Jill Jensen, "Negotiating a World Trade and Employment Charter: The United States, the ILO and the Collapse of the ITO Ideal," in *The ILO from Geneva to the Pacific Rim: West Meets East*, ed. Jill Jensen and Nelson Lichtenstein (London: Palgrave MacMillan, 2016), 83–109.

71. Vanni Pettinà, "Adapting to the New World: Mexico's International Strategy of Economic Development at the Outset of the Cold War, 1946–1952," *Culture & History Digital Journal* 4, no. 1 (2015).

72. UN Document A/RES/375(IV), "Draft Declaration on Rights and Duties of States," 6 December 1949, https://documents.un.org.

73. See Jorge Castañeda, *Mexico and the United Nations* (New York: Manhattan Publishing, 1958), 24–36.

74. Castañeda, *Mexico and the United Nations*, 65. The study was published in 1958 in English, but completed in fall of 1955, according to a preface by Daniel Cosío Villegas.

75. Philippe C. Schmitter and Ernst B. Haas, *Mexico and Latin American Economic Integration* (Berkeley: Institute of International Studies, University of California, 1964).

76. Vanni Pettinà, "Global Horizons: Mexico, the Third World, and the Non-Aligned Movement at the Time of the 1961 Belgrade Conference," *International History Review* 38, no. 4 (2016): 741–64.

77. Inter-American Committee on the Alliance for Progress, "International Monetary Reform and Latin America: Report to CIAP by the Group of Experts" (Washington, DC: Pan-American Union, 1966).

78. E. V. K FitzGerald, "The Financial Constraint on Relative Autonomy: The State and Capital Accumulation in Mexico, 1940-82," in *The State and Capital Accumulation in Latin America: Volume 1: Brazil, Chile, Mexico*, ed. Christian Anglade and Carlos Fortin (Pittsburgh: University of Pittsburgh Press, 1985), 210-40.

79. On Echeverría's repression, see Alexander Aviña, "'We have Returned to Porfirian Times': Neopopulism, Counterinsurgency, and the Dirty War in Guerrero, Mexico, 1969-1976," in *Populism in Twentieth-Century Mexico: The Presidencies of Lázaro Cárdenas and Luis Echeverría*, ed. Amelia Kiddle and María L.O. Muñoz (Tucson: University of Arizona Press, 2010), 106-21; and Alexander Aviña, *Specters of Revolution: Peasant Guerrillas in the Cold War Mexican Countryside* (New York: Oxford University Press, 2014).

80. See Keller, *Mexico's Cold War*.

81. UN Document A/PV.1952, "Address by Mr. Luis Echeverria Alvarez, President of the United Mexican States," United Nations General Assembly, Twenty-Sixth Session, Official Records, 1952nd Plenary Meeting, Tuesday, 5 October 1971, https://documents.un.org; original Spanish in "Discurso del Presidente de México en la Sede del ONU," 5 October 1971, in *Documentos de política internacional* (México, DF: Secretaría de la Presidencia, Departamento Editorial, 1975).

82. While one Mexico City newspaper considered Muñoz Ledo "a sort of Mexican Henry Kissinger," his politics were firmly on the Left. Muñoz Ledo considered himself a "man of the Third World" and would go on to be one of the founders of the Democratic Current, the left-wing group that split from the PRI and then became the Party of the Democratic Revolution after the fraudulent 1988 elections. Leopoldo Mendív, "Oficio: Reportero," *El Heraldo* (Mexico City), May 25, 1972; Porfirio Muñoz Ledo, James W. Wilkie and Edna Monzón Wilkie, *Historia oral, 1933-1988* (México, DF: Penguin Random House Grupo Editorial México, 2017).

83. "Discurso Pronunciado por el C. Presidente Constitucional de la República Mexicana, Lic. Luis Echeverría Álvarez," *Estudios Internacionales* 5, no. 18 (April-June 1972), 123. Echeverría forcefully added that international financing should not be made conditional on politics, and therefore should not be denied to those countries using revolutionary means to achieve progress—no doubt an allusion to the economic blockade being levied against the host country, Chile, under Salvador Allende's Popular Unity government.

84. As translated in "Summary of Address Given at the 92nd Plenary Meeting, 19 April 1972," in UN Document TD/180, *Proceedings of the United Nations Conference on Trade and Development, Third Session, Santiago de Chile, 13 April to 21 May 1972*, Vol. lA, Part One (New York: United Nations, 1973), 186.

85. "Discurso Pronunciado por el C. Presidente Constitucional de la República Mexicana, Lic. Luis Echeverría Álvarez," 126-27.

86. UN Document TD/L.62, https://documents.un.org.

87. After they came to consensus on a draft, it was to be sent to the member states for consultation, and then remitted for comment to the Trade and Development Board, the UNCTAD governing body, before going before the General Assembly. Revised draft TD/L.84 adopted as Resolution: 45 (III).

88. The working group included Alfonso García Robles, Permanent Representative of Mexico before the United Nations; Gustavo Petriccioli, Subscretary of Revenue; Eliseo Mendoza Berrueto, Subsecretary of Trade; and Porfirio Muñoz Ledo, Subsecretary of the Presidency. See Rabasa a Echeverría, 22 May 1973, Fondo Secretaria Particular, Exp. A-1117-1 (IV), SRE.

89. Documento de Trabajo: Que contiene un anteproyecto de Carta de Derechos y Deberes Económicos de Estados, 5 July 1972, Fondo Secretaria Particular, Exp. A-1117-1 (IV), SRE.

90. Documento de Trabajo. See also Antony Anghie, "Legal Aspects of the New International Economic Order," *Humanity* 6, no. 1 (2015): 145–58.

91. UN Document TD/180, *Proceedings of the United Nations Conference on Trade and Development, Third Session, Santiago de Chile, 13 April to 21 May 1972*, Vol. IA, Part Two (New York: United Nations, 1973), 124.

92. Partido Revolucionario Institucional, *México y el nuevo orden económico internacional: documentos* (México, DF: Comisión Nacional Editorial, 1976), 13.

93. In the original group of thirty-one, the subgroup of industrialized countries was, twice as big as any of the other groupings of countries from Africa, Asia, Latin America, or the Socialist bloc. See "Paises que integran el grupo de trajabo encargado de preparar un proyecto de Carta Sobre los Derechos y Deberes Económicos de los Estados," Fondo Secretaria Particular, Exp. A-1117-1 (IV), SRE. By agreement in November of 1972, nine more countries were added to the working group, bringing its total to forty.

94. For example, see Memorandum of Telephone Conversation, 18 October 1974, Digital National Security Archive (DNSA) collection: Kissinger Telephone Conversations, 1969–1977. The American Bar Association even went so far as to form a subcommittee to study the charter and passed a resolution against its approval without any mention of existing international law. See Charles N. Brower, Letter to the Editor, *New York Times*, 8 December 1974.

95. "Memoradum para información del Señor Secretario, Tlatelolco, 26 February 1973," Fondo Secretaria Particular, Exp. A-1117-1 (IV), SRE. On the various proposed alternatives, see the accompanying "Esquema de Carta de Derechos y Deberes Economicos de los Estado," Fondo Secretaria Particular, Exp. A-1117-1 (IV), SRE. In addition to the industrialized countries' opposition, the Socialist bloc had submitted its own proposal for consideration by the General Assembly, a resolution on a "UN Declaration on the Development of Cooperation in the Spheres of Economy, Trade, Science, and Technology," which some Mexican experts worried might hinder the ability to come to agreement on the charter due to confusion over competing projects. "Evolución de las Negociaciones sobre la Carta de los Derechos y Deberes Económicos de los Estados, 29 July 1972," Fondo Secretaria Particular, Exp. A-1117-1 (IV), SRE. For the attempts of Mexico to reconcile the Soviet proposal with their own, see Fondo Embajada de México en la URSS, Leg. 87, Exp. 2, SRE.

96. The third meeting draft is found in UN Document TD/B/AC.12/3, "Report of the Working Group on the Charter of Economic Rights and Duties of States in Its Third Session," 8 March 1974; the fourth is in TD/B/AC.12/4, "Report of the Working

Group on the Charter of Economic Rights and Duties of States in Its Fourth Session," 1 August 1974, https://documents.un.org.

97. "Documentos y comentarios en torno al viaje del Presidente Echeverría (Marzo-abril de 1973)," *Foro Internacional* 14, no. 1(53) (1973): 24–40. On British skepticism during Echeverría's visit, see Telegram, Secretary of State to U.S. Embassy in Mexico City, May 24, 1973, Wikileaks Document 1973STATE100257.

98. "Documentos y comentarios en torno al viaje del Presidente Echeverría," 40–54.

99. "Charlaron Tito y Echeverría," *El Informador* (Guadalajara), 14 February 1974.

100. "Necesaria Unión de Latinoamérica," *El Informador* (Guadalajara), 22 July 1974.

101. Transcript of Conversation No. 735-1, Cassette Nos. 2246–2248, 15 June 1972, 10:31 A.M.–12:10 P.M., Oval Office, National Security Archive Electronic Briefing Book 95, "The Nixon Tapes," 18 August 2003. An embassy memo noted Echeverría's "comments concerning mischief making of the communists, foreign and domestic," which "gave strong indication he has not forgotten his experiences in controlling their activities as minister of interior before becoming president"—a barely veiled reference to the repression of the student movement in the late 1960s. "As he has often done in the past," the embassy concluded, "he left no doubt as to his belief in a firm hand when dealing with extremists"; cable, United States Embassy, Mexico to Secretary of State, 19 May 1973, Digital National Security Archive (hereafter DNSA).

102. The translator interpreted this as "close to capitalism" to Nixon and Kissinger.

103. Quoted in Robert A. Mortimer, *The Third World Coalition in International Politics* (Boulder, CO: Westview Press, 1984), 37.

104. Mexico would eventually win the struggle to keep the reform effort within the IMF. See, for instance, "Impase en la CECLA," *Expreso* (Lima), 25 October 1971, Fondo SubSecretario, B1-415-1 (3a), SRE, and Summary Record of the Seventh Plenary Meeting, 1 November 1971, in *The Third World without Superpowers: The Collected Documents of the Group of 77*, vol. 2, ed. Karl P. Sauvant and Joachim W. Müller (New York: Oceana Publications, 1981), 129–46.

105. Mortimer, *The Third World Coalition*, 49.

106. Karen Hudes, "Towards a New International Economic Order," *Yale Journal of International Law* 2, no. 1 (1 January 1975), 102.

107. Memorandum para información del Señor Presidente de la Republica, n.d. Fondo Secretaria particular, Exp. A-1117-1 (II), SRE.

108. Hudes, "Towards a New International Economic Order," 114–16.

109. Memorandum of Conversation [Kissinger-Rabasa], Secretary's Office, 29 August 1974, 11:15 A.M., Kissinger Conversations: Supplement I, 1969–1977, DNSA; Telegram, Maw to Secretary of State, 1 July 1974, Wikileaks Document 1974STATE 141990_b.

110. Telegram, Secretary of State to USUN Geneva, 1 July 1974, Wikileaks Document 1974STATE142000_b. The compromise language concluded that states seeking to nationalize resources or regulate transnational corporations should

"fulfill in good faith their international obligations." When the Philippines' Hortencio J. Brillantes introduced the compromise proposal as his own at 2:00 A.M. on 28 June, however, he changed the language from "international obligations" to "international commitments and undertakings," which angered most of the developed countries, which thought it implied that only treaties, and not "customary international law as well," were relevant.

111. Memorandum of Conversation, Ford and Echeverría, 21 October 1974, DNSA.

112. Telecon, Percy and Kissinger, 18 October 1974, DNSA. Kissinger called U.S. businessmen "morons" repeatedly, in fact. See also Telecon, Mr. Maw/Secretary Kissinger, 21 June 1974, 9:40 A.M., Kissinger Telephone Conversations, 1969–1977, DNSA.

113. News Conference of the President and President Echeverria of Mexico in Tubac, Arizona, 21 October 1974, American Presidency Project, http://www.presidency.ucsb.edu/ws/index.php?pid=4497.

114. Quoted in Kathleen Teltsch, "New Declaration Voted in the U.N.," *New York Times*, 13 December 1974.

115. Informe del embajado Jorge Castañeda a la Segunda Comisión de la Asamblea General de las Naciones Unidas en su Caracter de Presidente del Grupo de 40 Países Encargado a Elaborar una Carta de Derechos y Deberes Económaicos de los Estados, acerca de las Labores de Dicho Grupo en Nueva York, NY, a 25 de Noviembre de 1974, en Partido Revolucionario Institucional, *México y el nuevo orden económico internacional: documentos* (Mexico City: Comisión Nacional Editorial, 1976), 83–97.

116. UN Document A/C.2/L.1419, https://documents.un.org.

117. Telecon, Rabasa and Kissinger, 6 December 1974, DNSA.

118. Memo, Secretary's Staff Meeting, 9 December 1974, DNSA.

119. Quoted in Teltsch, "New Declaration Voted in the U.N."

120. Nils Gilman, "The New International Economic Order: A Reintroduction," *Humanity* 6, no. 1 (2015): 10.

121. Alta Comisión Americana, Sección Nacional Mexicana, Memorandum (1931), L-E-201 (I), SRE.

122. Ramón Beteta, "Mexico's Foreign Relations," *Annals of the American Academy of Political and Social Science* 208, no. 1 (1940): 170. This, too, prefigures the NIEO, as Gilman writes: "Rather than accepting international law as a neutral device, NIEO legal theorists claimed that existing international law, unsuited to promoting structural reform, was biased toward economic incumbents and needed recasting in order to favor developing nations"; Gilman, "The New International Economic Order: A Reintroduction," 4.

123. Ogle, "State Rights against Private Capital," 211.

124. Ogle, "State Rights against Private Capital," 219.

125. Daniel J. Whelan, "'Under the Aegis of Man': The Right to Development and the Origins of the New International Economic Order," *Humanity* 6, no. 1 (2015): 93–108.

126. See Bradley Simpson's *The First Right: Self-Determination and the Transformation of Post-1941 International Relations* (New York: Oxford University Press, forthcoming). As Johanna Bockman has argued, "if we examine economic globalization

more closely and from the perspective of Second and Third World institutions, we can see that the Non-Aligned Movement, the Second World, and the Third World more broadly worked hard to create a global economy in the face of active resistance by the United States and other current and former colonial powers, which sought to maintain the economic status quo of the colonial system"; Bockman, "Socialist Globalization," 109.

13 Third Worldism and the Panama Canal
Liberating the Isthmus, 1971–1978

MIRIAM ELIZABETH VILLANUEVA

When Panama became an independent state in 1903, the United States obtained rights to build a canal with the Hay-Bunau-Varilla Treaty, which included a perpetuity clause. After its completion in 1914, the "in perpetuity" wording allowed the United States to maintain control of a 650-square-mile area, known as the Panama Canal Zone, that ran down the center of the nation, fifty miles long and five miles wide on either side of the completed waterway. The Canal Zone constituted a state within a state and impeded Panama's efforts at nation-building and exercising full sovereignty over its territory. Rising Panamanian nationalist sentiment over the U.S. presence erupted in protests in the 1950s, culminating on 9 January 1964, with anti-U.S. demonstrations and riots, which were followed by a series of failed treaty discussions in 1967. By 1968, a coup introduced an era of military dictatorship in Panama. At the time, not everyone believed that the Panamanian National Guard's leader, General Omar Torrijos Herrera, possessed the tenacity to pry loose Washington's grip on the canal, partly because the Guard itself was in many ways a creature of U.S. Southern Command Training. Since day one, the military's power rested on fulfilling the vision of a canal administered by and for Panamanians, and the general was running out of time. Despite U.S. obstacles and delays, the Panamanian military signed the Torrijos-Carter Treaties and staged a plebiscite for Panamanians to engage in the negotiations in 1977. The treaties guaranteed the transfer of the canal to Panamanian control by the end of the twentieth century. It was a landmark in Panamanian history, though the victory was muted by the twenty-two year period required before the final transfer.

In reconstructing Panama's military era and the canal negotiations, scholars have focused until recently on U.S. actors while ignoring Panamanians.[1] To remedy this oversight, Tom Long wrote a diplomatic history from the Panamanian perspective with attention to the country's leading diplomats.[2] In Panama, Omar Jaén Suárez has written on the Panamanian negotiators and their efforts to close the Canal Zone.[3] To contribute to the recent literature, this study moves beyond the key negotiators to illuminate how the Panamanian government gained approval for the treaties using a combination of Third Worldist and anti-imperialist rhetoric.

The process of ratifying the treaties was much more complex than what happened in Washington and Panamanian negotiation rooms. Using sources from repositories, Panama's Ministry of Foreign Relations, and private collections, this work explains how the government created broad popular support for the Torrijos-Carter Treaties, even in authoritarian circumstances, by channeling an anti-imperialist movement that was spreading across the Global South. Torrijos and his negotiators seized on Third Worldism to defend Panama's sovereignty before the United Nations Security Council (UNSC), the Non-Aligned Movement (NAM), the Organization of American States (OAS), and regional summits with Venezuela and Colombia. To help disseminate the military's rhetoric across the country, shift public opinion in favor of the Torrijos-Carter Treaties, and dismantle the Canal Zone, artists created theatrical performances and documentaries. For instance, the Universidad de Panamá's students in the Departamento de Expresiones Artística (DEXA, Department of Artistic Expression) and the Grupo Experimental Cine Universitario (GECU, Experimental University Film Group) drew on the military's nationalist dogma and Third World theory on cinema and performative art to assist the regime with its plebiscite. With the collaboration of the intellectual Left, the government presented the treaties as progress for Panamanian sovereignty and for all countries considered part of the Third World.

Panama participated in the second generation of countries that professed Third Worldism, defined as a theory that saw liberation struggles of countries in the Global South as the beginning of a widespread revolution not inspired by advanced capitalist or socialist world powers.[4] Alliances with neighboring countries and fellow dictators cemented Torrijos's place as a liberator and strongman against Washington. As early as 1971, Torrijos and his foreign minister channeled Panama's homespun ideology and adopted Third Worldism in speeches to global organizations and dignitaries. While abroad, the military regime adopted a position that strayed neither too far to the Left nor the Right so as not to appear ideologically compromised. Torrijos's unwavering decision to remain ambiguous was strategic, since it allowed him to experiment with Third Worldism and Cuban leader Fidel Castro's anti-imperialist rhetoric without ascribing to Communism. Throughout the 1970s, Torrijos's posturing and the international political climate helped him negotiate a treaty to dissolve the Canal Zone and hand over control of the canal to Panamanians.

Following Torrijos's lead, artistic groups at the national university embraced Third Worldist theory on the arts to produce theatrical performances and documentaries to support the canal negotiations. The artistic mechanisms employed allowed average Panamanians to imagine themselves as part of a patriotic movement to resist colonialism. The performative tactics of DEXA and GECU fomented a nationwide desire to fight as Torrijistas for the canal and for the closure of the Canal Zone. Artists embraced non-Western theories on theater and cinema in ways that were similar to Torrijos's employment of Third Worldism to promote Panama's cause and gain legitimacy for the state. DEXA's theater troupe, the Trashumantes (Nomads), staged nationalist plays written by Panamanian playwrights. GECU's filmmakers created a local cinema that drew on the historical and contemporary problems of the country—especially the fight for the canal—and ventured into rural and urban spaces to foster interaction with audiences. The groups' performative activism influenced Panamanians and received international attention that bolstered the regime's negotiating position.

The central argument of this chapter is that the regime capitalized on the change in international politics to safeguard its power and bring an end to U.S. control of the canal and Canal Zone. By the 1970s, the 1903 treaty was an anachronism that served to rally Panamanians and other Third World sentiment against the United States. Like Uruguay, Brazil, and Argentina, Panama also embraced Third Worldism as a tool to enter global conversations on anticolonialism and Third World liberation.[5] Likewise, artists delved into Third World cultural movements to generate a cultural policy geared toward the marginalized. As partners, Torrijos and Panamanian artists gained approval for a government threatened with illegitimacy. For everyday Panamanians, the mounting domestic and international fight for the canal included them in a transnational movement to combat imperialism.

The Canal Crisis before the 1968 Military Coup

Before Torrijos and President Carter signed the treaties in 1977, Panamanians had spent seventy-four years contesting the U.S. presence in the country because of the canal. The canal crisis dates to when Panama gained its independence with the assistance of the United States in 1903. For years, Panamanian nationalists had planned to secede from Colombia but had endured setbacks that impeded their success. The United States intervened on the condition that Panama consider a treaty to start construction on a waterway. The agreement, known as the Hay-Bunau-Varilla Treaty of 1903, signed by Frenchman Phillipe-Jean Bunau-Varilla and U.S. Secretary of State John Hay, was advantageous to the United States, but not to Panama. Articles 2 and 3 of the treaty signed away Panama's sovereignty and designated it a protectorate of the United States.[6] Article 3 further granted the United States rights to exercise authority in the Canal Zone and protect it without interference from the Panamanian government. In 1905, the United States acknowledged Panama's titular sovereignty over the Canal Zone. However, the wording of the treaty set into motion more than sixty years of continual conflict between the nations.

Part of Panama's dissatisfaction with the treaty had to do with the United States' interpretation of Article 3 as permission to house troops, settle American families, and employ a police force in the Canal Zone, thereby effectively enforcing a U.S. system within the country. According to Michael Donoghue, Panamanians rejected the Canal Zone's exclusivity, its discriminatory police, who routinely harassed locals living alongside the Canal Zone's perimeter, and Zonians (persons living in the Canal Zone) who were granted immunity from Panamanian courts.[7] Despite efforts to industrialize and modernize the isthmus, the U.S. operation of the canal and the privileges afforded to Zonians hindered progress outside the Canal Zone's borders.

In response to mounting local dissent, the United States agreed to revise the treaty twice, but without offering an end date to its administration of the canal or the Canal Zone. In 1936, the Hull-Alfaro Treaty abolished the protectorate status, prevented the United States from seizing territory without Panamanian consent, and allowed domestic merchants more rights to compete against commissaries in the Canal Zone.[8] In 1955, the Filós-Hines Treaty was signed to address Panama's grievances. U.S. President Dwight D. Eisenhower agreed to an increase Panama's annuity and to end Washington's monopoly over railroad and highway construction. Even though the 1936 treaty had stopped Washington from interfering in local affairs, the issue of sovereignty remained. The intensification of Panama's disdain over the Canal Zone led students from the university to mobilize demonstrations in front of the Canal Zone and U.S. embassy. In May 1958, Universidad de Panamá students and professors staged Operación Soberanía (Operation Sovereignty), during which protestors planted Panamanian flags in the Canal Zone. On 3 November 1959, students reenacted the protest from the previous year in violent demonstrations. The treaty's modifications were insufficient at quelling unrest on the isthmus.[9]

As students and laborers expressed themselves on the street, a Panamanian delegate to the United Nations Ninth and Twelfth Assemblies (1956 and 1957, respectively), George W. Westerman, advocated on behalf of the country to an international audience. Westerman did not use the term "Third World" or "Third Worldism," but the logic behind such theories was present in his thinking. For instance, he discussed Panama's dilemma with the United States within the context of two sovereign countries disputing land claims.[10] According to Westerman, Panama had never relinquished sovereignty over land within the Canal Zone, but instead had allowed the United States to operate on Panamanian soil. In contrast, the United States claimed that the Canal Zone, including the land and water inside its perimeter, fell under its jurisdiction. During his years as a UN representative, Westerman challenged U.S. attempts to categorize Panama and the Canal Zone as part of its territory as it did with Puerto Rico.[11] Panama's UN delegates had no interest in drawing comparisons between Panama and Puerto Rico. For instance, when the United States tried to designate the Canal Zone as a territory in the 1946 United Nations Committee on Information from Non-Self-Governing Territories, Westerman, along with Panamanian diplomat Ricardo J. Alfaro, asserted Panamanian sovereignty over the Canal Zone and distanced the isthmus from Puerto Rico.

Following Westerman's time as a delegate, a confrontation between Panamanians and Zonians on 9 January 1964, known as the Nueve de Enero (1964 Panama Flag Riots) devastated the isthmus. Gathered en masse, students from the university and Instituto Nacional peacefully entered the Canal Zone to protest the absence of their national flag at Balboa High School, where Zonian students raised the U.S. flag instead. They were responding to the Zonians' contempt for a U.S. order to fly the Panamanian flag at designated sites in the zone. When the Panamanian students walked into the Canal Zone, hostile Zonians greeted them in front of the school and reportedly tore the Panamanian flag, which encouraged Panamanian students to retaliate. Three days of rioting in Panama City and Colón ensued until the U.S. military silenced the demonstrations. Twenty-one Panamanians and four Americans died during these riots. These protests provoked President Roberto Chiari to break relations with the United States. The students pushed the country to act and seek new treaties that would end the U.S.-run Canal Zone and nationalize the canal. The event was a watershed moment in Panamanian history.[12]

The 1964 Panama Flag Riots spurred the Organization of American States (OAS) to become involved in the canal issue. To restore diplomatic relations between the nations, leaders of the Inter-American Peace Committee of the OAS mediated discussions on renegotiating the Panama Canal treaties.[13] Formed in 1948 to promote peace and security in the Western Hemisphere, the OAS was tasked with resolving conflicts between member states. However, since Washington dominated the organization, the OAS was often used as an instrument of U.S. power. After the 1964 Panama Flag Riots, however, the OAS recommended that U.S. President Lyndon B. Johnson renegotiate the treaty in late 1964. By 1967, three treaty drafts were presented to both governments. Under them, as Johnson requested, the United States would still have rights to protect the canal operations. In addition, the U.S. military would maintain its presence in the Canal Zone on sites currently occupied by the armed forces until 2004. Johnson tried to ease tensions between the two countries, but not to lose the waterway entirely to Panamanians. Washington wanted to maintain its strong presence in Latin America at the height of the Cold War. With neither side rushing to ratify the treaty, the negotiations failed to generate a suitable treaty for either nation.[14]

Since the construction of the canal, diverse working- and middle-class individuals attempted to assert Panama's dominion over the Canal Zone. As the years passed, workers, students, and merchants channeled their frustrations against the United States in protests, riots, and peaceful demonstrations. The inability to enact a pact that offered an end date to the U.S. control of the waterway became one of the most troublesome issues in the elections before the military coup. When the National Guard seized power in 1968, it presented itself as an alternative to the oligarchic political style that Panamanians had grown accustomed to during the previous half century. With Torrijos as its leader, the regime proposed to enter new treaty negotiations.

The 1968 Military Coup's Torrijista Project

On 11 October 1968, the Panamanian National Guard staged a coup and removed President Arnulfo Arias from office eleven days into his presidency. Arias faced retribution for threatening to replace and retire officers he saw as too powerful and a danger to his new government. A civilian-military junta, comprised of five citizens and a few officers, displaced the president and his supporters. The military's decision to take control came as no surprise; the move was symptomatic of its growing political power.[15] However, once in command, the officers lacked a clear agenda for the nation.[16] In droves, politicized masses challenged the Guard's unconstitutional coup, though not necessarily the displacement of the unpopular elite.

To unite the country, the government devised a populist ideology known as Torrijismo, named after its new ruler, General Torrijos. The ideology blended the general's charismatic persona with the isthmus's longstanding tradition of plebian republicanism. In December 1969, at the age of thirty-nine, Torrijos emerged as the nation's strongman. Young, easy going, machista, and attractive, the general exuded a brand of Panamanian masculinity rooted in military training, which differed from Arias's more compromised image as a career politician. The general exhibited a toughness instilled in him at the Academia Militar de San Salvador and the U.S. Army Training Center at Fort Gulick in the Canal Zone in the 1950s. Under President John F. Kennedy's Alliance for Progress, the U.S. Army Training Center changed its name to the U.S. Army School of the Americas in 1963. Torrijos's military persona and penchant for alcohol, women, and street vernacular added to his charm. Donoghue argues that Torrijos used his persona in an effort to "inject . . . self-reliance into the national psyche" to combat the United States and the elite.[17] Torrijos's celebrity contributed to the formation of the ideology, but Torrijismo also relied on plebian notions of equality, nationalism, and class. For over a century, Panamanians had fostered an egalitarian identity that united popular sectors, resisted U.S. imperialism, and demanded national sovereignty.[18]

On 5 September 1969, the regime designated an advisory commission, attached to the Ministry of Foreign Relations, to evaluate the three treaties proposed in 1967. Over a few months, the advisors drafted points the treaties needed to resolve. The treaties could be approved only if they ended the perpetuity clause, abolished the Canal Zone government, and returned the Canal Zone's land to Panama. Panamanians also wanted the United States to cease all construction projects unrelated to the maintenance, functioning, and protection of the waterway. Delegates especially wanted the removal of the U.S. armed forces.[19] At the OAS offices on 26 June 1970, the Panamanian commission met with President Richard Nixon's secretary of state, William Rogers, and Ambassador Daniel Hofgren, to share their points. After the meeting, Minister of Foreign Relations Juan Antonio Tack reported to Washington that Panama would no longer continue with the 1967 treaties and preferred to start new talks.[20]

By 1971 and 1972, the United States had agreed to six of the seven points the Panamanian advisors had devised in 1970. Under Nixon, Washington was willing to abandon the "in perpetuity" clause and agreed to set a date to transfer the administration of the canal to Panama. However, the conversations stalled when the United States insisted on controlling the canal for another fifty years until a sea-level waterway could replace the 1914 canal. Torrijos was in no position to accept any treaty that would extend foreign power on the isthmus beyond 2003, which marked the one-hundred-year anniversary of Panama's independence. The general halted treaty negotiations and prepared for a new round of talks contingent on the state's international diplomacy.[21] The possibility of failure weighed heavily on the military government, but the regime's commitment to gaining sovereignty over the canal shed a new light on the formerly despised Guard in the 1970s.

Third Worldism as Panamanian Policy

The geopolitical climate presented Panama with an opportunity to challenge the North American giant with support from the Third World movement in the 1970s. During the canal negotiations under Torrijos, the country found solidarity with other nations interested in removing colonial vestiges to exercise full sovereignty. With the United States entangled in a Cold War with the Soviet Union, Panama fostered relations with the Global South, which wanted to shift the balance of power in its favor and demand the nationalization of natural resources. With Torrijos at the helm, the isthmus entered a new series of canal negotiations as Torrijistas and members of the Third World.

Starting in 1971, Panama inserted itself into discussions on the Global South's development for fairer canal negotiations with the United States. During the 1970s, the United States was struggling with several factors that weakened its position but benefited Panama.[22] The United States was in a vulnerable position as the Soviet Union achieved military parity, and the war in Vietnam weakened U.S. military forces. As Tack pointed out, the Vietnam War demonstrated to Panamanians how "power through force and military technology cannot defeat a small country fighting for its independence."[23] The U.S. attention to the Vietnam War and ongoing criticism of its involvement in other countries' internal affairs placed Panama in a fortunate position. To find support for its cause, Panama joined the "third force" in politics (in support of neither the United States nor the Soviet Union), which began to emerge after 1945 and grew over time to wield considerable influence in the United Nations (UN) and Non-Aligned Movement (NAM).[24] The third force included countries that shared a similar desire to control their policymaking, economic systems, and use of natural resources without foreign intervention. These emerging postcolonial states built a bloc with like-minded nations interested in working together to achieve the benefits of modernity without the United States' or the Soviet Union's assistance.[25] As part of the movement, Panama found an international community with similar aspirations and a doctrine like Torrijismo. In missives and speeches, Panamanian diplomats and the general frequently described the isthmus as a Third World nation fending off imperialist control of its natural resources. The regime relied on this movement to pressure Washington in the largest international governing bodies of the world.

When Tack declared "a new image of Panama exists in the world" in 1971, he foreshadowed the isthmus's progress in the UN and its path to join the UNSC.[26] Before attending the Twenty-Sixth UN General Assembly meeting in New York City, the minister delivered a letter to UN General Secretary U Thant on Panama's efforts to negotiate with the United States. The organization translated the letter into five languages and delivered it to every member. Once the meeting began, Panamanian representatives gave a presentation to convince the delegates to demand fairer negotiations and treaties between Panama and the United States. Tack's speech stressed Panama's geopolitical position and importance in past international forums. For example, he drew on the 1826 Congreso Anfictiónico de Panamá (Amphictyonic Congress of Panama), convened by Venezuelan liberator Simón Bolívar, to claim the country had always exhibited the principles of the UN in terms of building alliances with other nations to promote peace.[27] Tack pressed on, saying that Panama had always been a center for international commerce and cultural exchange, and that U.S. control over the canal impinged on the nation's neutrality and sovereignty. In his presentation, Tack cited the Declaration on the Strengthening of International Security passed by the Third World meeting in Lusaka, Zambia, on 17 December 1971, which championed the idea of a collective and universal commitment from countries in the Global South to ensure a secure world without military alliances. Tack used the declaration to emphasize Panama's commitment to the Third World.[28] Despite objections from Washington, Panama won an overwhelming majority of votes to host the next UNSC meeting in 1973—a monumental achievement for Panama, which would have larger implications for negotiating the Canal Zone.

The meeting not only secured Panama the highest vote for any member to join the UNSC, but also fashioned Torrijos as a head of a generation interested in forging new partnerships outside of the East-West superpowers. At the UN General Assembly, Torrijos became more of a politician than a general. He had foregone his usual military regalia and wore a suit and tie, an outfit he would continue to wear during meetings with U.S. President

Jimmy Carter.[29] A year after the assembly, the newly drafted 1972 constitution contributed to legitimizing the general's rule with international allies. In the new constitution, Article 277 designated Torrijos as "Maximum Leader," but also the chief negotiator in all matters related to the canal.[30] Panama's induction into the UNSC in October 1971 and General Torrijos's legal status with the 1972 constitution cleared the way for the UNSC to convene in Panama City in 1973.

For seven days in March 1973, Panama was "the capital of the world."[31] Unions, students, workers, and other groups greeted delegates in Panama City. Panamanians were asked to show support and unite under Torrijos's message.[32] At the UNSC meeting, the general directed his attention to the Global South. He insisted that Panama wanted to resemble African states with resilient and dignified peoples, who fought for their natural resources. Egypt's nationalizing the Suez Canal impressed the isthmus.[33] The rousing speech was followed by a resolution to vote on discussing the canal question as a council, but the United States vetoed the proposal. At the meeting, India, Kenya, Sudan, and Yugoslavia sided with Panama. These countries continued to urge their colleagues in other parts of the world to side with Panama as a stance against U.S. imperialism.[34]

At the same time that Torrijos was courting the UN, he built ties with delegates from the NAM by arranging personal visits or offering monetary aid to countries where he could not schedule a trip. The NAM was established in 1961 to prioritize the interests of former colonies amidst the global tension of the Cold War. Self-determination was the founding principle of the movement. As a united bloc, the members used their influence within the UN General Assembly. The NAM included leaders from a wide geographical base, but was especially influenced by Gamal Abdel Nasser of Egypt, Kwame Nkrumah of Ghana, Shri Jawaharlal Nehru of India, and Josip Broz Tito of Yugoslavia. By the 1970s, many of the founders had passed away or been deposed, but Tito remained and was a staunch supporter of Torrijos. As early as 1972, Torrijos conversed with Tito to share updates on Panama's negotiations.[35] The intimate meetings influenced the NAM's decision to make Panama a priority in its convention in Guyana, held from 8 to 11 August 1972. At this conference, NAM adopted the "Georgetown Declaration," Which addressed Latin American initiatives for the region's absolute independence, specifically Puerto Rico's.[36] To prove its loyalty toward its new allies, Panama agreed to various missions in Africa and the Middle East, such as sending four hundred soldiers to observe and maintain peace after the Yom Kippur War between Egypt and Israel.[37] The NAM accepted Panama unanimously as a member in 1975.[38]

One of the most important NAM meetings for Panama took place in Colombo, Sri Lanka, in August 1976. In front of the eighty-six countries attending, Torrijos expressed himself freely without criticism from Washington. The visit to Sri Lanka provided unprecedented international exposure for the isthmus.[39] The goal was to present Panama's case to the NAM and get its support for Tack and U.S. Secretary of State Henry Kissinger's agreement at the UN's next General Assembly. The agreement, drafted in 1973 and signed by Kissinger in 1974, listed the following eight points: abrogate the 1903 treaty, eliminate the perpetuity clause, have an end-date for the United States in Panama, terminate U.S. jurisdiction, revert the Canal Zone to Panama, give Panama equal rights to canal earnings, allow Panama to participate in administering the canal, and jointly work together to protect and renovate the existing waterway.[40] Torrijos ordered the Panamanian press to cover every moment of his journey to Sri Lanka so Panamanians could connect with him and the Global South dimension of his trip. At the conference, the general argued that if Panamanians controlled the waterway, the canal would no longer serve as an instrument for U.S. hegemonic force. Rather, the canal would benefit countries also seeking modernity through interoceanic trade. His impassioned speech captivated the audience and ensured that eighty-one states voted in Panama's favor in a resolution on the canal at the next UN General Assembly in October 1976.[41]

While Torrijos fostered ties outside the region, he also worked toward building Latin American allies in the OAS. After encouraging new negotiations between Panama and the United States following the 1964 Panama Flag Riots, the OAS had proven its usefulness to the isthmus, even if the talks failed to bring anything to fruition. With that in mind, Panamanian delegates attended every OAS meeting between 1970 and 1973 in order to question the United States's control of the OAS and to encourage Latin American countries to side with the isthmus when discussing the Canal Zone and canal. In turn, Panama declared support for countries also resisting Washington. For instance, Panama requested Cuba's reintegration into the OAS as a direct challenge to Washington during the OAS General Assembly on 9 April 1973.[42] The isthmus also expressed solidarity with Puerto Rico's aspirations for national liberation.[43] Torrijos's team of diplomats impressed observers from the Global South with their attention to Puerto Rican and Cuban affairs. While Cuba had broken its ties to the United States, both Panama and Puerto Rico were both regarded as U.S. neocolonies by many developing states.

Panama's hard stance toward Washington received positive reactions from members of the OAS. For example, Argentina's president, Juan Domingo Perón, requested Torrijos's presence in Buenos Aires on 15 January 1974. At his home, Perón interviewed Torrijos and identified with Panama's cause.[44] The Colombian president, Alfonso López Michelson, and the Venezuelan president, Carlos Andrés Pérez, also defended Panama in the press, visited the general frequently, and championed Torrijos as a "flawless patriot."[45] These two countries had a lot to gain from new treaties. The general promised its neighbors (Venezuela, Costa Rica, and Colombia) that once they were passed, he would allow them to transport natural and industrial products for free though the waterway.[46] The region sympathized with the isthmus and rallied together for Panama in the UN.

The mounting pressure on the United States from international bodies set in motion the negotiations that took place between 1975 and 1977. Ellsworth Bunker and Sol Linowitz headed the talks for the United States. Juan Antonio Tack, Rómulo Escobar Bethancourt, Adolfo Ahumada, Jaime Arias Calderón, and Nicolás González Revilla led the Panamanian delegation. Key issues, however, such as the closure of U.S. military bases, the dismantling of the Canal Zone government, and a final end-date for U.S. administration of the waterway, dragged out the talks.[47] Nevertheless, the general continued to form relationships with states, and his negotiators stayed firm on drafting a treaty in Panama's favor. Panama's tactics and growing presence in the Third World were placing pressure on American negotiators. In the late 1970s, Bunker even admitted that Latin American endorsements on behalf of Panama had influenced the negotiations.[48] Torrijos's doctrine and progress with the negotiations motivated artists from the Universidad de Panamá to work alongside the military and to back the government's treaty efforts.

University Cultural Agencies and National Liberation

As Torrijos and the Foreign Ministry strove to create unity between Panama's cause and that of the Global South, artists at the university who identified with Torrijismo wanted to participate in convincing Panamanians to support the negotiations. To appease the students, the university rector approved the creation of fine arts programs for undergraduates to promote national culture. The Departamento de Expresiones Artisticas (DEXA)—which received government assistance to generate public support—and the Grupo

Experimental Cine Universitario (GECU)—which students formed to express their approval of the canal treaties and regime's social polices—emerged as two different types of cultural programs at the university. The fine arts students involved in these organizations worked in conjunction with other intellectuals to drive the United States from the isthmus. Even though the fine arts groups at the university originated from different intentions and expectations, both provided a form of propaganda for the regime.

In the first months following the coup, the university became a refuge of resistance for students who had devoted their lives to protesting government corruption and the U.S. administration of the canal. Distrustful of the regime, leftists, professors, artists, and multiple student organizations banded together to oppose the National Guard. The escalation of demonstrations motivated officers to imprison and exile protestors. Some students suffered severe torture and died from their wounds in prison. When a provisional government formed in December 1968, it shut down the university to deal with the crisis. Under a new administration and with close supervision from the Ministry of Education, the university reopened partially on 9 June 1969, to weary pupils.[49]

To make amends with students and professors, the state allowed exiled students to return to the country and to re-enroll in the university.[50] The institution also underwent a series of reforms that reorganized departments with a populist agenda. Under a new rector, the institution adopted as templates *The National Plan of Development* and *The Manifesto for University Reform*, written in the 1960s, to reinvent the school as a "revolutionary people's university."[51] The proposals altered the university's role in Panamanian society to make it a space for everyone, regardless of class status. *The Manifesto for University Reform* specifically gave the university a new mission statement to unify the country with strong national values. The university's involvement in a cultural movement fit within the acceptable parameters for change under Torrijismo. While the government never stopped surveilling university students, the military's commitment to reforming the university was sufficient for students who returned.

DEXA was the first fine arts program to open on campus with the regime's support. Created on 19 November 1969, DEXA fell under the direction of Torrijos's younger sister, Aurea "Baby" Torrijos Herrera. Multiple artistic groups, such as a university choir, a ballet company, a folkloric ensemble, and a theatrical troupe, formed under DEXA. Artists acknowledged that DEXA's purpose was to direct public attention toward the government's canal policy.[52] The university also funded DEXA's performance of Lucho

Bejarano's "Colonia Americana No!" in Argentina, which spurred Argentineans and Panamanians to sing and march to the anti-imperialist tune.[53] Torrijos's sister further ensured that DEXA's performances complied with the military's agenda.

An overview of the Trashumantes (Nomads) theatrical troupe highlights the multiple ways DEXA used Torrijos' nationalist and Third World doctrine to educate the populace on Panama's canal negotiations. In 1970, the student-led troupe started outside of DEXA, but after its first performance in El Chorrillo (an impoverished neighborhood near the Canal Zone and the site of the 1964 popular uprising against the U.S. enclave), Torrijos's sister hired Trashumantes.[54] As employees of DEXA, the group met and worked from 9 A.M. to 2 P.M. to compose plays and practice scenes. Performances were free of charge for everyone in attendance.

The Trashumantes appealed to the lower class by staging sociodramas—plays that addressed social ills and propounded nationalistic rhetoric in ways that were inspired by Polish director Jerzy Grotowski and the Argentine activist theater of Once al Sur. The troupe followed theories set forth by Grotowski's *Towards a Poor Theatre*, which suggested performers work in nontraditional spaces (buildings, rooms, parks, and streets), rather than mainstream theater houses, in order to achieve a greater impact. His experimental theater sought an elimination of excesses, such as elaborate costuming, lighting, and makeup, in order to build a relationship between actors and audiences for "poor theater."[55] The performative activism appealed to Trashumantes actors, who embraced Grotowski and adopted Once al Sur's uniform—jeans, sweaters, and shoes, which required no alterations.[56] The group's sociodramas capitalized on these influences and ruptured the traditional conventions of theater in Panama.

The Trashumantes' sociodramas borrowed from historical moments when Panamanians resisted the presence of U.S. servicemen and Zonians. The troupe performed plays by local playwrights José de Jesús Martínez, the general's closest confidant, and Rogelio Sinán. Their first self-composed play, *Alto a la Patria Boba* (An End to the Foolish Fatherland) presented three tragic conflicts between the United States and Panama: the 1856 Tajada de Sandía (Watermelon Slice Incident), the 1925 *Movimiento Inquilinario* (Renters' Strike), and the 1964 Nueve de Enero (Panama Flag Riots). The play ended with the Panamanian country's awakening from a stupefied slumber and embracing a decision to protect its sovereignty with Torrijos at the helm as a kind of deus ex machina. According to the play, the country, under military control, was no longer a *patria boba*, but a nation ready to fight for its resources. The term *patria boba* originated in the early twentieth century to describe "innocent developing states manipulated by powerful world powers."[57] Unlike in traditional theater, after each performance, the Trashumantes arranged a moment of dialogue with the audience to interpret the plays and explain the regime's canal negotiation strategies. The workshops and theater style of the Trashumantes worked well in regions without access to the government.[58]

The Trashumantes bare-bones activist performances on national liberation gained the group awards at international festivals held in Panama and Colombia in the early 1970s. The festivals, in turn, offered the regime an international platform on which to show that the state had no intention to suppress art, so long as the artists complied with the directives set forth by DEXA and the regime. If not, the regime quickly suppressed opposition movements and artwork. The troupe gained admirers such as Jorge Alí Triana, a Colombian theater director who served as a judge at the 1972 festival in Panama.[59] At the Theater Festival of Manizales, Colombia, the Trashumantes won another prize.[60] These festivals allowed Panama to engage with other Global South countries taking an interest in Panama's plight after having interacted with Torrijos.

In addition to DEXA, another university program, the GECU, aimed to stimulate an anti-imperialist consciousness among the masses. After the university hosted a weeklong festival on Cuban film, Panamanian students were inspired to learn more about guerrilla artistry. Cuban films such as *Lucía, Los Días del Agua, Memorias del Subdesarollo*, and *Las Aventuras de Juan Quin* were screened at the festival to major fanfare.[61] Leftist students embraced Cuba's cinematic approach, as well as various manifestos on creating a revolutionary cinema, such as Brazilian Glauber Rocha's "The Aesthetics of Hunger," Cuban Julio García Espinosa's "An Imperfect Cinema," and Argentineans Fernando Solanas and Octavio Getino's popular "Towards a Third Cinema."[62] Using these latest theories on creating documentaries, on 5 September 1972, Pedro Rivera started a student-led cinematography organization. Inspired by the Cuban Revolution, the majority identified as leftists and used the socialist state as an example of what Panama could achieve without the presence of the United States. Rather than an organ for explicit propaganda, the GECU was an independent group that participated in the Torrijista effort.[63] A decade later, Rivera and others claimed they never received government bribes.[64] Instead, the group was a willing collaborator in advocating for the treaties, so long as the negotiations strengthened the nation's independence.

Like their counterparts in the Global South, GECU started with little equipment but grew over time. At the GECU's founding, the university provided a Bolex 16-mm camera and sound equipment. As neorealists, the group's members preferred outside settings and nonprofessional actors for their documentaries. In their work, these Panamanians ventured outside their comfort zones and captured the daily lives of the poor to reveal that the isthmus drew few benefits from the U.S.-controlled canal. GECU's documentary mode fits Julianne Burton's description of a "realist, national, and popular" cinema that spurred viewers into political action in the Third World.[65] Every film served as a tool to enrage Panamanians and force them to question living in a semicolonized environment.

The crew produced thirty short pictures between 1972 and 1977, with Torrijismo and canal negotiations as the focus. One of their first five-minute shorts, "Ode to the New Nation" ("Canto a la Patria que ahora nace"), alludes to the contradictory presence of the United States as a peacekeeper for the canal and an imperialist in Panama. The film, with GECU cofounder Enoch Castillero's expertise as a writer and documentary poet, included images from the 1964 Panama Flag Riots. In 1973, Rivera and Castillero filmed *Ahora Ya No Estamos Solos*, a fifty-five-minute film that recorded the UNSC meeting held in Panama. The film captivated audiences and provided a positive image for the regime. Shown on national television, it offered Panamanians coverage of Torrijos's speech and the UN's favorable response. The crew filmed their most influential documentaries between 1975 and 1976. As the table indicates, in 1976, 60,274 people in 435 screenings across the country watched GECU's documentaries, and the numbers almost doubled in 1977.[66] These films and the discussions that followed the screenings strove to manufacture consent for the regime's proposed treaties.

The advances the GECU made at home to spread Torrijos's message paralleled its gains with international cinematographers. In 1977, members of the GECU attended two important festivals for filmmakers in the Global South. At the Fifth Committee of Latin American Filmmakers (Comité de Cineastas de América Latina) meeting in Mérida, Venezuela, Rivera was selected out of eighty delegates to serve on the roundtable. For his presentation, Rivera gave a presentation that covered the tense political climate in Panama and the immediate goal of producing shorts related to the anti-imperialist fight. GECU's presence at the festival impacted other delegates. In an interview, Rivera claims that, after watching "Man against the Wind" ("Hombre de cara al viento"), audiences were shocked by the footage of U.S. aggression toward Panama.[67]

TABLE 13.1 Documentaries screened by Panama's Grupo Experimental Cine Universitario, 1976

Documentary	Year Produced	Screenings	Attendance
Canto a la patria que ahora nace	1972	33	5,872
Ahora ya no estamos solos	1973	10	3,478
Los 505	1973	6	1,279
Un año depués	1973	12	2,871
Viva Chile mierda	1973	11	1,610
Who Is Peter?	1973	15	988
Aquí Bayano cambio: La quema	1974	7	2,485
Ligar al alfabeto de la tierra	1975	29	3,591
Aquí Bayano cambio: La producción	1975	20	3,156
María	1975	2	103
Noticero no. 1	1975	5	460
Noticero no. 2	1975	1	60
Noticero no. 3	1975	5	472
Bayano prioridad uno	1975	8	1,454
Unidos o dominados	1975	18	2,495
Soberanía	1975	21	1,801
Compadre vamos pa'lante	1975	11	1,621
Bayano Ruge	1976	104	12,284
La canción de nosotros	1976	35	4,145
Mi pueblo habla, mi pueblo grita	1976	42	4,842
El más opresor	1976	13	1,170
Como si a Maceo, Lorenzo diera Un apretón de manos	1976	23	3,778
Una canción a los mártires	1976	4	259
Total		435	60,274

Source: Pedro Rivera, "GECU: Cuatro años de trabajo continuo," Formato 16 (January 1976): 10.

Note: The table does not reflect all the screenings in the interior or documentaries that aired on national television.

Even though the GECU's mission reflected the Torrijista agenda, its young activists were not peons of the military. The musicians, writers, painters, and dancers who congregated in the studio and then GECU's new headquarters denounced policies that ran counter to their leftist ideals. On occasion, members of the organization would report to Torrijos any misgivings related to the administration of the university.[68] The relationship had to be mutual and serve the interests of the artists and the military. Since the National Guard worked toward continuing the generational struggle for sovereignty, the GECU's members were willing to act as Torrijistas. The cultural movement at home, with Torrijista and Third World influences, pacified and rallied people in favor of Torrijos's regime.

The university groups engineered a cultural movement that awakened the working-class consciousness of Panamanians in major cities and in the interior. Through cinema and theater, the artists reached out to individuals previously marginalized from politics and discussions on the canal, including many Panamanians of color whom the Torrijos regime embraced but the elites had long ignored. To maintain the dialogue on anticolonialism and Panamanian sovereignty in disparate communities, artists formed film clubs and impromptu theater groups after each screening and performance. The university students' ongoing cultural initiatives attracted many Panamanians and encouraged them to consider themselves as Torrijistas. Artists cemented popular support for the regime's nationalist program and cult of personality. In doing so, they readied Panamanians for the key 1977 plebiscite.

The 1977 Plebiscite

On 7 September 1977, Torrijos and President Carter signed the Panama Canal treaties at the OAS headquarters in Washington. The Torrijos-Carter Treaties were two separate accords that concerned the canal's operation and neutrality. The treaties guaranteed Panama control of the canal on 31 December 1999 and required the United States to train Panamanians to administer the waterway under a Panama Canal Commission. Rather than the all-American board of the Panama Canal Company, the new commission would start with five U.S. members and four Panamanians and continue to reduce the number of Americans, eventually replacing all of them with locals in 1999, after already appointing a Panamanian as the head commissioner in 1990. As for the Canal Zone, the United States reverted nearly 60 percent of the 648-square-mile area to Panama on 1 October 1979. The treaty eliminated the hated U.S. Canal Zone Police in 1982. Subsequently, the Canal Zone would shut down completely and revert to Panamanian hands. While one treaty dealt with nationalizing the canal, the other treaty focused on the canal's neutrality. It did, however, grant the United States unlimited access to transport warships through the waterway and to defend the canal with the continued use of military bases on Panamanian soil.[69]

Three days after the signing ceremony, the general announced a plebiscite for 23 October 1977, to a jubilant crowd in Panama.[70] The public that day danced on the streets, cried, and watched the Club Gallistico's "sovereignty" cock fights with the best roosters from around the country.[71] The crowd cheered Torrijos's adherence to the 1972 constitution's Article 274, which ordered a plebiscite for all treaties and laws related to the waterway. The Electoral Tribunal had forty-four days to plan, organize, and coordinate voting booths for approximately 787,251 Panamanians.[72] During the month of October, roundtables and lectures in favor of the treaties were scheduled throughout the country. This is not to claim that everyone in Panama supported the treaties. Fistfights often occurred with left-wing students in the Revolutionary Student Front (Frente Estudiantil Revolucionario, FER-29), who opposed the treaties. Leftist students in FER-29 were not afraid to paint its slogan, "Bases No!," all over public property and set fire to U.S. Ambassador William Jordan's car.[73] However, the government overpowered the opposition. Claiming he had nothing to hide, Torrijos invited the UN and the OAS to supervise the plebiscite.[74]

As the plebiscite went into effect, Torrijos continued to court heads of state, but paradoxically in Western countries allied with the United States. The trips Torrijos made between September and October of 1977 served two purposes: to appease U.S. allies weary of military states and to transmit messages at home of Torrijos's ability to function as a world leader. He began his trips in Israel and in Western Europe. The meeting with the Israel prime minister displeased the general's NAM allies, but pleased the U.S. Senate. As with his previous excursions, the general wrote reports on his interviews and urged citizens to mirror his campaign by convincing neighbors to vote yes.[75] Torrijos generated the largest electectoral turnout in Panama.

On the day of the plebiscite, mechanisms to influence the vote were minimal but present. UN observers noted minor irregularities, such as plainclothes National Guardsmen manning voting booths (the president of the Electoral Tribunal had emphasized that guards would not attend in uniform), Electoral Tribunal vehicles covered with pro-treaty stickers, and even officials at stations using megaphones to encourage the population to vote yes. Still, the referees considered these blatant displays of propaganda negligible in manipulating the vote.[76] With UN and OAS observers in attendance, the tallied votes were as follows: votes submitted, 766,232; yes votes, 506,805; no votes, 245,117; and null votes, 14,310.[77] Despite losses in certain districts, the regime's efforts ensured the treaties passed with a Panamanian majority. Following the results, UN representative Erik Suy commended Panama's plebiscite as an example of democracy.[78]

Conclusion

The plebiscite was a vote of confidence for the regime and the chief negotiators of the treaties. The cultural revolution that took place in the 1970s demonstrates the political impact of performative tactics to strengthen the legitimacy of the regime. The artistic mechanisms allowed everyday Panamanians to imagine themselves as part of a patriotic movement to resist colonialism. The performative tactics of DEXA and GECU fomented a nationwide desire to fight as Torrijistas for the canal and for the closure of the Canal Zone. When it came down to voting in the plebiscite, Panamanians already understood the severity of the conflict and voted as activists. In 1977, the county had made its decision clear with the plebiscite, and, after a grueling year of debates, the U.S. Senate ratified the treaties in April 1978. The cultural revolution and plebiscite afforded the military the legitimacy needed to maintain power without resorting heavily to violence.

Cultural mechanisms were essential in fomenting a movement to nationalize the canal and cement Torrijos's legacy as Panama's heroic leader, a legacy that to a considerable extent exists to this day. Artists and their commitment to the military regime impacted the way Panamanians conceived the rule of an authoritarian government. For lower-class Panamanians, the military, under Torrijos, liberated the nation and instilled an independent spirit in the people.[79] This chapter's reinterpretation of the negotiations shows that the regime relied on Third-World commonalities to foster international solidarity. In turn, artists transmitted blended messages of Torrijismo and Third Worldism with films and theatrical performances for Panamanians. During Panama's military era, its regime emerged as a leader for anti-imperialists and contributed in the 1970s Third World movement—albeit by manipulating Third Worldist discourse to sustain the populace's satisfaction with authoritarian rule.

Notes

1. George Priestly, *Military Government and Popular Participation in Panama: The Torrijos'Torrijos' Regime, 1968–1975* (Boulder, CO: Westview Press, 1986); Robert Harding, *Military Foundations of Panamanian Politics* (New Brunswick: Transaction Publishers, 2001); Carlos Guevara Mann, *Panamanian Militarism: A Historical Interpretation* (Athens: Ohio University Center for International Studies, 1996); Steve Ropp, *Panamanian Politics: From Guarded Nation to National Guard* (New York: Praeger, 1982); and Walter LaFeber, *The Panama Canal: The Crisis in Historical Perspective* (New York: Oxford University Press, 1979).

2. Tom Long, "Putting the Canal on the Map: Panamanian Agenda-Setting and the 1973 Security Council Meetings," *Diplomatic History* 38, no. 2 (2014): 431-55.

3. Omar Jaén Suárez, *Las negociaciones de los Tratados Torrijos-Carter 1970-1979* (Panamá: Autoridad del Canal de Panamá, 2005); Omar Jaén Suárez, "Historia de las negociaciones de los tratados Torrijos-Carter," *Revista Lotería* 57, nos. 473-74 (2007): 9-44.

4. Abdul Karim Bangara, "Toward a Pan-Third Worldism: A Challenge to the Association of Third World Studies," *Journal of Third World Studies* 20, no. 1 (Spring 2003): 95.

5. Germán Esteban Alburquerque Fuschini, "Third Worldism: Sensibility and Ideology in Uruguay—From the Third Position to the Thought of Carlos Real de Azúa," *Third World Quarterly* 36, no. 2 (2015): 306-32; Alburquerque Fuschini, "The Third-Worldism in the Argentinean Intellectual Field: A Hegemonic Sensibility (1961-1987)," *Tempo* 19, no. 35 (2013): 221-28; Alburquerque Fuschini, "Third World and Third Worldism in Brazil: Towards Its Constitution as Hegemonic Sensibility in the Brazilian Cultural Field, 1958-1990," *Estudios Ibero-Americanos* (Impresso) 37, no. 2 (2011): 176-95.

6. Walter LaFeber, *The Panama Canal: The Crisis in Historical Perspective* (New York: Oxford University Press, 1979), 30.

7. Michael Donoghue wrote the definitive work on the U.S. Canal Zone and the relationship between Zonians and Panamanians. Michael Donoghue, *Borderland on the Isthmus: Race, Culture, and the Struggle for the Canal Zone* (Durham, NC: Duke University Press, 2014).

8. Sheila Hamilton, "Panamanian Politics and Panama's Relationship with the United States Leading up to the Hull-Alfaro Treaty," MA thesis, University of Victoria, 2003, 26-77.

9. John Major, *Prize Possession: The United States and the Panama Canal 1903-1979* (New York: Cambridge University Press, 1993), 329-57.

10. George Westerman, "Los Territorios no Autonomos y las Naciones Unidas—1958," *Lotería* 8, no. 31 (1958): 2.

11. Westerman, "Los Territorios," 10.

12. Alan McPherson observes that the National Guard refused to pacify Panamanians and assist U.S. forces on 9 January 1964. The Guard's decision and the government's later diplomatic break with the United States signaled a shift in U.S.-Panamanian relations. Alan McPherson, "Rioting for Dignity: Masculinity, National Identity and Anti-U.S. Resistance in Panama," *Gender & History* 19, no. 2 (2007): 234.

13. Michael Hogan, *Panama Canal in American Politics: Domestic Advocacy and the Evolution of Policy* (Carbondale: Southern Illinois University Press, 1986), 77.

14. Major, *Prize Possession*, 329-57.

15. As Alan McPherson observes, the National Guard refused to pacify Panamanians and react to U.S. forces presence on the isthmus on 9 January 1964. The Guard's decision to stay in the barracks signaled a shift in military-Panamanian relations. For the first time, the military sided with civilian protestors and defied the government. McPherson, "Rioting for Dignity," 234.

16. Guevara Mann, *Panamanian Militarism*, 144.

17. Michael E. Donoghue, "Roberto Durán, Omar Torrijos and the Rise of Isthmian Machismo," in *Sports Culture in Latin American History*, ed. David M. K. Sheinin (Pittsburgh: University of Pittsburgh Press, 2015), 21.

18. "The Hay-Bunau-Varilla 1903 Treaty," reprinted in LeFeber, *The Panama Canal*, 256.

19. Ministro Juan Antonio Tack, *Memoria del ministerio de relaciones exteriores* (Panama: Ministerio de Relaciones Exteriores, 1970), 16–17.

20. Tack, *Memoria* (1970), 20.

21. LeFeber, *The Panama Canal*, 180.

22. LaFeber, *The Panama Canal*, 180

23. Ministro Juan Antonio Tack, *Memoria del ministerio de relaciones exteriores* (Panama: Ministerio de Relaciones Exteriores, 1971), 18.

24. Mark T. Berger and Heloise Weber, *Rethinking the Third World: International Development and World Politics* (New York: Palgrave Macmillan, 2014); Jeffrey J. Byrne, "Algiers between Bandung and Belgrade: Guerilla Diplomacy and the Evolution of the Third World Movement, 1954–1962," in *The Middle East and the Cold War*, ed. Massimiliano Trentin (Newcastle upon Tyne, UK: Cambridge Scholars Publishing, 2012).

25. Robert B. Rakove, *Kennedy, Johnson, and the Nonaligned World* (Cambridge: Cambridge University Press, 2012), xvii; Robert Vitalis, "The Midnight Ride of Kwame Nkrumah and Other Fables of Bandung (Ban-doong)," *Humanity: An International Journal of Human Rights, Humanitarianism, and Development* 4, no. 2 (2013): 277; Vijay Prashad, *The Darker Nations: A People's History of the Third World* (New York: New Press, 2007); Mark Atwood Lawrence, "The Rise and Fall of Nonalignment," in *The Cold War in the Third World*, ed. Robert J. McMahon (New York: Oxford University Press, 2013), 139–55.

26. Tack, *Memoria* (1971), 8.

27. Tack, *Memoria* (1971), 28.

28. Juan Antonio Tack's speech in Omar Torrijos, *Esta Victoria Pertenece al Pueblo* (Panama: Centro de Impresión Educativa del Ministerio de Educación, 1978).

29. Karen DeYoung, "Torrijos Restless in Statesman Role," *Washington Post Foreign Service*, 2 November 1977.

30. "The 1972 Constitution," quoted in *Organization of American States, Report on the Situation of Human Rights in Panama* (Washington DC: General Secretariat of the OAS, 1985), 11.

31. "Exposición en Honor del Consejo de Seguridad," *Crítica*, 15 March 1973.

32. "En apoyo al Consejo de Ceguridad se reunirán," *Crítica*, 15 March 1973.

33. Omar Torrijos "Discurso del General de Brigada Omar Torrijos Herrera ante el consejo de seguridad de la O.N.U. Reunido en la Ciudad de Panamá el 15 de marzo de 1973" in *Torrijos: Figura, tiempo, faena,* ed. Justo Arroyo (Panama: Revista *Lotería*,1981): 419–23.

34. Tack, "Annex 4," in *Memoria* (Panamá: N.A., 1973), 3.

35. Omar Torrijos, *La Quinta Frontera: Partes de la batalla diplomática sobre el Canal de Panamá* (Costa Rica: Ciudad Universitaria Rodrigo Facio, 1978), 26.

36. "Georgetown Declaration," in *A New International Economic Order: Selected Documents, 1945–1975*, ed. Alfred George Moss and Harry N. M. Winton (New York: United Nations Institute for Training and Research, 1976), 2:379–80.

37. "Egipto," *La Estrella*, November 16, 1973.

38. Ricaurte Soler, *La Invasión de Estados Unidos* (México: Siglo Veintiuno, 1991), 42; "Panamá observa cuarta conferencia de jefes de estado" *La Estrella*, 11 September 1973.

39. "Panamá observa cuarta conferencia de jefes de estado."

40. Ministro Juan Antonio Tack, *Memoria del ministerio de relaciones exteriores* (Panamá: Ministero De Relaciones Exteriores., 1974), 45–46.

41. Tack, *Memoria* (1974), 45–46.

42. Juan Antonio Tack, "Texto del discurso que pronunciara el sr. ministro de relaciones exteriores en la sesión del 9 de abril de 1973 de la asamblea general de la Organización de Estados Americanos," in *Memoria del ministerio de relaciones exteriores* (Panamá: Ministerio de Relaciones Exteriores., 1973), 102.

43. Jorge Aparicio, "Informe de la oficina de relaciones con países del tercer mundo y no alineados," in *Memoria del señor ministro de relaciones exteriores* (Panama: Ministerio de Relaciones Exteriores, 1977), 16.

44. Juan Antonio Tack, *Memoria del ministerio de relaciones exteriores* (Panamá: Ministerio de Relaciones Exteriores, 1973).

45. Alfonso López Michelson, "Mi amigo Torrijos," in *Comandante de los pobres* (Madrid: Centro de Estudios Torrijistas, 1984), 127.

46. "Declaración de Panamá," *La Estrella*, March 22–24, 1975.

47. Major, *Prize Possession*, 343–46.

48. Ellsworth Bunker quoted in Hogan, *Panama Canal*, 77.

49. Jorge Conte-Porras, *La rebelión de las esfinges: Historia del movimiento estudiantil panameño* (Panama: Litho Impresora Panamá, 1977).

50. Conte-Porras, *La rebelión de las esfinges*.

51. "Universidad de Panamá: Orígenes y evolución," Universidad de Panamá online, http://www.up.ac.pa/ftp/2010/principal/libros/Libro_Or%C3%ADgenes_y_Evoluci%C3%B3n_2010.pdf.

52. Manuel De la Rosa, interview by author, Panama City, Panama, 20 October 2015.

53. Rubén Darío Murgas, interview by author, Panama City, Panama, 20 October 2015.

54. De la Rosa, interview.

55. Jerzy Grotowski, *Towards a Poor Theatre* (New York: Routledge, 2002).

56. De la Rosa, interview.

57. Francisco Herrera, interview by author, Panama City, Panama, 20 March 2016.

58. De La Rosa, interview.

59. "I Took Panama," *El Panamá América*, 4 November 2003.

60. Manuel De la Rosa, "Research Notes," Personal Collection of Manuel De la Rosa.

61. Pedro Rivera, *Cine Cine?: La memoria vencida* (Panamá: Ediciones Fotograma, 2009), 216.

62. In 1965, Glauber Rocha wrote "A estética de fome," in the Brazilian journal *Revista Civilização Brasileira*. For a translated version, see Glauber Rocha, "The Aesthetics of Hunger," trans. Burnes Hollyman and Randal Johnson, in *Twenty-Five Years of Latin American Cinema*, ed. Michael Chanan (London: British Film Institute Books, 1983), 13–14. In 1969, Julio García Espinosa's "Por un cine imperfecto" appeared in the Cuban journal *Cine Cubano*; for a translated version, see Julio García Espinosa, "For an Imperfect Cinema," trans. Julianne Burton, *Jump Cut: A Review of Contemporary Media* 5, no. 20 (1979): 24–26. Octavio Getino and Fernando Solanas, "Hacia un tercer cine," *Tricontinental* 2, no. 13 (October 1969): 107–32.

63. Rivera, *Cine Cine?*, 130.

64. Pedro Rivera, "Testimonio: Omar Torrijos y el cine panameño," *Formato 16* 5, no. 10 (October 1981): 3.

65. Julianne Burton, *Cinema and Social Change* (Austin: University of Texas Press, 1986), 10.

66. Pedro Rivera, "Informe de panamá: V. encuentro del comité de cineastas de América Latina," *Formato 16* 1, no. 2 (1976): 3.

67. Stella Calloni, "GECU internacional el grupo experimental de cine universitario: una cinematografía nacional que comienza a proyectarse hacia el mundo," *Formato 16* 1, no. 2 (1976): 85–88.

68. Fernando Martínez, interview by author, Panama City, Panama, 29 January 2015.

69. Instituto Nacional de Telecomunicaciones, *Documento histórico: tratado y anexos, Torrijos-Carter* (Panama: Instituto Nacional de Telecomunicaciones, 1977).

70. Carlos J. Núñez, "Más de doscientos cincuenta mil panameños vitorearon al líder," *Crítica*, 10 September 1977.

71. "En el gallístico desafíoío de Gallos soberanía," *Crítica*, 6 September 1977.

72. República de Panamá Tribunal Electoral, *Memoria del Plebiscito 23 de octubre de 1977* (Panamá: Contraloría General, 1978), 1.

73. Franklin Barrett, interview by author, Panama City, Panama, 16 February 2015; "Discurso del Dr. Rómulo Escobar Bethancourt en inauguración del Encuentro nacional de Abogados," *La Estrella*, 20 October 1977; "Panamá pide disculpas a EEUU," *La Estrella*, 6 October 1977.

74. "Testigo de la ONU y la OEA invita Torrijos al plebiscite," *La Estrella*, 15 September 1977.

75. "Reporte no. 2 del general Omar Torrijos," *La Estrella*, 27 September 1977; "Conmovido por la emoción el general," *Crítica*, 24 October 1977.

76. United Nations General Assembly, "Report of the Mission by the Special Representative of the Secretary-General to witness the plebiscite on the Panama Canal Treaties held in Panama on 23 October 1977," Implementation of the Declaration on the Strengthening of International Security, Official Records, 32nd sess., agenda item 50. A/32/424 (New York: UN, 1977), 3.

77. República de Panamá Tribunal Electoral, *Memoria*, 37.

78. United Nations General Assembly, "Report," 3.

79. United Nations General Assembly, "Report," 3.

14 Isolating Nicaragua's Somoza

Sandinista Diplomacy in Western Europe, 1977–1979

ELINE VAN OMMEN

On 30 October 1978, the Central America Human Rights Committee (CAHRC) hosted a public lecture at the London School of Economics (LSE).[1] Approximately two hundred people attended this event, the purpose of which was to raise awareness about the increasingly violent situation in Nicaragua and to collect money for the left-wing revolutionaries of the Frente Sandinista de Liberación Nacional (FSLN, Sandinista National Liberation Front). Ángel Barrajón, the representative of the FSLN in Western Europe, was one of the speakers. His speech, according to a critical observer from the British Foreign Office, "consisted largely of revolutionary rhetoric and denunciations of North American imperialism."[2] Apart from blaming the United States "for all Nicaragua's present trouble," the civil servant noted that Barrajón called on the British people "for moral, economic and material assistance to enable the Nicaraguan people to continue their armed struggle against the regime."[3] Barrajón specifically underlined the importance of collecting money for weapons, stating that "the victors in the conflict would be those who had the most and best arms."[4]

This event in London is just one example of the massive international campaign the Nicaraguan Sandinistas and their supporters waged in the tumultuous period leading up to the fall of the Somoza dynasty on 19 July 1979. From 1977 onward, the FSLN broadcasted its message of Third World revolution and national liberation to thousands of solidarity activists, trade unionists, human rights campaigners, priests, business leaders, politicians, students, and journalists in Europe and the Americas. While doing so, it successfully mobilized and coordinated an international support base that strengthened the FSLN's legitimacy and provided Sandinista guerrillas with material and political support to overthrow the Somoza regime. The international campaign of the FSLN in the late 1970s was a crucial breakthrough for the Nicaraguan revolutionaries, who had fruitlessly tried to topple the Somoza dictatorship since the FSLN's foundation in the early 1960s.[5]

This chapter traces the origins of this international mobilization in support of the Nicaraguan struggle against Somoza by analyzing and assessing the efforts of the FSLN to shape public opinion and the foreign policies of Western European countries in the late 1970s. It argues that the key to the Sandinistas' successful targeting of Western European audiences and politicians in the two years leading up to the 1979 Nicaraguan Revolution was their ideological flexibility and pragmatism. Indeed, the 1977 decision to start working with individuals, governments, and organizations from all across the political spectrum proved remarkably effective, as it allowed the revolutionaries to create and coordinate an international anti-Somoza movement. In Western Europe, this led to the formation of a diverse alliance in support of the Nicaraguan struggle against the Somoza dictatorship, in which the Socialist International (SI) and Third World solidarity activists played a significant role.

Intimately related to the Sandinistas' change of revolutionary strategy was the new public image—or rather images—the FSLN adopted to mobilize supporters for its cause. Although Sandinista representatives consciously tailored their revolutionary message to fit their audiences' preferences and interests, there was a notable attempt to counter the idea that the FSLN was merely a group of Cuban-backed Marxist guerrillas. To challenge the historically negative portrayal of their movement, Sandinistas campaigning in Western Europe described the FSLN as the legitimate representative of a nationalist struggle for democracy and social justice, in which Nicaraguans from all political and socioeconomic backgrounds participated. By arguing that the revolutionary war could not be framed as a conflict between East and West, as well as by continuously stressing that the FSLN would adopt a nonaligned foreign policy once in power, the revolutionaries placed themselves outside of the Cold War and inside the long tradition of Third World national liberation movements.[6] At a time when Europeans were increasingly dissatisfied with the American tendency to frame international affairs solely in Cold War terms, and Western European social democrats started to develop an active interest in the Global South, this message resonated in an important number of ways.

Adding a crucial layer to the traditionally U.S.-centered narratives of the region's history, this chapter aims to contribute to the historiography of the Cold War in Latin America by integrating Western European perspectives into the history of the Nicaraguan Revolution.[7] This is not to suggest that the United States was a marginal actor in Central America during the Cold War, but rather that to fully understand the origins and impact of the Nicaraguan Revolution, we need to adopt a more global approach. What makes the late 1970s such an intriguing period in Central American history is that, for the first time in decades, actors beyond the Western Hemisphere developed a proactive interest in the region.[8] What is more, as this chapter shows, rather than being on the receiving end of outside interventions, Nicaraguans themselves encouraged Western European involvement in Central American affairs, as they hoped European governments could pressure the Carter administration to break ties with the Somoza regime. By incorporating Central American voices and perspectives, therefore, this chapter contributes to the growing body of literature that stresses the importance of Latin American agency in shaping the region's international history.[9]

Since the FSLN's international campaign targeted a range of state and nonstate actors, this chapter draws on a wide variety of sources. In addition to drawing on diplomatic archives in Germany, the Netherlands, Britain, and the United States, it is based on private papers, the archives of solidarity committees, and interviews with activists and politicians from Western Europe and Nicaragua. Combined, these sources shed light on the complex origins and impact of the international mobilization for the Nicaraguan struggle. Due to the nature of its source base, and inspired by, among others, the works of Matthew Connelly and Lien-Hang Nguyen, this chapter combines international and transnational history.[10] Western European solidarity activists and Nicaraguan guerrillas were not part of the state, but they participated in a struggle that was inherently political and shaped by the international Cold War system: they lobbied politicians, engaged with governments, and tried to overthrow an anti-Communist regime. To capture and assess the impact of the Sandinistisas' international campaign, it is important to integrate state and nonstate perspectives and actors. Looking at either one in isolation makes little sense when trying to understand the strategies and consequences of FSLN revolutionary diplomacy. In particular, this chapter discusses how Western European governments dealt with the Sandinistas' international campaign and how state officials juggled public pressure, traditional Cold War concerns, and the transatlantic relationship.

Sandinistas Go Global

The diplomatic campaign the FSLN launched in 1977 targeted primarily Latin America, Western Europe, and North America. In the years before the 1979 revolution, the international strategy of the FSLN was still rather unorganized and often lacked clear coordination. Nevertheless, Sandinistas around the globe had a solid idea about what their organization needed: material and political support for the military struggle and the isolation of the regime of Anastasio Somoza. With this in mind, Sandinista supporters organized themselves and presented their arguments to labor organizations, church groups, solidarity committees, governments, and political parties in their host countries. In particular, the FSLN's international strategy relied on the prestige and expertise of Nicaraguan intellectuals, such as the novelist Sergio Ramírez, the priest Miguel D'Escoto, and the liberation theologian Ernesto Cardenal.

The mobilization of a broad support base for the struggle against Somoza was rooted in the revolutionary ideology of one of the three factions of the FSLN. This insurrectional faction, better known as *tercerista*, became the most powerful of the three Sandinista factions after its foundation in 1977. The *terceristas* opposed the traditional foco theory of Che Guevara, which described rural guerrilla warfare as the most effective revolutionary strategy. Rather, *terceristas* believed in urban uprisings and, crucially, a temporary alliance with the country's other opposition forces.[11] Despite this pledge for a multiclass and politically diverse alliance, the *terceristas* were still principally inspired by Marxist ideas. Daniel Ortega, one of the leaders, clearly spelled out his faction's strategy in an interview in early 1979. *Terceristas*, according to Ortega, "aim at joining together all the anti-Somoza sectors and mass organizations of the country, including sectors of the opposition bourgeoisie."[12] In doing so, he continued, "we seek to conserve the political hegemony of the FSLN and . . . avoid the possibility of the bourgeoisie becoming the political leader of an anti-Somoza front."[13] *Terceristas*, then, disagreed with the proletarian faction, led by Jaime Wheelock Román, who argued that the key to a successful revolution was the recruitment and mobilization of workers. They also clashed with Tomás Borge, one of the three founders of the FSLN, who headed the prolonged war faction. This faction believed that the struggle should take place in the mountains, not the cities, and that it would take a long time before a coalition of peasants and workers would be able to overthrow the Somoza regime.

In the late 1970s, the pragmatic *tercerista* strategy of looking beyond the radical Left to build an anti-Somoza alliance was extended to the international arena. The FSLN looked for donors other than Fidel Castro's Cuba for financial aid, logistical support, and political backing. To achieve their goal, the FSLN employed several arguments and tactics. First, Sandinista representatives argued passionately against Somoza's claim that the only two options for Nicaragua were "himself or the communists."[14] To assuage fears that Nicaragua would become a second Cuba—isolated and dependent on the Soviet Union—Sandinistas tried to move beyond the ideological bipolarity of the Cold War.[15] Instead of being aligned to either the Soviet Union or the United States, they presented the FSLN as a national liberation movement, which fought for democracy, social justice, and political pluralism. According to U.S. sources, guerrilla commander Ortega "seemed to go out of his way to stress the moderate, democratic orientation of the Frente" in a meeting with U.S. officials in Panama in June 1979.[16] In that same month, Tomás Arguello Chamorro, a Nicaraguan student who also functioned as spokesperson for the FSLN in Britain, emphasized to the British Foreign and Commonwealth Office (FCO) "that it was quite untrue that the only alternative to Somoza or Somocismo was the extreme left and that it had been untrue for many years."[17] It was completely false, Sandinistas proclaimed, to compare the FSLN with Latin America's radical armed Left. One *tercerista* was quoted in the *Washington Post* pointing out that "while other revolutionaries enter banks to assault them, we were just received in Ecuador by the president of the central bank."[18] And the famous commander Edén Pastora, then known by his guerrilla name, Comandante Cero, denied claims that Fidel Castro's Cuba was funding and influencing the FSLN. Describing a successful raid of Nicaragua's National Palace in August 1978, Pastora declared the Sandinistas "did not need anyone" as "we are intelligent, we are capable, and we are revolutionaries."[19]

While playing down their connections with Cuba and international Communism so as not to provoke opposition from anti-Communists, the FSLN simultaneously highlighted the dependency of the Somoza regime on the United States.[20] When unidentified gunmen in Managua murdered the popular editor Pedro Joaquín Chamorro in July 1978, for instance, Ernesto Cardenal accused President Carter of trying to cover up Chamorro's murder, declaring publicly "Somoza knows who killed Chamorro and if Somoza knows, Carter knows, and if he doesn't know he has not wanted to ask."[21] Invoking memories of the early twentieth century, when U.S. Marines had occupied Nicaragua for several years, the FSLN also repeatedly warned the international community of the possibility of another "North American military intervention in Nicaragua" to prevent the FSLN from taking power.[22] In private meetings with U.S. government officials, FSLN negotiators toned down their anti-imperialist rhetoric and acknowledged that Carter's efforts were "being distorted by Somoza and the media."[23] Indeed, Ramírez and D'Escoto told Richard Feinberg in 1978 that "the Sandinistas were not anti-U.S." and pointed out that in the recently released FSLN manifesto "one of the references to the U.S. was favorable."[24] They did, however, stress the U.S. responsibility for Somoza's behavior, stating "the U.S. could remove him if it wanted."[25]

To bring across the message of democracy and nonalignment in a more convincing manner, the *terceristas* employed the support of a group of Nicaraguan intellectuals, known as the Grupo de los Doce (Group of Twelve). On 21 October 1977, citing the "repressive apparatus" and "irrational violence" of the Somoza regime, this respectable group of businessmen, politicians, priests, and academics publicly endorsed the Sandinistas' armed struggle in Nicaragua's main opposition newspaper, *La Prensa*.[26] In the two years leading up to the revolution, members of Los Doce skillfully used their prestige and international network to give the FSLN's revolutionary war momentum, legitimacy, and international press coverage. Sergio Ramírez, one of the founders of the group, played a particularly important role.[27] Taking advantage of his contacts with famous Latin American writers such as Gabriel Garciá Marquez and Julio Cortázar, Ramírez was able to get in touch with several sympathetic Latin American leaders and convinced them of the "moderate tendencies in the Sandinistas."[28] Ramírez and the Group of Twelve also tried to convince the U.S. government that the FSLN was not as radical as was generally believed. In 1978, for instance, he told Feinberg that the group's new manifesto was quite "moderate."[29]

The arguments FSLN representatives used to mobilize support, however, varied greatly depending on the audience and location. When talking to potential candidates in Western Europe, the Sandinista campaign strategy was to "avoid political discussions" and instead "look for common ground."[30] For example, if an organization or individual was unlikely to directly support the guerrillas' military struggle, but could perhaps be persuaded to denounce the human rights violations of the Somoza regime, the conversation's focus was on the latter. In meeting with Western European officials, the Sandinista leadership did not ask them to recognize the FSLN as the "diplomatic representative of Nicaragua." Instead, they focused on the crimes of the Somoza dynasty and asked Western European governments to officially "break off diplomatic relations" with the regime.[31] During a visit to the West German capital, Bonn, Cardenal called for "a suspension of all German investment and credits" in Nicaragua, arguing all aid would end up in "the pockets of the Somoza family."[32]

To mobilize the public, Sandinista representatives consciously adapted the style of their campaigns to suit the domestic situation in the countries they targeted. For example, in 1978, Barrajón wrote in a letter to a comrade that, unlike the Spanish, British people had little "sympathy for armed movements."[33] Therefore, he recommended that campaigns in Britain, in order to raise money for the FSLN, should have a "humanitarian" instead of a revolutionary and political character.[34] In letters to the Foreign Office and the Nicaraguan embassy, then, the abovementioned CAHRC focused on human rights violations. They accused Somoza of "imprisoning, torturing, and killing" and denounced the "atrocities perpetuated by the National Guard against ordinary people."[35] On their flyers, the CAHRC wrote that any money they received at fundraisings events would be used "for immediate relief work" and "items such as beds, blood, blankets, field hospitals, etc."[36] Most likely, however, this money was used for military means.

The new strategy the Sandinistas launched in the late 1970s appeared to be remarkably effective, as the FSLN was increasingly seen as the vanguard of the anti-Somoza movement, mobilized a range of people for its cause, and managed to obtain financial and political support from new sources. Latin American governments, such as those of Costa Rica, Venezuela, Panama, and Mexico, financially assisted the struggle of the FSLN. And by repeatedly asking the Carter administration when the United States "would be getting rid of Somoza," these governments contributed to Somoza's isolation.[37] Other Nicaraguan opposition groups such as the Frente Amplio Opositor (FAO, Broad Opposition Front) clearly worried about the growing popularity of the FSLN. In May 1979, one FAO representative reported to the Dutch Ministry of Foreign Affairs that the FAO was currently "sandwiched" between Somoza's army on the one hand and the increasingly powerful Sandinista guerrillas on the other.[38] Somoza too, noticed this trend, and complained to the U.S. ambassador, Mauricio Solaun, about the "new legitimization of the FSLN," adding there was clearly "a problem with the growing respectability of the Communists."[39] It needs to be noted that behind the scenes the Cubans continued to play a crucial role in the Nicaraguan struggle, particularly since Fidel Castro used his negotiating skills and prestige to ease the tension between the three FSLN factions.[40]

To understand why the FSLN's new campaign was so successful, however, it is important to look deeper than the general international strategy and analyze how Sandinista diplomacy played out on the ground. Individuals, political parties, and governments in Western Europe responded to the Sandinistas' diplomatic offensive in different ways. Solidarity activists, for example, were attracted to Nicaragua for a wide variety of reasons. The FSLN was also lucky to encounter an unusually receptive Socialist

International. Furthermore, clearly not all Western European governments were entirely convinced by the Sandinistas' apparent move toward the political center.

Transnational Solidarity Activism and the FSLN

A key aspect of the FSLN's campaign was the coordination of a transnational network of solidarity activists. Solidarity committees in Latin America, Western Europe, and North America cooperated with the Sandinistas to collect money, spread information about the situation in Nicaragua, and pressure governments to break off relations with the Somoza regime. In the years before the revolution, the network of Western European solidarity activists was still small, especially when compared to the 1980s, when hundreds of committees worked to "defend" the Sandinista Revolution against the Reagan administration and the counterrevolutionaries. Nevertheless, to understand the later functioning and importance of the solidarity movement, it is important to study how this network came into being.

As noted above, Cardenal visited Europe regularly to propagate the Sandinista message. The charismatic priest gave television interviews and was regularly quoted in newspapers.[41] Cardenal was a particularly well-known figure in Western European literary circles, and his books on liberation theology and Nicaraguan history were published in German, English, and Dutch.[42] His visits to Western Europe, however, had a purpose that went beyond mere publicity; he also traveled through the region to collect money for weapons, give messages and instructions to exiled Nicaraguans, and encourage Western European activists to set up solidarity committees. As a writer, priest, and activist, Cardenal established contacts with many grassroots organizations in Britain, the Federal Republic of Germany (FRG), and the Netherlands. The flyer from the CAHRC, for example, called upon the people of Britain to raise funds for the Nicaraguan people and send them "to the account of Father Ernesto Cardenal."[43]

Due to the nature of his work, Cardenal was never in one place long enough to become the official FSLN representative in Europe. To oversee and coordinate the foundation of a Western European network of solidarity activists, then, the Sandinista leadership appointed two official representatives. One was Ángel Barrajón, a Spanish ex-priest who had lived in Nicaragua since the 1960s, but was forced to move back to Spain because of his connection to the Sandinistas. Barrajón, based in Madrid, was appointed responsibility for the solidarity movement in Southern Europe and in Great Britain in September 1978.⁴⁴ The other representative was a Nicaraguan of German descent named Enrique Schmidt Cuadra, who had worked for the FSLN but had been living in exile in West Germany since 1977.⁴⁵ Schmidt Cuadra was responsible for the functioning of the solidarity movement in Northern and Central Europe. To instruct the solidarity committees and provide up-to-date information about the situation in Nicaragua to the press, Barrajón and Schmidt received monthly faxes from the International Department of the FSLN, which was based in Costa Rica. Additionally, on multiple occasions in 1978 and 1979, Barrajón and Schmidt traveled to Costa Rica and Nicaragua, carrying with them suitcases filled with thousands of dollars, which the solidarity movement had collected for the Sandinista struggle.⁴⁶

The primary task of the two Sandinista representatives in Western Europe was to encourage people to set up local solidarity committees and to simultaneously incorporate all these individual committees into a functioning transnational structure. To achieve the latter, the FSLN organized two Western European solidarity conferences in 1978, in Madrid and Utrecht. At the conference in Utrecht, the activists decided that the solidarity movement needed national representatives as well as one central Western European secretariat. Throughout most of the 1970s and 1980s, this secretariat, initially headed by the Dutch professor Klaas Wellinga and the German author and activist Hermann Schulz, coordinated campaigns on a Western European scale. The secretariat was also responsible for communication with Nicaragua, the International Department of the FSLN, and the national coordinating committees. In the late 1970s, the office of the Nicaragua Komitee Nederland (NKN, Dutch Nicaragua Committee) in Utrecht simultaneously functioned as the headquarters of the West European solidarity movement.⁴⁷

By 1979, it was clear that the Sandinista representatives had, to a large extent, succeeded in their task. In West Germany, dozens of solidarity committees campaigned for the Sandinista cause.⁴⁸ In most Dutch university cities, too, such as Groningen, Nijmegen, Utrecht, and Wageningen, local activists managed to set up active Nicaragua solidarity committees and promote the FSLN's cause.⁴⁹ In Britain, Nicaragua groups operated in at least twenty cities, such as Birmingham, Bristol, Leeds, Bath, and Oxford.⁵⁰ Nevertheless, as the Foreign Office noted, "despite two very disturbing television documentaries" about the violent situation in Nicaragua, "the campaign has failed to capture much public interest" in the United Kingdom.⁵¹ Solidarity activists such as George Black and Ángel Barrajón admitted the solidarity

In Western Europe during the late 1970s, Nicaragua's Sandinista rebels and their allies employed the imagery and language of national liberation and Third World solidarity, particularly in Western Europe. One of the most active support networks was the Nicaragua Komitee Nederland (NKN, Dutch Nicaragua Committee) in Utrecht. A few weeks before the revolution's success in mid-1979, the NKN circulated this poster calling for Dutch people to show solidarity for Nicaragua's Frente Sandinista de Liberación Nacional (FSLN, Sandinista Front for National Liberation). The poster reads "Steun het FSLN" ("Support the FSLN"), and it contains a bank account number along with contemporary rebel photographs superimposed upon an image of 1920s Nicaraguan revolutionary Augusto Sandino, namesake of the FSLN. (Image courtesy of the International Institute of Social History, Amsterdam, BG D10/698.)

movement in Britain had a slow start, but they became increasingly skilled at raising money for the FSLN during the 1980s.[52]

Before the revolution, then, the FSLN relied mostly on committees in the Netherlands and West Germany, where the Nicaragua solidarity groups were bigger and better organized.[53] In these countries, the movement succeeded in building an anti-Somoza alliance by establishing ties with human rights organizations, church groups, political parties, labor unions, and charities. The NKN, for instance, offered a petition to Nicaraguan consul in Rotterdam, stressing the right to "self-determination" of the Nicaraguan people. Political parties across the political spectrum had signed this petition, including not only the Partij van de Arbeid (PvdA, Labour Party) and the Dutch Communist Party, but also the center right Volkspartij voor Vrijheid en Democratie (People's Party for Freedom and Democracy) and the conservative Christen-Democratisch Appél (Christian Democratic Appeal).[54] In West Germany, committees also succeeded in creating a broad opposition front, as they had a good relationship with the Sozialdemokratische Partei Deutschlands (Social Democratic Party of Germany), and received support from politicians of the Green Party and the Communist Party, as well as from Christian groups inspired by the work of Sandinista liberation theologians, such as Ernesto Cardenal.[55] By contrast, the solidarity movement in Britain was not able to bridge the political divide in the country and received support only from the Labour Party, not the Conservatives.[56] Nevertheless, the British Secretary of State, David Owen, received dozens of letters asking the British government to support the "development of a democratic government in Nicaragua."[57] These letters were sent by a range of organizations, including the British Council of Churches, constituency Labour Parties, War on Want, the Justice and Peace Group for Prisoners of Conscience, and several student unions.[58]

In some cases, the competition and distrust between members of the three Sandinista tendencies spilled over to Europe. In November 1978, a German solidarity committee, based in Göttingen, wrote in a circular letter stating that they did not recognize the authority of Schmidt Cuadra and refused to accept the solidarity committee in Wuppertal as their national representative.[59] One reason the Göttingen committee gave for refusing to accept Schmidt Cuadra's position was that he gave favorable treatment to his "friends from the proletarian tendency" of the FSLN.[60] Overall, however, the FSLN succeeded in preventing Nicaraguan divisions from having a negative impact on the functioning of the transnational solidarity network. George Black, for instance, wrote to the FSLN that the British committee was "pluralist" and had been able to "avoid ideological conflict."[61] At solidarity conferences, FSLN representatives spoke openly about the ideological differences that existed between three tendencies but were conscious to stress that they now worked together to overthrow Somoza.[62] As Ángel Barrajón wrote to Miguel Castañeda, another Sandinista, in February 1979, "The struggle against the dictatorship is just more important than problems between the tendencies, particularly when this endangers the solidarity movement."[63]

Undoubtedly, the solidarity activists' personal determination to avoid ideological disputes was inspired by their earlier experiences with the Chilean solidarity movement, which started to disintegrate in the 1970s. Since the violent overthrow of the socialist Salvador Allende in 1973, Chilean exiles in Europe had worked hard to isolate and overthrow the military regime of the anti-Communist Pinochet. The Chile movement, however, was split between the radical Movimiento de Izquierda Revolucionaria (MIR, Revolutionary Left Movement), the Chilean Communist Party, and the Chilean Socialist Party. The inability of these parties to overcome their differences prevented them from working effectively for their cause. Furthermore, their movement was increasingly split between exiles and activists who continued to believe in the value of armed struggle and those who advocated the human rights narrative as a more effective strategy to overthrow Pinochet.[64] The internal divisions and debates within their network frustrated Chilean exiles and left many of their Western European and Latin American supporters confused and disenchanted. Nicaraguan exiles, and particularly Schmidt Cuadra, who had participated in the Chile solidarity campaign in Germany, naturally did not want history to repeat itself and therefore structured the Nicaragua solidarity campaign as a broad and inclusive anti-Somoza alliance.[65]

One group the FSLN targeted successfully, then, was the radical flank of the Chilean solidarity movement. As most Chilean solidarity activists preferred human rights, exiles and activists who advocated for armed struggle, such as the supporters of the MIR, ended up frustrated and without financial resources.[66] While armed revolution seemed increasingly unlikely in Chile, Sandinista guerrillas grew stronger and gained popularity. For some activists, therefore, Nicaragua was proof that guerrilla warfare was still a valuable strategy. In the years before the revolution, these people were the most likely to take up the Sandinista cause. Klaas Wellinga for example, was the Dutch representative of the MIR before he became a founding member of the NKN.[67] And George Black and John Bevan, the leaders of

British solidarity campaign for Nicaragua, stressed that Chilean exiles from the MIR and other militant groups played a key role in the early British mobilization for the armed struggle in Nicaragua.[68]

Not all solidarity activists were intrigued by armed struggle; many were drawn to Nicaragua due to a combination of cultural and political reasons. Here, too, the FSLN was able to build on earlier efforts. Indeed, since the 1970s, to encourage European interest in Latin American history and politics, Chilean solidarity committees in Britain, the Netherlands, and West Germany organized many cultural events, such as concerts by Latin American singers, art exhibitions, film showings, and literary nights. In the Netherlands, the Kultuur Kollectief Latijns Amerika (Culture Collective Latin America), which had direct ties to the solidarity committees, translated and distributed literature, poetry, and music.[69] These cultural events had a strong political undertone. For example, most musicians who played at the solidarity concerts were part of the popular Latin American Nueva Canción (New Song) movement. Returning to a more traditional folkloric style, New Song musicians such as the Uruguayans Numa Morales and José Carbajal addressed social tensions in their region and delivered political messages to their audiences.[70]

The Nicaragua solidarity campaign successfully continued the familiar strategy of linking political messages to cultural entertainment. They translated and distributed books by Cardenal, organized art shows, and invited Central American artists to perform at concerts. The Nicaraguan singers Carlos and Luis Enrique Mejía Godoy were particularly popular. They sang about social issues and romanticized guerrilla warfare. In "Guitarra Armada," for instance, the Godoy brothers explain how make explosives, handle small arms, and disassemble and reassemble an M1 Carbine, a weapon commonly used by the National Guard. And in the song "Venancia," Luis Enrique Godoy tells the story of a young female guerrilla from the mountains, whose brother was murdered by the army for joining a labor union. Next to records, Nicaragua solidarity committees also sold copies of the Costa Rican–made movie *Nicaragua: Patria Libre o Morir* (1979), which chronicles the FSLN's military struggle against Somoza.[71]

Thus, Sandinista representatives in Western Europe were able to build on existing networks of solidarity activists and capitalized on the frustrations and tensions that existed within these organizations. When Sandinistas started to broaden their horizon in the late 1970s and looked toward Western Europe for political and financial support, they encountered many left-wing activists with a strong interest in Latin America. After many years of fruitless solidarity activism against the anti-Communist dictatorships of the Southern Cone, these activists wanted, quite simply, a win. That the FSLN was able bring together such a diverse range of supporters from the radical Left, student unions, human rights organizations, and mainstream political parties, demonstrates the success of their pragmatic strategy. It also brought them in contact with Western European social democrats.

Social Democrats and the FSLN

Sandinista leaders considered Western European politicians an important target for their diplomatic campaign, as they believed European government policy could pressure the United States into an agreement with the FSLN. Although European politicians and activists had historically not been particularly involved in Central America, developments in Nicaragua slowly started to catch their attention in 1978 and 1979. Key in this context was the role of the Socialist International, through which the FSLN established contacts with prominent social democrats, such as François Mitterand (France), Olof Palme (Sweden), and Felipe González (Spain). Most important, however, was the influence and charismatic leadership of Willy Brandt, the leader of the Social Democrat Party, who was elected leader of the SI on a platform of human rights and North-South cooperation in 1976 and shifted the focus of the SI towards Latin America.[72]

The SI, founded in 1951, was an influential international organization that brought together socialist, labor, and social democratic parties. The SI aimed to challenge the bipolarity of the Cold War by presenting Western European social democracy as a "third way"—a suitable alternative to both Soviet communism and U.S. capitalism.[73] In the 1960s and 1970s, the SI's principal focus had been on Southern Europe, and the organization played a particularly important role in the democratic transitions in Spain and Portugal. Under Willy Brandt's leadership, the SI rapidly grew in membership and in scope. Stressing the need for greater economic cooperation between rich and poor countries, the organization started to develop activities outside of Europe, and this was particularly well received in Latin America.[74] Prominent Latin American leaders such as Carlos Andrés Pérez (Venezuela), José Francisco Peña Gomez (Dominican Republic), and Daniel Oduber (Costa Rica) joined the SI; others, such as Omar Torrijos (Panama) and Leonel Brizola (Brazil) regularly attended SI meetings.[75]

This was excellent news for the FSLN. As a result of their international campaign, Sandinistas from the Grupo de los Doce had already managed to establish friendly relationships with, among others, Pérez, Torrijos, and Oduber.[76] These connections, then, provided the FSLN with a good opportunity to put Nicaragua on the SI's agenda and, consequently, to increase the international pressure on Somoza. In 1978, Cardenal and several other Sandinista representatives were invited to speak at an SI conference in Vancouver, Canada, where they received a standing ovation.[77] In the final resolution of the conference, the SI called for international solidarity with the Nicaraguan struggle against the dictatorship and, implicitly referring to the United States, urged all governments "which have so long maintained the Somoza regime in power" to end their support for the regime.[78] Furthermore, the SI adopted concrete plans to assist the Nicaraguan opposition with financial and material aid, medical assistance, and political training.[79]

Because of the support of the SI for the Nicaraguan opposition, developments in Central America shaped political debates in Western Europe. Not only did European politicians voice their concerns about the Somoza dictatorship in their parliaments, urging governments to break ties with the regime, but some also endorsed the FSLN as the representative of the Nicaraguan struggle.[80] On 20 December 1978, the British Labour Party passed a resolution in which they extended "their warmest support to all the democratic opposition forces and particularly the Sandinista National Liberation Front."[81] In the resolution, Labour firmly rejected "the idea that the only alternative to Somoza is communist takeover in Nicaragua."[82] The PvdA, too, promoted the cause of FSLN in the Netherlands, criticizing Somoza, U.S. foreign policy, and Israeli arms shipments to Nicaragua.[83] The Dutch Labour leader, Joop den Uyl, emphasizing the "responsibility" of the Carter administration, urged his government to express "sympathy" for the struggle in Nicaragua.[84] The PvdA also called on the public to financially support the FSLN, "since you have to help the Frente, and not the dictator Somoza."[85] Through its connections with left-wing politicians, the FSLN could lobby Western European governments more directly. The Nicaraguan brothers Tomás and Humberto Arguello Chamorro, for instance, arranged a secret meeting with the British Foreign Office "through a British intermediary" from the Labour Party.[86] In that meeting, the Chamorro brothers asked the British government to break relations with the Somoza regime and recognize the new Junta de Gobierno de Reconstrucción Nacional (Junta of National Reconstruction), a provisional government that the FSLN, in cooperation with other opposition groups, had established in June 1979 to give the military struggle a civilian and moderate face.[87]

Again, the international strategy of the FSLN was effective. In less than two years, the FSLN was transformed from a marginalized group of guerrillas into an organization with connections to a respectable and influential network of Latin American and Western European politicians. Apart from giving the Sandinistas an international platform to voice their concerns, this shaped government policy. As the final section of this chapter demonstrates, Western European governments in the late 1970s were suddenly forced to engage with Nicaragua, a country where they historically had little direct economic or political interest.

Government Policies and the FSLN

As developments in Nicaragua captured the public's attention, European governments in the late 1970s became increasingly critical of Somoza. As we have seen above, the general sentiment in Europe was that Somoza's dictatorial behavior was unacceptable and that Nicaragua deserved democracy. On 29 June 1979, the foreign ministers of the nine member states of the European Community (EC) joined the debate by issuing a statement declaring "their very grave concern over the disturbing developments in Nicaragua and the steadily worsening sufferings being inflicted upon the Nicaraguan people."[88] They therefore called for "an immediate halt to the conflict" so that "free elections can be held without delay."[89]

This was the first time the Nine issued a joint statement on a Central American country, a region they considered of little political, economic, and strategic importance. Britain and the Netherlands, for instance, did not have embassies in Managua and depended on their ambassadors in Costa Rica, Mexico, and Panama for relevant information on the civil war in Nicaragua. Although this irritated the British ambassador in Costa Rica, who noted in September 1978 that "under the inefficient system of nonresident representation we tend to be two jumps behind events in Nicaragua," the FCO did not feel the need to change these arrangements.[90] John Shakespeare, for example, the head of the British Mexico and Caribbean Department (MACD), stated in November 1978 that Central America was an area where Britain "could close down all our missions without serious harm to the national interest."[91] West Germany did have an embassy in Managua and, according to the British ambassador, "relatively big commercial interests" in Nicaragua.[92] Nevertheless, the German Auswärtiges Amt (Ministry of Foreign Affairs), like its European counterparts, did not feel the need to become actively involved in the region. In fact, at an Anglo-German meeting to discuss European foreign policy in 1978, the German representative noted that West Germany "had no active policy towards Latin America."[93]

It is therefore remarkable to note that, a year later, despite the lack of direct interest, the European governments became opposed to the continuation of Somoza's regime and issued a joint statement.[94] What is more, together with the Netherlands and the FRG, the British government urged the International Monetary Fund to refuse the Nicaraguan government another loan.[95] And although Britain could not do much to directly put pressure on Somoza, Owen took the symbolic measure not to accredit the new British ambassador in Costa Rica to Nicaragua.[96] Also, Owen urged the United States in February 1979 to "pull the props out from under Somoza," and even said that he was willing to take "a lead in the EEC [European Economic Community] in support of any U.S. action against Somoza."[97]

To a large extent, the rising levels of European governmental interest in Nicaragua are evidence of the impact of Sandinista diplomacy on policy. Certainly, the FCO was aware of the growing public interest in Nicaragua and took this into account when making foreign policy decisions regarding Central America. For example, the MACD recommended that Owen make the U.S. administration aware of the "strong opposition to the Somoza regime within the Labour Party and amongst liberal and human rights groups in the UK."[98] Surely, the memorandum continued, there "would be some parliamentary and public criticism of the U.S. if, in spite of Somoza's rejection of the mediation proposals, they were to continue to give him any support."[99] In addition, as parliamentarians and the public pressured governments into issuing a statement about Nicaragua, European governments could no longer remain neutral. Even if they disagreed with public opinion, they had to come up with a response to justify this. In the late 1970s, therefore, although initially reluctant to get involved the region at all, European governments had to rethink their approach to Central America, and Nicaragua.

Nevertheless, to understand how European foreign policy toward Nicaragua was subsequently shaped, we need to take note of another actor that pressured Europe to get involved in the Nicaraguan conflict. In June 1979, several European governments, including Britain and the Netherlands, received a secret letter from the American president, Jimmy Carter, asking for European support for the United States' "general objectives" in Central America, most notably "a reduction of violence and the restoration of peace in Nicaragua."[100] Specifically, Carter asked his European allies to embargo "arms shipments to both sides in the Nicaragua conflict."[101] The letter also reflected the U.S. administration's fear of a Castroite takeover in Nicaragua, stating that "Western democracies less directly involved in Central American than the United States may have special advantages in helping to develop and strengthen centrist political forces in these countries."[102]

The initial European response to Carter's letter varied from passive to negative. The British diplomat Anthony Parsons' summarized the situation as follows: "The Americans have got rather a nerve. Since the 19th century they have treated the countries of Central America like a private estate and have resolutely discouraged any other powers from developing their interests on any significant scale there. Now the structure is coming apart and they are turning to us and presumably others for help."[103] The Dutch were equally unimpressed and concluded that the Carter administration was now "relatively powerless" since an "old-school intervention" was no longer politically acceptable. Also, the Dutch rejected Carter's suggestion that they could directly assist "moderate political groups" in Nicaragua since they considered this a task for political parties, not governments.[104]

The reluctance of European governments to support Carter's objectives does not necessarily mean that they were entirely convinced by the FSLN's argument that the Nicaraguan revolutionary struggle had nothing to do with the Cold War. Although the British foreign secretary, David Owen, wanted Somoza out as soon as possible, the FCO certainly shared some of the American concern about the possibility of Soviet involvement in Central America. The British ambassador, for instance, noted that the Costa Rican security service had discovered Sandinista propaganda and arms in a house in San Jose "not far from the Soviet Embassy."[105] And, in November 1978, a representative from the Overseas Information Department (OID) attended the Nicaragua solidarity event at the LSE. In a memorandum to the FCO, the OID compared Barrajón's speech to the language of the Cuban revolutionaries and concluded that it was "not clear" whether the FSLN "would follow Cuba's pro-Soviet party organization."[106] In fact, many in the FCO agreed with Carter that it was in the European interest to "bolster the moderates" in Nicaragua in order to prevent "a Castroite takeover."[107] And the Dutch Ministry of Foreign Affairs also acknowledged that the American fears "for escalation" and the "increase of Cuban/Marxist influence" in Central America were justified.[108]

This negative response in London and The Hague to Carter's letter needs to be placed in the wider context of transatlantic relations and the outbreak of the so-called second Cold War.[109] To summarize, transatlantic relations were extremely tense during the Carter presidency; European leaders were irritated by Carter's foreign policy toward the Middle East, the Soviet Union, and East Asia, which they saw as inconsistent, indifferent to the transatlantic alliance, and inconsiderate of European Cold War concerns.[110] The German chancellor, Helmut Schmidt, in particular, was known to disagree with Jimmy Carter on a wide variety of issues, most notably the correct response to the global economic crisis and nuclear arms control.[111] Additionally, as old Cold War tensions and rivalries heightened in 1978-79 and relations between the United States and the Soviet Union crumbled once again, Western Europeans were reluctant to start this new phase of the Cold War and remained committed to the continuation of détente.[112]

The reaction to Carter's letter, therefore, is reflective of the increasing frustration of Western European governments with the Carter administration. With regard to Nicaragua, Carter's apparent shift away from his earlier policy of prioritizing human rights only confirmed what many Western Europeans leaders already believed—namely, that Carter's foreign policies were vague, inconsistent, and contradictory. Indeed, when Carter showed himself unable to integrate human rights and Cold War concerns into a coherent and effective foreign policy toward Nicaragua, Somoza, and the FSLN, he alienated his Western European allies.[113] As the British ambassador in Costa Rica wrote in 1978, "The all-important United States are still obsessed with the fear of a second Cuba and have reluctantly concluded that Somoza is the only figure who can effectively subserve their desire to keep the region quiet."[114] The British ambassador in Washington, too, noted that the United States was once again "haunted by the memory of the Cuban Revolution."[115]

Despite these tensions, both sides of the Atlantic recognized that in the global Cold War they were on the same side. Indeed, Parsons concluded his memo by writing that there was "no point in rubbing salt in the Americans' wound" since "we all share the same objectives."[116] The main point of disagreement between the United States and its European partners was on the right methods for achieving these goals. West European officials believed that Carter's apparent refusal to push Somoza out would only worsen the situation, as this would bolster the FSLN. The nine EC member states, therefore, wanted Somoza to leave Nicaragua as soon as possible. This was based on the calculation that "the longer Somoza remains, the great the chance of the extreme left wing controlling the next government of Nicaragua and of it coming under Cuban influence."[117] The best strategy to keep Nicaragua away from Cuba and the Soviet Union, they argued, was to make sure Nicaragua's new regime would feel welcomed by the West.[118]

The situation in Nicaragua soon outpaced the development of European foreign policies; on 19 July 1979, Sandinista guerrillas succeeded in overthrowing the Somoza regime and installed a new revolutionary government. It is therefore difficult to assess the exact impact of the FSLN's revolutionary diplomacy on Western European foreign policy before the 1979 revolution. Nevertheless, we can conclude that, on the level of the state, the international campaign of the FSLN, combined with pressure from the Carter administration, put Nicaraguan developments on the West European political agenda and, in doing so, forced Western European governments to look closely at a region they had since the early twentieth century largely ignored. As they did so, these governments agreed with the Sandinistas that Somoza's regime should be brought to an end. Although they were not entirely convinced of the FSLN's noble intentions, they were frustrated by the apparent complacency of the United States.

Conclusion

In tracing the Western European mobilization for Nicaragua, this chapter has placed the origins of the Sandinista Revolution in a global context. It has demonstrated that the material, political, and financial support the Sandinistas received from its Western European allies strengthened the FSLN's position, both in Nicaragua and in the international arena. The solidarity network the FSLN set up in the late 1970s continued to be a valuable asset for it throughout the 1980s. As the new U.S. president, Ronald Reagan, set out to oust the Sandinistas in 1981, the solidarity committees raised large quantities of money for the FSLN, lobbied Western European governments, and presented public opinion with a positive image of the Nicaraguan Revolution. The FSLN's pragmatic and flexible international campaign in the late 1970s was therefore not only crucial for the international isolation the Somoza regime, but also set the stage for the tumultuous decade of the 1980s.

Regarding the SI, it needs to be mentioned that, although it criticized Somoza and supported the FSLN before the 1979 Nicaraguan Revolution, its relationship with Sandinistas became problematic in the 1980s. Brandt, concerned that the Sandinistas were not genuinely committed to democracy, wrote to González in 1981 that "many of our friends are communicating anxious thoughts about the latest developments there."[119] The SI's complaints about the lack of democracy and press freedom in Nicaragua frustrated the Sandinistas, who believed Western Europeans did not understand that their revolution was under attack. Ramírez, describing the relationship of the FSLN with the SI in his memoirs, concluded that when "push came to shove" the Western European social democrats "always aligned themselves with the United States in the end. They were part of their system."[120]

Finally, this chapter has been more than an international history of the Sandinistas' revolutionary diplomacy. Apart from adding to our scholarly knowledge of the origins of the Nicaraguan revolution, the history of the FSLN's campaign in Western Europe provides us with a new window into the international history of the late 1970s. By analyzing the impact of Sandinista diplomacy, this chapter has approached the transatlantic relationship from a new perspective. The FSLN's attempt to transcend the bipolar Cold War narrative was well received by many Western Europeans, who were genuinely frustrated with what they saw as the Carter administration's indecisiveness and inability to move beyond Cold War concerns. The FSLN's campaign resonated in Western Europe in a surprising number of ways, which provide insight into the concerns, ambitions, and interests of Western European actors in the final decades of the Cold War. By analyzing Sandinista diplomacy, therefore, this chapter has aimed to complicate and contribute to our understanding of the international system of the late 1970s.

Notes

1. Flyer, Central America Human Rights Committee (hereafter CAHRC), 27 October 1978, British Foreign and Commonwealth Office (hereafter FCO) 99/187, the National Archives, London (hereafter TNA).

2. Memorandum, Mexico and Caribbean Department (hereafter MACD), 1 November 1978, FCO 99/187, TNA.

3. Memorandum, MACD, 1 November 1978.

4. Memorandum, MACD, 1 November 1978.

5. For more on the early period of the FSLN, see Mathilde Zimmerman, *Sandinista: Carlos Fonseca and the Nicaraguan Revolution* (Durham, NC: Duke University Press, 2000).

6. For more on national liberation movements and the Third World, see Vijay Prashad, *The Darker Nations: A People's History of the Third World* (New York, New Press, 2007); Odd Arne Westad, *The Global Cold War: Third World Interventions and the Making of Our Times* (Cambridge: Cambridge University Press, 2008); and Matthew Connelly, "Taking Off the Cold War Lens: Visions of North-South Conflict during the Algerian War of Independence," *American Historical Review* 105, no. 3 (2000): 739–69.

7. There has been little historical research into Central America in the 1970s and 1980s. The most recent comprehensive accounts we currently have are William LeoGrande, *Our Own Backyard: The United States in Central America, 1977–1990* (Chapel

Hill: University of North Carolina Press, 1998) and Dirk Kruijt, *Guerrillas* (London: Zed Books, 2008).

8. Several historians have written about Western European solidarity activism with Nicaragua. See, for example, Kim Christiaens, "Between Diplomacy and Solidarity: European Support Networks for Sandinista Nicaragua," *European Review of History: Revue Européenne d'Histoire* 21, no. 4 (2014): 617–34; Christian Helm, "Booming solidarity: Sandinista Nicaragua and the West German Solidarity movement in the 1980s" *European Review of History: Revue européenne d'histoire* 21, no. 4 (2014): 597–615; José Manuel Ágreda Portero and Christian Helm, "Solidaridad con la Revolución Sandinista. Comparativa de redes transnacionales: Los casos de la República Federal de Alemania y España," *Naveg@merica* 17 (2017): 1–27, https://revistas.um.es/navegamerica/article/view/271921/198661; and Eline van Ommen, "La Revolución Sandinista en los Países Bajos: Los comités de solidaridad holandeses y Nicaragua (1977–1990)," *Naveg@merica* 17 (2016): 1–22, https://revistas.um.es/navegamerica/article/view/271861/198621.

9. See, for example, Tanya Harmer, *Allende's Chile and the Inter-American Cold War* (Chapel Hill: University of North Carolina Press, 2011), and Gilbert M. Joseph and Daniela Spenser, eds., *In from the Cold: Latin America's New Encounter with the Cold War* (Durham, NC: Duke University Press, 2008).

10. See Matthew Connelly, *A Diplomatic Revolution: Algeria's Fight for Independence and the Origins of the Post–Cold War Era* (Oxford: Oxford University Press, 2002); Lien-Hang Nguyen, "Revolutionary Circuits: Towards Internationalizing America in the World," *Diplomatic History* 39, no. 3 (2015): 411–22; and Ryan M. Irwin, *Apartheid and the Unmaking of the Liberal World Order* (Oxford: Oxford University Press, 2012).

11. David Close, *Nicaragua: Navigating the Politics of Democracy* (Boulder, CO: Lynne Rienner Publishers, 2016), 67.

12. Interview with Daniel Ortega by Pedro Miranda, *Latin American Perspectives* 6, no. 1 (1979): 114–18.

13. Interview with Ortega.

14. Telegram, Washington to FCO, 14 September 1978, FCO 99/186, TNA.

15. The truth about the intellectual foundations of the FSLN probably lies in the middle. As Donald Clark Hodges argued in his *Intellectual Foundations of the Nicaraguan Revolution* (Austin: University of Texas Press, 1986), the leaders of the FSLN were part of the New Left, influenced by Augusto César Sandino's writing, liberation theology, and Marxism.

16. Doc. 234, Telegram from the Embassy in Panama to the Department of State, 28 June 1979, in *Foreign Relations of the United States* [FRUS], *1977–1980*, vol. 15, *Central America*, ed. Nathan L. Smith and Adam M. Howard (Washington, D.C.: Government Printing Office, 2017).

17. Memorandum, MACD, 29 June 1979, FCO 99/340, TNA.

18. "Nicaragua's Rebels Hobnob with Bankers," *Washington Post*, 20 December 1978.

19. "Siege Gunmen Fly out of Nicaragua," *The Times*, 25 Augustus 1978.

20. Electronic Telegram, AmEmbassy Panama to SecState, 22 March 1978, Electronic Telegrams, Department of State, Central Foreign Policy Files (hereafter DOS/CFP), U.S. National Archives and Records Administration, Access to Archival Databases (AAD), http://.aad.archives.gov/add.

21. Electronic Telegram, AmEmbassy Panama to SecState, 22 March 1978.

22. Electronic Telegram, AmEmbassy Santo Domingo to SecState, 24 November 1978, DOS/CFP.

23. Doc. 85, Memorandum of Conversation, 29 August 1978, in *FRUS, 1977–1980*, vol. 15, *Central America*, ed. Nathan L. Smith and Adam M. Howard (Washington, D.C.: Government Printing Office, 2017).

24. Doc. 85, *FRUS*.

25. Doc. 85, *FRUS*.

26. Translation of Statement by "The Twelve" as published in *La Prensa*, 21 October 1977, FCO 99/44, TNA.

27. See, for more, Stephen Henighan, *Sandino's Nation: Ernesto Cardenal and Sergio Ramírez, Writing Nicaragua, 1940–2012* (London: McGill-Queen's University Press, 2014).

28. Mexico, Colombia, Venezuela, and Panama in particular showed enthusiasm for the Sandinista cause and supported the Group of Twelve with money, material, and political backing. Doc. 98, Memorandum from Robert Pastor of the National Security Council Staff to the President's Assistant for National Security Affairs (Brzezinski) and the President's Deputy Assistant for National Security Affairs (Aaron), 18 September 1978, in *FRUS, 1977–1980*, vol. 15, *Central America*, ed. Nathan L. Smith and Adam M. Howard (Washington, D.C.: Government Printing Office, 2017).

29. Doc. 85, *FRUS*.

30. Bericht und Ergebnisse des Europäische Treffens der Nicaragua Solidaritätskomitees, May 1979, not catalogued, Informationsbüro Nicaragua Wuppertal (hereafter INW), International Institute of Social History, Amsterdam (hereafter IISH).

31. Bericht und Ergebnisse.

32. Memorandum, British Embassy San Jose to McAD, 5 December 1977, FCO 99/34, TNA.

33. Letter, Barrajón to unknown, 1 December 1978, Ángel Barrajón Private Archive, Managua (hereafter AB).

34. Letter, Barrajón to unknown.

35. Letter, CAHRC to David Owen, 8 November 1978, FCO 99/187, TNA.

36. Flyer, CAHRC, n.d., FCO 99/187, TNA. Although it is impossible to trace the money raised by the CAHRC, it is safe to assume that Ernesto Cardenal, as a representative of the FSLN, used the money to support his organization's armed struggle.

37. Doc. 95, *FRUS*.

38. Memorandum, 17 May 1979, Inventarisnummer, 11838, Ministerie van Buitenlandse Zaken Archief (Dutch Ministry of Foreign Affairs Archive), The Hague.

39. Doc. 67, Telegram from the Embassy in Nicaragua to the Department of State, 8 February 1978, in *FRUS, 1977–1980*, vol. 15, *Central America*, ed. Nathan L. Smith and Adam M. Howard (Washington, D.C.: Government Printing Office, 2017).

40. For more information on the FSLN's relationship with Cuba, see Gary Prevost, "Cuba and Nicaragua: A Special Relationship?," *Latin American Perspectives* 17, no. 3 (1990): 120–39.

41. Henighan, *Sandino's Nation*, 129; Debra Sabia, *Contradiction and Conflict: The Popular Church in Nicaragua* (Tuscaloosa: University of Alabama Press, 1997), 60.

42. See Christian Helm, "Booming Solidarity: Sandinista Nicaragua and the West German Solidarity Movement in the 1980s," *European Review of History: Revue Européenne d'Histoire* 21, no. 4 (2014): 597–615, and Jan Hansen, Christian Helm, and Frank Reichherz, eds., *Making Sense of the Americas: How Protest Related to America in the 1980s and Beyond* (Chicago: University of Chicago Press, 2015).

43. Flyer, CAHRC, n.d., FCO 99/187, TNA.

44. Author interview with Ángel Barrajón, 8 August 2016, Managua, Nicaragua.

45. Between 1967 and 1974, Schmidt Cuadra lived in West Germany, where he studied and supported the Chile solidarity movement.

46. Interview with Barrajón.

47. "Concept Dutch Viewpoint for the 10th European Conference in Brussels," 23 November 1984, Box 17, Nicaragua Komitee Nederland Archive (hereafter NKN), IISH.

48. Such as, Munster, Berlin, Wuppertal, Göttingen, Frankfurt, München, Hamburg, Bremen, and Tübingen.

49. Annual Report, 1984, Box 1, Archive Nicaragua Komitee Amsterdam, Stadsarchief, Amsterdam (hereafter NKA).

50. Letter, George Black to Doris Tijerino, 30 October 1979, Nicaragua Solidarity Campaign Archive, London (hereafter NSC).

51. Memorandum, MACD to Keith Hamylton Jones, 22 November 1978, FCO 99/188, TNA.

52. Author interview with John Bevan, London, 20 March 2017.

53. Interview with Barrajón; Bericht und Ergebnisse.

54. "Om opmars Sandinisten te stuiten: Somoza beveelt bombardement van hoofdstad Nicaragua," *Leeuwarder Courant*, 12 June 1979; "Voorzorg evacuatie uit Nicaragua: Amerikaans leger naar Costa Rica," *Nieuwsblad van het Noorden*, 10 July 1979.

55. See Helm, "Booming Solidarity."

56. Letter, George Black to Doris Tijerino, 30 October 1979.

57. Letter, Council of Churches to David Owen, 20 September 1978, FCO 99/186, TNA.

58. For these and more letters, see FCO 99/188 and FCO 99/186, TNA.

59. Circular letter, Deutsche Solidaritätskomitee mit Nikaragua Göttingen, 20 November 1978, AB.

60. Circular letter, Deutsche Solidaritätskomitee mit Nikaragua Göttingen.

61. Letter, George Black to Doris Tijerino, 30 October 1979.

62. Bericht und Ergebnisse.

63. Letter, Barrajón to Casteñada, 28 February 1979, AB.

64. See Tanya Harmer, "The View from Havana: Chilean Exiles in Cuba and Early Resistance to Chile's Dictatorship, 1973–1977," *Hispanic American Historical*

Review 96, no. 1 (2016): 109–46; Patrick William Kelly, "1973 Chilean Coup and the Origins of Transnational Human Rights Activism," *Journal of Global History* 8, no. 1 (2013): 165–86; and Mariana Perry, "With a Little Help from My Friends: The Dutch Solidarity Movement and the Chilean Struggle for Democracy," *European Review of Latin American and Caribbean Studies*, no. 101 (April 2016): 75–96.

65. Hans Hübner, Werner Ley, Otto Oetz, Klaus Schmidt, Joachim Schmidt von Schwind, Hermann Schulz, and Helmut Wendler, eds., *Enrique Presente: Enrique Schmidt Cuadra—Ein Nicaraguaner Zwischen Köln und Managua* (Cologne: Schmidt von Schwind Verlag, 2004).

66. Author interview with Klaas Wellinga and Hans Langenberg, 6 August 2014, Utrecht, The Netherlands.

67. Interview with Wellinga and Langenberg.

68. Author interview with George Black, 21 November 2017, Skype; interview with Bevan.

69. Annual Report, 1984; interview with Wellinga and Langenberg.

70. Jan Fairley, "La Nueva Canción Latinoamericana," *Bulletin of Latin American Research* 3, no. 2 (1984): 107–08.

71. Letter, George Black to Doris Tijerino, 30 October 1979.

72. For more information on the SI and Latin America, see Fernando Pedrosa, "La Internacional Socialista y la Guerra de Malvinas," *Latin American Research Review* 49, no. 2 (2014): 47–67; and Giuliano Garavini, *After Empires: European Integration, Decolonization, and the Challenge from the Global South, 1957–1986* (Oxford: Oxford University Press, 2012).

73. As quoted in Michele di Donato, "The Cold War and Socialist Identity: The Socialist International and the Italian 'Communist Question' in the 1970s," *Contemporary European History* 24, no. 2 (2015): 196.

74. Garavini, *After Empires*, 236.

75. Pedrosa, "La Internacional Socialista y la Guerra de Malvinas."

76. Pedrosa, "Redes transnacionales y partidos politicos: La Internacional Socialista en América Latina, 1951–1991," *Iberoamericana* 13, no. 49 (2013): 37.

77. Henighan, *Sandino's Nation*, 129.

78. Electronic telegram, AmConsul Vancouver to SecState, 4 November 1978, DOP/CFP; "Willy Brandt: Geweld soms nodig tegen gewelddadige regeringen," 6 November 1978, NRC.

79. Electronic telegram, AmConsul Vancouver to SecState, 4 November 1978.

80. At least nine Constituency Labour Parties wrote the British Secretary of State about the situation in Nicaragua. See FCO 99/346, TNA.

81. Resolution, Labour Party, 20 December 1978, FCO 99/346, TNA.

82. Resolution, Labour Party.

83. Handelingen Tweede Kamer (hereafter HTK), 20 November 1978, Staten Generaal Digitaal, www.statengeneraaldigitaal.nl.

84. HTK, 5 October 1978.

85. Letter, Klaas Wellinga to European Solidarity Committees, 15 June 1979, INW.

86. Memorandum, MACD, 26 June 1979, FCO 99/340, TNA.

87. Memorandum, MACD, 26 June 1979.

88. Statement of the EEC Foreign Ministers, 29 June 1979, Archive of European Integration (hereafter AEI), http://aei.pitt.edu/.

89. Statement of the EEC Foreign Ministers, 29 June 1979.

90. Letter, Hamylton Jones to MACD, 8 September 1978, FCO 99/186, TNA.

91. Memorandum, MACD, 8 November 1978, FCO 99/112, TNA.

92. See, for instance, Thomas Schoonover, *Germany and Central America: Competitive Imperialism, 1821-1921* (Tuscaloosa: University of Alabama Press, 1995); Memorandum, British Embassy San Jose to MACD, 5 December 1977, FCO 99/43, TNA.

93. Record of conversation, 2 June 1978, FCO 99/116, TNA.

94. Apart from the abovementioned joint statement, however, European states did not coordinate their foreign policies towards Nicaragua in the 1970s.

95. Brief for EPC Latin America Working Group meeting, 22 September 1978, FCO 98/187, TNA.

96. Memorandum, David Owen to MACD, 27 February 1979, FCO 99/346, TNA.

97. Brief for visit by David Owen to Washington, 31 January 1979, FCO 99/350, TNA.

98. Brief for visit by David Owen to Washington.

99. Brief for visit by David Owen to Washington.

100. Letter, Brewster to Carrington, 19 June 1979, FCO 99/266, TNA.

101. Letter, Brewster to Carrington, 19 June 1979.

102. Letter, Brewster to Carrington, 19 June 1979.

103. Letter, Parsons to MACD, 28 June 1979, FCO 99/266, TNA.

104. Memorandum, Directie Westelijk Halfrond/Noord-Amerika en Caraïbische Zone to Directie Westelijk Halfrond, 19 June 1979, Inventarisnummer 11838, BZ.

105. Letter, British Ambassador in Costa Rica Keith Hamylton Jones to MACD, 5 December 1977, FCO 99/42, TNA.

106. Memorandum, Overseas Information Department, 1 November 1978, FCO 99/187, TNA.

107. Brief for Cabinet Meeting, MACD, 18 July 1979, FCO 99/347, TNA.

108. Memorandum, Directie Westelijk Halfrond/ Noord-Amerika en Caraïbische Zone to Directie Westelijk Halfrond, 19 June 1979.

109. See Matthias Schulz and Thomas A. Schwartz, eds., *The Strained Alliance: US-European Relations from Nixon to Carter* (Cambridge: Cambridge University Press, 2009).

110. See Mark Gilbert, *Cold War Europe: The Politics of a Contested Continent* (Lanham, MD: Rowman and Littlefield, 2015).

111. See Kristina Spohr, *The Global Chancellor: Helmut Schmidt and the Reshaping of the International Order* (Oxford: Oxford University Press, 2016).

112. John W. Young, "Europe and the End of the Cold War, 1979-1989," in *The Cambridge History of the Cold War*, ed. Melvyn P. Leffler and Odd Arne Westad (Cambridge: Cambridge University Press, 2010), 289.

113. William LeoGrande, *Our Own Backyard: The United States in Central America, 1977-1992* (Chapel Hill: University of North Carolina Press, 1998); Westad, *The Global Cold War.*

114. Letter, Hamylton Jones to MACD, 28 February 1978, FCO 99/186, TNA.

115. Telegram, British Embassy in Washington to FCO, 14 September 1978, FCO 99/186, TNA.

116. Letter, Parsons to MACD, 28 June 1979, FCO 99/266, TNA.

117. Memorandum, MACD, 22 June 1979, FCO 99/340, TNA.

118. Memorandum, DWH/NC to DWH, July 1979, Inventarisnummer 11838, BZ.

119. "Letter by the President of the Socialist International, Brandt, to the Chairman of the Committee of the SI for Defence of the Revolution in Nicaragua, González," 2 June 1981, History and Public Policy Program Digital Archive, Friedrich Ebert Foundation, Archives of Social Democracy, Willy Brandt Archive, A 11.15, 21, translated by Dwight E. Langston, published in *Berliner Ausgabe*, vol. 8, Cold War International History Project e-Dossier #22, http://digitalarchive.wilsoncenter.org/document/112717.

120. Sergio Ramírez, *Adiós Muchachos: A Memoir of the Sandinista Revolution* (Durham, NC: Duke University Press, 2012), 94–95.

Conclusion

The Third World in Latin America

ODD ARNE WESTAD

The Third World came to Latin America almost as an afterthought.[1] In the early twentieth century, Latin Americans on the left and right were preoccupied with the continent's own battles and with political and intellectual agendas that echoed those in Europe. Global anticolonial resistance and decolonization had only a very limited impact on the Latin American imagination. One reason, one suspects, was racial: concepts of "whiteness" and European heritage were supremely important to Latin American elites.[2] The idea of linking the region's development to liberation movements and to the newly independent states in Asia and Africa was far from what most Latin Americans had in mind for their countries' futures.

There were of course exceptions.[3] In the Caribbean, where real decolonization struggles were on the agenda, transcontinental anticolonial solidarity was already present since the late nineteenth century. Key anticolonial leaders such as Alexander Bustamante in Jamaica, T. U. B. Butler in Trinidad, Léon Damas in Guyana, and Aimé Césaire from Martinique built on these origins to create political and intellectual movements of great force. Seeing Caribbean anticolonialism as intimately connected with anti-imperial movements elsewhere, some activists—C. L. R. James and Frantz Fanon are, in different ways, great examples—went on to play major roles in the conceptualization of the Third World during the Bandung era.[4]

Early Communism in Latin America was another link with African and Asian anticolonialism.[5] Latin American Communists travelled to the USSR or elsewhere in Europe and met people from the colonized world who had been drawn to Communism through its anti-imperialist proclamations. Some Communists from European colonies went to Latin America on behalf of the Comintern: the Indian M. N. Roy, for instance, was a cofounder of the Mexican Communist Party.[6] All over Latin America, recent immigrants from the Middle East, South Asia, and East Asia provided links to radical organizations in their countries of origin, and sometimes to their Communist parties.

The third set of early links between Latin America and wider anti-imperialism was the resistance against U.S. domination that developed from the mid-nineteenth century onward in some areas of the Western Hemisphere. Parts of the Caribbean—Haiti, the Dominican Republic, and Cuba—fall into this category, as do Central America and to some degree Mexico and Venezuela. But even in areas of Latin America that were affected by U.S. pressures only much later on, such as the countries of the Southern Cone, opposition to U.S. hegemony within the continent gave rise to a sense of Latin American solidarity beginning in the late nineteenth century.[7] As Michel Gobat has shown, the very term "Latin America" came into use as a response to the occupation of Nicaragua by U.S. freebooters in the 1850s.[8] The sense that all of independent "Latin" America had much in common in the present and not just in the past of course goes back to Bolívar and San Martín. But it was the sense of a threat from the North that reactivated solidarities among Latin Americans as duties that went beyond mere lip-service to the concept of state sovereignty.[9]

In spite of these exceptions, most of Latin America played a marginal role in the early twentieth-century struggles against imperial rule. This started to change after World War II, when U.S. power became more predominant throughout the continent and when economic interest began to link many Latin American countries to their newly independent African and Asian counterparts. In addition, the international reach of the Cuban Revolution focused the attention of both its supporters and its enemies on the newly independent countries outside of Latin America. In this sense, as the contributions to this volume show, the 1960s and 1970s were the high point of Latin America's Third World imagination.

By the time World War II ended, U.S. power and influence had become paramount throughout Latin America. U.S. economic leverage was at a historic peak, pulling most Latin American economies toward the United States in ways that often skewed domestic development or outcompeted local producers (even while most consumers welcomed access to new U.S. products). The Cold War meant an intensification of U.S. security demands vis-à-vis Latin American states and created a political climate in which most U.S. policymakers equated nationalist radicalism with global Communism. Given the role that local Communist parties had played in Latin America, especially among intellectuals, it was not difficult to find "evidence" of

Communist influence, such as motivated the U.S. interventions in Guatemala in 1954 and in the Dominican Republic in 1965.

Whereas the United States had an increasing interest in controlling and manipulating Latin American politics, Latin American governments had an interest in preserving as much of their independence and sovereignty as possible. Even right-wing dictatorships, which flourished on the continent as the Latin American ideological Cold War intensified, were wary of giving up too much autonomy to Washington, whether or not they benefited from U.S. support against domestic left-wing enemies. Throughout the twentieth century, therefore, Latin American governments tried to socialize the United States into a framework of cooperation and mutual aid, which would help elites stay in power while respecting their countries' sovereignty. By the latter part of the century, with Latin America increasingly part of the global Cold War, states across the continent started looking for international allies in their attempts to temper U.S. power through what part I of this volume refers to as varying forms of Third World nationalism.

Coming out of the nineteenth century, state leaders and diplomats from all over Latin America attempted to bind the United States to frameworks of multilateralism and international organizations.[10] Much of this work dealt with international law and commercial treaties, in which Latin American diplomats, for reasons having to do with their countries' geographical proximity to the rising United States, became experts in the early twentieth century. These discussions continued at the League of Nations, where Latin American countries held significant numerical weight in a world still ruled by empires.[11] But the Union of American Republics (commonly known as the Pan-American Union, first organized in 1890), also played a significant role, both in developing Latin American cooperation and in regulating relations between the United States and the region. Some of these early twentieth-century interactions and mechanisms underpinned not only Latin American but also U.S. approaches to later changes in the wider world, such as the creation of the United Nations and its role in the processes of decolonization.[12]

The post–World War II transformation of the Pan-American Union into the Organization of American States (OAS) also helped to set a framework for Latin America's approach to multilateralism. The U.S. intention behind this transformation was primarily anti-Communism. At the founding conference in Bogota, U.S. Secretary of State George Marshall stressed the need to discuss "foreign-inspired subversive activities directed against institutions and peace and security of American Republics."[13] Latin American leaders readily agreed, though some of them may have had a different view from the secretary of state as to what such activities may have consisted of. Throughout the Cold War, the United States often saw the OAS primarily in terms of its global contest with the Soviet Union. But in part as a result of U.S. anti-Communism, Latin American leaders were also able to continue their attempts to bind the United States into a larger regional framework.

The Cuban Revolution changed both the U.S. approach to Latin America and the Latin American approach to the United States and the world. For the Latin American Right, Fidel Castro and Che Guevara were manifestations of a Communist threat inside their own region. The revolutionaries' appeals to Latin American solidarity and their alliance with the Soviets shook traditional elites who had long been combating the Left in their own countries, but had had less patience with U.S. claims of Soviet subversion (except when it suited their need for U.S. political and military support). The revolution in Cuba and the internationalist policies of the leaders in Havana made the Latin American and U.S. Right more united in their anti-Communism than they had ever been before.[14]

At the same time, Cuba's involvement with emerging Third World regimes in postcolonial states and its support for African liberation groups created a new playing field for Latin American interaction with the rest of the globe. In spite of its increasingly tight connections with the Soviet Union, Castro's Cuba became a founding member of the Non-Aligned Movement (NAM) at its first meeting in Belgrade in 1961. Through the NAM, Cuba was able to interact closely with a number of new states and assert its vanguard role for social and political change in all of Latin America. The Cuban Communists claimed to speak for the downtrodden and poor across the continent, and they portrayed leaders elsewhere as stooges of the United States. The fact that the Cubans followed up their stated support for anticolonial liberation with concrete action, sending supplies and soldiers to fight with liberation movements, massively increased Cuba's prestige in Africa and Asia.

Having discovered the Third World through Cuba, others in Latin America proceeded to involve themselves with the growing cooperation that took place among countries in what we now often call the Global South. As shown in this volume, concepts of Third Worldism took hold among Latin American students, intellectuals, and even nationalist elites during the 1960s and 1970s. Some on the Left began to see Latin America's dependence on the United States in similar terms to Africa and Asia's dependence on the former colonial metropoles. Just as in Europe and North America, the discovery of the Third World fed into a set of new left-wing movements, often critical of the established Communist and Socialist parties, and occasionally dedicated to a guerrilla struggle for which they found inspiration in Cuba, Algeria, Vietnam, and southern Africa.

As this volume also shows, it was not only the New Left that was inspired by Third World motives. Brazil under Juscelino Kubitschek, Peru under Fernando Belaúnde, Mexico under Luis Echeverría, and Chile under Salvador Allende began to formulate policies with regard to their countries' raw materials that were similar to those of the radical states in Africa and Asia. Under pressure from declining terms of trade in the early 1970s, even some Latin American military dictatorships—foremost among them Peru, Bolivia, and Brazil—began to think in similar terms as well. Concepts developed by the Left, such as "dependency," "import substitution," and "central planning," won adherents even among some supporters of right-wing regimes. For conservative nationalists, adopting a state-centric economic model made sense in a setting where they wanted to assert their freedom of action from what they saw as undue pressures from the United States and a global economy that served its interests.[15]

This broadening of the Third World concept inevitably led to strange bedfellows in international affairs. In terms of international economic policies, many raw material producers united from 1964 in the UN-based Group of 77. Just as often, consultations among Latin American and other postcolonial regimes took place within the Non-Aligned Movement. By the time of its 1973 Algiers conference, Chile, Cuba, Peru, and Jamaica had joined the movement, with Brazil, Colombia, Ecuador, Mexico, Uruguay, and Venezuela attending as observers. Moreover, by the end of the decade, Argentina, Bolivia, Grenada, Guyana, Nicaragua, Panama, Suriname, and Trinidad had officially signed up, while Colombia, Costa Rica, and El Salvador joined the growing list of Latin American observers. At the end of the Cold War a substantial number of Latin American states, of many political shades and colors, had signed up to a movement that, twenty five years earlier, had seemed the preserve of radicals only.

As I have discussed elsewhere, this turn towards economic demands and subsequent political broadening signaled the death of the Third World as a political project.[16] Once South American military dictators (or, for that matter, Saudi princes) could be seen as partners in promoting economic development in the Global South, radical redistributive politics went out the window. What remained more or less uninterrupted were links—not least of a personal kind—that assisted in furthering global capitalist markets as the Cold War came to a close. To point out one dramatic example, the Angolan government, headed by the Movimento Popular de Liberação de Angola (People's Movement for the Liberation of Angola) and coming out of a movement for which so many revolutionary Cubans (and Angolans themselves) fought and died, is today firmly tied to global energy producers and Western oil companies.[17]

Despite its deep historical origins, Latin America's Third World phase was an enchantment that did not last long. Nonetheless, it stimulated forms of thinking about potential overseas associations that are still with us today. As Latin American economies further internationalize, links with Asia, the Middle East, and Africa will become increasingly important. The image of the heroic guerrilla has long been replaced by the dream of lucrative contracts, but the future needs of the continent require a gaze beyond the Americas and toward the same global horizons that people saw a generation or so ago.

Notes

I am grateful to Thomas Field, Vanni Pettinà, Vanessa Freije, and Tanya Harmer for comments on a draft version.

1. For a discussion, see Jason C. Parker, "'An Assembly of Peoples in Struggle': How the Cold War Made Latin America Part of the 'Third World,'" in *Internationalism, Imperialism and the Formation of the Contemporary World: The Pasts of the Present*, ed. Miguel Bandeira Jerónimo and José Pedro Monteiro (London: Palgrave Macmillan, 2018), 307–26.

2. See Alan McPherson, "Anti-Imperialist Racial Solidarity before the Cold War: Success and Failure," in this volume, or, for a more extensive discussion, Edward Eric Telles, *Pigmentocracies: Ethnicity, Race, and Color in Latin America* (Chapel Hill: University of North Carolina Press, 2014).

3. In terms of postcolonial theory, see Mabel Moraña, Enrique D. Dussel, and Carlos A. Jáuregui, eds., *Coloniality at Large: Latin America and the Postcolonial Debate* (Durham, NC: Duke University Press, 2008).

4. James and Fanon of course also provide links to earlier Caribbean anti-imperialists, such as Marcus Garvey and Hubert Harrison. Another key figure is George Padmore. See Leslie James, *George Padmore and Decolonization from Below* (London: Palgrave Macmillan, 2014).

5. For overviews of Comintern policies, see Jürgen Mothes, *Lateinamerika und der "Generalstab der Weltrevolution": Zur Lateinamerika-Politik der Komintern* (Berlin: Karl Dietz, 2010); Leonardo Guedes Henn, *A Internacional Comunista e a revolução na América Latina: Estratégias e táticas para as colônias e semicolônias (1919-1943)* (Sao Paulo: Blucher Acadêmico, 2010).

6. The Comintern's organizational lumping of Latin America together with colonial areas of the 'East' prior to 1928 may also have played a role. (I am grateful to Tanya Harmer for this observation).

7. For an overview, see Tanya Harmer and Alberto Martín Alvarez, "Introduction: Writing the History of Revolutionary Transnationalism and Militant Networks in the Americas," *Estudios Interdisciplinarios de América Latina y El Caribe* 28, no. 2 (2017): http://eial.tau.ac.il/index.php/eial/article/view/1517.

8. Michel Gobat, "The Invention of Latin America: A Transnational History of Anti-Imperialism, Democracy, and Race," *American Historical Review* 118, no. 5 (1 December 2013): 1345–75, https://doi.org/10.1093/ahr/118.5.1345.

9. See Greg Grandin, *Empire's Workshop: Latin America, the United States, and the Rise of the New Imperialism* (New York: Metropolitan Books, 2006), esp. 11–50, and, from a different perspective, Max Paul Friedman and Tom Long, "Soft Balancing in the Americas: Latin American Opposition to U.S. Intervention, 1898–1936," *International Security* 40, no. 1 (2015): 120–56.

10. See Greg Grandin, "The Liberal Traditions in the Americas: Rights, Sovereignty, and the Origins of Liberal Multilateralism," *American Historical Review* 117, no. 1 (February 2012): 68–91.

11. A good introduction is Alan McPherson and Yannick Wehrli, eds., *Beyond Geopolitics: New Histories of Latin America at the League of Nations* (Albuquerque: University of New Mexico Press, 2015).

12. See, from different perspectives, Benjamin A. Coates, *Legalist Empire: International Law and American Foreign Relations in the Early Twentieth Century* (Oxford: Oxford University Press, 2016), esp. 107–35, and Arnulf Becker Lorca, "International Law in Latin America or Latin American International Law? Rise, Fall, and Retrieval of a Tradition of Legal Thinking and Political Imagination," *Harvard International Law Journal* 47, no. 1 (2006): 283–305. See also Arnulf Becker Lorca, *Mestizo International Law: A Global Intellectual History 1842–1933* (Cambridge: Cambridge University Press, 2014; Juan Pablo Scarfi, *The Hidden History of International Law in the Americas: Empire and Legal Networks* (Oxford: Oxford University Press, 2017); and Juan Pablo Scarfi, "La emergencia de un imaginario latinoamericanista y antiestadounidense del orden hemisférico," *Revista Complutense de Historia de América* 39, no. 1 (2013): 81–104.

13. The Secretary of State to the Acting Secretary of State, 30 March 1948, *Foreign Relations of the United States, 1948*, vol. 9, *The Western Hemisphere*, 24 (Washington, DC: Government Printing Office, 1972), https://history.state.gov/historicaldocuments/frus1948v09/d10.

14. See Aldo Marchesi, *Latin America's Radical Left: Rebellion and Cold War in the Global 1960s.* (Cambridge: Cambridge University Press, 2017) and Aldo Marchesi, "Escribiendo la Guerra Fría Latinoamericana: Entre el Sur 'local' y el Norte 'global,'" *Estudos Históricos* (Rio de Janeiro) 30, no. 60 (2017): 187–202.

15. Some of the perceived Left-Right division with regard to import substitution in the Global South is of course a red herring, since it assumes that new countries are following another strategy than what the Global North had already done. See

Ha-Joon Chang, *Kicking Away the Ladder: Development Strategy in Historical Perspective* (London: Anthem, 2002).

16. See Odd Arne Westad, *The Global Cold War: Third World Interventions and the Making of Our Times* (Cambridge: Cambridge University Press, 2005).

17. Such political metamorphoses are of course not unknown in Latin America either. Think, for instance, of the former Nicaraguan revolutionary Daniel Ortega's 2000s mutation into a market-oriented Catholic nationalist.

Contributors

THOMAS C. FIELD JR. is professor of social sciences at Embry-Riddle Aeronautical University. He is author of *From Development to Dictatorship: Bolivia and the Alliance for Progress in the Kennedy Era* (2014), which won the Thomas McGann Award from the Rocky Mountain Council for Latin American Studies and was named an "Outstanding Academic Title" by the American Library Association's *Choice* magazine. He is also the recipient of the Stuart L. Bernath Article Prize and the Betty M. Unterberger Dissertation Prize, both from the Society for Historians of American Foreign Relations.

SARAH FOSS is associate professor of Latin American history at Oklahoma State University, and she earned her PhD in 2018 from Indiana University's Department of History. Her research has been generously funded by numerous grants, including, a Fulbright-Hays Doctoral Dissertation Research Fellowship and an Oklahoma Humanities Council Research Grant. Currently, she is working on a book manuscript tentatively entitled "Making the Modern Indian: Development, Indigeneity, and Citizenship in Cold War Guatemala," based on archival research and oral histories in Guatemala and the United States.

ERIC GETTIG is Deputy Chair for Western Hemisphere Area Studies at the Foreign Service Institute of the United States Department of State and adjunct professor in the School of Foreign Service at Georgetown University. He is a specialist in modern Cuban and Latin American history, the history of inter-American relations and the United States in the world, and global energy history. He received his PhD in History at Georgetown in 2017, where his dissertation, "Oil and Revolution in Cuba: Development, Nationalism, and the U.S. Energy Empire, 1902–1961" won the university's Harold N. Glassman Award for Distinguished Dissertation in the Humanities. He has published articles in *Diplomatic History* and commentary in *Foreign Affairs* and *Americas Quarterly*.

MICHELLE GETCHELL (who now goes by Michelle Paranzino) is associate professor in the Strategy and Policy Department at the U.S. Naval War College. Having earned her PhD in history at the University of Texas, Austin, Getchell focuses on U.S. foreign policy, Soviet studies, Latin America, and the international history of the Cold War. She is author of *The Cuban Missile Crisis and the Cold War* (2018), and her work has also appeared in the *Journal of Cold War Studies* and in the edited volume *Beyond the Eagle's Shadow: New Histories of Latin America's Cold War* (2013). She has been the recipient of generous funding from the Society for Historians of American Foreign Relations, the American Councils for International Education, the Dickey Center at Dartmouth College, and the Kennan Institute at the Woodrow Wilson International Center for Scholars. She is currently working on a book about Reagan's wars on drugs and communism in Latin America.

STELLA KREPP is assistant professor of Iberian and Latin American history at Bern University, Switzerland. In 2013, she received her PhD in history at the University of Cambridge with the thesis "Contending Hemispheric Narratives in the Organization of American States, 1941–1982." Her book entitled *The Decline of the Western Hemisphere: A History of Inter-American Relations from 1941 to 1990* is currently under review with Cambridge University Press. Her current project, "The Real Road to Development: The Americas between Reform, Independence, and Revolution, 1954–64," examines emerging ideas of progress, modernity, and development in Brazil, Cuba, and the British Caribbean. In 2016, she won the D.C. Watt Prize of the Transatlantic Studies Association.

ALAN McPHERSON is Thomas J. Freaney Jr. Professor of History and director of the Center for the Study of Force and Diplomacy (CENFAD) at Temple University, where he specializes in U.S. foreign relations. He is the author or editor of eleven books, including *The Invaded: How Latin Americans and Their Allies Fought and Ended U.S. Occupations* (2014), which won the Ellis W. Hawley Prize from the Organization of American Historians and two other national prizes. His latest book is *Ghosts of Sheridan Circle: How a Washington Assassination Brought Pinochet's Terror State to Justice* (2019).

EUGENIA PALIERAKI is associate professor of Latin American history at the University of Cergy-Pontoise. Her PhD dissertation on the 1960s Latin American "New Left," jointly supervised by the Pantheon-Sorbonne University and the Pontificia Universidad Católica (PUC), was published as a monograph in Chile: *¡La revolución ya viene! El MIR chileno en los años 1960* (2014). She has also published or co-authored a series of articles, book chapters, and books on the history of Latin American and European revolutions, including *Révolution: Quand les peuples font l'histoire* (2013). Her current research interests focus on political connections between Latin America and the Mediterranean.

VANNI PETTINÀ is associate professor at Ca' Foscari University of Venice. He is author of *Historia Mínima de la Guerra Fría en América Latina* and has published scholarship in the *Journal of Latin American Studies*, *Cold War History* and the *International History Review*, as well as with the Wilson Center Cold War International History Project. He has been a visiting professor at the London School of Economics, Hebrew University of Jerusalem, Jagiellonian University of Krakow and Universidad Nacional Autónoma de México. His research has received funding from the Society for Historians of American Foreign Relations, the Latin American Studies Association, the Kluge Center at the Library of Congress, the Truman Presidential Library, and SciencesPo in Paris.

TOBIAS RUPPRECHT is senior lecturer in Latin American and Caribbean history at the University of Exeter. His research deals with the role of culture and religion in international relations, contacts between the Second and Third Worlds during the

Cold War, and the history of economic ideas. He is author of *Soviet Internationalism after Stalin: Interaction and Exchange between the USSR and Latin America during the Cold War* (2015), which explores Soviet intellectual and cultural encounters with Latin America during the Global Cold War, and co-author of *1989: A Global History of Eastern Europe* (2019).

MIGUEL SERRA COELHO holds a PhD in history from the European University Institute and an MA in international relations from the University of Lisbon's Instituto Superior de Ciências Sociais e Politicas. His research focuses on the history of Portuguese decolonization. His 2018 doctoral dissertation, entitled "The Crisis of Goa between Lisbon, Rio de Janeiro, and New Delhi (1947–1961): The Transnational Destiny of an Empire," analyzes the crisis of Goa from a transnational perspective.

DAVID M. K. SHEININ is professor of history at Trent University and Académico Correspondiente of the Academia Nacional de la Historia de la República Argentina. His most recent book is the edited volume *Making Citizens in Argentina* (2017), which he co-edited with Benjamin Bryce.

CHRISTY THORNTON is an associate professor of history at New York University. She is the author of *Revolution in Development: Mexico and the Governance of the Global Economy* (University of California Press, 2021), which won the Luciano Tomassini Latin American International Relations book award from the Latin American Studies Association.

ELINE VAN OMMEN is lecturer of Contemporary History at the University of Leeds. She received her PhD in international history at the London School of Economics and Political Science. Her dissertation work, under the direction of Tanya Harmer and N. Piers Ludlow, is on the international history of the Nicaraguan Revolution between 1977 and 1990. Her project draws on a wide range of sources from Nicaragua, Europe, Cuba, and the United States, including official state documents and the archives of transnational movements.

MIRIAM ELIZABETH VILLANUEVA is instructor in history at Phillips Academy. In 2017, she received her PhD in Latin American history from Texas Christian University. Her work concerns the legitimacy of authoritarian regimes in Latin America during the Cold War, particularly focusing on the Panamanian military's cultural and international policy for long-term governance.

ODD ARNE WESTAD is Elihu Professor of History and Global Affairs at Yale University. He is an expert on contemporary international history and on the eastern Asian region. Westad won the Bancroft Prize for *The Global Cold War: Third World Interventions and the Making of Our Times* (2005), which has been translated into fifteen languages. He served as general editor for the three-volume *Cambridge History of the Cold War* (2010) and is author of the *Penguin History of the World* (2012), now in its sixth edition, and *Restless Empire: China and the World since 1750*, which won the Asia Society's book award for 2013. His most recent book is *The Cold War: A World History* (2017).

Index

Note: Illustrations and tables are indicated by page numbers in *italics*.

AAPSO. *See* Afro-Asian Peoples Solidarity Organization (AAPSO)
Aboites Aguilar, Luis, 87
Afghanistan, 19, 120n20, 165–67, 266n21, 325
African Americans: Haiti and, 204–6, 211–13; Wilsonian ideals and, 306
Afro-Asian Latin American Peoples' Solidarity Organization (OSPAAAL), 6, 155, *156*, 159, 263
Afro-Asian movement, 1–3, 113–14
Afro-Asian Peoples Solidarity Organization (AAPSO), 113–14, 152, 155, 161, 164, 166, 262–63
agriculture, 80, 138–40, 244, 297n55, 309
Agüero, Carlos, 335n45
Ahumada, Adolfo, 354
Aja Castro, Ramon, 62
Aleman, Miguel, 77
Alencar, José Cochrane de, 31–32, 34–36
Alessandri, Jorge, 286
Alfaro, Ricardo J., 347
Algeria, 120n20, 155, 190; Brazil and, 110; Chile and, 274–93, 299n76; Cuba and, 245; equidistance and, 164; nationalism in, 277; Third Worldism and, 94
Algiers Charter, 320
Alianza de Sociedades Locales Colectivas, 87
Allende, Salvador, 2, 163, 274, 277, 286–87, 290–91, 293n1, 378, 398
Alliance for Progress, 45, 53–54, 57, 60, 105, 130, 349

Almeyda, Clodomiro, 298n69
Alvarez, Alejandro, 305
Amado, Jorge, 223–24, 226, 229
Ampuero, Raúl, 279
Anger-Egg, Ezequiel, 133
Angola, 4, 110, 165, 255, 399
Anti-Imperialist League, 205
anti-Westernism, 116, 222, 226–35
Arafat, Yasser, 2
Arana Osorio, Carlos, 132, 135
Araújo Castro, João Augusto, 110
Árbenz, Jacobo, 124, 142n6
Arévalo, Juan José, 129–30, 144n41
Argentina, 3; automobile production in, 174–75, 178–79, 182; beryllium in, 182; Brazil and, 174–75; Chile and, 186; China and, 181, 184, 190–91; Coca-Cola in, 182; Communism in, 183–86; coup in, 176; Cuba and, 174–76; developmentalism in, 29; Dr. Spock in, 178; Egypt and, 192–93; foreign policy of, 180–85; Guatemala and, 181, 183–84; India and, 34; Korean War and, 181, 183; marginalization of, 179; Middle East and, 185; nationalism in, 4, 175–77, 193; Non-Aligned Movement and, 116, 176, 190; nuclear policy and, 186–91; as outside of Cold War framework, 174; Panama and, 354; Peru and, 189–90; South Africa and, 189–90; Soviet Union and, 36, 79, 177, 190–92; Syria and, 190–91; Third World and, 186–87; Turismo Carretera in, 178–79; UFO culture in, 179;

Argentina (cont.)
  United States and, 174–89; Vietnam and, 184–85
Argentine Trade Promotion Institute (IAPI), 182
Arguello Chamorro, Tomás, 371
Arias, Arnulfo, 348
Arias Calderón, Jaime, 354
Armony, Ariel C., 179–80
Asturias, Miguel Angel, 226
Australia, 266n21
Austria, 301
automobile production, 174–75, 178–79, 182

Bandung Conference, 3, 6, 106, 108, 222, 316. *See also* Non-Aligned Movement (NAM)
Barberis, Victor, 284
Barrajón, Ángel, 367, 373–75, 378
Batista, Fulgencio, 148
Bay of Pigs invasion, 148, 152, 252
Bazykin, Vladimir, 80–81, 83–85, 91
Belaúnde, Fernando, 398
Belgrade Conference, 37, 46, 66, 79, 94, 106–12, *112*, 152, 155, 254–56, 304. *See also* Non-Aligned Movement (NAM)
Belize, 173n86, 211
Bellegarde, Dantès, 203, 209–10
Benavente, Saulo, 226
Ben Bella, Ahmed, 9, 279, 284, 286, 289
Benítez, Fernando, 231–32
Benkhedda, Benyoussef, 280, 282
Benton, Lauren, 3
Berle, Adolf, 130, 313, 336n57
beryllium, 182
Betancourt, Rómulo, 250, 257
Beteta, Ramón, 315
Bevan, John, 378–79
Bin Quej, Rogelio, 137
Birla, B. M., 24
Black, George, 375, 377–79
Blackwood, James, 204
Bockman, Johanna, 308, 341n126
Bolívar, Simón, 351

Bolivia: agriculture in, 297n55; aid to, from United States, 44, 51, 57; CIA and, 50, 58–60, 63–64; Communism in, 33–34, 44, 46, 48–55, 57–66, 160; Cuba and, 45, 48–57, 59, 61–62, 65–66; Czechoslovakia and, 45–48, 50, 53, 57–58, 62, 64–65; Guevara and, 160–61, 264; nationalism in, 33–34, 44, 47–49, 51, 64–66, 160; Non-Aligned Movement and, 54; nonalignment and, 48–54; Peru and, 45, 62–63; Soviet Union and, 60–61, 230–31; World Youth Festival and, 227
Bolshevik Revolution, 162
Borge, Tomás, 370
Borno, Louis, 205, 209, 211
Boumediene, Houari, 288–91
Bouteflika, Abdel Aziz, 32, 284I
Brandt, Willy, 380
Brandt Commission Report, 301
Brazil: Afro-Asianism and, 113–14; Argentina and, 174–75; Congress of Underdeveloped Countries and, 248–51; Cuba and, 113–14; Czechoslovakia and, 103; Eastern Europe and, 46; foreign policy of, 100; foreign policy of, after World War II, 18–19; foreign policy of, as independent, 103–5; foreign policy of, under Kubitschek, 29–30; Hungary and, 103; India and, 17, 19–37; nationalism in, 26–27, 36; Non-Aligned Movement and, 100–101, 103–12, *112*, 114–17; Operação Pan Americana (Operation Pan America) and, 29–30, 35, 249–50; Poland and, 103; presidencies of, during Cold War, 17; Soviet Union and, 103; Third World and, 101–3; Yugoslavia and, 108–9
Bretton Woods system, 301, 314–16, 326
Brezhnev, Leonid, 161, 225, 235
Briggs, Cecil, 204
British Guiana, 255, 260–61
Brizola, Leonel, 380

Bunau-Varilla, Phillipe-Jean, 346
Bunker, Ellsworth, 354
Burke, Roland, 305-6
Burma, 120n20, 266n21
Burtin, Julianne, 357
Bustamante, Alexander, 394
Butler, T. U. B., 394
Byrne, Jeffrey, 6, 94, 101, 276

Cairo Conference, 46, 79, 104, 114-17, 151, 154-55, 252, 261-62. *See also* Non-Aligned Movement (NAM)
Cairo Declaration, 320
Calle, La (newspaper), 48
Calvimontes, Jorge, 50, 227
Calvo, Carlos, 305
Calvo doctrine, 308
Cambodia, 120n20, 185, 266n21
Canada, 90, 186-90, 193-94, 257
Canal Ramírez, Gonzalo, 234-35
Caputo, Dante, 192
Carbajal, José, 379
Carballido, Emilio, 227
Cardenal, Ernesto, 370-71, 374, 377
Cárdenas, Héctor, 96n6
Cárdenas, Lázaro, 86-87, 92
Carlson, Ingvar, 191
Carlucci, Frank, 192
Carranza, María Mercedes, 237
Carranza, Venustiano, 309-10, 325
Carranza doctrine, 308
Carta Echeverría. See Charter of Economic Rights and Duties of States
Carter, Jimmy, 343, 345, 352, 360, 371, 373, 383-85
Castañeda, Jorge, 222, 316, 320, 324
Castañeda, Miguel, 378
Castillero, Enoch, 358
Castillo Armas, Carlos, 127-28
Castro, Fidel, 2, 9, 148, 150-51, 153, 157-59, 163-65, 176, 263. *See also* Cuba
Castro, Raúl, 263
Catholicism, 232-35

CCI. *See* Central Campesina Independiente (CCI, Independent Peasant Center)
Central Campesina Independiente (CCI, Independent Peasant Center), 87
Central Intelligence Agency (CIA): Bolivia and, 50, 58-60, 63-64; Cuba and, 47, 269n67, 318; Guatemala and, 124, 127; Mexican-Soviet relations and, 81; Soviet Union and, 81
Césaire, Aimé, 394
Cestero, Tulio, 201-2, 207
Ceylon, 30, 120n20, 243
Chakravarti, Anaya, 17
Chamorro, Pedro Joaquín, 371
Charter of Economic Rights and Duties of States, 301-3, 307-8, 312, 316, 318-26
Chauvet, Ernest, 204
Chevrolet Argentina, 174, 178-79
Chiari, Roberto, 347
Chile, 2, 34, 186, 227; agriculture in, 297n55; Algeria and, 274-93, 299n76; Arab community in, 278-79; Committee for the Self-Determination of Algeria, 278-81; Communism in, 378; coup in, 293n1; Cuba and, 284-85; Mexico and, 310-11; Nicaragua and, 378; Soviet Union and, 163, 287; Trotskyites and, 279-80
China, 149; Argentina and, 181, 184, 190-91; Brazil and, 20, 26; Charter of Economic Rights and Duties of States and, 321; Cuba and, 153, 155, 157, 164-65; Non-Aligned Movement and, 258; Soviet Union and, 6-7, 113
Chirac, Jacques, 190
Christiansen, Samantha, 293n6
cinema, 357-58, *359*
Clarke, Ellis, 117
CNC. *See* Confederación Nacional Campesina (CNC; National Confederation of Peasants)
Coca-Cola, 182

Index 409

Colombia, 155, 162, 226, 233–34, 250, 345–46, 354
colonialism, 253; Brazil and, 19, 28–31, 37, 110; Cuba and, 154, 161, 163–64, 248, 253, 255, 261; Mexico and, 318; Non-Aligned Movement and, 117; Panama and, 345; Puerto Rico and, 155; Soviet Union and, 81. *See also* neocolonialism
Comarca Lagunera, 87
Committee for the Self-Determination of Algeria, 278–81
Communism: in Argentina, 183–86; in Bolivia, 33–34, 44, 46, 48–55, 57–66, 160; in Chile, 378; in Guatemala, 127; in India, 20, 26; Latin American, 155; Latin American perceptions of, 221; in Mexico, 91, 394; in Peru, 232. *See also* Marxism
Communist Second World, 49
Cóndor II rocket, 192–93
Confederación General de Trabajo, 175
Confederación Nacional Campesina (CNC; National Confederation of Peasants), 87
Congo, 110, 115
Congreso Anfictiónico de Panamá (Amphictyonic Congress of Panama), 351
Congress of Underdeveloped Countries, 243, 246–52
Connelly, Matthew, 369
Conrad, Sebastian, 304
Cortázar, Julio, 226, 372
Cosse, Isabella, 178
Costa Rica, 121n48, 173n86, 210, 225, 311, 331n21, 354, 373, 375, 379, 383–85
Counterinsurgency (CI) Watch List, 61
coup: in Argentina, 176; in Chile, 293n1; in Guatemala, 127; in Panama, 343, 348–50
Crumb, Robert (R.), 178
Cuadernos del Tercer Mundo (news network), 1

Cuba: Afro-Asian Peoples Solidarity Organization and, 262–63; Algeria and, 284–85; Argentina and, 174–76; Bay of Pigs invasion in, 148, 152; Bolivia and, 45, 47–56, 59, 61–62, 65–66; Brazil and, 105, 113–14; Chile and, 284–85; China and, 149, 153; CIA and, 47, 269n67, 318; Congress of Underdeveloped Countries and, 243, 246–52; "export revolution" efforts by, 241; films from, 357; Guatemala and, 129; guerilla warfare and, 154; India and, 246–47; nationalism in, 252; Nicaragua and, 368, 370–71; Non-Aligned Movement and, 148–52, 155–57, 163–66, 242, 252–62, 397; Prague Spring and, 162; Soviet Union and, 149–54, 157–67, 227–28; Third World and, 150–51; United States and, 148–49, 242, 245–48, 255, 259–62, 269n67, 395; Venezuela and, 116, 162, 260–61; Vietnam and, 154
Cuban Missile Crisis, 148, 154, 167, 257–59
Cuban Revolution, 49, 53, 56–57, 75, 116, 129, 148, 150–51, 202
Cuban-Soviet Institute, 227
cultural agencies, universal, 354–60, 359
Cunha, Paulo, 27
Czechoslovakia, 33; Bolivia and, 45–48, 50, 53, 57–59, 62–65; Brazil and, 103; Guatemala and, 142n6; Mexico and, 87; Soviet Union and, 222, 225–26, 236

Dahomey, 30
Dalton, Roque, 232
Damas, Léon, 394
Dangond, Alberto, 233–34
Danza inmóvil, La (Scorza), 232
Danzós Palomino, Ramón, 87, 89
Dávila, Jerry, 17
Dawes Plan, 335n49
de Castro, Josué, 244

De Gaulle, Charles, 193
Departamento de Expresiones Artística (DEXA, Department of Artistic Expression), 344–45, 354–57
dependencia, 6
desarrollismo, 6
DESCOM. *See* Program of Community Development (DESCOM)
D'Escoto, Miguel, 370–72
developmentalism, 6, 10, 14n6, 29, 44, 66, 186, 302, 309, 318
DEXA. *See* Departamento de Expresiones Artística (DEXA, Department of Artistic Expression)
Díaz Ordaz, Gustavo, 317
Dominican Republic, 201–2, 206–8, 210–12, 215n27, 395–96
Dona, Pedro, 226
Donoghue, Michael, 346, 349
Dorticós, Osvaldo, 9, 111, 152, 162, 255, 260–61, 263, 269n67, 271n83, 272n100
Drago doctrine, 308, 312
Du Bois, W. E. B., 205
Dulles, John Foster, 32
Dumbarton Oaks, 316
Dutra, Eurico Gaspar, 17–18

Echeverría Álvarez, Luís, 2, 74, 93–94, 301, 318–19, 321, 323–24, 338n83, 340n101, 398
ECLA. *See* Economic Commission on Latin America (ECLA)
Economic Commission on Latin America (ECLA), 307, 317
Ecuador, 46, 109, 111, 133, 135, 152, 157, 227, 250, 254, 321, 371, 398
Egypt, 6, 120n20, 192–93, 251, 279, 352. *See also* Nasser, Gamal Abdel
Eisenhower, Dwight D., 346
Ejercito Revolucionario del Pueblo, 175
Ejidal Bank, 88–90
El-Sebai, Youssef, 263
entryism, 279

equidistance, 107, 164–66, 184, 256, 259, 261
Escobar Bethancourt, Rómulo, 354
Espinosa de los Monteros, Antonio, 314–15
Estrada Doctrine, 308, 333n36
Ethiopia, 120n20, 210, 266n21
European Common Market, 103
Exchange Stabilization Fund, 314
experiência democrática, 18

Falcão, Idelfonso, 23–25, 27–29, 31–33, 41n38
Fangio, Juan Manuel, 179
Fanon, Frantz, 293n7, 394
FAO. *See* Frente Amplio Opositor (FAO, Broad Opposition Front)
Felitti, Karina, 178
Fellman Velarde, José, 54–55
FER-29. *See* Revolutionary Student Front (Frente Estudiantil Revolucionario, FER-29)
fertilizers, 139–40
Filho, João Café, 17–18
film, 357–58, *359*
Filós-Hines Treaty, 346
First World modernization theory, 124–26, 129–30
Fletcher, Henry, 311, 335n47
FLN. *See* Front de Libération Nationale (FLN, National Liberation Front)
Fonseca, Carlos, 229–31
food production, 80, 138–40, 244, 297n55, 309
Ford, Gerald, 323–24
Ford Argentina, 174, 178–79
France, 110, 190, 194, 203, 231, 283, 324
Frank, Andre Gunder, 222
Frazão, Sérgio Armando, 117
Frei, Eduardo, 288
Frente Amplio Opositor (FAO, Broad Opposition Front), 373
Frente Nacionalista, 251

Index   411

Frente Sandinista de Liberación Nacional (FSLN, Sandinista National Liberation Front), 367–86, *376*, 389n28. *See also* Nicaragua
Freyre, Gilberto, 31, 110
Frondizi, Arturo, 29, 36, 317
Front de Libération Nationale (FLN, National Liberation Front), 277, 282, 290, 292
FSLN. *See* Frente Sandinista de Liberación Nacional (FSLN, Sandinista National Liberation Front)
Fuentes, Carlos, 225–26, 230

Gaddafi, Muammar, 2
Gagarin, Yuri, 229
Galarce, Alejandro A., 184
Galich, Manuel, 183
Gálvez, Oscar Alfredo, 179
Gálvez, William, 247
Gamboa, Alberto, 274
Gandhi, Indira, 37, 191
Gandhi, Mahatma, 19, 25
García Espinosa, Julio, 357
García Márquez, Gabriel, 225–27, 230, 372
García Moritán, Roberto, 192
García Robles, Alfonso, 339n88
Garvey, Marcus, 208–9
GATT. *See* General Agreement on Tariffs and Trade (GATT)
GECU. *See* Grupo Experimental Cine Universitario (GECU)
Gelman, Juan, 226
General Agreement on Tariffs and Trade (GATT), 316
General Motors Argentina, 182
Geography of Hunger, The (de Castro), 244
German Democratic Republic, 30, 33, 103, 256
Germany, Federal Republic of, 29, 324, 374–75, 377, 382–83, 385
Getchell, Michelle, 76
Getino, Octavio, 357

Ghana, 6, 30, 54, 105, 120n20, 247, 251, 259, *263*, 266n21
Ghioldi, Rodolfo, 228
Gilardi, Gilardo, 226
Gilbert, Gregorio Urbano, 210–11
Gil Gilbert, Enrique, 223
Gilman, Nils, 341n122
Global Cold War, The (Westad), 2–3
Global South, 2–3, 6–7; anti-imperialism and, 67; imaginary, 6–7; Panama and, 350, 352–54, 357; Soviet Union and, 164; as term, 293n6; Third Worldism and, 6; United States and, 124. *See also* Third World
Goa, 17, 23, 26–28, 31–32, 38
Gobat, Michel, 395
Godoy, Carlos, 379
Godoy, Luis, 379
Goebel, Michael, 213
Gonzales, José Luis, 223
González, Felipe, 380
González Gálvez, Sergio, 320
Gonzaléz Revilla, Nicolás, 354
González Rostgaard, Alfredo, *156*
Goulart, João, 38, 100–101, 113
Gouvernement Provisionel de la République Algérienne (GPRA; Provisional Government of the Algerian Republic), 280
Governing the World: The History of an Idea (Mazower), 305
GPRA. *See* Gouvernement Provisionel de la République Algérienne (GPRA; Provisional Government of the Algerian Republic)
Grandin, Greg, 306
Greece, 191, 246
"Green Revolution," 138
Grimaud, Nicole, 291
Gromyko, A., 83
Gromyko, Andrei, 161
Grotowski, Jerzy, 356
Group of 77 (G-77), 118, 163, 241, 260, 271n92, 308, 324

Group of Six, 191–92
Group of Twelve, 372, 380–81, 389n28
Grupo Experimental Cine Universitario (GECU), 354–55, 357–60, *359*
Guatemala: Argentina and, 181, 183–84; CIA and, 124, 127; coup in, 127; Cuba and, 129; Czechoslovakia and, 142n6; development in, 125–40; freedom fighters and, Communist support of, 155; human development indicators in, 123; Movimiento Nacionalista Revolucionario and, 49; MR-13 and, 129–30; Non-Aligned Movement and, 127–28; Program of Community Development (DESCOM) in, 131–40; Tactic community in, 126, 135–39; United States and, 396
guerilla warfare, 154, 318
Guevara, Ernesto "Che," 1, *8–9*, *112*, 150–51, 154, 157, 160–66, 243–44, 264, 307
Guillén, Nicolás, 223–24, 226
Guinea, 30, 120n20, 247, 251, 255, 266n21
Gumucio, Alfonso, 59
Gutiérrez, Joaquín, 225
Guyana, 253, 321, 352, 394, 398

Haiti, 155, 201–13, 395
Hale, Charles, 119n11
Harding, Warren G., 310
Havana Conference, 165, 250, 307
Hay, John, 346
Haya de la Torre, Víctor, 224, 232
Hay-Bunau-Varilla Treaty, 343, 346
Hellman, Lillian, 178
Herédia, Jaime, 27
Hill, Robert C., 176
histoire croisée, 275
Hodges, Donald Clark, 388n15
Hofgren, Daniel, 349
Holanda, Nestor de, 235
Honduras, 155, 211
Hoover, Herbert, 211
Hudicourt, Pierre, 210

Hughes, Charles Evans, 205, 212
Hughes, Langston, 204, 207
Hull-Alfaro Treaty, 346
Hungary: Brazil and, 30, 103; Soviet Union and, 222, 224–25, 229–30, 236
Hunton, Addie, 204
Hurston, Zora Neale, 204

IAB. *See* Inter-American Bank (IAB)
IAPI. *See* Argentine Trade Promotion Institute (IAPI)
Ibáñez del Camp, Carlos, 279
ICWDR. *See* International Council of Women of the Darker Races (ICWDR)
IDB. *See* Inter-American Development Bank (IDB)
illiteracy, 80, 123, 131, 229, 237
IMF. *See* International Monetary Fund (IMF)
import substitution, 75, 77, 316–17, 398, 400n15
India, 5–6, 54; Brazil and, 17, 19–37; Communism in, 20, 26; Cuba and, 246–47; equidistance and, 164; Non-Aligned Movement and, 269n63; nuclear explosion in, 188–89; overpopulation in, 21–22; Third Worldism in, 94
Indonesia, 30, 54, 105, 120n20, 151, 266n21
In From the Cold: Latin America's New Encounter with the Cold War (Joseph & Spenser, eds.), 3, 179
Ingersoll, Robert, 324
Inman, Samuel Guy, 334n45
Inter-American Bank (IAB), 312–14, 316, 326, 337n68
Inter-American Conference, 183, 302, 310–12
Inter-American Development Bank (IDB), 51, 317
Inter-American Peace Force, 158
Inter-American Rio Treaty, 36
Inter-American System, 30, 46, 48, 55, 104–5, 107, 112, 114, 116–17, 157, 242

Index   413

Inter-American Treaty of Reciprocal Assistance, 18, 31–32, 183
International Council of Women of the Darker Races (ICWDR), 204
International Institute for Rural Reconstruction, 134
Internationalism in the Age of Nationalism (Sluga), 305
International League of the Darker Peoples, 204
International Monetary Fund (IMF), 49, 314–15, 317, 321, 325, 340n104
International Trade Organization (ITO), 315–16
Iran, 135, 266n21
Iraq, 243, 266n21
Ireland, 266n21
Israel, 184, 353, 361, 381. *See also* Palestine
ITO. *See* International Trade Organization (ITO)
Ivory Coast, 30, 247

Jaén Suarez, Omar, 343–44
Jamaica, 116–17, 154, 394, 398
James, C. L. R., 394
Jansen, G. H., 120n20, 253
Jaudel, Pierre, 335n49
Johnson, James Weldon, 205–6
Johnson, Lyndon, 160, 348
Jolibois Fils, Joseph, 210
Jordan, 266n21
Joseph, Gilbert M., 179
Junta de Gobierno de Reconstrucción Nacional (Junta of National Reconstruction), 381

Karque, Luis, 299n71
Kazakhstan, 124, 227–29, 236
Kelley, Robin, 213
Kelsey, Carl, 203
Kennan, George F., 108, 148–49
Kennedy, John F., 45, 53–54, 57, 61, 108, 257–58, 349

Keynes, John Maynard, 314, 335n49
Khachaturian, Aram, 227
Khrushchev, Nikita, 73, 128, 152–53, 224–25, 227–30, 252, 257–58
Kissinger, Henry, 322–25, 353
Klein & Saks (consulting firm), 128
Korean War, 18, 79, 181, 183–84
Kosygin, Alexei, 158, 160
Krasner, Stephen, 332n35
Kreisky, Bruno, 301
Kubitschek, Juscelino, 17, 29–37, 102, 249–50, 317, 398
Kutejščikova, Vera, 225

Lafer, Horacio, 248
Laleau, Léon, 204
Laos, 120n20, 185, 253, 266n21
Lara, Jesús, 230–31
Last Utopia, The (Moyn), 304
Latin American Conference for National Sovereignty, Economic Emancipation and Peace, 113
Latin American Free Trade Association, 78, 317
Latin Americanization, 102, 179
Latin American Solidarity Organization (OLAS), 159–60, 252
League of Nations, 18, 209, 303, 305, 309–10, 331n21, 333n35, 334n45, 396
Lebanon, 120n20, 278
Lechuga, Carlos, 247, 250
Léger, Georges, 204
Lenin, Vladimir, 235
León, Carlos Augusto, 226
Liberia, 266n21
Libya, 4, 164, 266n21
Linowitz, Sol, 354
literacy, 18, 21, 80, 123, 131, 208, 229, 237
Loaeza, Soledad, 77
Logan, Rayford, 212–13
Long, Tom, 343
Lopérfido, Dario, 178
López, Carlos, 139

López Herrate, Mariano, 136–37
López Mateos, Adolfo, 29, 73, 76, 77–80, 83–85, 93, 95
López Michaelson, Alfonso, 354
López Portillo, José, 301

Magaelhães, Juracy, 115
Magloire, Clément, 204
Malay Federation, 266n21
Malaysia, 30
Malenbaum, Wilfred, 134
Mali, 109, 120n20, 256, 262
Malraux, André, 281
Mancisidor, José, 223
Mandela, Nelson, 2
Manela, Erez, 303, 306
Mao Zedong, 153
Marchesi, Aldo, 3
Márquez Sterling, Manuel, 334n45
Marrero, Leví, 247–48, 250
Marshall, George, 396
Marshall, Napoleon, 204
Marshall Plan, 29, 319
Martínez, José de Jesús, 356–57
Martinique, 293n7, 394
Marxism, 12, 44, 55, 61–62, 149, 163, 221, 230–31, 262, 263, 282, 368, 370, 384, 388n15. *See also* Communism
Masani, Minocher Rustom, 19
Mauritania, 30
Maw, Carlyle, 323
Maximilian Alliance, 87
Mazower, Mark, 305, 330n18, 331n19–331n20
McPherson, Alan, 363n15
Medina Silva, Pedro, 263
Mello Franco, Caio de, 20–21
Melo Franco, Afrânio de, 111
Méndez Montenegro, Julio, 132, 144n41
Méndez Montenegro, Mario, 144n34
Mendoza Berrueto, Eliseo, 339n88
Menon, Krishna, 27–28
"Mexican miracle," 77

Mexican Revolution, 44, 302, 309, 325, 327
Mexico: Charter of Economic Rights and Duties of States and, 302–3, 320–26; Chile and, 310–11; Communism in, 91, 394; Congress of Underdeveloped Countries and, 250; developmentalism in, 29, 77–78; diversification in, 77–80; foreign relations of, 79; import substitution in, 77; India and, 21; Indian diplomatic offices in, 33; Inter-American Bank and, 312–14; international order and, 308–9; nationalism in, 333n39; nationalization of economy in, 78; nationalization of petroleum industry in, 308; New International Economic Order and, 301–4, 322–23, 326–27; Nicaragua and, 373; Soviet Union and, 73–74, 76, 77–95; Third Worldism and, 74–75; United States and, 80–81, 310–11, 317–18, 323–25; World Youth Festival and, 227
Mi diario en la Unión Soviética. Un conservador en la U.R.S.S. (Dangond), 234
Mikoyan, Anastas, 73, 76, 77, 81–82, 84, 227–28
Mirault, Joseph, 204
Mitterand, François, 380
MLN. *See* Movimiento de Liberación Nacional (MLN; National Liberation Movement)
MNR. *See* Movimiento Nacionalista Revolucionario (MNR, Revolutionary Nationalist Movement)
Monjardín, Federico, 185
Monje, Mario, 62, 160
Monroe Doctrine, 3, 254, 310
Morales, Numa, 379
Moreira Salles, Walther, 36
Morel, Efrain, 228
Morgenthau, Henry, 313
Morocco, 4, 30, 246, 259, 280, 286
Moton, Robert, 204, 207

Moton Commission, 211
Movimento Popular de Liberação de Angola (People's Movement for the Liberation of Angola), 399
Movimiento de Izquierda Revolucionaria (MIR, Revolutionary Left Movement), 378
Movimiento de Liberación Nacional (MLN; National Liberation Movement), 87, 91
Movimiento Nacionalista Revolucionario (MNR, Revolutionary Nationalist Movement), 44, 46, 48–55, 57–66, 230–31
Movimiento Rebelde 13 de Noviembre (MR-13), 129–30
Moyn, Samuel, 304
MR-13. *See* Movimiento Rebelde 13 de Noviembre (MR-13)
Muñoz Cota, José, 223
Muñoz Ledo, Porfirio, 319, 339n88

NAACP. *See* National Association for the Advancement of Colored People (NAACP)
Nagy, Imre, 239n17
NAM. *See* Non-Aligned Movement (NAM)
Nasser, Gamal Abdel, 106, 108, 151, 193–94, 251, 258, 296n40, 352
National Association for the Advancement of Colored People (NAACP), 205–6, 212–13
nationalism: in Algeria, 277, 291; anti-colonial, 306; in Argentina, 4, 175–77, 193; in Bolivia, 33–34, 44, 47–49, 51, 64–66, 160; in Brazil, 26–27, 36; in Cuba, 252; decolonization and, 327; in Iran, 124; in Mexico, 333n39; in Panama, 345, 349, 356; and Third World concept, 3
NATO. *See* North Atlantic Treaty Organization (NATO)
négritude, 203, 210, 213

Nehru, Jawaharlal, 5, 27–28, 34–35, 54, 108, 269n63, 352
Nemours, Alfred, 204
neocolonialism, 6, 66, 117, 253, 255, 261, 276, 296n41
Neptune, H. Reuben, 332n29
Neruda, Pablo, 223, 229
Netherlands, 374–75, *376*, 377, 384
New International Economic Order (NIEO), 2, 301–4, 306–7, 311, 322–23, 326–27
New Zealand, 266n21
Nguyen, Lien-Hang, 369
Nguyen Van Tien, 263
Nicaragua: Canada and, 193; Chile and, 378; Cuba and, 368, 370–71; European Community and, 381; Gilbert in, 211; Haiti and, 212; Sandinista National Liberation Front and, 367–86, *376*, 389n28; social democrats and, 380–82; Somoza dynasty in, 367–69, 371; Soviet Union and, 230, 371; United States and, 212, 371, 373, 383–86
Nicaragua Komitee Nederland (NKN, Dutch Nicaragua Committee), 375, *376*, 377
Nicaraguan Revolution, 368–69
Nicaragüense on Moscú, Un (Fonseca), 230
NIEO. *See* New International Economic Order (NIEO)
Nieto Caballero, Agustín, 233, 235
Niger, 30
Nigeria, 30
Nixon, Richard, 29, 349
NKN. *See* Nicaragua Komitee Nederland (NKN, Dutch Nicaragua Committee)
Nkrumah, Kwame, 54, 110, 113, 251, 296n41, 352
noirisme, 203–4
Non-Aligned Movement (NAM), 1–2, 6, 8, 46–47; Argentina and, 116, 176, 190; Bolivia and, 54; Brazil and, 100–101, 103–12, *112*, 114–17; China

and, 258; Cuba and, 148–52, 155–57, 163–66, 242, 252–62, 397; Cuban Missile Crisis and, 259; Guatemala and, 127–28; India and, 269n63; Panama and, 350, 352–53
nonalignment, meaning of, 106–7
North Atlantic Treaty Organization (NATO), 103, 107, 193–94
North-South Summit on Cooperation and Development, 301
NPT. *See* Nuclear Non-Proliferation Treaty (NPT)
Nuclear Non-Proliferation Treaty (NPT), 187–88
nuclear policy, 186–91
Nueva Canción (New Song) movement, 379

OAS. *See* Organization of American States (OAS)
Objeto Volador No Identificado (OVNI), 179
Obregón, Álvaro, 310–11
Oduber, Daniel, 380–81
Ogle, Vanessa, 307, 326
oil embargo, in 1970s, 301, 322
OLAS. *See* Latin American Solidarity Organization (OLAS)
Oliver, María Rosa, 225–26
OPEC. *See* Organization of the Petroleum Exporting Countries (OPEC)
Operação Pan Americana (Operation Pan America), 29–30, 35, 249–50
Operación Manuel, 47
Operación Matraca, 62–63, 65
Operación Panamericana, 182, 250
Operación Soberanía, 346
Organization of American States (OAS), 105, 396; Bolivia and, 55, 57; Brazil and, 30; Cuba and, 115, 154, 157–58, 174, 260–61, 272n100; Non-Aligned Movement and, 259; Panama and, 347–48, 353–54
Organization of the Petroleum Exporting Countries (OPEC), 301, 307, 322

Ornstein, Roberto M., 191
Orona, Arturo, 88
Ortega, Daniel, 370
OSPAAAL. *See* Afro-Asian Latin American Peoples' Solidarity Organization (OSPAAAL)
OVNI. *See* Objeto Volador No Identificado (OVNI)
Owen, David, 377

Pablo, Michel, 279
Pakistan, 19, 21, 31, 123, 135, 186, 243
Palestine, 184, 261, 278. *See also* Israel
Palme, Olof, 191, 380
Pan-Africanism, 201–2, 205–6, 208, 212–13
Panama: Colombia and, 345–46, 354; coup in, 343, 348–50; Departamento de Expresiones Artística (DEXA, Department of Artistic Expression) in, 344–45, 354–57; Grupo Experimental Cine Universitario (GECU) in, 354–55, 357–60, *359*; Havana Conference and, 250; nationalism in, 345, 349, 356; Nicaragua and, 373; Non-Aligned Movement and, 350, 352–53; Organization of American States and, 347–48, 353–54; Puerto Rico and, 353–54; *Tercer Mundo* and, 4; Third Worldism and, 344–45, 350–54; Torrijismo in, 349; Tricontinental Conference and, 157; United States and, 349–52; university cultural agencies and, 354–60, *359*; Venezuela and, 351
Panama Canal: crisis, 345–48; plebiscite, 360–61; United States and, 343, 347–48, 353–54
Panama Canal Commission, 360
Panama Canal Zone, 343, 346
Panama Flag Riots, 347–48
Pan-Americanism, 49, 55–56, 305
Pan-American Union, 131, 133, 145n51, 302, 305, 310, 325, 331n19, 331n23, 335n45, 396

Index   417

Pan-Arabism, 279, 281, 290
Pani, Alberto J., 311, 326
Paraguay, 155, 228, 247, 331n21
Parsons, Anthony, 384
Partido Agrario Laborista (Agrarian Labor Party), 279
Partido Comunista de Bolivia (PCB, Communist Party of Bolivia), 55, 64
Partido Comunista de México (PCM, Communist Party of Mexico), 91
Partido de Indios Aymaras y Keswas (PIAK), 232
Partido Indio de Bolivia (PIB), 232
Partido Revolucionario Institucional (PRI, Institutional Revolutionary Party), 75, 80
Pasternak, Boris, 224, 229
Pastora, Edén, 371
Patriotic Union (UP), 205, 209–10
Paz, Octavio, 223
Paz Estenssoro, Víctor, 49–50, 52–55, 57–66
PCB. *See* Partido Comunista de Bolivia (PCB, Communist Party of Bolivia)
PCM. *See* Partido Comunista de México (PCM, Communist Party of Mexico)
Peace Corps, 144n34
Peña Gomez, José Francisco, 380
penicillin, 182
Peralta Azurdia, Enrique, 129–31
Percy, Charles, 323–24
Perera, Mena, Arturo, 92, 95
Pérez, Carlos Andrés, 354, 380–81
Perón, Juan Domingo, 3, 174–75, 177, 181, 193, 354
Peronism, 107, 175, 180–81, 185
Perovic, Leposava Lep, *8*
Peru: Argentinian nuclear reactor in, 189–90; Bolivia and, 45, 62–63; Communism in, 232; development in, 131
Petriccioli, Gustavo, 339n88
pharmaceuticals, 182
Philippines, 79, 130–31, 134–35, 266n21, 341n110

Philosophy of the Revolution (Nasser), 296n40
PIAK. *See* Partido de Indios Aymaras y Keswas (PIAK)
PIB. *See* Partido Indio de Bolivia (PIB)
Pinochet, Augusto, 293n1
Pinto, Luis Bastian, 35
Pio Correa, Manoel, 248–49
Poland, 30, 33, 87, 103
Portugal, 17, 23, 26, 28, 35, 103, 110, 380
Povic, Konstantin Koca, *8*
Prado, Abelardo Bueno do, 21
Prague Spring, 162, 224
Prashad, Vijay, 5–6, 241
Prebisch, Raúl, 307
Prestes, Luis Carlos, 29
PRI. *See* Partido Comunista de Bolivia (PCB, Communist Party of Bolivia)
Price-Mars, Jean, 203
Programa de Metas (Targets Plan), 29
Program of Community Development (DESCOM), 131–40
propaganda, 47, 49, 83, 111, 113, 157–58, 186, 229, 246, 248, 256, 355, 357, 361, 384
Puerto Rico, 155, 253, 255, 260–61, 347, 352–54
Puig Casauranc, José Manuel, 312, 326, 335n49

Quadros, Jânio, 1, 30, 38, 102–3, 106, 108–9, 111, *112*, 113, 251

Rabasa, Emilio, 322–25
race: in Brazil, 31, 110; in Dominican occupation, 207; in Haitian occupation, 202–3, 206, 212. *See also* whites
racial solidarity, 101, 201, 206–7
racism: of American occupiers, 202–3, 207–8; in Brazil, 21; Cuba and, 255; development and, 134; in Dominican Republic, 210–11; of empire, 202
Radhakrishnan, Sarvepalli, 28
Ramírez, Sergio, 370–72
Randolph, A. Philip, 204

418 Index

Reagan, Ronald, 301, 386
Reinaga, Fausto, 230-32
Republican Party, 206, 209, 309
Revolución Libertadora, 185
Revolutionary Student Front (Frente Estudiantil Revolucionario, FER-29), 361
Revueltas, José, 223-24, 239n17
Rivera, Diego, 223-25
Rivera, Pedro, 357-58
Roa, Raúl, 56-57, 109, 161, 244-45, 248, 250, 253-55, 260-62, 263, 268n56
Roa Kouri, Raúl, 244
Rocha, Gauber, 357
Rodrigues Valle, Henrique, 119n7
Rodríguez Adame, Julián, 90-91
Rogers, William, 349
Roosevelt, Franklin D., 311
Roumer, Émile, 203
Roy, M. N., 394
Rubottom, Roy, 84, 95, 245-46, 249
Ruda, José María, 185
Rumie, Tawfik, 299n71
Rumié Vera, Omar, 279
Rupprecht, Tobias, 46, 76
Rusk, Dean, 158
Russell, John, 202

Salum, Marco Antonio, 279, 289-90, 298n69, 299n71
Sánchez Azcona, Juan, 334n41
Sandinistas. *See* Frente Sandinista de Liberación Nacional (FSLN, Sandinista National Liberation Front)
Sandino, Augusto, 211
Sannon, Pauléus, 209
Santa Cruz, Hernán, 307, 320
Saudi Arabia, 120n20, 259, 398
Sauvy, Alfred, 3-4
Scali, John, 324
Scarlett, Zachary A., 293n6
Schlesinger, Arthur, 59
Schmidt, Helmut, 385
Schmidt Cuadra, Enrique, 375
School of the Americas, 349

Schulz, Hermann, 375
Schwebel, Stephen, 323
Scolari, Carlos, 178
Scorza, Manuel, 2332
Scott, William, 204, 211
Second Vatican Council, 235
Selcher, Wayne Alan, 18
Senegal, 30, 231
Serrano, Miguel, 34
Serviço Nacional de Informações (SNI, National Intelligence Service) (Brazil), 115
Shakespeare, John, 382
Shani, Varun, 17
Shelnov, A., 82
SI. *See* Socialist International (SI)
Sihanouk, Norodom, 185
Siles Zuazo, Hernán, 49, 230-31
Silva Gonçalves, Williams da, 17
Sinán, Rogelio, 356
Siqueiros, David, 223, 225
Sluga, Glenda, 305
social democrats, 368, 377, 380-82, 387
Socialist International (SI), 368, 380, 386-87
Sociedade Brasileira de Amigos da Índia (Brazilian Society of Friends of India), 22
Solanas, Fernando, 357
Soler, Eugenio, 246-47
solidarity, 101, 201, 206-7, 373-80, 376
Solzhenitsyn, Alexander, 225
Somoza Debayle, Luis, 367-69, 371, 381, 383, 385
Sosa, Jesualdo, 223
South Africa, 110, 189-90, 255
Souza Dantas, Rodolfo de, 40n30, 110
Soviet-Latin American Friendship Society, 227
Soviet Union, 6-7; Afghanistan and, 165-66; Algeria and, 283; Argentina and, 79, 177, 190-92; Bolivia and, 60-61, 230-31; Brazil and, 103; Chile and, 163, 287; China and, 6-7, 113; CIA and, 81; Cuba and, 149-54,

Index   419

Soviet Union (cont.)
157–67, 227–28; Czechoslovakia and, 222, 225–26, 236; Guevara and, 160–61; Hungary and, 222, 224–25, 229–30, 236; Latin American cultural figures in, 227–28; Latin American fascination with, 223–25; Latin American travelogues with, 228–29; Mexico and, 73–74, 76, 77–95; Nicaragua and, 371; Organization of American States and, 158; Prague Spring and, 162; Spaniards in, 227; Stalin and, 223–24; Third Worldism and, 222, 226–32, 236–37. *See also* Khrushchev, Nikita

Spain, 29, 53, 231, 374–75, 380
Spangenberg, Guillermo R., 181
Spanish Civil War, 227
Spenser, Daniela, 179
Spingarn, Arthur, 204
Spock, Benjamin, 178
Squibb Argentina, 182
Stalin, Joseph, 223–24
"States' Rights against Private Capital" (Ogle), 307
Storey, Moorfield, 205
Suárez, Eduardo, 315
Sudan, 120n20, 266n21, 352
Suez Canal, 193, 279, 352
Sukarno, 30, 54, 74, 151, 251
Sweden, 110, 191, 380
Sylvain, Georges, 205
Syria, 184, 190–91, 193, 278

Tack, Juan Antonio, 349, 351, 354
Tactic, Guatemala, 126, 135–39
Tagore, Rabindranath, 19, 22
Tanzania, 4, 164, 191, 307
Teceristas, 370–72
Tello, Manuel, 77, 85–86
tercermundismo. *See* Third Worldism
Tercer Mundo (magazine), 1–2, 4–5
Tettegah, John, 263
Thailand, 30, 134–35, 266n21
Thant, U, 184–85, 351

theatre, 356–57
"Third Force," 5
Third World: Argentina and, 186–87; Brazil and, 101–3; Cuba and, 150–51, 157; First World modernization theory and, 125; Latin America as left out of scholarship on, 304–6; origin of term, 3–5; positive connotation of, 274; as term, 293n6. *See also* Global South
Third Worldism, 2–3; in Algeria, 274; in Bolivia, 45, 55; defined, 6; Mexico and, 74–75; Panama and, 344–45, 350–54; Soviet Union and, 222, 226–32, 236–37
Thoby, Perceval, 205, 209
Tibet, 20
Tikhomirov, K. D., 88–89, 91
Tito, Josep Broz, 8, 54, 106, 108, 251, 258
Titov, German, 229
Toledano, Vicente, 223
Torrijismo, 349, 351, 354–55, 357–58, 362
Torrijos Herrera, Omar, 2, 343–45, 349–54, 360–61, 380–81
Touré, Sékou, 251
Towards a Poor Theatre (Grotowski), 356
transnationalization, 179–80
"Transnationalizing the Dirty War: Argentina in Central America" (Armony), 179–80
Trashumantes theatrical troupe, 356–57
Tratado Interamericano de Assistência Recíproca (Inter-American Treaty of Reciprocal Assistance), 18
travelogues, 228
Treaty for the Prohibition of Nuclear Weapons in Latin America and the Caribbean, 187
Trejo y Lerdo de Tejada, Carlos, 311, 325, 334n45, 335n46
Triana, Jorge Alí, 357
Tricontinental, 6, 263

Tricontinental Conference, 155, *156*, 157–59, 252, 262, *263*, 284
Trinidad and Tobago, 116–17, 154, 394, 398
Trotsky, Leon, 223
Trotskyites, 279–80
Trujillo, Rafael, 213
Tunisia, 30, 120n20, 246, 266n21, 286
Turismo Carretera, 178–79
Turkel, Harry, 84–85, 95
Tuskegee Institute, 203–4

UFO. *See* Unidentified Flying Object (UFO)
UGEMA. *See* General Union of Muslim Students of Algeria); Union Générale des Étudiants Musulmans Algériens (UGEMA)
UN Conference on Trade and Development (UNCTAD), 2, 6, 100, 116, 118, 160–61, 241, 290–91, 302, 307–8, 321
UNIA. *See* United Negro Improvement Association (UNIA)
Unidad Popular (UP), 274, 277, 280, 290
Unidentified Flying Object (UFO), 179
Unión Cívica Radical Party, 186
Union Générale des Étudiants Musulmans Algériens (UGEMA; General Union of Muslim Students of Algeria), 280–81
United Arab Republic, 106, 117, 287
United Fruit Company, 127
United Kingdom: Argentina and, 192; Bolivia and, 48–49; Cuba and, 242; Haiti and, 210; Mexico and, 314; Nicaragua and, 371, 375, 377, 379, 381–84
United Negro Improvement Association (UNIA), 201, 208–9
United States: Argentina and, 174–89; Bolivian aid from, 44, 51, 57; Brazilian aid from, 26, 33; Brazilian foreign policy and, 18, 30; Congress of Underdeveloped Countries and, 246–52; Cuba and, 148–49, 242, 245–48, 255, 259–62, 269n67, 395;
Guatemalan aid from, 132–33; Haiti and, 201–5, 207–13; Indian relations with, 25–26; Inter-American Bank and, 313–14; Mexico and, 80–81, 310–11, 317–18, 323–25; Nicaragua and, 312, 371, 373, 383–86; Panama Canal and, 343, 346–48, 353–54; Panamanian coup and, 349–52; Republican Party in, 206, 209, 309. *See also* Central Intelligence Agency (CIA)
United States Agency for International Development (USAID), 51–53, 57–59, 63–65, 124, 132–33
Universal Declaration of Human Rights, 320
Universal Postal Union, 305
university cultural agencies, 354–60, *359*
Upper Volta, 30
Urquidi, Víctor, 315, 317
Urrutia, Praxedes, 227
Uruguay, 116, 154, 223, 259, 311, 331n21, 345, 398
USAID. *See* United States Agency for International Development (USAID)
U.S. Army School of the Americas, 349
Uzbekistan. El espejo (Ghioldi), 228

Valcárcel, Gustavo, 221, 228–29, 231, 236
Varela, Alfredo, 223
Vargas, Getúlio, 17–19, 23
Vargas Llosa, Mario, 225
Vásquez Robles, Emilio, 135–36
Vazquez Cisneros, Pedro, 87–88
Velasco Alvarado, Juan, 2, 287–89
Velasco Letelier, Eugenio, 287, 298n62
Venezuela: attack on Nixon in, 29; Congress of Underdeveloped Countries and, 250; Cuba and, 116, 162, 260–61; India and, 42n64; Nicaragua and, 373; Non-Aligned Movement and, 155; Panama and, 351; World Youth Festival and, 226

Vera, Pedro Jorge, 225
Videla, Jorge Rafael, 1
Vietnam, 30, 51, 154, 157, 162, 165, 184–85, 260, 290–91, 398
Vietnam War, 115, 350
Vignes, Alberto, 174–76
Villafañe, Javier, 226
Villard, Garrison, 210
Villaseñor, Eduardo, 312–13
Villaseñor, Víctor Manuel, 223
Vincent, Sténio, 207, 209
Vitalis, Robert, 6, 118n3
Vitolo, Alfredo Roque, 185
Von Eschen, Penny, 213
Vrhovec, Josip, 165

Walker, Madam C. J., 204
Wallner, Woodruff, 36
Warsaw Pact, 107, 151, 166, 258
Washington, Margaret Murray, 204
Wasserman, Mark, 179
Wellinga, Klaas, 375, 378
Westad, Odd Arne, 2–3, 75
Westerman, George W., 347
White, Harry Dexter, 313–14
whites: in Algeria, 283; in Brazil, 110, 113; in Dominican Republic, 207; in Haitian occupation, 202–3, 205–6, 212; Latin American elites as, 102, 231, 394
Williams, Tennessee, 178
Wilson, Woodrow, 205, 207, 209–10, 309–10, 334n42
Wilsonian Moment, The (Manela), 306
World Bank, 307, 314–15, 317
World Youth Festival (Soviet Union, 1957), 226–27, 230–31
Worsley, Peter, 5
Wretched of the Earth, The (Fanon), 293n7

Ydígoras Fuentes, Miguel, 128–29
Yemen, 266n21
Yen, Y. C. James, 134
Yom Kippur War, 353
Yugoslavia, 6, 54, 106–9, 113, 164, 166, 251

Zannier, Víctor, 62
Zevada, Ricardo J., 84
Zhou Enlai, 321
Zimmerman, Andrew, 213
Zourek, Michal, 46

www.ingramcontent.com/pod-product-compliance
Lightning Source LLC
Chambersburg PA
CBHW030516230426
43665CB00010B/631